Robert Downey Jr.
from Brat to Icon

ALSO BY ERIN E. MACDONALD

Ed McBain/Evan Hunter: A Literary Companion (2012).

Robert Downey Jr. from Brat to Icon

Essays on the Film Career

Edited by ERIN E. MACDONALD

McFarland & Company, Inc., Publishers
Jefferson, North Carolina

LIBRARY OF CONGRESS CATALOGUING-IN-PUBLICATION DATA

Robert Downey Jr. from brat to icon : essays
on the film career / edited by Erin E. MacDonald.
p. cm.
Includes bibliographical references and index.

ISBN 978-0-7864-7549-0 (softcover : acid free paper) ∞
ISBN 978-1-4766-1703-9 (ebook)

1. Downey, Robert, 1965– —Criticism and
interpretation.   I. MacDonald, Erin E., editor.
PN2287.D548R63 2014   791.4302'8092—dc23   2014032850

BRITISH LIBRARY CATALOGUING DATA ARE AVAILABLE

© 2014 Erin E. MacDonald. All rights reserved

*No part of this book may be reproduced or transmitted in any form
or by any means, electronic or mechanical, including photocopying
or recording, or by any information storage and retrieval system,
without permission in writing from the publisher.*

On the cover: Robert Downey Jr. in *The Pick-up Artist*, 1987 (Photofest)

Printed in the United States of America

*McFarland & Company, Inc., Publishers
Box 611, Jefferson, North Carolina 28640
www.mcfarlandpub.com*

For two Roberts:
my husband, Robert Joseph Muhlbock,
who knows the importance of obsession,
and Robert Downey Jr.,
who knows the importance of balance.

Table of Contents

Acknowledgments ix
Preface 1
Chronology 3
Introduction: "You know who I am"
    ERIN E. MACDONALD 7

The Pick-Up Artist and the Failures of Virtuosity
    CHRISTIAN B. LONG 17

Delightful, Duplicitous and Flirting with Disaster: James Toback's Robert Downey Jr.
    THOMAS BRITT 29

"Mad as a box of frogs": Channeling Chaplin in the Role of a Lifetime
    ERIN E. MACDONALD 40

Facing Life with Face Off: Race and Identity in the Films of Robert Downey Sr. and Robert Downey Jr.
    TONY PRICHARD 64

Robert Downey Jr.'s Media Monsters: *Natural Born Killers*, *In Dreams* and *Zodiac*
    KAREN OUGHTON 75

Queering Downey Part 1: Queer as Catalyst in *Less Than Zero*, *Home for the Holidays* and *One Night Stand*
    ERIN E. MACDONALD 86

Queering Downey Part 2: Gender Identity and Cross-Dressing in *In Dreams*, *Wonder Boys* and *Sherlock Holmes: A Game of Shadows*
    ERIN E. MACDONALD 107

"This too too sullied flesh": The Resurfacing of Robert Downey Jr.
    JASON DAVIDS SCOTT 121

"Lie down with me Watson": Transgression and Fragile Masculinity in the Detective Films of Robert Downey Jr.
    RUTH O'DONNELL 136

Genre- and Gender-Bending in Shane Black's *Kiss Kiss Bang Bang* and *Iron Man 3*
    NILS BOTHMANN   153

Getting in Another's Shoes: Clashing Ethics in *Charlie Bartlett*
    FERNANDO GABRIEL PAGNONI BERNS   166

Robert Downey Jr. as Star: The Irreverent Hero of *Iron Man* and *Iron Man 2*
    F. E. PHEASANT-KELLY   176

Fragmented Relationships: Father-Son Dynamics in *Less Than Zero*, *A Guide to Recognizing Your Saints* and *Iron Man 2*
    JENNIFER HARRISON   191

"Welcome to the movie factory": *Tropic Thunder* as Postmodern Comedy
    BRIAN S. REINKING   205

Layers of Lazarus: Robert Downey Jr. Hits "true emotional pay dirt" Through Blackface
    DEREK ADAMS   218

Language and Power in *The Soloist* and *A Guide to Recognizing Your Saints*
    SAM LUNDBERG   235

Robert Downey Jr. as Detective: Sherlock Holmes Redux
    LINDA LEDFORD-MILLER   244

The Avengers in Post–9/11 America
    MIKE HERNANDEZ   255

Biography   269
Filmography   291
About the Contributors   295
Index   297

Acknowledgments

Comedy performer Dan Kamin kindly answered my multiple questions about his work on *Chaplin* over e-mail and allowed me to quote freely from the postscript to his book, *The Comedy of Charlie Chaplin: Artistry in Motion*. Acknowledgment must also go to the webmistresses, including GinaB, at *Downey Unlimited* for compiling such a comprehensive database of Downey articles, interviews, and videos, many of which were next to impossible to find in their original forms and were therefore consulted as research. Dandychick.com's *RDJ Film Guide* was also helpful, as were my colleague and friend Stefanie Ketley's kind comments on a couple of my chapters. To all the contributors whose insights and enthusiasm made such a collection possible, to Jason Davids Scott for organizing a great Downey panel at the Mid-Atlantic Popular American Culture Association conference in Atlantic City, and to all others who expressed interest in the project, a warm thank you. Finally, thanks as always to my family—to Rob, for helping with some of the technological aspects of the book, and to Emma and Rory (and our two cats, Tony and Pepper), for their patience.

"If only life was as easy as Hollywood. You basically get to start your life anew with every picture, if you like. If you're smart enough to shed those skins and keep peeling your own onion, you get what everyone gets and deserves in life, which is, every day, every second, right here in the moment is new."

—Robert Downey Jr. in Cannes, 2005

Preface

Robert Downey Jr. may be best known as Iron Man, but his career as an actor stretches back to the 1970s and features several Oscar-quality roles. He has worked with a wide range of innovative directors from Oliver Stone and Robert Altman to Richard Linklater and Shane Black and has played punk kids, detectives, journalists, and even a serial killer.

This fascinating collection of essays combines scholarly attention to detail with a highly readable style to examine, in roughly chronological order, more than twenty-five of Downey's best performances in films as diverse as *Less Than Zero*, *Chaplin*, *Natural Born Killers*, *A Scanner Darkly*, *The Soloist*, and *Tropic Thunder*. Including a biography, chronology, and filmography, the book overall highlights the inseparability of the actor's biography from his works and from the unique combination of talents that he brings to his roles.

Chronology

1965—Born April 4 in Manhattan to actress Elsie Ford and filmmaker Robert Downey. Sister Allyson born two years earlier.
1970—Appeared in first film, *Pound*, an absurdist comedy directed by his father.
1972—Moved to Sante Fe, New Mexico, to film Robert Downey Sr.'s *Greaser's Palace*.
1973—While living in Connecticut, became best friends with future musician, Moby.
1975—Moved to London, England; attended Perry House School.
1976—Moved back to the U.S., attended Stagedoor Manor summer acting camp in the Catskills.
1977—Lived in Woodstock, NY, teaching self to play piano; returned to Stagedoor for the summer; moved with his mother back to NYC when parents separated.
1978—Parents officially separated.
1980—After moving to L.A. to live with father, appeared in father's film *Up the Academy*. Joined Santa Monica High School choral group, learned tap dancing, and performed in school productions including *Oklahoma!*, *The Rivals*, and *Detective Story*.
1982—Moved back to New York after dropping out of Santa Monica High; father refused to support him. Worked as busboy, shoe salesman, and living art. Joined local theater group and earned roles in Off Broadway productions, at which an agent spotted him. Started auditioning.
1983—Appeared in plays *Alms for the Middle Class*, *Fraternity*, and Off Broadway musical, *American Passion*, produced by Norman Lear, at Joyce Theatre. Briefly appeared in first Hollywood film, *Baby It's You* (dubbed "Maybe It's You" by friends).
1984—Met Sarah Jessica Parker on set of *Firstborn*; began seven-year relationship.
1985—With friend Anthony Michael Hall, joined cast of *Saturday Night Live* for one season. Got supporting roles in *Tuff Turf* and *Weird Science* and also appeared in *Girls Just Want to Have Fun*, short film *Deadwait*, and TV miniseries, *Mussolini: The Untold Story*.
1986—Appeared in *Back to School* and *America*.
1987—First lead role opposite Molly Ringwald in *The Pick-up Artist*. Played drug addicted rich kid Julian Wells in adaptation of Bret Easton Ellis novel, *Less Than Zero*, earning first major critical acclaim.
1988—Played minor roles in *Johnny Be Good*, *Rented Lips*; co-starred with Kiefer Sutherland in *1969*. Entered rehab for first time, for cocaine addiction (28 days in a facility in Arizona).
1989—Appeared in *That's Adequate*; co-starred in *True Believer* with James Woods and *Chances Are* with Cybill Shepherd.
1990—Co-starred with Mel Gibson in *Air America*; appeared in father's film, *Too Much Sun*.
1991—Minor role in *Soapdish*; left by Sarah Jessica Parker; started researching role for *Chaplin*.

1992—Met and married (May 29) model/singer/actress Deborah Falconer after 42-day courtship. Featured in political documentary *The Last Party*, as narrator; starred as Charlie Chaplin in Richard Attenborough biopic, *Chaplin*.

1993—Starred in *Heart and Souls*; appeared in Robert Altman's *Short Cuts*. Nominated for Academy Award and Golden Globe for Best Actor in a Leading Role for *Chaplin*; won BAFTA award. September 7: son Indio Falconer Downey born.

1994—Appeared in *Hail Caesar*, *Natural Born Killers*, and *Only You*. Won Saturn award for Best Actor for *Heart and Souls*, Golden Globe for Best Ensemble Cast for *Short Cuts*.

1995—Starred in *Restoration*; co-starred in *Richard III*, *Mr. Willowby's Christmas Tree* (a Muppets special), *Home for the Holidays*—used heroin during filming for first time.

1996—Co-starred with Billy Zane in *Danger Zone*. April: Deborah left. Sean Penn broke into his house, kidnapped him, and took him to rehab in Arizona, which he fled. June: Stopped while speeding down Sunset Boulevard and arrested for possession of heroin, cocaine, and a "concealed" unloaded .357 Magnum handgun. July: Found passed out in child's bed in a neighbor's home in "Goldilocks" incident; revived by paramedics; ordered into rehab at Exodus in Marina Del Rey, escaped days later but captured and returned. November: Sentenced to six more months of rehab, three years of probation, and compulsory drug testing; received leave from rehab to host *Saturday Night Live*.

1997—Filmed *Two Girls and a Guy*; September: Missed a court-ordered drug test. December: Probation revoked for skipping drug tests; sentenced to four months in L.A. County jail. *One Night Stand*, *Hugo Pool* released.

1998—January: Allowed out of jail to film *U.S. Marshals*. February: Wounded in fight with other inmates, placed in solitary confinement; allowed out to do looping for *In Dreams*. March: Released from jail; entered 120-day rehab. *The Gingerbread Man* and *U.S. Marshals* released.

1999—June: Court violated his probation for missing more drug tests; taken to 24-hour rehab program. August: Told Judge Mira, "It's like I've got a shotgun in my mouth with my finger on the trigger, and I like the taste of the gun metal." Sentenced to three years in California Substance Abuse Treatment Facility and State Prison in Corcoran, California (a.k.a. "Corcoran II"). *Friends and Lovers*, *Bowfinger*, *Black and White*, *In Dreams* (co-starring with Annette Bening) released.

2000—Appeared in critically lauded roles in *Wonder Boys*, *Auto Motives* (short). Had served eleven months when judge freed him in August because total time spent in jail from previous arrests qualified him for early release. In fall, joined cast of *Ally McBeal* as lawyer Larry Paul. November: Spent Thanksgiving at Merv Griffin's Hotel in Palm Springs; police responding to anonymous call found him in possession of cocaine and Valium (and a Wonder Woman costume left behind by a friend).

2001—Nominated for Emmy Award; won Golden Globe, SAG awards for *Ally McBeal*; received standing ovation at Golden Globes. After years of separation, wife Deborah filed for divorce and requested supervised visits with Indio. April: While on parole, found by police wandering barefoot in Culver City under influence of cocaine. Fired from *Ally McBeal* and upcoming film *America's Sweethearts*; Mel Gibson shut down planned stage production of *Hamlet*. July: Pled no contest; sentenced to rehab and three years' probation after passing of new California law meant to keep nonviolent drug offenders out of prison. August: After getting out of rehab, hired by Elton John to star (lip-syncing) in his video for the song "I Want Love." Spent year at a live-in rehab residence in Malibu.

2002—Filmed *The Singing Detective* while on probation in L.A.; was reportedly clean for entire shoot. Appeared in *Lethargy* (short).

2003—*Whatever We Do* (short), *The Singing Detective*, *Gothika* released. Met and fell in love with producer Susan Levin on set of *Gothika*. July: Threw drugs into ocean; has reportedly been drug and alcohol free since. Won Chicago International Film Festival Career Achievement Award.

2004—Appeared in *Eros* (segment called "Equilibrium"). April 26: Divorced from Deborah Falconer. November: Released *The Futurist*, his debut musical album, on the Sony Classical label. Won Hasty Pudding Theatricals Man of the Year.

2005—Co-starred with Val Kilmer in *Kiss Kiss Bang Bang*; minor roles in *Good Night, and Good Luck*, *Game 6*, and *Family Guy* ("The Fat Guy Strangler" episode). August 27: Married Susan in Jewish wedding in Amagansett, NY.

2006—*A Guide to Recognizing Your Saints*, *The Shaggy Dog*, *A Scanner Darkly*, and *Fur: An Imaginary Portrait of Diane Arbus* released. Auditioned for *Iron Man*.

2007—Co-starred in David Fincher's *Zodiac*, *Charlie Bartlett* and cameoed in *Lucky You*.

2008—Starred in first blockbuster movies, *Iron Man* (April) and Ben Stiller's *Tropic Thunder* (August). Appeared in *Tropic Thunder: Rain of Madness* (short mockumentary); provided voice for *Iron Man* video game; had cameo in *The Incredible Hulk*. Canceled deal with HarperCollins to publish a memoir.

2009—Nominated for Academy Award, Golden Globe, BAFTA, SAG Award for Best Supporting Actor for role as Kirk Lazarus in *Tropic Thunder*. Won Irish Film and Saturn Awards for *Iron Man*. *The Soloist* released mid-year although completed in 2008. December 7: Had hands and feet immortalized in ceremony at Grauman's Chinese Theater. December: Guy Ritchie's *Sherlock Holmes* released on Christmas Day.

2010—January: Won Golden Globe for Best Actor in a Motion Picture Comedy or Musical for role as Sherlock Holmes. May: *Iron Man 2* released. June: Won Gene Siskel Film Center Renaissance Award and opened production company Team Downey with wife Susan as President. November: *Due Date* released in theaters.

2011—December: *Sherlock Holmes: A Game of Shadows* released. Received American Cinematheque award at special ceremony.

2012—February 7: Son Exton Elias Downey born to wife Susan. May: *The Avengers* released; achieved rank of third best-selling movie of all time.

2013—January: Won People's Choice Awards for Favorite Movie Actor and Favorite Movie Superhero; dedicated awards to late long-time fan, Joyce Schroeder. May 3: *Iron Man 3* released; achieved fifth best-selling movie of all time.

2014—January: Won People's Choice Awards for Favorite Action Movie Star, Favorite Movie Superhero, and Favorite Movie (Iron Man 3). Friend Jon Favreau's *Chef* released (May) and Team Downey's first production, *The Judge* (October).

2015—May: *The Avengers 2: The Age of Ultron* to be released, reprising role of Tony Stark.

Introduction

"You know who I am"

Erin E. MacDonald

Named Hollywood's most valuable star in 2012 and the highest paid actor of 2013, according to *Forbes* (Pomerantz), Academy Award–nominated and Golden Globe–winning Robert Downey Jr. has appeared in over 75 films, documentaries, and television shows since his first role at five years old in 1970. He is one of few actors to have consistently won high praise from critics and fans alike, for his intense, naturalistic performances. His roles in movies such as *Less Than Zero* (1987) (discussed in this book by Jennifer Harrison in "Fragmented Relationships"), *Chaplin* (1992), *Iron Man* (2008), *Tropic Thunder* (2008), and *Sherlock Holmes* (2009) have intersected with three decades of our culture's preoccupations with youth, celebrity, sexuality, and the rebel figure. Working with directors from Richard Attenborough, Oliver Stone, Robert Altman, and David Fincher to James Toback, Jon Favreau, Guy Ritchie, and Shane Black, Downey has played punk kids, gay characters, a superhero, and even a black man.

Tracing the progression of Downey's career through an in-depth analysis of his most important films allows us to measure the pulse of contemporary pop culture because he acts as a barometer of the zeitgeist by playing some of the world's most iconic, larger-than-life characters, including Chaplin, Iron Man, and Sherlock Holmes. Comparing his version of Holmes to the original great detective reveals, as Linda Ledford-Miller points out in her essay, that his "interpretation of Holmes is both modern and canonical." He has brought widespread popularity to works and genres that diversely aged and educated audiences might not otherwise have taken an interest in, through his trademark wit, irreverence, realism, and charm. Perhaps no other actor today has as much combined visibility, versatility, respectability, and license to court controversy as he. "You can't take your eyes off him" (Robbins, "Audio Commentary").

Known by younger fans as Iron Man and by older generations as a former troubled soul, Downey has most consistently been called one of the greatest actors of his generation by peers and critics alike. Critic Steve Vineberg wrote in 2001, "…there's no such thing as an uncomplicated moment in a Robert Downey performance. His impulse is always to play two emotions, usually opposite ones, at the same time, and when he's really swinging he can play three" ("Delivering Something Real"). Todd Phillips, director of *Due Date*, told Michael Fleming of *Playboy* in November 2010,

Mark Strong (back) as Lord Blackwood with Downey as Holmes on the set of *Sherlock Holmes* **(2009).**

> Actors who've been around bring baggage that leaves the audience with their arms folded, saying, "Show me" ... Robert has baggage, but the audience has always greeted him with open arms. He'd been this simmering talent, and during that period he gained the respect of so many of us just waiting for an *Iron Man* or a *Tropic Thunder* to see it fully realized. I love this guy more than any actor I've ever worked with. He made me a better director, and he is literally the greatest talent I've ever come across.

Phillips is not the only one to sing Downey's praises—from the beginning of his career, those who worked with him were quick to heap on the compliments. Director of Downey in three films, Robert Altman was quoted in 1999 saying, "There isn't a better actor in America," and in the same year, Neil Jordan, who had just directed Downey in *In Dreams*, agreed: "He's the best fucking actor in America" (qtd. in Garbarino, "Last Party"). While his lifestyle, roles, and bank account may have changed drastically over the years, directors from his early 1980s films to today have attested to Downey's raw talent, penchant for improvisation, and naturalistic acting style. Whatever image he may have courted in the past, his identity today is that of a great actor—fearless, hardworking, and innovative. Acting, for Robert Downey Jr., is a chance at a new life. With each new role, he peels the onion some more—explores his own identity and raises questions about gender, sexuality, and racial performance that audiences continue to be challenged and entertained by.

One of his most recent films, *Iron Man 3* (2013), is about addictions—Tony Stark's addictions to his suits and to the literal and metaphorical masks that he wears, and The Mandarin (Ben Kingsley)'s addictions to drugs and to celebrity. The film begins with the kind of voice-over narration that worked for the Black-Downey team previously on *Kiss Kiss*

Bang Bang (2005), and a glimpse of Stark's "old days," during which he was under the influence much of the time and prone to making "mistakes." "We create our own demons," he warns, and his past literally catches up with him in the forms of old flame Maya Hansen (Rebecca Hall) and AIM rival Aldrich Killian (Guy Pearce). Before leaving Hansen abruptly after a one-night-stand in 1999, Tony leaves a name tag for her with the message, "You know who I am." But does Stark know who he is? By the end of the film, he destroys several versions of the Iron Man armor and admits that he has been using his obsession with his suits as a "cocoon" rather than a "distraction or a hobby"—a way to shut himself off from the world and from the memory of what happened in New York. After an operation to remove the shrapnel from his heart, he stands on a cliff overlooking the ocean with a crumpled brown paper bag, slowly takes his old arc reactor out of the bag, and throws it into the ocean below. "I'm a changed man now," he says as he drives away in an expensive sports car, wearing sunglasses and looking very much like the man he always was. Dropping the bag into the ocean must have been a cathartic moment for Downey, who similarly dumped his bag of drug paraphernalia (or "cocoon") into the ocean nearly ten years earlier. Leaving behind a series of literally empty masks, their eye sockets filled with nothing human, Tony thinks he can leave his past behind and start again, with a "clean slate." This parallel to his own life may be meant to symbolically represent the actor's new sober, monogamous life or may suggest that Downey doesn't need to be a superhero anymore, that he can let go of the Tony Stark franchise security blanket at least temporarily, and return to smaller projects like Team Downey's first production, *The Judge* (2014).

However, "[k]ind of like Tony's obsession with the suit, this genre of movie, this and the 'Sherlock' stuff, it's addictive," Downey said in an interview with DailyFreeman.com (Germain). Tony is still the same guy at the end, needing to endlessly repeat the traumatic events of his life, some of his own creation and some not, through "therapy." The hidden scene after the credits, featuring Tony retelling his entire story to Bruce Banner in a framing narrative, not only provides a tidy connection to *The Avengers* but also continues the parallel with Downey's life. As Stark, he thanks Banner (who hasn't actually been listening) for hearing him out, because "putting it out there in the atmosphere" is healthier than "holding it in" but the one-sided conversation seems to have no end, as Tony/Downey launches into a humorous explanation of his "original wound." Both characters, Tony Stark and the Downey persona, are clearly emotionally injured and unable to ever completely get over whatever it is about their pasts that tortures them. Is acting a kind of talk therapy for Downey, a "working through of trauma," as Jason Davids Scott writes in his essay? Are the filmmakers banking on audiences making connections between the star's real life and the filmic narrative? Statistics prove that "the Marvel movies in which Downey appears perform far better than those in which he doesn't" ("Marvel Cliffhanger"). With images of the shattered Iron Man mask and of Tony kissing "himself" (one of his Iron Man drones) and the overall metanarrative of an actor playing the part of a terrorist, the postmodern layering of the film is at least as impressive as its digital effects. In *SciFiNow*, Downey even compared the film's reference to media creations of terrorism to his own role as a crazed TV journalist in Oliver Stone's 1994 movie, *Natural Born Killers* (24), which is discussed in the essay by Karen Oughton. Nils Bothmann writes of Stark as a "traumatized hero." Whether the Iron Man films are an example of his desire to infuse each character with something of himself or of contemporary film's use of society's obsession with celebrity as a postmodern technique, they are certainly not the only films in which Robert Downey Jr. plays some aspect of himself.

Always well known as an improviser, Downey said in 1987, "Things are always funniest when you play them as real as you can.... I love just seeing people in the act of being themselves. I think at best my work seems like a documentary" (Soriano). James Toback, who directed Downey in his first starring role, opposite Molly Ringwald in 1987's *The Pick-Up Artist*, says, "He doesn't act a role, he embodies it" (Garbarino, "Last Party"). In his essay, Thomas Britt acknowledges Toback's indebtedness to Downey, his muse. Toback has frequently commented on the power of Downey's facility with language, an idea that Sam Lundberg revisits in his essay on *The Soloist* and *A Guide to Recognizing Your Saints*. Part of Downey's technique of embodying a role involves improvising as often as he's allowed to, and even sometimes when he isn't. Jodie Foster, Downey's director for *Home for the Holidays* (1995) (discussed in one of my essays, "Queering Downey 1"), explains what she calls "typical Robert Downey improvisation—where he always takes it one step further than it ever should go" ("Commentary"). Foster was open to the actors improvising their dialogue during rehearsal, but generally dislikes improv during filming. "Downey's the only one who somehow could make that useful," she attests. Although Downey famously digresses from the script and makes sure that "[e]ach take is different," he "always come[s] back to whatever the line [i]s that the other actor need[s] in order to get back to the text. He has just an amazing brain.... He's somebody who can't say the same thing twice and he comes up with everything that he says." According to Foster, he does this because "[h]e gets bored. He's an actor who's sort of so smart that he gets bored and so he has to create a little fun for himself and basically change all the lines every time around." *Singing Detective* director Keith Gordon in his commentary on that film calls Downey "a very sweet and wonderful guy" who works from "intuition" and "from his heart," improvising as much as possible. Even the director and writer of Disney's *The Shaggy Dog* acknowledge that their film contains "a lot of Robert Downey improvising, just sort of letting him go and letting him do his thing" ("Audio Commentary").

When asked for his own explanation of his improv style, Downey says, "Well to me, improvisation is when you take something, you add other elements to it, and then you go and shoot that and if something also happens to come up, that's it, but to me, an improvisation usually has to start from upping the wit factor in what you're doing. It's not like I'm just bangin' out one-liners in the moment" ("Movie Star"). Downey told Howard Stern in 1995 that he likes to ad lib because, "If I don't do that, I feel like I haven't really brought all I could to the part." While filming his more recent movies such as the *Iron Man* and *Sherlock Holmes* films, he has worked with writers and directors to contribute his own ideas to the original scripts. Despite his insistence on teamwork, however, he still trusts his own ideas. Even while making *Iron Man 3* with Shane Black, Downey says,

> I respect him so much that I did not respect his day to day writing at all and I just looked at scenes at the beginning of the day as, well, they had to put a bunch of words on this or they couldn't have a call sheet. These are called sides. I call them three-piece. Three pieces of paper with print on them. Which must be annoying to an excellent writer, but that's just the way I've been conditioned. I get a good script and go, "This is good! I mean, we're not going to shoot it, but..." [Lussier].

Directors like Phillips, Altman, Toback, Foster, and Black value and appreciate Downey's improvisations. Others, such as Richard Attenborough, Michael Hoffman, and Mike Figgis had to deal with the actor during times when he was unsuccessfully struggling with addiction, but they all speak highly of him and of his acting style. Downey himself admits, "There've been times when I've been treated by directors—critics, even—better really than I might have deserved" (qtd. in Garbarino, "Last Party"). Even though he made a few of his movies on autopilot, those he worked with never stopped being impressed.

Even in 1994, before such diverse roles as *A Scanner Darkly* and *The Soloist*, he was called "Hollywood's hardest actor to pigeonhole" (Sanello). Despite the wide range of roles he has played and the different approaches and styles of the directors, all praise his uncanny ability to embody a character. "I don't know anybody who does as many things well as Robert does," says *Air America* screenwriter John Eskow ("Commentary"). In this book, Christian B. Long compares Downey's "virtuosity" to a political strategy that offers charm as a "solution" to real-world problems. Diana Hawkins and Sir Richard Attenborough, who made *Chaplin* with Downey, thought he was an eccentric genius. In Germany in June of 1992 to record voice-overs, Downey

> scann[ed] his page of dialogue for less than ten seconds before casting it contemptuously aside ... then proceed[ed] to deliver every one of his lines; each exquisitely timed, totally in character and, amazingly, word-perfect.... Staring at the disappearing tail lights, Dick [said]: "Would you believe it? The little bugger can act, sing, dance, play the piano and compose like an angel. And, as if that wasn't enough, he's got a photographic memory" [Hawkins qtd. in Attenborough 233–234].

When Scott Rudin, former president of production at Fox, told a journalist, "I think of all his peers Robert seems to be the one with the widest range and the most natural electricity. Very few actors have that combination of mercurial energy and emotional depth. He's now the guy that everybody in Hollywood wants," it was 1989 (Hoban). Not much has changed. Admired for his ability to simultaneously disappear into and bring life to roles like Julian in *Less Than Zero* and Charlie Chaplin, Downey has always been well liked by both critics and directors.

Nevertheless, by the late 1990s, Downey had become miserably disenchanted with his career, realizing he had appeared in flop after flop while trying either to do something creative and artistic (such as the 1995 period piece *Restoration* which sent him into a major downward spiral in terms of drug use) or to simply pay the bills for his lifestyle ("Interview"). Now, he can afford to be pickier about the roles he signs on for. He tries to do something different, not "derivative," even within his genre-confined franchises. He doesn't want to sell "the same soap over and over again" ("Movie Star"). He respects the audience and tries to put himself in moviegoers' place, as a fellow film lover.

At first glance, Downey's roles seem to have little in common—a rich-kid drug addict, an English vaudevillian and filmmaker, a journalist, a serial killer, a lawyer, a detective, a writer, a principal, a black army sergeant, a superhero—but a closer study reveals that most of the characters he has portrayed on film tend to raise similar issues concerning identity. Many of them are dual roles—characters who, either deliberately or subconsciously, occupy at least two different identities at once. Some of these portrayals of duality, such as the basic superhero premise of the *Iron Man* films, films like *Restoration* (1995) in which Downey's character, Lord Merivel, is basically a beard for the king's relationship with his favorite mistress, or the bad-guy-posing-as-a-good-guy of *U.S. Marshals*, are obvious but others, including Kirk Lazarus/Lincoln Osiris of *Tropic Thunder*, Dan Dark of *The Singing Detective*, and even Nathan Gardner of *Charlie Bartlett* (the ethics of which are explored in this collection by Fernando Gabriel Pagnoni Berns) are more complex.

In almost every film he's been in, Downey has played a character with an ambiguous or deceptive identity. In *Chaplin, Two Girls and a Guy, A Scanner Darkly, The Singing Detective, Kiss Kiss Bang Bang, Tropic Thunder,* and the Iron Man films, Downey's characters all struggle with questions of identity and help to destabilize identity categories. For *Chaplin*, he is sometimes the Little Tramp, sometimes a poor Victorian boy, and sometimes a Hollywood tycoon. In *Two Girls and a Guy*, he is leading a deceptive life, telling each of two women that he loves only her and when he does tell the truth about his mother, no one believes him. *A Scanner Darkly* features Downey as a type of double-agent: a paranoid, drug-addicted snitch who turns in his friend (who is an undercover cop). *The Singing Detective* is actually a pulp fiction writer who escapes from his diseased body into a fantasy world in which he plays a stereotypical private eye. In *Kiss Kiss Bang Bang* (a movie that, according to Ruth O'Donnell, highlights Downey's expertise with portraying "fragile masculinity"), Harry Lockhart is a thief pretending to be an actor pretending to be a private detective. And as Iron Man, he is, of course, both Tony Stark, a brilliant but self-absorbed inventor, and Iron Man, a superhero in a suit who sacrifices his own pleasure for the sake of others. As Mike Hernandez writes in his essay, "*The Avengers* in Post–9/11 America," in many ways the Tony Stark character as Downey plays him is about acknowledging his responsibility—to himself as well as to others. Even in *Tropic Thunder*, Downey "make[s] use of a category that can be called into question, made to account for what it excludes" (Butler, "Imitation" 311). Through the vehicle of racial satire (and blackface), he and the film's creators make use of a black stereotype in order to question it. Kirk Lazarus is an Australian actor who becomes so confused about his identity that he almost believes he *is* his character—a black army sergeant named Lincoln Osiris.

Derek Adams writes in his essay that "Downey's exceptional skill in negotiating the one-man-plays-two-distinct-yet-interconnected-roles-in-the-same-film character labyrinth is affirmation of his acting greatness. He captures the intricacies of black speech and mannerisms through Lazarus to a degree that makes Sgt. Osiris believable as a black character." He had actually done the same thing several times before, for example while playing Chaplin playing the Little Tramp; or in *Heart and Souls* (explored by Tony Prichard in "Facing Life with Face Off") in which he plays a man who is temporarily partly possessed by several other characters; or in *Chances Are*, in which he plays a man who has been reincarnated but remembers his previous life, essentially playing two characters in one body; or even in *The Shaggy Dog*, in which he plays an evil genius and a canine simultaneously. Directors tend to ask for Downey specifically to play these complicated roles because he has this unique ability. Ron Underwood, director of *Heart and Souls*, said, "I honestly don't know if the film could have been made without him" (qtd. in Falk 92). When asked about his method on this complicated film, Downey self-mockingly said, "It's hard to explain my creative process" ("VH1 Interview").

Further complicating the theme of identity in these works, the actor's personal life and own issues with his public image contribute an undeniable presence to his roles. Perhaps more than any other actor, Robert Downey Jr. seems to merge his own identity with that of his characters, not like a Method actor who "becomes" the character, but more like someone who's peeling away at layers of his own identity, both causing in the other characters and

Downey (left) in makeup as Dan Dark and Mel Gibson as his psychiatrist Dr. Gibbon in *The Singing Detective* (2003), directed by Keith Gordon.

embodying in his own the catalyst for change. Downey told Charlie Rose in 1995 that for him, making a movie "really is also about the personal journey of making the film and that there are lessons that, you know, that I have as a man that ... sometimes can be in the script, in the kind of films you do." Making *The Singing Detective*, for example, was a good lesson for the actor, who saw the parallels between his character Dan Dark's self-hatred and his personal experience with addiction: "The idea of someone who has a disease that's so humiliating, because it's worn right on the surface of his skin—in my own way, I can relate to that" (qtd. in Udovitch). In the movie, Dark learns how much his own negativity affects his disease. Similarly, talking to a Dutch interviewer about his character in *Kiss Kiss Bang Bang*, Downey said, "I think about Harry and I having basically the same challenges, which is we're the makers of our own problems and but also, you know, like him, essentially just a hardworking guy who wants to do the right thing." Harry ends up being given the opportunity to be someone new in the future, someone who "doesn't have to be so desperate, and doesn't have to be so immoral to survive" ("Dutch Interview"). When he recorded his album *The Futurist* in 2004, Downey's struggles with his own identity became visually apparent. He created the artwork for the cover—a portrait of Downey made up of a photograph of him (by Davis Factor) covered over by his own paintings and doodles. When Jay Leno expressed confusion about the CD having a more palatable, traditionally posed cover photo inserted over the case, Downey explained, "That's who I really am.... I did the freakazoid one and they said, 'Robert, that's very artistic of you. Now we're gonna put this one over it so we can sell it.' And little Bobby was very hurt for a moment."

In his essay on *Tropic Thunder* as postmodern comedy, Brian S. Reinking quotes Linda Hutcheon's comment on postmodernism: "the most important boundaries crossed have been those between fiction and nonfiction" (251). This statement can easily be applied to most of Downey's films, especially recent ones, in which the blurring of the line between his own life and the roles he plays is most apparent. In this sense, Robert Downey Jr. is the personification of postmodernism. In his films, he speaks to audiences about his own life, his past, and his character flaws, through the characters he plays. He identifies with Tony Stark's injury and with his need for moral rehabilitation. As F.E. Pheasant-Kelly points out in "Robert Downey Jr. as Star," whether he's playing Iron Man, Sherlock Holmes, or any other "injured" or flawed character, viewers read his performances not just as enactments of a script or a role, but as part of an ongoing meta-dialogue in the cinema and in the press, about the man himself. Downey said in 2003, "I'm very tangible to people because my fallibility is my forte" (Fischer). Audiences lap up his down-to-earth, self-mocking style and his willingness to lay his own vulnerabilities bare, on screen. Together, this book's analyses of his work demonstrate that it is Downey himself, rather than the roles as they are originally written, who brings poignancy and complexity to his films.

During the Moscow Press Conference for *Iron Man 3*, Sir Ben Kingsley answered a question directed to Downey about what makes the Iron Man franchise so successful:

> I think the reason why this franchise is such an enormous success is that Robert brings to his work a degree of humanity, an understanding of mythology, a kindness, a constant self-questioning, which makes Tony so accessible. There is no arrogance, there is no pomposity; there's always that very touching grain of self-doubt that includes all the audience and therefore it's a very embracing portrayal that always connects with the audience and the reason why Robert can't answer your question is he's too modest so I'm answering for him. He's just a brilliant actor and brings layer and layer and layer and layer to his work and he's a joy to work with.... When you look at the extraordinary range of roles that Robert has played—*extraordinary* range of roles—it's because they're all inside him, layered inside him, and it just takes a little alarm call or wake-up call to bring that amazing character out of him.

Works Cited

Attenborough, Richard. "Strolling into the Sunset." Special Features. *Chaplin*. 15th Anniversary Edition. Dir. Richard Attenborough. Maple Pictures, 1992. DVD.

Attenborough, Richard, and Diana Hawkins. *Entirely Up to You, Darling*. London: Hutchinson, 2008. Print.

The Avengers. Dir. Joss Whedon. Paramount, 2012. Blu-ray.

Butler, Judith. "Imitation and Gender Insubordination." *The Lesbian and Gay Studies Reader*. Ed. Henry Abelove, Michèle Aina Barale, David M. Halperin. New York: Routledge, 1993. Print. 307–320.

Chances Are. Dir. Emile Ardolino, TriStar, 1989.

Chaplin. 15th Anniversary Edition. Dir. Richard Attenborough. Maple Pictures, 1992. DVD.

Charlie Bartlett. 2007. Dir. Jon Poll. *The Robert Downey Jr. Collection*. Fox Home Entertainment, 2009. DVD.

The Charlie Rose Show. PBS. 20 Dec. 1995. Television.

Downey, Robert, Jr. *The Futurist*. Sony Classical, 2004. CD.

Due Date. Dir. Todd Phillips. Warner Bros., 2010. DVD.

"Dutch Interview." *Cannes Film Festival*. May 2005. Audio and Video Index. *Downey Unlimited Forever*. Web. 6 Jan. 2014.

Eskow, John. "Commentary." *Air America*. Special Edition. Dir. Roger Spottiswoode. Lions Gate Home Entertainment, 1990. DVD.

Falk, Ben. *Robert Downey Jr.: The Fall and Rise of the Comeback Kid*. London: Portico, 2010. Print.

Fischer, Paul. "Interview: Robert Downey Jr. for *The Singing Detective*." *Dark Horizons.com*, 3 Mar. 2003. Web. 1 Aug. 2013.

Fleming, Michael. "The Real Robert Downey Jr." *Playboy*, Nov. 2010: n. pag. Articles and Interviews. *Downey Unlimited Forever*. Web. 3 Aug. 2013.

Foster, Jodie. "Director's Commentary." *Home for the Holidays*. 1995. Dir. Jodie Foster. *The Robert Downey Jr. Collection*. Fox Home Entertainment, 2009. DVD.

Garbarino, Steve. "Robert Downey's Last Party." *Detour*, Feb. 1999: n. pag. Articles and Interviews. *Downey Unlimited Forever*. Web. 8 Aug. 2013.
Germain, David. "'Iron Man 3' Stars Robert Downey Jr. Gwyneth Paltrow Enjoy Ironclad Friendship." *Daily Freeman*, 7 May 2013. Web. 6 Jan. 2014.
Gordon, Keith. "Director's Commentary." *The Singing Detective*. 2003. Dir. Keith Gordon. Paramount Home Entertainment, 2004. DVD.
A Guide to Recognizing Your Saints. 2006. Dir. Dito Montiel. First Look Home Entertainment, 2007. DVD.
Heart and Souls. 1993. Dir. Ron Underwood. Universal, 1998. DVD.
Howard Stern. 1995. MP3. Audio and Video Index. *DowneyUnlimited Forever*. Web. 6 Jan. 2014.
In Dreams. Dir. Neil Jordan. Dreamworks, 1999. DVD.
Iron Man Ultimate 2-Disc Edition. Dir. Jon Favreau. Paramount, 2008. DVD.
Iron Man 3. Dir. Shane Black. Disney, 2013.
"*Iron Man 3* Moscow Press Conference." *You Tube*, 11 Apr. 2013. Web. 6 Jan. 2014.
The Judge. Dir. David Dobkin. Warner Bros., 2014. Film.
Kiss Kiss Bang Bang. 2005. Dir. Shane Black. Warner Bros., 2006. DVD.
Less Than Zero. 1987. Dir. Marek Kanievska. Fox Home Entertainment, 2001. DVD.
Lussier, Germain. "Interview: 'Iron Man 3' Star Robert Downey Jr. Opens Up About Contracts, Phase Two, and His Colleagues." *Slash Film*, 7 Mar. 2013. Web. 6 Jan. 2014.
"Marvel Cliffhanger: Robert Downey Jr.'s $50 Million Sequel Showdown." *Hollywood Reporter*, 7 May 2013. Web. 6 Jan. 2014.
"Movie Star Bios: Robert Downey Jr." Narr. James Tobin. *You Tube*, 30 Mar. 2011. Web. 11 Aug. 2013.
Natural Born Killers: The Director's Cut. 1994. Dir. Oliver Stone. Warner Bros., 2009. DVD.
The Pick-up Artist. 1987. Dir. James Toback. Fox Home Entertainment, 2009. DVD.
Pomerantz, Dorothy. "Robert Downey Jr. Tops Forbes' List of Hollywood's Highest-Paid Actors." *Forbes*, 16 July 2013. Web. 17 Aug. 2013.
Restoration. Dir. Michael Hoffman. Miramax Home Entertainment, 1995. DVD.
Robbins, Brian, and David Hoberman. "Audio Commentary." *The Shaggy Dog*. Dir. Brian Robbins. Disney Home Entertainment, 2006. DVD.
"Robert Downey Jr. Interview." *Hollywood Conversations*, 20 Aug. 1998. Narr. Mike Figgis. *You Tube*, 6 May 2013. Web. 11 Aug. 2013.
Sanello, Frank. "Natural Born Talent." *Cosmopolitan*, Jan. 1994: n. pag. Articles and Interviews. *Downey Unlimited Forever*. Web. 5 Aug. 2013.
A Scanner Darkly. Dir. Richard Linklater. Warner Bros., 2006. DVD.
The Shaggy Dog. Dir. Brian Robbins. Disney Home Entertainment, 2006. DVD.
Sherlock Holmes. 2009. Dir. Guy Ritchie. Warner Bros., 2010. Blu-Ray.
The Singing Detective. 2003. Dir. Keith Gordon. Paramount Home Entertainment, 2004. DVD.
The Soloist. Dir. Joe Wright. Paramount, 2009. Blu-Ray.
Soriano, Camille. "Face to Face." *In Fashion*, Jan./Feb. 1987: n. pag. Articles and Interviews. *Downey Unlimited Forever*. Web. 11 Aug. 2013.
Tropic Thunder. Dir. Ben Stiller. Dreamworks Home Entertainment, 2008. DVD.
Two Girls and a Guy. 1997. Dir. James Toback. Fox Home Entertainment, 2000. DVD.
Tyley, Jodie. "The End of the Iron Age." *SciFi Now* 79 (Spring 2013): 22–27. Print.
Udovitch, Mim. "The Sobering Life of Robert Downey Jr." *New York Times*, 19 Oct. 2003: SM34. *Proquest*. Web. 31 Oct. 2013.
U.S. Marshals. Dir. Stuart Baird. Warner Bros., 1998. DVD.
"VH1 Interview on *Heart and Souls*." 1993. Audio and Video Index. *Downey Unlimited Forever*. Web. 6 Jan. 2014.
Vineberg, Steve. "Delivering Something Real To 'Ally McBeal.'" *New York Times*, 18 Mar. 2001. Web. 2 Jan. 2013.

The Pick-Up Artist and the Failures of Virtuosity

Christian B. Long

James Toback's 1978 film *Fingers* opens with a ninety-second shot of Jimmy Fingers (Harvey Keitel) behind a piano, practicing Bach's *Toccata and Fugue in E Minor*. Fingers longs to be a concert pianist, but is caught between this desire and his job as a debt collector for his mobbed-up father, and he would appear to be very different from Robert Downey Jr.'s middle-class Jack Jericho in another Toback film, *The Pick-Up Artist* (1987). Nevertheless, the latter film functions as a sort of sequel to *Fingers*. *The Pick-Up Artist* also begins with its protagonist alone, honing his craft, as Jack Jericho practices his pick-up patter in the bathroom mirror. But whereas *Fingers* investigates and queries musical virtuosity, *The Pick-Up Artist* investigates and queries verbal virtuosity. Jimmy Fingers hopes that his virtuoso job skill, as it were, will provide him an exit from debt, and his failure is very much a product of the reduced circumstances of late–1970s New York. Jack Jericho puts his virtuosity to a different use, to create the appearance of abundance so identified with the Reagan era. *The Pick-Up Artist's* opening sequence alternates between Jericho's patter in the mirror and the Manhattan this patter seems to create, one full of gorgeous, scantily-clad women, embodying the dream that speaking and believing in a narrative can create it. In this manner, *The Pick-Up Artist*, like *Fingers*, confronts the key virtuosity of its cultural and political moment. In the cultural sphere, the film reflects and refracts the heightened cultural profile of pick-up artistry, detailed most famously in Ross Jeffries' *How to Get the Women You Desire Into Bed: A Down and Dirty Guide to Dating and Seduction For the Man Who's Fed Up With Being Mr. Nice Guy*, which was rooted in a Neuro-linguistic programming (NLP) model that claims, "Problems will always be with us. The problem is not the problem; the problem is the way people cope" (Andreas & Andreas 183). Ronald Reagan deployed this very thinking (material conditions are not the problem, the way the nation thinks about them is) to great effect in his two terms as president. But for all Jack Jericho's pick-up artist virtuosity, he cannot change the material conditions that matter; his verbal facility cannot erase the debt Randy (Molly Ringwald), his romantic interest, faces. The film's recourse to a *deus ex machina*-derived happy ending reveals the shortcomings of Jack's—and the era's—particular virtuosity. The moment a neuro-linguistic programming approach fails, it ceases to paper over the cracks it has obscured and instead reveals them too clearly. This essay takes up David Palmer's call to "rethink both the rhetorical and ideological roles of virtuosity in social interaction" (354). For Palmer, "[e]xamining how virtuosic display operates as a personification of a community's values might provide vital insight into the practices and performance strategies operating within the system" (354). In *The Pick-Up Artist*, and in *Fingers*, we see that virtuosity—both in failure and in success—offers a great deal to film makers, who can wrestle with the ways in which total mastery might operate. However, even the fictional characters within Toback's movies come to see that virtuosity represents the triumph of fantasy as a way to deal with concrete problems, not a way to solve them.

Ross Jeffries, Ronald Reagan, Robert Downey Jr.

James Toback's films invite not just auteurist criticism, but also biographical criticism. His lifelong fascination with and implication in the world of not-quite-legitimate gambling, for example, figures prominently from the first film he wrote, *The Gambler* (1974), through his writer-director projects *Fingers*, *The Pick-Up Artist*, *Black and White* (1999), and *Harvard Man* (2001) to his screenplay of Las Vegas film, *Bugsy* (1991). *Black and White* also reveals Toback's interest in African-American culture, especially its masculinities. He co-wrote football star Jim Brown's memoir and then cast him in *Fingers*; thirty years later he cast another iconic African-American athlete, Mike Tyson, in *Black and White* before directing a documentary on him, *Tyson* (2008). In addition to his compulsive gambling, Toback is also well-known as a pick-up artist (of sorts). In the same 1989 issue of *Spy Magazine* that details Toback's sleazy pick-up attempts in a fold-out insert—a formulaic combination of I'm-a-director, name drop, making a film, call me, Harvard Club, numerology and danger (Demetz)—Paul Simms provides a handy chart, "Will The Real James Toback Please Pipe Down," that compares the real Toback and the fictional Jack Jericho in order to offer "special insight into how he sees himself. Or how he wants us to see him. Or how he wants credulous video-renting women to see him" (88). In short, *The Pick-Up Artist* is something of a *film-à-clef* that arrived in theaters at the same time that "Ross Jeffries, who described himself as unattractive and frustrated, wrote a small book called 'How to Get the Women You Desire in Bed.' His method was based on an adaptation of neuro-linguistic programming, a school of hypnosis holding that one can communicate with the subconscious through seemingly normal conversation" (Strauss).

Toback's interest in debt and pick-up virtuosity underpins *The Pick-Up Artist*, in which the director again cast Keitel as a collector, Alonzo. Whereas public debt was the cause of New York's near-downfall, private debt grew throughout the decade, fuelled by the increased degree of financial deregulation. As Paul Krugman summarizes the decade and its repercussions, "The change in America's financial rules was Reagan's biggest legacy. And it's the gift that keeps on taking" (Krugman). *The Pick-Up Artist*, like *Fingers*, resolves its narrative conflict by choosing the dominant economic and cultural model. Jack and Randy lift a moment out of cinema history (more on this moment later) to repay their debt. In this way, *The Pick-Up Artist* ends with a critical engagement with Reagan's impact on political life, presenting a forced happy ending drawn from film rather than history.

To discuss the film's conclusion, it is necessary to spend some time getting to know how Jack Jericho works and looking in some detail at two figures key to the rhetoric of virtuosity in the 1980s: President Ronald Reagan and Ross Jeffries, author of *How to Get the Women*

You Desire in Bed. Jeffries' 1992 book functions as a summary of pick-up artists who had been (self-) publishing since at least the 1970s, as with Eric Weber's book and cassette "seminars," *How to Talk to Girls* (1971), frequently advertised in, among others, *Spy Magazine* and many pornographic magazines. Jack Jericho occupies the intersections of Reagan's and Jeffries' deployment of the rhetoric of virtuosity, revealing not just that pick-up artistry pervades the decade's cultural and political life, but also that this pervasive presence creates undesirable limits on everyday economic life.

Much like pick-up artists Jeffries or Toback or Jack Jericho, politicians lean on formula in making their case to voters. Before the twenty-four-hour news cycle and the advent of cable news (CNN started in 1979), it was a little easier for a politician to repeat him or herself from town to town. As Nelson Polsby, Aaron Wildavsky and David Hopkins note in *Presidential Elections: Strategies and Structures of American Politics*:

> Most candidates are likely to follow Kennedy and Nixon, Johnson and Goldwater, and Carter and Ford in using just a few set speeches. Ronald Reagan's virtuoso shuffling of his well-worn index cards, with their anecdotes of questionable accuracy, seems to have served him well enough. In view of the pervasive inattention to public affairs and political talk in our society, this approach may have the advantage of driving a few key points home (as well as driving mad the news correspondents who must listen to the same thing all the time) [201].

What distinguished Reagan was his ability to make the most of his limited number of examples; the specious content didn't convince, Reagan's delivery did. While the factual basis of Reagan's claims was often shaky, such an approach fits within the NLP approach to confronting problems. As Richard Bandler explains in Using Your Brain—for a CHANGE, in NLP, "we deliberately make up lies, in order to try to understand the subjective experience of a human being. When you study subjectivity, there's no use trying to be objective" (Bandler 19). Ross Jeffries exhorts his pick-up artist trainees to combine formula and fiction repeatedly; How to Get the Women You Desire in Bed contains not just the six-step process of "How To Install The Super Get Laid Attitudes In Yourself So You Use Them Automatically" (Jeffries is a fan of all caps) and the five rules for "phone pitching" a date, but also an advertisement for more Jeffries material, including "the 4 major attitudes of the 'super studs' and how to make them part of your own personality automatically" and "The AIRIP formula for meeting and picking up women anywhere!" (76). Bandler sums this NLP approach up as "If you make really vivid images in your mind—especially if you can make them externally—you can learn how to be a civil engineer or a psychotic. One pays better than the other, but it's not as much fun. What people do has structure, and if you can find out about that structure, you can figure out how to change it" (15). Like a politician polishes a speech, finding the applause lines and the bum notes, The Pick-Up Artist returns to Jack's mirror practice over and over, showing him installing the attitude—and its upgrades—key to his formulaic pick-up script.

The appearance of caring appears in Ross Jeffries' pick-up manual in chapters like "FAKE LIKE YOU ARE WARM AND FRIENDLY." To put across how important being nice is, Jeffries charmingly compares women to children and animals: "Even the nastiest person finds it hard to react fearfully or angrily to someone who makes them feel loved and appreciated.... Conveying warmth and affinity isn't so tough—just think of how you look and sound when you see a niece or nephew, or even a pet that delights you" (Jeffries 17–18). *The Pick-Up Artist* in fact goes out of its way to make Jack a fairly decent young man who exhibits genuine warmth and friendliness—he takes care of his grandmother, teaches grade school, and foils muggings by singing Elvis songs. However, Jack also performs niceness in his pursuit of phone numbers and hook-ups, his patter full of fawning praise, "greats," and "excellents." President Reagan had a way of conveying sincerity that Garry Wills describes in terms of a by-rote performance: "[Reagan] lacks the vocal idiosyncrasy of Presidents Kennedy or Johnson, Nixon or Carter. Even his trademark opening—'Well...'—is not John Wayne's 'Waal,' or Gary Cooper's 'Wul,' or Jimmy Stewart's up-and-down-the-scale 'We-e-e-l.' It is just a vocal intake of breath, done as part of Reagan's choreography of candor: eyes down, eyes up, smile, slight dip of head to the right, and begin" (162). Jeffries also advises combining acting like you care with saying one thing and meaning another as a route to sex. Most of Jeffries' "First Date Screw Techniques" involve generating a link between the pick-up artist's voice or touch and a pleasant memory or sensation in the woman he's talking to. On the surface it's harmless bar banter and party tricks, but "Anchoring" or "Sensory Overlap," Jeffries promises, can turn ordinary phrases into passports to sex.

The NLP pick-up artist approach closely resembles what has come to be known as "dog-whistle politics." William Safire, who worked in the Nixon White House and also wrote the *New York Times'* "On Language" feature, defined dog-whistle politics in a 2005 column: "The idea behind the political metaphor—dog-whistle politics—is not who hears your signal, but who does not have the special sensitivity to catch the message. Your whistle is pitched high enough to rally your "base" without running the risk of turning out your opposition's base. Nice turn of phrase" (Safire). While it's true that Democratic politicians use dog whistles, in the 1980s the Republican Party, and its standard bearer President Ronald Reagan, put dog whistles to the most effective use. Examples of this effectiveness include Reagan's Cadillac-driving Welfare Queen, and his speech on states' rights in Neshoba County, Mississippi. Rather than confronting the root causes of the nation's economic distress—globalization, deregulation, deindustrialization, and so on—Americans opted for a different approach throughout the 1980s. As Jefferson Cowie concludes *Stayin' Alive: The 1970s and the Last Days of the Working Class*, dog-whistling "figures like George Wallace, Richard Nixon, and Ronald Reagan offered *psychic* salve to the wounds of pride" working-class whites felt most painfully in their pocketbooks (217, my emphasis). One of the mantras of the American right credits Reagan with restoring American pride; after all the strife of the late 1960s and the 1970s, he made Americans feel good about being American again. Or, to use NLP and pick-up artist lingo, Reagan (like many politicians) made up lies, using vivid images like a city on a hill, in order to improve the subjective experience—the feelings—of late-twentieth-century American voters. Such an approach does not generate long-term solutions, but a pick-up artist like Jack Jericho doesn't mind.

"Hi, I'm Jack Jericho": Copia in The Pick-Up Artist

The anonymous and fleeting nature of Jack's pick-ups, even the successful ones, embodies the two factors that Paulo Virno identifies as key to a virtuoso performance—"an activity which finds its own fulfillment (that is, its own purpose) in itself" and "an activity which requires the presence of others" (53). Jack consistently exhibits a particularly verbal sort of virtuosity in his near-monologue pick-up attempts. To be more specific, Jack's virtuosity takes the form of what Erasmus would call "copia." Although they may have a great deal to say, say it well, and even tailor it to their audiences, young people like Jack Jericho, untrained virtuosos, too often substitute quantity for quality. "I am instructing youth," Erasmus writes, "in whom extravagance of speech does not seem wrong to Quintilian, because with judgment, superfluities are easily restrained, certain of them even, age itself wears away, while on the other hand, you cannot by any method cure meagerness and poverty" (14). That is, copia can be an effective approach, but it requires a great deal of effort to make copia work. For Erasmus, reading and study are essential to creating the background to facilitate copia:

> It not infrequently happens that we have to say the same thing several times, in which case, if destitute of copia we will either be at a loss, or, like the cuckoo, croak out the same words repeatedly, and be unable to give different shape or form to the thought. And thus betraying our want of eloquence we will appear ridiculous ourselves and utterly exhaust our wretched audience with weariness [Erasmus 16].

The Pick-Up Artist's opening sequence simultaneously casts shadows over Jack's use of copia in his pick-up artistry. On the one hand, Jack's film-opening recitation to the mirror betrays his want of eloquence; he practices a formula—(Hi) + (face of artist A) + (body of artist B) + (chat up line) + (name?) + (phone number + photographic memory)—that becomes ridiculously, abundantly, and even wearyingly clear. As with *Fingers*, the film confronts not the characters of the film's fictional world, but its audience with the shortcomings of virtuosity: Downey's copia reveals Jack's lack. On the other hand, within the film's narrative, Jack's copia works, when it does, because a woman hears his patter only once.

The first five minutes of *The Pick-Up Artist* set up Jack Jericho as an immensely charming and handsome young man, with the doo-wop soundtrack providing a hint of innocence to prevent his compulsive pick-up artist habits from rendering him grotesque (it features "Da Do Run Run" by The Crystals, a song Spitting Image turned into the mock campaign song "Da Do Run Ron," in 1984). As the opening credits finish, Jack watches from across the street as a man pinches a woman's butt. She kicks the man, chasing him away. A cut to a close-up of Jack, in a flashback of sorts, practicing in the mirror indicates that Jack will try to pick her up. Even a seasoned pick-up artist like Ross Jeffries admits that

> One of the toughest places to pick-up women is right on the street, and that's why I love it; it's a real challenge.... The absolute *key* to street pick-ups is to be very upbeat, happy, warm and friendly. Do NOT come on heavy on the street. Women are naturally (and justly) cautious in the big city [31].

Jack, though, charges ahead, rushing down the sidewalk toward the woman as she walks away. As he catches up to her, he starts talking and doesn't stop for the next fifty seconds: "Excuse me, my name's Jack Jericho" he says as she rolls her eyes and looks away, "and I saw what you just did and I just wanna say one thing to you and then I'll disappear and we'll probably never see each other again as long as we live on this planet. OK?" When she replies with a completely uninterested "Uh huh," Jack maintains his manic energy, saying, "Great I love the way you said that. What's your name?" She replies, again in a monotone, "Karen." At this point, Jack delivers a very upbeat, happy, warm and friendly cascade of words:

> Karen. That's a phenomenal name. Ok here's what was on my mind. I think you should get a medal. I'm totally serious. You were brave, you were graceful, you were totally right. I wish I had

a camera. Guys like that give meeting strangers a bad name. That's a personal affront to me personally because I have a vested interest in meeting strangers you know see, every woman that I've ever liked or communed with or given great satisfaction to always started off as a complete stranger and only became known to me because I followed the impulse I felt when I saw her and I went up to her and I said, politely with a smile, hi, I'm Jack Jericho and I like you do you like me. Anyway, in the name of men who truly appreciate desire and respect women allow me to apologize for that buffoon and to wish you great luck and good fortune.

This pick-up shows copia working because Jack smuggles the pick-up inside a torrent of well-delivered off-kilter praise. The purposely clunky construction of "personal affront to me personally" choreographs candor, and the "politely" to describe how he talks to women builds on that signal to show that he's not a sleazy pick-up artist. The moment that underscores Jack's pick-up artistry and Downey's acting skill (and perhaps Toback's blocking) comes when Jack slows down his patter to say "great satisfaction" while he makes eye contact with Karen even though they're crossing the street at the time. On this score, he's implementing a version of the "anchoring" plan Jeffries lays out, coming close to Jeffries' view of women as people to be duped, to be spoken to in dog-whistled code. Anchoring seems to work; Jack's slowed-down speech and mention of pleasure intrigues Karen, drawing her first smile in the scene. After delivering his speech, Jack feigns to walk away, satisfied that he has set the hook. Karen calls him back, and the look of smug satisfaction on Jack's face as he turns is almost unbearable. Jack's face reveals that his patter succeeds not because of the words, but because of their delivery. Karen's response of calling Jack back is motivated by a clever bit of poststructuralist pick-up artistry: Jack betrays his "want of eloquence" and then walks away to convince Karen that he's genuine. Or, as Jeffries puts it, "The important principle to apply here is that the meaning of your communication is the response it gets. If you use a tone of voice or a facial expression that makes women fearful or suspicious, then no matter how clever your words are, the message you convey to her is that she should be afraid and suspicious of you" (18). Going by the book—both Jeffries' and Erasmus'—leads Jack to pick-up success.

Jack's successes turn out to be relatively rare and necessarily short-lived. In the same moment that Karen gives him her phone number, Jack spots another beautiful woman, Rae, and he stops paying attention to Karen to dash off to his next pick-up. *The Pick-Up Artist* makes clear that copia demands further study to be consistently effective. As Erasmus puts it, "Elegance consists partly in words used by suitable authors; partly in using the right word; and partly in using it in the right expression…. Accordingly, they err greatly who think that it matters nothing in what words something is expressed, provided only it is in some way understandable" (18).

When Jack chats up Rae she doesn't even break her stride or look at him as she dismisses his formula patter. Once Jack arrives at work, he receives another lesson in the importance of study to copia. His principal asks, "Did you tell Stephen Merchant's mother she had the face of a Chagall and the body of a Reuben?" After they discuss the need for Jack to be a little less flirty, the principal adds, almost as an afterthought, "and another thing: Chagall's women aren't beautiful and Reuben's women are fat." In the place of a cut to a close-up of Jack that would indicate that he'd learned and internalized the lesson, the film cuts to Jack practicing in the mirror again, asking, "Anyone ever tell you you have the face of a Botticelli and the body of a Degas?" He gets the artists right this time—Venus faces and ballet dancer bodies—and the next shot proves as much, cutting to Lulu's (Victoria Jackson) smiling face. The only reason Jack is not successful with his new and improved vocabulary for seduction is that Lulu's gangster boyfriend Alonzo (Harvey Keitel) shows up. If you're planning on going by the book to pick up women, studying clearly pays off.

But an audience that studies can undo Jack's pick-up artistry. Randy, a museum docent, understands the art world that Jack invokes, giving her an advantage when Jack tries to use his usual shtick. Thus when Jack repeats his "has anyone ever told you you have the face of a Botticelli and the body of a Degas" line, Randy, who also happens to be carrying a book on Botticelli, replies, "My tenth grade art teacher" before warning Jack, "I think with an opening like that there's nowhere to go but down." Even after Jack has successfully picked her up, and they're having sex in his car, Randy deflates his use of copia. Over a shot of Jack's car parked in Central Park, Jack's voice narrates, "Is there anything in the whole cosmos that could make this moment any more perfect than it is right now?" Randy answers, "Uh huh. Just one. If you could keep absolutely quiet for the next fifteen seconds, I'll come." Randy is the witness who rejects the basis of Jack's pick-up artist virtuosity, his use of copia. In other words, Randy's decision to talk to Jack, to have sex with Jack, and later, to get help from Jack, thus only makes sense in terms of the generic conventions of a romantic comedy starring Robert Downey Jr. a charismatic lead who can turn more or less sleazy lines into something charming.

The Last Hamburger on Earth

The Pick-Up Artist builds its resolution to show that Jack's charm and verbal virtuosity cannot pay back Flash and Randy's debts. To find twenty-five thousand dollars, Jack helps in the only way he can—by being Robert Downey Jr. super-charming film actor. Thus, the film leaves more or less comfortable Manhattan for the more economically disadvantaged spaces of the subway, Coney Island, and Atlantic City at the same time that it changes its attention from Jack Jericho's virtuosity within the film narrative to Robert Downey Jr.'s virtuosity in the creation of that narrative. In this manner, *The Pick-Up Artist* establishes a strong connection between Randy and real economic distress, and Jack and fantasy. Even before the film leaves Manhattan, Randy's appearance signals financial troubles. When the audience first sees Randy, Alonzo the mob debt collector threatens her. Immediately after, Alonzo's girlfriend Lulu tries to convince Randy to go out with mobbed-up Fernando, acknowledging the financial character of the situation: "I'd call it trying to talk somebody into going out with someone rich for their own good. I mean rich is better than poor no matter what, isn't it?" The next time Randy appears, it's in an off-track betting parlor, where a fellow gambler sees her betting on long shots and asks, "Flash in trouble again?" Randy answers, "Like everybody else." And the Coney Island place where Randy looks after her alcoholic father, Flash (Dennis Hopper), looks like a single-resident occupancy, quite unlike the Manhattan brownstone Jack shares with his grandmother.

Somewhat curiously, and to the film's loss, *The Pick-Up Artist* also switches from a sense of the danger within the fictional world (the money Flash and Randy owe and the danger they face are real) to a sense of comfort with the way film-generic conventions can solve problems. It's here that the film evokes Reagan's ability to convince Americans that fantasy can solve real-world problems. Reagan's political aim of improving the feelings of

Americans ran up against the real world and, judging by approval ratings, the concrete won out over the abstract, at least briefly. John Ranelagh, in his history of the CIA, criticizes Reagan's approach to intelligence in terms that apply to his pick-up artist approach to domestic policy: "what Reagan sought was an administration of tone. His themes were resistance to enemies, support of allies, trade, relief for natural disasters, and resistance to terrorism and subversion. They were all relatively 'easy' issues: very few people are for terrorism or subversion.... It was an administration of atmosphere rather than of substantive policies" (705, 710).

Reagan shares with Jeffries a preference for the telling details that "convince" the audience. Jeffries' step three in Appendix Three's "INDUCING TRANCE STATES IN YOUR DATE USING THE STORY TELLING METHOD" is to "Weave elements of your current situation into the story that are based on your dates [*sic*] current sensory experience" (Jeffries 80). When speaking to a crowd of working-class whites, Reagan could invoke the *Cadillac*-driving welfare queen and her mind-boggling *eighty* identities and four fake dead *veteran* husbands. The people had just driven to a political event in a non-luxury car, intent on solidifying their voting choice/identity as, possibly, a Reagan voter. As for veterans, Reagan once (or perhaps more than once) used part of the plot from the movie *Wing and a Prayer* (1944) as if it were a real event, in a number of campaign speeches. The urban legends reference/debunking page Snopes.com notes that an April 1980 *Los Angeles Times* "news report about a Reagan campaign swing through Wisconsin demonstrates how frequently and effectively the actor-turned-politician made use of it." As the *Los Angeles Times'* Roger Simon relates the story:

> In Racine, Reagan told a large crowd about a B-17 bomber pilot in World War II whose plane was hit over France. The belly gunner was wounded and trapped in his gun turret. And, when the pilot told everyone to bail out, the gunner knew he was doomed. Reagan's face grew thick with emotion. "The kid in the turret cried out with tears," Reagan said. "And so the pilot sat down on the floor of the plane and said: "We'll ride it down together, son." "And that pilot," Reagan said, his voice actually breaking, "was given the Congressional Medal of Honor, posthumously!" What matter to the wildly applauding crowd that Reagan's voice had cracked perfectly each of the three times that he had told the story before. What matter? The crowd knew what Reagan was saying to them. It may look like our plane is on fire, it may look like we are trapped, Ron may look old and tired, but he will see us through. He will sit on the floor of the plane and hold our hands. He will be with us [qtd in Snopes.com].

Here we see the newspaper reporter, familiar with the story from its repetition in town after town, revealing the results of practiced, one might say virtuosic performance. Lou Cannon, who covered Reagan as California's governor and as president, noted that Reagan's aids "adopted Reagan's own standard of judging stories by their impact rather than their accuracy" (40). Just as Jack's pick-up of Karen generates its impact by using fake-clumsy phrasing to communicate honesty ("a personal affront to me personally"), Reagan's Wing and a Prayer story generates its impact by subverting the rules of standard spoken English in an otherwise conversational style. Reagan's story finishes with, "Medal of Honor, posthumously," closing not on the Medal, but "posthumous," an indication that the nation, with Reagan in charge, will once again recognize heroism. This rose-colored use of a fictional event shows that the meaning of Reagan's speech was the response it was designed to generate: tone and atmosphere, rather than concrete/factual acts will change how American political culture conceives of problems. *The Pick-Up Artist*'s critical stance on this approach reassesses the efficacy of managing reactions to the world through audience-specific comforting (and deal-closing) details rather than managing the world itself.

The wheels come off of Jack's ability to change how people think about the world when *The Pick-Up Artist* hits Atlantic City. For all the hard work Randy does—when she first meets Jack she's carrying gambling guides like *The Atlantic City Gamble* and *Blackjack: A Winner's Handbook* in addition to the art book—she loses at the blackjack table; it seems the house always wins. Jack's failed negotiation when he tries to sell his car highlights how pick-up artist skills are of little use when it comes to fixing financial problems. At the used car lot, Jack, Randy, and the used car salesman Marty self-consciously work through a used-car-sale script. Jack starts the negotiation for his Camaro at $6,000, but Marty's counter-offer turns Jack's purposely clunky honesty-signaling sentence construction back on him: "Interest in a Camaro convertible happens to be at an all-time historical low. At this point in time." Jack disputes Marty's description of the Camaro, using the sort of vocabulary that has worked in his pick-ups, calling it, "a phenomenal car … a collector's item." When Marty disagrees, Randy plays her part, saying, "Come on Jack, let's just go," but Marty remains unimpressed. "Forgive me young lady," he says, "that's the oldest trick in the business," and makes a counter-offer of "not a penny over four." Again, Jack follows the script, acting as if he's going to drive away in a huff, only to find that the car won't start. After three tries, Jack leans on the door and, using the same bluff confidence, smiles and tries to sound as nonchalant as possible: "Four thousand sounds reasonable." Much like the politicians Polsby, Wildavsky, and Hopkins describe above, Jack's approach has "served him well enough," but it depends on a version of "the pervasive inattention to public affairs and political talk in our society" (Polsby, Wildavsky, Hopkins 201). Even with Randy's help, Jack can't work his magic on Marty because Marty sees such performances all day, every day.

However, although this setback indicates the more realistic tone of the movie when it shifts to Atlantic City, even this realism erodes into wish-fulfillment as the film moves toward its conclusion. Narrative conventions rescue the film while echoing one of the best-known film romances. Just as *Casablanca's* Annina fends off Renault's sexual advances instead of encouraging them in order to gain money, Randy resists the chance to "date" a Mafioso in place of $25,000 to pay off Alonzo. And just as Annina is rescued by Rick, who rigs a roulette game so that Annina's husband will win their passage money out of Casablanca, Randy is rescued by Jack. Jack gambles everything on one spin of the roulette wheel, and the wheel stops on his lucky number, 13. Jack responds to his roulette win as if it were the most natural, expected outcome: He saunters off to cash in his chips, and not even Randy passionately kissing him fazes him. The big win severs the film's connection with the grimy world of debt and danger and ushers it into the realm of wish-fulfillment. This turn makes the focus of the film's conclusion not the fictional Jack Jericho, but the cinematic apparatus, especially Robert Downey Jr. In Jack's greatest moment of triumph, Downey is restrained. Such underplaying calls attention to Downey's range and leaves room for the shock Randy feels to register in reaction shots.

This quiet is short-lived, as Jack loudly and publicly shames Alonzo for refusing to release Flash. Here Jack projects all of his shortcomings as a pick-up artist onto Alonzo, and then disavows them. In the "Hot Lonnie" speech, Downey over-acts in such a way that it makes clear that Jack is shooting for the cheap seats, much like Judy Garland overacts in character when putting on her corset in *Meet Me in St Louis* (Ray 317–8). The sequence

Jack Jericho (Downey) and Randy Jensen (Molly Ringwald) contemplate their winnings in *The Pick-Up Artist* (1987), written and directed by James Toback.

begins with a long shot of Jack isolated from the gamblers in the casino, shouting at Alonzo, "You're worse than a crook because you're a cheap lying crook!" A cutaway shows a table full of heavies taking notice, and some other casino patrons looking around. Then, still in long shot, Jack says in a loud and clear voice, "I've seen your kind all my life. Everyone has—Hot Lonnie Scalera. He's a pick-up artist, he hits on women everywhere he goes, he walks, he talks, jumps 'em in the back of his car practically breaks their back on the gearshift then takes their number and never calls." During this portion of the speech, Toback cuts to show the casino manager looking unhappy, and then there's a cut into a close up of Jack when he says, "Admit it, Hot Lonnie. Does your mother have to do your dirty laundry? Does your mom have to wash the lipstick off your underpants? Does your mother—" At this point the casino manager interjects, affected by the sordid atmosphere Jack's speech has created, to tell Alonzo to do as Jack says. Jack's speech shows that a virtuosic verbal performance can allow a speaker to control and change a hostile, unfamiliar space. But in changing the room, Jack renounces the very source of his strength, his pick-up artist past. Accordingly, when Jack leaves the casino to profess his love to Randy, she rejects him. After the underplaying at the roulette wheel and the overplaying with Alonzo, Downey for the Oscar reel stand-by: tears. Asserting that the two of them together are not a gamble, Jack finishes his big speech in tears, and rips up his sheet of phone numbers to demonstrate that he has changed for the better and can be part of a monogamous romantic couple, as the generic conventions demand. But Randy remains unconvinced of their suitability, and Jack walks away, teasing that *The Pick-Up Artist* will have a 1970s-style down ending. It doesn't. Virtuoso pick-up artistry creates the conditions for its own obsolescence. The next day, after unconvincingly practicing "Hi. I'm Jack Jericho" in front of the mirror, Jack sees Randy in front of his place, and, after a short conversation, they walk off arm-in-arm, a romantic couple.

This switch from Jack Jericho's virtuosity to Robert Downey Jr.'s virtuosity, informed by narrative necessity, echoes the shift that occurs at the end of *Fingers*. To return to the David Palmer formulation, "[e]xamining how virtuosic display operates as a personification of a community's values might provide vital insight into the practices and performance strategies operating within the system" (354). *Fingers* recognizes how difficult success is to attain—virtuosity seems the only route for Jimmy—and how difficult debt is to escape, ideas that carried a great deal of currency in the Seventies' economic downturn. *Fingers* resigns itself to cinema as the system that can represent escape, as in its ability to represent compelling, violent, narratives. Jimmy finds the debt-flaunting Riccamonza (who has killed Jimmy's father) and fights him in a stairwell, eventually shooting him twice in the face and killing him. *Toccata and Fugue in E Minor* returns as a sound bridge into the film's final shot; rather than performing music, as in the film's first scene, Jimmy kneels with his back to the piano, staring vacantly out the window, and then directly into the camera. Whereas Jimmy used to provide his own diegetic soundtrack, the film ends with non-diegetic music playing. For a musician who fails in front of an audience, Jimmy's look into the camera acknowledges that a different sort of performance in front of a different, and larger, audience takes precedence. The look into the camera acknowledges the cinema audience who has just watched a brutal fight and killing, one that moves from hand-held documentary immediacy to a more stylized jump cut and new-to-the-film sound bridge. For all his resistance, killing a connected guy in the stairwell cements his place in a cinematic and cultural cycle of collecting—and paying back—debts. But this virtuosity is built on and in fiction.

Jack's success within the narrative is based on the power of fiction to change perception. Actually fixing financial troubles emerges out of fantasy—in the generic conventions of the romantic comedy and in Robert Downey Jr.'s performance. This ambivalence makes *The Pick-Up Artist* very much an Eighties film, one with significant Seventies roots. Like *Fingers*, it's interested in the clash between reality and fantasy that virtuosity can mediate. And like *Fingers*, *The Pick-Up Artist* depicts virtuosity as, ultimately, failed. But while in *Fingers* failure leads to the grimness common to Seventies cinema, in *The Pick-Up Artist* failure leads to fantasy solving all problems, aligning *The Pick-Up Artist* with Reagan's approach, which proved so popular as a way of not dealing with real problems but rather wishing them away. *The Pick-Up Artist* likewise recognizes how difficult virtuosity is to attain, and shows that the solutions movies offer ring hollow in light of economic troubles. Jack admits that when it comes to him and Randy as a couple, "It's not worth it. We'd annihilate each other…. We would. Wouldn't we?" Downey is key to this shift because of his persona as a middle-class, attractive young actor able to manipulate people, and also because of how *The Pick-Up Artist* crafts layers of virtuosity into the film—Jack's virtuosity is undergirded by Downey's virtuosity. *The Pick-Up Artist* may not be entirely convinced of the approach pick-up artists and Reagan take, but it cannot conceive of another way to address the world. In much the same way a later Downey film, *Iron Man*, holds out hope that One Great Man can wield the terrible power necessary to set things right, *The Pick-Up Artist*, because it has Robert Downey Jr., reluctantly accepts Reagan as the best the 1980s has to offer.

Works Cited

Andreas, Conniraw, and Steve Andreas. *Heart of the Mind: Engaging Your Inner Power to Change with Neuro-Linguistic Programming.* Moab, UT: Real People Press, 1989. Print.
Bandler, Richard. *Using Your Brain—for a CHANGE.* Ed. Steve Andreas and Connirae Andreas. Moab, UT: Real People, 1985. Print.
Black and White. 1999. Dir. James Toback. Sony Pictures Home Entertainment, 2000. DVD.
Bugsy. 1991. Dir. Barry Levinson. Sony Pictures Home Entertainment, 2006. DVD.
Burt, Martha. "Causes of the Growth of Homelessness During the 1980s." *Understanding Homelessness: New Policy and Research Perspectives.* Washington, D.C.: Fannie Mae Foundation, 1997. 169–203. Web. 31 Jan. 2013.
Cannon, Lou. *President Reagan: The Role of a Lifetime.* New York: Public Affairs, 1991. Print.
Casablanca. 1942. Dir. Michael Curtiz. Warner Home Video, 2003. DVD.
Cowie, Jefferson. *Stayin' Alive: The 1970s and the Last Days of the Working Class.* New York: The New Press, 2010. Print.
Demetz, Vincenza. "The Pick-Up Artist's Guide to Picking Up Women: A Case-By-Case Look at Movie Director James Toback's Street Technique." *Spy Magazine* Mar. 1989: 82–87. Print.
Dempsey, Michael. "Love and Money, Ecstasy and Death." *Film Quarterly* 34.2 (1980): 24–35. Print.
Erasmus. *On Copia of Words and Ideas* (De Utraque Verborum ac Rerum Copia). Trans. Donald King and H. David Rix. Milwaukee: Marquette University Press, 1963. Print.
Fingers. 1978. Dir. James Toback. Turner Home Entertainment, 2002. DVD.
The Gambler. 1974. Dir. Karel Reisz. Paramount, 2002. DVD.
Harvard Man. 2001. Dir. James Toback.. First Look, 2008. DVD.
Iron Man. Dir. Jon Favreau. Paramount, 2008. DVD.
Jeffries, Ross. *How to Get the Women You Desire into Bed: A Down and Dirty Guide to Dating and Seduction for the Man Who's Fed Up with Being Mr. Nice Guy.* Culver City, CA: Jeffries Publishing, 1992. Print.
Krugman, Paul. "Reagan Did It." *New York Times*, 31 May 2009: n. pag. Web. 31 Jan. 2013.
Madrick, Jeff. *Age of Greed: The Triumph of Finance and the Decline of America, 1970 to the Present.* New York: Knopf Borzoi, 2011. Print.
Meet Me in St. Louis. 1944. Dir. Vincente Minnelli. Warner Home Video, 2004.
Newport, Frank, Jeffrey Jones and Lydia Saad. "Ronald Reagan from the People's Perspective: A Gallup Poll Review." Gallup, n. d. Web. 31 Jan. 2013.
OECD. "Income Distribution—Inequality." *OECD StatExtracts*, n. d. Web. 31 Jan. 2013.
Palmer, David L. "Virtuosity as Rhetoric: Agency and Transformation in Paganini's Mastery of the Violin." *Quarterly Journal of Speech* 84:3 (2009): 341–57. Print.
The Pick-Up Artist. 1987. Dir. James Toback. Fox Home Entertainment, 2009. DVD.
Polsby, Nelson, Aaron Wildavsky and David Hopkins. *Presidential Elections: Strategies and Structures of American Politics.* Lanham, MD: Rowman & Littlefield, 2008. Print.
Ranelagh, John. *The Agency: The Rise and Decline of the CIA.* Revised and Updated. New York: Touchstone, 1987. Print.
Ray, Robert. *The ABCs of Classic Hollywood.* Oxford: Oxford University Press, 2008. Print.
Reagan, Ronald. "Address to the Nation on the Iran Arms and Contra Aid Controversy." White House. Washington, D.C. 13 November 1986. Speech. Ronald Reagan Presidential Library Archive. Web. 31 Jan 2013.
_____. "Address to the Nation on the Iran Arms and Contra Aid Controversy." White House. Washington, D.C. 3 March 1987. Speech. Ronald Reagan Presidential Library Archive. Web. 31 Jan 2013.
Safire, William. "On Language: Dog Whistle." *New York Times*, 24 Apr. 2005: n. pag. Web. 31 Jan. 2013.
Shapiro, Robert. "Even Reagan Raised Taxes." *Forbes*, 3 Feb. 2010. Web. 31 Jan. 2013.
Simms, Paul. "Will the Real James Toback Please Pipe Down?" *Spy Magazine* Mar. 1989: 88. Print.
Strauss, Neil. "He Aims! He Shoots! Yes!!" *New York Times*, 25 Jan. 2004. ST1 +. Print.
Tyson. 2008. Dir. James Toback. Sony Pictures Classics, 2009. DVD.
Virno, Paulo. *A Grammar of the Multitude: For an Analysis of Contemporary Forms of Life.* Trans. Isabella Bertoletti, James Cascaito, Andrea Casson. Los Angeles: Semiotext(e), 2004. Web. 31 Jan 2013.
Wills, Garry. *Reagan's America: Innocents at Home.* New York: Penguin, 2000. Print.
A Wing and a Prayer. 1944. Dir. Henry Hathaway. Twentieth Century–Fox. Film.

Delightful, Duplicitous and Flirting with Disaster: James Toback's Robert Downey Jr.

Thomas Britt

Writer/director James Toback cites a couple of key figures in his development as a person and an artist. One is Russian author Fyodor Dostoyevsky and the other is American multi-hyphenate Norman Mailer (Toback and Mailer 75). Toback's filmography reveals the influence of both men on his obsessions with philosophy, gambling, sex, race, and death. A chronicler of various social intersections, Toback is interested in the meeting points of high culture with low, in men who are infatuated with calculating women, and in hustlers of all stripes. Though excessively talky, Toback's films are always hopping with conflict because his characters are constantly on the make.

Cut from a similar cloth as Toback, and very much in the continuum of Mailer's "American existentialist" but with a "Brat Pack" twist, Robert Downey Jr. arrived as a film star with his own potential for hustling and testing limits. Two decades Toback's junior, Downey (born 1965) is generationally perched between the hippies and the yuppies. 1987 was a breakthrough year for the young actor, as two timely films showcased two very different sides of his personality. Whereas Marek Kanievska's *Less Than Zero* revealed Downey the hopeless addict, forever disappointing his friends and family through deceit and drug use, Toback's *The Pick-up Artist* featured Downey the charmer, talking his way into the hearts of female passersby. Certainly based on the writer/director's own exploits with women and gambling, *The Pick-up Artist* allowed Toback to fashion an actor into his own image, or perhaps to discover that they were already kindred spirits.

Toback is particularly indebted to Mailer in his evocation of a conflicted character type Mailer described in his 1957 essay, "The White Negro." Commenting on the postwar emergence of "the American existentialist," Mailer laid out the self-contradictory path of preservation for the "twentieth century man." This is a way of life that accedes to the immediacy of death:

> In short, whether the life is criminal or not, the decision is to encourage the psychopath in oneself, to explore that domain of experience where security is boredom and therefore sickness, and one exists in the present, in that enormous present which is without past or future, memory or planned intention, the life where a man must go until he is beat, where he must gamble with his

energies through all those small or large crises of courage and unforeseen situations which beset his day, where he must be with it or doomed not to swing [339].

What follows is an attempt to characterize Toback and Downey as once inseparable creative forces, whose personal indiscretions and artistic inspirations have fueled (to date) three examinations of "twentieth century man." Their collaborative lens renders this character a hustler, drawn from the philosophy of Dostoyevsky, the "psychic havoc" of Mailer, and most immediately from both filmmaker's and actor's self-destructive tendencies. Are their womanizing, risk-taking and drug use insecure inheritances of the postwar, post-free love, post–Wall Street eras? Perhaps, yes. But their passive placement within socio-historical contexts is merely exposition for their active attempts to contribute to (and exercise those personas within) Hollywood film culture.

This chapter is specifically concerned with the positive and negative effects of turning those destructive tendencies into cinema. *The Pick-up Artist*, *Two Girls and a Guy* (1997), and *Black and White* (1999) form a collective crucible for this filmmaker and actor, who have since come out on very different sides of the Hollywood gamble. In retrospect, their mutual artistic ascendency was a trajectory dependent on exploiting Downey's capacity for delight, duplicity, and disaster. Coinciding with his fall(s) from grace, the actor's work for Toback could be read as creatively fecund but psychologically consuming, with a dimension of vampirism that fed the director as it drained the actor. Though both talk about their experiences on these films as reciprocally sustaining, their individual pathways in the years since they last collaborated make known whose blood most fed these gambles of energy. Downey without Toback is a box office behemoth. Toback without Downey is a filmmaker in retreat.

The oft-repeated self-mythology of James Toback could well be considered a dramatic adaptation of Mailer's character. Based on various accounts, the filmmaker was a son of privilege, with parents whose status in the political and business worlds ensured his access to the best education (The Fieldston School, from which he graduated in 1963, and Harvard College, from which he graduated in 1966). Toback's formative years took place in between Mailer's "White Negro" and the birth of the hippie subculture. Almost as if by design, Toback counts one experience from each camp as having a transformative effect on his personal philosophy. The definitive "hippie" moment of Toback's college years was his ingestion of a massive amount of LSD, chronicled (among many other places) in a 2009 interview by Jeremy Hatch for *The Rumpus*: "I took a massive dose of LSD when I was nineteen and completely flipped out, and that was the end for me. The real reason I flipped was not just the amount, but that I was unafraid of death, and acid makes you aware that you're going to die, that you're nothing. And I wasn't ready to handle that."

Later, as a young journalist, his "White Negro" self flourished while living on assignment with football star Jim Brown, a period of time that resulted in *Jim: The Author's Self-Centered Memoir on the Great Jim Brown*. The *Kirkus* review of the book describes the author as "a tortured Jewish intellectual from New York testing his manhood against Brown's athletic, moral, political and sexual stature, searching through his hero for his own confused identity." When Toback describes the experience, he focuses almost exclusively on the constant sexual orgies that took place.

In contrast to Toback's collegiate descent into his own chosen vices, Downey was groomed for drug use by his father from a very young age. Robert Downey Sr. was a radical filmmaker who tried to bond with his son by giving him drugs, opening up the doorway for his son's teenage addiction. By the time Downey reached the age at which Toback took his single defining LSD trip, he was a veteran at taking drugs of all sorts, and "his drug use only increased with his stardom" (Gliatto). As a result, *Less Than Zero* (adapted from the novel of the same name by Bret Easton Ellis) was an ideal star vehicle for the young actor all too acquainted with the darker corners of 1980s excess. Though the casting of Jami Gertz and Andrew McCarthy in the lead roles remains debatable, none would argue against Downey as the perfect avatar for the wasted transgressions of a selfish decade.

As the product of classicism and crassness, Toback the young filmmaker made a handful of films about crime (1978's *Fingers*), money and infidelity (1982's *Love and Money*), and—less predictably—fashion modeling and terrorism (1983's *Exposed*). These early films are united by a theme of characters going "in too deep," with subtexts doubtless informed by Toback's own compulsive gambling and sexual fixations. In fact, his earliest professional film credit (as writer, not director) was 1974's *The Gambler*, directed by Karel Reisz. Though Toback did find a number of effective on-screen surrogates in these films, his true cinematic counterpart emerged in the most innocuous entry of his early filmography. A romantic comedy is rarely the stuff of artistic inspiration and career invention, but *The Pick-up Artist* united Toback with his muse. Toback's past belonged to Dostoyevsky, Mailer, and Brown. His future belonged to Robert Downey Jr.

Less Than Zero

Though not a Toback film, *Less Than Zero* deserves some mention in the tale of this creative partnership, especially as it introduces Downey's readiness to expose his demons to cinemagoers. Audiences at the time (November 1987, only a couple months after the release of *The Pick-up Artist*) wouldn't have necessarily understood the connection between Julian, Downey's troubled character, and the actor's off-screen habits. But in the 25 years since the movie's release, Downey's arc—from promising young actor to addicted, repeatedly incarcerated has-been, to box office champion—brings the film's prescience into sharp focus. It's a testament to his inherent star power that the actor steals the film from its supposed leads.

Nearly all of the dramatic action revolves around Blair (Gertz) and Clay (McCarthy) attempting to help their drug-abusing friend get sober. Clay is the straight man, having left Los Angeles for his freshman year of college and returned home to a concerned Blair. Eventually setting aside his own misgivings about the romantic attraction between Blair and Julian, Clay jeopardizes his own safety in order to get Julian back on the straight and narrow. For Julian's friends and family, such sacrifices are largely thankless tasks. The troubled young man ends up dead in a convertible, seated upright and sandwiched between his two well-intentioned friends.

Ellis has long claimed that the film adaptation of his work was not faithful to the book. The film does suffer from an identity crisis, abruptly transitioning between tones. The dominant tone seems to be romance, especially in the beginning, as Clay and Blair's relationship is expressed via a dramatic orchestral score, black and white flashbacks, and overwrought emotional reactions. For the film's extended party sequences, dozens of twenty somethings conservatively dance and mingle. That cocaine is present doesn't even signal a threat. The exquisite production design and cinematography make the decadence of young, wealthy Angelenos look like a consequence-free snapshot of early MTV. The film plays all of these elements so safely, that Downey stands out for the charged energy he contributes to the environment. His interpretation of Julian is the only aspect of the movie that suggests danger.

In its treatment of masculinity, *Less Than Zero* was anemic when compared to the concurrent film trend of late–1980s Hollywood blockbusters. One of the defining statements of action cinema arrived less than a year later, with a plot also set in Los Angeles, also at Christmastime. In John McTiernan's *Die Hard* (1988), New York City police officer John McClane (Bruce Willis) "performs a series of feats that demonstrate his mastery of what film and gender-studies scholar Steven Cohan has called the 'traditional manly virtues': '[f]ortitude, courage, perseverance, loyalty, sacrifice, and honor' (Cohan 206). He climbs down elevator shafts, jumps off buildings, explodes bad guys and, ever at the threshold of death, wins every fistfight and gun battle in the film" (Cohen 75). Compared to this 1980s action hero characterization, Downey's Julian could hardly be more opposite. Defined by dependency (on substances, on attention, and on friends), Julian on his own is like a wraith. He passes out on park benches, hides like an animal among rocks, trees, and water, and sells his body to other men to pay off debts. He, too, embodies a masculinity that is "ever at the threshold of death," but squarely in the Mailer/"hipster" sense of the phrase, rather than the McClane.

The Pick-up Artist

In *The Outsider*, Nicholas Jarecki's feature length documentary about Toback, the director describes his recurring protagonist in language one might use to describe Downey/Julian circa 1987: "Going to the limit. Discovering through uninhibited curious behavior, what they're capable of." As much as Toback admitted to his own share of "uninhibited curious behavior" well before writing and directing a version of his experiences in *The Pick-up Artist*, his first outing with Downey is surprisingly soft and sentimental. Downey says in *The Outsider* that his character of Jack Jericho is a thinly veiled version of Toback. Though *The Pick-up Artist* is comparatively inconsequential as a work of either man's art, it does have worth as the beginning of a process of reflections in which Toback tests Downey's boundaries and explores their synchronized obsessions.

Toback is fixated on sex. *Salon*'s Catherine Getches profiled the director in 2002, and a considerable portion of her account of their time together is devoted to his attempts to meet young women for sex. The article, called "The Original Pick-up Artist," details Toback's peculiar form of seduction. He tells Getches, "I want to show you something. This is an example of how I get a bad reputation." He approaches an unsuspecting blond woman in the park and aggressively propositions her, bragging about his status as a director, disarming her with his strange sense of humor, and using the phrase "Would you be interested?" like a form of hypnosis. After getting her phone number, he says to the journalist, "I do that 15 times a week. Well, OK, maybe 50 times a week. Forty girls and 10 guys."

The image Getches paints of Toback the pick-up artist is decidedly sleazy—that of a dirty old man. But in *The Pick-up Artist*, with that same spirit filtered through the fresh face and quick wit of young Downey, the effect is all charm. He's a walking, talking, manifestation of Toback's desire to extend his own self-image as a 1970s ladies' man, whom Jim Brown himself praises for his powers of "intellectual seduction" (*The Outsider*). Therefore Toback's first use of Downey might be understood in Brechtian terms: "If art reflects life it does so with special mirrors. Art does not become unrealistic by changing the proportions but by changing them in such a way that if the audience took its representations as a practical guide to insights and impulses it would go astray in real life. It is of course essential that stylization should not remove the natural element but heighten it" (203–4). *The Pick-up Artist* literalizes Brecht's mirror. The film begins with Jack/Downey in the bathroom, looking at his own reflection as he practices pick-up lines. In a bit of stylization that does depart from the stalking quality connoted by Getches' *Salon* article, the action cross-cuts from bathroom "rehearsals" to street "performances" as Jack scopes out girls on the city street. The cross-cutting casts the activity in a youthful, innocent light, also differentiating Jack from other would-be Lotharios by having him critique another, more aggressive suitor: "Guys like that give meeting strangers a bad name" (*The Pick-up Artist*).

There are additional softening features. Jack is sensitive to older and younger generations. He takes care of his elderly grandmother, feeding her and giving her medicine. At his job as an elementary school teacher, he's popular (and a bit of a rebel) in his efforts to entertain young students. Such an awareness of those who came before him and those who will come after him contrasts with Mailer's characterization of a man who "exists in the present, in that enormous present which is without past or future." Although Jack does fulfill (to a degree) the "twentieth century man's" equation of security with boredom, Toback is also careful to create a character whose ambitions and talents exceed the immediate limits of his life experience.

The plot of *The Pick-up Artist* builds up Toback's ideal self through a delightful protagonist for whom (to borrow a phrase from The Flaming Lips) "enthusiasm for life defeats existential fear" (Coyne). Jack becomes infatuated with Randy Jensen (Molly Ringwald), a guarded girl who is trying to right her father's gambling debts. Randy is a hardened character—emotionally unavailable and therefore Jack's supreme challenge. The risky circumstances of her father (Dennis Hopper's "Flash Jensen") and his antagonist (Harvey Keitel's "Alonzo Scolara") do inject the film with irresponsibility and the criminal, psychopathic fringe. However, in *The Pick-up Artist,* these are forces to fight against, not to embrace, and Jack is determined to rescue Randy from peril.

As executed, *The Pick-up Artist* is (like all of Toback's work) a bit of a mess. Randy never quite blends into the world of the story to a degree that justifies Jack's level of obsession/pursuit. That the film attempts to energize his fixation with a premature sex scene only highlights the lack of character development. The gangsters in the film are inconsistent in the threat they represent. Most absurd is the delay of information that keeps Jack from realizing that Flash is Randy's father and not (as he misunderstands) her boyfriend. Yet despite all this, *The Pick-up Artist* is significant for being Toback's last narrative film to engage in romanticism without overwhelming/defeating it by cynicism or deviancy. In one of the film's best vignettes, Randy asks Christine Baranski's Harriet, "Why depend on them? Why trust them? Just so they can let you down?" She's projecting her relationship with Flash onto her potential romantic partnership with Jack and with men, in general. It's language that equates emotional availability with gambling. Toback uses Downey to create an ideal self, one that eventually delights Randy as he defies her certainty that there's no such thing as a man worth the risk.

As if being rewarded for the romantic optimism of *The Pick-up Artist*, both Toback and Downey met temporary critical and commercial acclaim in the early 1990s. Toback's screenplay for *Bugsy* (1991), directed by Barry Levinson, was nominated for an Academy Award. After a series of roles in forgettable late 1980s films, Downey also received an Academy Award nomination for his portrayal of Charlie Chaplin in Richard Attenborough's *Chaplin* (1992). Seemingly poised to become industry players, both men instead stalled. Tellingly, Toback dropped off the map entirely, without another professional credit until his next collaboration with Downey. The actor fared somewhat better, with supporting roles in some defining films of the period, including Robert Altman's *Short Cuts* (1993) and Oliver Stone's *Natural Born Killers* (1994). Yet any professional traction he hoped to make was undone by his personal struggle with substance abuse. Rebecca Winters summarized the effects of his addiction in her 2008 *Time* article, "Why is this Man Smiling?": "In 1996 he was arrested driving his Porsche naked down Sunset Boulevard, throwing 'imaginary rats' out of his window. Another night, he mistook a neighbor's house for his own and fell asleep in a child's bedroom. His life was a series of court dates and drug relapses."

Two Girls and a Guy

Logic might dictate that a late–Nineties reunion of filmmaker and actor would provide an opportunity to prove to the industry and to moviegoers that there was more to Toback and to Downey than professionally-backfiring personal behavior. But the product of their reunion, *Two Girls and a Guy*, is a fascinating refusal to disavow the root causes of their lean/lewd years. Forever closing the door on the sanguine delight of *The Pick-up Artist*, *Two Girls and a Guy* reaches back to Dostoyevsky to justify the inherent duplicity of a protagonist directly confronted with the chaos wrought by his bad behavior, yet still not moved to repentance or change. *Two Girls and a Guy* aligns Downey with the narrator of Dostoyevsky's *Notes from the Underground*, specifically this passage referenced in Toback's script for *The Gambler*:

> But man is a frivolous and incongruous creature, and perhaps, like a chess player, loves the process of the game, not the end of it.... In fact, man is a comical creature; there seems to be a kind of jest in it all.... But yet mathematical certainty is after all, something insufferable. Twice two makes four seems to me simply a piece of insolence. Twice two makes four is a pert coxcomb who stands with arms akimbo barring your path and spitting. I admit that twice two makes four is an excellent thing, but if we are to give everything its due, twice two makes five is sometimes a very charming thing too [20].

Downey is Blake, an actor, a Mama's boy, and a cad who lives in a massive New York City loft he inherited. One day, two young women, Lou (Natasha Gregson Wagner) and Carla (Heather Graham) stand outside of Blake's building, waiting for their boyfriends to return home. When they realize that they're both waiting for Blake, they decide to break into his loft and ambush him. The ensuing 24 hours find Blake, to quote the film's trailer, "trapped like a rat."

There is some continuity with Downey's performance in *The Pick-up Artist*, insofar as Blake has a reputation for using language to seduce. Before Blake enters the picture, Lou says, "He has a way with words. He could talk you into buying a house without a roof." There's humor in the fact that both women are able to recite Blake's lines to each other. He's clearly a man of manipulative, memorized, and melodramatic language that functions "as if it were a mantra" (*Two Girls and a Guy*). *Two Girls and a Guy* is a film fixated on performance, subjective truth, and the fuzzy/faulty logic of which Dostoyevsky's narrator was enamored—all of this in the name of excusing duplicity.

Downey enters the film like a force of nature. With both women hiding, Blake is unaware that he has an audience, yet he performs anyway. He sings Ray Charles' "You Don't Know Me" and "Cum Sancto Spiritu" from Vivaldi's *Gloria*. He attempts to cover all of his bases with a succession of phone calls, leaving voice messages for both girlfriends, calling his mother, and weighing a job offer in the Catskills. Once Carla pops out of the background and surprises him, he immediately starts to rationalize his behavior but repeatedly interrupts his own rationalizing with questions about how she got into his home. Downey has the paranoid/defensive/aggressive cocktail down to a science. His body language communicates that he wants to get away, to back away, or to disappear. All the while, he doubles down with his words, asking her if she's been unfaithful and asserting that he hasn't been with anyone else in the ten months they've been dating. The audience, Carla, and Lou know this to be patently untrue. All of this behavior has an undeniable subtext of Downey's real-life self-destruction and denial. To watch Blake alone is to be privy to a volatile manic energy. To hear his pathetic attempts to cover his transgressions is to witness a man who knows all too well the feeling of being trapped. There's an uncomfortable degree of closeness to the actor's tabloid persona that Toback is clearly exploiting, and unfortunately, not to a restorative end.

When Lou makes her presence known, Blake insists there is a "legitimate explanation" and that he is "not lying." But try as he might to persuade the scorned women that two and two make five, so to speak, they remain unconvinced. Blake resorts to self-pity, staging a suicide scene (Downey's invention) and later excusing his deceit with his profession: "You name me one good actor who doesn't lie." The dramatic arc of the film becomes so intertwined with Downey's own documented cycle of duplicity that one could be forgiven for losing the distinction between Blake the character and Downey the man.

This blurring of the line between artifice and actuality comes to a head in the film's other warped reference to *The Pick-up Artist*. Smeared with fake blood from the suicide scene he staged to arouse pity and to make his point, Blake stares at himself in the mirror. It's a far cry from Jack Jericho's reflected banter and is devastating in its evocation of the damage of a decade on the leading man. He interrogates himself about the damage he inflicts on others, then instructs, "Shape your ass up. Stop bullshitting everyone." The monologue ends wordlessly, with a grotesque facial expression smashed against itself—a reflection of a man attempting to reconcile the irreconcilable.

While the entire premise of the film could be read as a stand-in for a drug intervention, the scene that explicitly conjures that encounter is an extended group discussion in a tub. Co-written and improvised by the actors, the scene starts to achieve Blake/Downey's exhortation to "stop bullshitting everyone." After some additional prodding of Blake, both Carla and Lou reveal that they too have been unfaithful. Blake explodes in disbelief, but Carla maintains that her indiscretion is not as bad as his because she didn't have to be *forced* to tell the truth. In other words, because she chose to be honest, the admission retroactively allays some guilt.

In an interview with the director that appears on the Blu-ray release, Toback says the film is about the "tension between monogamy and romantic impulse," but the tub scene suggests that the stronger theme of the film is the comparative morality of truth-telling. Had he followed through on this more substantial dramatic idea, then *Two Girls and a Guy* might have contributed to a greater honesty, or at least a greater value of honesty or of much needed accountability, for Downey himself. Unfortunately, the narrative lets him off the hook, as Carla stays around to fulfill his physical and emotional desires, and Lou makes herself available if they ever want to involve a +1. *Two Girls and a Guy* caters to the needy Blake instead of keeping him in that tub and in front of that mirror long enough to arrive at some uncomfortable truths about his lifestyle.

Black and White

In August 1999, Downey hurtled toward rock bottom. He received a jail sentence of "three years for repeatedly breaking the terms of his parole for a previous conviction on a drugs charge" ("America's Addicted Downey Jnr Jailed"). Sensing Downey rationalizing his addiction and rebuking him in the spirit of Carla and Lou in the bathtub, "Judge Lawrence Mira said: 'I don't believe your client is committed to not using drugs. You may call that addiction. But there is some level of choice'" ("America's Addicted Downey Jnr Jailed"). Almost exactly one month after his sentencing, *Black and White* premiered at the Telluride Film Festival. In the wake of two more years of trouble following *Two Girls and a Guy*, Toback had reached whatever step follows rock bottom. He wanted to see if Downey was willing to die on camera.

Black and White is Toback's most investigational film, in the sense that he's dynamically uniting individuals from vastly different popular culture spheres in order to examine how popular culture (specifically hip-hop culture) has transformed conceptions of race and sexual expression. His findings, or rather the way he expresses them, are alternately revelatory and frustrating. The plot is scattershot, with threads involving a basketball player (Allan Houston) asked to throw a game for money, his anthropologist girlfriend (Claudia Schiffer) and her machinations, and the pervasive influence of a group of rappers (played by members of the Wu-Tang Clan) as they personify dual identities as gangsters and artists. The thread relevant to this essay is that of a documentary filmmaker (Brooke Shields' Sam Donager) making a film about white teenagers who want to be black. Robert Downey Jr. plays her gay husband, Terry. He weaves in and out of the picture as an irrepressible cruiser, courting danger with each romantic proposition. Any apparent link to the romantic juggling act of Jack Jericho or Blake exists only in the basic activity of flirting. His demeanor here is more insidious and his targets more often than not carry a high potential for negative response. As he chats up a young, defensive guy on a ferry and rubs his finger against a rapper, the chances grow more likely that he will invite a violent response.

In a similar manner to the ambush-as-intervention metaphor that props up *Two Girls and a Guy,* Downey's scenes in *Black and White* convey his real-life thirst for risk. The same BBC News article that chronicled his jail sentence reported his description of addiction: "It's like I've got a shotgun in my mouth, with my finger on the trigger, and I like the taste of the gun metal" ("America's Addicted Downey Jnr Jailed"). Toback takes advantage of Downey's dance with death in the film's most memorable and most exploitative scene.

The setting is familiar. It's the same loft that housed *Two Girls and a Guy,* but this time it is populated with fresh-faced young actors (Bijou Philips, Gaby Hoffman, and Elijah Wood) and veteran rappers (The Wu-Tang Clan). Shields (as Sam) is wandering around with a camera. Boxer Mike Tyson, former undisputed heavyweight champion of the world, appears as himself. Recently released from what he repetitively refers to as "the penitentiary," Tyson appears to want nothing more than to stay out of trouble. It's clear that Toback has not warned Tyson about the specifics of the impending interaction with Downey, a fact that the director proudly asserts was necessary to achieve the ambush that occurs when Downey (as Terry) strolls into Tyson's personal space. Having directed Downey to flirt with Tyson, Toback essentially sends his troubled muse into the lion's den. In his director's commentary on the DVD release, he recalls his speech to a nervous Downey: "How many better ways would there be to die, than to be killed on camera by Mike Tyson? People would talk about it and see it for as long as civilization exists. You're going to go anyway…" (*Black and White*). The joking manner in which Toback recalls his pep talk with Downey is evidence that he didn't actually intend for his actor to perish right then and there. Yet the gallows humor that surrounds his and Downey's awareness of the actor's perilous lifestyle suggests that the potential for death is nearby, be it at the hands of the wrong mark or an overdose in a hotel room.

What transpires is not too far off from Toback's speech. After trying his best to ignore Terry/Downey's advances, Tyson loses control when Downey recalls a dream in which Tyson is "holding" him. Tyson smacks him in the face and chokes him, bringing the actor to the ground. If *Black and White* is remembered as a touchstone in late–Nineties American independent cinema, it is due to this scene, in which the scripted narrative feature begins to resemble an unadulterated documentary for a few terrifying minutes. Certainly the scene is more authentic in its documentary style than anything else from Sam's supposed documentary, and it only has visual continuity because Shields stays in character and continues to film with her digital video camera, which at one point entirely replaces the coverage of the standard film camera. Downey is injured but walks away. Tyson appears humiliated, pleading to Shields to stop shooting him, as "this is not a study of animals"—one of his many vividly improvised bits of dialogue in the film. Shields' choice to confront Tyson rather than comfort Downey isn't the most humane decision, but it produces compelling footage. Essentially, no one comes out of the encounter innocently, but ironically, Tyson, the supposed aggressor, is the least culpable. Much could be written of how Toback undermines his own thesis about racial accord and complexity, but by this point in his career, such a contradiction is unsurprising. He's betting on his performers' dependency, up to and including that of his longtime leading man, who may be seen to be reduced to expendability in the service of preserving Toback's reputation as a provocateur.

Mined by Toback for delight, duplicity, and proximity to death, Downey the "twentieth century man" entered the next century on a precipice. Additional arrests, drug charges, and rehab stays sabotaged any forward motion he made in the industry. But the collective impact of spending nearly a year in prison, being fired from his comeback role on television series *Ally McBeal*, becoming known as "an uninsurable serial relapser famous for being pulled out of hotels or other people's homes in an addled, disheveled state" (Carr), and meeting future wife Susan Levin caused Downey to finally take sobriety seriously: "On or around Independence Day in 2003, he stopped at a Burger King on the Pacific Coast Highway and threw all his drugs in the ocean" (Carr).

The road to *Iron Man* (2008), *Sherlock Holmes* (2009), and beyond would involve the help of friends such as Mel Gibson and the forgiveness/goodwill of others in the film industry. Downey paid his dues anew with a number of well-regarded supporting roles. Perhaps the most interesting aspect of his transformation into a twenty-first century action hero is his belated acquisition of those qualities that defined screen heroes past, but eluded him in the first phase of his career. His professional success skyrocketed only after he channeled his personal capacity for "fortitude, courage, perseverance, loyalty, sacrifice, and honor" (Cohan 206) into positive directions and purposes, as opposed to using such traits to maintain his negative lifestyle during the years of drug dependency that coincided with his films for Toback. Downey has also grown into a way of reflecting on his life that (perhaps by coincidence) echoes Mailer's language as a way to cast off his old persona. He rejects "the decision ... to encourage the psychopath in oneself" (Mailer 339), saying, "It has struck me lately that I don't have to talk about last century at all" (Carr). He resists the temptation to dwell or capitalize on his past prison time and drug abuse, saying such reminiscence is "the sociopath using his trauma as currency" (Hedegaard).

Downey's newfound philosophy sharply contrasts with twenty-first century Toback. Presently, the director seems lost and damned to circle the drain of the past. Jarecki's *The Outsider*, a documentary that ostensibly praises the man's rogue nature, also reveals his refusal to evolve beyond the character he's been playing since the 1970s. Roger Ebert observes that he's perpetually "attracted to gambling, he's attracted to women, he's attracted to sins of the flesh" (*The Outsider*). Toback doesn't let us forget any of this, as he again recounts his past glories with LSD and Jim Brown. His new muse is Mike Tyson, with whom he has now made three films and who offers Jarecki a most succinct assessment of his director: "Toback: deviancy. Toback: deviancy" (*The Outsider*).

Downey's account of his relationship with Toback is that they "evoked in one another the ability to evolve, even if it's not seeming that way to the outside world" (*The Outsider*). He says that without their creative partnership, Toback might've been killed over gambling debts and that he himself might've "taken the biggest snort of coke ever and blown [his] brain up" (*The Outsider*). Gracious as the actor is in crediting Toback with that intervention, a close reading of the three films they made together uncovers an actor being pushed toward indulgence and self-destruction, not steered away. Given his resistance to reliving the past, it makes sense that Downey chooses to remember only the initial spark of his time with Toback rather than the decade-plus dance with personal demons.

In his *Two Girls and a Guy* Blu-ray interview, Toback regrets that the wild version of Downey that played Blake is now "a more sober, elder statesman, still with great skills" but lost to the last century, thus leaving Toback alone, now nearly seventy years old, right where he started—cruising the street for girls. His exploits have become a recurring punchline on the website *Gawker*, with women submitting detailed narratives (and corroborating evidence such as voicemails) that describe their encounters with a dirty old man who tries to impress them with stories of Harvard, LSD, and his career as a filmmaker. Two and a half decades since *The Pick-up Artist*, with his old protégé now a marquee name, Toback seems lost in pursuit of a mythical winning hand, in which two and two will someday equal five.

Works Cited

"America's Addicted Downey Jnr Jailed." *BBC News*, 6 Aug. 1999. Web. 28 Feb. 2013.
Black and White. 1999. Dir. James Toback. Sony Pictures Home Entertainment, 2000. DVD.
Brecht, Bertolt, and John Willett. *Brecht on Theatre; The Development of an Aesthetic*. New York: Hill and Wang, 1964. Print.
Carr, David. "Been Up, Been Down. Now? Super." *New York Times*, 20 Apr. 2008: n. pag. Web. 28 Feb. 2013.
Cohan, Steven. *Masked Men: Masculinity and the Movies in the Fifties*. Bloomington: Indiana University Press, 1997. Print.
Cohen, Paul. "Cowboys Die Hard: Real Men and Businessmen in the Reagan-Era Blockbuster." *Film & History: An Interdisciplinary Journal of Film and Television Studies* 41.1 (2011): 71–81. Web. 28 Feb. 2013.
Coyne, Wayne. "Enthusiasm for Life Defeats Existential Fear." *20 Years of Weird: Flaming Lips 1986–2006*. The Flaming Lips. Warner Bros., 2006. CD.
Dostoyevsky, Fyodor. *Notes from Underground and The Double*. DigiReads. DigiReads, 2010. Web. 28 Feb. 2013.
Ellis, Bret Easton. *Less Than Zero*. New York: Simon & Schuster, 1985. Print.
Getches, Catherine. "The Original Pick-up Artist." *Salon.com* RSS, 2 July 2002. Web. 28 Feb. 2013.
Gliatto, Tom. "Hitting Bottom." *People.com*, 19 Aug. 1996. Web. 28 Feb. 2013.
Hatch, Jeremy. "The Rumpus Interview with James Toback." *Rumpus*, 15 May 2009. Web. 28 Feb. 2013.
Hedegaard, Erik. "The Arrest of the Hollywood Hellraiser." *Sunday Times* [London], 31 Aug. 2008: n. pag. Web. 28 Feb. 2013.
Juzwiak, Rich. "James Toback Strikes Again." *Gawker*. n. p., 31 Aug. 2012. Web. 28 Feb. 2013.
Keegan, Rebecca Winters. "Why Is This Man Smiling?." *Time* 171.17 (2008): 77–79. Military & Government Collection. Web. 28 Feb. 2013.
Less Than Zero. 1987. Dir. Marek Kanievska Fox Home Entertainment, 2008. DVD.
Mailer, Norman. *Advertisements for Myself*. Cambridge, MA: Harvard University Press, 1992. Print.
The Outsider. Dir. Nicholas Jarecki. Westlake Entertainment, 2009. DVD.
The Pick-up Artist. 1987. Dir. James Toback. Fox Home Entertainment, 2008. DVD.
"Rev. of Jim: The Author's Self-Centered Memoir on the Great Jim Brown." *Kirkus Reviews* 1 Mar. 1971: n. pag. Web. 28 Feb. 2013.
Toback, James, and Norman Mailer. "A Certain Grim Pleasure." *Variety* 6.12 (Dec. 2004): 75. LexisNexis Academic. Web. 1 Mar. 2013.
Two Girls and a Guy. 1997. Dir. James Toback. Twentieth Century–Fox, 2009. Blu-ray.

"Mad as a box of frogs": Channeling Chaplin in the Role of a Lifetime

Erin E. MacDonald

When he heard that director Richard Attenborough of *Gandhi* (1982) fame was making a movie about the life of Charlie Chaplin, "the first million dollar artist" (Robinson, "Most Famous Man"), young Robert Downey Jr. jumped at the chance to play the lead role. Based on Chaplin's 1964 book, *My Autobiography*, as well as a biography by David Robinson, the film was to cover every major stage of his life, from childhood to old age—not a small task. When Attenborough told people he wanted to make a movie about Chaplin, they said, "Who can play him? You'll never find anybody who can play him" ("Strolling"). He not only had to find an actor who could play ages 18–83, physically resemble Chaplin, and be an agile, excellent mimic, but who could also communicate Charlie's emotional turmoil. As Robinson said, "It's one thing to impersonate Chaplin in real life; that's okay, but to impersonate Chaplin as Charlie, the actor, is really asking a lot because he was unique" ("Strolling"). Attenborough remembers his introduction to Downey: "But into the CAA offices came a madman one day. He had spiky black hair and rushed into the room and said, '... my name's Robert Downey. You may not know me, but I shall be more famous than you've ever been, ultimately, because I shall play Chaplin. You realize I'm going to play him, do you not?'" ("Strolling"). The director then "lied through his teeth extremely courteously, promising that, when the time came, he would be considered" (Hawkins 226), never expecting to be bowled over by the young man's audition. His determination to succeed and the intense connection he felt with Chaplin enabled Downey to merge his own identity with the role and ultimately to create the most critically acclaimed performance of his career.

Every scholar of literature or film warns against mistaking the narrator or the character for the author or director, and no one past about ten years of age would confuse an actor with his or her role. There are, nevertheless, times in an actor's life when a role speaks to him or her so clearly and intimately that some identity confusion must result. In his role as the Method-acting Kirk Lazarus in *Tropic Thunder* (2008), Robert Downey Jr. pokes fun at performers, like himself, who may have confused their own identities with those of the characters they played. Although he is not a Method actor and does not tend to remain "in character" when off set, certain roles have, throughout his career, threatened to confuse the man with the character. So well-known are his past troubles and the seemingly endless coin-

Charlie (Robert Downey Jr.) learns the film business in *Chaplin* (1992).

cidences with characters and situations reflecting, before or after the fact, events in his own life, that many moviegoers think he doesn't act—he just plays "himself" in every role. In a way this is true—although he has played a variety of characters with a wide range of emotions and traits and is infallibly described by directors as a consummate professional, he always brings something of himself to the role. Talking about both *Chaplin* (1992) and *The Singing Detective* (2003), Downey told Charlie Rose in 2003, "I think that actors do the films they're meant to do, on a certain level." In *Less Than Zero* (1987), Julian Wells' addicted desperation was a bit too close to home and in the Iron Man franchise (2008–present), Downey and his friends and coworkers have all, at times, commented that Robert Downey Jr. *is* Tony Stark. But although Wells and Stark bear more than a superficial resemblance to the actor (he has commented on their reflections of his own personality flaws), perhaps no character has captured Downey's emotions as strongly as the one who was a real man—Charlie Chaplin.

The Reincarnation of Charlie Chaplin

Chaplin himself believed that a great actor is one who has the ability to "feel a character's soul instinctively, to know under all circumstances what his reactions will be" (Chaplin 255) and in *Chaplin*, Robert Downey Jr. seems to do just that. When Kevin Kline (as Douglas Fairbanks) says to Downey (as Chaplin), "It's remarkable. Your timing in work is flawless. In life, it's the reverse," today's audience can't help but think of Downey's history—the combination of talent and personal turmoil, the dedication to work and the deep insecurities that he also shares with Chaplin. One magazine's description of Chaplin as "film's premiere comic actor, the man who forced the world to take him seriously, who insisted upon living his own life—complete with scandals and nervous breakdowns—as unconventionally as he wished" (Schneller) sounds more than a little like a description of Downey himself. Roger Ebert writes in his review of the film that "Robert Downey Jr. succeeds almost uncannily in playing Chaplin; the physical resemblance is convincing, but better is the way Downey captures Chaplin's spirit, even in costume as the Tramp." Attenborough agreed, saying, "I don't think there was a gesture or finger or anything that he attempted to convey in terms of the persona of Chaplin which was not absolutely right on, absolutely true. He became Chaplin, in the most extraordinary way" ("Strolling").

According to Diana Hawkins, who wrote the storyline for *Chaplin* and co-wrote Attenborough's biography with him, an agent in their building at Creative Artists "had a client who was desperate to meet" the director. Hawkins remembers seeing "a bizarre American youth" with a punk look attempting to convince Attenborough that he alone was capable of portraying Chaplin (Attenborough 225–226). This bizarre youth was Robert Downey Jr. and he set about trying as hard as he could to land the role. "In some ways my whole life had led up to that opportunity," said Downey (Interview): "I just knew, like, you had better go for this…. I almost felt like you know, like everyone who'd ever supported me in any way was in the back of my mind—a chorus of people saying, you know, go." He "went after it like someone would go after a missing child" ("Biography, Famous"), despite the fact that

Downey as Charlie Chaplin clowning for his first film as the Little Tramp in Richard Attenborough's *Chaplin* (1992) (co-star Marisa Tomei is back row, fourth from right).

no one was, at that point, interested in casting him. Comic masters Dustin Hoffman, Billy Crystal, and Robin Williams all coveted the role (Stivers); so did young Matthew Broderick and Emilio Estevez (Spitz). The filmmakers considered and dismissed for various reasons everyone from Kenneth Branagh to Michael Jackson, then finally tested Downey, "[a]lmost as an afterthought" (Attenborough 226). Hawkins writes:

> At the end of a long and dispiriting day, he was the last to stand in front of the camera. With his dark hair now waved in a reasonable facsimile of the young Chaplin, he gave an excellent reading in a totally believable English accent. Concealing his surprise, Dick said he'd get back to his agent after viewing the rushes, but the young actor asked if he could be granted a little more time.
>
> He left the stage and came back with a stepladder. As the camera started to turn, he embarked on an extraordinary silent routine; clowning his way through a series of ham-fisted attempts to set up the ladder, tripping, trapping his hand, getting his head stuck between the rungs and, when he did finally reach the top, swaying alarmingly before performing an amazingly acrobatic pratfall.
>
> "Cut." Dick was laughing so hard the tears were running down his face.
>
> He knew it. I knew it. The whole crew knew it. He might be mad as a box of frogs but Robert Downey Jr. was as close to a reincarnation of Charlie Chaplin as we were ever likely to encounter. We never had any doubts [Attenborough 226].

Attenborough agreed: "He had a touch of genius. He was a remarkable, remarkable performer. And he worked—I mean, his ability to capture the Chaplin mannerisms, the walk, the manner in which he spoke, and so on, was miraculous" ("Strolling"). The director chose Downey over all others because "[h]e provided the fire in the belly and the turmoil behind the eyes. Robert had the ability to convey that driving, unqualified determination to achieve what he set out to achieve" (Attenborough qtd in Falk 76), that was common to both men. "And once [Robert had] done a [screen] test," Attenborough says, "the money came straight away. It really was because of Robert Downey" ("Strolling").

Downey's passion for the role, his determination to get it right, and his willingness to take the risk of being compared to the cinema god and found wanting made the film possible. In his autobiography, Chaplin writes of his belief that "[t]he basic essential of a great actor is that he loves himself in acting.... [He] is mainly preoccupied with his own virtuosity.... Just a fervent love of the theatre is not sufficient; there must also be a fervent love of and belief in oneself" (254). Downey may not have loved every aspect of himself, but acting was one sphere in which he knew he could shine.

Director Mike Figgis has said that he's never seen another actor so able to become another person. Robert looked at a photograph of Figgis' friend, a man dying of AIDS, and became the physical and emotional embodiment of him for the film *One Night Stand* (1997) (Hoggard). Figgis told Liz Hoggard, "I remember coming on the set and he had utterly absorbed the photograph. I had never seen an actor become someone to that extent before. It was quite shocking." He did something similar for Chaplin, not so much becoming Charlie as absorbing him into his own identity. Attenborough, who compared Downey's involvement in the iconic role to Ben Kingsley's commitment to his portrayal of Gandhi, remarked on Robert's ability to capture Chaplin's spirit, above and beyond his physical movements. He said, "Robert looked at the very early black and white comedic stuff and brought into it elements of the almost ingénue feeling that Charlie had when he was a clown, as it were, and Robert found that. Beyond the pure impersonation." Although the performance "was such a copy of the actual man and his mannerisms..." ("Strolling"), Downey went beyond mimicry to an almost spiritual level of understanding. The actor's physical comedy trainer, Dan

Kamin, was similarly impressed: "One day when we were rehearsing in his motel room Robert went into character, and I was startled by how he suddenly submerged himself into the role" (Message to Erin E. MacDonald). Although be "became" Chaplin for the screen, Kamin says, "Robert is such an experienced pro that he could drop in and out of character at the drop of a hat" (Message). Chaplin biographer David Robinson similarly described Downey's ability to capture the character of the Tramp as "astounding" and said that "he gave the impression that he was inventing these things" as Chaplin did ("Strolling"). Chaplin's childlike joy and enthusiasm when his inventive antics evoked laughter from the crowd resonated with Downey, who could relate to both his pureness as an artist communicating the human condition and the depths of his emotional pain.

Reincarnating Charlie Chaplin would be more difficult than the actor knew, however, because the more muscular Downey did not possess Chaplin's shorter, thinner body type. Kamin explains how RDJ's natural talent and hard work enabled him to overcome both the difference in body types and the lack of the old-fashioned, sped-up film:

> Robert is obviously a brilliant comic actor. Chaplin's body type made it easier for him to do the delicate movements that offset his ragged costume and more acrobatic comic falls. For Robert— for virtually anyone—it takes a lot of hard work to do Chaplin. Don't forget, Chaplin's silent film performances, along with Buster Keaton's and Harold Lloyd's, are always seen at faster than life speed, which makes their actions seem impossibly precise. In the context of naturalistic scenes in a biopic we couldn't speed up the action in an obvious way, except for the films-within-the-film. However, Attenborough did subtly speed up the action by shooting some of the comedy sequences at 22 frames per second, giving Robert's movements a bit more springiness [Message].

A reporter who was on set to interview the star during filming also commented, "Downey doesn't look much like Chaplin; his body is huskier and more striking than the Little Tramp's. And yet, as he approaches the camera, Downey's face seems to transform. That unctuous Tony Curtis look of his, with its shameless smirk, takes on a certain stately vintage. He uses charm to ward off the impulse to caricature" (Spitz). Even Chaplin's son and daughter agreed that Downey's recreation of their father's movements was nothing short of miraculous. Michael Chaplin (Chaplin's son) admitted, "Robert Downey, physically, he wasn't the same as my father, who was kind of slim and not very broad shouldered. When I first saw Robert Downey, I thought how could he possibly move in the same way? But he did. He really succeeded in putting that across" ("Strolling"). Chaplin's daughter, Geraldine, said, "I think he actually became Charlie Chaplin. I mean I really do. Completely" ("Biography, Famous"). When a black and white scene from *The Immigrant*, featuring Downey as the Tramp on a ship docking in New York City, was recreated for the film, Geraldine "thought she was seeing an actual clip from *The Immigrant*" (Kamin, "Postscript" 452). Although the film's director and the legend's own relatives were behind Downey, the task with which he was confronted was enormous, and it took its toll.

"Facing the daunting challenge"

Partly because of his known drug problem, the first studio with the rights to the film didn't want Downey and planned to cast an A-list star instead, but Attenborough insisted on Downey (Attenborough 227). He found a new backer and cast the young American "because he understood creative passion" ("Biography, Famous"). When Downey heard of the director's dedication to him, he said, "It doubled my respect; it also doubled my feeling of responsibility" ("Biography, Famous"). He was thrilled but terrified, later telling an interviewer, "[W]hen Dickie came up to me to tell me I had the part I was stunned. I started crying. It was probably the most exciting thing that's ever happened to me" (Leftwich). In a behind-the-scenes special made in 1992, he talks about the "petrifying responsibility of portraying [Chaplin] in ... the first film ever made about his life" ("The Perfect Charlie"). He said, "It was like winning the lottery then going to prison. I realized that nothing that had worked for me before was going to work here. I'd watch one of Charlie's films, but by the end of it I was wildly depressed, because I realized that what he'd done in this twenty-minute short was more expressive and funnier than everything I've thought about doing my whole life" (Schneller). Because the film took so long to get funding, he had 18 months to research, watching the silent star's films over and over, finding the idea of replicating them more and more "intimidating" ("Perfect Charlie"). He also convinced staff at the Museum of the Moving Image in London to allow him to try on a pair of Chaplin's shoes, which fit him perfectly (Diamond), cementing the idea in the actor's mind that he was meant to play this role. In 2006, Downey told James Lipton on *Inside the Actor's Studio* that he read Chaplin's autobiography several times, backwards and forwards, "went to every other biographical source," and watched all his films "repeatedly." "They freaked me out," he said, because Chaplin "had this thing that he never lost but his ability to innovate and communicate and how practiced and loose it was, I mean, you know, it was just the ultimate, ultimate education." As Thomas Doherty writes in a 1993 review of the film in *Cinéaste*, "Few actors have dared to tread among talents in the light of whom they would only wilt..." (Doherty 75). Downey dared, and he came through the experience having learned much.

As part of his preparation, he scoured numerous sources and, through one, found a man he thought could help him. Dan Kamin, a physical comedy performer, had written a book called *Charlie Chaplin's One-Man Show* (1984) and when Downey tracked him down, he told Kamin, "I think you may be the only person in the world who can help me pull this off" (Kamin, "Postscript" 447). Kamin, who became Downey's "movement-acting coach and comedy choreographer" (Kamin, "Postscript" 451) for the film, believes that, during both preparation for the role and filming, Downey was "[v]ery focused on the task at hand. Very excited by the challenge. Humbled by the responsibility—the more he watched Chaplin's work the more in awe he was of the man" (Message). Despite his determination, Downey was scared people would think he was an imposter, "an absolute sham" (Downey qtd. in Falk 82). In a 1992 article, he acknowledges his own "imposter-complex," explaining it as the feeling that "I don't know what I'm doing and everyone's gonna find out" (Bishop). As Kamin writes in the postscript to his book, *The Comedy of Charlie Chaplin* (2011):

> Facing the daunting challenge of portraying the man who was arguably the greatest comedian, filmmaker, and, some would say, actor of the twentieth century, Downey, even then notorious in Hollywood as a brilliant but undisciplined bad boy, realized that for once he couldn't get by on chutzpah and native ability. This time he needed a number of highly specific physical acting skills, many of them discussed in my book. Playing Chaplin in a major motion picture was the opportunity of his lifetime; to succeed would move his career to a new level, and to fail would confirm many industry people's worst opinion of him. Within a couple of weeks he flew to Pitts-

burgh, and we began the task of preparing him for his role. Our work went well, and I was hired by the production to train Downey and create several of the film's comedy sequences [447].

This training included "daily postural alignment exercises" to change Downey's typical slouch to something more closely resembling Chaplin's "grace and fluidity" (Kamin, "Postscript" 448). As Kamin points out, "Chaplin's style is not easy for anyone to mimic, because he moves so fluidly he makes the rest of us look arthritic" (Message). Taller and more muscular than the real Chaplin, Downey had to learn how to move like the silent film star. He told a press conference at the time, "There's not a day that's gone by that I haven't had to do something that I couldn't do. Or rather, that I couldn't do before we started" (Aldridge, "Charlie's Angels"). "Luckily," Kamin writes, "Robert proved to be an eager and hard-working student" ("Postscript" 448), and the two worked together well. According to David Robinson, "Robert would come onto the set and know how to do it. Obviously there'd be a lot of takes and a lot of discussion, but he obviously prepared" ("Strolling"). In fact, he prepared himself for the role in every possible way.

As Hawkins remembers, "Robert, convinced of his spiritual affinity with Chaplin, went on to approach the task of reincarnating him for the film with a dedication which, at times, bordered on fanaticism" (235). She adds, "he'd learned to play tennis and the violin left-handed, as Chaplin had done," and he had spent the months of production delay closely studying "the work of all the great stage and film mime artists. Then, weeks before the start of shooting, he'd travelled to London with the express intention of acquiring Charlie's original accent, spending hours with Dick's cockney chauffeur, Bill Gadsdon, until he could mimic him perfectly" (Attenborough 235). Hawkins calls him a "brilliant and endearing boy [who] was, to say the least, a little bit strange" (234), as they knew from going to dinner at his house in the Hollywood Hills to find a dummy dressed like the Tramp seated at the table and "the entire place glowing with hundreds of candles. A violin recording of the romantic theme music Chaplin had composed for *Limelight* was spilling into the narrow street, accompanied by an amazing voice, not unlike that of Nat King Cole—Robert singing, 'I'll be loving you eternally...'" (235). Such rituals were necessary to the actor's state of mind.

Downey felt enormous pressure from the moment he took on the role. As Kamin points out, "Attenborough wanted Robert to inspire both cast and crew by becoming the familiar Tramp character at the outset. Accordingly, one of the first things we shot was Chaplin putting on his costume for the first time, then 'discovering' his walk as he strides toward the set" ("Postscript" 450). Such an iconic moment must have been daunting for Downey to attempt to replicate, knowing that everyone involved in the picture was counting on his performance. He needed to carry the entire movie from that first scene shot, to the last. Downey was obsessed with getting his part right, telling Kamin, "I want you to correct me when I'm eating. How would he hold a fork?" (Kamin, "Postscript" 447) and Kamin also "was determined that Robert resemble Chaplin more than superficially" (Kamin, "Postscript" 449). Acting had come so naturally to Downey that he at first wasn't used to the hard work that *Chaplin* brought. "The amount of repetition required to master some of these movements surprised and discouraged Robert, an excellent but instinctive actor," said Kamin ("Postscript" 449), who encouraged the actor and was in turn impressed by his work ethic. Downey tried everything he could to relax and de-stress when not on set, including listening to Debussy "because [he] thought there was [sic] some sacred geometric rhythms coming out of the music." He admits, "But I was pretty off my rocker; I was doing everything I could to get into a zone that would loosen up this really tough gig. After work, I'd listen to Tom Petty and pretend that I didn't have anything to worry about" ("Tracks of His Years"). He was determined to succeed and terrified of being exposed as a fraud, "But," he says, "every day I just sat with the fear, because, underneath it all, more than anything, was a great desire to be a catalyst in the reigniting of Chaplin's spirit" (Bishop).

Dan Kamin was both aware of the pressure his student felt and confident that Downey could master it. He recalls, "Robert always seemed very confident. During pre-production, when we'd be walking around L.A., fellow film actors would come up to him, look at him gravely, and say, basically, 'You're really brave'" (Message). Although the actor proved unable to stay sober for the entire shoot, Kamin and others give the impression that Downey did not descend further into drug use because he couldn't handle the role. Kamin insists:

> Robert never used any drugs in my presence.... He worked very hard with me during pre-production on his physical transformation into Chaplin and the business of the various routines I created for him. For five weeks we worked hours every day. What I did become aware of was the intense pressure his stardom imposed on him, from the family members who depended on him financially, to a small entourage that he supported, to the fans who pressed in upon him whenever we were out in public. Robert was invariably gracious towards all these people, and I was struck by his generosity and kindness [Message].

Downey himself told Peter Bart and Peter Guber on *Sunday Morning Shootout* that it wasn't the pressure of making *Chaplin* that drove him further into addiction once it was completed—he just wanted to take some time off after the film wrapped because he was "exhausted."

During filming, the young actor tried to stay clean as long as he could, but fell back into old habits partway through. Attenborough and Hawkins knew that Downey was emotionally disturbed by his breakup with his girlfriend of seven years, Sarah Jessica Parker, and

> also knew from telltale sources that he went home at the end of the shooting day and drank a whole bottle of vodka in an effort to get a full night's sleep. Waking only a short time later, he would drive round one of the less salubrious areas of Los Angeles until he managed to hook up with an alley dealer. Then, having had his fix, he again tried to sleep until it was time for the fifty-mile drive out to the location and another long day in front of the camera [Hawkins in Attenborough 234].

While they were shooting in California, Diana Hawkins remembers, "The sun was only a glow on the horizon when 26-year-old Robert arrived promptly for his dawn call. I remember watching in dismay as the most multitalented artist I had ever encountered emerged from the chauffeur-driven car, unshaven and glassy-eyed; a stumbling wreck falling into the waiting arms of our second assistant director" (Attenborough 234). He never put the film in jeopardy, though, as Hawkins relates: "An hour and a half later, costumed, made up and bright as a button, the other Robert was on set, ready to rehearse" (234). She begged Attenborough to speak to him but the director refused, not wanting "to bring everything to a halt by having a showdown" (234). Like many others who would work with Downey in the years to come, he was prepared to accept the actor on his own terms, drug addictions and all, because his performance never seemed to suffer. He didn't throw fits or shout at the crew or pass out in the middle of scenes and, according to these directors, whatever he did in his personal life was his own business.

Despite his relationship troubles, his problems with drugs and alcohol, and the pressure of having taken on such a difficult and high-profile role, Downey overcame it all. He poured all his considerable energy into *Chaplin*, asking "for additional takes more often than Attenborough" (Schneller). The director remembers, "He was miraculous. Quite miraculous. Very difficult, because he hadn't freed himself of all his drug problems and so on, and he had to battle through those and the old makeup, you see, took hours and hours and hours and he went mad playing the old man" ("Strolling"). After sitting through six to eight hours of delicate makeup application, he couldn't eat anything and could only drink through a straw (Stivers). "Come early afternoon," Hawkins recalls, "when it became evident he was quietly going mad under the latex, Dick would announce a wrap and Robert would immediately claw at his face, tearing it off in strips" (Attenborough 236). The old man makeup nearly drove him to distraction "[b]ut his concentration was such, an actor's concentration, that he managed that" (Attenborough, "Strolling"), using his determination and drive (and possibly some artificial enhancements) to get him through the shoot.

A Spiritual Affinity

Downey gave the performance his all not only because of what it might mean for his career. He told the *New York Times*, "Chaplin has been an undercurrent my whole life" (Diamond), and he believed that he was meant to play him. Whether Charles Chaplin Jr. and Robert Downey Jr. actually had much in common or not is irrelevant. Although one man grew up in poverty-stricken Victorian London and went on to become the most recognizable figure in the world whereas the other grew up in the avant-garde environs of Greenwich Village and achieved early fame as a drug offender, Downey, in his twenties, felt an intense connection to the foreigner. In *The Last Party* (1992), a documentary which he filmed while preparing to be Chaplin, Downey says, "I'm taking you into my hero's church. We're goin' to Charlie Chaplin's studios which is now A&M Records ... to ask questions and get answers, I won't say who from." He felt a "spiritual affinity" with Chaplin (Hawkins qtd. in Attenborough 235), who is portrayed in Attenborough's film as a tortured soul who acts like a clown to hide his emotional scars. Jodie Foster said the same thing about Robert Downey Jr. (Commentary) and even Geraldine Chaplin seemed to believe that Downey and her father were kindred spirits, saying, "He's heartbreaking and he has my father's sense of melancholy" (qtd. in Falk 79–80). Above and beyond their early troubles and their personalities, Downey felt he could relate to Chaplin's art. "My point of identification with Chaplin was the intense desire to show the humor in the sadness," he told one interviewer (qtd. in Haldeman). Chaplin had written in his autobiography that to be creative, "One must have a capacity to suffer anguish and sustain enthusiasm over a long period of time" and that humor "heightens our sense of survival" (210). A reviewer of the film writes that "Downey captures the rebellious outrage of Chaplin's comic spirit" (Byrge), possibly because his own rebellious spirit is so similar. Press at the time noticed other similarities, writing:

> There are, amazingly, some strange coincidences between the life of Robert Downey Jr. and the silent screen hero he is portraying. They both started acting at the age of five, and both are known for their passion for music. But perhaps the strangest coincidence is that Robert bought a

house that had once belonged to Charlie Chaplin just a few years ago. The pink art deco house was designed by one of Cecil B. De Mille's set designers. Downey, who believes that there is meaning to all these things, says, "I have a feeling that a large part of my lessons in life are to be derived from my experiences on this film. If there is any role model that I could ever have had on this planet for the kind of work or the general kind of energy I would like to work with—it's him" [Leftwich].

Having (or wanting to have) a similar "energy," Downey hoped that playing the part of Chaplin would allow the legend's greatness to rub off on him, to help him move from a teen draw to a serious artist in both his professional and personal lives. His perceived connection to Chaplin (in addition to his skills as an actor) allowed him to merge with the character and to create the most critically lauded performance of his career.

Interviewers have always brought Downey's personal life, including his inner journey to emotional maturity, into their assessments of his career. "Making *Chaplin* represents Downey's coming of age, not just as an actor but as a man," insists Johanna Schneller. A *Harper's Bazaar* article that came out after the film wrapped is even titled, "A new and improved Robert Downey Jr. takes on the role of a lifetime and grows up in the process" (Bishop)—a bit on the nose, perhaps, but nevertheless true. After gaining the role, he literally buried the party-boy clothes he'd saved from the set of *Less Than Zero* (1987) (Schneller), to clear the way for a new beginning. The challenges of the role made him finally realize that preparation might be as valuable to the art form as spontaneity. As Kathy Bishop writes, "Downey's spiritual maturity coincided with the fine-tuning of his acting." The piece describes Chaplin as having taken on the roles of both mentor and savior, for Downey, who decided it was his destiny to play the part. His description of his mentor sounds like one of the many similar descriptions of himself that he had become known for admitting: "Chaplin was desperate but charming. He had a great sense of self-esteem, knew right from wrong, yet was still a bit of a goat at times, not above picking up a cigarette from the floor if he wanted it. I don't think there has ever been another time when the whole planet could relate to one thing." That "one thing" was Chaplin's (and perhaps Downey's) ability to heal not only himself through entertainment, but the audience as well. Filming Chaplin made him "recognize the tertiary, healing element to art. I have to believe," he said, "that there's something, some greater purpose for my doing it, because, really, nobody has any business playing Charlie Chaplin" (Bishop).

It's easy to guess which parts of Chaplin's autobiography Downey felt a spiritual affinity with. For example, on achieving fame, Chaplin says, "I wanted to enjoy it all without reservation, but I kept thinking the world had gone crazy! If a few slapstick comedies could arouse such excitement, was there not something bogus about all celebrity? I had always thought I would like the public's attention, and here it was—paradoxically isolating me with a depressing sense of loneliness" (Chaplin 177). When Downey first rose to fame, he thought that being a movie star was similarly bogus: "Acting is the most wildly overpaid position imaginable. 'How much did you make for eight weeks sitting in your trailer?' 'More than the President.' It's really silly." In the early parts of his career, he felt like a con artist, swindling people out of money and attention with nothing but charm. He also "fe[lt] like a whore sometimes" and said, "They deify people in this business.... I think it's people's own lack of connection with themselves" (Turan). This statement is ironic considering that Downey thought of Chaplin as a god, and as someone who helped him connect with his true self. Chaplin also admitted about the rapid rise of his fortunes, "Investing money was a problem and I knew little about it" (190). Both men saw fame and the attention it brought as insincere, and both were clueless with money. When Chaplin describes the vanity he perceives in the great pianist Paderewski and how he wanted someone to pull the piano stool out from under him (Chaplin 191), a reader can easily imagine Robert Downey Jr. doing or thinking the same. Chaplin admired Godowsky instead, "a greater pianist," because he was "simple and humourous" (Chaplin 191). Chaplin was always attracted to "unique personalities" more than to success (Chaplin 47), another predilection he shared with Downey, who made as many lifelong friends among the working class as among the Hollywood elite. In their childhood scars, confidence in their abilities to succeed, and philosophies of naturalistic acting, Chaplin and Downey shared much.

Childhood Deprivation

Charlie Chaplin and his half-brother spent their childhood foraging for food and trying to keep out of the poorhouse while their mother quietly went mad from malnutrition. Forced, out of destitution, to live in a workhouse in Lambeth and then an orphanage at the tender age of six (Chaplin 25–27), Chaplin the boy was shuffled back and forth from workhouse to orphanage to workhouse to a small room reunited with his mother, to the care of his drunk father and resentful stepmother when his mother was sent to a lunatic asylum (Chaplin 33). "I was not yet eight years old, but those days were the longest and saddest of my life," he writes (35), later adding that he developed a strong sense of "the combination of the tragic and the comic" (40) early in life. He didn't really have a childhood, was forced to grow up too fast, and spent his days hatching schemes to make money. Even after he achieved fame and fortune beyond his wildest dreams, Chaplin remained damaged by "deep-hidden psychological scars" (Robinson, "Introduction" 7). In his introduction to Chaplin's autobiography, Robinson wonders, "Was it necessary therapy, essential to his confidence, always to tell himself that he had conquered the world and raised himself from poverty and nonentity to universal fame and affection unaided?" (7). Charlie was sometimes "not particularly popular" with everyone in the crew and seen as "a precocious brat" (Chaplin 88) for seeming like a know-it-all when giving advice about the theater. His pride and whims were often self-destructive for him, as when he didn't like the way an important woman he was to meet with treated him condescendingly so he turned down a part "and was out of work for ten months" (Chaplin 91).

A childhood inferiority complex caused by being a transient misfit from a strange family similarly scarred the young Robert Downey Jr. who felt it "essential to his confidence" to brag about his filmmaker father to other kids and to tell press in the 1980s such ego-inflating gems as, "There's no stopping me!" (Hirschberg). Like Chaplin, whom he called a "stranger in a strange land," "Downey, too, consider[ed], himself an outsider," not fitting into either the California rich-kid crowd or the so-called Brat Pack that the media attempted to lump him in with (Bishop). In 1991 he confessed that he used to feel the need to persuade everyone "that [he was] the funniest, most original person they [had] ever met." He told *Playboy*, "I used to have this feeling that unless I had gone nine steps further than was necessary to convince everyone of my comedic genius and spiritual insight, I was invalid" (Rensin). Like Chaplin, he was (and is) possessed of a "mouthy arrogance, irony, flippancy, insecurity, [and] charm" (Rebello). Having virtually no parental guidance or stability at home and being allowed to partake in his parents' drug-fueled lifestyle at an early age also traumatized the boy, who has spoken as recently as 2013 about the massive effect that this lack of discipline in his formative years had on the next few decades of his life (Showbiz). "I don't think he had a childhood," said Moira Kelly, who plays two of Chaplin's loves in the film. "I suppose that's why he's such a boy now" (Diamond). She was talking about Downey, but she might just as easily have been in character as Oona O'Neill and talking about her husband, Charlie. Shane Black, Downey's director years later, also drew a parallel between the actor's Peter Pan complex and that of his mentor: "It's the Chaplin thing: the boy in the man and the man in the boy" (qtd. in Hudson 69).

The Downeys were certainly never reduced to the level of poverty to which Charlie Chaplin was subjected, but Robert did face intermittent power shut-offs and the embarrassment of having to wear hand-me-down clothes (Cozzone). Downey's pride also tended to get in his way on occasion, such as the time he went for an audition and the director asked how he supported himself when he wasn't acting. "My spine," he quipped (Hirschberg). Of course, many people experience childhood trauma, but not all of them display this inner pain and vulnerability in their art, for all to see. As a result, Chaplin and Downey both maintained a sympathy for the human condition that is easy to see in the silent films of the Little Tramp and in the eyes of every character that Robert Downey Jr. plays.

Throughout *Chaplin*, Downey plays a man who is haunted by poverty and class. He starts the film as Chaplin started his life, with a lower-class, Cockney accent that changes (like the real Chaplin's) by the end of his career. The young Charlie once got a taste of luxury when a friend of his mother's invited them to stay with her for the summer (Chaplin 51), but it wasn't to last—much like Downey's family constantly yo-yoed between near-poverty and wealth with the instability of his father's work. This lifestyle gave both a hatred of poverty and a desire for luxury, but made them feel like imposters (Chaplin 52, 261). Seeing the huge fancy houses and towers of New York City on his first trip to America, Chaplin felt "inadequate" (Chaplin 123), associating his own background and identity with destitution and hopelessness (Chaplin 266). The Chaplin family went from pawning his brother Sydney's one suit every week for a year, so the family could use the money during the week while Sydney had his work uniform to wear (Chaplin 55), to living in luxuriously appointed apartments once Charlie became a star. But although his accent and his fortunes changed, Chaplin retained a preoccupation with class that found its way into his characters and his films.

Downey has maintained a similarly conflicted view of his own income level, indiscriminately buying expensive clothes in the late Eighties and early Nineties because he finally could but later checking the price tags even once their numbers didn't matter to his bank account anymore (Fleming, 2010). As soon as he could afford to, he became "one of Hollywood's sharpest dressers, which he said was a reaction to years of wearing hand-me-downs…" (Fallon). Like Downey would decades later, Chaplin "enjoyed the nonsense" of going on "spending sprees" and dressing in luxurious clothes (135, 261). During the filming of *True Believer* (1989), for example, James Woods (who appears in *Chaplin* as a prosecutor) took to calling Robert "Binky" because of his needless habit of showing up to the set every day in expensive suits (Turan). Because of their experiences as children, both men enjoyed the finer things—or wanted to. Each would discover that money could not adequately compensate for the intense sadness caused by his childhood deprivations.

Chaplin scholars believe, and Attenborough demonstrates in his film, that Chaplin felt guilty starting his life so poor and becoming so rich so quickly (Schinkel, "Most Famous Man"). He tells his editor (Anthony Hopkins) that he couldn't "just enjoy" his success because "it meant too much." During the Depression, when unemployed, hungry people approach him on the street, he hopes they're going to ask him for money but they ask him for autographs instead. When Charlie sees millions out of work, replaced by machines, he makes *Modern Times*, becoming obsessed with it and ignoring his wife and kids. At one point in the movie, Woods, as the lawyer filing an undeserved paternity suit against Chaplin, asks the court, "What good has all his money done Chaplin?" He is still, and always will be, a "cheap Cockney." Robert Downey Jr., now one of the richest and most powerful players in Hollywood, similarly albeit jokingly calls himself "an animal" and "an ugly American" in comparison to a more finely bred costar, Gwyneth Paltrow ("Gwyneth"). Downey says his first few films "felt like a scam," because he was good enough without really trying (Schneller). "He wouldn't let himself feel like an artist" (Schneller), in much the same way that Chaplin always felt like the little Cockney boy dressed up in a rich man's clothing.

Both men's interests in performance were sparked by their mothers, women who virtually gave up their own show business careers of acting and singing to raise their children while their husbands fell deeper into addiction (alcohol in the case of the mostly absent Chaplin Sr. and alcohol and cocaine in the case of Downey Sr.). Chaplin writes in his book that his mother "stimulate[d] [his] interest in the theatre" and "imbued [him] with the feeling that [he] had some sort of talent" (Chaplin 41), much as Downey's mother did for him. Forced to commit his mother to an asylum when her mind went from starvation, Chaplin always felt guilty about abandoning her. Downey likewise felt guilty enough about his mother's situation to stay with her in New York when his father and sister left for L.A.. He tells a young boy in *The Last Party* that he needed to look after her, but within a couple of years he had left the squalor of their walk-up for the party life of California.

Their flair for performance acted as a defense mechanism for both men. As a boy at school, Chaplin received laughs and fame and went from being "an obscure and shy little boy" to "the centre of interest of both the teachers and the children" (Chaplin 42). "Chaplin had little formal schooling" (Robinson, "Introduction" 2) and was self-taught, like Downey, who dropped out of high school but whose natural intellect likewise urged him to read a wide variety of books on multiple subjects. Throughout years of odd jobs, Chaplin "never lost sight of [his] ultimate aim to become an actor" (Chaplin 76) and finally got his start playing a page-boy in *Sherlock Holmes* (Chaplin 88–89). Chaplin reflects, "Everyone was delighted and smiled beamingly at me. What had happened? It seemed the world had suddenly changed, had taken me into its fond embrace and adopted me" (Chaplin 77). The praise he received from performing must have filled a little of the hole in his heart. Now he was able to make his mother's and brother's dreams come true. Though a successful comedian by nineteen, Chaplin writes that he "grew melancholy and dissatisfied," wanting adventure and "enchantment" instead of the daily grind of "just grubbing for a living" (103). Progressing from bussing tables to being a working actor did not satisfy Robert Downey Jr. either, who started to see acting as a grind that often took too much away from his down time. He even considered giving up acting entirely, saying he'd be happy to stay at home while wife Deborah ventured out into the spotlight (Schneller). Both men lived for applause but felt empty even when they received it.

Downey is aware that an unstable upbringing can be well mined by a sensitive actor. "I think Chaplin had about as tragic a life as God would allow someone," he told *US Magazine*, "[b]ut I'm almost sure that it provided some of the most raw and best material for his movies." Thinking of the similarities between the two men, the interviewer felt compelled to add, "The irony is not lost on Downey, whose own face once wore the barbed-wire stare of too-much-too-soon" (Spitz), and whose movies since *Chaplin* have used his own emotional turmoil as fuel for his passionate performances.

On Art and the Artist

Chaplin's and Downey's ideas about acting also seem remarkably similar. Like Downey, who only took a drama class in high school and went to an open-admission acting camp for a couple of summers, Chaplin writes that he had no formal training as an actor, but luckily "it came naturally to [him]" (Chaplin 78–79). He felt a "glow of satisfaction" from pleasing the director and cast but "accepted their enthusiasm as though it were [his] natural birthright" (Chaplin 79). Also like Downey, Chaplin quickly became known as the best thing about the productions in which he appeared and was singled out for critical praise even in unsuccessful shows (Chaplin 81). When discussing acting, Chaplin stresses the primacy of emotion over intellect (Chaplin 252–253) and his preference for improvisation over method.

Chaplin was a perfectionist in his working life, despite believing that his talent came to him naturally. "I do not believe acting can be taught," he writes in his autobiography; "acting essentially requires feeling…. But when intellect and feeling are perfectly balanced, then we get the superlative actor" (Chaplin 254). A great performer, like the Russian ballet dancer Nijinsky, can convey emotion "in a few simple gestures without apparent effort" (Chaplin 193). Similarly, Downey's best performances seem effortless, but both men worked hard to be professional technicians, timing moves perfectly so no one would get hurt (Chaplin 188; Foster). Downey's desire for artistic perfection in many ways matches Chaplin's. As Attenborough attests in an article on the film, "When Robert is committed, the house could fall down, his favorite aunt could die, but it would be utterly irrelevant." He adds, "Robert is identical to Charlie that way, his extraordinary search for what an artist believes to be perfection" (Schneller). The astute interviewer comments, "Without knowing it, Attenborough has hit on Downey's shameful secret. He wants to be an artist. A real artist. If only he can figure out what that means" (Schneller). Years later, Downey admitted that if and when he were to direct, he would "probably be a bit like Chaplin": "I'd probably be a fucking basket case about the details" (qtd. in Falk 198), he confessed. Shane Black, director of Downey in *Kiss Kiss Bang Bang* (2005) and *Iron Man 3* (2013), also compares his combination of intense work ethic and playfulness to Chaplin's, stating, "He's a fireball…. Really, the challenge is to make sure that everyone is ready to work as hard as he does. He's so in command that you have to match that level of commitment. He has so much nervous power. But that's his appeal. It's based on his playfulness" (qtd. in Hudson 69). Downey, like Chaplin, uses his "nervous power" to relentlessly pursue the emotional truth to be found in art.

Despite Downey's frequent mislabeling as a Method actor for his ability to portray emotional realism on screen, both he and Chaplin favored a method that was less Method, more intuition. Chaplin writes in his autobiography, "Stanislavski, for example, strove for 'inner truth,' which I understand means 'being it' instead of 'acting it.' This requires empathy, a feeling into things: one should be able to feel what it is like to be a lion or an eagle, also to feel a character's soul instinctively, to know under all circumstances what his reactions will be. This part of acting cannot be taught" (255). Stanislavski wrote in *My Life in Art*, "I am not interested in a truth that is without myself; I am interested in the truth that is within myself..." (qtd. in Perry 153). Although Stanislavski's system became much more complex than this quotation suggests, compensating for the fact that most actors are unable to achieve such "truth" intuitively (*An Actor Prepares* 77), Chaplin maintained that a great actor relies more on him- or herself than on a method: "The theory that one must know a character's life story is unnecessary. No one could write into a play or a part those remarkable nuances ... [that a great actor can instill in a character]. They must have been dimensions beyond the concept of the author" (Chaplin 255). Downey admired the way Chaplin used his own experiences as material for his films (*Sunday Morning Shootout*), and would later do the same when getting into his characters for films like *The Singing Detective* and *Iron Man*. Although Downey has sometimes used painful memories from his childhood to create psychological realism in his roles (Felperin), he would likely agree with Chaplin's comment, "I abhor dramatic schools that indulge in reflections and introspections to evoke the right emotion. The mere fact that a student must be mentally operated upon is sufficient proof that he should give up acting" (Chaplin 255). Downey's thoughts on Method acting, told to *Rolling Stone* in 1988, are worded in a less gentlemanly way but reflect the same belief that "...if you get into a method.... [I]t's like you're always working at this big plateau to be able to say six words on camera and then walk to your next mark. Fuck it man" (Hirschberg). Always shying away from questions asking him to describe his process, Downey has instilled directors with the idea that "Robert just kind of does stuff" (Gordon qtd. in Falk 182). Parts of Chaplin's biography sound like a description of Robert Downey Jr.'s acting method, or lack thereof. Both men seem to agree with Stanislavski's emphasis on empathy (that magical "if"—what would I do if I were in this situation? question with which an actor uses his or her own emotional reality to make a character believable (Sawoski 7)) but reject his early insistence on the use of "affective memory" exercises (Dewey 55), which Lee Strasberg turned into "emotional memory" (Dewey 58) and popularized as the Method.

The Method came to be mocked for paralyzing actors who were so fixated on their characters' psychological motivations that they couldn't perform simple physical actions (Dewey 59). Stanislavski himself had noticed this problem decades earlier in Russia (Dewey 58) and moved on, focusing instead on creating naturalism through a combination of the emotional and the physical. In employing this technique, a great actor combines the most realistic movements with the truest emotional response for the most natural-seeming performance (*AAP* 77). Experimentation, also known as improvisation, determines which combinations work best. Downey also shares with Chaplin a love of such improvisation. In his memoir, Chaplin describes getting big laughs for ad-libbing during live theatre when he first started working for Fred Karno (Chaplin 100). The creation of the Tramp was another improvisation, which Attenborough reflects in his depiction of the cinema-changing event, in his film. Gaining confidence from this creation, Chaplin began to improvise and express his own ideas more and more (Chaplin 145–147), quickly realizing that he wanted more control over his filmic endeavors. Although he was full of respectful admiration for Attenborough and fairly humbled by the entire project of making *Chaplin*, Downey was never one to keep his opinions to himself. From the beginning of his career, Downey tended to see scripts more as guidelines than prescriptions. Having been raised in a creative family, he always had his own ideas on how to make a scene or a line of dialogue better. Kamin says, "We improvised all the time when we were working. Robert is a natural improviser, as is evident from the wonderful, offhand way he delivers lines in all his movies" (Message). Robert and Kamin "both gave Attenborough a lot of script input, both before and during the shoot, and Attenborough received [their] ideas graciously if not always gladly" (Kamin, Message). Downey also performed all of the film's stunts himself, including Chaplin's vaudeville act as a drunk, in which he "accidentally" acrobatically flips over a railing. The Nijinsky ballet scene that impressed James Lipton (*IAS*) so much was totally improvised, as Kamin remembers: "Robert came up with that himself, gibberish and all—and executed it beautifully" (Message).

Chaplin and Downey both hold appeal to audiences not only because of their talent, but because their intuitive understanding of the universal human condition transcends the lines on the page. Attenborough believes that Chaplin wasn't just a great actor and comedian. He was "the one who actually had something to say. The one who felt the difficulties and deprivations and humiliations of the little man and to convey those and to break your heart, silently, those are moments of true, true genius" ("Chaplin: The Hero"). Schinkel agrees, "If you show a Chaplin film to a little kid, they are simply delighted by it. They don't care that it's not in color, they don't care that it's not talking. They see what that figure is because he has a certain childlike quality—it is innocence" ("Hero"). Even without words, "[h]e could talk with his body" (Michael Chaplin, "Hero"). Directors such as Mike Figgis have similarly relied on Robert Downey Jr.'s non-verbal communication, especially with his eyes (Commentary). While filming *Fur* (2006), director Steven Shainberg and co-star Nicole Kidman were entirely confident in Downey's ability to convey sensitivity and sensuality through layers of hair and prosthetics ("Commentary"). In addition to being able to speak without talking, the silent Tramp is also "an inspirational character" who survives "against every obstacle" (Robinson, "Hero"). Likewise a survivor, "Downey is unsinkable," as critic Stephen Schiff wrote early in Robert's career (qtd. in Hirschberg). Downey overcame box-office failures, drug addiction, prison, and divorce, all under the public eye. Peter Travers has talked about viewers' enjoyment of watching Downey "face his demons," on screen and off ("Best Performances"). Just as Michael Chaplin believed that "[e]veryone could understand ... what the Tramp was fighting for—it was immediately recognizable and people could identify with it and sympathize with it because it's a universal character that he created" ("Hero"), viewers have rooted for Downey, perhaps connecting with his confessed "fallibility" (Fischer). The struggles faced by both Downey's characters (on film and in his public persona) and the Tramp humanize films that would have remained at the level of basic entertainment in the hands of lesser actors. Like Downey, "Charlie was so malleable," people could claim him as anything they wanted to (Louvish 358).

Despite their abilities and the praise they received for them, both men remained acutely, cynically aware of the hypocrisy and superficiality of Hollywood. In his autobiography, "Chaplin is ... shrewd about himself, humorously deriding and deflating his own vanities, aware of their deep roots in the ineradicable heritage of early deprivation and sense of inferiority" (Robinson, "Introduction" 5). Downey is similarly self-deprecating, often drawing attention to his own narcissism and commerciality and to the relative insignificance of the entertainment industry, compared to the harsh realities that most people in the world face (Fleming). Nevertheless, as Robinson says about Chaplin, "He was an artist. He was making art and this in the lowest form of cinema which is slapstick comedy. And this shocked people and amazed people and I think gave a special self-respect to the cinema" ("Hero"). Chaplin ironically achieved artistic greatness within the mass media and helped to elevate it as an art form (Louvish 361), much as several critics believe Robert Downey Jr. did for the superhero film, with his genre-elevating depiction of Tony Stark in *Iron Man* (Travers, "Best Performances").

When asked by Charlie Rose in 2003 to explain Chaplin, Downey offered this analysis: "He was a hard, hard working man who invited a time into his life where he had a training that no one else will ever be afforded again. Nobody." But, "[i]f you strip all of that away and watch what he was communicating with no other instrument than his heart and his mind, and then the body was just dancing as directed, I mean that's just, it's so transcendent, it makes you wanna quit." Film scholar Constance B. Kuriyama writes in her review of *Chaplin* that he is an understandably difficult figure to make a conventional film about: "His charm, humanity, and acute sensibility were completely genuine, yet no artist, as he candidly admitted, could be more completely devoted to himself. Simultaneously or alternately, he was a visual poet, a balletic dancer, a consummate pantomimist, a robust buffoon, a sardonic ironist, and a morose, perfectionistic self-tormentor." She adds, "The more famous (or infamous) he became, the more difficult it was for everyone, including Chaplin, to define Chaplin" (Kuriyama 43). With the Tramp, Chaplin "was in search of simplicity, believing that the complexities of life begat confusion, despair and conflict" (Louvish 357). Downey understands how complex and difficult life is, "[i]f you're at all sensitive" (qtd. in Raab), and applauds Chaplin's desire to cut through the confusion to provide something pure for his audience.

Months after the picture came out, Downey still "[found] himself obsessing, watching Chaplin movies at night and constantly finding new links to his mentor." He told Bishop, "A lot of people think that I have to let this Charlie thing go, so I can move on with my life" but admitted that likely wouldn't happen, because "There's still so much to learn." His own affinities with Chaplin aside, though, Downey now believes that his friend Ben Stiller "is the closest living thing to Chaplin we have today as an actor and a director. He's devoted to detail but also loves the feeling of a loose fish in his hand" (Fleming, 2010). At the 2011 Britannia Awards, he presented Stiller with the Charlie Chaplin Award for Excellence in Comedy, quipping, "This is humiliating, to present this award, when by any metric I should be receiving it."

Critical Reception

When *Chaplin* was released in December 1992, it received mixed reviews. Critics were fairly consistent in their lukewarm-to-downright-nasty assessment of Attenborough's direction, of the script, and of the film overall, but nearly all singled out Downey as the diamond in the rough. Peter Travers of *Rolling Stone* summed it up: "All the nuances Robert Downey Jr. invests in playing Charlie Chaplin, the clown prince of the silent screen, are blunted by a skim job of a script and inert direction from that Madame Tussaud of film biographers, Richard Attenborough" ("Chaplin"). Downey's reaction to the film's bad London reviews reveals his loyalty to the director: " 'It really makes me mad,' says Downey, even though his virtuoso performance as Chaplin has been universally exempt from any criticism. 'There seems to be this requirement that you denigrate your heroes, and those people who have some sort of reputation' " (qtd. in Aldridge, "Chaplin's Defence"). Hawkins and Attenborough insist that the film would have been better if they had been allowed to make it the way they wanted to. However, the movie had been put in turn-around and almost didn't get made at all (Attenborough 227). After seeing "Downey's terrific test" (Attenborough 228), Mario Kassar became interested in backing the film and, fresh from the success of *Terminator 2*, decided he wanted control over the script and to "include the last chapter of Chaplin's life" (Hawkins in Attenborough 230). Says Hawkins, "We should have stuck to our guns and refused" (230), but their fear that the production would be cancelled ultimately won out. The editor (played by Anthony Hopkins) was fourth screenwriter William Goldman's idea, in order to allow the inclusion of the elderly Chaplin, to satisfy Kassar (230). This script change brought about the least-critically-liked elements of the play: the attempt to convey Chaplin's entire life and the addition of Hopkins' character.

Despite Hopkins' abilities as an actor, critics found his part too awkwardly contrived. As a device forced onto the script in order to string the packed narrative together, it probably did more harm than good. Attenborough says he was also forced to put in the scene of the elderly Charlie at the 1972 Academy Awards although he didn't want to. Some of the special effects were not looked upon favorably, either. Attenborough admits, "There was a certain theatricality about parts of it which I regret now.... It certainly wasn't as profound a film as it might have been" ("Strolling"). Vincent Canby agreed, writing in the *New York Times* that *Chaplin* is

> windy, courtly, full of names and dates but never terribly revealing about either the film maker's life or his art. In view of the fact that the autobiography was harshly criticized for its superficiality, the narrative device employed by the screenplay is so idiotic as to seem self-destructive. The conceit used to introduce the film's flashbacks is to have the aging Charlie, while working on the book in Vevey, discussing the manuscript with his editor, a fictional character named George Hayden (Anthony Hopkins).

George's awkward connect-the-dots place in the script comes under much fire from Canby, who notes that "George's comments are ... used to shovel in information, as in this unlikely expostulation: 'My God, Charlie, you weren't even 30. You had your own studio. You were the most famous man in the world. Couldn't you slow down?'" Canby's overall assessment of the film, that "[w]ith the exception of the moving episodes involving Ms. Chaplin, the film makers never transform Charlie's life into significant drama," echoes the opinion of many critics. Geraldine Chaplin received critical applause for convincingly playing her own grandmother, Hannah, "whose slide into madness provides the movie with its only emotional weight" according to Canby. Duane Byrge calls it "the film's most layered and touching portrait."

Film scholars gave the movie as similarly mixed reviews as did the critics, again highlighting Downey's performance. According to Constance B. Kuriyama, Attenborough tries hard to say everything but the script "remains unfocused" (43). She complains about the underdeveloped minor characters, "especially the women" (Kuriyama 43), as well as "[t]he fictitious editor of Chaplin's autobiography (Anthony Hopkins) [who] becomes a ghostly doppelgänger for the director, wantonly posing inane questions as the film slogs relentlessly through more than 70 years of Chaplin's life" (Kuriyama 43). She believes the film sensationally exaggerates Chaplin's liking for teenaged girls while it should have focused more on his political unconventionality (Kuriyama 44). However, Attenborough "insistently emphasizes the behind the camera anguish and dedication that went into the cinematic expression of Chaplin's performance art," according to Thomas Doherty (77). Doherty says *Chaplin* "displays ironic distance from its subject and shows self-conscious awareness of the tortuous and duplicitous turns of memory, the tendency to self-romanticize and omit, to construct a narrative out of one's own past in the present presentation of self" (77). Although Chaplin says in the film, "If you want to understand me, watch my movies," Doherty says, "*Chaplin* does not define the artist by his work" (77). Doherty believes, in opposition to Kuriyama, that the film tries to be too political (77), but his review is much more positive overall.

Others, including Michael Chaplin, also defend the film: "I think it's a very honest film. It doesn't make anything up. It sticks to the story of his life, and it tries to give a picture of his life and I think a lot of people who saw the film said to me, 'Well, I never knew he had that kind of life.' ... You do get a picture of his life and his whole career" ("Strolling"). David Robinson insists in a DVD interview included with an anniversary edition of the film, "Everything is totally researched. I don't think there's any inaccuracy there. Lord Attenborough was incredibly conscientious in wanting to get it right" ("Strolling"). Attenborough himself insisted, "It is not ... a whitewash in any sense whatsoever" ("A Right Charlie").

All agree, including *Time* film critic Richard Schinkel, that "[t]he big saving grace of the movie *Chaplin* is Robert Downey's performance" ("Strolling"). Schinkel continues, "There was, in that performance, something else, I thought. There was a kind of wistfulness in the performance, a kind of almost stunned quality sometimes as he sort of embraced this rapid rise to gigantic stardom, gigantic celebrity. There's a kind of puzzled, looking around quality in the performance that's very nice. I mean, it was kind of humanizing ("Strolling"). Canby wrote that in *Chaplin*, Downey "is good and persuasive as the adult Charlie when the material allows, and close to brilliant when he does some of Charlie's early vaudeville and film sketches. His slapstick routines are graceful, witty and, most important, really funny." Even Travers raved, "Everything you see Downey do in it—from how Chaplin moved, how he behaved as a mime—you could put that in a time capsule and use it to teach people about acting" ("Best Performances").

In discussing Downey's portrayal of Chaplin, Kuriyama concedes that he copies the Tramp well,

> but this superficial mimicry is not what makes his performance remarkable. Somehow—perhaps by studying Chaplin's films—Downey has burrowed deep into a forbiddingly difficult character, and at times actually seems to merge with him. He is surprisingly adept at recreating Chaplin's private moods—brooding self-absorption, physical and emotional exhaustion, irritability, icy anger, gritty determination shading into obsession.... Good actors can sometimes compensate for a weak script, but Downey humanizes and sublimates Chaplin in spite of a sleazy tabloid script—a far more impressive achievement [Kuriyama 44].

Thomas Doherty reiterates the high praise given by nearly all commenters on the film when he, like Kuriyama, stresses Downey's ability to move beyond mere copy: "Stripped of his Tramp persona, mimicked by a second-rater, Chaplin might have seemed merely mortal. Downey's double achievement is not only to reveal the private man behind the artist but also to do credit to his public artistry" (76). Doherty writes, "In truth, he is terrific.... Downey's mastery of a theatrically derived style that was equal parts buffoonery and ballet is the more impressive because there is simply no training ground of even rough equivalence to the lifelong apprenticeship on the vaudeville boards that Chaplin and Keaton served from childhood" (76). When the film ends with a montage of clips of real Chaplin films watched by Downey as Chaplin at the Oscars, "It is a tribute to Downey's performance that the recent memory of his Chaplin bears such worthy comparison with our deeper memory of the real one. At the end it's a seamless match" (Doherty 77).

Film critics and scholars weren't the only ones impressed by Robert's abilities. Dan Kamin remembers, "I was very proud of Robert. His hard work and native ability resulted in a brilliant performance" (Kamin, Message). Diana Hawkins notes in Attenborough's autobiography, "Deservedly, he received a Best Actor Oscar nomination for his reincarnation of Chaplin. That he didn't win was our fault," she admits, but explains their limitations defensively: "Had we stood out against Mario Kassar and refused to tell Charlie's story in flashback, the film would have been far more coherent—although it would almost certainly never have been made at all. And had we fulfilled expectations by including more of the comedic Little Tramp and less of his progenitor's dark and complicated life story, we would undoubtedly have attracted better reviews" (Attenborough 236). Although Downey did not win the Academy Award or the Golden Globe for Best Actor, he was nominated and he did win a Best Actor BAFTA from the British Academy of Film and Television. The film also received several other nominations, including John Barry's Academy and Golden Globe nominations for Best Music and Original Score, nominations by the British Academy for Best Costume Design, Best Make-Up and Best Production Design, and a Golden Globe nomination for Geraldine Chaplin for Best Supporting Actress (*IMDb*).

Only Human

Although he believed "Chaplin is God.... He's an ideal, something the world created because they desperately needed him" (qtd. in Diamond) and although he had been praised at the highest levels for his portrayal of this "God," Downey was characteristically both proud of and humble about his own performance. In a 1992 interview, he said about his Oscar nomination, "It's largely due to Attenborough's direction and to Chaplin giving us something to make a film about anyway, a great artist." He did admit to being disappointed by not winning, though, saying on *Sunday Morning Shootout*, "I can be kind of a sour grapes guy on occasion I guess, too. I didn't even want to go to the parties after. I was like, that son of a bitch Al Pacino, he took my Oscar." Downey finally conceded, "it was his turn" (*SMS*). At the time, he told press, "I'm just so happy I made it through without having a nervous breakdown or really disappointing everyone" (Stivers). *Chaplin* gave him some self-respect because, as he explained, "For the first time, I am at a place where I demand respect. People used to perceive me as some kind of fucking idiot savant who needs to be led around by the hand. Which took the edge off being a grown-up, whether or not I wanted to admit it" (Schneller).

Hawkins muses, "Would winning an Oscar have provided the impetus Robert needed to kick his drug habit? I doubt it…. [But d]espite many setbacks after his release [from prison], this most captivating, infuriating and creative of actors, has continued to work ever since. He is now … remarried and, hopefully at long last, clean" (Attenborough 236–237). Downey himself admits that not winning the Oscar for his performance was probably a good thing. Even taking ten more years to get sober wasn't so bad, he believes, because it taught him humility. He told *Playboy* in 2010,

> Let's say Chaplin had come out and I'd busted all the right moves, gotten on Antabuse or something, and done the stuff I'm doing now back then. I guarantee you I'd have a hangar filled with vintage this and that and maybe even a bronze of myself—flagrant artifacts of success, a real squander-fest. Now a splurge to me is getting a bunch of T-shirts or sneakers. And I still look at the prices, because I think everything is ridiculous.

He wouldn't have been able to handle, in 1993, the degree of success that he has now.

Despite not winning the Oscar and falling into heroin addiction a couple of years later, Downey was able to use what he learned from Chaplin, both the man and the movie. On the set and in training with Dan Kamin, he honed his physical skills to perfection, using them again in films like *Heart and Souls* (1993). "Over the course of filming [*Chaplin*], Downey changed his posture and the way he moved his mouth" (Schneller), and became even more adept with physical comedy. His timing and agility had always come naturally to him but perhaps without *Chaplin*, they would not have evolved to the level they did. Norman Jewison, who directed him in *Only You* (1994), cast Downey for being "like Tony Curtis: charming with great comedic timing" (Fallon). Although Kamin refuses "to claim credit for any changes in Robert's performance style" (Message), audiences can easily see the effects of his *Chaplin* education on his posture and poise in wildly different films such as *Iron Man* (2008) and *Due Date* (2010). Even the writer and director of *The Shaggy Dog* (2006) believed that Downey carried a bit of Chaplin with him in many of his physical comedy scenes ("Commentary"). Having spent a couple of years intently studying Chaplin's movements, it's not surprising that some of the Tramp's style became amalgamated into Robert's own repertoire. It is visible in recent films such as *Sherlock Holmes* (2009) and its 2011 sequel, *A Game of Shadows*, in which the bare-knuckle boxing fight sequences and action scenes, mixed as they are with Guy Ritchie-driven violence, Eric Oram-taught Kung Fu, and Downey's own old-fashioned balletic, self-mocking goofiness, showcase a unique combination of skills and habits, some of which the actor no doubt acquired while attempting to channel Chaplin.

But did Chaplin become the role model Downey was looking for? In 1992 he told *Sky Magazine* (whose unimpressed interviewer called him a prat), "I'm really starting to realise what this experience was about for me. It was like someone saying, 'You have no excuse not to try after this. You have the ability, you have the information, you've had the experience, you've relived the life of someone who did it right.' Career-wise, Chaplin nailed it" (Sweeting). The film's production notes quote Downey explaining that the movie "changed [his] life," giving him "a whole different perspective on communication, art, humor and the sadness behind humor." It also furthered his desire to have more "creative autonomy" (7), as Chaplin did. Now with his own production company helmed by his wife, Susan, he has finally reached that stage. *Chaplin* obviously didn't completely heal Downey, but maybe it began the long process. He said in 1993, "[E]verything was a lesson in this film. The dialect was about discipline; the movement was about restructuring; and the makeup was about patience, a virtue I just didn't possess in any way." Chaplin the man taught him much about hard work and slowing down and the Tramp further brought out in him what he already instinctively knew—that the kind of ironic yet innocent, silly but sad persona that both artists shared connected with audiences in a powerful, universal way. Remembering his own reaction to Chaplin's *The Gold Rush* as a child, biographer Louvish writes,

> Existence, of course, is the teetering cabin, poised in a blizzard over the cliff. Aware of something amiss, inside the cabin, Charlie and Mack Swain try jumping up and down, to figure out whether it's just the stomach cramps, or external reality. When both walk to the wrong side, reality swiftly tips over, held by a rope caught in a cleft. Every child knows this feeling, that derives from nature, not nurture. It is the human condition, that Chaplin understood instinctively, derived no doubt from his own childhood, but also, and perhaps more so, from the very fact of being alive, of being vulnerable in a void filled by the self and perception, and which becomes a sharper dilemma as we grow older, and realize our temporary sojourn on earth [363].

Feeling this vulnerability too keenly, Downey was unsuccessful in his early Nineties attempts to get free from addiction but no matter how far he fell, he remained able to bring an overwhelming likeability to the characters he played. We are all vulnerable in "the teetering cabin," but a great artist can embody and communicate that feeling—that humanity—in a way that seems to make the struggle all right. Chaplin depicts Charlie as a dissatisfied clown who wants to do something more and seems to be his own worst enemy. In the film, he expresses what Downey must have felt after losing that Oscar: "It's when you feel you're getting really close but you can't make it the rest of the way. You're not good enough. You're not complete enough. And despite all your fantasies, you're second rate. You're human. That's very hard." Like Chaplin, Downey covered his inferiority complex with a deliberate confidence and determination that made audiences unable to look away. His recent self-deprecating comments about his starring role in a blockbuster franchise ("It's not that serious and it's not that artistic," he told Chris Heath in *GQ*) echo Chaplin's final thoughts on the Tramp, in Attenborough's film: "End of the day, you're not judged by what you didn't do, but what you did.... I didn't change things, I just—he just cheered people up. Not bad, that."

Works Cited

Aldridge, David. "Chaplin's Defence." *Film Review* Feb. 1993: n. pag. Articles and Interviews. *Downey Unlimited Forever*. Web. 5 Jul. 2013.
_____. "Charlie's Angels." Film Review Mar. 1992: n. pag. Articles and Interviews. *Downey Unlimited Forever*. Web. 5 Jul. 2013.
Attenborough, Richard, and Diana Hawkins. *Entirely Up to You, Darling*. London: Hutchinson, 2008. Print.
Bart, Peter, and Peter Guber. "Robert Downey Jr." Episode #1.14. *Sunday Morning Shootout*. 18 Jan. 2004, AMC. Television.
"Biography, Famous." 2006. Audio and Video Index. *Downey Unlimited Forever*. Web. 2 Aug. 2013.
Bishop, Kathy. "A New and Improved Robert Downey Jr. Takes on the Role of a Lifetime and Grows up in the Process." *Harper's Bazaar* Dec. 1992: n. pag. Articles and Interviews. *Downey Unlimited Forever*. Web. 1 Aug. 2013.
Byrge, Duane. "Review of *Chaplin*." *The Hollywood Reporter* 7 Dec.1992: n. pag. Downey Review Archive—*Chaplin*. *Downey Unlimited Forever*. N.p. Web. 2 Aug. 2013.
Canby, Vincent. "Robert Downey Jr. in Charlie Chaplin Life Story." *New York Times,* 25 Dec. 1992: n. pag. Downey Review Archive—*Chaplin*. *Downey Unlimited Forever*. Web. 2 Aug. 2013.

Chaplin. 15th Anniversary Edition. Dir. Richard Attenborough. Maple Pictures, 1992. DVD.
"Chaplin." *IMDb*, n. d. Web. 11 Jan. 2014.
Chaplin, Charles. *My Autobiography*. 1964. London: Penguin, 2003. Print.
"Chaplin the Hero." Special Features. *Chaplin*. 15th Anniversary Edition. Dir. Richard Attenborough. Maple Pictures, 1992. DVD.
The Charlie Rose Show. Host Charlie Rose. PBS. 23 Oct. 2003. Television.
Cozzone, Camille. "Cover Story: Robert Downey Jr. and Virginia Madsen." *In Fashion* Oct. 1988: n. pag. Articles and Interviews. *Downey Unlimited Forever*. Web. 30 July 2013.
Dewey, Donald. "150 Years with Stanislavsky." *Russian Life* 56.1 (Jan-Feb 2013): 52–59. Print.
Diamond, Jamie. "Robert Downey Jr. Is Chaplin (on Screen) and a Child (Off)." *New York Times*, 20 Dec. 1992. Web. 1 Aug. 2013.
Doherty, Thomas. "Chaplin." *Cineaste* Fall 1992: 75+. *Academic OneFile*. Web. 2 Aug. 2013.
Due Date. Dir. Todd Phillips. Warner Bros., 2010. DVD.
Ebert, Roger. Review of *Chaplin*. Chicago Sun-Times, 8 Jan. 1993: n. pag. Downey Review Archive—*Chaplin. Downey Unlimited Forever*. Web. 2 Aug. 2013.
Falk, Ben. *Robert Downey Jr.: The Fall and Rise of the Comeback Kid*. London: Portico, 2010. Print.
Fallon, James. "Upside Downey." *W* Sept. 1994: n. pag. Articles and Interviews. *Downey Unlimited Forever*. Web. 1 Aug. 2013.
Felperin, Leslie. "Robert Downey Jr.: Marlon Brando on Acid, Anyone?" *Independent News* 2003: n. pag. Articles and Interviews. *Downey Unlimited Forever*. Web. 6 June 2013.
Fleming, Michael. "The Real Robert Downey Jr." *Playboy* Nov. 2010: n. pag. Articles and Interviews. *Downey Unlimited Forever*. Web. 1 Aug. 2013.
Figgis, Mike. Director's Commentary. *One Night Stand*. 1997. New Line Home Video, 1998. DVD.
Fischer, Paul. "Interview: Robert Downey Jr. for *The Singing Detective*." *Dark Horizons.com*. Dark Futures Pty Ltd., 3 Mar. 2003. Web. 1 Aug. 2013.
Foster, Jodie. "Director's Commentary." *Home for the Holidays*. 1995. Dir. Jodie Foster. *The Robert Downey Jr. Collection*. Fox Home Entertainment, 2009. DVD.
Gandhi. Dir. Richard Attenborough. Columbia, 1982. Film.
The Gold Rush. Dir. Charles Chaplin. United Artists, 1925. Film.
"Gwyneth Paltrow Shows Up Robert Downey Jr. with Fluent French." *Express*, 22 Apr. 2013. Web. 7 Jan. 2014.
Haldeman, Peter. "It's the Tramp! It's the Great Dictator!" *Mirabella* Dec. 1992: n. pag. Articles and Interviews. *Downey Unlimited Forever*. Web. 1 Aug. 2013.
Heart and Souls. 1993. Dir. Ron Underwood. Universal, 1998. DVD.
Heath, Chris. "RD3." *GQ*. May 2013. 90–97, 144–146. Print.
Hirschberg, Lynn. "Robert Downey's Weird Science of Acting." *Rolling Stone* May 1988: n. pag. Articles and Interviews. *Downey Unlimited Forever*. Web. 1 Aug. 2013.
Hoggard, Liz. "Figgis with Attitude." *Guardian*, 26 Oct. 2003. Web. 1 Aug.2013.
Hudson, Greg. "The Man in the Iron Mask." *Sharp* May 2013. 66–71. Print.
Iron Man. Dir. Jon Favreau. Paramount, 2008. DVD.
Kamin, Dan. *Charlie Chaplin's One-Man Show*. Metuchen, NJ: Scarecrow Press, 1984. Print.
_____. Message to Erin E. MacDonald. 14 Jan. 2013. E-mail.
_____. "Teaching Charlie Chaplin How to Walk." *The Comedy of Charlie Chaplin: Artistry in Motion*. Lanham, MD: Rowman & Littlefield, 2011. Print.
Kuriyama, Constance B. "Chaplin." Review. *Film Quarterly* 47.2 (1993/94): 42–48. Web. 29 June 2013.
The Last Party. 1992. Dir. Mark Benjamin and Marc Levin. Live Home Video, 1993. VHS.
Leftwich, Lynda. "Robert Downey Jr.—The New 'Little Tramp.'" *Movie Extra* Spring 1992: n. pag. *Downey Unlimited Forever*. Web. 5 July 2013.
Less Than Zero. 1987. Dir. Marek Kanievska. Fox Home Entertainment, 2008. DVD.
Louvish, Simon. *Chaplin: The Tramp's Odyssey*. London: Faber and Faber, 2009. Print.
"The Man in Chaplin's Boots." *Chaplin Production Notes*. TriStar Pictures, 1992. 5–7. Print.
Modern Times. Dir. Charles Chaplin. United Artists, 1936.
"The Most Famous Man in the World." Special Features. *Chaplin*. 15th Anniversary Edition. Dir. Richard Attenborough. Maple Pictures, 1992. DVD.
Only You. Dir. Norman Jewison. TriStar, 1994. Film.
"The Perfect Charlie." Audio and Video Index. *Downey Unlimited Forever*. Web. 2 Aug. 2013.
Perry, John. *Encyclopedia of Acting Techniques*. Cincinnati: Betterway Books, 1997. Print.
Raab, Scott. "The Second Greatest Actor in the World." *Esquire* Dec. 2009: n. pag. Articles and Interviews. *Downey Unlimited Forever*. Web. 1 Aug. 2013.

Rebello, Steven. "Young Hollywood—Rockin' Robert." *Movieline* Mar. 1991: n. pag. Articles and Interviews. *Downey Unlimited Forever*. Web. 1 Aug. 2013.

Rensin, David. "20 Questions." *Playboy* Aug. 1991: n. pag. Articles and Interviews. *Downey Unlimited Forever*. Web. July 2013.

"A Right Charlie." *Academy* 21 Mar., 1992: n. pag. Articles and Interviews. *Downey Unlimited Forever*. Web. 1 Aug. 2013.

Robbins, Brian, and David Hoberman. "Audio Commentary." *The Shaggy Dog*. Dir. Brian Robbins. Disney Home Entertainment, 2006. DVD.

"Robert Downey Jr." *Inside the Actor's Studio*. 12.15.06. *You Tube*, 15 May 2013. Web. 2 Aug. 2013.

"Robert Downey Jr. Attends Los Angeles 2011 Britannia Awards." *You Tube*, 5 Dec. 2011. Web. 2 Aug. 2013.

Robinson, David. "Introduction." Charles Chaplin. *My Autobiography*. 1964. London: Penguin, 2003. Print.

Sawoski, Perviz. "The Stanislavski System: Growth and Methodology. Second Edition." http://homepage.smc.edu/sawoski_perviz/Stanislavski.pdf. Santa Monica College, n. d. Web. 25 July 2013.

Schneller, Johanna. "What a Tramp!" *GQ* Jan. 1993: n. pag. Articles and Interviews. *Downey Unlimited Forever*. Web. 11 July 2013.

Shainberg, Steven. Director's Commentary. *Fur*. New Line Cinema, 2006. DVD.

Sherlock Holmes. 2009. Dir. Guy Ritchie. Warner Bros., 2010. Blu-Ray.

Sherlock Holmes: A Game of Shadows. 2011. Dir. Guy Ritchie. Warner Bros., 2012. Blu-Ray.

Showbiz, Bang. "Robert Downey Jr.—Robert Downey Jr.: 'I wish I'd had discipline.'" Contactmusic.com, 10 June 2013. Web. 2 Aug. 2013.

The Singing Detective. 2003. Dir. Keith Gordon. Paramount Home Entertainment, 2004. DVD.

Spitz, Bob. "On the Set: Ladies and The Tramp." *U.S. Magazine* Jan. 1993: n. pag. Articles and Interviews. *Downey Unlimited Forever*. Web. 1 Aug. 2013.

Stanislavski, Constantin. *An Actor Prepares*. 1936. Trans. Elizabeth Reynolds Hapgood. New York: Routledge, 1989. Print.

Stivers, Cyndi. "Trampled." *Premiere* Jan. 1993: n. pag. Articles and Interviews. *Downey Unlimited Forever*. Web. 7 July 2013.

"Strolling into the Sunset." Special Features. *Chaplin*. 15th Anniversary Edition. Dir. Richard Attenborough. Maple Pictures, 1992. DVD.

Sweeting, Adam. "A Right Charlie?" *Sky Magazine* Dec. 1992: n. pag. Articles and Interviews. *Downey Unlimited Forever*. Web. 1 Aug. 2013.

Terminator 2: Judgment Day. Dir. James Cameron. TriStar, 1991.

Travers, Peter. "Chaplin." Review. *Rolling Stone Archives*, 7 Jan. 1993. Web. 5 July 2013.

_____. "Robert Downey Jr.'s Best Performances." *You Tube*, 17 Apr. 2010. Web. 30 July 2013.

Tropic Thunder. Dir. Ben Stiller. Dreamworks Home Entertainment, 2008. DVD.

Turan, Kenneth. "Cinema Scion." *Interview Magazine* Apr. 1989: n. pag. Articles and Interviews. *Downey Unlimited Forever*. Web. 1 Aug. 2013.

Untitled. MP3 Interview on Chaplin. 1992. Audio and Video Index. *Downey Unlimited Forever*. Web. 2 Aug. 2013.

Virtue, Graeme. "Tracks of His Years." *Sunday Herald* [Edinburgh], 17 Apr. 2005. Institute for Robert Downey Jr. Studies—Required Reading. *Robert Downey Jr. Film Guide*. Web. 1 Aug. 2013.

Facing Life with Face Off: Race and Identity in the Films of Robert Downey Sr. and Robert Downey Jr.

Tony Prichard

"I don't drop character until I record the DVD commentary."
—Downey as Kirk Lazarus as Lincoln Osiris, *Tropic Thunder*

Robert Downey Jr. in the summer of 2008 became something new— the most respected and popular star of his generation. Such an event was hardly a novel experience for his career, which started when he was five starring in his father's film *Pound* (1970). Downey had been here before nearly two decades prior after his performance in *Chaplin* (1992), a role that moved him out of the place of just another brat pack star trying to survive in the '90s and into the Hollywood elite. With his role as Tony Stark in the adaptation of Jack Kirby and Stan Lee's classic comic *Iron Man*, Downey had his very own profitable action franchise. Ironically, his other film that came out during that summer presents a critique of Hollywood and the paths to success or failure—Ben Stiller's *Tropic Thunder*. In the works of Robert Downey Jr. the consequences of the debt his family owed to film and performance are worked out in a variety of films, most notably *Heart and Souls* and *Tropic Thunder*. However, it is essential to consider this legacy as one which passes through the films of his father, Robert Downey Sr., who gave Downey Jr. his first starring roles. Downey Sr.'s films, many of which interrogate concepts of race, politics, and performance, specifically inform and shape this legacy.

In *Tropic Thunder*, Downey plays Method actor Kirk Lazarus who is famous for his devotion to each role that he plays. Downey, in preparing to play Lazarus, apparently modeled his performance on actors such as Russell Crowe and Colin Farrell, as well as on his own career. Consequently, very little of the screen time in *Tropic Thunder* consists of Downey as Kirk Lazarus. Instead, Downey's time on screen is dominated by the character that Lazarus is playing—Sergeant Lincoln Osiris. In the film, Lazarus as Osiris observes that he doesn't "drop character" until the last phase of the production—when the DVD commentary is completed. On the DVD release for *Tropic Thunder*, Downey performs the commentary as Osiris. In this way, Downey follows through on Osiris's promise and breaks the fourth wall in a way that complicates many of the rules of film but works in the context of the film and its satire of Hollywood.

Performance is all in the world presented in *Tropic Thunder*. All of the work in the film, whether it borders on the self-consciousness of satire or is just physical humor, has to deal with the fact of being in a world of performances. What works or doesn't work in the film does so because of its relationship to performance. It is only once the performance is "in the can" that it is seen as succeeding or failing. Downey Jr. plays his role as the example of how to succeed. Kirk Lazarus is the epitome of the Method actor, down to the bouts of strange public behavior and trappings of fame such as armfuls of acting awards; however, in a very real sense, Lazarus points to Downey's own career—one filled with critically praised roles and infamous encounters with the law.

In Downey's world, there has always been a connection between film and life. Robert Downey Sr. gave his son his first roles in his films *Pound* and *Greaser's Palace* (1972). Downey Sr.'s films were from the beginning a family affair with his wife, Elsie Downey, typically starring. However, this connection between film and life began for Downey Jr. even before his roles in his father's films, when Downey Sr. made a movie so that he could have a son: "I actually did *Sweet Smell of Sex* to pay for the birth of my son [actor Robert Downey Jr.], because when my daughter was born it was tough, it was in Bellevue. Because of *Sweet Smell of Sex*, I was able to put his mother [Elsie Downey] in a decent hospital, and that's what that was really about" (qtd. in Dixon, "No More Excuses" 5).

Simply put, a film paid for Robert Downey Jr. to be born. The film's production was not a job that Downey Sr. was interested in from an artistic point of view but was instead a necessity for the growth of his family. Born to a father who saw film both as an artistic outlet and as a means of financial survival, Junior must have been aware at an early age of the unstable nature of performance and its relationship to identity. The evolution of representations of race in film that influenced Downey Sr. and led up to Senior's film *Putney Swope* (1969) in turn influenced Downey Jr.'s performances of race and identity.

Sound Histories

From its beginnings, narrative film in America has been bound up in the country's racial problems. It is old news that the history of the KKK forms a foundation text for Griffith's *The Birth of a Nation*, narrative cinema's first blockbuster. The dawn of popular sound cinema in the late 1920s inaugurated many things: the pioneering of new genres and possibilities for the medium, a new phase in the technology of illusions, and the beginning of a social transformation. At the core of this development stood one fundamental operation—the cutting off of voices from bodies and the reattaching of them by technical means. Typically this was a means by which the technology allowed for the voice and image to be recorded separately and then integrated. By the time of Downey Sr.'s films, the technique could be used by filmmakers to replace all the voices and sound in a film by recording them over the original soundtrack. There was for a very long time no means of having the two recorded by the same medium. The separating of voice from body in film always potentially references race—or at least the way in which identity is represented in American cinema. With the talkies, the technological capability to cut a voice off from a body and replace it with another became possible.

Race relations in Ishmael Reed's *Mumbo Jumbo* play out as an ongoing clandestine war.

The borrowings in the work from various sources make Reed's novel a complex text that works in many ways like a film. Much like William S. Burroughs' Nova Trilogy a decade before it, *Mumbo Jumbo* shows forms of media such as newspaper articles as means of control. Reed gets at the fear of possession by the racial other that forms a basis of American culture. From the first American bestseller, George Lippard's *The Quaker City*, up to the present day, this trope has been worked and reworked in novels and films. From the hips of Elvis to films like Warren Beatty's *Bulworth* and Spike Lee's *Bamboozled,* the trope of whites being possessed by blackness still fuels opinions about culture.

Specifically in *Mumbo Jumbo*, the threat of possession takes the form of the Jes Grew, a plague that threatens all things white. Ishmael Reed in his narrative constantly shifts point of view between characters so that the Jes Grew sometimes appears as a plague, for example when the narrative is being told by secret societies of the white characters, such as the Atonists, The Wallflower Order, and the Templars, and at other times appears as an anti-plague, when the black characters narrate. As in the films of Robert Downey Sr. and Robert Downey Jr. identity and performance have to be revised to suit the situation of the story by any technical means necessary. Reed in his presentation of the power of newspapers and books points to the idea that prior to sound cinema there was still a container to culture that can be seen in the reliance upon print and physical encounters with actual performances. The world of the novel is one where radio, newspapers and films act as new weapons in the war between races. In this way Reed's book presents mass media as on the rise in its powers to fashion and recreate identities. But in Reed's novel the ultimate move of being able to separate voice from body has not yet happened. Once sound cinema arrives on the scene and makes possible the separation, it marks a point of no return for the presentation and crafting of identity.

The specific plan of the Atonists involves a key point that connects to film's power to remove voice from body. In order to stop the spread of Jes Grew, the Wallflower order tries to strike specifically at the carriers of Jes Grew by using "a Talking Android who will work within the Negro, who seems to be its classical host; to drive it out categorize it analyze it expel it slay it" (17). It is not enough to keep a culture separate but the ultimate power lies in co-opting one culture and making it speak its opposite from within itself via technological means. This is a power that will be taken up in forms of twentieth century culture as diverse as film, literature, and advertising; however, this is also a power that will be critiqued from within those same forms. In the performances of Robert Downey Jr. such as *Heart and Souls* and *Tropic Thunder*, the actor's abilities take the place of the technological means of reconnecting different voices with bodies.

Heart and Souls: *The Return of the Repressed*

Downey's performance in Ron Underwood's *Heart and Souls* puts forward a different strategy with respect to voice and actor. Because Thomas Riley (Downey Jr.) is haunted by the victims of an accident in which a bus driver, played by David Paymer, swerved to avoid hitting Riley's parents-to-be, his role involves him playing the majority of characters in the film. After the crash, the driver's ghost ascends into heaven; however, his four passengers, Harrison Winslow (Charles Grodin), Penny Washington (Alfre Woodard), Julia (Kyra Sedgwick), and Milo Peck (Tom Sizemore), are not so lucky. They find themselves attached to the boy—

literally tethered to Riley by six feet of ectoplasmic chain, following him both willingly and unwillingly.

The ghosts try to make the most of the situation by advising Thomas and keeping him company. The spirits influence him to such a degree that his parents and teachers see him as having mental problems. Instead of dooming the seven-year-old Thomas to a life in clinics, the ghosts collectively make a decision to abandon him by making themselves invisible to him. When the scene changes from the Sixties to the early Nineties, the damage done by the spirits' choice becomes clear. Thomas Riley is a successful businessman who has emotional attachment issues that the audience can only assume he developed from being abandoned by his spirit guides at such a young age. The ghosts are informed by the bus driver that they were left on Earth to get the help of the boy Riley in order to clean up their accounts and set things straight. They will need to reappear to Riley and get his help. By returning, the four will also need to set things straight with Riley and emotionally heal him.

The first soul to possess Riley is Milo. When Milo died, he was attempting to become a reformed thief. From a narrative point of view there are many reasons that Milo is first to possess Riley. First, the adventure or screwball comedy tropes that a heist-gone-wrong offers to the film present a logical choice, given Downey's roles in the 1980s in films like *Weird Science* (1985) and *Back to School* (1986), to get the audience accustomed to the concept of Downey Jr. being possessed by these souls. Showing Downey acting as a wisecracking criminal falls within the roles that he had already played, such as Jimmy in *Tuff Turf* (1985) or Ian in *Weird Science*, and so Downey's performance of being possessed by a streetwise thief works as a low risk way to introduce the idea. Milo appears to be simply trying out Riley's body the way he would borrow a car.

The process of resolving the narrative requires that the others take turns possessing Riley. As an actor, Downey must take on the roles of most of the members of this ensemble cast. His identity as a character in the film exists as a hybrid of the four other main characters. After Milo succeeds, Riley is possessed by Penny Washington to get backstage so that Harrison Winslow can sing in front of a crowd. Interestingly, Penny announces that she had trained as an actor—so an African-American woman possessing a white man is framed within the rules of performance. Once backstage, the ghosts force Harrison Winslow into Riley's body. We see Downey performing on stage as Riley possessed by Winslow to sing the national anthem. The performance pleases the crowd and eventually becomes a duet with B.B. King. Of course, Riley is trespassing and is brought before the law. As these adventures with the spirits make him break the rules of traditional film performance, they also frequently cause him to break the law and get arrested. Riley continually faces the opportunity to admit to someone that he is haunted and sees ghosts, but to do so would be to admit the impossible. He does not choose to do this and instead talks his way out of jail to a sympathetic police officer who eventually is revealed to be Penny Washington's son.

In the final scene in which Riley is possessed by Penny and she speaks to her son, Downey delivers a performance during which he takes on not only a different race and gender but, more challengingly, the role of a mother meeting her long-lost son. Downey's skilled performance as a hybrid character who throughout the film has played the role of all of the major characters results in the power of this scene. Riley as a role for Downey requires him to be an ensemble of one.

With Julia, the final ghost, it turns out that her lost love has passed away so she cannot resolve her matter simply by writing a letter and delivering it to her old boyfriend. Julia then interprets this turn of events to mean that she is supposed to fix things in Riley's life, so that he does not make the same romantic mistakes that she did. In this way, Riley reconciles with his estranged girlfriend and Julia boards the bus. The plot wraps up neatly and this fact is remarked upon by Hal the bus driver: "I like that it has unity." In his performance, Downey not only performs all the roles of the major characters in the film but, more importantly, presents a hybrid character that combines different classes, genders, and races.

Black No More / White No More

George S. Schuyler's novel *Black No More* presents the idea of technology as being used to end discrimination by the invention of a process that can make blacks look the same as whites. Resulting from this technology is the hope that the narrator's future would contain "no more expenditures for skin whiteners," "no more discrimination," and " no more obstacles in his path" (14). The continuum voiced by the narrator shows how the process of attempting to appear white required a vigilant effort prior to the invention of the machine. The countless cosmetic procedures that he no longer has to perform after the operation illustrate how the machine and its procedure will meet a specific need. In the book's first chapter, the machine's creator, Dr. Junius Crookman, justifies his creation by explaining that "[t]here is no such thing as Negro dialect, except in literature and drama." Furthermore, the difference between blacks and whites relies only upon constructions. It is the ear that offers proof of this fact for the Crookman who states, "you can't tell over the telephone when you are talking to a white man or a Negro"(11). These observations by the doctor present several interesting and conflicting ideas. The idea that dialects are sectional is a widely known fact that linguistics has spent much ink verifying. The other is that the technology of the telephone with its ability to sever voice from body makes race not an issue—or at least makes it impossible to discern race. Finally, the judgment put forward is that literature and drama are the place where the ideas of Negro dialect live and gain value. In this work of fiction, it is fiction itself that is being indicated as the cause of the problem. This combination of factors made in this novel from 1931 connect significantly to the way in which sound cinema was changing how race was presented.

Roughly two years before Schuyler's novel, Jolson put blackface on in *The Jazz Singer*. In it, Jack (Jolson) prepares nervously for the dress rehearsal. His goal is to stop the show by putting on the best performance he can. Jolson is in blackface for about 12 minutes (about a tenth) of the film. No other place in the film focuses upon the preparation for a role in as minute detail as the blackface scene.

The application of the makeup takes place alongside a discussion about Jake preparing for another role, that of star. Unlike Downey Sr.'s situation, in which the creation of work is a means of providing for and growing a family, in his exchanges with Mary Dale (May McAvoy) Jake boldly states that nothing holds more importance than his career. After this important claim, the sort that typically brings about the negotiation of a Faustian pact, Jake's mother appears backstage. Jake, who has just spoken that performance is all and claimed that nothing can stand in his way, is haunted by his mother and his old life.

At first, the performance and the makeup are so good they fool his mother—if the audience hadn't been walked through the process of seeing Jolson turn into someone else, they might have been fooled as well. It is tempting to put forward the idea that sound technology and the ability to separate voice from image allowed for a shift away from race but such a statement smacks of naivete—the sort that probably would make one's mother show up backstage. The evidence, however, is strong not only in the sense that the technology breaks the chains of literature and drama proposed by the good doctor in Schuyler's novel but also in the sense that the technology shifts away from the identifiable presence of a performer.

At this same time, Harry Smith was in the process of collecting the records that would comprise his *American Anthology of Folk Music*. Smith as a record collector took two segregated histories of recordings (Race records and Hillbilly records) and recombined them in a way that it was hard for listeners to tell the race of the performer. In many cases people were later surprised to discover the race of the performers. The technologies of recording and film, specifically their abilities to disconnect voices from bodies, have an impact upon how race is not only perceived but also how it is thought about and lived. In *Tropic Thunder*, this idea takes a unique shift in that we see the reaction of Kirk Lazarus after his racial reassignment surgery. He, like Jake's mother and the listeners of the *Anthology*, isn't at first able to form a connection between what he sees and hears. However, in the sense that the person who is speaking is him, the situation is like that of the narrator of *Black No More*. Instead of following the seductive idea of the talkies ending race, the concept of sound film as destabilizing the relationship between what is seen and heard with regards to race and identity offers a means of investigating how the work of both Downeys uses hybrid performances that make the viewer question what is seen and heard.

Out of Synch

While the use of sound is a breakthrough, the predominant history of film in America has in many cases replicated Jim Crow laws that segregated blacks from whites, by creating separate films and distribution networks. A film like *Cabin in the Sky* (1943) provides an example of this replication by allowing the new director Vincente Minnelli to work at a fantastical musical with African-Americans before taking on the other major Freed produced musicals for MGM. Also, the birth of rock and roll, in which Elvis took the moves and sounds of black music and presented them in whiteface presents a key example of how dominant culture repackages non-dominant culture as white. But other non-dominant legacies exist that produce counter-movements and different narratives for race.

One of these legacies passes through American underground film. Robert Downey Sr.'s films, in particular, take on these issues or, as Wheeler Winston Dixon notes, "In all of Downey Sr.'s work as a filmmaker, one finds a cheerful and confident glee in the manner in which he deconstructs the sites of power in 1960s cultural production, both as consumerist and/or colonialist zones of haptic transcendence, in which the self may triumphantly reassert its individuality outside the realm of social constraint" (*The Exploding Eye* 62).

In the early work of Robert Downey Sr. such a situation comes about—where, by the use of previously shot footage and the incorporation of underground rock, pop, and jazz, the image and the sound are linked but rarely ever synchronize completely. Moments in his early films such as *Babo 73* or *Chafed Elbows* use the tenuous connection between sound and image to emphasize aspects of the performance that break the seductive power of film. In Downey Sr.'s films, there is a consistent feeling that what is on screen is not really happening—and that the viewer needs to contend with this instability that undermines the traditional connection between sound and image.

Putney Swope, which Downey Sr., made in 1969, attacks the idea of representation and performance from a variety of angles. Specifically, each commercial made in the film by Putney's ad agency Truth and Soul complicates the typical performance of certain codes—ones that the firm violates in every conceivable way. For example, the ad for the pimple cream Face Off features an interracial couple singing the story of their courtship in a park:

> It started last weekend
> At the Yale-Howard Game.
> Girl, I saw your beaver flash
> I'll never be the same. Oh-no.
>
> You gave me a soul kiss,
> Boy it sure was grand.
> You gave me a dry hump
> Behind the hot dog stand. Oh yes.
>
> I used to have pimples
> But I made them disappear.
> He faced life with Face Off
> It made his skin so clear. mmm-mm mm
>
> A pimple is simple
> If you treat your pimples right.
> My man uses Face Off
> He's really out of sight ... and so are his pimples.

This ad presents the couple in a way that initially takes the cultural norm and subverts it. The song contains all of the saccharine of a generic jingle but after the first couple of lines, it deliberately unmasks the subtext of advertising. The ad stays true to the norm, despite the blatant stating of the couple's physical desire for each other, because the actors sing the lines as though without recognition of their potential to be shocking. Within the last two verses, the banalities of ad copy and the typical logic of advertising take over the song: Shock the audience in order to grab attention and then deliver the message of the ad.

From a practical point of view, Downey Sr., in dubbing the voice of Putney Swope, saves his film, but the resulting on-screen performance is unique. The character of Putney Swope exists as a hybrid performance between Arnold Johnson (a black man) and Downey (a white man)—a performance that not only lets the director speak directly through his character but additionally presents a complex picture of race in the film. Because of actor Arnold Johnson (Putney)'s inability to remember the lines of dialogue, Robert Downey Sr. dubbed the dialogue for the film. Downey Sr. explains:

> Arnold [Johnson; the actor who played Putney] never learned his lines. He couldn't. He just didn't, he couldn't, so the cameraman [Gerald Cotts] one night said to me ... he knew I was upset ... I said, "Jesus, I can't make any fucking sense out of this," and he said "well look through here," and I looked through the viewfinder. He said, "You see that beard moving?" I said "yeah," and he said "you can put *anything* in there. Including what you *wrote*. But you gotta do it later, Don't waste your energy now getting upset." So I would come in every night ... we shot most the film at night ... and [Arnold] would say, "I've got the lines." And I would say, "oh good," and

then I knew he didn't. He would just get pieces of it. But we just kept shooting after that, and then I dubbed the whole thing in later. But it was my voice all the way through. It had to be. [Laughs]. It sounded like it was coming from Canada [because it was so obviously dubbed in]! ["No More Excuses" 7]

While this deconstructing and challenging of race may not have been deliberate, it must also take into account the particular ways in which Downey Sr. makes films—typically on the shoestring budgets that define underground film. With this film, the needs of production unfolded into a complex situation with respect to identity and performance.

With Swope, who is introduced to the audience in a corporate boardroom, we find that the narratives of culture are being exploited in ways that work both with and against the grain of accepted culture. Swope, the only African-American on the ad agency's board, is voted in to replace the recently deceased president because none of the other members of the board could vote for themselves and they all drew the conclusion that no one else would vote for Swope. The film starts with the embracing of this "great mistake" that many of the board members insist that they must "stand by." Other members try to persuade Swope from taking the job by informing him of how awful of a job it is.

In *Putney Swope's* dialogue, the ability to distinguish truth from satire is, wonderfully, nearly impossible. Downey's time working in an ad agency makes the script of the film so close to the real boardrooms of Madison Avenue. One example of this verisimilitude occurs in the film's first scene when the firm's chairman, Mario Elias Sr. (Elias was Downey's real last name), addresses his board members with the fact that "[e]very consumer has a small box in his head" and that it is the job of the ad agency to fill that box.

A scene about three-quarters through the film mirrors one that happened in real life while Downey was working in an advertising agency that served as the impetus for making *Putney Swope*. However, for the film, he reverses the races of the two participants in the dialogue. In the film, Truth and Soul's sole white executive presents his case that he should be paid as much as everyone else and so he should get a raise. Swope offers the line back that if he gives him a raise then everyone else will want a raise and nothing will change. The white executive replies with, "I never thought of it that way," to which Swope responds, "and that is why you make less money!" The conversation's logic demonstrates how in racist discourses a claim works because it appears to activate common sense—no matter how nonsensical or unjust the claim may be.

The performance in the film, in which Downey's dubbed voice delivers the lines, complicates the logic's appeal to sense even more because it is the voices of two white men that we are hearing. Like the logic of the commercials that Truth and Soul produces, the truth of the situation is exposed in a way that still allows for a mask to function and offer meaning to the viewer. The audience can read this as a simple reversal in which the satire presents a political message about the hypocrisy and injustice of racism in the workplace. However, with Downey providing the voice for the black boss, such a simple and expected position doesn't completely hold. The audience sees a black man tell a white man that he cannot have a raise but the voice that is doing the telling is not just that of a white man but the voice of the director of the film—the figure that was typically, even in American underground film in the '60s, a white male.

Downey also deals with the issue of dubbing Swope's voice by making a great number of shots in the film from behind Johnson's back. In this way, Downey's voice need not match

Johnson's moving lips. Additionally, much of Johnson's performance involves remaining silent and reacting to others as they pitch ideas to him. Since the performance of Swope never exists entirely in the moment of filming nor in the post-production dubbing of Downey's voice, both pitch and the diegetic consistency of the sound can change in an instant. Downey uses his own voice, as Swope, to change scenes throughout the film. In most cases of this in the film, it is Swope's voice addressing a large group of people. The voice of the director here guides the film not only in its post-production but in the way that Downey as Swope's voice has the last word. Many of these scenes work from a technical point of view because they allow Downey to use a reverse shot so that we don't need to see the disconnect between the actor's mouth and his director's voice.

In the final act of the film, Swope dresses in fatigues like Fidel Castro, and Truth and Soul's offices are constantly beset by protesters. These scenes employ loud non-diegetic music as a means to reinforce the tense mood—with the added bonus of not having to overdub lines. The protestors in the film's last stages have been put there by the President of the United States to protest that Swope discriminates against war toys and cigarettes by not producing ads for those products. Swope decides to cave to this pressure and appears to sell out. However, in a film like *Putney Swope* where everyone acts corruptly, Swope's selling out can be easily reframed as cashing in on the situation. By taking the money and corrupting the corrupt system further, Swope makes the best ethical choice available to him and exits.

"The story of the men who attempted to make that movie"

Unlike *Heart and Souls* in which Downey Jr. needed to perform the identities of all of the main characters, in *Tropic Thunder* he only plays one role; however, that role is potentially more complex because his character is an actor not unlike himself. The role as Kirk Lazarus as a composite performance inspired by the leading contemporary Method actors of the past decade, specifically Russell Crowe, Colin Farrell, and Downey (not quite a Method actor but often taken for one) himself, presents an even greater challenge because *Tropic Thunder* is a satire. Like his father's film targeted advertising, *Tropic Thunder* takes aim at another powerful form of identity construction, cinema. *Tropic Thunder* as a narrative is in no way as clear cut as *Heart and Souls*. It is not a linear narrative or about a historical event but about the moments where film meets a historical event and fails. After a slew of fake trailers and an advertisement, the DreamWorks logo appears. The establishing of a fictional world of films prior to the epic battle scene that follows the studio logo grounds that battle as an illusion—not an illusion that viewers of a fiction film expect, but instead the audience expects the battle scene to be revealed as part of a film production, because it features all of the actors that appear in the trailers prior to the DreamWorks logo.

A key instance of the fragility of the levels of narration happens after the actors have been dropped in the jungle and have encountered live fire. It is still a point of contention between the actors if they are actually making a film or simply trying to survive in a hostile environment. As the characters set out from their drop point, Credence Clearwater Revival's "Run Through the Jungle" begins to play. The inclusion of this song complicates the reality in the scene in that the song has become an obligatory feature of films about the Vietnam War. As the men head out, Downey as Lazarus as Osiris looks back and does a double take.

Such a gesture in a typical film could act as a foreshadowing of danger to come or provide a deal of insight into Osiris's character as one who knows that in the jungle you need to be wary not only of what lies ahead but also of what might come from behind. *Tropic Thunder* as a satire about performance and film raises the stakes of Osiris's glance. Downey performs the double take that questions the whole reality of the thing—not just the way that the reality of the film is up for grabs, but the way in which it is Downey looking at the audience and presenting the idea that all of film as a form of presenting narrative is up for grabs. In that moment the break created makes it hard to decide if we are seeing the concern from the position of Lincoln Osiris's character, the worry of the stranded actor Kirk Lazarus, a silent breaking of the fourth wall by Downey, or some combination of these identities.

Downey as Lazarus as Osiris offers advice to the other characters about acting throughout the whole film. Specifically, in discussing with Tugg Speedman (Ben Stiller) Speedman's recent career choices, Lazarus as a character seems to partially break out of his role as Osiris. As he informs Speedman that Tugg's performance in *Simple Jack* was too realistic because an actor "never goes full retard," he highlights what is ultimately important to Lazarus as a character, the complex navigation of performance and verisimilitude in the performance of a role. With Downey's performance in the film and on the DVD commentary, he shows that the real performance seems to always be about identity and the means by which the actor is able to perform it.

Unlike Jolson who, in blackface, appears in *The Jazz Singer* as a performer working in a tradition that allows for him to bring attention to the black artists that inspired him, Downey's performance points at how performance itself is an essential component of our lives in the twenty-first century. Downey functions as the most popular actor of our times not only because of his powers as an actor but because he connects to the popular narrative of the time concerning performance. Technological media allow for new possibilities for performance. People can, with very little effort, become anyone. Downey, in his professional and personal lives, has illustrated this fact throughout his career. Whether it is as the boy playing a dog in *Pound* or the man playing Iron Man or Sherlock Holmes or Downey as reformed Hollywood troublemaker, he speaks to the idea that technology does indeed change us in the way that it opens up more possibilities for role playing. But it isn't as though we can be anyone—there are rules and responsibilities or at least limits to the kinds of performances that we can pull off even when our face is off.

Works Cited

Babo 73. 1964. Dir. Robert Downey Sr. Criterion, 2012. DVD.
Back to School. Extra-Curricular Edition. 1986. Dir. Alan Metter. Fox Home Entertainment, 2011. Blu-ray.
Bamboozled. Dir. Spike Lee. New Line Cinema, 2000. Film.
The Birth of a Nation. Dir. D. W. Griffith. Epoch Producing Corporation, 1915. Film.
Bulworth. Dir. Warren Beatty. Twentieth Century–Fox, 1998. Film.
Cabin the Sky. Dir. Vincente Minnelli. MGM, 1943. Film.
Chafed Elbows. 1966. Dir. Robert Downey Sr. Criterion, 2012. DVD.
Chaplin. 15th Anniversary Edition. Dir. Richard Attenborough. Maple Pictures, 1992. DVD.
Dixon, Wheeler Winston. *The Exploding Eye: A Re-visionary History of 1960s American Experimental Cinema*. Albany: SUNY Press, 1997. Print.
_____. "No More Excuses: An Interview with Robert Downey Sr." *Post Script* 21.1 (2001): 3–13. Print.
Greaser's Palace. Dir. Robert Downey Sr. Cinema 5 Distributing, 1972. Film.

Heart and Souls. 1993. Dir. Ron Underwood. Universal, 1998. DVD.
The Jazz Singer. 1927. Dir. Alan Crosland. Warner, 2007. DVD.
Lippard, George. *The Quaker City: Or, The Monks of Monk Hall*. Philadelphia: Leary, Stuart & Company, 1845. Print.
Pound. Dir. Robert Downey Sr. MGM, 1970. Film.
Putney Swope. 1969. Dir. Robert Downey Sr. Criterion, 2012. DVD.
Reed, Ishmael. *Mumbo Jumbo*. New York: Scribner, 1996. Print.
Schuyler, George S. *Black No More*. Mineola: Dover, 2011. Print.
Sweet Smell of Sex. Dir. Robert Downey. Adelphia Pictures, 1965. Film.
Tropic Thunder. Dir. Ben Stiller. Dreamworks, 2008. DVD.
Tuff Turf. 1985. Dir. Fritz Kiersch. Image Entertainment, 2012. DVD.
Weird Science. 1985. Dir. John Hughes. Universal, 2008. DVD.

Robert Downey Jr.'s Media Monsters: *Natural Born Killers*, *In Dreams* and *Zodiac*

Karen Oughton

Robert Downey Jr. is known to millions as the charismatic and cantankerous Tony Stark in the *Iron Man* and *Avengers* franchises and for his slightly crazed action-hero take on Sherlock Holmes. However, this essay examines Downey's darker characters, focusing on his depictions of gender, immaturity, and self-obsession in Oliver Stone's *Natural Born Killers* (1994), Neil Jordan's *In Dreams* (1999), and David Fincher's *Zodiac* (2007), in the context of the social and media gaze.

Natural Born Killers

Firstly, Robert Downey Jr.'s display as the over-zealous, morally questionable, manic journalist Wayne Gale in *Natural Born Killers* shows how the media depicts the mass murderer as a masculine hero. Borrowing from Shaun Kimber's research, this section will chart how Gale is paradoxically in a position of social power, yet is in crisis due to a lack of emotional fulfillment resulting from professional obsession. Gale's character experiments with different conceptions of masculinity expressed by those around him, from his desk-bound colleagues through to his collaboration with mass murderer, Mickey Knox. Only by rejecting contemporarily-promoted male power models does his character find peace in a death scene in which he acts as a controlled yet submissive sacrifice to the hungry global audience.

Natural Born Killers tells the story of Mickey and Mallory Knox. The pair come from abusive families, fall in love and begin killing soon after meeting, leaving a witness to retell their story at every scene. Naturally, they attract media attention, specifically that of journalist Wayne Gale. Soon Gale is tracking them, stoking the public fervor for their deeds and consciously turning them into celebrities in the process.

The appearances of both Gale and Mickey and Mallory establish the central themes of the film: the relationship between media and violence and expectations of social class and of gendered behavior. Indeed, Shaun Kimber's recent research into serial killer films shows the popular imagination's link between notions of violence, masculinity, and working-class culture. These suggested links are illustrated by the initial café scene and highlighted by what director Stone calls "vertical cutting"—the insertion of black and white film to indicate the characters' "inner moments" (Commentary). The first example of this technique is seen with the cashier, Mabel, whose "inner moment" shows her flirting with Mickey and reinforcing the female stereotype of romanticism. The male equivalent is inscribed on Mickey's face when the other customers make amorous advances toward Mallory, a challenge to his masculinity that, culturally, could be solved by the ensuing violence. The film plays with these stereotypes when the action becomes an exaggerated brawl in which the feminine-looking Mallory, complete with a long blonde wig and figuring-hugging costume, attacks her voyeurs and vertical cutting illustrates her with masculine gestures and associated working-class status as she yells, "How sexy am I now, fucker?" Repetitions of such aggressive behavior thus depict violence as masculine regardless of the perpetrator, as Stone's commentary states.

Robert Downey Jr.'s reporter, Wayne Gale, is contrasted with Mickey and Mallory's violence. He is introduced presenting his television show, *American Maniacs,* and is therefore shown as someone with a career, but who also peddles images of "masculine" aggression such as kicking down doors during crime-fighting shots. Downey's performance completes the class paradigm within the film. As Stone comments, Gale condescendingly views Mickey and Mallory as "zombie" media consumers, while he is supposedly educated and therefore unaffected by the violence. Nevertheless, the contrast between his TV show and the first scene in which he talks to his colleagues shows that his life is largely sedentary, leaving intimidating his male co-workers with an overarching sense of frustration as his outlet for aggression.

This aggression (barring his vertical-cut moments) is depicted via Gale's frantic movements of his hands, shoulders, mouth, and eyebrows that cause his billowy hair to bounce around comically. He speeds through scenes without seeming to consider the consequences of his actions. Downey also adopts an Australian accent for the role. Often, Gale appears to be talking for the sake of being heard to talk and to justify himself and speaks so quickly as to be periodically unintelligible. He doesn't care if he is understood as long as he gets the coverage he wants. Stone sees this performative hyperactivity as "false" hyper-masculinization (Commentary), but it is actually more akin to what is culturally considered feminine behavior as it constantly demands reciprocation. Furthermore, Gale's accent and speed raise the pitch of his voice to an excited squeal that sounds childlike and almost girlish when he feels he is losing control and becomes exasperated. To be manly is to be powerful and in his class this power is achieved by having influence via high ratings and pay, regardless of what he shows to get them. Gale therefore represents the immaturity and irresponsibility of the media during the film, which is comically parodied when he is shown being feminized before his television interview with Mickey. At that point, he is "girled" (to use gender expert Judith Butler's term) as he shows no understanding of what violence (in the form of Mickey) is or does. His naivety is shown in their interview when the lighting changes from normal daylight to red and white as Gale presents alternate arguments to prompt Mickey's most dramatic responses and leads to his misreading of the situation and to his ultimately being taken hostage by Mickey during the prison riot.

However, Gale's interaction with Mickey ultimately forces him to confront both his and the media's immaturity and self-obsession during the riot. Being a target of the violence allows him to experience the masculinity he had been promoting and thus the violence becomes his personal rite of passage. His participation in this rite is shown graphically when he wears a piece of cloth as a bandana, resulting in him looking like a schoolboy parody of action hero Rambo, particularly when compared to the bald Mickey. As a hostage, his necessary allegiance to Mickey gives him some understanding of blue-collar perspectives of masculinity, and he literally and metaphorically pays for his rite of passage when he witnesses his team being killed and contributes to the scene by firing back in retaliation. Yelling that he "feels alive," he becomes evidence of the corrupting effect his own output has had on him.

Having completed his first "schoolyard" rite-of-passage fight, he is handed the rather safer option of a camera by Mickey, allowing his character time to consider his actions in an emotional test in a green-hued scene that Stone describes as one of "death and rebirth" (Commentary). While acting as the alpha male at work, Gale has nevertheless been shown to be unable to manage his private life successfully. He has married his boss's daughter while also having a girlfriend and emotionally mistreats them both. It is in this scene that Gale's wife and girlfriend tell him (over the phone) that their relationships with him are over, forcing him to witness the increasingly strong bond between Mickey and Mallory that defies the shallow way he previously characterized them.

Gale's murder by Mickey and Mallory represents him finally gaining peace by discarding his previous perceptions of masculinity. He, Mickey, and Mallory have escaped the prison when Mickey terminates the post-riot interviews they appear to have instigated to tell Gale they are going to kill him. Gale becomes aggressive and accuses Mickey of hypocrisy after Mickey professed belief in love while recounting the couple's experience with a Native American he accidentally shot while the man was attempting to heal them. When the couple ignore Gale's argument and pleas for his life, Gale begins to cry and attempts to run away. His movements are physically unbalanced and childlike, mimicking his mental desperation until Mickey, his quasi mentor, tells him to have some dignity. Gale duly returns and reverts temporarily to his nurtured type, as indicated by vertical cutting, and attempts to save his life by suggesting he can help them capitalize on their notoriety.

The film then presents the two concepts of his life: the seemingly professional yet immature and irresponsible man seen by the camera he clutches in his hands, and the man who sees the camera and chooses the masculine power he finally decides to represent. In a vertical cut, Gale discards his aggression and intellect, spreads his arms and makes a meditative sound, recalling the iconography of the Native American man. The repetition thematically bestows some of the Native's qualities on Gale, yet at the same time references uncontextualized globalization by also recalling the position of Christ on the cross. In this pose, therefore, he also represents his communities' "sin" as Jesus is biblically considered to have done and similarly pays with this ritualized finish. It represents a shallow appropriation of the signifiers of Native spirituality that are nonetheless stripped from their contextual denotations. Gale is assuming the image of the Native American because Native Americans are often used in mass media representation as icons of localized spirituality and survival. However, in this instance the image of the particular Native American person Gale is assuming was also little more than a public relations act which in turn led to his death through his misreading of the danger present when tackling the Knoxes' "demons." This section is swiftly followed by a repeated image of Gale as a demon, grinning in apparent acceptance of his nurtured monstrosity before being gunned down.

The audience's final glimpse of Gale is shown from the camera's point of view and sees him crumpled and powerless against a tree. Its low resolution contrasts against the colorful and frenetic display of seconds previous. It shows the arrogant, yet exhilarating character as a suitable and terrible final victim for the couple who have taught him the meanings of maturity, masculinity, and media violence before moving on to what the credits suggest are the rest of their notably non-murderous lives.

In Dreams

Five years following Robert Downey Jr.'s role as murder accessory, he turned to primary antagonist in Neil Jordan's *In Dreams*. In this film, he plays Vivian Thompson, a serial killer who preys on children and on book illustrator Claire's sleeping moments before spiriting them away to become his constructed family after his own deserted him in a flood when he was young. As well as the story slipping between dreams and waking reality, Vivian moves between genders, as is suggested by his name. He dresses in women's clothing and wears makeup—fingernail polish—while wearing men's clothing. Unlike the notion of Vivian as an atypical transvestite discussed in Erin E. MacDonald's work within this volume, this section considers Vivian as a representation akin to metrosexual gender-queerness. It will argue that Vivian uses social personae and stereotypes to gain power by appropriating what has been called the "realness" of the characters he interacts with.

It's firstly necessary to examine the different identities Vivian uses during the film. He is initially described by Claire from the memory of her dreams as either a woman or a man. Consequently, the audience's first sighting of him is within a dream sequence, where a close-up reveals what appears to be a man's hand, but with silver polish visible on the thumb nail. He is then shown from behind abducting a child, his hair flowing long, but with a manly gait and what appear to be men's sneakers and trousers. He is then also shown as a young boy in one of Claire's dreams. However, gender fluidity becomes apparent when the same long-haired figure is seen dressed in red and emitting a forcibly-feminine shriek. From this feminine position, the audience then sees Vivian androgynously, before being dressed entirely (and convincingly) as a female nurse in order to escape from the hospital undetected with Claire. After this instance, when he has brought Claire to the cider factory, he is dressed in an almost cowboyish fashion, complete with his hair tucked into a wide-brimmed hat. The variety of costume changes indicates that clothing to Vivian represents a range of identities including social roles, stereotypes, and finally individuals, such as the red "bad mommy" dress he dons when pretending to be his highly disgruntled mother.

The film suggests there the reason for Vivian's behavior, namely that having been brought up within a sanatorium rather than with his mother, he has issues with abandonment. Indeed, the narrative's use of the Snow White fairy tale suggests both the danger that can befall the child forced to flee his or her home as he was, but also the danger of jealousy that Vivian inflicts on his victims in order to reassemble a family for himself. In both readings, however, the traditionally accepted family model is paramount. Therefore, it's important to ask if Vivian's cross-dressing is the adoption of an additional personality to act as "mother" until he can get Claire, or if it represents something else.

As the next examples show, by trying to be the different aspects of the persona expected of him depending on how he dresses, Vivian begins to succeed at fulfilling the personas he feels he should be by configuring them to suit his own needs. As gender expert Judith Butler has stated, "hegemonic forms of power which fail to repeat loyally [...] open possibilities for resignificating the terms of violation against their violating aims" (84). That is to say, human relationships and indeed "types" of person are based on ideals rather than realities and are therefore practically impossible to achieve. However, by using some of the aspects associated with those types and relationships, it is possible to make them recognizable so that other people respond to them and acknowledge these stereotypes and relationships due to the social power of expectation they wield. However, just as these stereotypes are based on ideas rather than realities, they are alterable. This means that Vivian can use the roles of caregiver mother and nurse that he temporarily inhabits to his own ends, creating new versions of both to get what he wants. The other characters within the film simply respond to what they see and act accordingly.

To understand these roles, it is important to differentiate how Vivian dresses in terms of the distinction between drag and what has been called post-gay drag—taking on aspects of the persona of a social role, rather than simply aspects of the role of the opposite sex. The importance of his persona can be seen in the way Vivian changes his clothing and moves between his social roles. The most obvious role he uses is that left vacant by his mother, whose clothes he wears when "playing" her. However, the audience is told by Ruby, the "adopted" child he kidnaps but does not kill, that he wears his mother's clothes when being the "bad mommy" who chastises her family in the way Vivian's mother chastised him in his father's absence. His attempted reformulation of the family unit throughout the film is what Judith Butler calls "the effect of a love embittered by disappointment or rejection; the incorporation of the Other whom one loved, but now hates"—a "displacement and appropriation of 'woman'" (87). That is, Vivian wants the hierarchical structure, nurturing, and supposed love that the parent role is associated with, while also hating the woman who was his mother precisely because she did not live up to the ideal. It is thus as her that he kills Claire's husband in order to establish and nurture his own family unit. In this sense, he is using and altering his mother's "violation" (to use Butler's term) of what a mother should be in his own conception of the care provider.

But Vivian does not just act the mother role, or as his mother as a person for that matter. His other method of attempting to gain control of his situation is less to do with being a controlled method of establishing his own identity as unashamedly utilizing others' perceptions of gender to achieve his aims. An instance of this technique can clearly be seen when he helps Claire to escape from the sanatorium. After showing her to the nurses' station, he kills the nurse and Claire follows his lead in dressing up in a female nurse's outfit and applying makeup while looking in the mirror.

As any girl (male or female) will tell you, lipstick is important. As performer and gender critic Kate Bornstein has said, to be accepted as a person rather than simply as a role requires character, particularly if it is going to involve speaking to people. There is a question of what kind of person one needs to be to be accepted by other people. In Bornstein's case, the example is a particularly fetching scarf. In Vivian's case, bright red lipstick is the item to hand and it, coupled with his otherwise demure appearance, suggests a quietly assertive femininity rather than simple femaleness.

This representation is useful in terms of Vivian's role as the combined hero and villain of the piece and Judith Butler's theories on the social construction of identity here are useful to explain the section, particularly as the example she uses is a police officer and potential criminal. Referring to interpellation theories (which talk about how individuality is "produced" socially), Butler states that, "it is the police who initiate the call or address by which the subject becomes constructed" (81). As Butler explains, if the police officer is the first to initiate contact, the other person—Vivian—is forced to define himself in relation to the police officer because the police officer represents the socially established force of the law. However, as Vivian is dressed as a woman in preparation for avoiding the police officer's suspicion, the officer doesn't recognize him as the escapee and murderer he now is. As a result, the person with the more contextualized knowledge of his social position—the disguised Vivian—is more able to gain power and the force of law that Butler discussed and can reflect that law and the duties of upholding it back onto the policeman. Vivian therefore lifts a shapely leg in the officer's direction and as the policeman has no obvious law to enforce on the apparently innocent female before him, he instead reverts to the police officer's role of social guardian. As Butler would say, the relationship of cop vs. convict is then "forced into a rearticulation" (82) and he invites Vivian into his car to offer "her" a safe ride.

In Dreams then takes this theory a stage further. The waif-like Vivian develops the policeman's role as chaperone beyond his control with friendly glances. Displaced from his position of social power, the lawman's guardian role becomes perverted and devolves into the stereotype of the corrupt cop who sees his passenger as property. While this is happening the audience is shown medium close-ups of Vivian (played as a teenager by Geoff Wigdor) as the nurse and while he is partially obscured by shadow, it is still clear to the audience who the person is as his facial structure is particularly profiled and he begins to flirt. The longer the camera emphasizes that Vivian and the officer continue to behave like this, and the longer the officer's reactions become amorous rather than protective, the more tense the audience becomes as they wait to see if Vivian's secret will be discovered. As the tension increases, sympathies begin to transfer from the inappropriate and increasingly sleazy lawman to the criminal but audacious Vivian. It softens their potentially negative reaction when Vivian kills the officer as his actions are an inventive means to escape capture and victimization due to his assumed gender identity. The audience's approval for Vivian's action is further bolstered after this section when the adult version of the character is played by the famously charismatic and chameleon-like Downey. It is easy to believe that he could do the same.

The next persona Vivian adopts in the film is that of a hippy hunter-gatherer. In the beginning of the film and in the final section when he takes control, he wears sneakers, trousers, a sweater, a t-shirt, and a long and masculine coat and hides his long hair in a wide-brimmed man's hat. Played by Downey, he looks dashing and almost cowboy-like. He has picked the costume that he feels will be suited to his new role and acts on a completely constructed basis as he establishes his new family unit around him. He tells Claire that he will "work real hard" to make the new family a functional unit, with the factory refigured as a rambling squat-come-homestead. Vivian does not adopt full feminine mannerisms at this point because he simply does not need to. Now that he has brought Claire to be the biologically traditional mother to the child, he can play the father's role. What is more, because the social roles he plans for himself, Claire, and Ruby are devised from his idea of an appropriate family and reflect their character histories, he can break away from traditional conceptions of gender because these rules are less needed as a method of stabilizing his new family's social unit. Therefore, he instructs Claire to take time to bond with Ruby while he cooks dinner. In giving these instructions he performs a mixture of the masculine breadwinner role and a nurturer role that promotes interaction rather than pure caregiving between the new parent and the child he has procured for her. Ruby even highlights the meaning of his actions, stating, "Daddies can be just like mommies Vivian said [...] they can cook, too" as she, too, adjusts to his social order.

This social interaction produces the effect of "realness." Butler argues that to be "real" or accepted as something is "symbolic" (89) and based on arbitrary signs. These arbitrary signs, she argues, become social constructs—such as gender—that are then interpreted by society as facts with inherent truths. In this sense, gender norms as an operational force within society are based on what people look like, which is essentially an illusion of fashions. Vivian, however, shows that his chosen roles are not simply based on what he looks like.[1] In Vivian's conception, being "real" and being accepted is actually iconic as he is being part of what is expected of the role he is playing, but isn't actually reproducing it exactly and is therefore making it his own.

As this point in *In Dreams*, Vivian is at his most heroic, having assembled the family unit from the nightmarish fairytale. He has brought them together and in doing so has stabilized his own identity by understanding how he wishes to interact with them. As a result, he is not overly emotional when he is finally convicted of his crimes and instead calmly walks into the prison cell and over to the mirror to look at himself and understand his change in circumstance. Indeed, now knowing himself, he sees his shorn hair and comments, "I can live with this, too." While the film's continued (and unexplained) shifts between dream, fantasy, and reality render Claire's final attack difficult to comment on conclusively, the audience can conclude that his final realization of her image acts to convince him that he was wrong about the potential for the new family unit. It was not that the alternative family type was unworkable (as many Americans will attest), but that his construction of it from unwilling characters who simply shared experiences was. This realization destabilizes his identity. Within modern metrosexuality, communication rather than coercion is key. The audience understands this fact as they witness Vivian's failure to force Ruby and Claire to remain with him and validate his world view and instead watch as his mental state dissolves into madness.

Zodiac

Finally, Robert Downey Jr.'s role as newspaper reporter Paul Avery shows how self-obsession and aggression have affected history. In stark contrast to *Natural Born Killers* and *In Dreams*, the film is based on the actual people involved with the serial killings that occurred in America in the 1960s and 1970s, for which the culprit was never convicted. *Zodiac*, in its themes of creativity and madness, suggests that Avery is vain and portrays him as a mirror image of the notional serial killer as an enigmatic, aggressive creator. Unlike the Zodiac killer, however, Avery's ability to maintain personal control is shown as ultimately and dangerously lacking. Like the other roles discussed in this chapter, the role of Avery shows Downey as a shape-shifting Hollywood star whose casting, professional branding, and somewhat troubled personal history thematically compare with and highlight that of his on-screen character to comment on the media's relationship with masculinity, social expectation, and violence.

As the Zodiac killer was never caught, the film concerns the police investigation into the murders. Examining the role that the police played in the case automatically focuses the narrative on the supposedly-known facts rather than a development of suspense that would otherwise lead nowhere. As a result, the killer's "appearances" are limited to re-enactments of his crimes, encounters with suspects, and, most importantly, his interactions with law enforcement and the media via letters through which he seeks to publicize his crimes.

To show how Avery, an investigative reporter, is depicted as a mirror to the historical Zodiac, the characteristics associated with serial killers must be detailed. FBI agents including Roy Hazelwood developed the criminal profiling practices that deduce the killers' identities from the clues they leave behind. Typical killer traits include narcissism and the presence of the *modus operandi* or signature method of operating, which represents the psychological purpose of their action (Knight). Serial killers are able to function within society, which enables their crimes to go undetected, sometimes for many years. However, in the Zodiac's case, the actual villain of the piece is effectively absent. Popular (if fictitious) serial killer narratives, such as *The Silence of the Lambs*, nevertheless normalize a narrative focus on investigators catching the killer using criminal profiling. To do this, characters such as Hannibal Lecter have popularized the (undoubtedly inaccurate) assumption that investigators must share some of the killers' characteristics in order to replicate their thought patterns. Therefore, as the Zodiac killer uses news media in his *modus operandi* to gain attention, it theoretically follows that a writer who does not despise detailing grisly crimes and indeed writes as a boost to the ego is arguably promoting violence. This suggestion of shared characteristics is a central concern of the film and of the original case and reflects Downey's role as Wayne Gale in *Natural Born Killers*. His Avery is thus placed in that role in this film.

Indeed, writerly concerns and obsessions with language shared between the reporter and the serial killer are highlighted early in *Zodiac* in the first words Avery delivers in the editorial meeting in which the killer's first letter is received. On being asked for the local news report, Avery answers, "Janice in Datebook left the fondue party before everyone got naked." The script focuses the audience's ear initially on the repeated "a"s of "Janice" and "Datebook," then the "e"s of "left," "fondue, and "everyone" before finally uniting the "a" and "e" in "naked." Downey emphasizes these nuances by lingering on the word "fondue" then quickening his pace for the final words while turning toward the camera. In doing so, he emphasizes the scandalous nature of the "news," thus indicating his skills as a wordsmith.

The Zodiac's own obsession with words and meaning is then graphically illustrated as the camera's close-up shot focuses on his first letter to the newspaper, particularly his alliterative coupling of the "s" consonants in the words "teenagers" and "Christmas." This alliterative emphasis on the sound of the name for this celebrated time of the year differs from his use of the specific date (the 4th of July) to discuss when he next attacked. Because of this fact, the camera's close-up shot thematically marries together the concepts of family and celebration and suggests that Zodiac's communication is intended to have a chillingly emotive and fear-inspiring rhetorical impact, a fact emphasized when the letter is passed to the editor to read, instead. The Zodiac's famous ciphers, purposeful misspellings, allegedly disguised handwriting, and word games also draw attention to the alleged killer's rather malignant ingenuity. His malice is shown particularly in his letter of October 14, 1969, in which he writes that he will "just shoot out the front tire & then pick off the kiddies as they come bouncing out." The language emphasizes the comic way he views his murders, with the "i"s of "pick" and "kiddies" alliteratively linking to emphasize the youngsters' smallness. To complete the effect, the "o"s in "come bouncing out" contain more alliteration as well as constructing a sustained, onomatopoeic representation of the sound the children would make when moving as he shot them.

Character traits are also emphasized between Avery and the killer, most notably a level of aggression. Despite David Fincher's assertion on the DVD's audio commentary that the film is not about "aggrandizing a mass murderer" and that he wanted to depict the facts of the case as closely as possible, Downey states that he carried out little research for his role. The real Paul Avery had died and Downey could interpret the role as he saw fit. It is in Downey's choices in playing Avery that the reporter is made to represent a mirror to the killer. Footage of the real Avery in *Graysmith UNMASKED* shows a hesitant and somewhat contemplative-looking man who stares habitually into the middle distance.[2] These personal traits are not replicated in Robert Downey Jr.'s depiction of him. Downey's characterization revels in the actor's charisma combined with a spiky, bullying aspect and Avery is indeed described as "derisive" in the film's Cannes Festival press pack. Downey's Avery introduces himself to the famously young-looking Gyllenhaal's "boy scout" Graysmith by leaning over Graysmith's table to shake his hand rather than waiting for Graysmith to stand. Furthermore, the camera focuses on Graysmith to emphasize the height difference as Avery tells him, "The guy who used to sit there was a great cartoonist," leaving Graysmith to state that he has worked there for nine months. The directing and acting in this exchange suggest that Avery's actions appear to be an attempt to belittle him. Furthermore, Avery's bullying behavior is emphasized later when he angrily (and rudely) wags a finger to reprimand Graysmith for "looming" over him when sitting on the desk, yet frequently does the same to Graysmith.

However, the most interesting departure from recorded reality is Avery's professionalism. The *San Francisco Chronicle*'s obituary (written by Michael Taylor) describes Avery as a man who ended his days dragging his medical equipment to the bar to discuss the local news with his former colleagues and who was survived by a wife and children. Such interest in his journalistic calling and personal commitment to his family are not depicted in the film. Beginning from his first speaking appearance in the editorial meeting in which he has to be commanded to report on crime in Vallejo (the murder in question), to where he is reprimanded for not filing his reports, the Avery of the film is portrayed as vain and lacking in professionalism as well as in an interest in the mechanics of his supposed vocation. Indeed, Avery often appears most enthused about his role in the proceedings when he is shown attempting to use his job to gain status on television interviews or in front of colleagues rather than using it as a means to report on or solve crime. As a result, Downey's representation of Avery contradicts indications of the reporter's character and instead portrays him as having a practical inversion of the behaviors and characteristics typically expected from a journalist.

This negative characterization is further developed in relation to Avery's demise. The real Avery's health may also have been ruined by his addictions, but in the obituary he is depicted as collegiate and is remembered fondly. Downey's Avery is not collegiate or remembered fondly, and here his casting is important. The actor is known for his personal battle with addiction and it would be folly to think this background did not impact on casting him in a role in which personal problems threaten the brilliance of the professional.[3] While the Zodiac killer is obsessed with his "work" (and evades arrest through attention to detail in covering his tracks), Downey's Avery is obsessed with his own ego, or as Fincher describes it, the standard journalist's "incredible, grandiose self-image." This trait is coupled with self-destructive impulses and Avery is repeatedly seen visibly drunk in comparison to the coherent Graysmith, becomes an alcoholic, breaches his remit, attends work in casual dress and walks out of his job when his "excellent work" is not rewarded by his editor.

Moreover, after Avery is seen to leave his job, he carries the film's menace. When Graysmith visits him at home, a medium close-up looks into his darkened houseboat over Graysmith's shoulder. Avery did share the boat with a fellow writer while working on a book project (Taylor), but this fact is not mentioned and instead the action leads to a claustrophobic sequence that is depicted similarly to one in which Graysmith unwittingly visits a possible suspect's home.

Robert Downey Jr.'s Avery is wearing a heavily stained t-shirt and moth-eaten dressing gown as he ushers Graysmith into the darkened houseboat and immediately begins to drink alcohol straight from a bottle. The audience hears the diegetic sound of a primitive computer game playing to itself in the background, a metaphor for the lack of meaningful activity in the once-creative journalist's brain. As Graysmith tries to cajole Avery into talking about the Zodiac case, the tension is increased by silences when the game beeps loudly and defaults while ominous extra-diegetic music begins quietly in the background and Avery sarcastically thanks Graysmith for his desire to "reinvigorate" his "sense of purpose." Robert Downey Jr. then leans forward menacingly, asking Graysmith if he is being "unkind" and belittling Graysmith's own work on the case. Downey's enigmatic renegade has become a drunken, friendless loser. Yet, even in his disheveled state, the actor's charisma serves as a reminder of the heights from which the journalist has supposedly fallen.

As a result, Avery's depiction in the film and Downey's portrayal of him serve to compensate for the lack of a conclusion to the case. As Fincher's commentary states, "I think that's kind of ultimately the need. We wanna find out who [the Zodiac] is because he loses his fangs, he loses his aura, he loses his myth...." Therefore, as the real Graysmith comments in archival footage in *Graysmith UNMASKED*, from the murders of Jack the Ripper, the media—people such as Avery—have fed the mythos of murderers with lip-smacking descriptions of the killers, apprehended or not, ensuring a depiction of the killer has become a concluding requirement of the public and popular imagination.[4] We and the media are left to fill in the blanks to understand what these crimes mean for our society. Avery's depiction provides part of the catharsis of the story as he remains visible and carries some of the villain's qualities, thus acting as a partial bridge to the killer's mindset and as a journalist who provided for the popular imagination's need for descriptions of the killer's crimes.

Robert Downey Jr.'s complex personal branding as a previously self-destructive media delinquent and as a charismatic actor enables audiences to consider their fascination with murder through his characters. This dynamic has been shown through his roles in *Natural Born Killers*, *In Dreams*, and *Zodiac*. However, these films also ask audiences to question what the media states are the acceptable limits of the self. The boundaries between Downey as a person and as the characters he plays merge, suggesting the extents to which the media, gender, society, and indeed the unrestrained ego can make monsters of us all.

Notes

1. This chapter uses Charles Peirce's conception of the semiotic modes.
2. While *Graysmith UNMASKED* is not a professionally-produced documentary, it is directed and produced by Michael Butterfield, consultant for a number of television productions. It has therefore been used as suitable source material as it contains archival footage of the people involved in the case.
3. His later performance as the drug-addicted Sherlock Holmes also invites audiences to read truth into his portrayal.
4. Fincher states the following in the film's Cannes Festival press pack: "The one thing about the Zodiac story too is there are so many people out there who are convinced Robert (Graysmith) is wrong about some things and that their version or interpretation is right and there are so many myths that sprang up so you have to keep all of that in mind when you are dealing with the story of Zodiac. That is why we chose to tell the story the way we did, through Robert's eyes. My goal was to capture the truth of those books." The lexical slippage between factual information and one person's subjective perception requires no further explanation.

Works Cited

Bornstein, Kate. "Preface." *PoMoSEXUALS: Challenging Assumptions About Gender and Sexuality*. Ed. Carol Queen and Lawrence Schimel. San Francisco: Cleis, 1997. Print.
Butler, Judith. *Bodies That Matter: On the Discursive Limits of "Sex."* New York: Routledge, 1993. Print.
Cannes Film Festival. *Zodiac Production Notes*. Cannes Film Festival, n.d. Web. 22 July 2013.
Fincher, David. Commentary. *Zodiac*. Warner Bros., 2007. DVD.
Graysmith UNMASKED. Dir. Michael Butterfield. *Zodiac Killer—Robert Graysmith Unmasked*. N.p., n.d. Web. 24 July 2013.
In Dreams. Dir. Neil Jordan. DreamWorks SKG, 2001. VHS.
Kimber, Shaun. *Henry: Portrait of a Serial Killer*. Ed. Julian Petley. Basingstoke: Palgrave Macmillan, 2011. Print.
Knight, Zelda G. "Some Thoughts on the Psychological Roots of the Behavior of Serial Killers as Narcissists: An Object Relations Perspective." *Social Behavior and Personality: An International Journal* 34.10 (2006): 1189–206. Print.
Natural Born Killers: Special Edition. Dir. Oliver Stone. By David Veloz and Richard Rutowski. Trimark Home Video, 2003. DVD.
Stone, Oliver, dir. "Director's Commentary." *Natural Born Killers: Special Edition*. Trimark Home Video, 2003. DVD.
Taylor, Michael. "Paul Avery, Longtime Newspaper Reporter." Editorial. *San Francisco Chronicle*. n. pag. *SFGate*, 13 Dec. 2000. Web. 23 July 2013.
The True Story: The Silence of the Lambs. Dir. David Hickman. The History Channel. *YouTube*, n.d. Web. 18 May 2013.
Zodiac. Dir. David Fincher. Warner Bros., 2007. DVD.

Queering Downey Part 1: Queer as Catalyst in *Less Than Zero*, *Home for the Holidays* and *One Night Stand*

Erin E. MacDonald

The word "queer" has many possible meanings: strange, gay, bisexual, or, as in queer theory, it can be used to describe any person, text, or film that questions identity categories more than he/she/it reinforces them. Robert Downey Jr. is not gay, nor is he bisexual by most definitions of the term. However, his comments in interviews and, above all, his strikingly believable performances in gay and bisexual roles combine to make him a poster boy for queerness. The films *Less Than Zero*, *Home for the Holidays*, *One Night Stand*, *In Dreams*, *Wonder Boys*, *Sherlock Holmes*, and *Sherlock Holmes: A Game of Shadows*, among others, showcase his ability to meld sexual confidence, identity insecurity, flamboyance, subtlety, and naturalism in a way that, many directors seem to believe, only he can. In life and in film, Robert Downey Jr. professes and enacts the queer theory belief that sexual identity is not essential, definite, or fixed—it is as much a performance as any other aspect of gender identity. Through costuming, disguise, performance of bisexuality, a subtle portrayal of gayness, and a personal anti-homophobic approach, Downey has consistently demonstrated queerness throughout his decades-long career. In three of his early movies, *Less Than Zero*, *Home for the Holidays*, and *One Night Stand*, Downey's "queer" characters act as catalysts for change, forcing friends and family members to examine their own lives in a different way.

Queer Theory

According to David M. Halperin, queer "is by definition whatever is at odds with the normal, the legitimate, the dominant. There is nothing in particular to which it necessarily refers. It is an identity without an essence" (*Saint Foucault* 62). Queer theory can therefore be used to destabilize or deconstruct identity categories, whether the work deals with sexual preference or not. Queer theorists tend to believe that identity is a social construction—there is nothing (or at least, very little) biological, inherent, or "essential" about being a woman, a man, gay, or straight, although these categories are used in society. Starting in about 1990, critics from Teresa de Lauretis to Judith Butler and Eve Kosofsky Sedgwick have used the term "queer" in their writing. To "queer" heterosexuality means to challenge its accepted status as natural, "normal." In addition to questioning the continued dominance of heteronormativity and all the gender assumptions that go along with it, queer theory can also point out that so-called "normal" sexuality and/or gender/identity performance is actually not as straightforward and uncomplicated as mainstream society might believe. Therefore, even works considered to be definitely "heterosexual" can be "queered." In her 1990 book, *Gender Trouble*, Judith Butler proposes to reject stable identity categories altogether. Other theorists, such as Alexander Doty, discuss the pleasure straight audiences can derive from watching queer or homosocial character interactions in popular culture. For example, heterosexual women or men might enjoy the sexual tension that Downey and Jude Law consciously play with in the *Sherlock Holmes* movies. In "Imitation and Gender Insubordination," Judith Butler writes, "If it is already true that 'lesbians' and 'gay men' have been traditionally designated as impossible identities, errors of classification, unnatural disasters within juridico-medical discourses, ... then perhaps these sites of disruption, error, confusion, and trouble can be the very rallying points for a certain resistance to classification and to identity as such" (309–310). From the beginning of his film career, Robert Downey Jr. has always stirred up trouble.

The Androgynous Eighties

Downey tended to play "the weirdo" in his early films. In *Firstborn* (1984), he is the sole punk of his small group of friends, wearing an earring and sporting a spiked up hairdo and cutting-edge clothes while the others fade into the background in their jeans and t-shirts. At one point when his character, Lee, tries to intervene after his friend bumps into another boy in the cafeteria by saying it was an accident, the friend shouts hurtfully, "*You're an accident!,*" drawing attention to Lee's misfit status within the group. In *Weird Science* (1985), he plays a punk again, this time a bully, and although his character in *Back to School* (1986) is a likeable outcast and a radical socialist, it is more of the same—they are all brash, witty teenagers with spiked hair, New Wave clothes, and a demeanor meant to compensate for an inner vulnerability. Charles Taylor writes of Downey in *Back to School* that

> with his lace cravats, new-wave hair (a few blue spikes added for dash) and big, fey doe eyes, he looked like some parody of a kid in a Keane painting, a college boy who couldn't decide whether he wanted to be Lord Byron or join Duran Duran. His manner was smiling, ingratiating—at times he seemed so eager to please he practically [and actually, in *Weird Science*] batted his eyes—yet there was also something secretive about his pleased little smile; you couldn't be sure what he was laughing at, but he wore his amusement like a snug, comfy coat. He was an alluring and not particularly trustworthy puppy [Salon].

None of his characters in any of these early films is gay (at least not openly so), but they are all outsiders, misfits—"queer" in the original sense of the word. One of his favorite films is *Little Miss Sunshine*: "When I see that dysfunctional family, demonstrating to us how we can all be okay," he says, "I kind of feel like it's a triumph for weirdos" (Hofler). Here and in many other interviews, it's clear that Downey has always considered himself a "weirdo," primarily because of the artsy, movie-making family he was raised in. Performance was all around him. Director Mike Figgis mentions in his commentary on *One Night Stand* that Downey was raised in the atmosphere of underground cinema via his parents' work and that he seems to have been, rightly or wrongly, raised without the typical rigid boundaries (sexual or otherwise) that most parents attempt to instill in their children. Feeling free to try whatever he wanted to, Robert applied this idea of impulsive experimentation to not only drug use and sex but to acting, as well. Nevertheless, in 1987, he said of the characters in *Less Than Zero*, "no one can blame their family…. You're not a product of your environment. I mean, you're a product of yourself" ("Biography, Famous").

Personally, in the Eighties, Downey was experimenting—not only with drugs and with sexuality, but primarily with identity. He said, "I hesitate to fully admit how androgynous and freaky things were getting," when he and his fellow Durannies were wearing spandex, lace, and makeup and taking "the same amount of time getting ready" as the girls (Virtue): "I mean, I was a pretty straight-shooter but it was funny when you looked in the mirror and suddenly realised you were wearing a shirt with a lace collar on it" (Virtue). He also pierced one ear with a yin-yang symbol which he said represented "the masculine and feminine aspects of individuality" ("What's Up"). He told *Rolling Stone* in 1988, "I have no reservations," and,

> A lot of my peer group think I'm an eccentric bisexual. That's OK. Being relaxed about sexuality is something you're born with…. [My bisexuality] was manufactured. I didn't have an identity. I was playing around. I expressed it. I grew up in the Rocky Horror Picture Show world, where even my butch friends turned out to be androgynous on Saturday nights [qtd. in Hirschberg].

He doesn't just mean that he/they dressed androgynously, though, as he revealed in a *Detour* article in 1999: "When I was like 15, I had something go on with a trannie. It was in New York City at a Rocky Horror show. There were all these other Addams Family characters of dubious gender around us." When asked about his own homosexual experiences, Downey told the interviewer, "I think that everybody is bisexual," but added, "I've acted upon gay situations less than practically every other man I know. As much as I consider myself a sexual person—and not without a fairly rich fantasy life—I'm not very sexually motivated. I'm not sexually addicted or compulsive." His sexual philosophy goes something like this: "I'd say 25 percent of the men I know have a serious addiction to sex. The other 25 percent are bisexual, but are in complete and utter vowed silence about it—which is really weird. The other 25 percent are gay. And the other 25 percent are vehemently heterosexual with leather queen undertones" (Downey qtd. in Garbarino, "Last Party"). Whether or not he still considers "everybody" bisexual today, Robert Downey Jr. clearly never had the sexual hang-ups and homophobia that most young men his age would have been hampered by.

Less Than Zero

Despite Downey's known penchant for looking strange and acting out, "Nothing in those [mid–Eighties] movies prepared you for his work in *Less Than Zero* (1987), the first evidence of his willingness to lay himself bare" (Taylor). During his 2006 *Inside the Actor's Studio* interview, Downey avoids making eye contact with host James Lipton and admits about his role in the film, "At that point in Los Angeles, um, save for the fact that I wasn't a wealthy kid, I wasn't from Los Angeles, I wasn't about to start selling my ass for crack money, and I didn't drive a $60,000 Avanti, I was kind of living the lifestyle of that character and so when I came in to audition, I kind of looked like I'd just come from a nightclub." When Lipton tries to bring up the reported concern of his *Less Than Zero* cast mates that Downey was "playing the part too realistically," he attempts to dismiss his decade-and-more of Julian Wells–like struggles with addiction with a joke—"I actually researched the role of Julian for ten years following the completion of the movie"—before confessing, "Yeah, there was some concern because we'd like, you know, finish doing the party/club scene and they'd be like, all right, that's a wrap, time to go home, and I'd be like, no, now it's time to like, do the party scene, for real. And they'd be like okay, but it's kind of an early call." Looking down, he says quietly with a cross between shame and pride, "but I uh, I made it."

He took the part specifically because he knew that most of his peers would not take the risk of playing Julian Wells (Morice). After the film came out, he told a reporter for *Rolling Stone*, "I'm not an exhibitionist, really, but I have no reservations, either. Otherwise, why, in *Less Than Zero*, would I agree to do a scene about somebody going down on some guy in Palm Springs for coke?" (Hirschberg). Others would have had reservations, not wanting to be typecast or thought of in Hollywood as a gay or bisexual actor. In addition to thriving on the challenge of playing such a risky and difficult role, Downey probably also saw some of himself in Julian. He told *Elle Magazine* in 1987, "I took the part because this kind of guy hasn't really been done before on film—a potential artist who slips really low" (Caruso). Although many people think he has changed enormously over the years, anyone reading his interviews from the 1980s through to today can see how strikingly similar his comments and beliefs are, then and now. Many of the roles he has taken, from Charlie Chaplin to Dan Dark in *The Singing Detective* to Tony Stark and Sherlock Holmes, have involved immersing himself in the lives of characters whose own brilliance and eccentricity has led them to near-self-destruction.

In *Less Than Zero*, Downey plays Julian Wells, a crack-addicted former rich kid whose father, who gave him money to become a record producer, has had enough and kicked him out. Now spending his nights scoring and his mornings sleeping it off on park benches, Julian is literally on the outside, looking in. While protagonist Clay and his extended dysfunctional family are celebrating Christmas at their gigantic, perfectly decorated mansion, Julian sneaks onto the grounds and looks through the floor-to-ceiling windows at Clay, his eyes begging his friend to come out and join him as he sits by the pool in a huddled, exhausted heap. Julian also literally looks in in at least two other scenes: Rip (a drug dealer played eerily well by James Spader) finds him smoking up on his balcony while the wealthy guests party in the comfort of his well-appointed home, and Julian also breaks into his own house, using a credit card to jimmy a door so that he can grab some CDs to sell for drug money. Climbing over fences and balconies to catch a glimpse of the "good life" going on inside, Julian is no longer a part of that life. He is the unwanted intruder whose illegitimate lifestyle was bred by the same society that now shuts him out.

Julian doesn't cross-dress in this film, but he does cross gender lines. He is, in effect, the damsel in distress—the traditional position of a female character like Clay's ex-girlfriend Blair, but in this case it is Blair who seeks to rescue him. Julian is feminized in more ways than one. To pay back the fifty thousand dollars he owes his drug dealer, Rip, he is forced to enter into prostitution with several wealthy male clients. In contrast to the novel, in which

Julian and Clay are both openly and willingly bisexual, in the film they are both heterosexual. Despite Downey's 1987 comment that "Julian is really a nice guy who goes about three ways sexually" (Caruso), Julian is represented as being in love with Blair (Although he tries to deny it to Clay, it is written on Downey's face) and shows no interest in his own sex except for the platonic, nostalgic friendship he shares with Clay. Clay and Blair are a couple until Clay goes away to college and returns home at Thanksgiving only to find Julian and Blair in bed together. Later, it is Julian who catches Clay snuggling up to Blair on a dance floor. This love triangle adds some dramatic tension to the film, but it is absent in the book—the novel by Bret Easton Ellis upon which the movie was based. In Ellis' novel, Julian does not sleep with Blair. Like Clay, he probably sleeps with both women and men, but mostly men once he is forced into prostitution. In the novel, no one seems to care who is sleeping with whom. Like the men in Ellis' later work *American Psycho*, Clay has trouble telling one face from another or remembering who left what party with whom, because none of it matters.

Ellis said in an interview that the movie became "compromised" after a new studio head took over Twentieth Century–Fox (Buchanan). Leonard Goldberg was a family man (Buchanan) who, presumably, thought America didn't want to see a movie about bisexual drug addicts, most of whom got away with their "immoral" behavior. Julian shoots heroin in the book, but not in the film. In the novel, Clay eagerly plays voyeur for Julian and a john in a hotel room—in the film, he rescues Julian, pulling him out of a same-sex encounter instead of watching it. Although many people thought the film should have stuck more closely to the disturbing realism of the novel, Janet Maslin of the *New York Times* was happy

Julian (Downey, left) nods as Rip (James Spader) tells him he must entertain some male friends, to pay off his drug debt.

that it didn't, because, "[f]or all its shock value, Mr. Ellis's story of bored, jaded, affluent California teens-agers would have been paralyzingly downbeat on screen, if not worse. Indeed, by the time it got to the book's scenes of ultimate depravity—the snuff film watched as casual entertainment, the gang-rape of a 12-year-old girl—a faithful film version would have cleared the house." According to Taylor, "The movie is a ridiculous example of Hollywood's playing it safe, a late Brat Pack vehicle cum anti-drug tract fashioned out of Bret Easton Ellis' cold, repellent novel." However, some critics believed that Downey's talents compensated for the film's flaws, allowing him to play Julian more as Ellis envisioned him:

> Despite the screenplay's watered-down insistence that Downey and McCarthy are competing for the favors of [Jami] Gertz's character, Downey instead slyly plays his part like it's torn from the scorched pages of the novel, where the two boys are lovers, not just friends. It's a bold choice that brings his desperate character to vivid life: In addition to all the other emotional ravages he evokes, he shows us with his panicky, sad eyes that he knows he's losing McCarthy to Gertz [Hennesey].

Julian makes a joke out of everything, to cover his sensitivity, such as asking a waiter at a party to bring Clay a shotgun so his friend can "quench that thirst for revenge" that Julian assumes Clay must feel after essentially losing Blair to his best friend. Clay says he's not angry and he doesn't seem overly emotional about anything, which perhaps results in a bit of a lackluster performance by Andrew McCarthy but actually fits well with the protagonist of Ellis' book.

With scenes full of palm trees, mansions, TVs, and fancy cars, the empty materialism portrayed in the novel comes across well. As Rip says to Clay, "These people are assholes. Who gives a fuck about these people." Unfortunately, everyone is included in the category of "these people." The parents of Clay, Blair, and Julian are just as messed up, shallow, and drug-addicted as their children. When Julian stops by his Uncle Bob's salesroom to ask him to invest in a club he wants to buy, Uncle Bob offers him "a bump" in his office. Blair's father is so busy in the bedroom with his new woman that he can barely manage to say Merry Christmas to his daughter through the door, and Clay's mother appears to heavily medicate herself to get through the tedium of her existence. The décor is meticulous (according to 1980s tastes) and huge bowlfuls of festive-colored candy are waiting for Clay and Blair whenever they return home, but their actual families are not. Julian and his friends party hard to fill the void but the drugs are not enough to make them happy and they end up reducing Julian to desperation, prostitution, illness, and finally, death.

Fans of the novel were disappointed by the Hollywood-like anti-drugs message of the film although the novel could hardly be considered to be pro-drugs. The most radical departure between novel and film is the representation of queerness: All the bisexuality and moral ambiguity of Ellis' novel was removed and replaced, in the film, with forced gay sex as a representation of the lowest fate to which one can sink. Although Ellis did not portray his characters' lifestyles in a positive way, either, they were, at least initially, experimenting sexually because they chose to.

Downey, though, humanizes Ellis' character. Whereas all of the characters in Ellis' novel and the entire novel itself are devoid of any real human sentiment and are instead unique in their distinct lack of true emotion, their utter coldness, Downey's portrayal of Julian as a vulnerable, messed up kid who tries to cover his pain with gaiety creates sympathy for him and provides a believable rescue narrative—Clay and Blair want to help him not only because they feel a nostalgia for the good times they shared together in high school but because they care what happens to him. When Julian fails to get any money to pay off his debt, he tells Rip with pleading eyes, "Man, I had it all worked out. Christ, I thought I did. I fucked up.... Please don't cut me off. I'll do whatever you want me to do." The full reality of what Rip wants him to do doesn't hit him until he's told that Bill, Rip's ominous-looking thug, is going to take him to a party to meet some "very important people." Julian swallows his terror and nods with resignation as Rip puts an arm around him and coos silkily, "Everything's gonna be just fine." Bill takes him to a motel and when Julian comes out of the door looking traumatized, Bill asks if he enjoyed the party. As Charles Taylor writes, "The look of shame and fear on his face after he turns his first trick is of the intensity that registers in the pit of your stomach. You feel like you know what it means to be inside Julian's skin, breaking out in cold sweats and shaking with nausea." When Bill turns his back to use the payphone, Julian runs.

He runs to Clay's house, where he looks in through the window at the artificially warm scene he can't be a part of. No longer the life of the party, he quietly tells Clay he's "just watching" and then adds, "I feel like Tiny fucking Tim." He's the doomed, lame boy, tired of pretending that everything is fine, looking in the store windows at all the things he can't have while the rich and the healthy enjoy a fat Christmas goose. When Clay tries to pull him up to join them inside, Julian recoils from his touch, protesting, "No, no, it's too crowded." Downey communicates not only Julian's financial desperation and drug-induced physical sickness but also his paranoia, his depression and loneliness, and his psychological trauma at being, essentially, sexually abused. Clay half-heartedly talks to him like a counselor attempting to get him into rehab, but Julian tries to stress that he has reached the end of his rope: "I don't need a discussion on the finer points of morality. Spare me." Having not wanted to ask Clay for help in the first place, he sees his friend's reluctance and gives up hope, deciding instead to sneak into the house and steal Clay's mother's jewelry. Clay next finds his friend at a motel in Palm Springs, pants down, performing fellatio on another of Rip's important guests.

"[E]veryone should like me until that one scene," Downey told *Elle* in 1987. Knowing that mainstream viewers would react to Julian's prostitution by thinking, "Damn, he's a fag!" (Downey qtd. in Caruso), he did it anyway, probably *because* of that scene. Always eager to push the boundaries, Downey has never shied away from controversial roles, as he proved not only by playing a porn star named Wolf Dangler in his father's 1988 film *Rented Lips*, but also by appearing in blackface for the bulk of *Tropic Thunder* (2008) and by playing up the "bromance" aspect of Holmes and Watson's relationship in *Sherlock Holmes* (2010) and *Sherlock Holmes: A Game of Shadows* (2011).

Although Clay "rescues" Wells by taking him out of prostitution and driving off with him and Blair into the desert, the drugs catch up to Julian. When he dies, he is the catalyst for Clay and especially Blair to change their lives. Clay tells Blair, who is apparently now his girlfriend again, that he is going back to school up north and he expects her to go with him. She nods in acceptance—Julian's death has finally convinced her that she has reached a dead end in the L.A. party scene and that there is no other solution but to radically change her location and her lifestyle.

Critics disliked the film and its preachy tone overall (in the book, Julian doesn't die and Blair doesn't leave sin-filled L.A. with Clay) but raved about Downey's performance in it, calling it disturbingly, painfully real (Ebert, Weinberg, Maslin). The actor himself was so disturbed by the experience that he eventually buried Julian's clothes in the backyard

(Schneller), literally trying to bury his past identity. Even in the early Nineties, he realized that living the lifestyle of a Julian Wells was not, ultimately, going to be productive for him. He hoped that marrying Deborah Falconer and having a child (Indio) with her would fill whatever needs he was trying to meet through using drugs, but even family life and an Oscar nomination for *Chaplin* (1992) couldn't stop the train wreck from coming.

Too Much Sun

Downey has always been somewhat sensitive to the cultural depiction of homosexuals. In 1990, he joined a talented cast to make another of his father's kooky yet touching movies, *Too Much Sun* : "It's about a gay brother and lesbian sister—Eric Idle and Andrea Martin—whose father is dying and says he's going to leave his money to whoever has a kid first. It doesn't deal with homosexuality responsibly, but it's not supposed to. That makes me a little uneasy, but I know that my father is so accepting it's not like he's not aware" (Downey qtd. in L'Ecuyer). The politically incorrect treatment of homosexuality in *Too Much Sun* can be compared to much more recent movies such as *The Kids are All Right* (2010), in which a woman in a committed lesbian relationship has an affair with a man. In terms of the mainstream cinematic portrayal of queerness, the Downeys, both Senior and Junior, were ahead of their time.

In her 1980 essay, "Compulsory Heterosexuality and Lesbian Existence," Adrienne Rich wrote of the need for feminists of all colors and sexual orientations to recognize their common bonds and join forces in the fight against societal acceptance of forced heterosexuality, since all women (and, one might argue, many men) are oppressed by compulsory heterosexuality's lack of options—not only homosexuals. Instead of male-identifying and alienating themselves from each other, women should see that they are all part of a "lesbian continuum" of "woman-identified experience" (217) and that a person's emotional and sexual experiences can change and develop over time. She asks feminists to "take the step of questioning heterosexuality as a 'preference' or 'choice' for women" (216) and to consider that many of the beliefs and acts we consider "normal" and "natural" have actually been beaten into us by centuries of submission to the patriarchy. It is not only women who can benefit from questioning compulsory heterosexuality, however. As *Too Much Sun* points out, the dying father's patriarchal assumption that he has a right to expect his children to marry (someone of the opposite sex) and to have children of their own is illogical. Although his gay son and his lesbian daughter enjoy brief sexual encounters with those of the opposite sex, the film represents the old man's wish as a silly, farcical demand that comes from an old-fashioned world that is out of touch with reality. As Rich calls for in her essay, *Too Much Sun* also promotes "the breaking of a taboo and the rejection of a compulsory way of life" (Rich 217).

Downey seems to believe that everyone—straight or gay—should question their assumptions about sexual identity and realize that most people actually fall somewhere in between those two poles. In 1991 he told an interviewer that he was turned down for a role in *Three of Hearts*, "about a male escort who comes between a lesbian couple" (Rebello). Downey took it upon himself to "completely rewr[i]te the script outline," saying,

> Let's be responsible to the gay community, but let's also shock them out of thinking that a lesbian would never sleep with this guy. That's bullshit. Most lesbian women I know have a guy

that they have slept with or sleep with now and then. I said, "Let's go beyond the righteousness of 'a gay woman would' to 'a person would.' Why not have the male escort and the lesbian have a kid together?" They said, "Ohhhhh, that's another can of worms." Well, call me crazy, guys, but I kind of like to open a can of worms when I do a movie [Rebello].

As the interviewer points out, "Downey had been opening cans of worms on the project all along. During a production meeting, he confronted one of the producers by asking, 'Are you gay? Do you like the idea of another man's hand on your penis? Can you accept the fact that everyone's bisexual?'" (Rebello). In the same interview, he also says about Hollywood, "It's a very homophobic business" despite the fact that some of the people in powerful positions are gay. When asked to address rumors about his own possible bisexuality, Downey answers, "Although I guess, at least in my actions, I've been heterosexual, I think 'heterosexuality' and 'homosexuality' are overspecifications" (qtd. in Rebello). Rather than label everyone, he believes, we should be "relaxed" about sexual identity and not attempt to force people into categories.

In 1992, he filmed a documentary about the presidential campaigns, called *The Last Party*, perhaps hoping again, symbolically, to leave Julian Wells behind him and move on to more serious things than the L.A. nightclub scene. When asked by Arsenio Hall in a 1993 interview, "What did you learn?" from the experience of making a political film, he replied,

no one's right and no one's wrong and everyone is a product of their environment and where they were raised. We were in Houston for instance and they were like, those guys are from the queer press. And they didn't want to let us into their God and Country rally. They're like, those guys are with MTV. They are gay. They didn't want to let us in their place and I experienced, maybe for the first time, discrimination. And uh, I got really really mad. And then I said, you know what, this guy couldn't have reacted any other way than the way he did. And yeah, it's not right, but it's almost like it just makes you realize how much footwork we have to do.

Being a member of liberal Hollywood and, before that, a part of the New York bohemian scene, Downey was shocked by the homophobia he encountered in the American South, but even then he expressed a tolerance for ambiguity and for diverse lifestyles that, along with a belief in the ability of individuals to determine their own identities, seems to have stuck with him through the years.

Home for the Holidays

Home for the Holidays (1995), the first film on which Downey used heroin on set (*Inside the Actor's Studio*), includes some similarities to *Less Than Zero*: Both Julian Wells and Tommy Larson (Downey's character in the 1995 film) childishly joke around and act out as a defense against their own vulnerabilities, both characters are catalysts for the other characters to get together and to change themselves, and both characters are misfits within dysfunctional families. Just as *Less Than Zero* is about more than drugs, *Home for the Holidays* is about more than the cliché of the dysfunctional family. It's about miscommunication, misunderstanding, and even mistaken identity.

At the Hollywood premiere, the actor told an interviewer that working with director Jodie Foster was "like a real big breath of fresh air." He may have meant by that not only that Foster instilled confidence in her actors but also that she freed him from feeling the usual

Claudia (Holly Hunter) and Tommy (Robert Downey Jr.) are the outsiders of the Larson family in Jodie Foster's *Home for the Holidays* **(1995).**

pressures of a film set by letting him improvise his scenes—although being high probably also helped him relax. He speaks elliptically in the same television interview about being pleasantly surprised that Foster didn't fire him. Fellow cast member Steve Guttenberg appears beside Downey, both literally and figuratively propping him up, speaking for him, and offering his prediction that Downey will win an Academy Award for his performance (in the film). "Yeah," Downey pretends to agree, "for best ham." Somewhat deceptive and leading a double life of sorts with his personal problem with addiction, the actor at the same time plays a character who is somewhat closeted and misleading, in a film about a whole family of people who need to "come out" to each other in one way or another. It's a film about secrets, and letting go of them.

Although the script originally focused on the American Republican identity and the effects of Reaganomics (Foster, Commentary), it eventually morphed into a story about the bond between a quirky, artsy sister and her unconventional brother. Foster

> quickly realized during the rehearsal process that the movie was really about Holly [Hunter] and Robert—Tommy and Claudia—and that it was about these two outsiders—not just her, but two outsiders that didn't belong in this family and that had—their bond had been that they were the ones that disappointed their parents and that their parents couldn't relate to and that they formed a sort of subset family with each other of the alienated ones, the ones who spend Thanksgiving eating in the kitchen, together [Commentary].

She adds, "It just became clear to me the more I watched Downey and the more I watched their relationship, that it was about the two of them" (Commentary). "Rather than concentrating on the love story," she decided to make the brother-sister relationship the central "focus of the film." Setting the narrative in the time and place of a family's Thanksgiving dinner allowed the secondary theme of the questioning of the traditional American Dream to develop organically. Foster says the fantasy of the American Dream and the fact that everyone shares it is both the problem with America and what makes it great: "We really rely on the American Dream in order to function" but if everyone realized they were having the exact same experiences as everyone else, "we'd kill ourselves" (Commentary). Although Foster insists that fantasies are what's great about America, the Larson family's (and by extension, every American family's) fantasy of the perfect family, perfect home, perfect holiday, perfect life keeps people like Tommy and Claudia, the "queer" people, from fitting in. Foster's characters are "not heroes"—they are "very complicated and ugly" because she was able to make *Home for the Holidays* with "no studio influence whatsoever" (Foster, Commentary). Given Foster's recent "coming out" speech at the 2013 Golden Globe Awards, it's not surprising that she reports in her commentary, "my goal and my challenge in this film was to take my feelings about my family, which are very conflicted, which are also very bitter and very sweet, and to try and find a theme or a focus that kind of brought all of them together." She also wanted "to create characters that were complicated and not just loveable" and a "film that was messy and that just really didn't have any solutions at all"—like queer theory. The film doesn't "make any apologies" for its characters, including Claudia's obnoxious brother, Tommy.

During the developmental phase, Foster decided to make Tommy gay and, as she comments, "Robert brought so much to it." Talking about Tommy, she adds, "Of course he's the character who doesn't want to come home because his life isn't accepted." And of course he's the clown "because that's his way of coping with it and coping with the fact that his family and his parents turn a blind eye to who he really is and that a long time ago they disappointed him as a family and so he chose to create another family. Which I think is pretty common in the gay community." She chose Downey for the role because she needed Tommy to be complex—more than just "the obnoxious brother." Foster calls Downey "a tortured soul" who's "just one step from being out of control and falling off the barstool." In describing the character as Downey plays him, she conflates the two men, describing him/them as "a happy-go-lucky guy but underneath that is somebody who's really hiding the fact that he's disappointed by all of them and that he's just biding his time by making them laugh because he knows that he can't get another reaction from them that's gonna be appropriate" (Foster, Commentary). Foster seems to apply her view of Tommy to her view of Robert, in explaining why he was so perfect for the role.

Viewers are only introduced to Tommy elliptically, as we hear his sister talking to him over a telephone. At the beginning of the film, Holly Hunter's character, Claudia Larson, is on her way home (the film was shot in Baltimore) to spend Thanksgiving with her family and calls her beloved brother, Tommy, from the plane. Through tears caused by an odd series of events including being fired, she tells his answering machine, "I really wish you were gonna be there, kiddo.... Give Jack a big hug from me." Claudia obviously feels close to Tommy and has no issues with the fact that he is, so she believes, living with his lover—a man. Until we meet the rest of the Larson family, Tommy's queerness is treated nonchalantly. As Downey said when the film was released, "He's gay. That's his sexual orientation. So what? Do you like the character? Do you like the movie?" ("Biography, Famous"). During an interview with Howard Stern on the day the film premiered, Stern asked Downey if he was "afraid that being in a gay movie, people start to say maybe he's bi or something." The actor replied, "It's not a gay *movie*; the character's just gay." When asked about the process involved in learning to play a gay man, he told Stern that he did not need to act any differently in terms of his voice or mannerisms: "Like my friends who are gay, they're just, that happens to be their [sexual preference]" and added, "My friend Sam who plays my husband in the film is gay and I also kind of based it on him because he's an incredibly hilarious person and ... kind of macho himself."

The audience's second introduction to Tommy is not so straightforward. Two presumably young men, their faces mostly unrevealed to the audience, pull up outside the Larson family home in a GTO, the sounds of the theme from *Shaft* furthering the non-conformist, anti-suburban vibe that rides into town with them. His face shielded by a pair of goggles, the driver and his male friend get out of the car and sneak up to the house, spying through the window Claudia's father stealing a bite of pumpkin pie. Even when they enter the house, the audience can't be sure if these men are burglars or welcome guests, good guys or bad guys. The driver creeps into Claudia's bedroom, throws back her covers, and snaps a Polaroid of her in her underwear before she wakes up and wrestles him to the floor. "Tommy, you asshole!" she shouts, but she's clearly happy to see him. Hearing the ruckus and venturing into the hall with a baseball bat to investigate, Claudia's father is about to take a swing at the intruder when Tommy's friend, Leo Fish (Dylan McDermott), tells him, "Whoa, whoa—it's your son!" as though Tommy's identity within the family might not be recognized otherwise.

For a substantial amount of the film, Tommy innocently (or not) leads his sister and the audience to believe that he and Leo are a couple. Whether putting his arm around Leo's shoulders or hopping onto his back in the street, Tommy is apparently entirely comfortable with being physically friendly with this man. Claudia is cold toward Leo, thinking that he has somehow replaced Jack, Tommy's long-time partner and someone she has considered to be a part of her family. When Tommy teases that Claudia has been staring at Leo, she dismisses the idea that she would look at a man who is obviously gay, "a pretty boy" with a pretty face. When Tommy counters that his friend was "born that way" and it's "not his fault," he works to destabilize assumptions about gender and sexuality. The siblings' mother (played by Anne Bancroft) willfully denies her son's sexual identity by describing Tommy and Leo to Claudia as swinging bachelors. From Claudia's reaction, the audience knows that her mother (and, we later discover, her sister) is well aware of Tommy's proclivities but prefers to leave that "secret" unacknowledged.

Although viewers are meant to know, without a doubt, that Tommy is gay, the only character who suggests some sort of stereotypical representation of his homosexuality is his other sister, Joanne (Cynthia Stevenson). Through her depiction as the epitome of the uptight, perfect middle-class suburban wife and mother who disapproves of the sympathetic main character, the audience sees Joanne's accusations of Tommy's perversity and effeminacy as not only reprehensible but also very strange, almost ironically aberrant. Downey does not play Tommy as gay in any stereotypically visible sense; like in *Less Than Zero*, he plays the character as a complex man, not a one-dimensional caricature of queerness. *Variety* called it an unusually "multi-nuanced portrayal of a gay man" (Levy) and Owen Gleiberman declared in his review in *Entertainment Weekly*, "The most arresting person on screen is also the most irritating: Tommy, played by Robert Downey Jr. with a kind of showboating obnoxiousness that renders the character's gayness a secondary issue—for Hollywood, a real breakthrough—and, at the same time, marks him as a selfish cad." Tommy is hyperactive, a joker, and a typical annoying but loveable little brother who happens to be in love with a man. In fact, Tommy's words to Claudia upon learning how concerned she is about his relationship with Jack ("This is a projection. You see, I'm fine, Jack's fine, everything's fine") underline his portrayal of a normal person. Claudia, the heterosexual, is the one who has problems with men—not him.

Tommy does have a problem that he tries to keep others' attentions away from, however. He loves to provoke a reaction and to reveal and revel in revealing the secrets of others including his sisters and his eccentric aunt (played by Geraldine Chaplin), but his sly smile and his wisecracking come to an abrupt end when two-dimensionally "evil" sister Joanne outs him to his parents, at the dinner table. In fact, Joanne reveals not only that he has not come out overtly to his mother or father but also that he has secretly married Jack without telling even his closest family confidante, Claudia.

Joanne's entrance into the film furthers the dichotomy set up between the "normal" people and the "freaks"—with the gay brother and single-parent sister as the normal ones and the superficially successful sister and brother-in-law as the freaks. Joanne's husband, Walter, is a successful banker, a conservative capitalist who believes the health of the nation rests on making more "stuff," while the recently fired artist Claudia and Leo, who also seems unable to hold down a job, agree with each other that America already has "too much stuff," including, as Claudia points out to her father, unnecessarily large TVs. Joanne and Walter (whose last name is "Wedman," perhaps to highlight their conventionally acceptable heterosexual union) and their children (a girl and a boy, of course) have just pulled up in their vehicle when Tommy runs over, jumps onto the hood, bangs on the windows, and roars, pretending (in classic Downey style) to be the T-Rex from *Jurassic Park*. Tellingly, Joanne locks the doors in an attempt to block Tommy's nonconformity out of their lives. One of the children cries, "Mom, tell him to stop!" because although other children might enjoy this bit of fun propagated by a slightly manic uncle, Joanne and Walter's entire family here symbolizes the repression, denial, and suffocating pose of heteronormative perfection that Foster presents as a contrast to the warm, loving, offbeat unconventionality of Tommy, Claudia, Aunt Glady, and father Henry. Tommy even attempts to panic the perfect family by suggesting that they have missed dinner and Walter (Steve Guttenberg) takes the bait, but Joanne sees through the lie. Claudia takes her sister aside to say, "I think something awful's happened between Tommy and Jack" and Joanne snidely replies, "Yeah. And everybody in town knows it." Inside, her vain, ballet-dancing daughter garnishes a plate of sweet potatoes and asks, "Isn't this too perfect, what I did?" Walter, Joanne, and their kids need external validation and seem to care more about what others think of the family than they do about their own happiness. Joanne plays the role of doting daughter, helping out her parents even though she doesn't enjoy it and resenting Claudia because she was able to escape.

Tommy continues to disrupt Joanne's image of perfection throughout the film, pointing out that the tag of her dress is showing, encouraging Aunt Glady to make an embarrassing confession about her decades-old love for her sister Adele's husband (Tommy's father), provoking his parents to argue, and giving Joanne's son a turkey leg instead of the lean white meat his mother has insisted on. Tommy even takes a picture of the boy holding the leg like a "cave man"—the opposite of Joanne's idea of proper, civilized society. She is so rigidly entrenched in her own inflexible identity that when Tommy accidentally flings the turkey carcass onto her lap, she refuses to change her dress because it is an outward symbol of the starched conventionality she has convinced herself she loves.

This physical messing up of Joanne's careful façade brings on the climax of the narrative, what Foster calls "people's unconscious motivations coming to the forefront" (Commentary). She is so horrified and angry with Tommy that she screams at him, "You cocksucker! You goddamn bastard!" Her daughter cries, "You ruined my mommy," not "You ruined my mommy's dress" because even she realizes that Tommy has finally broken through Joanne's illusion of perfect respectability. Smiling, he takes a Polaroid of her, Henry laughs, and Joanne gets up to leave. Tommy calls her a "drama queen" and she has no choice now but to retaliate: "*You're* calling *me* a drama queen, Mr. Pervert?!" While Henry films the whole scene with a video camera, Tommy forces Joanne to confront her own image in his Polaroid. After he calls her a "product of baboon lovin'" in "typical Robert Downey improvisation—where he always takes it one step further than it ever should go" (Foster, Commentary)—she warms up by calling him "sleazy" and a "freak." Walter, anxious to avoid further scenes, tries to stop her but Joanne screams, "No, don't muzzle me! You and I both know I am the only normal person here!" "Your secret's safe with us," Tommy quips, taking another photograph. Joanne then reveals Tommy's secret, calling him "Mrs. Gordon" and asking him if he wore a dress at his wedding to Jack. Tommy is finally visibly hurt. His own strategy has been used against him.

Joanne envisions Tommy's wedding, based partly on the report of some acquaintance and partly on her own stereotypes, as an orgy of effeminate men "prancing around," wearing dresses, and physically demonstrating their affection in a public and therefore inappropriate way. For Joanne, being gay is bad enough, but being openly gay in public is far worse. "I could throw up," she seethes, sick more at the thought of the scandal than of two men kissing. When their bewildered father asks, "Tommy, did you wear a dress?" Tommy simply answers, "No," invalidating Joanne's homophobic assumptions but not denying the marriage. He looks upset but does not engage with her, walking instead to Leo and Claudia, who will support him.

Tommy does not spare even his favorite sister, though: When she asks him to tell the family something "glamorous" about her fabulous life, he instead tells them all the dirt—that she was recently fired, that she kissed her boss, and that her teenaged daughter is planning to have sex. Claudia seems relieved to have her secrets exposed, and the two curl up together smoking, physically together and distanced from the rest of the family. Claudia has never taken sides before but now, she "goes on the bad side" (Tommy's), according to Foster, who adds, "This is the side that will alienate everyone" (Commentary). The magic of Downey and Hunter together totally changed the scene for the director, who decided to focus on revealing "what the two of them have together" (Commentary). Tommy had planned to stay away but showed up at the house specifically to save her; in return, she dares her parents to disapprove of her and defends him, aligning herself with the outsider, the unaccepted one—the "queer" one in the most general sense of the term.

When Aunt Gladys kisses Henry (on whom she has secretly had a crush since they were teens), Adele retreats into the pantry to smoke, preferring to hide. "Tommy's somebody's wife!" she exclaims to Claudia, who goes after her mother, but Claudia shakes her head, "No. No, no. Everybody's growing up." She won't let Tommy's marriage be defined in that way and insists instead that her mother accept it as a healthy, normal development. Adele says brusquely to her son, "I hope you're happy, Thomas. I hope it was a nice wedding and I hope one of these years you'll send your poor devastated mother some pictures." "We didn't take any pictures," Tommy admits, because "[e]veryone takes pictures like no one fuckin' remembers anything." These are strange statements coming from a person who has spent the entire day thus far taking pictures, but Tommy uses his Polaroid to provoke others, to catch them off guard in their worst moments and perhaps to reveal their secrets to everyone including themselves. He doesn't use photography in the traditional, accepted way, to capture carefully contrived poses so that people remember typical events in perfect ways. Foster says in her commentary that the film is about those "wordless moments that nobody ever got on a camera or on a Polaroid or on a picture—those are the ones that define you, and yet you can't really share that with the people that claim to understand you." Although Tommy has been reticent with his family at least regarding his unconventional relationship, he still desires approval. His marriage "had nothing to do with you," he tells his mother. "Is that all right? Tell me that's all right." He also feels like he needs his mother to know that he is "not unhappy"—that people who live in unconventional ways are not necessarily to be pitied. Foster says about this scene, "Downey finally puts his hand out and says, 'Love me for who I am' ... and unfortunately she responds by saying, 'I still can't accept you.' I think because of fear—the fear that it's different from the life that they lead and that their children will be unhappy." The director believes that children have to choose their own identity, not the one their parents want them to have. In a society of compulsory heterosexuality, telling parents that you need them to accept you as you are is "a brave gesture and Tommy is the bravest person in the family" (Foster, Commentary).

By the end of the film, the audience pities Joanne more than it does Claudia, who has a loving, open relationship with an intelligent daughter; or Tommy, who has a whole "*real* family" of people who accept him as he is, back in Boston, and who seems "impervious" to Joanne's homophobic comments. When he and Claudia hug, it's clear that they have each other, but Joanne doesn't seem to have that kind of bond with anyone. Henry, the father, congratulates Jack over the phone because he is too self-conscious to overtly tell Tommy that he loves and accepts him, gay marriage or not. He touches Tommy's face as he says it, though, and Tommy is visibly moved. The next morning, Claudia thinks she let Leo get away and regrets it but he shows up on her flight home, saying, "This really weird guy I work for said he'd cover for me." Tommy is not only the "really weird guy," he is again the catalyst for positive change in Claudia's life, as well as for a small, but important change in his father's attitude toward queerness. The film ends with a series of home video clips of family members in memorable moments from childhood to adulthood, including Tommy and Jack embracing on the beach, presumably just after their wedding. The Larsons have not moved to a place of perfection by the end of the holiday, but some progress has been made. The family may be dysfunctional but, for the most part, they love each other. What's more dysfunctional, Foster and her actors suggest, is a society that treats deception and secret-keeping as normal and noble while vilifying those whose lifestyles or sexualities don't conform to the traditionally accepted norm.

One Night Stand

Like his portrayal of Tommy in *Home for the Holidays*, Downey's depiction of a gay man in *One Night Stand* (1997) does not artificially highlight the character's sexual preference (or the fact that he is dying of AIDS) above his complexity and humanity. Charles Taylor says of his performance in *One Night Stand* that "Downey passes one of the crucial acting tests with flying colors. Given the chance to revel in the part of a man falling apart physically, Downey chooses to play the character and not the disease" (Salon). British director Mike Figgis based Downey's character, Charlie, on his own friend, Steven. Figgis said of his friend, "When he was dying I took his portrait—and later I gave the photograph to Robert. At the point, Robert's drug problem was terrible, he was a sick puppy, and I remember coming on the set and he had utterly absorbed the photograph. I had never seen an actor become someone to that extent before. It was quite shocking" (Hoggard). Like in *Less Than Zero* and *Home for the Holidays*, he plays a character who "has a great influence on his friend" (Downey qtd. in *IAS*). Charlie is the catalyst for Max and Karen (Nastassja Kinski) to change their lives, just as Julian was a catalyst for Clay and Blair. Also like in *Less Than Zero*, art imitated life—Downey's.

Downey in character as Charlie, in Mike Figgis' *One Night Stand* (1997).

Written and directed by Figgis, maker of the critically acclaimed, award winning *Leaving Las Vegas*, *One Night Stand* was considered, shortly after its 1997 release, either "a masterpiece" or "one of the worst films ever made" and overall received a "catastrophically negative critical response" in America (Figgis, Commentary). Part of the reason for the film's critical failure surely rests with its defamiliarizing effect, its inability to be pinned down to one genre (although the two huge coincidences in the plot do seem gimmicky to most viewers). It begins with protagonist Max (played by Wesley Snipes) talking to the camera in a type of "Shakespearean prologue" (Figgis, Commentary). In it, he clearly sums up his relationship with Robert Downey Jr.'s minor character, Charlie, who is a gay choreographer former best friend with whom Max had a trivial argument and a falling-out that both men now regret. Upon hearing that Charlie has been diagnosed as HIV positive, he goes to see him in New York. Max tells the audience, "Charlie is gay. I'm not gay." This extremely and atypically straightforward stating of the facts gets the background details out of the way so the viewer can focus on the characters' developments rather than on what may otherwise have been their stereotypically defining characteristics.

When we first see Charlie, he is working as a choreographer, holding his arms out in a

Christ-like pose to demonstrate something about the combination of the lighting with the movement. Downey is distressingly thin and although Charlie tells Max that he is not yet sick, he looks sick. In fact, Downey was at the time becoming increasingly physically exhausted by his addictions. He admits that he "was in pretty bad shape and probably weighed about 140 pounds and was carrying a firearm and didn't have any shoes on" when he first met the director (*Inside the Actors Studio*). In a 1998 interview with the actor after the film was released, Figgis mentions the trouble that Downey was going through during the making of *One Night Stand*, that he was "arrested a couple of times while [they] were making the film ... [and] finally got locked up." Downey remembers that, at that first meeting, he had expected Figgis to offer him the romantic lead role (of Max) and adds, "When you said no, I think you should play Charlie, the guy who's dying of AIDS, I think I went in the bathroom to get high and I looked at myself and I said, 'You know, I may never look this ready to play someone really sick than I do right now.'" He was also impressed that the director didn't pretend that his drug problem didn't exist but neither did he attempt to enact any kind of self-righteous intervention. Instead, Downey says, Figgis "just seemed to acknowledge what was going on and honor the fact that I was willing myself into a very bad place hopefully for some higher reason than just, uh, death. Unfortunately, I took that as ... I didn't see there was any direct request to alter my course of action." He admits he had been "plummeting" since the "calamity" of *Restoration* (1995), a supposed "art film" that failed to live up to its promise. Amidst this depression, he saw *One Night Stand* "as this opportunity to really kind of explore [his] dissatisfaction with life and with being an actor and a lot of stuff." Downey adds, "and I was filmed kind of doing it, you know." The movie was not, for him, just a movie. It was a cathartic event into which he could pour all of his self-destruction and pain. When Charlie sits down with Max at a streetside café and tells him, "Everything's fine," Downey's eyes speak the lie. Everything is clearly not fine, for Charlie or for Downey.

Bits of the dialogue hint at Charlie's sexual preference (such as when he playfully asks Max if he is "still in the closet"), but the emphasis in Charlie's scenes is never on his gayness and always on the emotional connection between the two characters. When Max shows Charlie photos of his children and reveals that he named his son Charlie, Charlie is visibly touched. At a birthday party for Charlie that takes place in his hospital room days before he dies, Charlie rests his head on his lover's shoulder and kisses him, clearly at ease with the man physically and much in love. Downey plays Max's friend as Charlie, not as a gay man. Although the film is not about sexual orientation as a theme, even the way Max speaks and behaves when he's not around Charlie raises questions about society's misguided assumptions about queerness. During a dinner party at which Max is increasingly annoyed by the shallowness of his companions, he is asked, "Have you ever kissed a man?" and he responds, "Yeah. Now does that make me any less of a man?" With this question, Figgis is not only countering mainstream homophobia but at the same time raising a host of other possible questions about masculine identity: Does experimenting with (bi)sexuality, does being gay, does being HIV-positive or sick, does being a drug addict make a man less of a man?

In fact, Figgis deliberately inserted the in-some-ways-incidental plot of a gay man dying of AIDS into his comedy of manners about marriage in order to question the typical Hollywood approach: Why do we tend to only see gayness represented in films that focus on the topic of gayness? According to Figgis, death, homosexuality, and AIDS are marginalized in cinema in much the same way that black actors have tended to mostly appear in films focusing on the issue of race. Figgis wanted "to have these things as givens within a story" rather than using them "to make a cause film" (Commentary). Why not, within a "politically incorrect" film about adultery, have a minor character who happens to be gay, dying of AIDS, and asking for pot?

The film can be considered politically incorrect or at least unusual partly because most movies about a gay man dying of AIDS would have made Charlie's brother Vernon a much more clearly reprehensible character for implying that his dying brother is essentially getting what he deserves. At one point, Vernon says, "You know, with the lifestyle these guys [meaning these gay guys] lead, it's ... I mean, you don't watch someone out playing in the middle of a minefield and not expect to hear an explosion, right?" Charlie is not getting what he deserves for being gay, but he is, the film and Downey imply, suffering the consequences of some careless behavior. When he accepted the role, Downey saw it as a chance to experience some kind of catharsis or learn a personal lesson. He saw the film in "a larger context, which was, I'm really struggling with something right now, and it was kind of cathartic to play that part in the film because it was someone whose own proclivities and own sexual promiscuity and own desire to eat life and live fast was the reason why he wasn't going to be there for his friend when he might have enjoyed him most" (Downey qtd. in *IAS*). Charlie is not absolved of all personal responsibility just because he is dying, because he is gay, or because he is a sympathetic, likeable character.

A year after he cheats on his wife with a one night stand, Max returns to New York to visit Charlie who is now hospitalized with full-blown AIDS and is weeks or even days away from dying. Downey's appearance as a man knocking on death's door is disturbingly realistic. When Charlie, curled on a hospital bed and forced to breathe through an oxygen mask, tells Max, "I'm really tired but I can't sleep," viewers who are aware of the actor's personal history cannot help but assume this statement is coming as much from Downey as it is from his character. Charlie asks Max to visit him just before dawn, at about 5:30 or 5:45, because it's the scariest time of day for him: "I shit my pants for fear of death," Charlie admits, through watering eyes. When Max breaks down and cries at Charlie's bedside, Charlie comforts him: "It's okay, baby. It's okay. This is a lot harder for my friends than it is for me." It's a performance eerily reminiscent of *Less Than Zero*, another film in which Downey was able to naturalistically convey the combination of humor, sadness, and vulnerability that continues to draw audiences to him. Although a small number of critics considered his performance to be "melodramatic," Figgis says that such a wrongheaded sentiment only provides him with "an overwhelming temptation to grab somebody by the throat" since, according to both the director and others who have observed AIDS patients in their final stages, these are actually some of the most realistic scenes on film (Figgis, Commentary). Downey even won an award for third place for Best Supporting Actor from the Boston Society of Film Critics in 1997 (*IMDb*).

Coincidentally, Max's one night stand turns out to be Charlie's sister-in-law and Charlie sees them kissing in the darkened room when they think he is asleep. "The gamble was on ... Robert Downey's eyebrows," Figgis admits, because the rest of his face was covered by the oxygen mask, he was confined to a bed, and the room was in near darkness. He had to convey his surprise, curiosity, concern, and belief that Max and Karen had bonded emotionally, not just sexually. When Max asks his friend what he should do about his marital situation, Charlie tells him a story about a father who tells his son, "Life is an orange" and, when asked years later to explain this bit of folk wisdom, says, "I haven't a fucking clue." Charlie adds, "You gotta work out your shit, Max." Life is short and there are no easy answers, Charlie implies, but if you aren't happy, you need to put in the work to solve your own problems. Statements like these are frustrating to an audience that knows that Downey spent the next six years following the making of this movie failing to work out his own shit. In another instance, an older man walks into the room while Charlie sleeps and looks down at him silently, then leaves. We know instinctively who this man is, and Max confirms it just before Charlie dies when he tells him that his father had visited him. Max's line, "Your dad was here," is the most emotionally provoking line in the film for Mike Figgis, who says in the DVD commentary that "Robert's response was brilliant." The camera focuses on Charlie's eyes as they briefly, subtly but clearly, register surprise, hope, resentment, and bitter disappointment.

Although Downey's character is only "the catalyst" for the two main characters (Figgis, Commentary), his performance is the best thing about the movie and his portrayal is so striking and haunting that the audience and, presumably, the filmmaker, are not willing to leave Charlie when he leaves them, by dying. Although Figgis reluctantly cut a long funeral scene short because "The truth is the film is not, essentially, about Robert Downey," he couldn't resist filling the funeral scene with a large photographic portrait of Charlie and having him appear to Max after death, as his inner voice. In this genre-crossing tragicomedy about marriage, Charlie functions as "the voice of Max" and "the audience's entry or potential to enter into the emotion of the film" (Figgis, Commentary). One reviewer writes that "Downey and Snipes's partnership is the focal point" (Wickliffe), even though Charlie's scenes take up only a small portion of the movie's 102 minutes. Downey's character is not the central figure of the film, but he supplies nearly all of its emotion.

His role in *One Night Stand* revels in the ambiguity of a gay minor character who is incidentally dying of AIDS. In *Less Than Zero*, Julian Wells may or may not be bisexual, but, like Charlie, his "desire to eat life" and his outsider status as a *persona non grata* combine to bring about his own destruction. In the film, Julian's death is a tragedy only because it deprives the audience of their most vibrant character; his demise necessitates the miraculous resurrections of both Clay and Blair. In *Home for the Holidays*, Tommy Larson teaches Claudia not to assume that his male friend is gay just because he's "pretty," teaches Joanne that not all gay men fit into her stereotyped image of queerness, and teaches his parents that he can be happy and fulfilled in an unconventional relationship. In each of these films, Downey plays a character who, partly because of his queerness, functions as a catalyst in the lives of the film's protagonists. These roles demonstrate his willingness, ability, and desire to portray queerness with realism and compassion. Figgis' image of Robert Downey Jr. as a martyr on a cross (a pose he can also be seen striking in other films including *Natural Born Killers* and *Iron Man 3*) may be ludicrously unsubtle, but it may also be a fairly accurate depiction of his place not only in these separate narratives, but also in American pop culture in general. Through roles like these, he can pay penance for and therapeutically work through his own sins, make statements about the complexity of identity, and provide audiences with a vicarious experience of what it's like to be the damaged outsider. If America can't yet handle queerness as a "normal" part of life, perhaps Downey and the characters he plays can be a window between worlds—the homosexual and the heterosexual, the deviant and the embraced.

Works Cited

Arsenio Hall. 1993. Audio and Video Index. *Downey Unlimited Forever*. Web. 17 Dec. 2013.
Back to School Extra-Curricular Edition. 1986. Dir. Alan Metter. Fox Home Entertainment, 2011. Blu-ray.
"Biography, Famous." 2006. Audio and Video Index. *Downey Unlimited Forever*. Web. 2 Aug. 2013.
Buchanan, Kyle. "Bret Easton Ellis on *Less Than Zero*, Its Adaptation, and Its Sequel Imperial Bedrooms." *Movieline*. PMC, 17 May 2010. Web. 26 Aug. 2013.
Butler, Judith. *Gender Trouble*. Routledge: New York, 1990. Print.
_____. "Imitation and Gender Insubordination." *The Lesbian and Gay Studies Reader*. Ed. Henry Abelove, Michèle Aina Barale, David M. Halperin. New York: Routledge, 1993. Print. 307–320.
Caruso, "Kid Controversy." *Elle Magazine* 1987: n. pag. Articles and Interviews. *Downey Unlimited Forever*. Web. 17 Dec. 2013.
Chaplin. 15th Anniversary Edition. Dir. Richard Attenborough. Maple Pictures, 1992. DVD.
Doty, Alexander. *Making Things Perfectly Queer*. Minneapolis: University of Minnesota Press, 1993. Print.
Ebert, Roger. "Review of *Less Than Zero*." *Chicago-Sun Times*, 6 Nov. 1987: n. pag. Downey Review Archive. *Downey Unlimited Forever*. Web. 17 Dec. 2013.
Ellis, Bret Easton. *American Psycho*. New York: Vintage, 1991. Print.
_____. *Less Than Zero*. New York: Simon & Schuster, 1985. Print.
Figgis, Mike. Director's Commentary. *One Night Stand*. 1997. New Line Home Video, 1998. DVD.
_____. "Robert Downey Jr. Interview." *Hollywood Conversations*. 20 Aug. 1998. Narr. Mike Figgis. *You Tube*, 6 May 2013. Web. 11 Aug. 2013.
Firstborn. Dir. Michael Apted. Paramount, 1984. Film.
Foster, Jodie. "Commentary." *Home for the Holidays*. 1995. Dir. Jodie Foster. *The Robert Downey Jr. Collection*. Fox Home Entertainment, 2009. DVD.
_____. "Golden Globes Acceptance Speech." *YouTube*. You Tube, 13 Jan. 2013. Web. 12 Jan. 2014.
Garbarino, Steve. "Robert Downey's Last Party." *Detour* Feb. 1999: n. pag. Articles and Interviews. *Downey Unlimited Forever*. Web. 8 Aug. 2013.
Gleiberman, Owen. Review of *Home for the Holidays*. EW.com, 10 Nov. 1995. Web. 17 Dec. 2013.
Halperin, David M. *Saint Foucault: Towards a Gay Hagiography*. New York: Oxford University Press, 1995. Print.
Hennesey, Kevin. "Role Models." *Moveline* Mar. 1992: n. pag. Articles and Interviews. *Downey Unlimited Forever*. Web. 26 Aug. 2013.
Hirschberg, Lynn. "Robert Downey's Weird Science of Acting." *Rolling Stone* May 1988: n.pag. Articles and Interviews. *Downey Unlimited Forever*. Web. 1 August 2013.
Hofler, Robert. *Variety's The Movie That Changed My Life*. Philadelphia: Da Capo Press, 2009. Institute for Robert Downey Jr. Studies—Required Reading. *Robert Downey Jr. Film Guide*. N. p. Web. 5 Aug. 2013.
Hoggard, Liz. "Figgis with Attitude." *Guardian*, 26 Oct., 2003. Web. 1 Aug. 2013.
Home for the Holidays. 1995. Dir. Jodie Foster. *The Robert Downey Jr. Collection*. Fox Home Entertainment, 2009. DVD.
"*Home for the Holidays* Hollywood Premiere." 1995. Audio and Video Index. *Downey Unlimited Forever*. Web. 1 Aug. 2013.
Howard Stern. 1995. MP3. Audio and Video Index. *DowneyUnlimited Forever*. Web. 6 Jan. 2014.
In Dreams. Dir. Neil Jordan. Dreamworks, 1999. DVD.
Jurassic Park. Dir. Steven Spielberg. Universal, 1993. Film.
The Kids Are All Right. Dir. Lisa Cholodenko. Focus Features, 2010. Film.
Kiss Kiss Bang Bang. 2005. Dir. Shane Black. Warner Bros., 2006. DVD.
The Last Party. 1992. Dir. Mark Benjamin and Marc Levin. Live Home Video, 1993. VHS.
Leaving Las Vegas. Dir. Mike Figgis. MGM/UA, 1995. Film.
L'Ecuyer, Gerald. "Turns of Endearment." *Egg* Jan. 1991: n. pag. Articles and Interviews. *Downey Unlimited Forever*. Web. 7 June 2013.
Less Than Zero. 1987. Dir. Marek Kanievska. Fox Home Entertainment, 2001. DVD.
Levy, Emanuel. Review of *Home for the Holidays*. *Variety* 30 Oct. 1995: n. pag. Downey Review Archive. *Downey Unlimited Forever*. Web. 26 Aug. 2013.
Little Miss Sunshine. Dir. Jonathan Dayton, Valerie Faris. Fox Searchlight Pictures, 2006. Film.
Maslin, Janet. "Young Lives." Review of *Less Than Zero*. *New York Times*, 6 Nov. 1987: n. pag. Downey Review Archive. *Downey Unlimited Forever*. Web. 5 Aug. 2013.

Morice, Laura. "Acting—Or Just Acting Up?" *Mademoiselle*, Nov. 1988: n. pag. Articles and Interviews. *Downey Unlimited Forever*. Web. 3 Nov. 2013.

Natural Born Killers. 1994. Dir. Oliver Stone. Warner Bros., 2009. DVD.

One Night Stand. 1997. Dir. Mike Figgis. New Line Home Video, 1998. DVD.

Rebello, Steven. "Young Hollywood—Rockin' Robert." *Movieline*, Mar. 1991: n. pag. Articles and Interviews. *Downey Unlimited Forever*. Web. 1 Aug. 2013.

Rented Lips. Dir. Robert Downey Sr. International Video Entertainment, 1987. VHS.

Restoration. Dir. Michael Hoffman. Miramax Home Entertainment, 1995. DVD.

Rich, Adrienne. "Compulsory Heterosexuality and Lesbian Existence." 1980. *Adrienne Rich's Poetry and Prose*. Ed. Barbara Charlesworth Gelpi and Albert Gelpi. New York: Norton, 1993. Print. 203–224.

"Robert Downey Jr." *Inside the Actor's Studio*, 15 Dec. 2006. Narr. James Lipton. *YouTube*, 15 May 2013. Web. 2 Aug. 2013.

"Robert Downey Jr.—Awards." *IMDb*, Inc., n.d. Web. 24 Jan. 2014.

Schneller, Joanna. "What a Tramp!" *GQ*, Jan. 1993: n. pag. Downey Review Archive. *Downey Unlimited Forever*. Web. 4 July 2013.

Shaft. Dir. Gordon Parks. MGM, 1971. Film.

Sherlock Holmes. 2009. Dir. Guy Ritchie. Warner Bros., 2010. Blu-Ray.

Sherlock Holmes: A Game of Shadows. 2011. Dir. Guy Ritchie. Warner Bros., 2012. Blu-Ray.

The Singing Detective. 2003. Dir. Keith Gordon. Paramount Home Entertainment, 2004. DVD.

Taylor, Charles. "Robert Downey Jr." *Salon*, 10 Apr. 2001. Web. 13 Jan. 2014.

Three of Hearts. Dir. Yurek Bogayevicz. New Line Cinema, 1993. Film.

Too Much Sun. 1990. Dir. Robert Downey Sr. RCA/Columbia Pictures Home Video, 1991. VHS.

Tropic Thunder. Dir. Ben Stiller. Dreamworks Home Entertainment, 2008. DVD.

Virtue, Graeme. "Tracks of His Years." *Sunday Herald* [Edinburgh], 17 Apr. 2005. Institute for Robert Downey Jr. Studies—Required Reading. *Robert Downey Jr. Film Guide*. Web. 1 Aug. 2013.

Weinberg, Scott. "Review of *Less Than Zero*." *Apollo Movie Guide, 1998–2008*. Downey Review Archive. *Downey Unlimited.com*. Web. 4 Aug. 2013.

Weird Science. 1985. Dir. John Hughes. Universal, 2008. DVD.

"What's Up with Robert Downey Jr.?" *WOW*, Aug. 1987: n. pag. Articles and Interviews. *Downey Unlimited Forever*. Web. 4 Aug. 2013.

Wickliffe, Andrew. "One Night Stand." *Zimbio*, 18 Apr. 2011. Web. 9 Sept. 2013.

Wonder Boys. Dir. Curtis Hanson. Paramount, 2000. DVD.

Queering Downey Part 2:
Gender Identity and Cross-Dressing in
In Dreams, Wonder Boys and
Sherlock Holmes: A Game of Shadows

ERIN E. MACDONALD

Robert Downey Jr.'s first instance of cross-dressing on film was for a scene in *Chaplin* (1992) in which Charlie disguises himself as a woman in order to sneak his latest film reels out from under the prying eyes of a divorce lawyer. "Robert did a very Chaplinesque female impersonation" in the Salt Lake City scene (Kamin, Message). Since then, he has played slightly gender-bending characters in several movies, including James Toback's *Black and White* (1999) in which he plays a quite flamboyant gay man married to a woman and the Sherlock Holmes movies, which are full of homosocial jokes about Holmes being in love with Watson (Jude Law).

In *Sherlock Holmes: A Game of Shadows* (2011), Downey even dresses in drag (his idea). Paraphrasing Esther Newton, Judith Butler writes that..." drag enacts the very structure of impersonation by which any gender is assumed. Drag is not the putting on of a gender that belongs properly to some other group.... There is no 'proper' gender, a gender proper to one sex rather than another, which is in some sense that sex's cultural property" ("Imitation" 312–313). Downey's performances in *In Dreams, Wonder Boys*, and *A Game of Shadows* highlight the performativity of gender identity and its inability to be pinned down by categorization.

In Dreams

In *In Dreams*, released in January of 1999, Downey plays a transvestite serial killer—not a new idea (see *Psycho, Silence of the Lambs*, etc.) but one given slightly more of a sympathetic treatment here. Co-written and directed by Irish writer Neil Jordan of *Michael Collins* and *The Crying Game* fame, the film is a cross between a fairy tale, a sociological study of deviance, and a clichéd horror movie. The color red and apples present themselves not too subtly as recurring motifs throughout but the underlying theme of childhood gives these overused visual cues their interest. Just before her own daughter disappears after a performance as a fairy in her school's version of *Snow White*, illustrator Claire Cooper begins having prophetic dreams about a person who is kidnapping and possibly killing little girls. At first, Claire can't tell if the long-haired person in a room filled with apples is a man or a woman, and this confusion signals the second interesting aspect of the movie—its challenging of gender categories.

Of course, making the serial killer the one who cross-dresses and plays with gender because he is clearly mentally disturbed does not make for a positive queer political strategy, and Jordan could be accused of using the same tired queer-character-as-villain stereotype that stretches back to the early days of Hollywood. Jordan describes his villain as "a horribly damaged child … an utterly unpredictable, amoral person" (qtd. in Garbarino, "Last Party"). The way that both Bening and Downey play their characters, though, Vivian Thompson is in some ways as much of a victim as he is a criminal. In an oddly ironic parallel to his own life, Downey plays a man whose childhood of neglect caused his psychological development to become stunted at an early stage and whose resulting inappropriate behavior eventually lands him in prison, right before the actor himself was actually sent to prison—Corcoran 2—for nearly a year. Vivian's mental growth stopped at such an early age that he apparently still plays with dolls and his only desire is to construct the loving family he never had (or perhaps to get revenge on the mother who abused him and left him for dead)—not to enact the twisted sexual fantasies that audiences tend to associate with villainous queers and child abductions.

Although most scholars believe that male transvestites dress as women because doing so sexually excites them (Garber 323), Vivian does not attempt to have sex with Claire and does not appear to be sexually aroused by his identification with her. In fact, the audience does not see him dressed as a woman but is told, through Ruby, that he often wears his mother's (red) dresses. Although he has a gender-ambiguous name (Claire's roommate says "Oo-la-la" when she hears it) and long hair and cooks for his new "family" just like a Mommy, Vivian does not really look like a woman until the end of the film, when he is shown with shorn locks, entering his prison cell. With this new short, red hair and his blue eyes (obviously added deliberately since Downey's eyes are brown), Vivian at the end looks most like Claire—the two have switched positions. *In Dreams* is unusual in its lack of phallocentrism and in its use of a female hero; no man comes to save Claire Cooper—she saves Ruby herself and ends up exactly where she has been trying to go along—joined with her daughter in death. Unlike *Psycho*, in which Norman Bates kills a naked, sinful woman in a shower, *In Dreams* makes no sex and violence connection.

Instead, Jordan emphasizes the mental anguish of two characters—Claire and Vivian—who seem opposite in every way but one: they are both misfits who seek a loving family. Claire tells a psychiatrist, "I'm not obsessed. I'm possessed. He's feeding me dreams bit by bit.… Maybe he's lonely" and "He wants to stop. He wants me to stop him. I've got to let him possess me. Surrender. Let him take me to him." She is sympathetic to him until he tries to kill her with a scythe when she tries to escape with the little girl. Robert Stoller believed that transvestitism is "a rather efficient method of handling very strong feminine identifications without the patient having to succumb to the feeling that his sense of masculinity is being submerged by feminine wishes" (*Sex* 1:186). Vivian identifies with his mother and with Claire. He wants the nurturing that a "good Mommy" provides but is full of anger from being abused by the "bad Mommy." Fairy tales and nursery rhymes, children's games and play and the way Vivian repeats things in a childlike way are all about mimicry—children learning to mimic the ways of adults, and specifically of men or women.

Through her psychic connection to Vivian, Claire sees flashes of his past as a child, chained to his bed by his abusive mother who left him there to drown when the Northfield Reservoir was flooded in 1965. She also discovers, in her dreams and in her room in the Stapleton Mental Hospital, that before he escaped from the same room in 1972, Vivian had scrawled on the walls a nursery rhyme that keeps haunting Claire, along with the Andrews Sisters' song, "Don't Sit Under the Apple Tree," which turns out to have been his mother's favorite song. Claire escapes through the ductwork the same way she knows that Vivian did and sees that he killed a nurse and disguised himself in a clean nurse's uniform and lipstick stolen from a locker, in order to walk out the front door unnoticed. When the police officer who gives him a ride shows interest in the "nurse," staring at "her" stockinged legs, Vivian plays along, telling him "her" name is "Vivienne," flirting with a high voice, until the cop's wandering hand discovers a surprise between the boy's legs, Vivian's voice goes back to normal, and he shoots the cop. Claire does the same, using the piggishness of the man who picks her up as an excuse to get close enough to take his gun and then his car. She stops on the road and Vivian comes toward her, face obscured by a wide-brimmed hat and long hair hidden in a doubled-up ponytail. The audience is not clearly shown Vivian's/Downey's face until Claire herself sees him. "You wanna come over to my house, Claire?" he asks, sounding a bit menacing but more like a little boy arranging a playdate. She's sitting in the car and his reflection can only be partially seen in the lowered car window. Then he gets in beside her and removes his hat and the audience and Claire can clearly see his face close up for the first time. He acts nonchalantly, as though they're just going home for dinner.

When they arrive at what Claire had thought was an apple orchard but turns out to be a cider factory called The Good Apple (where apples are chewed up and spit out in machines instead of grown in pastoral orchards), he says, "You thought it was a real orchard, huh? That's the thing about dreams. They're always right and always wrong"—much like her image of him as both a woman and a man. Whereas the unseen Vivian/Downey was creepy and menacing, the seen version is childlike and vulnerable, like a hurt puppy. What other actor could make a killer of children seem human? He puts old-fashioned music on the car stereo and pulls her close, trying to dance with her. He tells her in a tear-choked voice,

> I am so, so sorry, sorry, sorry, Claire. All I wanted was a family. And I knew there was a dreamer out there like me, 'cause I was dreamin' of her. I wanted her to be my family. Then I took her little girl. And the little girl cried and hollered and I punished her, like any dad would. And she was lying, quiet, beautiful, but like the doll now. That's what I'm sorry for. But I'm gonna make it up to you. I'm gonna work real hard to make it perfect. I'm not gonna get upset anymore, now that I've got you here. And I've got us Ruby for a daughter now. Claire and Vivian and Ruby.

Claire sees that he hasn't harmed Ruby. He decorated the room with stuffed animals and gave her his old doll, Marge (who also wears red), to play with. She doesn't seem to be scared of him. He gives her piggyback rides and calls her "Sweetums." He offers to make them both "pasghetti." Ruby says, "Daddies can be just like mommies, you know that?" "That's what Vivian says. They can cook, too." He keeps his mother's red dress on a mannequin "for when he's playing Mom." According to Ruby, "[h]e's very good at it. You know, you should hear

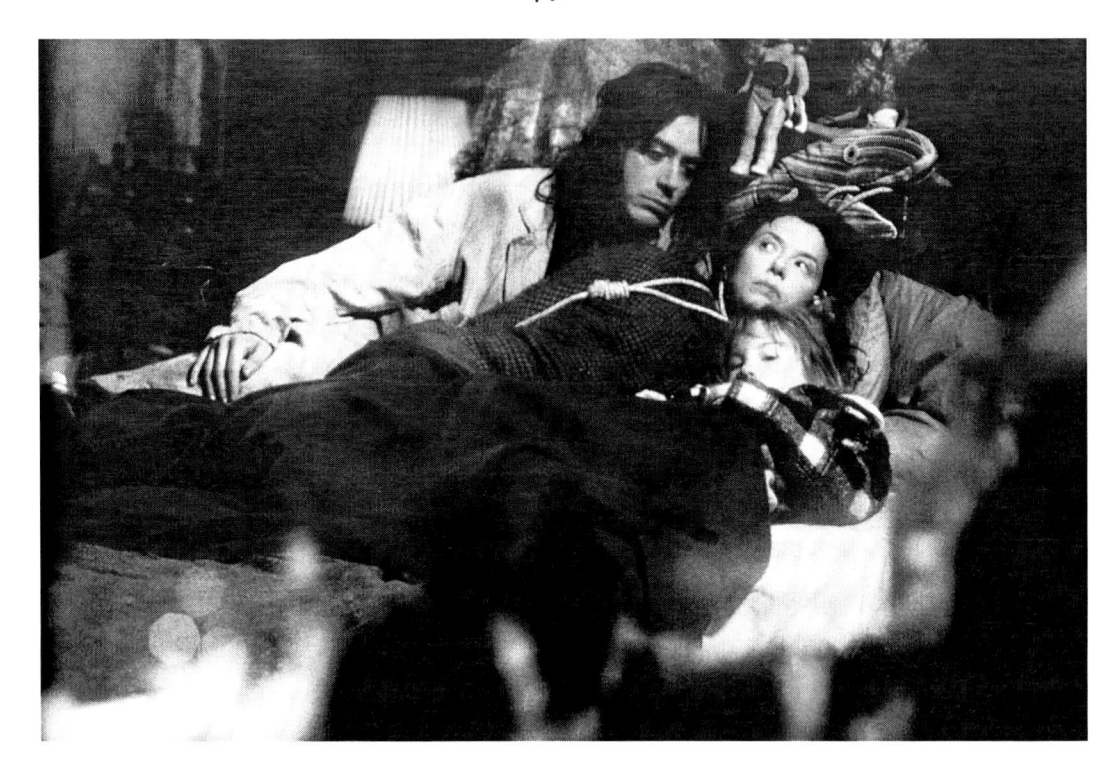

Downey, Annette Bening (center, as Claire) and Krystal Benn (as Ruby) in a scene from *In Dreams* (1999).

the way his voice changes." She appears to be convinced that he could make a good Mommy/Daddy.

This sympathetic treatment only goes so far, however. Claire tells Ruby, "Vivian's sick, honey. He needs help. There's a possibility that he could hurt you." In her role as mother figure to this girl, she doesn't want to scare her. She tries to escape with Ruby but Vivian catches them, hits her with a can, then casually continues his conversation: "You know, sometimes Mommy and Daddy fight and that's bad. Sometimes Mommy and Daddy fight and it's good." While Claire is out cold, he dresses her in "Bad Mommy's clothes" and tells her when she wakes up, "I thought you'd be a better mommy. My mom was no good either." When he kisses her goodnight on the cheek, the action is totally asexual. Like a child, he wakes up crying and calling for Claire, telling her he had a nightmare in which his mother, with Claire's face, was lying dead in the lake. She talks to him like he's a child needing to be nurtured and he calls her Mom but this reminder of his own mother makes him want to destroy her. When he turns violent again, Claire uses herself as a decoy and tells Ruby to run. During the police chase, they both fall into the reservoir and she drowns, happily reunited with her daughter, but he survives and is sent to a "secure mental facility," saying, "I can live with this." He looks in the cell's mirror at his new short red hair, claiming, "I can live with this, too," but when Claire starts haunting him, he can't live with that. He has gone from possessing her to being possessed by her and the film ends with the image of Vivian in prison, mentally tortured in a kind of psychic poetic justice.

The imagery, use of color, and fairy-tale exaggerations of gender roles work together to give the film the atmosphere that filmmaker Neil Jordan desired. The flooded, underwater

Vivian (Downey) realizes his mind is being possessed by Claire, whose looks his now resemble. *In Dreams* **(1999) was directed by Neil Jordan.**

town is a metaphor for both the past (Vivian's hidden past of abuse) and the unconscious (revealed through dreams that start to seep into Claire's waking hours). Jordan notes, "The visualization of dreams allowed me to deal with multiple levels of reality, and afforded me the opportunity to tell the audience something that the central characters don't know. Only Claire and the audience see the terrifying truth of her visions" ("Production Notes"). The director admits that he got his inspiration for the setting and style of the film from his own Irish childhood:

> I grew up in a respectable, lower-middle-class home. Our family was quite educated; my mother was a painter, and stuff like that. And I didn't chop up my next-door neighbour. But I remember those emotions. It was a very strange world. Ireland is very grey, and it seems like nothing has changed for centuries. The only bits of colour were in churches, with statues and gaudy religious vestments. It was a very insanely Catholic country. And, you have an educational system run by celibate men in skirts, which is bizarre in itself. But, there's just a sweet irrationality to the whole place ["Biography for Neil Jordan"].

The "only bits of color" in Jordan's film are the reds of the fairy tale that stand out against the muted, washed-out tones of the rest of the film. The "celibate men in skirts," the priests of Jordan's childhood, may be embodied in the character of Vivian, simultaneously identifying with and seeking to destroy the feminine within himself.

In her essay "Spare Parts," Marjorie Garber posits the idea that a transvestite man dressed in a woman's clothing is performing "a man's idea of what 'a woman' is; it is male subjectivity in drag" enacted for the purpose of reassuring the male of his maleness in the face of potentially feminizing articles such as clothing and makeup (324). Because he is afraid of being destroyed by, or consumed by, a woman (in Vivian's case, his mother),

> the male transvestite represents the extreme limit case of "male subjectivity," "proving" that he is male against the most extraordinary odds. Dressed in fishnet stockings, garter belt, and high heels, or in a housedress, the male transvestite is the paradoxical embodiment of male subjectivity. For it is his anxiety *about* his gendered subjectivity that engenders the masquerade [Garber 324].

Whether Vivian is heterosexual or not isn't really the point. He desperately wants to create the idyllic heteronormative family, with himself as Daddy, Claire as Mommy, and Ruby as Child, even though, as he has told Ruby, "Daddies can be just like Mommies" and even though, when things don't go as he'd planned, he instinctively refers to Claire as though she is *his* Mommy. He is confused, wanting to supply himself with the happy childhood and the mother he never had, but realizing on some level that it can never happen.

The role of the transvestite does not, according to Garber, work to destabilize gender categories. Most transvestites perform their notion (stereotype) of one gender or the other—their goal is not to be genderless (334). *In Dreams*, however, complicates this notion because Vivian is both Mommy and Daddy at once (and even Child—genderless and sexless) and because Vivian is played by Robert Downey Jr. (both the androgynous pretty boy from *Less Than Zero* and the macho stud who is Tony Stark/Iron Man). In this "absolutely impressionistic performance" (Jordan qtd. in Garbarino, "Last Party"), Downey helps Neil Jordan uncover, whether he intended to or not, the instability and ambiguity of gender.

Wonder Boys

Downey won the 2001 Screen Idol Award from L.A. Outfest for his role in *Wonder Boys* (*IMDb*), Curtis Hanson's 2000 film based on the 1995 novel by Michael Chabon. Downey plays Terry Crabtree, editor to author and creative writing professor, Grady Tripp. At the opening of the movie, Terry travels from New York to meet with Tripp, who hasn't published a book since his critically lauded *Arsonist's Daughter*, seven years prior. While Tripp has been hiding the reality of his "new" book (that it is thousands of pages long, aimless and unpublishable), Terry has never hidden his queerness from the author. Downey doesn't dress in drag for *Wonder Boys*, but Crabtree is attracted to ambiguous gender identities and to those who play with gender assumptions. Downey and his character seem to agree with Judith Butler's statement, "I'm permanently troubled by identity categories, consider them to be invariable stumbling blocks, and understand them, even promote them, as sites of necessary trouble. In fact, if the category were to offer no trouble, it would cease to be interesting to me..." ("Imitation" 308). Hanson's film overall provokes multiple questions about our perceptions of both feminine and masculine identity, arguing that men and women can both be either fertile or stagnant.

Tripp meets Crabtree at the airport and takes both him and his newfound friend Antonia to a party at the English department Chair's house because Terry and Antonia got along so well on the plane. Crabtree explains the situation this way: "You know how many times I've boarded an airplane just praying that some gal like her would be sittin' down beside me?" Tripp replies, "She's a transvestite." The two men know each other very well. Crabtree knows all about Tripp's history of falling quickly for "young, beautiful" women and Tripp is familiar with Terry's tendency to "collect freaks" as Antonia herself (one of the "freaks") puts it. Antonia is the first and ironically the most glamorous image of femininity in the film. At the party, the Chair, Walter Gaskell (who happens to be married to Tripp's mistress), says to Antonia "that every woman in some way desires to be Marilyn Monroe." "Oh, I couldn't agree more," she gushes, while he appears to have no idea that this particular woman has the genitalia of a man. Not every woman wants to be Marilyn Monroe, but the Chair's assumption stems from what Butler points out as "the very structure of impersonation by which any gender is assumed" ("Imitation" 312). In other words, Monroe herself was acting female, in the same way that Antonia acts female. Neither performance is based on a "real" gender identity. As Chabon writes in his novel, Antonia has mastered the "woman" performance: "This person had long black curls, wore a smashing red topcoat over a black dress and five-inch black spikes, and was laughing in sheer delight at something that Crabtree was whispering out of the corner of his mouth. It didn't appear to me, however," narrates Tripp, "that this person was a woman, although I wasn't entirely sure" (7). Chabon describes her as "intolerably flirtatious" and capable of "a creditable Mae West" imitation (16). Antonia's imitation of "woman" is creditable, but not entirely believable.

Tripp's secret girlfriend and the next image of femininity in the film, Sara Gaskell (Frances McDormand), is the university Chancellor, a 42-year-old powerful career woman who is pregnant, loves her greenhouse, and is often shown working there, helping to build the film's collection of images of fertility and growth. In one scene, Sara stands over Tripp as he comes to from one of his "spells" outside the lecture hall; she's in a white light, angelic, with a statue of the archetypal mother and infant above them. Mary's face dissolves into her face, casting Sara as the nurturing and powerful mother figure. When Crabtree helps carry an inebriated student (James Leer) out of the lecture, obviously high for the first time, Terry sees the Chancellor's look of disapproval and says, "He's fine." Sara says to Tripp, "Terry Crabtree and James Leer. Leave it to you to make that mistake." She goes to make sure he's okay, like she gets rid of the cop who later comes to Tripp's house looking for Leer. She's competent and capable, unlike Tripp and unlike Terry who says "Competence!" when Tripp asks what the editor's bosses are looking for in a new breed of employees. Sara takes care of herself, making her own decision about her baby, and takes care of most of the men in the film, as well.

Other female characters include Hannah (Katie Holmes), a young, seductive student-temptress with a crush on her older professor and Oola, a pregnant cocktail waitress who, by the end of the movie, walks off with Marilyn Monroe's jacket. Hannah says about Grady's book, "It sort of reads in places like you didn't really make any choices. At all." She recognizes Tripp's lack of meaningful editing in his work and in his life, and thinks she can save him. Her adolescent obsession with Tripp is excessive but believable. Images and metaphors of excess and fertility abound in *Wonder Boys*, but women are not the only ones capable of possessing this ripe abundance. Tripp is too fertile with his endless book; James is fertile in the right way, writing something "true"; and James gives Terry new life by "impregnating" Crabtree's career with his book.

Representations of masculinity in the film are more complex and more explored than those of femininity. Although Tripp announces, "We had decided to rescue James Leer," Tripp and Crabtree, and possibly most of the males in the story, are in need of rescuing, as well. The Chair of the English department, Walter Gaskell, is a parody of an intellectual's ideal of masculinity: He demonstrates his prowess through excessive spontaneous lecturing at parties and is obsessed with both Marilyn Monroe and Joe DiMaggio, her macho "slugger" husband. He is an object of derision possibly because of his insistence on the polarity of the feminine and masculine. Grady Tripp, constantly smoking pot in his deviant pink woman's bathrobe, can be seen as either unproductive or *too* productive, writing volumes every day but getting nowhere until his editor (mostly accidentally) forces him to "edit" his life.

Terry Crabtree in some ways represents the typical male mid-life crisis, although he is not the typical male and not yet middle-aged. He is on the verge of being tired of his youthful partying ways but still clings to drugs, alcohol, and affairs with interesting people (Antonia/Tony calls it "collecting weird tricks") because he doesn't know what else to do with his crumbling career and lonely life. Forcing himself to have fun, Terry attempts to feed off the ambiguous energy and passion of people like Antonia and James. Tripp admits that his friend is "going through the motions a little bit"—he sees that Terry is acting a role, performing an identity. Tony says, "[maybe] cause his career's ruined and all.... He said he hasn't had a success in over five years and everyone in New York thinks he's kind of a ... loser." When Crabtree glimpses James Leer, the young, brooding student writer for the first time, he quickly abandons Antonia and pressures the boy into going out after the lecture. When James protests that he'd rather go home, Terry insists, "Don't be silly. No one your age just wants to go home. Besides, faculty will be present—just consider it a field trip." He looks mischievous and James looks worried, as he should be. The field trip Terry has in mind will teach James as much about himself as it will about life. Already moving on to the next item in his collection, Crabtree adds another confused identity to his portfolio, perhaps as a way of avoiding examining his own. Crabtree's queerness makes him atypical, although *Wonder Boys* does not sensationalize this aspect of his identity and treats it instead as an unremarkable fact. While Tripp searches Terry's bag for drugs (finding some codeine pills to take care of the pain caused by a dog bite), James asks if Terry is gay. Tripp replies, in a very casual, accepting way, "Most of the time he is, James. Some of the time he isn't." Crabtree exceeds the boundaries of the masculine stereotype.

James Leer's excess lies in his mysterious sensitivity—it often goes unexplained but he clearly has more of it than any "normal" man would reveal in public. When Tripp shows James Marilyn Monroe's jacket in Walter's bedroom (accompanied by reverential music highlighting the museum-like nature of the artifact collection the Chair has assembled in his safe), James

Downey as Terry Crabtree in Curtis Hanson's *Wonder Boys* (2000).

becomes emotional staring at it, and says, "It just looks kind of lonely, hanging there in the closet." He is a loner, a misfit who thinks that the other students in Tripp's creative writing class hate him, but he finds happiness and artistic fulfillment, or at least identity transformation, with Terry.

The relationship between Terry and James renews Crabtree, who feeds off of Leer like a vampire and pushes Leer into self-realization. James represents innocence, trying drugs, getting drunk, and having sex for the first time, while Terry, who calls Tripp "killjoy" and "den mother," represents an excess of experience. When Tripp goes to rescue James from Terry at the pub where everyone has gone after the lecture, he sees the two sitting close together in a booth. James looks passed out when Terry tells Tripp he's going to read James' book. Tripp tries to protest, "He's one of my students, for Christssakes. Besides, I'm not sure if he's ... uh..." Tripp believes that Terry is opportunistic, only taking an interest in Leer's work because he thinks it will lead to his bed. Crabtree replies, "He is. I'm sure. Take my word for it. I see myself in him," but Tripp wants to protect James: "It's a little more complicated than that. Besides, he's a little scattered right now ... I don't think he needs sexual confusion to mix up the stew a little more." "On the contrary—I think it might be just the ticket," Crabtree comments, then looks seductively at their pregnant waitress, Oola, suggesting he's open to both genders. Butler writes,

> What remains permanently concealed by the very linguistic act that offers up the promise of a transparent revelation of sexuality? Can sexuality even remain sexuality once it submits to a criterion of transparency and disclosure, or does it perhaps cease to be sexuality precisely when the semblance of full explicitness is achieved? Is sexuality of any kind even possible without that opacity designated by the unconscious, which means simply that the conscious "I" who would reveal its sexuality is perhaps the last to know the meaning of what it says?" ["Imitation" 309]

To Terry, ambiguity and identity excess are exactly what an artist like James needs.

The viewer sees Crabtree sleeping angelically at Tripp's house and later entering Tripp's study in boxers, looking sleepy. "Morning, boys," he says, then looks at James specifically: "G'morning, James." Terry smiles and whispers mysteriously, "Jimmy, Jimmy, Jimmy. I'm gonna take a shower." When he walks out, James asks Tripp, "Did I do anything bad [last night]?," implying that sex with Crabtree would be something "bad." However, by the time a later scene shows Terry and James comfortably naked, in bed together (Crabtree reading Leer's manuscript while the younger man sleeps), James has changed his mind about what is "bad." Just like Tripp provides Leer with his first opportunity to get high, Terry provides him with his first chance to let his guard down, physically. James is at one point taken away in a police car and Sara quips to Tripp, "I wonder if this is what the university has in mind when it promises a liberal education." Both Crabtree and Tripp contribute to James Leer's "liberal education," in different ways.

A clue to Crabtree's role in the narrative can be found in the clip from *The Picture of Dorian Gray*, the 1945 (and arguably the best) film version of Oscar Wilde's 1891 novel, that plays on the television in Tripp's wife's parents' home. Lord Henry Wotton explains to young Dorian Gray,

> There's no such thing as a good influence, Mr. Gray. All influence is immoral. The aim of life is self-development. To realize one's nature perfectly. That's what we're here for. A man should live out his life fully and completely. Give form to every feeling and reality to every dream....

> There's only one way to get rid of a temptation and that's to yield to it. Resist it and the soul grows sick with longing for the things it has forbidden to itself.

In Wilde's novel, Lord Henry continues,

> The body sins once, and has done with its sin, for action is a mode of purification. Nothing remains then but the recollection of a pleasure, or the luxury of a regret. The only way to get rid of a temptation is to yield to it. Resist it, and your soul grows sick with longing for the things it has forbidden to itself, with desire for what its monstrous laws have made monstrous and unlawful. It has been said that the great events of the world take place in the brain. It is in the brain, and the brain only, that the great sins of the world take place also. You, Mr. Gray, you yourself, with your rose-red youth and your rose-white boyhood, you have had passions that have made you afraid, thoughts that have filled you with terror, day-dreams and sleeping dreams whose mere memory might stain your cheek with shame—[18].

Wilde's homosexual subtext works well here, as Terry tempts James to give in to his true nature. Crabtree is the corrupting influence of Wilde's novel: Lord Henry's words inflame young Dorian just as Terry provokes James to action. If Terry is Lord Henry, then Tripp is Basil, the artist who is helpless to prevent the corruptor's influence over the innocent boy. Although in the film Lord Henry is seen as a decadent hedonist who encourages Dorian to abandon all decency and become almost evil, Crabtree is portrayed as slightly more benign, in Hanson's film, and the Wilde reference contributes to the darkly humorous tone of the movie.

The implication, however, is not only sexual—even Tripp must realize that he has been sacrificing his true self to someone else's ideal. Just as Dorian cries, "I wish I could love.... But I seem to have lost the passion, and forgotten the desire. I am too much concentrated on myself. My own personality has become a burden to me" (205), Grady must stop denying himself the woman he loves, and must let go of the narcissistic burden—specifically, the book—that has kept him on a treadmill of dissatisfaction. His pink bathrobe is a symbol of incompetence—his inability to move forward with his life. Terry, too, needs to move forward, and in transferring his professional and personal attention from Tripp to James, whose personality has also been his own burden, succeeds in fulfilling himself. When Crabtree reads aloud James' latest novel that he finds in the typewriter and Tripp realizes the old man described is himself, the comparison between the aging artist and the innocent and beautiful young protégé continues.

James writes, "His hero's true injuries lay in a darker place. His heart, once capable of inspiring others so completely no longer inspired so much as itself. It beat now only out of habit. It beat now only because it could." Tripp realizes not only that the book is about him, but that he is in the same place, mentally, as Crabtree. The book that never ends is a metaphor for stagnation, for their lives. Oola asks what it's about, and Grady says he doesn't know. In the car, when discussing how Tripp only has one copy of his book, Crabtree says, "All I'm saying is that sometimes, subconsciously, a person will put themselves in a situation, perhaps even create that situation, in order to have an arena in which to work out an unresolved issue—all right? It's a covert way, if you will, of addressing a problem." This idea proves prescient when, while Terry attempts to flee from someone he believes to be a crazed gunman, Tripp's manuscript flies away. James has a VHS tape of *Written on the Wind* (starring gay but closeted Rock Hudson) in his backpack and when Terry loses Grady's manuscript, the pages are literally "written on the wind."

Terry Crabtree is the catalyst for both James and Grady to change their lives. James admits his homosexuality and has a shameless, fulfilling experience with Terry and moves out of his parent's house and on to a bigger and better future, getting his book published by Terry's company and saving Terry's career in the process. Tripp, because Terry has forced him to literally let go of the manuscript and the "script" (as metaphor) that was holding him back and keeping him trapped in a go-nowhere situation, realizes what's important to him—Sara, starting a family, and writing. He is cleansed (by Terry) of the book that's been dragging him down and endangers his career by helping James and by admitting his love for Sara. He gets rid of both the manuscript and the marriage that did nothing for him. James decides to give in to his temptations and eat life in the form of drugs, alcohol, gay sex, and getting published, courtesy of Crabtree's improvisation skills. Charles Taylor calls Downey's appearance in *Wonder Boys* a "sly, wily performance" that "bursts the boundaries of the character; it's the triumph of an actor who, in his craft, has not been smoothed over or made salable." Downey's own excessive identity bleeds into the film, merging yet again with a character whose queerness shakes the foundation of the status quo.

Sherlock Holmes: A Game of Shadows

Continuing his tendency to represent an excess of identity, Downey in 2009 took on the role of Sherlock Holmes and deliberately exceeded the gender expectations of the traditional character. Although Arthur Conan Doyle did not intend for his famous detective to be considered an object of sexual attraction, fans from the Victorian period onward have, partly because of Holmes' appearance in illustrations, plays, and films, seen the great detective as a dashing, desirable figure. Several different incarnations of Sherlock Holmes have, since at least the 1970 Billy Wilder film *The Private Life of Sherlock Holmes*, taken this sex appeal and added a queer complication. Now, whether in the BBC version of *Sherlock* starring Benedict Cumberbatch or in the Guy Ritchie films starring Downey, it has become commonplace for the audience to question Holmes' sexual orientation. Recent media adaptations are responding to (mostly female) fans' desire to play with the notion of Holmes and Watson's romantic friendship, as evidenced by internet fan fiction sites (Graham and Garlen 24–30). Several of these sites also feature homoerotic imaginings about Downey and Law, not just Holmes and Watson. The "bromance" between Downey's Holmes and Law's Watson, as Kayley Thomas points out, has been purposely highlighted from the start by "Downey's prefilm hype [which] effectively created a ready-made framework through which audiences were encouraged to view the film" (35).

As Graham and Garlen write, "Ritchie and his screenwriters develop Holmes' sexuality in several directions simultaneously" (30) and are able to do so partly because of the history of Holmes adaptations and their audience reception but also partly because of the persona of Robert Downey Jr. "Popular culture has amply demonstrated that audiences adore the complicated, rebellious, Byronic type of hero much more than the straight arrow," and Downey's notorious past therefore helps, rather than hinders, his sex appeal as Holmes (Graham and Garlen 31). Holmes' relationship with Watson (Jude Law), with its "strong homosexual undertones" (Graham and Garlen 31), takes center stage in both Holmes films over the detective's supposed love for the mysterious Irene Adler. Nevertheless, the inclusion of two possible romantic partners for Holmes positions him as "a bisexual rogue" (Graham and Garlen 31)—a queer Sherlock Holmes.

During multiple press interviews for the films, Downey broadly played up the potential sexual tension between Holmes and Watson, Law and himself ("On Jude Law"). Thomas argues in her article, "'Bromance is so passé': Robert Downey Jr.'s Queer Paratexts," that Downey deliberately queers Holmes, taking Ritchie's oft-repeated inspiration of *Butch Cassidy and the Sundance Kid* and running with it. She writes, "The actor's own (re-) interpretation and (re-) creation of Ritchie's conception, textually and paratextually—both in his performances in the films and ... his proclamations in the press—employ a queer framework through which to view Ritchie's adaptation" (37). Thomas uses the example (43–44) of an instance on *The Late Show with David Letterman*, when Downey suggested that Irene Adler "could be a beard" and introduced the film by saying, "Why don't we observe the clip and let the audience decide if he just happens to be a very butch homosexual. Which there are many. And I'm proud to know certain of them" (Letterman 2009). In another interview, Downey refuses to reduce Watson's and Holmes' "love" (his term) for each other to mere "bromance" because the word and its implications "cheape[n]" and "simplif[y]" a complex, potentially ambiguous relationship (qtd. in Thomas 45). Thomas writes, "Thus Downey's comments work to establish within the popularity and subsequent categorization of the bromance a queer space of potentiality, an essence to be filled and multiplied with meaning" (46). Just as he attempted to do when attached to *Three of Hearts* (see "Queering Downey Part 1"), Downey, in his interviews for and performances in the Holmes films, promotes queerness by resisting simplified or polarized interpretations of gender or sexuality.

A queer subtext is deliberately suggested most strongly in the second Holmes film, *A Game of Shadows* (2011). References range from the subtle (Watson taking a cigar out of Holmes' mouth and placing it in his own; Holmes referring to his friendship with Watson as a "relationship" and then, when John objects, changing the term to "partnership"; Holmes telling Watson, "Unlike you, I repress nothing") to the broadly comic (Holmes' suggestive command, "Lie down with me, Watson"; Holmes and Watson dancing hand in hand together at the Peace Summit at Reichenbach Falls to the raised eyebrows of some elderly gentlemen; Mary's comment to John after Holmes' supposed death that he "would've wanted to come with [them]" on their honeymoon). Aside from being saddened by his friend's marriage (the main "crisis" of the film, according to Downey and Law—qtd. in Thomas 39) and repeatedly trying to sacrifice himself to save Watson (which he arguably would do with or without any kind of same-sex attraction), Holmes also establishes a queer identity for himself by repeatedly using disguises and other physically altering techniques such as "urban camouflage." He successfully "passes" as an Asian opium-smoker (in his first appearance in the film), a porter, an Einstein-like student, and an armchair, to name a few instances. At the end of the film, when Watson asks Mary if the postman who delivered the parcel containing Mycroft Holmes' breathing apparatus looked like "the usual chap, or did he look peculiar?" and Holmes inserts his own question mark into the end of Watson's narrative, the peculiar, questioning nature of the detective figuratively frames the story.

The most obvious and most Tony Curtis–like (see *Some Like It Hot*) comedically queer scene, of course, features Downey as Holmes, dressed and made up like a woman. Irene Adler has been pushed out of the narrative by this point and Watson's wife, Mary, has been forcibly removed from it by Holmes himself. While dressed in drag, he throws Mary off a moving train, ostensibly clearing the way for the two men to be together, but actually just removing her from harm—or possibly the other way around. The sexual energy of the film, then, becomes focused on the two men "grappling with their complex feelings for one another. The homosexual undertones are emphasized by Sherlock's brief appearance in drag, although he ends up looking rather like Tim Curry in *The Rocky Horror Picture Show*, delivering innuendo-laden lines to Watson while shirtless, tussled, and bedecked with eye shadow" (Graham and Garlen 31). Unlike his transvestite date in *Wonder Boys*, Downey's Holmes in drag does not look remotely like a woman—he simply looks deviant; he looks like trouble. The drag scene (and possibly its *Rocky Horror* overtones, considering Downey's childhood love for the film—Raab, "Second Greatest") was his own idea. He reasoned that Watson's bride would be most upset not only to be interrupted by Holmes on the way to her honeymoon but especially to see him force his way into their relationship once again, dressed as a woman ("Maximum Movie").

The term "bromance" usually contains within it a specification that the central male bond of the bromance is non-sexual and often homophobic. Although Ritchie's Holmes and Watson qualify as a homosocial "buddy" couple in terms of modern cinema, they break with convention when Watson expresses no fear of Holmes' advances and when Holmes does not make any effort to confirm his own (supposed) heterosexuality. Instead, partly due to Downey's influence both on set and off, *A Game of Shadows* embraces a "homosocial continuum" (Sedgwick) that does not exclude the possibility of homosexuality. Drag, for Downey, is not just a gag—it is an opportunity to push audience reactions to the limit and to question the nature of Holmes and Watson's relationship, "letting the audience decide" how they choose to interpret it.

In 1999, Downey told an interviewer, "It's so crazy that nowadays people have to consider closeting themselves.... Because I'm not leading a double life—because I don't have a quote-unquote documented past—because I'm not using some foot soldier to keep me clamped down from any sort of exposés—I have no reservations about putting to word my thoughts, projections, beliefs. I don't have those fears" (Garbarino, "Last Party"). Although there may have been times in his life when he was closeted in terms of his drug use, he has candidly admitted to many of his indiscretions and all of his opinions, on everything from filmmaking to sex. Having the confidence and the open-mindedness to have never hidden his tolerance for multiple lifestyles and identities, Downey will hopefully continue, with his recent superstar status, to influence pop culture to embrace and accept the queer as normal.

Works Cited

"Biography for Neil Jordan." *IMDb*, n. d. Web. 3 Nov. 2013.
Black and White. Dir. James Toback. Columbia TriStar, 1999. DVD.
Butch Cassidy and the Sundance Kid. Dir. George Roy Hill. Twentieth Century–Fox, 1969. Film.
Butler, Judith. "Imitation and Gender Insubordination." *The Lesbian and Gay Studies Reader*. Ed. Henry Abelove, Michèle Aina Barale, David M. Halperin. New York: Routledge, 1993. Print. 307–320.
Chabon, Michael. *Wonder Boys*. 1995. New York: Random House, 2008. Print.
Chaplin. 15th Anniversary Edition. Dir. Richard Attenborough. Maple Pictures, 1992. DVD.
Charlie Bartlett. 2007. Dir. Jon Poll. *The Robert Downey Jr. Collection*. Fox Home Entertainment, 2009. DVD.

The Crying Game. Dir. Neil Jordan. Miramax, 1992. Film.
Garbarino, Steve. "Robert Downey's Last Party." *Detour*, Feb. 1999: n. pag. Articles and Interviews. *Downey Unlimited Forever*. Web. 8 Aug. 2013.
Garber, Marjorie. "Spare Parts: The Surgical Construction of Gender." *The Lesbian and Gay Studies Reader*. Ed. Henry Abelove, Michèle Aina Barale, David M. Halperin. NewYork: Routledge, 1993. Print. 321–336.
Graham, Anissa M., and Jennifer C. Garlen. "Sex and the Single Sleuth." *Sherlock Holmes for the 21st Century: Essays on New Adaptations*. Ed. Lynnette Porter. Jefferson, NC: McFarland, 2012. Print.
In Dreams. Dir. Neil Jordan. Dreamworks, 1999. DVD.
Jordan, Neil. "Production Notes." *In Dreams*. Dreamworks, 1999. DVD.
Kamin, Dan. Message to Erin E. MacDonald. 14 Jan. 2013. E-mail.
The Late Show with David Letterman. CBS. Dec. 2009. Television.
"Maximum Movie Mode." *Sherlock Holmes: A Game of Shadows*. Dir. Guy Ritchie. Warner Bros., 2011. Blu-Ray.
Michael Collins. Dir. Neil Jordan. Warner Bros., 1996. Film.
The Picture of Dorion Gray. Dir. Albert Lewin. MGM,1945. Film.
The Private Life of Sherlock Holmes. Dir. Billy Wilder. United Artists, 1970. Film.
Psycho. Dir. Alfred Hitchcock. Paramount, 1960. Film.
Raab, Scott. "The Second Greatest Actor in the World." *Esquire*, Dec. 2009: n. pag. Articles and Interviews. *Downey Unlimited Forever*. Web. 4 Aug. 2013.
"Robert Downey Jr.—Awards." *IMDb*, n. d. Web. 3 Nov. 2013.
The Rocky Horror Picture Show. Dir. Jim Sharman. Twentieth Century–Fox, 1975. Film.
Sedgwick, Eve Kosofsky. *Between Men: English Literature and Male Homosocial Desire*. New York: Columbia University Press, 1985. Print.
Sherlock. Crea. Mark Gatiss, Steven Moffat. BBC Worldwide, 2010-. Television.
Sherlock Holmes. Dir. Guy Ritchie. Warner Bros., 2009. Blu-Ray.
Sherlock Holmes: A Game of Shadows. Dir. Guy Ritchie. Warner Bros., 2011. Blu-Ray.
The Silence of the Lambs. Dir. Jonathan Demme. Orion Pictures, 1991. Film.
Some Like It Hot. Dir. Billy Wilder. United Artists, 1959. Film.
Stoller, Robert J. *Sex and Gender*. 2 vols. London: Hogarth, 1968–75. Print.
Thomas, Kayley. "'Bromance is so passé': Robert Downey Jr.'s Queer Paratexts." *Sherlock Holmes for the 21st Century: Essays on New Adaptations*. Ed. Lynnette Porter. Jefferson, NC: McFarland, 2012. Print.
Three of Hearts. Dir. Yurek Bogayevicz. New Line Cinema, 1993. Film.
Wilde, Oscar. *The Picture of Dorian Gray*. New York: Oxford University Press, 1994. Print.
Wolf, Jeanne. "Robert Downey Jr. on Jude Law: 'We Should Be Doing Romantic Comedies Together.'" Parade.com, 24 Dec. 2009. Articles and Interviews. *Downey Unlimited Forever*. Web. 2 Nov. 2013.
Wonder Boys. Dir. Curtis Hanson. Paramount, 2000. DVD.
Written on the Wind. Dir. Douglas Sirk. Universal, 1956. Film.

"This too too sullied flesh": The Resurfacing of Robert Downey Jr.

Jason Davids Scott

In the wake of the blockbuster success of the work of Robert Downey Jr. one dismissive interviewer wrote, "By 2006 Downey was longtime clean, but he was still playing the sixth lead in a remake of *The Shaggy Dog*, the thespian equivalent of opening for a puppet show" (Rodrick). This broad comment ignores the impressive and (in retrospect) significant work that Downey did in three less-seen independent films shortly after his stint in rehab: *The Singing Detective* (2003), *A Scanner Darkly* (2006), and *Fur: An Imaginary Portrait of Diane Arbus* (2006). These performances ultimately point toward Downey's subsequent blockbusters in which his character's compromised/resurfaced body leads to unlikely acts of heroism and bravery—the deeply "Method" Kirk Lazarus/Lincoln Osiris in *Tropic Thunder* (a comic turn which earned Downey an Academy Award nomination) and the mechanized Tony Stark, powered by a mechanical heart to become Iron Man.

Actors are, by definition, required to be something that they are not. From the earliest traditions of performed drama, that has meant literally disguising the actor's true identity, initially through the use of mask, eventually extending to costume and makeup. Although actors have had recognizable public personalities dating back to the 1700s with the likes of Charles Macklin and David Garrick, the notion of "personation" (or "impersonation") of the character has for the most part remained as the ultimate goal of the actor's craft. How an individual performer achieves this effect has fluctuated historically, but the intent has always remained the same: In order to be effective, the audience must see the character functioning as an agent of the narrative, and not see the "actor" behind the mask.

This is a particularly vexing problem with film stardom, which has just as much relied on a celebrity's individual persona for narrative function as it has the actor's technique. Particularly in the so-called "Golden Age" of Hollywood studio filmmaking, the carefully honed images of the stars almost always matched the parts they played on screen. Thus, the actor John Wayne, no matter which part he was playing, almost always conveyed the same persona and used the same acting techniques over the course of nearly forty years of filmmaking. The same could arguably be said for Hollywood icons such as James Cagney, Humphrey Bogart, Gary Cooper, Bette Davis, Katharine Hepburn and Marilyn Monroe. However, other stars have traditionally pursued versatility in their roles: In Wayne's generation, actors like Fredric March, Spencer Tracy, and Paul Muni were well respected for their ability to "disappear" into any role. In the present day, many stars seem to represent both traditions. Robert DeNiro and Meryl Streep, for example, are at times unrecognizable or "invisible" in their parts, particularly earlier in their careers; at other times, however, they seem to be performing almost as parodies of themselves or characters they have made well-known, as if foregrounding their own skills as actors over the meaning and purpose of the characters they are representing. Finally, there are stars who seem to be playing "themselves," as if they are inseparable from their on-screen personae: Judy Garland is perhaps the most notable example in this regard, someone known off-screen as emotionally fragile and insecure who seemed to thrive when playing characters of similar quality (notably in the 1954 version of *A Star is Born*). It has become impossible to see a Judy Garland performance without superimposing Garland's own life as a kind of critical filter, allowing us to see the "real" Judy underneath whatever mask she has appropriated.

Contemporary audiences, then, often read star performances through a complex arrangement of critical filters that seem to combine our expectations and understanding of three separate but interrelated entities: the function of the character being represented in the singular film text, the function of the star persona as related to the other characters that the actor has portrayed most memorably, and the function of the star's own personal/private biography.[1] At various points in his or her career, an actor's performances might be read through one filter more dominantly than another, or through a combination of all three. In the case of Robert Downey Jr. he is now almost entirely read in regards to the second category—that of the star persona. After early success as a "Brat Pack" juvenile, he began to demonstrate versatility, culminating in his performance in 1992's *Chaplin*. Today, Downey has evolved into a "superstar" capable of playing larger-than-life superheroes like Tony Stark/Iron Man and Sherlock Holmes—this despite (or perhaps because of) the fact that his signature "technique" is to "underplay" emotional extremes. He creates his characters through a combination of snarky asides, reaction shots, and understated (often mumbled) thoughts, drawing attention to himself by being the quietest and calmest figure in otherwise "loud" and dynamic films.

Critic Roger Ebert notes that "Tony Stark is created from the persona Downey has fashioned through many movies: irreverent, quirky, self-deprecating, wise-cracking," later noting that "the screenplay seems almost to have been dictated by Downey's persona. He's flippant in the face of disaster, casual on the brink of ruin." At the end of this review, however, Ebert makes a cogent point: "You hire an actor for his strengths, and Downey would not be strong as a one-dimensional mighty-man. He is strong because he is smart, quick and funny, and because we sense his public persona masks deep private wounds" (Ebert, *Iron Man*).

Ebert's last comment references the period of Downey's career when his performances were primarily read not through the second filter of star persona, but an unusual combination of the first and third, when predictable technique took a back seat to character as a result of Downey's off-screen, biographical experience. The most unique performances of Downey's career are the ones in which he literally (and in radically different ways) offers up his own skin as a space representing trauma, compromise, disconnection and displacement.[2] The key performance in this regard is in *The Singing Detective* (2003), the first film Downey made after his (hopefully) final stint in rehab, in which he plays a delusional medical patient who must go through a rehab-like process in order to battle a crippling skin condition. While it is certainly conceivable that other actors could have taken on this role, Downey's own (then) recent battles with drug abuse and his process of recovery make his presence in this film more than just an example of "good casting." Along with his performances in *A Scanner Darkly* and *Fur*, one can see Downey "disappearing" into the skin of the character by literally resurfacing his own skin (with psoriatic sores, animation, and bodily hair), and yet character and actor are both magnified by the presence of the other, resisting any simplistic reading of the performances that might be the case with another actor.

Celebrity Performance and Public Addiction

There is, sadly, a long tradition that connects Hollywood stardom to substance abuse. Silent film star Wallace Reid, prescribed morphine to combat injuries he suffered in an accident, became addicted, and died within four years despite attempts to kick his habit. In the decades since, Judy Garland, Marilyn Monroe, Lenny Bruce, Dorothy Dandridge, Elvis Presley, John Belushi, River Phoenix, Chris Farley, and Heath Ledger are just a few of the most famous film stars who died as a result of abuse and misuse of both legal and illegal substances. Many of these deaths were sudden and shocking: Of the above stars, Garland was the oldest when she died at age 47, and the average age at time of death was 36. When one considers the number of careers ruined by performers who battled drug problems and the lives of colleagues, families, and friends devastated by addiction, the impact of substance abuse on the film industry cannot be minimized.

At the same time, there is a historical record of actors and celebrities surviving substance abuse, or at least mitigating and minimizing the effects of substance abuse enough to continue their careers. In the golden age of Hollywood, to be sure, there were a number of stars and executives who would (by most contemporary standards) be considered alcoholics or addicts, their dependencies well-hidden by studio publicists and journalists willing to keep these addictions secret. In a comprehensive account of the life of Spencer Tracy, long regarded as one of the most beloved and respected screen actors in history, biographer James Curtis relies on Tracy's personal diary and medical records to recount Tracy's lifelong battle with alcohol, which eventually led to a dependency on highly addictive prescription drugs like Seconal. Convinced that his alcoholism was a sign of spiritual weakness that ultimately manifested itself in the deafness of his first son, John, Tracy, at least early in his career, was one of Hollywood's most unreliable contract players. While establishing himself as a generic leading man type at Fox, he frequently disappeared for days at a time on blackout-inducing benders, causing massive delays in shooting. Later in life, as he became a more publically recognizable star, he would have extended periods of sobriety, only to fall spectacularly off the wagon as a result of emotional turmoil connected to his career or his private life. Though his public image as a hard-nosed but ultimately loveable Irishman would have afforded him some leeway with his public in terms of his alcohol use, the extent of his dependency and his addiction to sleeping pills until his death would have likely been a shock (Curtis).

Thus, for the most part, the public history of celebrity substance abuse typically follows one of these two narratives: a life and a career tragically cut short, or a long-held "secret" that remains as such as long as the celebrity remains functional, productive, and profitable. There are other narratives that are all too familiar but perhaps less compelling: minor stars or "B-list" celebrities who die before achieving top-tier status (Brittany Murphy, Anna Nicole Smith, Robert Pastorelli, Christopher Penn); stars who slowly drink themselves to death (Richard Burton, Errol Flynn) after years of alcohol abuse; performers who may have briefly been famous, but who admit to or succumb to drug use long after their star has faded (former child stars Scotty Beckett, Corey Haim, Dana Plato); or stars with personal problems (often including chemical dependency) who commit suicide by drug overdose (Jean Seberg, Inger Stevens, Charles Boyer).

What is remarkably rare in Hollywood is the star who suffers publicly, but then successfully goes through recovery and reestablishes him- or herself as a viable screen commodity. Robert Downey Jr. is by far the most high-profile actor ever to achieve this unique personal history. Remarkably, just about a decade removed from a personal and professional "bottom" that seemed insurmountable, his current status as an A-list movie star and one of the most respected actors of his generation is barely tainted by the memory of his very public battle with addiction. It is safe to say that most of Downey's younger fans, who know him from the *Iron Man* and *Sherlock Holmes* films, have little or no memory of his troubled past, and no longer automatically associate him with drug use or identify him as a "rehabilitated" celebrity. Although Downey himself does not preclude the subject from being discussed, it is rarely mentioned in the popular discourse surrounding his films. Discussing Downey's complex celebrity history with his younger fans, a helpful point of comparison is to ask them to look ten years into the future and imagine Lindsay Lohan as one of the biggest and most respected stars in Hollywood: that is how remarkable and unlikely Downey's turnaround has been.

Downey's public battle with drugs was well documented in the popular press, who were quick to highlight the dramatic and extreme nature of Downey's addiction against the backdrop of a career that seemed to be spinning out of control. After peaking at the age of 27 with his Academy Award-nominated role in *Chaplin*, his drug-influenced behavior became more and more erratic. His career likewise seemed to veer from the potential of perpetual leading man stardom to a string of bad misses and box-office failures. Softer comedies like *Heart and Souls* (1993) and *Only You* (1994) failed to connect with big audiences despite Downey's presence as a lead in front of a strong supporting cast. The same could be said of the underrated period drama *Restoration* (1995), which barely earned $4 million in the United States (on a budget of five times that amount). He appeared in supporting roles in acclaimed films such as *Short Cuts* (1993), *Natural Born Killers* (1994), *Richard III* (1995), *U.S. Marshals* (1998), and *Bowfinger* (1999), but also in notable failures such as *Home for the Holidays* (1995), *The Gingerbread Man* (1998), and *In Dreams* (1999). (It would be a stretch to consider any of these previous eight films as "Robert Downey Jr." films, another indication of his fall from the "A-list.") Finally, there are a host of films featuring Downey that for one reason or another barely got released: *Hail Caesar* (1994), *Danger Zone* (1997), *One Night Stand* (1997), *Hugo Pool* (1997), *Friends and Lovers* (1999), and *Black and White* (1999). Even the critically acclaimed *Wonder Boys* (2000), which arguably offers Downey's strongest performance of the post-*Chaplin*/pre-rehab films, did not earn back its $35 million budget.

Of course, by the year 2000, Downey's career had been interrupted several times by the legal problems related to his drug abuse. Arrests, parole violations (including one incident where he was found sleeping in a neighbor's home after breaking and entering), and failure to abide by a court-ordered drug test resulted in a brief prison stint in 1997. Two years later, another missed drug test earned him a three-year sentence at the California State Prison in Corcoran (which has a drug rehab facility). In a celebrity-friendly environment where it seemed like high-priced lawyers could get their famous clients off with minimum punishment—his legal team had recently and famously defended murder charges against O.J. Simpson—Downey's sentence to prison was a shock. He was allowed to end his incarceration after several months thanks to a hefty bond and a sympathetic panel of judges who agreed that the actor's sentence had been miscalculated by the trial judge ("Actor Robert Downey Jr. Released from Jail").

At that point, Downey's addiction would have already been notable because of the many actual prison stints (not just home-based rehab or house arrest). He began appearing on the Fox television series *Ally McBeal*, which had been struggling, and the combination of his "comeback" and natural talent helped boost the program's ratings. But he continued to use drugs secretly—or at least until another series of public incidents that threatened his parole, including a charge of possession of Valium and cocaine following an incident in Palm Springs in November 2000, and an April 2001 arrest for being under the influence of cocaine while aimlessly wandering the streets of Culver City in his bare feet. He was fired from *Ally McBeal*, and preparations to star in a Mel Gibson-produced stage version of *Hamlet* also were scrapped, along with plans for Downey to star in films for Joe Roth (*America's Sweethearts*) and Woody Allen (*Melinda and Melinda*) ("Robert Downey Jr.'s Drug 'Deal'"; Lax). He eventually pled no contest in July 2001, promising to enter a three-year detox/rehab program under the guidelines of California's new Proposition 36, which sought to get drug addicts help instead of prison time ("Actor Downey Given Three Years' Probation"). The probation was reduced after several months by the trial judge impressed with Downey's dedication, effort, and desire to work again ("Judge to Downey: Keep up the Good Work"). Though the legal system was giving him yet another chance, he seemed to have burned his final bridge in Hollywood: In addition to being considered unreliable because of his erratic behavior, he was for all intents and purposes unemployable, since no insurance company would back a project that he was involved in. His public battle with addiction lasted over five years, and his once-promising talent was reduced to being a cautionary tale and the subject of late-night comedians' jokes.[3]

The Compromised Body in Public Recovery: The Singing Detective

One of the more widely quoted definitions of "trauma" comes from Cathy Caruth, who writes that trauma is "an overwhelming experience of sudden or catastrophic events in which the response to the event occurs in the often delayed, uncontrolled repetitive appearance of hallucinations and other intrusive phenomena" (11). Such a description might be apt for Dan Dark, the character played by Robert Downey Jr. in *The Singing Detective*. Dark is suffering from both a catastrophic case of psoriasis that has covered his body with painful, crippling sores, as well as "uncontrolled repetitive" hallucinations that encompass both his personal past and his present ambitions as a writer of *noir* fiction.

The critical literature surrounding issues of trauma and performance often focuses on the psychological process of both audience and subject identifying the trauma and "working through" the event as it exists in both fact (what actually happened) and memory (what prompts emotional turmoil in the present). "We suggest," writes Patrick Duggan, "that the survivor-sufferer is caught in a structure cognate with performance insofar as it is a *mise-en-abyme* in which the symptom is a representation or rehearsal of the original event but at the same time itself is a traumatic event—and that this may give performance a particular purchase on trauma" (Duggan and Wallace 5). He writes elsewhere, "Both [performance and trauma] share a destabilising power so it would seem that theatre, more than any other art form, is perfectly placed to attempt a dialogue with, if not a representation of, trauma" (Duggan). Representations of trauma survival—on either an individual level, such as a character surviving rape or abuse, or on a collective one such as a community processing the aftermath of war or genocide—then seem to specifically have the potential to unite spectator and performer.

This "working through" of trauma can certainly be seen in Dan Dark, who, as he begins to (reluctantly) engage in productive psychotherapy with Dr. Gibbon (Mel Gibson), sees the trauma to his skin abate and recede into the past, just as the traumatic memories from his past become more vivid in the present and allow him to confront the issues of abandonment and confusion inflicted upon him as a child. However, when one considers Downey's presence on camera as Dan Dark—particularly in the context of 2003, when the film was released, so close on the heels of Downey's public battles with drugs and rehab—the identification between the audience and Dark is mitigated. The knowledge that Downey's own suffering was self-inflicted rather than forced upon him potentially alienates Downey/Dark from any easily assumed identification—the audience might theoretically root for Dark's recovery, while simultaneously being suspicious of Downey's authority to represent such recovery. Downey himself seemed to acknowledge this contradiction and potential suspicion of his recovery to the press during his publicity appearances for the film, saying he had "subjected [him]self" to drugs "for a heartbeat [but] signed up for a lifetime" (Pevere), therefore implying that his own "disease" was self-inflicted.

The contemporary readings of his performance were no doubt further complicated by the facts surrounding the production of *The Singing Detective*, which (at times by coincidence) reflect an almost uncanny self-reflexivity. Originally a BBC miniseries created by Dennis Potter (*Pennies from Heaven*), *The Singing Detective* had been a potential Hollywood property for a number of years. Potter—who himself suffered from crippling psoriasis and considered Dan Dark a representation of his own lived experience ("*The Singing Detective*: Infirmity")—adapted the British work to run at conventional feature length, switching the locale from Britain to America (initially Chicago), and suggesting that musical numbers be drawn from the 1950s and 1960s (as opposed to earlier decades in the television production) (Gordon). Potter died in 1994, but the project lingered in various Hollywood studios, at times with major stars and huge budgets attached, only to be scrapped as too risky.

Ultimately, actor Mel Gibson, who had established himself as a successful producer, acquired the rights to the screenplay. Having worked with Downey in the 1990 film *Air America*, Gibson thought that the role of Dark would be ideal for Downey to reestablish himself as a leading man. The fact that Gibson also plays the part of Dr. Gibbon (the similarities in their names are purely coincidental, as the character was also in the 1986 miniseries) further overshadows any reading of the film, as the established and successful mentor (Gibson/Gibbon) proves to be the key to recovery for the compromised and traumatized young artist (Downey/Dark). As any picture with Downey was uninsurable, Gibson put up his own money as a bond (several million dollars), and agreed to shift the film's location from Chicago to Los Angeles because Downey was on probation and not allowed to leave the state of California (Gordon). "Every two weeks I send him [Downey] a Polariod of my pecker lying across the chopping block," Gibson told one reporter visiting the set. (The reporter noted of Gibson's comment, "He's smiling but not joking.") (Millar).

Furthermore, the critical discourse surrounding the film seemed to ubiquitously require a kind of confession tour for Downey—a very public performance of the process of recovery that allowed critics and audiences to establish a connection to the performer's lived experience that could then extend to their reading of Dan Dark. Just as viewers had to confront the painfully alive surface of Dan Dark's skin on screen, so too did they need to acknowledge the most obvious element of Downey's life, his recent addiction visible on his celebrity "skin." Feature articles discussing Downey as Dark link the role and his real life. "This movie saved my ass in so many ways," Downey told *The Guardian*. "It wasn't difficult for me to relate to a character in so much deep denial. It's fair to say that I understood the emotions going on." Later in the article he claims that the film allowed him to establish a new standard for himself, something that had benefits both professionally and personally: "For a long time, I've needed to make a movie that edged *Chaplin*. With *The Singing Detective*, I think I've finally edged it. It's made me realize that I've too much to lose to fuck up again and go back to the mess I was" (Wilde). Other interviews and profiles followed suit, with Downey indicating that public contrition was part and parcel of the recovery process: "I was talking to a friend who said that public humiliation had been a really big part of my karma. But now that part is over. Now you just get to do what you do for a living every day, like every other sad motherfucker on earth" (Byrnes).

The relationship between Dark and Downey was not missed by critics of the film. Overall, reactions were mixed, but many cited Downey's performance as something above and beyond the standard leading man performance, and something that can only be understood through his personal experience. Critics who didn't make explicit connections between the character and the actor still felt compelled to mention Downey's addiction: "Personal problems notwithstanding, Robert Downey Jr. is one of the best under–40 actors working today, as his multi-faceted performance here illustrates" (Berardinelli). Another reviewer mentions both the addiction and Downey's effective performance without explicitly connecting the dots between the two: "Downey, a splendid actor whose troubled personal life has too often overshadowed his talent, spends much of the movie in a hospital bed…. He has to act around all those flakes [skin makeup] and miraculously registers some moments of energy" (MacDonald).

Critics who probed deeper into the performance mentioned Downey's rehab experience in connection with his reputation as an actor who underplays his roles with sarcasm and casual close-jawed snarkiness. "What horrors Downey has endured during his struggle with addiction we can easily imagine," wrote Roger Ebert: "Dan Dark's sardonic view of the world and his insulting, sarcastic manner of speech is a defense mechanism familiar to anyone who has known a user" (Ebert, "*The Singing Detective*"). Disagreeing with the performance's value, Jami Bernard still connects and conflates biography and technique:

> Robert Downey, Jr … must have looked perfect for this part on paper. Having gone through his own hell in revolving-door drug rehab, Downey could draw upon his own experience of

being locked inside himself, furious at a world that sees him as a hopeless case. The casting misfires. I suspect that Downey has indeed brought to the role his own method of coping—the quicksilver smart aleck who is painfully self-aware while running for his life. His game face doesn't have the authority, pain, and fury that [BBC series star Michael] Gambon summoned with a single scowl.

Only the occasional critic frames the performance in terms of Downey's acting technique: "Downey's lockjaw delivery makes most of it intelligible," wrote Leslie Camhi, echoing the descriptions of Downey's technique from Ebert and Bernard without equating it to Downey's public reputation as a user.

With very few exceptions, critics seem, in these reviews, forced to analyze and critically process both Downey as a real-life biographical entity—someone whose psychic scars from drug abuse are tangible (though not visible)—and his role as Dark, whose skin condition renders him "like sausage and mushrooms with extra tomato sauce and an occasional eruption of cheese" (Ebert, "*The Singing Detective*") or "like Krispy Kreme glaze" (MacDonald). Dan Dark's skin, described as consumable as junk food, thus serves as a compelling reflection of Downey's persona and reputation as a larger-than-life Hollywood burnout, equal parts appealing and revolting. That Downey must actually engage in the actor's craft is secondary to his seemingly necessary subjugation to therapy in the form of "public humiliation," or at least conciliation on Downey's part that his own trauma and compromise, unlike his character's, is self-inflicted. In order to author the performance of the character, he must also acknowledge the authorship and responsibility of his own lived experience.

Because *The Singing Detective* was a low-budget film with an unusual premise, it received only minimal distribution in the United States, playing in "arthouse" cinemas in major cities, and in a maximum of 46 theatres for two weeks in November 2003 (*Box Office Mojo*). Fans of Downey who may have been eager to welcome his comeback—after all, his two most recent stints were the successful run on *Ally McBeal* and the supporting role in *Wonder Boys*—likely never had the chance to appreciate the unique relationship between the character and the role. Thus, although for critics within the industry *The Singing Detective* marked the point from which Downey began his comeback, his image with the public was likely little changed.

Resurfacing: A Scanner Darkly *and* Fur

Such was also the fate for two subsequent films that Downey made (both released in 2006) that employ his standard acting techniques in combination with the drastic alteration of the surface of his skin. *A Scanner Darkly*, like *The Singing Detective*, was based on a previously much-beloved (if not necessarily well-known) property, in this case the novel by fantasist Philip K. Dick. Just as a number of critics and observers (notably Jami Bernard, quoted above) found the film version of *The Singing Detective* lacking in comparison to the original Dennis Potter miniseries, so too did fans of Dick and some film critics complain that Richard Linklater's animated version of *Scanner* took too many liberties with the text and ultimately was not as enjoyable or provocative as the novel upon which it was based. "Linklater has robbed Dick's novel of the intensity that made it a cautionary classic," wrote critic Jeff Shannon of the *Seattle Times*. Similarly, many critics took issue with *Fur: An Imaginary Portrait of Diane Arbus* for taking extensive liberties with Arbus' life by essentially framing her in an entirely fictional circumstance: "The problem with this vision of the real Arbus' life isn't that it's myth; it's that it's crap," states Dana Stevens for Slate.com. Curiously, then, the critical discourse surrounding each of these films featuring Downey often read the filmed text "against" the "original" or "true" version of the stories. Just as Downey's skin is mitigated, disguised, and transmuted into the characters,' so too are the films themselves read as reflections, adaptations, or translations of texts considered by some to be more authentic.

The critical discourse surrounding both *Scanner* and *Fur* also represents a shift in the way in which critics read Downey's performance as complicated by his own personal history, as compared to the reception of *The Singing Detective* three years earlier. Part of this change can be explained by Downey's film work between 2003 and 2006, in which, although he still fell far short of the critical and popular acclaim that accompanied *Chaplin*, he had not proved a liability. *Gothika* with Halle Berry was a box-office hit but critically panned (and is notable for being the film on which Downey met his future wife, Susan Levin); *Kiss Kiss Bang Bang*, co-starring Val Kilmer, about broke even at the box-office and earned some favorable reviews; while *Good Night and Good Luck*, in which Downey played a supporting role, earned great acclaim and several Academy Award nominations. Without the backdrop of battling a drug addiction, however, these films were read more as typical "blips" in an actor's career, rather than as indicative of the direction of Downey's career or reputation. In short, he had stayed out of prison, stayed out of rehab, and stayed out of the headlines, which meant at the very least that he could work on a film without worrying about the implications for his producers in terms of completion bonds or insurance costs. And despite his presence in *The Shaggy Dog*, he was hardly reduced to the level of ignominy suggested by Stephen Rodrick a few years later.

A rotoscoped Downey as James Barris with Rory Cochrane (right) as Charles Freck in Richard Linklater's *A Scanner Darkly* (2006).

Too, although he is an important character in both *A Scanner Darkly* and *Fur*, Downey is not the "star" attraction as he was in *The Singing Detective*, so much of the critical attention was instead focused elsewhere. In *Scanner*, Downey shared the screen with three contemporaries who also had unusual and difficult reputations in Hollywood circles. Keanu Reeves had a career that vacillated between early teen idol status (*Bill and Ted's Excellent Adventure*), arthouse films with drug-related overtones (*River's Edge, My Own Private Idaho*), laughable attempts at blockbuster genre films (*Johnny Mnemonic, The Devil's Advocate, Point Break*) and legitimate blockbusters (*Speed, The Matrix*). Long dogged by false rumors of drug addiction and a "secret" homosexual marriage to David Geffen (or, in a later iteration, actor Alan Cumming), Reeves was (and is) one of Hollywood's more inscrutable and private stars. Winona Ryder had a similarly peripatetic career, beginning as a surprisingly effective actress as a teenager (*Heathers, Beetlejuice*) but becoming gossip column fodder when she was arrested in 2001 for shoplifting $5,000 worth of merchandise in Beverly Hills, which lead to revelations of prescription drug abuse and eventually to a suspended sentence and several years of probation (Silverman). Woody Harrelson, though quite successful both on television (*Cheers*) and in film (*White Men Can't Jump, The People vs. Larry Flynt*), was considered by many in Hollywood to be unreliable and problematic because of his open support of marijuana legalization, including serving on the board of NORML (National Organization for Reformation of Marijuana Laws) since 2003 ("Woody Harrelson Joins NORML Advisory Board"). Along with Downey, the cast of *A Scanner Darkly* off-screen seemed to exemplify the kind of paranoia and suspicion of the "druggie" community that underscores the on-screen narrative of the film.

"All the main actors—adept at playing slackers—are inspired casting," wrote critic Claudia Puig, one of the few major critics to specifically discuss the acting in the film, "but Downey is a stand out. Perhaps fueled by his own drug problems, Downey's portrayal feels the most real and multi-faceted. He is also often hilariously funny, as if he's poking a bit of fun at his drug-addled past." Puig isn't the only one who finds humor in Downey's self-deprecating performance: NPR critic Bob Mondello notes that when Downey "spends much of the movie doing terrific hopped up druggy riffs, things are great fun." Mondello does not, significantly, connect the "fun" druggy riffs with Downey's past drug abuse. J. Hoberman of *The Village Voice* also praised Downey without making any such connection to the actor's life: "Having grasped that he's playing a cartoon character, [Downey] delivers the most animated performance. (Midway through 2006, this supporting turn is the performance to beat in what seems the year's American movie to beat.)"

The ability to read Downey's performance "through" the layer of animated rotoscoping (as well as the performances of the other actors) is vexing to some critics (Shannon writes that the animation "seems like a pointless distraction, robbing performances of nuance") while inspiring to others (as Hoberman indicates above). Still, for a film that is explicitly about drug use, identity, secret lives, and careers on the line, Downey's performance cries out for more than just a skin-deep reading of "his mind in perpetual overdrive" (Hoberman) or his ability to fit into the "slacker" aesthetic frequently found in Linklater's films.

So, too, does his performance in the mostly poorly reviewed *Fur*. The second collaboration between screenwriter Erin Cressida Wilson and director Steven Shainberg, who had caused something of a sensation with their kink-themed *Secretary* (2002), *Fur: An Imaginary Portrait of Diane Arbus* uses the real-life character of Arbus, imagining her early married life before she took up photography. Her interest in photography—and specifically the imaging of the unusual, marginalized, and "freakish"—is prompted when a new neighbor, Lionel (Downey) moves into her apartment building. Lionel is a former circus attraction with a rare disease that causes his bodily hair to grow excessively (he looks like a "wolf man"); his presence and gentle friendship eventually lead Arbus (Nicole Kidman) to seek out other "freaks" as a way to liberate herself from her conventional marriage to a successful commercial photographer. Viewed as a work of fiction (as the subtitle clearly claims), *Fur* is the story of "two masked, hidden creatures liberating each other" (Hornaday), the quotidian and the bizarre intersecting and melding as Lionel and Arbus eventually develop romantically (albeit briefly, as Lionel eventually reveals that he doesn't have long to live).

Again, Downey assumes a character who must be read through a layer of trauma and bodily compromise that is embodied on the surface of his skin. Although the film itself was not well received by critics, his performance (in what is decidedly a supporting role) is often cited as the strongest aspect of the film: "Only an actor of his prodigious gifts would be able to create such an indelible character while completely hidden behind a curtain of hair. He's the original sexy beast, sinister and alluring" (Hornaday). Another critic echoes Downey's ability to communicate intensity through the makeup: "In one of the most challenging roles of his career, [Downey] is captivating as Lionel. Even though he spends most of the film covered in hair the actor hypnotizes Arbus and the screen with just his eyes" (Goodridge).

In her extended (and extremely hostile) review, Dana Stevens also acknowledges the power of Downey's eyes:

> There is no one more capable of projecting a tormented inner life than Robert Downey Jr. but what director in his right mind takes an actor this expressive and hides his face under a solid mask of foot-long hair? … Downey is reduced to a pair of eyes (admittedly, wonderfully sad ones) and a voice which, for some reason, delivers lines in the breathy stop-start diction of John Malkovich.

Stevens' remark is particularly curious given that the "stop-start diction" that Downey employs as Lionel is (for the most part) the same kind of approach he employs with his voice in most of his films. If the volume is a bit softer here ("breathy"), it's mostly in service of the film's overall aesthetic, which "Shainberg deliberately paces … like a dream" (Goodridge). Kidman also gives a "quiet, whispery performance" (Hornaday), and the potentially "shocking" content of the film—Lionel's group of "freak" friends, or Arbus' visit to a nudist colony—are all treated with both a visual and aural gentleness, with soft filters, delicate sounds, and other formal elements that tend toward the prosaic and lyrical.

Lazarus Come Forth: A Star Is Reborn

Perhaps what Stevens' remark indicates is the potential frustration a viewer might feel at not seeing the "real" Downey—as if the actor, cloaked in fur, was hiding something or hiding from some recognition of his own identity. Significantly, the marketing campaign for the film does not reveal Lionel's hirsute state, only Lionel "in disguise" and then after he is shaved by Arbus (see the film's promotional one-sheet). If the post-rehab Downey initially needed to be resurfaced in order to represent his compromised identity as an actor and drug addict, *Fur* at least symbolically represents the need for his viewers and his characters to

Downey (as Lionel) is shown shaved and bare-chested with Nicole Kidman (as Diane Arbus) in this movie poster for *Fur* (dir. Steven Shainberg, 2006).

begin to emerge from that resurfacing with a less compromised, sober, and more authentic identity.

Indeed, one can see from these three performances the trajectory toward the character of the appropriately named Kirk Lazarus in *Tropic Thunder*, an ice-blue-eyed Australian "Method" actor (and "five time Academy Award winner") who dons blackface and a comically urban accent to play the part of "Lincoln Osiris" (another name overloaded with meaning in regards to Downey, referencing both a murdered American icon and the Egyptian God of the afterlife). Arguably for the first time since *Chaplin* fourteen years earlier, Downey had found the perfect combination of character and vehicle: the film was a box-office sensation, well-reviewed by critics, and his multi-layered, broadly comedic turn as an actor struggling with his own persona (as if addicted to a self-destructive process that bordered on self-parody) was almost universally recognized as the film's strongest performance. Here, too, is another performance in which Downey must disappear into the skin of the character and resurface himself, something he had by this point perfected through his work in the earlier films.

It was during the release of *Fur* in the fall of 2006 that word of Downey's participation in the Marvel Studios long-awaited production of *Iron Man* was announced to the press. Only three years removed from his lowest personal and professional point, it is remarkable how quickly his fate had turned and his reputation had been restored. An uncredited wire story in *The Guardian* noted that "Downey has had a golden streak recently, garnering rave reviews in *Kiss Kiss Bang Bang*, *Good Night and Good Luck* and Richard Linklater's animation experiment *A Scanner Darkly*." His failures behind him, the article also noted something about his role in *Iron Man*: "Interestingly it is understood the screenplay will sidestep the issue of Stark's alcoholism. Downey Jr. famously has a history of substance abuse" ("Downey Jr. to don Iron Man suit"). In just a few short years, these unique performances of Robert Downey Jr. had allowed him to engage with his audience and film critics through a symbolic and therapeutic "working through" of his addiction as reflected on the surface of the skin of his characters. Whether the character ultimately shed the grotesque scars of abuse and trauma through an extended period of therapy (*The Singing Detective*), remained shrouded in a layer of animation as if to admit to the secretive and destructive nature of his past behavior (*A Scanner Darkly*), or shaved the freakish residue of an uncontrollable disease and emerged anew *(Fur)*, Downey's work in his immediate post-rehab career showcases a performer not only dedicated to improving his craft after almost losing his life but also one reclaiming his reputation through a series of performances of public contrition and through a literal shedding and resurfacing of his skin.

Notes

1. James Naremore's excellent *Acting in the Cinema* addresses this complex reading of star performances in a more elaborate fashion, notably in regards to James Cagney's performance in *Angels with Dirty Faces* (1938).
2. I am cautious of using the words "trauma" or "traumatized" in the formal sense to describe Downey's ordeal with drugs, though informally it may be appropriate (certainly the events of his life felt traumatic to him and those around him). "Traumatized" typically implies both violence and victimhood, an implication that is problematic with someone whose abuse is largely self-inflicted, such as a drug addict. I am offering the word "compromised" to describe Downey's condition during and after recovery, reflective of self-inflicted damage that he was forced to assume responsibility for.
3. To illustrate the perception of Downey's reputation at the time: I was employed in Hollywood as an assistant and later executive between 1996 and 2002. Around the time of Downey's firing from *Ally McBeal*, some executives in a company affiliated with mine circulated a "death pool" where you bid on the famous person you expected to die first: Downey was far and away the most popular choice on a list that included elderly stars such as Marlon Brando, Milton Berle, Billy Wilder, Bob Hope, and Katharine Hepburn.

Works Cited

"Actor Downey Given Three Years' Probation." *CNN*, 17 July 2001. Web. 8 May 2013.
"Actor Robert Downey Jr. Released from Jail." *CNN*, 2 Aug. 2000. Web. 8 May 2013.
Ally McBeal. Crea. David E. Kelley. 20th Century–Fox Television, 1997–2002. Television.
America's Sweethearts. Dir. Joe Roth. Columbia, 2001. Film.
Angels with Dirty Faces. Dir. Michael Curtiz. Warner Bros., 1938. Film.
Beetlejuice. Dir. Tim Burton. Warner Bros., 1988. Film.
Berardinelli, James. "*The Singing Detective*." Review. *Reelviews*, 2003. Web 8 Mar. 2013.
Bernard, Jami. "*Singing*, Alas, Is Way Off Key." *New York Daily News*, 24 Oct. 2003: 54. *LexusNexis*. Web. 9 Mar. 2013.
Bill and Ted's Excellent Adventure. Dir. Stephen Herek. Orion, 1989. Film.
Black and White. Dir. James Toback. Columbia TriStar, 1999. DVD.
Bowfinger. Dir. Frank Oz.. Universal, 1999. DVD.
Byrnes, Sholto. "I'm Absolutely Normal, Really." *Independent*, 8 Mar. 2005. *LexusNexis*. Web. 8 Mar. 2013.
Camhi, Leslie. "A Noir's by-the-Musical-Numbers Remake Hits a Sour Note." *Village Voice*, 21 Oct. 2003: n. pag. *LexisNexis*. Web. 8 Mar. 2013.
Caruth, Cathy. *Unclaimed Experience: Trauma, Narrative and History*. Baltimore: Johns Hopkins University Press, 1996. Print.
Chaplin. Dir. Richard Attenborough. Maple Pictures, 1992. DVD.
Cheers. Crea. James Burrows, Glen Charles, Les Charles. NBC, 1982–1993. Television.
Curtis, James. *Spencer Tracy: A Biography*. New York: Knopf. 2012. Print.
Danger Zone. Dir. Allan Eastman. Live Video, 1997. VHS.
The Devil's Advocate. Dir. Taylor Hackford. Warner Bros., 1997. Film.
"Downey Jr. to Don Iron Man Suit." *Guardian*, 29 Sept. 2006. *LexisNexis*. Web. 10 Mar. 2013.
Duggan, Patrick. "Feeling Perforrmance, Remembering Trauma." *Platform* 2.2 (Autumn 2007): n. pag. Royal Holloway University of London. Web.12 Mar. 2013.
Duggan, Patrick, and Wallis, Mick. "Trauma and Performance: Maps, Narratives and Folds." *Performance Research: A Journal of the Performing Arts* 16.1: 4–17. *Taylor and Francis Online*. Web. 10 Mar. 2013.
Ebert, Roger. "*Iron Man*." Review. *Chicago Sun Times*, 1 June 2008.Web. 17 Mar. 2013.
_____. "*The Singing Detective*." Review. *Chicago Sun Times*, 7 Nov.2003. Web. 8 Mar. 2013.
Friends and Lovers. Dir. George Haas. Lions Gate Home Entertainment, 1998. DVD.
The Gingerbread Man. 1998. Dir. Robert Altman. Universal, 2002. DVD.
Good Night and Good Luck. Dir. George Clooney. Sony Pictures Home, 2006. DVD.
Goodridge, Mike. "*Fur: An Imaginary Portrait of Diane Arbus*." Review. *Screen International*, 9 Oct. 2006. *LexisNexis*. Web. 12 Mar. 2013.
Gordon, Keith. Audio Commentary. *The Singing Detective*.. Paramount Home Video, 2004. DVD.
Hail Caesar. Dir. Anthony Michael Hall. Prism Entertainment Corporation, 1994. VHS.
Heart and Souls. 1993. Dir. Ron Underwood. Universal, 1998. DVD.
Heathers. Dir. Michael Lehmann. New World Pictures, 1989. Film.
Hoberman, J. "Brain Candy." *Village Voice*, 27 June 2006: n. pag. *LexisNexis*. Web. 9 Mar. 2013.
Home for the Holidays. 1995. Dir. Jodie Foster.. *The Robert Downey Jr. Collection*. Fox Home Entertainment, 2009. DVD.
Hornaday, Ann. "*Fur*: Strange Fiction Reveals a Real Truth." *Washington Post*, 17 Nov. 2006: n. pag. *LexisNexis*. Web. 12 Mar. 2013.
Hugo Pool. 1997. Dir. Robert Downey Sr. Wellspring, 2002. DVD.
In Dreams. Dir. Neil Jordan. Dreamworks, 1999. DVD.
Iron Man. Dir. Jon Favreau. Paramount, 2008. DVD.
Johnny Mnemonic. Dir. Robert Longo. TriStar, 1995. Film.
"Judge to Downey: Keep Up the Good Work." *CNN*, 20 Mar. 2002. Web. 8 May 2013.
Kiss Kiss Bang Bang. 2005. Dir. Shane Black. Warner Bros., 2006. DVD.
Lax, Eric. *Conversations with Woody Allen*. New York: Knopf Doubleday, 2007. Print.
MacDonald, Moira. "*The Singing Detective* Lacks Harmony." *Seattle Times*, 7 Nov. 2003: n. pag. *LexisNexis*. Web. 9 Mar. 2013.
The Matrix. Dir. Andy Wachowski and Lana Wachowski. Warner Bros., Film.
Melinda and Melinda. Dir. Woody Allen. Twentieth Century–Fox, 2004. Film.
Millar, John. "Review Cinema; *The Singing Detective*." *Sunday Express*, 19 Oct. 2003: 58. *LexisNexis*. Web. 8 Mar. 2013.

Mondello, Bob. "*A Scanner Darkly* Looks Odd, and That's Good." *All Things Considered*. NPR. 7 July 2006. Broadcast. Transcript retrieved 9 Mar. 2013.
My Own Private Idaho. Dir. Gus Van Sant. Fine Line Features, 1991. Film.
Naremore, James. *Acting in the Cinema*. Berkeley: University of California Press, 1990. Print.
Natural Born Killers. 1994. Dir. Oliver Stone. Warner Bros., 2009. DVD.
One Night Stand. 1997. Dir. Mike Figgis. New Line Home Video, 1998. DVD.
Only You. Dir. Norman Jewison. TriStar, 1994. Film.
Pennies from Heaven. Writ. Dennis Potter. Dir. Piers Haggard. BBC, 1978. TV Mini-series.
The People vs. Larry Flynt. Dir. Milos Forman. Columbia, 1996. Film.
Pevere, Geoff. "Robert Downey High on Praise." *Toronto Star*, 14 Sept. 2003: D02. *LexisNexis*. Web. 8 Mar. 2013.
Point Break. Dir. Kathryn Bigelow. Twentieth Century–Fox, 1991. Film.
Puig, Claudia. "Clarity Emerges from a Murky *A Scanner Darkly*." *USA Today*, 10 July 2006: n. pag. *LexisNexis*. Web. 8 Mar. 2013.
Restoration. Dir. Michael Hoffman. Miramax Home Entertainment, 1995. DVD.
Richard III. 1995. Dir. Richard Loncraine. *The Robert Downey Jr. Collection*. Fox Home Entertainment, 2009. DVD.
River's Edge. Dir. Tim Hunter. Island Pictures, 1986. Film.
"Robert Downey Jr's Drug 'Deal.'" Wired.com, 31 May 2001. Web. 8 May 2013.
Rodrick, Stephen. "Robert Downey Jr.'s Cosmic Punishment." *Men's Journal*, May 2011. Web. 20 Mar. 2013.
Secretary. Dir. Steven Shainberg. Lions Gate, 2002. Film.
The Shaggy Dog. Dir. Brian Robbins. Disney Home Entertainment, 2006. DVD.
Shannon, Jeff. "*Scanner* Not as Intense as the Book." *Seattle Times*, 7 July 2006: n. pag. *LexisNexis*. Web. 8 Mar. 2003.
Sherlock Holmes. Dir. Guy Ritchie. Warner Bros., 2009. Blu-Ray.
Short Cuts. Dir. Robert Altman. FineLine Features, 1993. Film.
Silverman, Stephen M. "Winona Ryder Gets Three Years' Probation." *People*, 6 Dec. 2002. Web. 8 May 2013.
The Singing Detective. 2003. Dir. Keith Gordon. Paramount Home Entertainment, 2004. DVD.
"The Singing Detective." *Box Office Mojo*, IMDb, n.d. Web. 8 May 2013.
"*The Singing Detective*: Infirmity. Exploring Dennis Potter's Thematic Preoccupations." *British Film Resource*, n. p., n.d. Web. 8 May 2013.
Speed. Dir. Jan de Bont. Twentieth Century–Fox, 1994. Film.
A Star Is Born. Dir. George Cukor. Warner Bros., 1954. Film.
Stevens, Dana. "Arrested Development: A Lame Take on Photographer Diane Arbus." *Slate*, 10 Nov. 2006. Web. 12 Mar. 2013.
Tropic Thunder. Dir. Ben Stiller. Dreamworks Home Entertainment, 2008. DVD.
U.S. Marshals. Dir. Stuart Baird. Warner Bros., 1998. DVD.
White Men Can't Jump. Dir. Ron Shelton. Twentieth Century–Fox, 1992. Film.
Wilde, Jon. "More Than Skin Deep." *Guardian*, 7 Nov. 2003. Web. 8 Mar. 2013.
Wonder Boys. Dir. Curtis Hanson. Paramount, 2000. DVD.
"Woody Harrelson Joins NORML Advisory Board." *NORML.org*, 3 Apr. 2003. Web. 8 May 2013.

"Lie down with me Watson": Transgression and Fragile Masculinity in the Detective Films of Robert Downey Jr.

Ruth O'Donnell

Introduction: The Robert Downey Jr. Persona

Bad Boy Downey: cocky yet vulnerable, honorable yet transgressive—this is the persona of actor Robert Downey Jr. Ironically, his historical brushes with the law and struggle with illicit drugs both fed the screen persona while threatening to overshadow his acting career at the time. Moreover, given the actor's transgressive connotations, one might consider it odd that his star image has come to be associated with that ubiquitous symbol of law and justice: the detective. In this paper I will show that although the detective figure may seem to contradict the persona traits we have come to associate with the star Downey—both on and off the screen—these characters explore and develop certain themes that support and extend his dominant star image.

Robert Downey Jr.'s persona was established with his break-out role as the titular *Chaplin* in Richard Attenborough's 1992 film. The figures of Charlie Chaplin and Downey draw parallels: the irreverent clown up against the establishment who wins by luck or by pluck; the craft element of their artistry as star; the self-aware performance, which emphasizes the body and its potential for comedy. There is also an element of transgression attached to both: In Chaplin's case this was demonstrated in his personal life, such as his fourth marriage to the much younger Oona O'Neil, as well as in his defiance of the ruling classes—demonstrated in his communist political leanings, which led to his eventual exile in Switzerland. Finally, there is an overwhelming sense of both characters' almost childish vulnerability, enhanced by the specter of childhood neglect. I argue that Downey demonstrates all of the above, in terms of his off-screen persona as well as the characters he plays. Here, I will focus on his detective films: *The Singing Detective* (Keith Gordon, 2003), *Kiss Kiss Bang Bang* (Shane Black, 2005) and the *Sherlock Holmes* (Guy Ritchie, 2009, 2011) series, although these traits are present throughout his filmography to varying degrees.

The figure of the detective, in classical Freudian psychoanalysis, is associated with the exercise of the "super-ego" and restraint of the "id." (Freud, "The Ego and the Id"). The superego draws from the parental "imago"; it is the part of the mind that has internalized the father and mother's moral law and is responsible for inhibiting the id, which manifests one's instinctive impulses and drives. The third aspect of the mind is "ego," which is based on the reality principle, meeting the needs of the id without bending too far to the restrictions of superego, while evaluating the demands of each real-life scenario. Robert Downey Jr.'s star persona and personal history play out this struggle between superego and id. Downey, with his past drug consumption, could be considered to be in thrall to the id's demands. His eventual incarceration by the state of California can be read as punishment by the superego (note that this psychodynamic reading does not negate the reality of historical fact but merely offers an analytical interpretation). This dynamic structures many of Downey's movies. The *Iron Man* (Jon Favreau, 2008 and 2010; Shane Black, 2013) films offer a protagonist, Tony Stark (Robert Downey Jr.), consumed by his id impulses, indulging in fast cars, women, and drink. The *Iron Man* suit represents the rigidity—literally—of the superego. Only after three films is Stark's ego sufficiently evolved to give up the suit and the playboy lifestyle, to manage the conflicting demands of the superego and id. The figure of Sherlock Holmes also evokes superego and id: The superego in Holmes is displayed by his devotion to justice as well as his supercilious and judgmental nature, which is part and parcel of an overactive superego; the id, by his cocaine addiction.

The Detective Figure and Downey

The model of superego, ego, and id is useful in considering both Downey's persona and the detective figure for a number of reasons. The superego is a punitive force—most commonly punishing the ego through feelings of guilt but also lashing out externally. The detective symbolizes self-mastery and control—often over events themselves (in so far as he is able to find an explanation for circumstances cloaked in mystery) and others (controlling the eventual fate of wrong-doers). A psychoanalytic interpretation of film noir, perhaps the most famous of cinema's detective genres,[1] suggests that the detective is often preoccupied with ascertaining the femme fatale's guilt, which can be read as the (masculine) superego's punishment of the feminine—guilt is bound up in one's very femaleness. This problematic view of femininity is typical of the noir genre and symptomatic of the tensions related to women's growing emancipation and men's uncertain place in society following the Second World War. Beyond the social reading is a psychodynamic interpretation, which suggests that the femme fatale operates as an archetypal mother figure. In the Freudian framework, the male child must work through his oedipal impulses of aggression toward the father and desire for union with the mother, to progress to the mature genital stage. If he shies away from the oedipal threat posed by the father figure, he is threatened with regression to an earlier psychosexual stage, in which he is more attracted to the father and dominated by the mother. It is a model of psychosexual development that can easily be mapped onto the film noir genre, which is characterized by strong women, terrifying patriarchs, and weak male protagonists. Indeed, the unstable sign of the detective is useful for considering Robert Downey Jr.'s depiction of masculinity across his body of work, and how that informs the dominant persona.

Downey's detective films divide into two distinct categories: the "neo-noir" films that cite post-war film noir—*The Singing Detective* and *Kiss Kiss Bang Bang*—and the *Sherlock Holmes* films. Each has quite different influences. Nevertheless, all of the films work through common themes of mastery over self, woman, and environment and scrutinize the unstable masculine sign that the detective figure presents. Performance, disguise, and altered bodily states contribute to a sense of the male body under attack, or at the very least subject to unpredictable change: Corporeality cannot be relied on to shore up the masculine sense of self. This theme is a feature of the film noir genre, which often involves a character who is physically wounded prior to or during the course of the film. Physical damage reflects psychological trauma and, in the Freudian framework, castration.

The theme of mastery in relation to the detective figure remains key when considering the neo-noir films of Downey, for neither character—Dan Dark in *The Singing Detective* nor Harry Lockhart in *Kiss Kiss Bang Bang*—is actually a detective.[3] Dark is a writer, suffering from a terrible skin disease, who has been hospitalized for treatment. In great pain, he starts to hallucinate, inventing fantasies in which he plays a detective who often tries to wreak revenge on those who have crossed him. These revenge fantasies are interspersed with musical numbers performed by the hospital staff treating him. In *Kiss Kiss Bang Bang,* Lockhart is a small-time crook who stumbles into an audition while on the run from the police. So convincing is his performance that he is cast for the part of a detective. In each film, Downey plays a character not typically associated with masculine strength: respectively, a writer and actor (albeit a law-breaker in disguise). Both are "wordy" professions and it is perhaps significant that the Downey persona is especially "talky" by modern Hollywood standards. His high verbiage points both to intelligence in his characters—particularly in Holmes and his verbal revelation of his deductions—and nervousness or neuroticism. This combination is most evident in the figures of Lockhart and Tony Stark in the *Iron Man* films (the third of which was also directed by Shane Black). A highly verbal man is considered somewhat suspect, juxtaposed with the strong silent masculine types in cinema (such as Clint Eastwood), and points toward a defense strategy against attack. Verboseness distracts from a sense of emasculation and powerlessness in the speaker, and indicates a lack of self-possession. In the Freudian schema, a favoring of the verbal mode represents a withdrawal from the challenge of oedipal struggle and retreat to the earlier psychosexual stage of orality.

The Singing Detective

This precarious position threatens to be destabilized even further in *The Singing Detective* which shows Dan Dark break into garbled rants, shouts, and eventually descent into fantasy, switching between episodes of him inhabiting his own novel, paranoid fantasies involving his wife defrauding him, and singing sequences. His breakdown is reflected by a plot structure characterized by flashbacks, echoing the genre of noir that it draws from, and the "detective's" position as narrator—albeit one who is highly unreliable. Storylines are split between Dark in the hospital, Dark as a private eye involved in an investigation of two men who have killed a prostitute (based on Dark's novel, *The Singing Detective*), and Dark's flashbacks to his unhappy childhood, which he recounts to his psychotherapist Dr. Gibbon (Mel Gibson).

Robert Downey Jr. as Dan Dark and Jeremy Northam (right) as Mark Binney in *The Singing Detective* (2003), directed by Keith Gordon.

    Dark is almost entirely powerless. Rendered prostrate on a hospital bed, his skin disease eats into his flesh, his very body under attack. Weak and vulnerable, his defense is to lash out at those around him, shouting at and threatening his wife who visits him and the hospital staff who tend him. The psychotherapist who treats him recognizes Dark's hatred of women, reading aloud excerpts of his novel that demonstrate Dark's squeamish attitude to sex. Dr. Gibbon concludes that his misogyny stems from his relationship with his mother and the promiscuity that led to the break-up of her marriage (with the young Dan witnessing her having sex at least once). This diagnosis seems supported by a series of flashbacks that shows the same actress (Carla Gugino) play both Dan's mother and the prostitute who is drowned in a bathtub in the opening of the film. (His wife, played by Robin Wright-Penn, also appears as a prostitute.) Gibbon notes to Dark the parallels between that scene, which comes from his book *The Singing Detective*, and his mother's suicide by drowning. His is one of many neglectful and/or abandoning mothers in Robert Downey Jr.'s films, evident in his filmography as early as *Chaplin* (who was separated from his mother at the age of seven, following her mental breakdown and entry into a local London workhouse) (Robinson 19). The trope of absent mothers—physically or emotionally—contributes to the trait of childish vulnerability and neglect present in Downey's star persona, perhaps echoed by his own life—his parents divorced when he was 13 and after a short time with his mother in New York, he moved to Los Angeles to live with his father.

    Yet the film in offering this pat explanation for Dark's condition, psychological as well as physical, and the psychotherapist's preoccupation with Dark's childhood to explain his current circumstances undermine the whole enterprise of biographical truth-seeking. This moment in the movie alludes to the genre of star biography that attempts to offer an explanation of why a star is as he or she is—a comprehensive tale of origins—as well as mocking the simplicity of the psychoanalytic project (it even includes a version of the primal scene). Nevertheless, the figure of the psychotherapist does recall one aspect of the Robert Downey Jr. persona: the attempt to understand oneself and one's often self-destructive behavior. Remember, Downey's early break-through role was *Chaplin*, a biographical account of one of the first Hollywood stars, which seeks to understand the man behind the tramp's outfit and moustache. The desire to understand one's self is part of a larger project to comprehend human nature more generally and this is something that actors, in their study of various roles, are believed to excel at. The other type of person that takes human behavior as their subject of study is, of course, the detective. It is perhaps fitting that an actor such as Downey, who has had so much cause in his personal life for introspection, as well as the connotations of Method acting in his persona, should align himself to the aspect, especially in his embodiment as the genius Sherlock Holmes, that the detective figure excels at: reading people.

Returning to the biographical potential of *The Singing Detective* and the use of the psychotherapist's diagnosis to "explain" the patient's character, it extends the idea of Dark as a vulnerable and damaged man, alluding to similar traits in the actor Downey himself (whose own history reveals a socially irresponsible father who exposed him to drugs at a very early age). One can draw parallels between the skin condition suffered by Dark and the star's own drug addiction (the topic of which forms another chapter in this volume), both physical symptoms of psychological trauma. Downey himself has been candid in admitting his attraction to roles in which the characters' weaknesses reflect his own. *The Singing Detective,* Downey's first film after his time in prison, may only be the most extreme example of the biographical parallels to his work as well as his willingness to draw attention to his fragile masculinity, often in a tongue-in-cheek way: For example, the closing credits of *Kiss Kiss Bang Bang* feature the song "Broken," from Downey's own album *The Futurist* (2004).

Kiss Kiss Bang Bang

If Dan Dark, in his physical and psychological state, cannot "control" the story he tells, Harry Lockhart does a better job, though he is equally suspect of being an unreliable narrator. Lockhart, like Dark, is the neo-noir detective, framed as such by the opening moments of the film: He is shot from below through the rippling waters of a swimming pool, which recalls a similar shot of the narrator of *Sunset Boulevard* (Billy Wilder, 1950), though that one is already dead, floating face-down. The opening tells the spectator that *Kiss Kiss Bang Bang* will provide a parody of the genre and the hard-boiled detective novel that film noir draws from. Lockhart is the most self-aware of narrators, directly addressing the spectator, apologizing for his failure to tell a vital part of the story. He even mocks the conventions of cinematic storytelling itself, indicating that certain scenes are significant for the information they are "planting" for exposition at a later point. Harry's proclivity for self-conscious posturing suits his characterization as a smart-assed but ultimately loveable rogue. He is marked from the outset as a transgressive figure, and in this way echoes what we know of Downey's real life (*Kiss Kiss Bang Bang* was released in 2005, only five years after the star's year in jail for drug possession). Lockhart is a petty crook, but not without redeeming features: The film opens with him breaking into a toy store at night, on the phone to his nephew in order to secure his Christmas present of choice. On the run from the police with his partner, who is shot dead by a vigilante neighbor, he stumbles into a film audition. There, his performance of grief is so convincing he is immediately given the part.

Considerations of heroism are self-consciously bandied about in *Kiss Kiss Bang Bang*–Lockhart is chastised by his nephew for thinking that the character "Protectocop" is still in vogue, and a fully dressed Protectocop wanders into the heroine Harmony's (Michelle Monaghan) living room before stumbling over her balcony to his death. This scene is surely a reference to Downey's own nocturnal wanderings: In 1996 there was the infamous "Goldilocks" incident, in which the intoxicated star stumbled into a neighbor's house and fell asleep on her eleven-year-old son's bed. We later learn that the actor playing Protectocop was suffering from depression following the cancellation of his TV show. Other manifestations of the heroic ideal include references to the "White Knights," the football team of Harmony and Harry's school. There are also frequent mentions of Johnny Gossamer, a hard-boiled detective figure from a popular book series. Harmony read the Gossamer books as a child, telling her little sister Jenna that her real father was a hero who would come to rescue her. She went as far as telling Jenna that the actor playing Gossamer on a film shoot that passed through town, one Harlan Dexter, was her real father, a lie that would have tragic consequences. Gossamer features in such titles as *You Wouldn't Want to Live Here, Little Girl Lust,* and *You'll Never Die in this Town Again.*[4] He is the hard-boiled detective so loved by film noir, whom Dan Dark of *The Singing Detective* wishes to emulate. But it is clear in *Kiss Kiss Bang Bang* that this hero belongs only in fiction.

If heroism is under threat, Harry Lockhart is not the man to take up its banner. In an early scene at a party held by Hollywood actor Harlan Dexter (Corbin Bernsen), he sees a sleazy guest approach a sleeping young woman. He tells the would-be molester to leave, eloquently issuing him a number of threats for what will happen if he fails to desist. The next scene shows Lockhart being physically beaten on the front lawn. Adding insult to injury, the sleeping beauty ends up leaving the party with her attacker. It is another depiction of a prostrate, physically damaged Downey, further proof that his verbal defense cannot protect him, or those around him. Instead, coming to his rescue, is private investigator Perry van Shrike, aka "Gay Perry."[5] Played by Val Kilmer, made famous by that paean to filmic homoeroticism, *Top Gun*, Gay Perry subverts notions of heteronormative masculinity: That is to say, the most heroic of men in this film is a gay man. It is Perry who allows Harry to shadow him in his preparations for his acting audition as a detective character, so demonstrating a form of masculinity that Harry may wish to live up to. It is also while on a case with Perry that the pair stumble into real trouble: Hired by an Alison Ames to investigate an incident at a local lake, they witness a corpse being dumped in a car and driven into the water.[6] They are unable to report the murder to the police, as Perry shoots the woman in an attempt to open the trunk, thinking she may still be alive. The standard forces of patriarchal protection, signified by the police, cannot be appealed to. Equally negligent is that other symbol of paternal protection, the father, for most of the men in this film, including fathers, are predatory, abusive, or ineffectual. The terrifying patriarch of the oedipal phase posited by Freud seems relevant here, dominating the figural son.

Mothers, by contrast, are absent, abandoning their children to these harmful patriarchs.

Dexter, the party host, has spent the last ten years feuding with his daughter Veronica over his late wife's inheritance, another absent mother in the Downey filmography. The apparent resolution of their feud is later discovered to have a sinister explanation. Abusive men seem to lurk around every corner: We are told by Lockhart that Harmony's Hollywood ambition is predicated on a drive for financial success, hoping she can return home to rescue her little sister Jenna from the clutches of their sexually abusive father. No mention is made of their mother. Powerful men are exploitative and abusive of those who are weaker than them, especially women. This vulnerable position of women and girls is magnified by the backdrop of Hollywood, an exploitative industry, especially for young actresses. Harry is also exploited: Perry finally explains to him that the Hollywood execs were only promising him the detective role as a bluff in order to knock a few dollars off Colin Farrell's price tag. He is emasculated by his inability to defend himself—and protect women—against these men, but more than that, he identifies with their victims. As in *The Singing Detective,* the prostrate position is indicative of powerlessness. This is demonstrated in the opening of the film, when the young Harry (played by Downey's son, Indio Falconer Downey), as the magician "Harold the Great," performs the act of sawing young Harmony (Ariel Winter) in half: It is a theatrical performance of the passive, powerless position of the feminine in relation to the violent aggression of the masculine. The gag is that Harmony is such a good actress, that when she starts screaming they think the stunt has gone wrong. Only when her father (Harrison Young) rushes over and they open the box do they discover that she is perfectly safe: She was just pretending. Her father raises his hand to strike her: a prediction of the paternal abuse that will form the theme of the film. The vulnerability of girls and women is often shown in their horizontal placing in the *mise-en-scène*, such as in the aforementioned magic scene, in which Harmony's little sister is taken from her bed, and in the scene of Harmony passing out/sleeping at the party.

This is also the resting position of corpses, of which there are a number in the film, all women: Harmony's sister, Veronica Dexter, and an anonymous pink-haired girl that Harry witnesses being killed. This vulnerable, "feminine" position is one that Harry continually adopts, huddling in a corner of a cupboard, hiding under a bed, slumped on the floor of a car. Most often he slumps, huddles, or lies when under great emotional and/or physical stress such as when discovering a corpse in his shower (when the first thing he does is to call Perry), hearing the news that Harmony has killed herself (untrue), hiding from a killer, or in physical shock from his injuries. This association with the feminine is both emasculating and identificatory: Harry demonstrates great empathy for the plight of the women in the film. He objects to Harmony's casual acceptance of the sexually predatory nature of men and is an unexpected emissary of modesty; when he and Perry pull the girl from the car trunk at the lake side, the first thing he does is pull her skirt down over her legs.

Harry's association with the feminine is advanced by the physical abuse that he suffers, assaulted at the Dexter party and injured by Harmony, who accidently severs his finger by slamming it in a door. The moment is a tongue-in-cheek homage on the part of writer-director Shane Black to the noir genre, which often sees its heroes maimed in some way to reflect their emasculated position, and is a symbolic castration. Physical injury of the hero is also common in later film noirs, such as *Chinatown* (Roman Polanski, 1974) in which the hero Jake Gittes (Jack Nicholson) has his nose sliced for being too nosy. This is a noir film that uses the theme of incest as a metaphor for the ruthlessly exploitative nature of the patri-

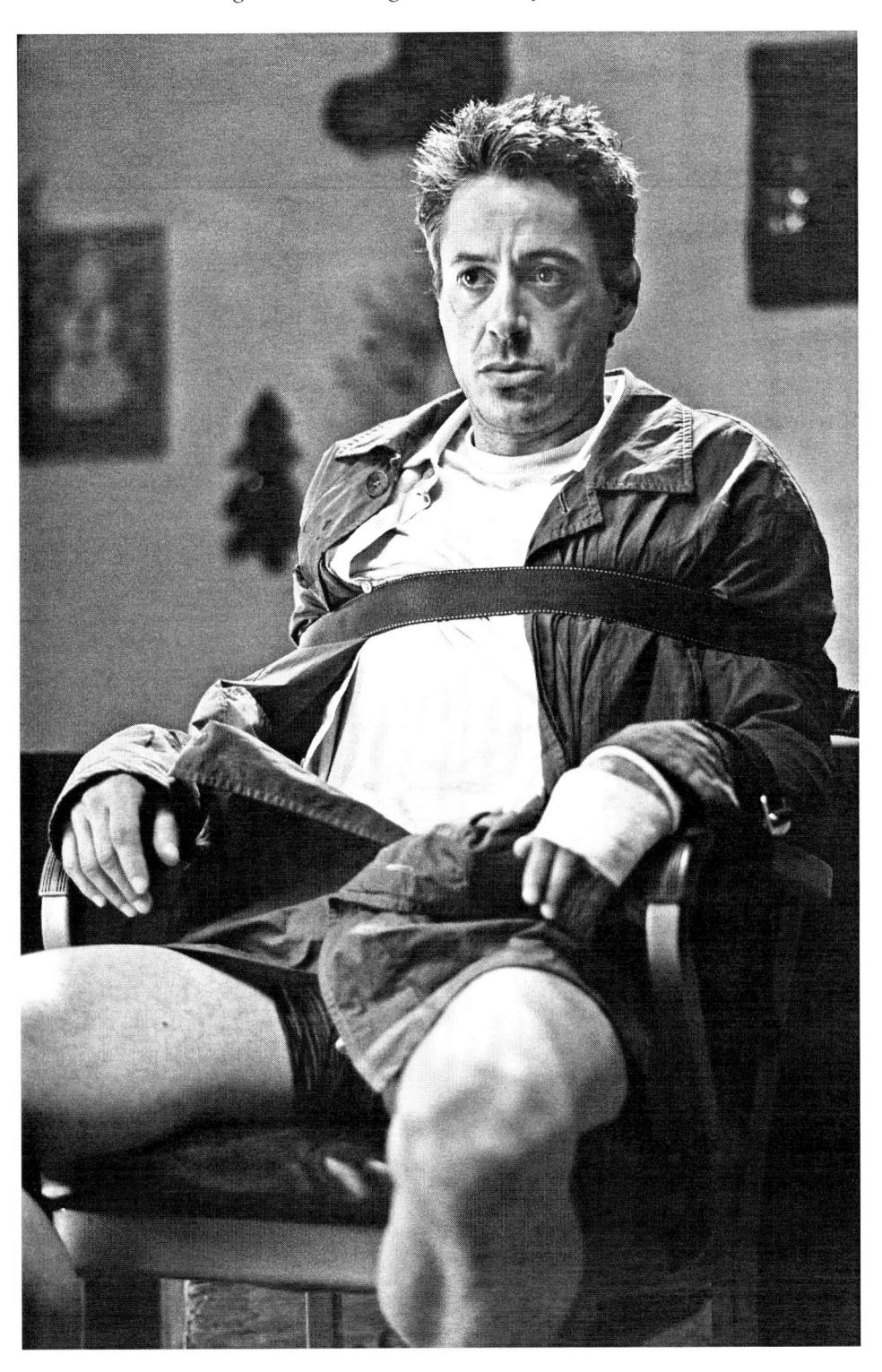

Harry Lockhart (Robert Downey Jr.) is strapped to a chair and tortured during a scene in Shane Black's *Kiss Kiss Bang Bang* (2005).

archal elite, one that is echoed in *Kiss Kiss Bang Bang*. Harry's finger suffers further mistreatment, being re-severed after it is stitched back on and almost eaten by a dog. He continues to be the target of attack: Approached at a party by the killers he has witnessed at the lake, he is kidnapped, then interrogated and beaten, his finger re-severed. (If he is playing at "detective," then this role reversal only shores up his lack of authority.) Let go by his captors, it falls to Harmony to take him back to the hospital to have his finger sewn on again, the repeated hospital trips perhaps echoing Downey's real-life recurring visits to drug rehabilitation programs.

Allusions to the star's own history are pronounced in this sequence: Dosed up on painkillers that make him spaced out and giggly, he falls asleep in the back of Harmony's car as she drives off to intervene on Perry's behalf, when she realizes he has been set up in a stake-out. Harmony rushes across traffic to save Perry from the two killers, while Harry sleeps in the car. The "plant" of the stake-out—a pink-haired young woman—runs away when Harmony intercepts the pair and saves Perry from being killed. She flees in Harmony's vehicle, taking the now unconscious Harry with her. Waking up in a garage, he wanders into what appears to be a safehouse and hides under the bed when he hears people coming (an oblique allusion to the Goldilocks incident?) He hears the pink-haired girl being shot and sees her slump to the floor, her body falling beside his own as he hides. It is this callous act of murder of an exploited young woman that moves Harry to action: He takes the pistol left by the killer on the bed and on his return shoots him several times in the chest. He apologizes to the woman, "Sorry sweetheart, you deserved better," as he wipes the fingerprints from the gun and places the pistol in her hand.

Yet, as indicated by the finger-severing incident, Harry's physical assault is as often a cause for comedy as the abuse of women is cause for pathos. When Perry and Harry realize there has been a plot by Harlan Dexter to incarcerate his daughter Veronica in a mental institution while an actress impersonated her, they take a visit to the health clinic owned by Dexter (a further nod to the drug dependency rehabilitation industry that resonates with Downey's own experience). Although they overcome the clinic guard, whom Harry kills in a moment of jubilant bravado by playing Russian roulette, they are intercepted by Dexter and his thugs. Dexter reveals that his daughter's body—the one that they tried to dispose of in the lake—will be cremated to conceal any evidence of his crimes. Perry and Harry are left to the tender mercies of one of his men, who clamps electrodes to Harry's genitals before proceeding to electrocute him. This grossly comic moment is reminiscent of the earlier film *Lethal Weapon* (Richard Donner, 1987) that Shane Black penned, which featured a visceral scene of the semi-clothed star Mel Gibson being electrocuted by the film's villains. It is a hysterical pastiche of the writer's earlier work, sending up the moment of cruel spectacle that emasculates the hero once and for all.

The two films should be considered in tandem, as the earlier work provides an example of the homophobic banter which attempts to diffuse homosexual anxiety in the pairing of the police duo. The pairing of black and white cops is one way of distracting from this bond, in the working through of "difference"—the same can be said of the difference of sexual orientation, though this becomes an excuse for drawing attention to the potentially sexualized nature of their bond. In the *Lethal Weapon* series, some labor is undertaken to highlight, then dispel, these homoerotic impulses through the *mise-en-scène* and dialogue. Sharon Willis suggests that "*Lethal Weapon 2* [Richard Donner, 1989] exhibits a particularly—and jocularly—anxious fascination with its own homoerotic subtext, expressed in Riggs's jokes on two occasions." In the second example she cites, at the close of the film, "we find Murtaugh holding the wounded Riggs in his lap, as they wait for the police to arrive. Riggs quips 'Give us a kiss before they get here'" (28–29). In one moment of *Kiss Kiss Bang Bang*, when Perry and Harry are attempting to dispose of Veronica's corpse in their car trunk, their only way of distracting the police patrol car that passes them is by embracing in a romantic clinch. Perry plays a similar card with Harry's torturer: He accuses him of being a closet homosexual, desperate for Perry's sexual advances. The ruse works, distracting him long enough for Perry to wiggle free the small revolver he keeps stuffed down his pants for such occasions ("Homophobes never search there"), fire a round through his crotch, and shoot his assailant dead. It is a hysterical (in both senses of the word) assertion of the absolute power of phallus, here belonging indubitably to the gay man.

Nevertheless, it is Harry who finally saves the day, with the same combination of innocent surprise and good luck that characterizes his persona in Downey's other films. By the time Harry and Perry finally escape their assailant at the clinic, Harmony has driven off in the van holding the coffin of Veronica, due for cremation. Pursued by Dexter's men, she drives the vehicle off the road: The van crashes and she rolls down a grassy verge toward the freeway, the coffin meanwhile hanging off an intersection road sign. In the subsequent shootout both Harry and Perry are shot, Perry fatally. As Harry huddles crying over the body of Perry, Harmony rings from her cell phone, reciting the familiar command of "Harold the Great," a desperate plea for rescue. Springing into action, he grabs a gun and shoots at the oncoming car about to knock him down. Jumping out of the way, he is hurled across the bridge, sliding down the coffin lodged there, and finally grabs onto the corpse's dangling arm which saves him from falling into the oncoming traffic below. The morbidly comic moment is reminiscent of Harold Lloyd hanging off a clock tower in *Safety Last!* (Fred C. Newmeyer and Sam Taylor, 1923) (Keaton was a contemporary of Chaplin). In a move reminiscent of his childhood magic tricks, he catches the gun that slides off the coffin, shooting Dexter as he shoots at Harry from the bridge above. He then fires at the thugs on the freeway below, falling onto the car of one and shooting the driver as he hangs onto the vehicle's roof. Seeing that all of the bad guys are dead, he declares, "All done," and lies back on the car top. Like Downey, Harry has "won the game" by the most fortuitous combination of luck, charm, and naivety. The character's—and by extension—Downey's association with the figure of the magician also points to an alternative conception of masculinity—one that transcends hegemonic ideas of masculinity that are based on hard logic and reason, relying instead on intuition and stealth, one more closely aligned with the 'Other.' It is a trope that is extended in Downey's later films, including the *Sherlock Holmes* series.

Following Harry's unlikely rescue efforts, Perry soon regains his status as the most masculine of men. Only Harry is relegated to the position of lying in a hospital bed: Perry remains mobile in a wheelchair, recovering from his near-death experience—furthermore, he is the only one who is able to mete out justice. In a final scene "for your viewing pleasure," declares Harry, Perry goes to visit Harmony and Jenna's father, after Jenna's funeral. The father is now bed-bound, hooked up to a ventilator. Entering the room without announcing himself, Perry challenges him on his sins of the past, slapping him several times across the face. Enraged, he demands to know who Perry thinks he is, mockingly calling him a "big tough guy"—to which the latter can only reply, "Yeah, big tough guy." These are the only words Perry can find to acknowledge his disgust at the horrible power such a man can have over the young and vulnerable. It is an empty, overdue, punishment of an abuser, for in the real world there are no white knights—only a gay hard-boiled detective can come close.

Meanwhile, his straight counterpart wraps up the story—the body of the film that we have seen is a flashback with Harry's voiceover; the present day is presented as a direct-to-camera commentary, with Harry explaining that he now works for Perry. The setting is domestic, suggesting an easy familiarity. The sense of their set-up is underscored by Perry's interruption of the scene and a demand that the camera is turned off—he tells the audience to leave, reminding them to validate their parking, a further tongue-in-cheek reference to this being a movie and to the presence of an audience. But it is the homoerotic bond between the pair—for where is Harmony?—that the spectator is left with, suggesting that masculine heroics no longer need to be straight. It is further proof of the "queer" aspect of Downey's persona, defined as "whatever is at odds with the normal, the legitimate, the dominant. There is nothing in particular to which it necessarily refers. It is an identity without an essence. 'Queer' then, demarcates not a positivity but a positionality vis-à-vis the normative" (Halperin 62). It can be argued that Robert Downey Jr.'s persona and film characters are positioned in relation to, at odds with, the normative—most apparently in his misdemeanors with the law, and also with his reliance on drugs and/or alcohol. A further marker of Downey's association with the extra-normative is the frequent hint of sexual transgression in his films—a "queer" demeanor in relation to his attachments to the same gender.

Sherlock Holmes

These themes come together in the *Sherlock Holmes* series of films. Although the detective Holmes is on the right side of the law, his unorthodox methods deviate from correct police procedure; nowhere is this more evident than in the lengths he will go to in the pursuit of suspects or information-gathering. Holmes is a master of disguise, a fact indicated in Conan Doyle's novels, but in Ritchie's films the disguises are frequently ridiculous in concept: He dresses as a Chinese opium addict (an allusion both to Holmes' cocaine habit and Downey's own drug addiction?), a bell boy, an aging academic, and a woman, among others. He even experiments with camouflage, dressing himself in painted undergarments to blend in with the interiors of his apartment—to be tested out on Watson (this brings up the question of Holmes passing as a straight man in his environment). This willingness to submit himself to such indignities in the pursuit of his detective work is suggestive of the star who goes to great ends for his acting, for example Downey himself. Ever since *Chaplin*, he has been considered in this category, as an actor who applies himself conscientiously to his work; Downey's association with craft was further shored up by playing Charlie Chaplin, who took his comic art seriously and was a great innovator. This sense of clownishness in his physical persona, as well as physical versatility, has never left Downey. It reaches its hiatus—or perhaps self-parody—in the Ben Stiller comedy *Tropic Thunder* (2008) in which he plays Method actor Kirk Lazarus, who goes as far as injecting himself with melatonin in his preparations to play an African-American soldier in a Vietnam film. Holmes' facility for disguise also points to his association with the figure of the magician: Although as a detective his role is to strip back the illusion and deceit created by others to reveal the truth—indeed, in the first film his opponent is the aristocratic black magician Lord Blackwood (Mark Strong)—there is something of the preternatural in his abilities. The performance he engages in presenting his deductions is itself breathtaking and magical. Performativity of the sleuth in such expositional set pieces does seem to be an established part of the detective genre, e.g. Agatha Christie's Belgian detective Poirot. Furthermore, Holmes' mental virtuosity can be paralleled to Downey's equivalent acting talents, which the Lazarus figure in *Tropic Thunder* is sending up. The detective's association with the "Other" is further evidenced by his much greater ease than Watson in accepting the help of a band of gypsies in *A Game of Shadows*, once they have committed to hunting down the brother of Madame Simza Heron (Noomi Rapace), one of Moriarty's pawns.

The instability of Downey's physical performance, its reliance on disguise and clownishness, supports the extra-normative gender positioning of the star, a transgression of gender. This is most explicit in the *Sherlock Holmes* series of films. It should be noted that the dynamic between the detective Sherlock Holmes and his companion and aide Dr. Watson in their original literary form has historically been interpreted as solidly homosocial in origin, lacking the homoerotic charge present in the Guy Ritchie movies. Eve Kosofsky Sedgwick considers the representation of male bonds in Victorian literature, coining the term "male homosocial desire." She suggests the phrase is an oxymoron, created to divulge the ideological contradictions inherent in the phrase. "Male homosocial" refers to masculine bonds, which are characterized in Western society by homophobia. Her intention, in coining the phrase "homosocial desire," is to "draw the 'homosocial' back into the orbit of 'desire,' of the potentially erotic, ... to hypothesize the potential unbrokenness of a continuum between homosocial and homosexual—a continuum whose visibility, for men, in our society, is radically disrupted" (1–2).

In his film adaptations, director Guy Ritchie depicts Holmes' and Watson's friendship as existing somewhere upon the continuum that for Sedgwick is ruptured in modern culture, both in its emotional compulsion and in the implication that Holmes may in fact be gay. In press and publicity for the first film, Downey took great pleasure in alluding to Holmes' homosexuality: When pressed by David Letterman (*Letterman*, 2009) he suggested, "Why don't we observe the clip and let the audience decide if he just happens to be a very butch homosexual. Which there are many. And I'm proud to know certain of them." Rumors followed on the Hollywood gossip circuit that production of the sequel could be threatened due to the intervention of nervous studio executives (*IMDb*).

In spite of such rumors, in the second Sherlock Holmes film, *Sherlock Holmes: A Game of Shadows*, subtext has become text. Dr. Watson is played by Jude Law, complete with handlebar moustache and top hat, a Victorian prototype for the Village People. Law's persona is not only that of "pretty boy" but with some "queer" associations, typically as the (often straight) muse of a gay companion. This association grew from his casting as "Bosie" Douglas, the young aristocrat who finally proves to be Oscar Wilde's undoing, in the film *Wilde* (1997). (The playwright sued Douglas's father, the Marquess of Queensbury, for libel, when he accused him of being homosexual. Not only did Wilde lose, but he was eventually tried for "gross indecency" and sentenced to two years' hard labor.) Note also that the actor who plays Wilde, Stephen Fry, later appears as Sherlock Holmes' brother Mycroft in *A Game of Shadows* (Fry is also famously "out" about his sexual orientation, unlike many actors in Hollywood). This positioning as an out-of-reach love object to gay men is repeated in the later film *The Talented Mr. Ripley* (Anthony Mingella, 1999) in which Law plays the role of playboy Dickie Greenleaf, whom the sociopath Tom Ripley falls in love with, and whom the latter eventually kills. Thus, where the dynamic of straight-gay homoerotically inflected friendship is hinted at in *Kiss Kiss Bang Bang*, in the Sherlock Holmes films it finds its most overt demonstration—and note that it is now Downey who is playing the homosexually inclined figure.

While Holmes is presented as nominally straight—he conducts a relationship with a female criminal, Irene Adler, played by Rachel McAdams—there is little sense of an emotional connection between them: this he saves for Watson. Adler's transgressive character both suits an association with the Robert Downey Jr. persona and echoes the femme fatale figure that features as the cornerstone of the later noir detective genre; indeed, Adler can be considered a proto- femme fatale, deserving of the scrutiny and suspicion she evokes in Holmes. Her fate for transgressing convention and the law is punishment, not by the police or by Holmes, but by his nemesis, Professor Moriarty (Jared Harris), for whom she works. Holmes retains an element of rule-flouting himself, which extends back to his air of sexual transgression, so Adler is an ideal companion for the detective, in spite of being on the opposite side. Downey's personal history cannot help but be alluded to: Drawn into conversation with Holmes, Irene declares, "I've never woken up in handcuffs before." He responds, "I have. Naked." The in-joke for the audience familiar with Downey's repeated arrests is unequivocal.

Adler may indeed be a diversion, for Holmes demonstrates considerable jealousy toward Watson's relationship, engagement, and subsequent marriage to his sweetheart Mary, all but stopping him from attending his own wedding ceremony (he successfully sabotages the honeymoon). He remains suspicious of women: This distrust is naturalized in the relationship with Irene, but shown as a symptom of his misogyny when presented with a normal woman like Mary. Nevertheless, it is telling that the actress Kelly Reilly plays Mary as a cool, restrained character, lacking the warmth one would expect to see between her and Watson. Thus, in the world of Sherlock Holmes there are no women with whom a man would really want to have an intimate connection; they are all cold, victims and criminals alike.

Women indeed do not have an easy time of it in this environment: In *A Game of Shadows*, Adler is poisoned by Moriarty (a mode of death most often associated with the feminine, specifically the maternal). Holmes goes as far as throwing Mary from a moving train as it crosses a gorge, sending her plummeting hundreds of feet into the river, ostensibly to protect her from Moriarty's henchmen. Moments after Mary re-emerges from her dive, Holmes' brother Mycroft appears in a rowing boat to fish her out of the water and return her to the safety of his stately home. Nevertheless, the fact remains that Holmes pushes her from the train. Interestingly, this is also the fate that is assigned to both Holmes himself and the archvillain Moriarty: At the film's denouement, Holmes pulls Moriarty over a cliff-top ledge into the Swiss Reichenbach Falls, killing them both. One might argue that Mary is assigned the role of villain that Holmes wishes to dispatch, just as Moriarty is (note also that both have red hair!). Alternatively, in each instance Watson is faced with the loss of his love object: When Mary is thrown from the carriage, he thinks her dead—only the spectator and Holmes know otherwise. Likewise, when Moriarty and Holmes plunge into the waterfall, we assume both drown. In the Sir Arthur Conan Doyle story, "The Final Problem," on which this scenario is based, both hero and villain do in fact die. However, such was public opinion at the killing off of Holmes that Doyle was forced to bring him back—both for *The Hound of the Baskervilles* (set before "The Final Problem") and "The Adventure of the Empty House." The assumption that Holmes has died in his plunge over the falls is supported in *A Game of Shadows*, which shows a desolate Watson in the last scene, writing "The End" to his adventures with Holmes. Only once he has left the room, does Holmes sit up from the chair he has been hiding in—apparently camouflaged in a ridiculous painted undergarment—revealing to the spectator, but not Watson, that he is still alive. This ending suits Holmes,' and by extension the film's, evasion of intimacy: the detective substitutes the serious for the ridiculous at every turn, perhaps in evasion of the tender bond that exists between him and the doctor.

If the homoerotic nature of the relationship between Holmes and Watson is largely subtextual (in spite of Downey's extra-textual allusions in interviews) it is "outed" in the sequence in which Mary is thrown from the train. Holmes disguises himself as a woman, in one of his many ridiculous disguises, to get his way past Moriarty's men who are, or are at least dressed as, soldiers, that most patriotic and patriarchal symbol of masculinity (that Holmes, in spite of his demonstrations of masculinity in the arena of boxing, clearly transgresses). As the enemy loads up a machine gun several carriages along but with the power to blast through the wooden interiors, Holmes declares, "Lie down with me Watson." The instruction comes moments after Watson attacks Holmes with the cry, "You killed my wife!" while wrestling the cross-dressing detective over the carriage seating in a moment of farcical, self-parodying homoerotic spectacle in which both participants struggle, red-faced and panting, to defend themselves. Watson does indeed lie down with Holmes: Flat on their backs, Holmes smoking (!), the position is suggestive of post-coital intimacy, following their athletic tumble—indeed, it is another moment of Downey in a prostrate position, though this time he is in control of proceedings.

That is not to say that Holmes is not physically vulnerable. In both *Sherlock Holmes* and *A Game of Shadows*, he finds himself up against opponents of atypical strength and stamina against whom there seems to be no possibility of winning. He triumphs in the boxing ring, not through pure brawn (though his bare-chested boxing reveals a developed musculature) but through brains, mentally playing out his fight tactics for himself and the spectator before he commits himself to action. Unfortunately, with Moriarty he meets his match: The older, less physically capable man is able to defeat him due to his own tactical brilliance and exploitation of Holmes' injuries, which he has himself previously caused. Like Downey's previous detective characters, Holmes finds himself physically exposed: He finally tracks Moriarty down to a munitions factory in Germany but is captured. Moriarty, the ultimate terrifying patriarch, strings him up on a phallic-looking meat-hook, where he proceeds to swing on Holmes' body, further exasperating his injuries. In a typically astute observation of his persona's appeal, Downey remarked of this scene, "Audiences like to see me bleed. I don't know why. It started with *Kiss Kiss Bang Bang* and it's progressed right up through this second Sherlock movie" ("Maximum Movie Mode"). The comment reveals an awareness of the masochistic nature of his star image, present to some degree since his early career, but exaggerated in his later films following his years of drug abuse and time in prison.

Watson finally comes to Holmes' rescue by blowing up the factory chimney (another phallus), which falls on the part of the building where he is held, allowing him to escape. By the time the pair board a cargo train, along with their allies, Holmes is at the point of death.

Once again, the Downey persona is subject to physical vulnerability and the prostrate position, symbolizing his weakness. Watson is inconsolable, fearing he will lose his closest friend. (This incident is handled much more tenderly than the moment when he fears he has lost his wife, which is played for humor.) He finally remembers the adrenaline shot that Holmes has given to him—as a wedding present!—and injects him in the heart. Holmes comes to, bolt upright, ready for a fight. The moment recalls *Pulp Fiction* (Quentin Tarantino, 1994), in which Vincent (John Travolta) injects Mia (Uma Thurman) after an accidental overdose—suggestive perhaps both of Holmes' reputation as a cocaine addict and Downey's own drug history, including the "Goldilocks" incident during which paradernics revived him (Garbarino, "Star") (His return to consciousness also gives embodiment to the resurrection Downey's career has undergone since 2003.) The episode of Holmes' return from the dead in this sequence brings us back to a crucial facet of Holmes' character, one which resonates with the persona and history of Downey: his drug habit. The casting of Downey as this character only emphasizes what we already know: that Holmes' genius is a peculiarly tormented one, a struggle between superego and id, one that reflects the torments of the actor himself. Both *Sherlock Holmes* films make a number of references to Downey's history in their representation of Holmes' drug use; for example in *Sherlock Holmes* we are first introduced to the detective as he crawls along the floor of his bedroom, avoiding the sunlight, apparently intoxicated.

Conclusion

As we have seen, the detective films of Robert Downey Jr. provide a particularly apt thematic framework for the working through of certain key aspects of the star's screen persona. The fragile masculine identity, typical of the film noir detective, reappears in the self-conscious homage provided by both *The Singing Detective* and *Kiss Kiss Bang Bang*, whose heroes are physically assaulted and emasculated at every turn. Terrorized by the avenging oedipal patriarch and his agents, the latter film's hero finds comfort only in compelling male friendships, indicative of his retreat from oedipal challenge. Equally, in the *Sherlock Holmes* films, it is men not women who provide the greatest sense of emotional intimacy and relief from the terrifying archetypal father embodied by Moriarty. The clownishness of the Downey persona points to a childish streak—one method of evading paternal competition—and a certain unwillingness to grow up. This childishness is typified by many of his characters' love of dressing up, including Sherlock Holmes and Iron Man (who is at the end of the day, a just a little boy in a suit of armor). In dressing up, the young boy can also play at being a man, which is what Dan Dark does in his fantasy as the hard-boiled private eye. However, such role-play, evident also in *Kiss Kiss Bang Bang*, only highlights the artificiality of the masculine performance. It also provides a platform for the transgression of sexual norms, most apparent in Holmes' drag act in *A Game of Shadows*, which points out the queer nature of his friendship with Dr. Watson. Beyond the transgression of heteronormative heterosexuality, not only in sexual orientation but also in a failure to live up to the demands of masculinity, lies a wider transgression against patriarchal law and its internalized agent, the superego. While the persona of Robert Downey Jr. addresses the performative nature of masculinity, and its inherent fragility, it also explores punishment of transgression against the law. Thus, as a detective figure, the persona of Downey is associated simultaneously with the upholding of the law and the flouting of it, both superego and id. This struggle against one's darker impulses, one apparently lost by the actor for a number of years, is perhaps best embodied by detective Sherlock Holmes, and his plummet over the Reichenbach Falls with his arch-enemy Professor Moriarty into the watery abyss. Even this act of self-abnegation does not guarantee the death of Holmes who, like Downey, demonstrates his unequivocal talent as a come-back kid. Holmes rewrites both Watson's story ("The End?") and the star's own, as the spectator is assured that there will be a sequel for the detective and for Robert Downey Jr.

Notes

1. Freud formalizes his thoughts on the structural model of the human psyche in *The Ego and Id*, first published in 1923.
2. There is some debate amongst critics over whether film noir can even be considered a genre, as the term was applied retro-actively by French film critics to films which at the time of release were labeled by the Hollywood Industry as melodramas, crime thrillers or detective films, indicating that it was more of a film movement or trend rather than a genre per se (Gates 10).
3. The literal nature of both characters' names indicates that each film has a self-conscious relation to the noir genre that inspired it.
4. This is comic allusion to the famous memoir *You'll Never Eat Lunch in this Town Again*, by Hollywood producer Julia Philips.
5. Perry is the first name of Perry Mason, a popular day-time television detective character of the same series.
6. The woman is later revealed to be Dexter's daughter, Veronica. Her attempted disposal in the lake suggests a tongue-in-cheek allusion to Veronica Lake, a famous actress of film noirs in the 1940s.

Works Cited

Chaplin. Dir. Richard Attenborough. Maple Pictures, 1992. DVD.
Chinatown. Dir. Roman Polanski. Paramount, 1974. Film.
Conan Doyle, Arthur. "The Adventure of the Empty House." *The Return of Sherlock Holmes*. New York: McClure, Phillips & Co., 1905. Print.
_____. "The Final Problem." *The Memoirs of Sherlock Holmes*. Strand Magazine Dec. 1893. Print.
_____. *The Hound of the Baskervilles*. Strand Magazine Aug. 1901 to Apr. 1902. Print.
Downey Jr., Robert, Perf. "Broken." *The Futurist*. Sony Classical, 2004. CD.
Freud, Sigmund. "The Dissolution of the Oedipus Complex." *The Standard Edition of the Complete Psychological Works of Sigmund Freud, Volume XIX (1923–1925): The Ego and the ID and Other Works*. London: The Hogarth Press, 1957. 174–179. Print.
_____. "The Ego and the Id." *The Standard Edition of the Complete Psychological Works of Sigmund Freud, Volume XIX (1923–1925): The Ego and the ID and Other Works*. London: The Hogarth Press, 1957. 1–59. Print.
Garbarino, Steve. "The Star in Cell 17." *Vanity Fair*, Mar. 2001. Institute for Robert Downey Jr. Studies—Required Reading. *Robert Downey Jr. Film Guide*. Web. 3 Aug. 2013.
Gates, Phillippa. *Detecting Men: Masculinity and the Hollywood Detective Film*. Albany: SUNY Press, 2006. Print.
Halperin, David. *Saint Foucault: Towards a Gay Hagiography*. Oxford: Oxford University Press, 1997. Print.
Kiss Kiss Bang Bang. 2005. Dir. Shane Black. Warner Bros., 2006. DVD.
The Late Show with David Letterman. 20 Dec. 2009. Television.
Lennard, Dominic. "Wonder Boys: Matt Damon, Johnny Depp and Robert Downey Jr." *Shining in Shadows: Movie Stars of the 2000s*. Ed. Murray Pomerance. New Brunswick, NJ: Rutgers University Press, 2012. 12–31. Print.

Lethal Weapon. Dir. Richard Donner. Warner, 1987. DVD.
Lethal Weapon 2. Dir. Richard Donner. Warner, 1989. DVD.
"Maximum Movie Mode." *Sherlock Holmes: A Game of Shadows.* 2011. Dir. Guy Ritchie. Warner Bros., 2012. Blu-Ray.
Phillips, Julia. *You'll Never Eat Lunch in This Town Again.* New York: New American Library, 1992. Print.
Pomerantz, Dorothy. "Robert Downey Jr. Tops Forbes' List of Hollywood's Highest-Paid Actors." *Forbes*, 16 July 2013. Web. 17 Aug. 2013.
Pulp Fiction. Dir. Quentin Tarantino. Miramax, 1994. Film.
Robinson, David. *Chaplin: His Life and Art.* New York: McGraw-Hill, 1985. Print.
Safety Last! Dir. Fred C. Newmeyer, Sam Taylor. Pathé, 1923. Film.
Sedgwick, Eve Kosofsky. *Between Men: English Literature and Male Homosocial Desire.* New York: Columbia University Press, 1985. Print.
Sherlock Holmes. Dir. Guy Ritchie. Warner Bros., 2009. Blu-Ray.
Sherlock Holmes: A Game of Shadows. 2011. Dir. Guy Ritchie. Warner Bros., 2012.
Sherlock Holmes: A Game of Shadows. IMDb, 3 Jan. 2010. Web. 17 Aug. 2013.
The Singing Detective. 2003. Dir. Keith Gordon. Paramount Home Entertainment, 2004. DVD.
Sunset Boulevard. Dir. Billy Wilder. Paramount, 1950. Film.
The Talented Mr. Ripley. Dir. Anthony Minghella. Miramax, 1999. Film.
Thomas, Kayley. "'Bromance is so passé': Robert Downey, Jr's Queer Paratexts." *Sherlock Holmes for the 21st Century*. Ed. Lynette Porter. Jefferson, NC: McFarland, 2012. 35–47. Print.
Top Gun. Dir. Tony Scott. Paramount, 1986. Film.
Tropic Thunder. Dir. Ben Stiller. Dreamworks Home Entertainment, 2008. DVD.
Wilde. 1997. Dir. Brian Gilbert. Sony, 1998. Film.
Willis, Sharon. *High Contrast: Race and Gender in Contemporary Hollywood Film.* Durham: Duke University Press, 1997. Print.

Genre- and Gender-Bending in Shane Black's *Kiss Kiss Bang Bang* and *Iron Man 3*

Nils Bothmann

Genre definitions are always open for interpretation and change over time, yet they still provide for viewer expectations. A film is placed in a generic context through paratexts such as advertising, star images, and reviews. Thereby, viewers know what they can roughly expect from the movie they might want to see—this concept is often called the genre contract.[1] In film studies, genres are often discussed with regard to their gender constructions. This essay will therefore take a look at the ways in which *Kiss Kiss Bang Bang* works with the (gendered) genre expectations of the action movie, the hard-boiled novel, and the film noir, especially the conceptions and crises of straight white masculinity, which are important issues in all these genres. Black's movie subverts classic notions of hegemonic masculinity and offers progressive roles for gay and female characters, thereby making clear that gender-bending is an important tool for genre-bending, yet it still negotiates the anxieties of straight white manhood, which are also central to *Kiss Kiss Bang Bang*'s genres.

In 2005 *Kiss Kiss Bang Bang* provided a comeback opportunity for writer/director Shane Black, who had not received a movie credit for nearly ten years, as well as for the two stars Robert Downey Jr. and Val Kilmer, pairing small-time thief Harry Lockhart (Downey) with gay private eye Perry Van Shrike (Kilmer). While running from the police, Harry bursts into a movie audition, is mistaken for an actor, and is even considered for the part of a detective. He is flown to Los Angeles, where Perry, nicknamed Gay Perry, is supposed to give him detective lessons, but already on their first job they stumble across a murderous conspiracy. Another plot strand concerns Harry's high school friend Harmony Faith Lane (Michelle Monaghan), an actress trying to make it in L.A., with whom he is still in love although she never requited his feelings and who is also tangled up in the web of conspiracy.

Action Movie Associations

Shane Black has shaped the genre of the buddy cop movie as a screenwriter with the groundbreaking *Lethal Weapon* (1987), *The Last Boy Scout* (1991), *Last Action Hero* (1993), and *The Long Kiss Goodnight* (1996). This filmography as a paratext in turn influences fans' and moviegoers' expectations when watching *Kiss Kiss Bang Bang*. The heyday of the classic buddy cop movie was already over in 2005, but Black takes a fresh look on the genre by twisting its traditional structure in this postmodern variation.[2] *Kiss Kiss Bang Bang* references the film noir and the hard-boiled novel as well as the (buddy cop) action movie. The movie's title alludes to a name given to James Bond by viewers, Mr. Kiss Kiss Bang Bang, which was also an unused alternative title for *Thunderball* (1965) (*IMDb*). While this title pays homage to spy action movies, the two alternative titles considered during production make the movie's generic heritage even clearer: *L.A.P.I.* is an abbreviation reminiscent of the departments in cop action films (L.A.P.D., N.Y.P.D. etc.) and also quotes the term P.I. for private investigator, marking the link to the hard-boiled detective novel; *You'll Never Die in This Town Again* is a title in the vein of the fictional hard-boiled Johnny Gossamer books that are part of the movie (*IMDb*).

References to these genres abound on the diegetic[3] level, usually playing with stereotypes and clichés. Standard action movie situations are acted out, but with different results from the usual: the torture of the heroes (during which Perry points out the homosexual tones of such an undertaking to their torturer), the Russian roulette to frighten a criminal (which immediately ends with Harry executing the goon with the first bullet), or the object forgotten in the hero's breast pocket as he is shot in the chest (only this time the object, a paperback of a hard-boiled novel, is incapable of stopping the bullet).

Hierarchies Among Buddies

A majority of buddy duos consists of a tough leading male, often portrayed by action stars such as Bruce Willis or Mel Gibson, and a comedic sidekick, with the tough male star

Robert Downey Jr. as Harry Lockhart in Shane Black's *Kiss Kiss Bang Bang* (2005).

usually being the more important of the two protagonists. Some scholars claim that the black partners in cop movies such as *Shoot to Kill* (1988), *Die Hard* (1988), and *Lethal Weapon* have often been portrayed as inferior and less manly than their white counterparts (Ames 52–61), while the cop action movie remains a "politically charged, wonderfully brutal, and straight-white-male centered genre" (King x). In his seminal study on cop action movies, *Heroes in Hard Times*, King extends the concept of a cop to different types of investigators, including private eyes (28), labeling these types of investigating characters "working-class community protectors" (2). Harry and Perry fit this description in nearly all respects: By solving the central murder case in *Kiss Kiss Bang Bang* and killing all the criminals involved, they rid the community of gangsters action-movie-style and although Harry starts off as a thief, he joins Perry's detective agency in the end, holding down a legal, working-class job. Moreover, the main villain turns out to be a rich, powerful, but also (morally) corrupt white man: movie producer Harlan Dexter (Corbin Bernsen)—exactly the type of villain cop heroes most often struggle against (King 66–69).

Contrary to the dominant power structure of buddy cop movies, though, Perry is the man of action, carrying guns, talking back while being held at gunpoint, showing competence and tough-guy-attitude. Harry is the protagonist, since the film follows his adventures (this is also made clear by Harry's frequent voiceover narration), although Downey takes on a role that would usually have been the one of the comedic sidekick. He is often incompetent as a detective, is verbally abused by Perry, the bad guys, and nearly everyone he encounters and, although he kills a couple of criminals during the film's course, these scenes are staged as moments of pure fluke, like the semi-conscious Harry rolling around on top of the villains' car and shooting the thugs as a reflex action. Although these occasional moments of taking action or brilliant thought occur, Harry is more often portrayed as inferior and subordinate. His skills in detecting are limited as well: He notices an important detail for solving the case, the fact that a murder victim doesn't wear any underpants, but it is Harmony and Perry who draw the right conclusions from this observation. Whereas many cop action heroes are at least masters in one discipline, the killing of bad guys (King 28–34), Harry claims that he has never finished anything he has started in his entire life and has always stopped halfway. In typical action sidekick fashion, he not only develops skills in killing villains during the movie (King 42–45), he also matures in other respects and earns at least some admiration from tough guy Perry. As a result he may be the hero and narrator of *Kiss Kiss Bang Bang*, but it is a perspective that would have usually been the sidekick's. This change of perspective is also a strategy of genre-bending.

Perry's sexual orientation twists the classic hierarchical logic of the buddy movie even further. Whereas the traditional straight-white-male heroes of the genre had to experience the feeling of "losing ground" (King 1), meaning that they had to share their formerly exclusive privileges with representatives of the Other, much of that ground seems to be already lost in *Kiss Kiss Bang Bang*: The film's tough alpha male is a gay person of higher social standing than the whiny, criminal protagonist. Moreover, this arrangement of protagonists picks up on the notion that traditional buddy movies place "the male couple between the representational poles of homoeroticism and homophobia" (Fuchs 195). Cynthia J. Fuchs and other scholars refer back to Eve Kosofsky Sedgwick's concept of homosociality, a form of kinship among men, which could pass over into homosexuality in cultures such as ancient Greece, but nowadays is coupled with strong notions of homophobia (3–

4). Furthermore, these male homosocial structures exclude women from the male sphere of power/agency and turn them into pure objects in male-male relationships; Sedgwick calls these acts "traffic in women" (13), implying a strong bond between the concepts of heterosexuality, homosociality, and patriarchy. Many scholars view buddy (cop) movies as a contemporary expression of male, homophobic, and misogynist attitudes: While the strongest bond on screen is the one between men, homophobic jokes and the presence of inactive wives or girlfriends assure the viewer of the protagonists' heterosexuality (Fuchs 194–210; Ames 52–61; Pfeil 1–36).

Kiss Kiss Bang Bang undermines this concept in various ways. First, one of the main characters actually is a gay man, who is also able to make jokes at the expense of his own sexual orientation, in much the same way that many action film heroes joke about themselves (Tasker 98–90). Moreover, in one scene Harry and Perry kiss: While hiding a dead body, they encounter a police car and Perry starts to make out with Harry, in order to deceive the cops about what they are actually doing in the dark alley. Still, Perry shows no real desire for Harry, thereby avoiding the cliché of the homosexual male trying to seduce every attractive man he meets. While most homosexuals in action films are stereotypically portrayed as overly effeminate (Purse 135), "Perry is matter of fact about his homosexuality, and [...] it does not result in his visual representation being obviously stereotyped" (Purse 139). This lack of stereotyping represents a big difference from the few earlier movies about gay investigators, such as *Partners* (1982), in which homosexual police officer Kerwin (John Hurt) is not only the weaker sidekick to the heterosexual cop Benson (Ryan O'Neal), who is portrayed as macho, but also tries to hide his sexual orientation in public, especially on the job, and constantly does things that are connoted as "womanly" in private, including doing housework and cooking for his cop buddy. Purse criticizes *Kiss Kiss Bang Bang* for partnering Perry "with a male character who is permitted to be sporadically but openly homophobic" (140). However, at the same time, Harry is ridiculed throughout the movie, while Perry is constantly shown to be in control, so the film undermines Harry's homophobic outbursts. In one of the last scenes, Harry also seems to have overcome his homophobia as he helps the injured Perry to take a closer look at (and possibly pursue) a male nurse the gay detective has laid his eyes upon. Harry is also awarded traits that are typically connoted as feminine: He resentfully complains about Harmony having slept with a former friend of his although she promised years ago that she wouldn't, and he is whiny when talking about his injuries and is often very emotional. When he hears about the supposed suicide of Harmony, he is the one who breaks down and cries, while the gay but not effeminate Perry unfeelingly tries to push the grieving Harry away from his car, so he can head home.

The perceived relationship between toughness, maleness, and sexual orientation is also consciously addressed within the movie. Assassins Mr. Frying Pan (Dash Mihok) and Mr. Fire (Rockmond Dunbar) ask Harry during an interrogation, "Now, me and my man, we're puzzled lately by your behavior, such as—"—"Such as why is a savvy, stand-up cat like yourself consorting with gay men? Frolicking in the lake and shit together. What is that?" They threaten Harry by undermining his maleness, implying that straight men should not work with homosexuals, beat him up, and tell him, "L.A. don't want you no more, tough guy." The irony of course is the fact that Harry is not actually a tough guy, although the assassins treat him as one. For a moment Harry gives in to this illusion, as when he is hitting Perry in a fit of rage and challenging him: "You sissy bitch!" But Perry ends these illusions of grandeur, when he easily overpowers the attacking Harry and in a demeaning gesture forces him to pick up the glasses he has knocked off of Perry's face.

Harmony: Not Your Typical Damsel in Distress

The film also ridicules the stereotypical portrayal of women as objects in a male sphere. In contrast to the male heroes, Harmony is never captured by the bad guys, whereas wives, lovers, and girlfriends are constantly kidnapped and threatened in most action movies (including Black's own *Iron Man 3* (2013)), usually in order to provide additional motivation for the heroes (Ames 52–61). Harmony even warns Perry as he is about to walk into a trap set up by the film's villains, overpowers assassin Mr. Fire in that same scene (although she is unable to execute the unconscious killer afterward), and later comes to the rescue of Harry and Perry, when they have been captured by Dexter's henchmen during the finale. Although she never shoots a gun or kills a villain in contrast to Harry and Perry, she nevertheless possesses great skill in handling cars as the final chase scene demonstrates. The fact that the baseball bat she uses to attack an intruder in her apartment has the inscription "Wonder Girl" parallels her to Roy Hobbs (Robert Redford), the male protagonist of *The Natural* (1984), whose bat carries the inscription "Wonder Boy"—another hint that Harmony possesses attributes traditionally connoted as masculine. Her status as an object of male desire remains problematic, however. Although Harmony and Harry discuss the meaning of sex in more than one scene and also her status as a potential object of male interest, *Kiss Kiss Bang Bang* at times implies that Harmony might be promiscuous, causing Harry to express his wish that she isn't "that kind of girl." At the same time, *Kiss Kiss Bang Bang* makes clear that the narrative is filtered through Harry, who might be overprotective and likely to deny Harmony any sexual agency due to his idealized image of her. As often as Harmony disputes Harry's claim, the film remains vague about the extent to which Harmony subdues herself to male desire in order to make it in Hollywood and to what extent she is a strong, self-determined woman, choosing her sexual partners and openly challenging the double standard for men and women in society. *Kiss Kiss Bang Bang* also debates the double standard: On the first night of their reunion, Harry does not end up in bed with Harmony but with Marleah (Ali Hillis), a friend of hers. While Harry tries to brush the incident off as a misunderstanding and points out that he has no memory of actually sleeping with Marleah, he seems to be embarrassed by the idea of Harmony having sex with people other than him. A similar revelation occurs when Harry calls the girls in Los Angeles "damaged goods." He claims, "I'm telling you, you take a guy who sleeps with 100 women a year, go into his childhood—dollars to doughnuts, it's relatively unspectacular. Now, you take one of these gals, who sleeps with 100 guys a year, and I *bet* you if you look in their childhood, there's something rotten in Denver." Thereby, Harry implies that it is normal for a man to be promiscuous, while a woman doing the same thing has to be driven by some sort of trauma, declaring himself once more a believer in the double standard.

The Shane Black Factor

While consciously avoiding stereotypes in the depiction of heroic buddy duos, gay people, and women in action movies, *Kiss Kiss Bang Bang* also presents a classic duo of black

Shane Black (left) directing Robert Downey Jr. as Harry Lockhart in *Kiss Kiss Bang Bang* (2005).

and white men, reminiscent of the so-called salt 'n' pepper duos of movies such as *Die Hard*, *The Last Boy Scout*, or *Lethal Weapon*. But while those were the heroes of classic cop action movies, white Mr. Frying Pan und black Mr. Fire in *Kiss Kiss Bang Bang* are a self-confident duo of hitmen, ruthlessly gunning down witnesses and expendable accomplices at Dexter's order. They are not only marked by their status as an interracial duo but also by their tough and professional demeanor—indicators that align them more to classic images of action manhood than the Harry/Perry duo. Then again, such conceptions of bad guys as the heroes' reflections are common to the action genre and to Shane Black's work: General McAllistair and Mr. Joshua in *Lethal Weapon* function as mirror images to Riggs and Murtaugh, and the greatest nemesis of former elite government assassin Charlene in *The Long Kiss Goodnight* is her former target and male counterpart, Timothy, to name a few examples.

At the same time, the ruthless assassins are also ridiculed by the film: Shortly after their introduction, Mr. Fire is gunned down by the drugged Harry, and Mr. Frying Pan dies in a shootout with Perry, but not by the detective's hand—instead, he is shot in the back by an armed, angry hot dog vendor, whose tables were overturned in Mr. Frying Pan's previous effort to run Perry over. Their nicknames are also made fun of, which is striking, since the viewer is never told their real names. While interrogating Harry, Mr. Frying Pan calls himself, his partner, and Harry "Ike, Mike and Mustard," which leads to a disagreement about whether this labeling is adequate or witty, before settling on the names Mr. Frying Pan and Mr. Fire, which are also the ones they are awarded in the film's credits. "Ike, Mike and Mustard" jokes are vulgar jokes, often about sex, racial minorities, or gender. Ike and Mike are also terms for salt and pepper shakers in diners, once again hinting at their status as an interracial (salt 'n' pepper) duo. These puns with their names also point out that henchmen's names in action movies usually don't matter. Black had already made fun of this aspect in *The Last Boy Scout*: As Milo, the main villain's right-hand man, asks the hero Joe Hallenbeck "Can we do a formal introduction here?," Hallenbeck simply replies, "Who gives a fuck? You're the bad guy, right?" Milo answers, "I am the bad guy." The movie also contains a scene in which the heroes are roughed up by a well-spoken thug, causing sidekick Jimmy Dix to claim that they are beaten up by the inventor of Scrabble. The film credits actor Jack Kehler also as "Scrabble Man"—showing to what extent *The Last Boy Scout* is in on such jokes: Most bad guys just serve the narrative purpose of providing conflict for the heroes and aren't fully rounded characters.

There are more references to Shane Black's other work in *Kiss Kiss Bang Bang*: The image of Harry dangling from a coffin while shooting bad guys during the finale is an ironic inversion of similar scenes in other action movies, including the Black-penned *The Long Kiss Goodnight*, in which the heroine fires at a helicopter while dangling from a rope. *Kiss Kiss Bang Bang* takes place during Christmas, like *Lethal Weapon*, *The Last Boy Scout*, *The Long Kiss Goodnight*, and *Iron Man 3*. The first sentence Harry has to read during the audition is "Go spit!" which is one of Roger Murtaugh's catchphrases from the *Lethal Weapon* series. Perry tells Harry "Thrill me!" which is the catchphrase of cop Ray Cameron (Tom Atkins) in *Night of the Creeps* (1986), written and directed by Black's old friend Fred Dekker, in which Black has a small role as another cop. The screenwriters Black, Dekker, Ed Solomon, Chris Matheson, Ryan Rowe and Gregory Widen shared a house in the 1980s, the so-called "Pad o' Guys" (Nashawaty 82).

Black also works his own experiences into the film, commenting on them ironically.

When he was asked to write the sequel for *Lethal Weapon*, he wrote a screenplay in which Riggs dies. This and other differences about the tone of the movie led to Black quitting the production before he was fired (Nashawaty 83). As a result, he is only credited for writing the characters and the story for *Lethal Weapon 2* (1989), but not the screenplay. Perry in *Kiss Kiss Bang Bang* suffers a seemingly fatal wound during the showdown, but the epilogue reveals that he has survived the injury.[4] In his voiceover Harry comments on the practice of studios and producers interfering and meddling with endings, bringing dead characters back to life to appease the audience. As he makes this comment, characters who were killed during the film (Mr. Frying Pan, Mr. Fire, and the girl with the pink hair) start entering the room, followed by historical personalities like Abraham Lincoln and Elvis Presley. As Harry ends his speech with "But the points is, in this case, this time, it really happened. Perry, like, lived. Yeah, it's a dumb movie thing, but what do you want me to do, lie about it?," these characters are ushered out of the room by a nurse, while Perry stays with Harry and Harmony. Despite ridiculing a need for happy endings in contemporary mainstream cinema, this scene is one of the many instances in which *Kiss Kiss Bang Bang* displays its own fictionality and status as a postmodern narrative text. This notion is usually conveyed by the voice over, despite some visual markers (like the pausing or rewinding of certain scenes) which function to underscore Harry's off-commentary.

Hard-Boiled Tough Guys, Femme Fatales and Good Girls

Off-commentary isn't a typical narrative feature of action movies, but it is a feature of the other two important sources of inspiration for *Kiss Kiss Bang Bang*: the hard-boiled novel and the film noir. Black had already worked notions of these genres into previous movies, like the character of hard-boiled private eye Joe Hallenbeck in *The Last Boy Scout*. Paul Werner also counts Black's cop action movies *Lethal Weapon* and *The Last Boy Scout* as neo noirs (284–285). *Kiss Kiss Bang Bang* is inspired by Brett Halliday's hard-boiled novel *Bodies Are Where You Find Them* (1941), while the chapter titles refer to Raymond Chandler's work, namely his hard-boiled classics *The Lady in the Lake* (1943), *The Little Sister* (1949), and *Farewell, My Lovely* (1940), the short story "Trouble Is My Business" (1939), all of them starring his famous private eye Philip Marlowe, and his essay on crime fiction, "The Simple Art of Murder" (1950). Black pays homage to and ironically reflects on the genres of film noir and hard-boiled novel, which are closely intertwined, the same way he does with the action genre.

Classic hard-boiled detectives like Philip Marlowe usually work alone and get only occasional help from sidekicks, creating a lone-wolf-attitude, which they also convey in their function as first-person narrators, exceptions like Dashiell Hammett's seminal *The Maltese Falcon* (1930) (which is told by a third-person-narrator) notwithstanding. This time it is not the hard-boiled detective but the "soft-boiled" sidekick telling the story. While Harry projects the same cynicism and world-weariness as hard-boiled protagonists on the level of voiceover, his intradiegetic performance as a character within the plot stands in contrast to that attitude. The difference between Harry's hard-boiled veneer and soft-boiled core is also constantly addressed by the plot: Harry's threats against a man touching the sleeping Harmony are proven empty as the guy beats up Harry in response and when Harry tries to wrap up the movie in the last scene, in which his functions as character in and narrator of *Kiss Kiss Bang Bang* merge, he is interrupted by Perry as soon as the detective joins the room, is bossed around and has his mouth held shut by Perry, who takes over as narrator and bids farewell to the audience. Shane Black remarks that "our guy can't even do the narration right, he keeps flubbing it [...] It's like he's ruining his own detective movie" ("Kiss Kiss Bang Bang").

Common to the genre of the film noir is also the femme fatale, an enticing woman who often hires the private eye or seduces an innocent man into committing a crime (Blaser). To restore the "natural" (patriarchal) order, the femme fatale has to die by the end of the movie (Mulvey 840). The femme fatale is often opposed to the character of the nurturing woman, who is an ideal that is unavailable for the hero, and the marrying woman, who threatens the hero's status by trying to domesticate him and place him in his socially prescribed role as breadwinner (Blaser). These typical film noir depictions of women as either saints or whores are deconstructed in *Kiss Kiss Bang Bang*. Harmony's sister Jenna hires Perry to tail Harlan Dexter, but is not setting him up as a witness to murder (thereby endangering him), as Harry and Perry think for most parts of the movie, but to film Dexter having sex with a girl that the little sister believes to be his daughter. Jenna kills herself after hiring Perry, making her a victim of a patriarchal society ruled by people like Harlan Dexter and her father. She is no femme fatale; her demise does not restore order or bring justice—quite the opposite. Still, the role of the victim is a common one for women in crime narratives (Gates 19).

The character of Harmony plays with these stereotypes even more. She asks "private eye" Harry to solve her sister's murder, "hiring" him in a way. Harry also wants to help her because of his feelings for her and the sexual attraction she displays when asking for his assistance. This is a major difference to the femme fatale, who uses her seductive skills actively, whereas an accidental showing of her breast is the only form of aggressive sexual attraction that Harmony displays. Harry and Perry face dangers and imminent death when trying to solve the case of Jenna's murder, but in contrast to the femme fatale, the imminent demise of the detectives is not intended by Harmony—quite the contrary: She actively warns the heroes and comes to their rescue. But Harmony is also neither a nurturing woman nor the marrying kind. As it turns out, Harry can begin a relationship with her, although she has to be won over during the narrative, so she is not as unreachable as film noir's good girls. She actively questions her status as Harry's dream girl: "I am so not who you think I am," thereby challenging her role as the good or nurturing woman of the classic film noir. Some of her actions also deny her status as an idealized, nurturing woman: She accidentally cuts off Harry's finger, does not bring him to the hospital afterward and, on another occasion, leaves the wounded Harry in the back of her car, when she tries to warn Perry. In a darker twist she is also, involuntarily, partly responsible for her sister's death since her lie that Jenna's real father was a movie star set the tragic events in motion. Furthermore, she does not try to pressure Harry into any socially prescribed roles. It is actually Perry who turns to him and says, "Don't steal any more shit. You're not a punk." The fact that Harry announces that their relationship didn't last long also implies that she is not the marrying kind. Thereby *Kiss Kiss Bang Bang* places Harmony in all three classic female roles of film noir at times but ultimately refuses to turn her into any stereotype of the genre, making her a character who challenges these roles, instead.

From Kiss Kiss Bang Bang *to* Iron Man 3

Prior to *Kiss Kiss Bang Bang* Robert Downey Jr. had starred as a sidekick to mentoring characters in films like *True Believer* (1989) and *Air America* (1990). After *Kiss Kiss Bang Bang* he frequently took on leading roles in buddy movies such as *Sherlock Holmes* (2009), *Due Date* (2010) and *Sherlock Holmes: A Game of Shadows* (2011). The hit franchise of the *Iron Man* movies also contains some buddy elements, partnering Downey's Tony Stark with Colonel James Rhodes, played by Terence Howard in *Iron Man* (2008) and Don Cheadle in *Iron Man 2* (2010) and *Iron Man 3*. After doing some uncredited consulting work on the first two installments of the franchise, Shane Black directed *Iron Man 3* and co-wrote the script with Drew Pearce, adapting traits from his earlier movies.

Tony Stark starts off as a traumatized hero in *Iron Man 3* due to his awareness of the existence of entities more powerful than him, such as gods and aliens, and his near-death experience in *The Avengers* (2012), putting him in line with previous heroes of Shane Black movies, including suicidal Martin Riggs from *Lethal Weapon*, who is broken up over his wife's death; drunk and burnt-out private eye Joe Hallenbeck from *The Last Boy Scout*; seemingly cool, but lonely action-movie hero Jack Slater in *Last Action Hero*; amnesiac housewife/former assassin Samantha Caine/Charlene Baltimore in *The Long Kiss Goodnight*; and of course Harry, who is responsible for his partner's death at the beginning of *Kiss Kiss Bang Bang*. Like all of these heroes, Tony Stark manages to cope with his problems and to reintegrate into his social role by the end of the movie. As Black says,

> One of the things I'm most passionate about is the sense that it's never over. No matter how low you go, no matter how long it takes, there's always a chance to bounce back from any adversity, there's always a chance to completely reverse your misfortune, turn your life around, no matter what. And I like to write stories about people who have given up on their lives and then how they gradually acquire a determination, or a knowledge that this is not the end for them, that they still have another chapter ["Shane Black Int."].

Iron Man 3 also focuses more on Tony Stark than on Iron Man: He spends much of the movie not wearing his robotic armor, using guns and other weapons instead, which is more reminiscent of classic action heroes, since they usually rely on physical strength and muscular masculinities (Tasker 73–90), not only on technical gadgets. Black says that *Iron Man 3* succeeds "as a thriller with real characters and real suspense [...] the thriller version, the Tom Clancy/Michael Crichton version of an *Iron Man* movie" ("Iron Man 3"). The movie's finale once again evokes the tropes of action movies of the 1980s and 1990s: It is set in a container harbor, like the showdowns of films such as *Lethal Weapon 2*, *Double Impact* (1991), and *Back in Action* (1993). Also the way that Tony uses his Iron Man suits is paralleled to the use of guns in action movies: They are weapons utilized for a purpose and dropped if they don't function anymore; similarly, Tony isn't bound to one suit as in the previous *Iron Man* movies.

There is also the buddy duo Stark/Rhodes, a salt 'n' pepper team battling the bad guys together. Rhodes had already been Stark's sidekick in *Iron Man* and *Iron Man 2*, providing the occasional banter and comedic interplay in the first two movies. *Iron Man 3*, like its predecessors, uses Rhodes only for parts of the movie, since two thirds of the narrative are basically concerned with Tony being on his own, finding himself and realizing his potential outside of and apart from the Iron Man suit. Like Murtaugh, Rhodes is there to guide the slightly crazy white hero, offering advice in the beginning of the movie, while being a rule-abiding team player: Whereas Tony claims that he has "privatized world peace" in *Iron Man 2*, Rhodes uses his Iron Man suit in service of the government, first as War Machine (in *Iron Man 2*), then as Iron Patriot (in *Iron Man 3*). He listens to Tony's problems, offering free therapy like the sidekicks of cop action films (King 50–54), until he and Tony team up for the last third of the film, which leaves room for buddy movie characteristics: They bicker while fighting villains with or without their suits and save each other's life frequently. Cheadle claims that *Iron Man 3* provided "more opportunity for us to bust each other's chops" (White). He goes on, "The conscience for Tony is kind of what Rhodey provides, and Tony for Rhodey kind of provides someone trying to get him out of his shell" (White). In classic sidekick fashion, Rhodes must complete an important but secondary goal during the showdown (saving the president's life), while it is Tony's duty to defeat the main villain and his band of genetically enhanced super-soldiers.

Here, Black again plays with audience expectations and gender stereotypes: Tony's love interest, Pepper Potts (Gwyneth Paltrow), is abducted prior to the showdown and treated with the same drugs as the villain's soldiers. She falls to her supposed death during the climax, appearing to be just another typical damsel in distress, although she had been awarded some agency in the *Iron Man* trilogy. But Tony cannot defeat the evil genius he is faced with and it is Pepper who comes to his rescue, since she has survived the fall and developed powers of her own, due to her prior treatment with the Extremis virus. She is the one who finally takes out the villain, implying that she is now the more powerful of the two, even on the level of physical strength. As of now it is unclear how this dynamic will develop in possible sequels. A cure for the drugs that empower but also endanger Pepper is mentioned in the film's epilogue, but Tony also destroys his arsenal of Iron Man suits. The film implies that it is not the suit, but his personality that makes him a hero. Robert Downey Jr. has signed on for sequels to the *The Avengers* and the credits of *Iron Man 3* promise, "Tony Stark will return," but it remains uncertain in what way Stark (not Iron Man) will reappear.

Conclusion

Robert Downey Jr. has taken on roles as a team player, as a sidekick, and as a hero in action oriented movies throughout his career, while Shane Black's scripts have shaped, but also played with the buddy cop formula, reflecting different dynamics, hierarchies, and power structures in their various duos; therefore, both Black and Downey are familiar with different facets of the buddy (action) genre. Other cop action movies have cast characters who would traditionally have been sidekicks as their hero (King 47–48) and have played with the conventions of the genre, but none of these films has taken the self-referential negotiations of gender and sexual orientation as far as *Kiss Kiss Bang Bang*. While depicting progressive characters like a gay action hero or a strong female love interest and contrasting them with a male protagonist who is inferior to them in many respects, it also hints at the problems that straight white males, like Harry Lockhart, have when encountering those characters, showing that the conflicting messages of the cop action genre may have taken a new shape—but still dispute the crisis of (white, straight) masculinity which also shapes action movies like *Lethal Weapon* and *Iron Man 3*. While Black subversively reflects on genre and gender in all of his movies, he still cannot escape the genre's dominant ideological concerns.

Notes

1. The rules of this contract are not set in stone: Movies can also violate the genre contract in some ways and still be accepted by the audience as long as they keep up with the genre's general parameters. If a number of genre movies violate a rule frequently, it may also bring about a change of this particular rule within that genre.
2. There is dissent about what exactly constitutes a postmodern movie, although the term is frequently used by film critics and film fans (Eder 9–10). There are, however, certain strategies that have been identified as being typical for postmodern movies such as double coding, intertextuality, anti-conventional narrative structures, self-reference and aestheticization (Eder 11–25). Since *Kiss Kiss Bang Bang* employs a lot of these strategies, it will be viewed as a postmodern movie in the course of this essay without delving into the debate mentioned above.
3. The term diegesis means the level of the narrative within a fictional text. The opposite of the intradiegetic level is the extradiegetic level, which means events that are not described or pictured in the narrative of a fictional text.
4. The concept of the Other refers back to Jacques Lacan, who in his seminar on the mirror stage pointed out that children learn to distinguish between their own body/identity (Self) and those of others (Other) in that stage, which they were previously incapable of (Lacan 1285–1290). This concept can also be applied to a society or social group, in which certain bodies/identities are marked as (an ideal) Self, deviant ones as Other. Regarding cop action movies, King writes, "People in such straits tend to resent 'others': members of the other sex, of another race, nation, religion, or sexuality" (7).

Works Cited

Air America. Dir. Roger Spottiswoode. Kinowelt, 1990. DVD.
Ames, Christopher. "Restoring the Black Man's Lethal Weapon." *Journal of Popular Film & Television* 20.3 (1992): 52–61. Print.
The Avengers. Dir. Joss Whedon. Paramount, 2012. Blu-ray.
Back in Action. Dir. Steve DiMarco, Paul Ziller. One World Entertainment, 1993. DVD
Black, Shane. "Iron Man 3 Director Shane Black Interview." Interview for RedCarpetNews Extra. *You Tube*, 2013. Web. 8 Aug. 2013.
Black, Shane. "Shane Black Int." Interview for LA Shorts Fest. *You Tube*, 2010. Web. 8 Aug. 2013.
Black, Shane. "Shane Black Interview—Kiss Kiss Bang Bang." Interview for ShowbizJunkies. *You Tube*, 2013. Web. 8 Aug. 2013.
Blaser, John J. "No Place for a Woman: The Family in *Film Noir*." *Film Noir Studies*. Ed. John J. Blaser and Stephanie L.M. Blaser, 2008. Web. 13 Jul. 2013.
Chandler, Raymond. *Farewell, My Lovely*. New York: Knopf, 1940. Print.
_____. *The Lady in the Lake*. New York: Knopf, 1943. Print.
_____. *The Little Sister*. Boston: Houghton Mifflin, 1949. Print.
_____. "The Simple Art of Murder." *The Simple Art of Murder*. Boston: Houghton Mifflin, 1950. Print.
_____. "Trouble Is My Business." *Dime Detective Magazine*, Aug. 1939: n. pag. Print.
Die Hard. Dir. John McTiernan. 20th Century–Fox, 1988. DVD.
Double Impact. Dir. Sheldon Lettich. Columbia Tristar, 1991. DVD.
Due Date. Dir. Todd Phillips. Warner, 2010. DVD.
Eder, Jens. "Die Postmoderne im Kino. Entwicklungen im Spielfilm der 90er Jahre." *Oberflächenrausch: Postmoderne und Postklassik im Kino der 90er Jahre*. Ed. Jens Eder. Münster: Lit Verlag, 2002. 9–62. Print.

Fuchs, Cynthia J. "The Buddy Politic." *Screening the Male. Exploring Masculinities in Hollywood Cinema*. Ed. Steven Cohan and Ina Rae Hark. London: Routledge, 1993. 194–210. Print.
Gates, Philippa. *Detecting Women. Gender and the Hollywood Detective Film*. New York: SUNY Press, 2011. Print.
Halliday, Brett. *Bodies Are Where You Find Them*. New York: Dell, 1941. Print.
Hammet, Dashiell. *The Maltese Falcon*. New York: Knopf, 1930. Print.
Iron Man. Dir. Jon Favreau. Concorde, 2008. DVD.
Iron Man 2. Dir. Jon Favreau. Concorde, 2010. DVD.
Iron Man 3. Dir. Shane Black. Concorde, 2013. Film.
King, Neal. *Heroes in Hard Times. Cop Action Movies in the U.S.* Philadelphia: Temple University Press, 1999. Print.
Kiss Kiss Bang Bang. Dir. Shane Black. Warner, 2005. DVD.
"*Kiss Kiss Bang Bang*." Trivia. *IMDb*, n. d. Web. 13 Jul. 2013.
Lacan, Jacques. "The Mirror Stage as Formative of the Function of the I as Revealed in Psychoanalytic Experience." Trans. Alan Sheridan. *The Norton Anthology of Theory and Criticism*. Ed. Vincent Leitch. New York: Norton, 2001. 1285–1290. Print.
Last Action Hero. Dir. John McTiernan. Columbia Tristar, 1993. DVD.
The Last Boy Scout. Dir. Tony Scott. Warner, 1991. DVD.
Lethal Weapon. Dir. Richard Donner. Warner, 1987. DVD.
Lethal Weapon 2. Dir. Richard Donner. Warner, 1989. DVD.
The Long Kiss Goodnight. Dir. Renny Harlin. Warner, 1996. DVD.
Mulvey, Laura. "Visual Please and Narrative Cinema." 1975. *Film Theory and Criticism: Introductory Readings*. Ed. Leo Braudy and Marshall Cohen. New York: Oxford Unversity Press, 1999. 833–844. Print.
Nashawaty, Chris. "The Vanishing." *Entertainment Weekly*, 28 May 2004. 80–85. Print.
The Natural. Dir. Barry Levinson. Columbia Tristar, 1984. DVD.
Night of the Creeps. Dir. Fred Dekker. Sony, 1986. DVD.
Partners. Dir. James Burrows. Paramount, 1982. Film.
Pfeil, Fred. *White Guys: Studies in Postmodern Dominance and Difference*. London: Verso, 1995. Print.
Purse, Lisa. *Contemporary Action Cinema*. Edinburgh: Edinburgh University Press, 2011. Print.
Sedgwick, Eve Kosofsky. *Between Men: English Literature and Male Homosocial Desire*. New York: Columbia University Press, 1985. Print.
Sherlock Holmes. Dir. Guy Ritchie. Warner, 2009. DVD.
Sherlock Holmes: A Game of Shadows. Dir. Guy Ritchie. Warner, 2011. DVD.
Shoot to Kill. Dir. Roger Spottiswoode. Touchstone/Buena Vista, 1988. DVD.
Tasker, Yvonne. *Spectacular Bodies: Genre, Gender and the Action Cinema*. London: Routledge, 1993. Print.
Thunderball. Dir. Terence Young. MGM, 1965. DVD.
True Believer. Dir. Joseph Ruben. Columbia Tristar, 1989. DVD.
Werner, Paul. *Film-noir und Neo Noir*. München: Vertigo, 2005. Print.
White, Brett. "'Iron Man 3' Interview: Don Cheadle Buddies Up with Robert Downey Jr." *MTV.com*, 2013. Web. 8 Aug. 2013.

Getting in Another's Shoes
Clashing Ethics in *Charlie Bartlett*

Fernando Gabriel Pagnoni Berns

In 2007, Jon Poll directed his first (and so far only) feature film, *Charlie Bartlett*, a sophisticated comedy that revolves around a little-worked topic in mainstream cinema: Teenagers do have problems, and they do not revolve solely around sex. Their problems are more related to existential angst manifested in attitudes as "running away from problems, not speaking, brooding, shutting one-self in the bedroom" (Tomas 177) or identity crisis since "adolescence is, by nature, a chaotic time. It is a normal developmental issue. The teen is beginning to form his or her own identity, and in order to do this successfully, the teen begins to resist parental rules" (Stabno and Nagle 75). This denial about adolescence and its problems is striking if we take into account that contemporary Hollywood films are "teen-driven" (Winston Dixton 357) and specially formulated to please a younger audience (Schatz 23), but it is also clear that the studies are prone to a kind of uncommitted cinema which, although it proves profitable, "shr[inks] the author aspirations" (Bordwell 5) and hides the complexities that require more active viewers. Jon Poll's film not only raises questions about the complexities of adolescence, but also shows that the differences between teenagers and adults can be based on ethical differences. Furthermore, the film speaks of the ethical responsibility that comes with every stage of life and every social position and provides a possible solution to the problems created by the clashes between different points of view: putting one momentarily in another's shoes through empathy, which in turn seems to be the basis of any ethics or at least, "relevant to morality" (Slote 127). Poll uses not only the narrative structure, but also the presence of Robert Downey Jr. as the main adult lead to express two clashing ethical viewpoints.

By the time the movie was filmed, the actor's addiction problems were already known worldwide. For that reason, his presence and his portrayal of a character who instructs against the use of substances and asks for responsibility could be seen almost as an ironic postmodern gesture since Nathan's problems mirror those of Robert Downey Jr. Particularly complex is the relationship between the actor's persona and the sense of responsibility that is attributed to public figures by virtue of being public. Are celebrities loaded with an extra quota of ethical responsibility since they "have prominent positions in society" and "clearly exercise power, patronage and influence?" (Crook 99). A highly popular actor followed by millions of fans should give an example of conduct, and perhaps Downey's erratic behavior could be considered non-exemplary. Richard Myatt, for example, does not understand the "ovations" (133) offered to public figures like Robert Downey Jr. since the actor seemed unable to cope with his problems. Many people believe that actors have a responsibility of "good behavior" since they are taken by some viewers as examples of how to behave to be successful, but many forget that celebrities are, above all, individuals, with strengths and weakness. That's when we, as audience members, should try Charlie Bartlett's proposed solution and put ourselves in the other person's shoes and assume, momentarily, the celebrity's position for a better understanding of his or her life's problems. That, of course, is not an easy task to do, because the world which Hollywood's stars inhabit is too far from the immediate reality of most people in the audience, but this is in fact Charlie's proposal: to make such an effort to build a bridge between one's own subjectivity and the subjectivity of others to better understand individuals, for a better society. Nathan Gardner, the character played by Robert Downey Jr., agrees with this idea, but he also suggests that ethics come in part from the sociocultural position that each person holds, and that each position has its own set of responsibilities which, once assumed, allow everyone to begin to understand the subjectivities of others.

Thus, Robert Downey Jr. seems to challenge his audience by telling it that he has assumed his responsibilities, or by admitting (as Nathan Gardner) that he is trying to cope with his problems. Thus, both ethical points of view, rather than being antagonistic, are complementary. When the character assumed by Downey recognizes his faults, he admits them not just to Charlie, but also to the viewers while asking them to, as Charlie proposes, put themselves in the other's shoes before making value judgments.

Reading Charlie Bartlett

Charlie Bartlett (Anton Yelchin) is a young upper-class student who, after being expelled from most of the best private schools, must go for the first time in his life to a state school, the Western Summit High School. There he falls for the beautiful student Susan Gardner (Kat Dennings), who has the disadvantage of being the daughter of Nathan Gardner (Robert Downey Jr.), the school's principal. The relationship between these two men is one of caution at the beginning, but later becomes one of "frenemies," "friends, yet enemies" (Peckham 111). In the case of Charlie and Nathan, it can be further defined as two people who have more in common than not but who nevertheless are antagonistic by virtue of the points of view from which they think and act. Charlie Bartlett and Nathan Gardner embody different ethics but want the same thing: to be appreciated by people.

However, although Charlie and Nathan are not really that different, they can not act together, not just for personal reasons, but because Nathan embodies, in his job, an institution which, like any other "law-making bod[y]" (Graham 12), has rules and regulations that transcend the individuals who work in it. In short, Charlie and Nathan want the same acceptance by and affection of the people with whom they live every day, but they try to get to the same result from different ethical conceptions: Charlie will listen to the people around him, but he will come to understand that listening is not enough of a serious commitment, while Nathan will be obliged to use coercion, only to later understand that a community cannot be settled down by force. The film is far from presenting a simplistic dichotomy, and therein its richness lies. There is no perfect ethical position, especially when dealing with teen problems, largely because teenagers tend to hide their problems from adults, and on many other occasions, adults do not tend to take teens seriously. Even if the adults try to get close and do have knowledge about teen affairs, the problem pointed out by Stabno and Nagle remains, because if part of the construction of identity in adolescence is based upon rebellion against parents and, by extension, all authority figures, then adults cannot successfully find a place from which to provide or suggest solutions. These gaps between different points of views are reinforced by the ethical thinking of the film's characters, by their ways of understanding life, by their actions, and by their faces. In this way, the face of Robert Downey Jr. becomes an admonition about how to behave in life. Nathan Gardner / Downey presents a position that goes beyond the filmic text, which thus becomes what Stephen Mulhall (2007) calls a philosophical exercise.

Gilles Deleuze's concepts about ethics and film can help shed light on the ethics of *Charlie Bartlett*. For the author, ethics are the different views that the characters have in a particular film. These conflicting moral views lead to a confrontation which will serve as an engine for the narration in movement-image based cinema (at least, it is the motor of a narrative film, not necessarily an experimental or avant-garde film). For Deleuze, the long form of the movement-image (which Deleuze contrasts to his much better known formula of time-image) is made up of four ingredients: the milieu, the modes of behavior, the duel, and ethics. The milieu is equivalent to the setting or the situation of a film which tries to "determine the 'situation' of a film, the sense of 'what is going on?' and 'what is at stake?'" (Rushton and Bettison 116). For Deleuze, what happens in the film, the characters' actions, are constantly updated in "determinate, geographical, historical and social space-times" (141) that give meaning to those actions. For its part, the modes of behavior are broadly reducible to the actions of the characters. Then, "the action-image is the relation between the two" (141), the milieu and the modes of behavior. The milieu will provide a challenge to the main character and he or she will respond "to the situation, to modify the milieu, or his [or her] situation with the milieu, with the situation, with other characters" (141).

These ideas are closely related to two others: duels and ethics. According to Rushton and Bettison, "Typical of films of the large form is the conflict between one character or group of characters and another. Often the large form gives rise to a series of duels, that is, a series of conflicts or showdowns between opposing forces which ultimately culminate in a final duel which is designed to settle things once and for all" (117). Here the ethics and their importance appears, since these duels frame "not merely a grudge between two people or groups, but a battle between opposed world views—in short, an *ethics*" (Rushton and Bettison 118). This clash of opposing ethics is the key to any reading of *Charlie Bartlett*. The film is structured on the confrontation between Charlie and the director of the Western Summit High School, an ethical confrontation of two individual views that, deep down, want the same thing.

Charlie lives with his mother, but in this relationship, he is the one who fulfills the mature role, while his father spends some time in jail due to a series of tax crimes. When the film begins, Charlie has been expelled again from a luxury private school and now, with no more places to be sent, will end the year at a public school. The construction of Charlie's character is based on a series of contradictions that combine to form a series of private or internal duels in the boy's subjectivity: brilliant (the director of the school from which Charlie is expelled at the film's beginning recognizes this) but a misfit, unpopular but not shy, self-centered but in a permanent search to interact with others and always ready to help, and teen son but father of his childish mother, Marilyn (Hope Davis). Charlie oscillates between various identifications without getting anywhere, but always with a single purpose: to be popular. Charlie's big fantasy, with which the film opens, shows him standing on a big stage under the glare of several reflectors, while a large audience acclaims his name. In reality, Charlie is expelled from school for having forged a number of driving licenses which he has sold to his companions. His intention, as expressed explicitly by him, was not to make money, but to be loved and accepted by his schoolmates. As Charlie will express later, there is no bigger motivation at his age than popularity. This is Charlie's ethic: the important thing is to be integrated and to be the center of attention; in short, to be popular. This ethic knows no other moral commitments, such as distinctions between right and wrong. If any action helps him become popular, then it is a good action. To Charlie, popularity is the axis around which morality rotates.

It is this ethic that will cause the confrontation with Nathan Gardner, who has passed from being a history teacher to being principal of the institute, but in that action has lost the focus of his life. Nathan is no longer loved by his students because Nathan is now the law within the institution: it is he who embodies it. This new role has alienated him from his daughter who sees that her own place within the school has been predetermined by her father's status. Being the daughter of a teacher is not the same thing as being the daughter of the man who embodies the law within a school, the least popular man. Nathan wants the same thing as Charlie: to be loved. But this does not mean that, like Charlie, Nathan will find any action acceptable if it guides him to obtain this benefit. He, from his position of authority, recognizes that he has a number of responsibilities to fulfill and although to be loved is his ultimate goal, what he, or at least the institution, understands as the greatest benefit for the students must take precedence over his personal desires. Because of what Sarah Wright calls an "agent's social role" (96), the commitments and obligations that come with a certain job or profession chosen by a particular person, and within that profession, the hierarchy of those who practice these obligations, Nathan will always place his obligations before his own desire for popularity.

Charlie, on the other hand, has no moral compass at home who can place his ethics under a critical framework. His mother is his only companion and she is addicted to pills, alcohol, and especially, denial. Charlie constantly asks his mother if she is angry with him, because he knows that she won't show signs of anger: actually, Charlie is asking his mother to get angry and to take responsibility as the only adult at home, but Marilyn is very comfortable in her infant role that depends on Charlie to remind her of the medication schedule. The only time Charlie can act as a teen within his family is in his refusal to visit his father in prison. For the rest of the time, at least at home, Charlie assumes the adult role.

Charlie's presentation in the film's opening scenes is followed by the presentation of his nemesis, Nathan. If the boy belongs to a high class in which money is not a problem, Nathan represents the American middle class. These two presentations work as inverse mirrors: Charlie is responsible for the care of his mother, with whom he does not have an exemplary relationship because she does not recognize her responsibilities as an adult, even if she is always open to dialogue with her son. In fact, the communication between mother and son is excellent. Marilyn just does not want to assume her role. Nathan does recognize his responsibilities as a parent, but Susan, his daughter, will not listen to him, so he cannot act as one. If Charlie's mother is alienated from her role as parent by pills and alcohol, Susan separates herself from her father through the technology that takes her away from the house: to speak with her, Nathan must pass through an always-lit television, blaring music, and a cellular telephone that never rests. Although Susan is in the house, she is always connected with the outside world—not with the only person who lives with her, her father. However, the relationship between father and daughter clearly was not always bad, but was deteriorated by two events: first, Nathan's new position within the institute and second, Susan's mother's abandonment of them. This situation, together with the pressure of his new position, has led Nathan to an incipient alcoholism, a dependence which in turn has expanded the gap between father and daughter. The use and abuse of alcohol and medications to avoid responsibilities or to better support them is, therefore, central in the film.

While Nathan and Charlie seem to be very different, they both desperately seek acceptance. For Charlie, this is his ultimate goal. Not so for Nathan who accepts, reluctantly, his new position as a hated character, especially considering that he is responsible for communicating the news to the students that the school board has decided to place cameras in strategic positions to monitor the students when they are not in class. The intention of this idea is to place the students under a constant surveillance, a sort of panopticon (Foucault 201) which obliges them to behave. If Charlie has not been popular before, now in his new school his relationship with his peers will be more troublesome, since his status as a new rich kid will cause an even bigger gap between him and his classmates. Also, Charlie must confront the school's bully and dealer, Murphy Bivens (Tyler Hilton) and only with the school's fool, Len (Dylan Taylor), will he be able to begin a friendship.

This alienation and lack of empathic relationship between adolescents and adults explodes when Charlie is diagnosed with an attention deficit disorder and, as a solution, Dr. Weathers (Stephen Young), Charlie's psychologist, prescribes him Ritalin, since "a lot of the kids at the colleges are taking this stuff." The tablets are the only solution that the adult world can offer to the teens' problems as a substitute for hearing or understanding them in all their complexity. This recipe will also be Charlie's path to achieve the so-desired popularity. When the pills fill him with unprecedented euphoria, he decides to sell them at school. He will have Bivens' help, who will distribute the drugs in exchange for money. Again, Charlie's intention is not economic, but social. Due to the success of this sale, Charlie will start selling psychotropics to his schoolmates. At first it will be only Ritalin, which causes disinhibition, and *Charlie Bartlett* here may fall into the typical teen film in which the only goal of youth is to have more sex. But when Kip Crombwell (Mark Rendall), a student with serious depressive problems, asks for Charlie's help, Charlie will perform an action that no adult has hitherto done: listen and try to put himself in another's shoes for better understanding. Charlie will notice that Ritalin is not the drug that can cure Kip's problems and, narrating Kip's symptoms to his own psychologist, Charlie gets a better solution: Prozac. Charlie finally finds a solution to his enduring unpopularity: distributing pills in the school. To each student, he provides a different set of drugs. This may be the closest that the students have so far gotten to being listened to, since Charlie doesn't just sell the same drug (such as Ritalin) to everyone, but, after hearing each case, comes up with an individualized drug specific to each teen's problem.

Charlie's solutions to teens' problems can be differentiated from those of Dr. Weathers in two points: First, Charlie takes time to actually listen to others. In addition, he is really interested in their varied problems and, most of all, he tries to relate to others' problems. Consequently, a parade of teenagers begins visiting Charlie's "office" (one of the school's men's toilets) with a wide array of social problems: parents who do not listen to them, chronic depression, sexual identity crises, needs to be loved and respected, promiscuity, anxiety. For each, Charlie obtains a different set of pills after consulting with psychiatrists to whom he narrates the problems of his schoolmates as if they were his own in what could be considered almost a literal way to *put oneself in the place of others*. However, it is possible to observe a significant similarity between Charlie and Dr. Weathers: Both try to solve very complex problems with pills.

While Charlie's popularity grows, so do Susan's feelings for him, attracting the attention of Nathan, who is naturally suspicious of Charlie, given the boy's record. Soon, both men are competing for Susan's attention, with Charlie easily winning the duel. In his willful blindness as far as Charlie is concerned, Nathan ignores the fact that the boy is genuinely interested in Susan and that, as her father, he could do better, and try to put himself in Charlie's place to understand him better. For Nathan, Charlie is a threat because the students begin to rely too heavily on him, thus threatening the discipline of the school. He is both a threat to Nathan's relationship with his daughter and to his authority, which is already questioned from the film's beginning, since Superintendent Sedgwick (Derek McGrath) believes that Nathan needs his presence during the announcement of the cameras so that Nathan will be "taken seriously." The crisis of authority can be observed when, during the announcements about the placement of the cameras, the students rebel in the face of the authority that both the principal and the superintendent represent. After observing that the students do not respect them, the difference in the two men's ethics is clear: Nathan is concerned that the students do not appreciate him, while for the superintendent, the idea that students do not love him is unimportant and almost alien: what he looks for is respect. Nathan also wants respect, but for him, respect is necessarily linked to love. The views of both men are opposed and form a second duel between different sets of ethics which seek the same thing: student welfare.

Both men seek a contractualist rational logic which can serve as a basis for their different ethical postures. The superintendent tries to ensure the social contract using "coercion to advance and protect the general good by compelling individuals to act in accordance with rules whether they want to or not. And this enforcement applies to all, regardless of their rationality because the general good to be realized is in the longer-term interests of everyone" (Graham 172). This logic is not necessarily bad, but it does not work since once again the teens' needs are canceled. This idea of community works if individuals agree to behave under certain rules and regulations that they see as beneficial to their development. Teenagers, however, by reason of their age, understand these rules as harmful and, because of their nature, rebel. They are not interested in being part of a contract, at least until they have been able to establish their own requests too.

Unlike the superintendent or Nathan, Charlie is successful because he actually listens to others' problems and tries to understand them, and that's what they appreciate. In this implicit contract, Charlie wins popularity while teens achieve being heard. The importance of these mutual benefits becomes clear when Charlie ceases selling drugs but his schoolmates continue coming to his "office" in large numbers. Being heard was always what mattered to them. The sale of drugs stops when Kip can no longer dominate his chronic depression and attempts suicide. It is then that Nathan discovers Charlie's role as a supplier of drugs and his antagonism toward the boy reaches its highest level. However, it is not Nathan that really stops Charlie from selling drugs but Charlie's realization of the naked truth: what he provides is not that different from what Dr. Weathers provides as a solution—drugs. Charlie makes a difference when listening to others and placing himself momentarily in another's shoes, but the solution that he provides is ultimately the same one that the adults provide: drugs that mask the source of the problems while not really solving them. Thus, the ethical conflict explodes.

Charlie Bartlett *as a Philosophical Text: Robert Downey Jr.'s Face*

Charlie Bartlett presents two contrasting ethics. For Charlie, all ethics are contingent upon obtaining popularity while Nathan tries to avoid typical authoritarian coercion but doesn't ignore his own position as an agent of authority, his social role. Charlie has achieved his dream to be popular for the first time in his life and has even managed to establish a serious romantic relationship with Susan but to accomplish this, he has had to understand that listening to the problems of others is not always enough if the responsibilities created by listening are not assumed. With Charlie's popularity comes a series of new responsibilities, since his schoolmates are increasingly relying more and more on him, even to make a decision about what to do with the cameras. The speech that Charlie gives to his partners at the end of the film is eloquent: they must make their own decisions and accept the responsibilities attached to these decisions. Furthermore, they must begin to listen to adults. Charlie reminds them that he is just an adolescent, the same as those that follow him, and implicitly calls on them to establish a better relationship with adults. In order to do so, they must find a suitable context of mutual respect in which the dialog can take place. The film therefore works as a philosophical text that speaks about ethics and their conditions.

Charlie Bartlett also works by exceeding the simple enunciation of moral ideas and thinking about itself philosophically. Julian Baggini argues that films, "like philosophy, can offer a reason-giving way of seeing the world truthfully and (locally) coherently" (209). That is, films can be philosophical texts themselves. Although Baggini analyzes in his text the films of the Coen brothers, some ideas in his conclusions can apply to this film. Baggini understands that a film can display ethics and that "morality requires empathy and understanding," since "empathy forms the basis of good ethics" (213). This is in fact the position that Nathan and the film both assume, to try to find a neutral place from where it is possible to listen to and empathize with others. Only then is it possible to maintain a sense of real community or, as Deleuze would define it, a healthy community as opposed to a "pathogenic" (147) one, which comes to degradation by a lack of consent and a superficial illusion of understanding. This is what happens in the first half of *Charlie Bartlett* when adults supplant true understanding with psychotropic drugs that neutralize, but do not solve, teenagers' problems. In fact, for Baggini, "to not listen is to not extend a basic civility which fully recognizes the humanity of others, to act precisely in such a way that leads to evil, because it dehumanizes" (214). The only way to recognize others and their ethics is to listen and understand their positions, even when we do not ideologically share them. To not listen to others denies their moral standpoint.

Baggini continues, in his argument, the ideas of Stephen Mulhall when he says that certain films think philosophically and do not just limit themselves to showcasing the director's ideas. They are capable of reflecting on and evaluating points of view and arguments, and thinking about them in just the ways that philosophers do (209). To do this, a film should consistently establish its ethics (or opposed ethics) and support them with the image editing or some formal element of the film itself. In *Charlie Bartlett*, it is the presence of actor Robert Downey Jr. that transcends the film's ethical positions and makes of *Charlie Bartlett* an ethical exercise.

After Kip's suicide attempt, Nathan visits Charlie and demands of the boy responsibility in his actions since he is now the most popular boy in the school. If Charlie is willing to hear the problems of his schoolmates, he must take responsibility and act like an adult. Nathan makes clear that Charlie's ethics are wrong, at least in some respects, if all his actions are based on whether they help him become popular or not. Charlie has a new social role in the school, a prominent one, and he must make good use of it. Nathan requires maturity from Charlie and maturity means understanding our responsibilities for our own actions. But Charlie denies maturity, arguing, correctly, that he is just a boy and that for him, there is nothing more important than being popular. Here he collides with Nathan's ethics since he too wants to be popular with the kids, but this desire will not prevent him from fulfilling his responsibilities, even when he does not entirely agree with them (the security cameras, for example). In fact, Nathan will only recover a position of empathy with the students in the film's last scene, when he is seen not as a principal but again as a teacher, lecturing and interacting with students after the school superintendent has decided to dismiss him from office.

Downey's presence creates new textures and readings on the film, especially in the scene in which he confronts Charlie about the use and abuse of drugs or alcohol as means of escape: Charlie, who knows of Nathan's alcoholism, confronts him. What moral status does Nathan have to give lectures about dependencies when he himself depends on alcohol to evade pressure? The implications are clear. By the time the film was made and released, Downey's drug dependency and eventual sobriety were well known to most audiences. Therefore, when Nathan instructs Charlie about drug use, this caution order is embodied in Robert Downey Jr. especially in his very expressive face, which is framed in close shots during his speech. According to the philosopher Emmanuel Levinas, it is in the face—"the very beginning of philosophy" (103)—where subjectivity is grounded. For Levinas, all individuals constitute themselves in their sense of responsibility toward others, rather than in their own egos. In other words, a person constructs his or her subjectivity in encounters "face-to-face" with others with whom he or she has a relationship of responsibility. Our responsibility, as individuals, to others, registers on our faces and this sense of responsibility is on the face of Robert Downey Jr. playing the role of Nathan, who ceases to be a character and becomes, by the actions and face of the actor and by his situation, a transcendence that challenges not only Charlie, but also the audience, asking for accountability in our actions.

Furthermore, Deleuze distinguishes, in film, between a "reflecting face" and an "intensive face" (92). Robert Downey Jr.'s face fits into this second category. While the character is reflecting on his own individual responsibilities, the actor's face is intensive because it only refers to himself (the character and the actor), and not to the world, as the reflecting face does. This intensive face functions as the framing of subjectivity (again, that of Nathan / Downey), which is pure affection, severity, recognition of his identity and his personal hell in a "face-to-face" encounter with the viewers. Nathan / Downey are not hypocritical because they recognize that what they do, their dependence, is a weakness. If Charlie's ethics are based on a principle of pleasure (popularity) deciding what is right and what is wrong, Nathan and Downey can recognize their own errors, even if for the moment they cannot cope with them. Mainly, Nathan and Downey must recognize their weaknesses to assume properly their responsibilities, whether these be of an adult in charge of a group of teens, or of a highly popular film star being watched and admired worldwide. Eventually, both Nathan and Robert Downey Jr. will face their problems and overcome them. Robert Downey Jr. will gain immense popularity in his role as Tony Stark in the *Iron Man* saga playing a friendly billionaire playboy prone to alcohol abuse. However, this self-parody role can only take place after the actor's encounter with his own personal hell and after an amount of time that invites proper reflection. Currently, the role of Stark in Robert Downey Jr.'s life mirrors the end of *Charlie Bartlett* when Nathan can now continue his life interacting again with others.

Downey's presence turns Jon Poll's film into a philosophical text that reflects ethically on different points of view on conflict. Through Nathan, Charlie comes to understand his responsibilities as the most popular boy in school, while Nathan eventually understands that the practice of ethics is impossible without first listening to others since that is the basis of morality, as Baggini argues, and, most of all, without first addressing one's own problems. Only placing oneself momentarily in another's shoes and understanding the position of others as one's own (as the most popular kid in school or as a highly popular Hollywood actor) will work as the basis of true ethics.

Works Cited

Baggini, Julian. "Serious Men: The Films of the Coen Brothers as Ethics." *New Takes in Film-Philosophy*. Ed. Havi Carel and Greg Tuck. Hampshire: Palgrave Macmillan, 2011. 207–222. Print.
Bordwell, David. *The Way Hollywood Tells It: Story and Style in Modern Movies*. Los Angeles: University of California Press, 2006. Print.
Charlie Bartlett. Dir. Jon Poll. MGM, 2007. DVD.
Crook, Tim. *Comparative Media Laws and Ethics*. New York: Routledge, 2010. Print.
Deleuze, Gilles. *Cinema 1: The Movement-Image*. Trans. Hugh Tomlinson and Barbara Habberjam. London: Athlone, 1986. Print.
Foucault, Michel. *Discipline and Punish: The Birth of the Prison*. 1975. Trans. Alan Sheridan. New York: Vintage Second Edition, 1995.
Graham, Gordon. *Eight Theories of Ethics*. New York: Routledge, 2004. Print.
Levinas, Emmanuel. *Entre Nous*. Trans. Michael. B. Smith and Barbara Harshav. New York: Columbia University Press, 1985. Print.
Mulhall, Stephen. "Film as Philosophy: The Very Idea." *Proceedings of the Aristotelian Society (Hardback)*. 107.1 (2007): 279–94. Print.
Myatt, Richard. *A Fool's Guide to Wisdom: Finding Discernment in an Age of Fear and Folly*. Xulonpress, 2011. eBook.
Peckham, Aaron. *Mo' Urban Dictionary: Ridonkulous Street Slang Defined*. Kansas City: Andrew McMeel, 2007. Print.
Rushton, Richard, and Gary Bettinson. *What is Film Theory? An Introduction to Contemporary Debates*. Berkshire: Open University Press, 2010. Print.
Schatz, Tom. "The New Hollywood." *Film Theory Goes to the Movies*. Ed. Jim Collins, Hilary Radner, and Ava Preacher Collins. London: Routledge, 1993. 8–36. Print.

Slote, Michael. *The Ethics of Care and Empathy.* New York: Routledge, 2007. Print.
Stabno, Carolee, and Sarah Nagle. "Foster Care: A Developmental Problem." *Art, Angst, and Trauma: Right Brains Interventions with Developmental Issues.* Ed. Doris Banowsky Arrington, IL: Charles C Thomas, 2007. 63–77. Print.
Tomas, Angela. *Youth Online: Identity and Literacy in the Digital Age.* New York: Peter Lang, 2007. Print.
Winston Dixon, Wheeler. "Twenty-Five Reasons Why It's All Over." *The End of Cinema as We Know It: American Films in the Nineties.* Ed. Jon Lewis. New York: New York University Press, 2001. 356–366. Print.
Wright, Sarah, "Virtues, Social Roles, and Contextualism." *Virtue and Vice, Moral and Epistemic.* Ed. Heather Battaly. Malden, MA: Blackwell, 2010. 95–113. Print.

Robert Downey Jr. as Star: The Irreverent Hero of *Iron Man* and *Iron Man 2*

F.E. Pheasant-Kelly

Robert Downey Jr. has been variously described as charismatic, Niven-esque (Wilde), and a performer who has a "humanizing, wiseacre wit" and is drawn to "kooks and oddballs" (Gilbey). His qualities might also be articulated as encompassing vulnerability and resistance to authoritarian figures. Typifying this eclectic polysemy, accounts of the actor range from "perennial bad boy" (Ressner) to "one of the greatest actors of his generation." Certainly, Downey's troubles are well documented and include a childhood during which he was exposed to drugs and, thereafter, parental divorce (CNN). For a while, he lived with his father, who was also a filmmaker, an aspect reflected in the *Iron Man* films in that the father of Downey's character, Tony Stark, is portrayed as an influential figure for his son and is also (like his son) a scientist. Following a succession of successful films, including *Chaplin* (Attenborough, 1992), for which he was nominated for an Academy Award for Best Actor, Downey's life took a downturn and during the late 1990s, he was arrested numerous times for drug and firearms offenses, and eventually imprisoned (Scott).

As Jon Wilde observes of Downey, "so many great, indelible movie performances. So many scandalous, drug-fuelled interludes. For the greater part of the past decade, the focus on him as been fairly evenly split between (1) his reputation as the finest actor of his generation, and (2) his status as the ultimate poster boy for a particularly epic form of Hollywood self-destruction." A number of additional arrests for drug charges ensued, for which he potentially faced further imprisonment and, as David Carr reports, "by 2003 he was an uninsurable serial relapser famous for being pulled out of hotels or other people's homes in an addled, disheveled state," although after rehabilitation, he successfully returned to acting.

Downey's portrayal of Tony Stark in Jon Favreau's *Iron Man* (2008) and *Iron Man 2* (2010) displays features closely corresponding to this image in the presentation of an unconventional superhero who enjoys an extravagant lifestyle and exhibits general qualities of irreverence toward figures and institutions of authority. This rendering of Stark thus reflects Downey's own turbulent personal life, and his star image, public personality, and "real-life persona" therefore seemingly coincide. Using Richard Dyer's study of stars, this essay analyzes

Downey's star persona, drawing on aspects of him as star and as "real person." It focuses on the correspondence of the *Iron Man* narratives with Downey's own experiences, namely Stark's descent into alcoholism, while *Iron Man 2*'s theme of "palladium" toxicity corresponds with Downey's history of drug dependence. Stark's relationship with Pepper Potts (Gwyneth Paltrow) in the third film of the franchise (as opposed to his one-night liaisons in the earlier films) also mirrors Downey's recent personal commitment. Taking into account Dyer's categories of promotion, publicity, criticism and commentaries, and film appearances, this essay examines Downey's structured polysemy as an acclaimed Hollywood star, centering on his characterization in, and audience reception of, *the Iron Man* films.

Star Theory

In his theorizing of celebrity, Dyer explores the concept of the star through both the star image and the star's lived social reality. He proposes that the term "star" encompasses a range of aspects that "consists of everything that is publicly available about stars" (*Heavenly Bodies* 2). Dyer categorizes these aspects into several areas, namely, the films themselves, associated publicity and promotional material produced by the studios, and criticism and commentaries from external sources, as well as the afterlife of the star in other contexts. He thus considers how the concept of the star extends well beyond his or her filmic appearances, noting, "Star images are always extensive, multimedia, inter-textual" (3). In addition, Dyer explains that the elements of a star's persona are not fixed, but are liable to change and a star's history "may outlive the star's lifetime" (3). Indeed, while a 2002 anthology, *Stars in Our Eyes*, focuses on "the tragic drug ordeals of Robert Downey Junior" (Ndalianis and Lenry x), recent accounts are more interested in the fact that Downey is the highest paid actor in Hollywood (Pomerantz), thereby illustrating the shifting signification of a star's image. In differentiating stars' images from their social reality, Dyer proposes stars as economic products in terms of the value that they have in relation to the film, themselves, the studio, and the agent who employs them (5). In short, the celebrity actor is a commodity that is marketed in ways to exploit his or her specific characteristics and qualities. Indeed, as Paul Scott reports, "Downey [...] admits he is now considered not so much an actor but a 'strategic cost' to the big money corporations who employ him—and rake in billions from his films."

Nonetheless, the star is different from the ordinary performer because his or her attributes move beyond merely being commodities and carry an extensive range of meanings. Dyer describes these connotations through the concept of a "structured polysemy" which points to "the multiple but finite meanings and effects that a star image signifies" (*Stars* 72). He goes on to explain that these signifiers are structured because of their relationship with each other, and the fact that they may be mutually reinforcing. Alternatively, "the elements may be to some degree in opposition or contradiction, in which case the star's image is characterized by attempts to negotiate, reconcile or mask the difference between the elements, or else simply hold them in tension" (72). The associations attached to the star's image may be either convergent with his or her private existence, or, in other cases, may be opposed. In respect to Downey's role in the *Iron Man* franchise as Tony Stark, this essay locates a convergence between the character of Stark and Downey as performer, a crossover that seems a perfect "fit" and has led to widespread critical acclaim and commercial success for both Downey and the *Iron Man* trilogy.

Audience Reception

The first film of the franchise, *Iron Man*, followed several other commended works for Downey, including *The Singing Detective* (Gordon, 2003), *Good Night and Good Luck* (Clooney, 2005), *A Scanner Darkly* (Linklater, 2006), *Fur* (Shainberg, 2006), *Kiss Kiss Bang Bang* (Black, 2005), and *Zodiac* (Fincher, 2007). However, *Iron Man* outperformed each of these at the box office, having the third highest grossing opening weekend of 2008 behind *Indiana Jones and the Crystal Skull* (Spielberg) and *The Dark Knight* (Nolan) and the twenty-sixth highest opening weekend of all time (boxofficemojo.com). Its sequel was released in 2010 with a third production in 2013. *Iron Man 2* outperformed the first film, becoming the fourth highest grossing film of 2010, and currently twelfth in the highest grossing weekends of all time (*boxofficemojo*). It presently ranks at position 74 in all-time highest grossing worldwide box office while *Iron Man 3* (Black, 2013) is the most lucrative of the franchise, having the second highest opening weekend of all time and now the status of being the fifth highest grossing film worldwide (boxofficemojo.com).

These achievements may in part reflect the more generalized box office dominance of superhero films in the new millennium. However, audience blogs indicate that Downey has been instrumental in the films' successes, with IMDb revealing widespread audience praise for his performance. This reception corresponds with earlier sentiments in 2001 when an article in the *Wall Street Journal* (Satel), which criticized Downey's "decision" to take drugs, prompted strong, defensive reactions from readers in support of Downey. Equally supportive of Downey are audience blogs in response to *Esquire*'s feature about him in May 2012, with comments such as, "Downey's resurrection following his incarceration is the greatest second act in motion picture history. While no-one questioned his extraordinary talent, the fact that he is now the cornerstone of two phenomenally successful franchises: *Iron Man* [...] and the *Sherlock Holmes* films, is simply remarkable"; "Downey was a revelation"; and "I thank god every day that Mr. D has embraced recovery so we can continue to see his amazing work on the big screen. And NO-ONE gives better interviews. He makes me laugh more than any other entertainer" (Fussman). While the third film was the highest grossing of the trilogy, the first film remains the most popular according to IMDb, which rates it at 7.9/10, and, of 982 viewer responses, 645 were positive. *Iron Man 2* ranks at 7.0/10, and of 680 reviews, 390 viewers gave positive responses. *Iron Man 3* is rated at 7.4/10, but of 1045 viewers, only 341 enjoyed the film. However, even where reviews of the films are negative, criticism centers on narrative flaws and plot implausibility, with Downey remaining popular, indicated by comments such as "Downey is magnetic." These commentaries about Downey invariably take into account his troubled past and his ability to recover from it, these aspects persistently emerging in blogs, publicity, and promotional material.

Promotion

Indeed, studio publicity and promotion strategies have not attempted to disguise Downey's past, but have capitalized on it. In differentiating publicity from promotion, Dyer explains that the latter generally includes "i) material concerned directly with the star in question—studio announcements, press handouts (including potted biographies), fan club publications [...] pinups, fashion pictures, ads in which stars endorse a given merchandise, public appearances [...] and ii) material promoting the star in a particular film—hoardings, magazine ads, trailers" (*Stars* 68). In the case of *Iron Man*, promotion was tied closely to product placement which targeted an "all-ages, but largely male audience [but] the title character, a multimillionaire inventor played by Robert Downey Jr. was a key selling point in partner deal making for Paramount" (Stanley). The film's promotion began with a Super Bowl and extended "through broad-based promotions at 6400 7-Eleven convenience stores and global campaigns with Burger King and Audi" (Stanley). Its release was planned for May 2 to avoid clashes with other blockbusters scheduled including *Indiana Jones and the Kingdom of the Crystal Skull* and *The Dark Knight*.

The promotional trailer for the first film also includes product placement, with a zoom to close-up of an Audi opening the visuals. Thereafter, the preview addresses various facets of Downey's star persona through a montage that first sees Stark dressed in a black dinner suit and then descending from a private jet, these aspects emphasizing Stark's (and Downey's) charismatic, "playboy" persona. The "Jericho" scene follows, after which we see Stark drinking a glass of whisky. An edit to a stylized extreme close-up of Stark's anxious-looking eyes then

Tony Stark (Downey) perfects the Mark II suit in the first *Iron Man* (2008), directed by Jon Favreau.

conveys his (and Downey's) vulnerability, accompanied by a voiceover that states, "I should be dead already." Thereafter, rock music accompanies digital imagery of Iron Man in flight. The trailer briefly features other protagonists but focuses mostly on the diverse aspects of Downey's persona as mediated through his portrayal of Stark. In fact, a 2006 press release by Kevin Feige of Marvel Studios comments that "Downey's versatility sets him apart and makes him an ideal fit to play such a complex character as Iron Man" (*Breaking News.ie*).

As an established product, *Iron Man 2* attracted yet more marketing partners, with one executive justifying their investment on the grounds that "Tony Stark is this likeable fun human character who doesn't take himself overly seriously but takes his work very seriously. He has fun doing it but yet the products he creates are the very best of the best" (qtd. in Hampp). The cast of *Iron Man 2* promoted the film at Comic Con in San Diego in 2009 where the first of two trailers was exhibited. A second preview accompanied the film *Sherlock Holmes* (also starring Downey), when it was released in 2009. The trailers feature quotes from Tony Stark, including "It's good to be back" and "I am Iron Man—the suit and I are one," these statements ironically relating to Downey's own life. Stark's "playboy" aspects are still evident, but these visuals intercut with imagery of him wearing a vest while welding. The latter image not only accentuates his muscular physique, but also conveys him as ordinary and hard working. This ordinariness, together with the diverse range of characteristics and associations that constitute Downey's real persona—such as his healthy lifestyle preoccupations, an inclination for humor and wit, repeated mention of bodily function, and fine art appreciation—are also consistently evident in, and central to publicity material.

Publicity

Downey has undertaken numerous interviews, appearing in newspapers, high-profile journals directed at women, such as *Vogue*, and more male-oriented sources such as *Esquire* and *GQ*. In distinguishing this more generalized publicity from promotional material, Dyer explains that it "is not, or does not appear to be, deliberate image–making. It is 'what the press finds out,' 'what the star lets slip in an interview,' and is found in the press and magazines" (*Stars* 69). In other words, it is controlled information that does not appear to be. According to Dyer, such material gives the audience the impression that they are afforded "a privileged access to the real person of the star" (69). This often seems to be the case in interviews with Downey, where there is candor about and consistent reference to a troubled past that he has left behind, though he mostly refuses to give details of his prison experiences. Even so, in a much earlier interview in *Time* in 1998 shortly after his release from his first prison sentence, he was more unguarded about his tribulations and reveals that "it was awful, it was highly personal, it had a direct correlation to the effects of a disease" (qtd. in Ressner). Downey concludes the interview by saying, "I'm enjoying life again. I can't tell you what a pleasure it is just to take a nice shower. It's so cool—using a hairdryer again, good towels." Such comments convey Downey's ordinariness and a sense that we are accessing the "real" person. In conversation with David Carr, Downey also states, "You can't go from a $2,000-a-night suite at La Mirage to a penitentiary and really understand it and come out a liberal. You can't. I wouldn't wish that experience on anyone else, but it was very, very, very educational for me and has informed my proclivities and politics ever since." In a round table interview with David Ansen in *Newsweek* (2009), Downey further elaborates on his criminal past, though cloaks it in humor when describing a press visit to Japan after the opening of *Iron Man*. Stopped at immigration for his "incredible criminal activity," Downey reports, he was told never to return to Japan. In the same interview, as in others, there are references to bodily function, which lends a corporeality to Downey not usually associated with stardom. Often these references are linked with his prison experience. Additionally, in interview with *Guardian* reporter Jon Wilde in 2003, Wilde describes him as "touchingly modest about his talents and achievements [...] ask him for a list of his worst movies and he'll say 'If I get started on that one, I'll never stop." Wilde details how Downey has changed with the help of holistic therapies and yoga, though Downey qualifies this by saying, "That's not to say I'm in the clear yet. I might be shifting out of it, but I'm still the same guy that did all that crap" (qtd. in Wilde).

Despite his prison history, *Vogue* has featured Downey several times, once in 2006 under the headline "an exceptional talent" (Buck) and later, in 2009, when he was photographed by Mario Testino and interviewed by Sophie Dahl with the headline, "From superhero to Sherlock, Robert Downey Jr. has been on a tear, propelled by a tireless work ethic and a dedication to the simplest details." Like Wilde, Dahl also notes Downey's self-deprecation and wit, and comments on his "cornucopia of naturopathic remedies" (Dahl). In a similar vein, Mim Udovitch of the *New York Times* describes Downey as "a warm presence, and the extraordinary charm of his conversation, full of quicksilver feints away from ego, is almost impossible to render in print." Udovitch goes on to comment on the apparent normalcy of Downey's current domestic life, and concludes the interview with a quote from Downey: "I know I am currently embracing a much more authentic and much less complex me. One that doesn't have to hold on to that thing, the part of my whole package that is that I'm this wild, unpredictable, tragic and self-destructive guy. It's so passé but it did work for me. Now I am culpable and accountable for things that got me to the impasse where I was just running, running, running with nothing to show for it." In a more recent interview (April 2013) at Downey's Malibu home, Chris Heath also notes Downey's pill bottles containing "anti-parasitics and anti-virals," again accentuating his preoccupation with physicality and health. Here, Downey discusses his role in the *Iron Man* franchise and his determination to get the role of Tony Stark despite Marvel's statement that "under no circumstances are we prepared to hire him for any price" (qtd. in Heath). Downey's ordinariness is further manifest when he states, "Nothing pleases me more when somebody who was awe-inspired to be working with me realizes I'm just another schmuck that they're bored of hanging out with on a set. I love that moment. I like it when that persistent illusion is smashed." This ordinariness surfaces again when, partway through the interview, he asks his wife, with regard to their one-year-old son, "How did my diaper hold up?" At the opposite end of the "real person" spectrum, the interview also discloses Downey's appreciation and collection of fine art, a detail that emerges in his characterization of Stark. Overall, therefore, publicity sources emphasize Downey's turn to a healthy lifestyle, his charm and ordinariness, his art appreciation, and a sense of his physicality. These attributes, which illustrate Downey's complexity as real person, consistently channel into his star image, especially in his portrayal of Stark.

Critical Reception and Commentaries

Dyer's third category includes material "said or written about the star in terms of appreciation or interpretation by critics and writers [...] and is found in film reviews, books on films [...] [and] film, radio and television profiles of stars" (*Stars* 71). Dyer indicates that criticism and commentaries are aligned with audience reception rather than the industry, and often express a commonly held view of the star. He adds that "More frequently, however, they contribute to the shaping of 'public opinion' about a star" and thus differentiates between criticism and commentaries and promotion and publicity. He contends that the gap between the two "accounts both for the complexity, contradictoriness and 'polysemy' of the star image and also for the capacity of critical opinion to contribute to shifts in careers" (72). If commentaries about Downey repeatedly address his troubled past, critical reception of his role in the *Iron Man* films is universally positive and generally mirrors audience responses. For instance, the *Mid-Devon Gazette* comments that "The magic ingredient in both Iron Man movies [1 and 2] is Robert Downey Jr." while the *Financial Times* considers that "Robert Downey Jr. [is] an intriguing, even bold piece of casting"; Kim Newman of *Sight and Sound* remarks of *Iron Man* that "it has Downey's spirited turn going for it"; of *Iron Man 3*, Philip French of the *Observer* describes "standout performances from Robert Downey Jr. and Ben Kingsley"; and the *Telegraph*'s Robbie Collins comments, "Downey too has quips on quick-draw, and is utterly at home in the part of Stark. At this point, Downey is as important to the franchise as Sean Connery was to Bond." Such observations typify critical reception of the films, and even where reviews are unfavorable, a common refrain is that Downey is ideally suited to the role because of his own history.

Films

If promotional materials and publicity help to shape a star's image, films are pivotal to it, and indeed, may be constructed around the star's persona. When this is the situation, Dyer explains that the film is essentially a vehicle for the performer, and "[s]tories might be written expressly to feature a given star [and] sometimes, alterations to the story might be effected in order to preserve the star's image" (*Stars* 70). This is precisely the case in the *Iron Man* franchise, in which aspects of *mise-en-scène*, narrative, and characterization were adjusted to accommodate Downey's persona, with Downey himself often improvising on the script. Specifically, the way in which the trajectory of the trilogy traces the changed attitudes of Tony Stark resembles Downey's own past because, for Thomas Ambrose, "in many ways, Downey Jr. is the perfect Tony Stark. He's suave, intelligent and charismatic, he's done the hell raising thing" (69). The first *Iron Man* film particularly seems to re-enact Downey's life in the way that Stark, a wealthy industrial entrepreneur and weapons designer, spends three months in captivity and then re-evaluates his existence and moral values. As Gilbey observes, "The preening smugness [Downey] lends Stark draws on his own complacency in the years leading up to that protracted fall from grace [...] He has tasted a world beyond privilege, and it shows." Indeed, the franchise's overall success and the particular accomplishments of the third film mirror the concurrent upturn in Downey's personal life and confirm him as a significant box office attraction. In this sense, he fulfills Dyer's concept of star as commodity and, as Tim Robey states with respect to *Iron Man 2*, "with his newfound bankability and knowingly debauched charm, [Robert Downey Jr]'s absolutely the right star to do this. He's essential to everything that's pretty entertaining about Jon Favreau's [film]—basically its winking awareness of what an obscenely expensive corporate product is in itself."

One might argue that any actor could have played Iron Man, since the armored suit effectively effaces performer identity. However, this is not the case, since Downey as Stark spends more time not in the suit, and even when wearing it, there is still a sense of his resistance to authoritarian figures, his sardonic wit, and his pushing of boundaries—for instance, during *Iron Man*, he instructs Jarvis (his robotic computerized assistant, voiced by Paul Bettany) to propel him higher into the stratosphere despite the knowledge that dangerous ice problems might imperil his flight. As previewed in the trailer, the film opens with Stark promoting a new missile called the "Jericho" in Afghanistan when his team comes under attack from a group of insurgents who attempt to kill him with one of his own explosive devices. Initially, Stark is portrayed as "an entertaining but unpleasant fellow, smarmily dismissing interview questions about the ethics of arms dealing and then seducing the reporter, strutting into a war zone with a drink in his hand, and exploiting his admiring but skeptical gal Friday" (Newman 60). However, if it resembles other new millennial fantasies in its allusions to 9/11, Iron Man's opening departs from them in its realistic effects and semblance to a war movie, mediated through handheld camera and a *mise-en-scène* of military vehicles and U.S. army personnel set against a backdrop of Afghanistan. These aspects initially immerse the viewer in a seemingly realistic version of the war on terror, until the diegetic sound of loud rock music and a close-up of a whisky glass, followed by an edit to Stark holding the glass, evidence his unconventional sensibilities. Just as the camera cuts to frame Stark, we observe a young soldier studying him closely, leading Stark to comment, "I feel like you're driving me to court martial. This is crazy. What did I do?" (a question ironically relevant to Downey's own history of repeated arrest). His comments to another marine (who is wearing full combat gear, and therefore leads Stark to assume the soldier is a man) also prove amusing if contentious: "Good god, you're a woman! You have excellent bone structure, there. I'm having a hard time not looking at you now," he quips, his sexist observations rendered humorous because the female soldier to whom he addresses the comments appears flattered and also laughs. The spectator, who has been led to make a similar assumption concerning the soldier's gender, is also compelled to look at her, and so identifies with Stark. Mention of Stark's association with *Maxim*'s cover models further alludes to his "playboy" tendencies and his obliviousness to their war zone situation. This lighthearted tone, however, quickly dissipates as a roadside explosion kills most of the army personnel within the vehicle. Kinetic, unsteady cinematography with rapid editing and sounds of gunfire set against imagery of fireballs and explosions continue to enforce its realism. As the sole survivor from the vehicle, Stark escapes, only to see a missile land close by. The camera rapidly zooms into a close-up of the device, disclosing the words "Stark Industries" etched on its side, before it detonates and fires shrapnel at him. In emphasizing the irony of being wounded with one's own weapons, the close-up inevitably acknowledges general perceptions of Western complicity in arming Iraq and Afghanistan, corresponding metaphorically with Downey's self-destructive behavior concerning drugs and alcoholism.

Following the missile detonation, an overhead camera perspective reveals Stark's bleeding wounds before the screen cuts to white, and the distant muffled sound of foreign voices becomes audible, indicating his loss of consciousness. Slowly coming into focus, a cut to close-up shows Stark's face, now disheveled and unshaven before the film rewinds to Las Vegas thirty-six hours earlier. Here, a montage video sequence, which is being projected to celebrate Stark's meteoric rise to success, appropriates a style of exaggerated excessiveness that parodies show-time celebrity culture, and informs the spectator that "Tony Stark has changed the face of the weapons industry by ensuring freedom and protecting America and her interests around the globe." The montage incorporates an image of Stark as a child (actually a real photograph of Downey as a child), followed by one of his father, and we learn that he is a "chip off the old block," an aspect that would not be lost on Downey's fans who realize that his father was also a drug addict. Stark's upward trajectory is also indicated by an image (within the video montage) of a front cover of *Forbes*, a finance and business magazine, which ironically recently reported Downey's top earnings (2013). There is therefore sustained narrative congruence between Stark as character and Downey as star. Although Colonel Rhodes (Terrence Howard), friend and military colleague of Stark, announces Stark as the recipient of an award and the entire event centers on Stark, he fails to appear. Just as Obadiah Stane (Jeff Bridges), who accepts the award on Stark's behalf, says, "the best thing about Tony is also the worst thing. He's always working," a camera edit reveals Stark gambling in a casino, surrounded by a host of glamorous women. Thereafter, Stark seduces *Vanity Fair* reporter, Christine Everhart (Leslie Bibb), again more than coincidental given that Downey has been interviewed by *Vanity Fair* on several occasions. The reporter awakens in Stark's technology-controlled Malibu mansion (also the location of Downey's home) which reflects not only on the excesses of Western culture, and on the West's affinity for technology (and weaponry), but also mirrors the hedonism of Downey's earlier life. The setting is a particular example of how the *mise-en-scène* was tailored to Downey's star image. J. Michael Riva, the production designer, explains that "Robert Downey Jr. comes with a certain vulnerability with him and it may sound strange but we redesigned the notion of the house after casting him. I thought that he would be more suitable in something that architecturally mirrored who he was, a little softer inside, a little more susceptible, a little more vulnerable. There was a certain vulnerability about him so I thought, round is nice […] and it just seemed a little bit more womb-like."

An indication of Stark's preoccupation with excess and technology is furthered when Pepper Potts, his personal assistant, reminds him that his private plane was due to leave several hours earlier. Stark's response of "That's funny, with it being my plane and all..." not only indicates his extravagance, but also his irreverent attitude toward friends (since Rhodes is waiting to accompany him on the flight). Just as Stark is about to leave, Potts also asks him if he wants to buy a "Jackson Pollock" that is "incredibly overpriced." Stark whimsically instructs her to "buy it, and store it," suggesting it merely as an investment and display of wealth rather than exhibiting any knowledge of, or interest in its artistic merit. The scene thereby highlights his unpleasant materialistic inclinations and serves to further shore up notions of him as decadent and money-oriented. It also has a connection to Downey as real person in the latter's interest in collecting fine art.

Stark then speeds to the airstrip in an Audi sports car, the cinematography first deploying an extreme low angle long shot of the approaching vehicle before cutting to show it disappearing into the distance, thereby emphasizing its speed (and hence accentuating Stark's thrill-seeking, profligate tendencies). His playboy associations specifically materialize when aboard his private jet with Rhodes when he instructs one of the hostesses to "heat up the sake" and, despite Rhodes' protests, a further edit then discloses the two men drinking, the plane now accommodating a large video screen as backdrop, and their conversation barely audible above loud diegetic music. A slow zoom out subsequently reveals the previously demure and polite air stewardesses with their shirts tied up to expose their abdomens drinking and dancing provocatively around a central pole. (Favreau consistently encouraged improvisation and this scene provides another example of the way in which the *mise-en-scène* was adapted to reference Downey's 'bad boy' image).

Aside from keeping Rhodes waiting for three hours and being entertained by the pole dancing stewardesses, Stark continues his show-time behavior on arrival in Bagram by his display of the destructive capacity of his new weapon, the Jericho. As he begins his presentation of the weapon to the troops, he comments, "I prefer the weapon you only have to fire once. That's how Dad did it. That's how America does it [...] Find an excuse to let one of these off the chain and I personally guarantee you the bad guys won't even want to come out of their caves." Once more, the film references Tony following in his father's footsteps while the camera then cuts to a close-up of the soldiers as they turn their heads in unison to watch the weapon's performance. The rocket launcher rises up and a low camera angle looks upward at the missiles as they launch. As the camera then cuts back to Stark, the missiles still travelling mid-air, he announces dramatically, "For your consideration, the Jericho" and spreads his arms in a cruciform shape (implying that he perceives himself as a savior) just as the weapons crash behind him in the mountains. Stark's behavior is consistently exaggerated and the film's reflexive nature suggests Downey's own performance as Stark. If Stark's fascination with weaponry reflects U.S. preoccupations, it also calls to mind Downey's arrest in 1996 for firearms possession (Smith) and his words may remind viewers (or industry insiders) of the "For your consideration" ads taken out for actors during awards season.

After detonating the missile, Stark then nonchalantly opens a chiller cabinet and pours himself a whisky, narratively indicating his lack of regard for the implications of the missile's destructive capacity but also alluding to Downey's history of alcoholism. This style of deliberate excess serves to convey how far Stark's personality changes during the narrative, reflecting accounts of Downey that describe him as "The star who came back from the depths" (Smith). Indeed, these opposing representations, which materialize as the narrative progresses, distinctly resemble Downey's changed behavior and fortunes.

The ensuing scene subsequently reverts to the present and to a disturbing sequence as Stark experiences flashbacks and intermittent consciousness. A montage of dark shadowy images of a wounded Stark, seen from directly overhead, includes close-ups of his bloody injuries, "double-vision" images, bright lights, and out-of-focus, unsteady camerawork accompanied by screaming and other distorted sounds. The scenes provide a distinct contrast with the confident, self-assured celebrity of the previous sequence and, when Stark regains consciousness, he discovers that an electromagnet has been inserted into his chest to keep him alive. He is being held prisoner by Afghani insurgents, and, while reflecting Post–9/11 political issues, such scenes also call to mind Downey's real-life incarceration. When Stark refuses to reconstruct the Jericho missile, the insurgents "water-board" him, echoing the interrogation techniques deployed at U.S. terrorist detention camps and involving Stark in near-death experiences that also resonate with Downey's past. Certainly, the motif of physical vulnerability and bodily contamination recurs throughout the franchise. Here, the notion of toxicity corresponds with reports of Downey's addiction to drugs and alcohol, especially since, when Dr. Yinsen (Shaun Toub) (who saves Stark) tells him they had met previously, Stark replies, "I don't remember." "Oh, you wouldn't. If I had been that drunk I wouldn't have been able to stand," Yinsen responds. (Clearly, this comment is grounded in reality since, despite Downey's addictions, he successfully performed roles in films including *Home for the Holidays* (Foster, 1995) while under the influence.)

The insurgents continue to demand that Stark recreate the Jericho missile for them, and provide him with the materials to do so. With the aid of Yinsen, who has implanted the arc reactor into his chest and saved his life, and, under pretense of building the missile, he instead constructs a prototype weaponized suit and uses it to blast his way out of the cave. The sequence, which renders him as a manual worker—he arc-welds and casts various devices—indicates his ordinariness, ingenuity, and ability to recover from impossible situations with the minimum of resources, again corresponding with Downey's own reversal from dire circumstances. While Stark escapes after three months, Yinsen is fatally wounded, and his dying words to Stark when he goes back to rescue him (in one of Stark's first acts of selflessness and humility) are, "Don't waste your life." Stark's changed persona further surfaces when he is airlifted by his army friend, Rhodes, and, whereas previously he has been rude and arrogant to him, he now embraces him. He abandons the weapons program, telling the press in an informally convened press conference, "I saw young Americans killed by the very weapons I created to defend and protect them and I saw that I had become part of a system that is comfortable with zero accountability." Stark's moral epiphany is further highlighted when he tells Potts, "I shouldn't be alive unless it was for a reason. I just finally know what I have to do" (meaning that he intends to destroy all the weapons that he has manufactured), while he informs Stane that he is "being responsible. That's a new direction for me." The implication of this statement is identical to that noted in interview with Udovitch when Downey stated, "Now I am culpable and accountable."

Although Stark has survived his three months in captivity, his physical vulnerability becomes apparent when he asks Potts to assist him with replacing the original arc reactor in his chest with a more sophisticated version. Potts has to remove the wire from inside the reactor shell within Stark's chest but accidentally touches the sides, thereby triggering an electric shock. She then mistakenly takes out the magnet, causing Stark's heart to dysfunction though, as she inserts the replacement reactor, Stark jumps up, appearing fully restored, the arc burning brightly. This wounding scenario recurs toward the end of *Iron Man* when it transpires that his work colleague, Stane, is still secretly supplying Stark weapons to the Ten Rings insurgents and has conspired with them to assassinate Stark. Stane attacks Stark, temporally paralyzes him (again, ironically, with a device designed by Stark), and then removes the arc reactor from Stark's chest, incapacitating him. Close-ups of Stark disclose his ashen face as he gasps for breath and his clothes are drenched with sweat. He barely manages to survive by replacing the stolen reactor with the original prototype device, yet, even though his physical vulnerability is therefore repeatedly accentuated in each of these near-death experiences, he makes a complete recovery. Downey himself comments, "Probably the biggest thing that Tony Stark and I have in common is the hardware of conflict, the courage under fire" (qtd. in Carr).

As a weapons expert, Stark is incongruously accorded celebrity status, and when he "crashes his own party" at a firefighters fundraiser (because Stane is trying to exclude the morally reformed Stark from the public face of Stark industries), allusions to Hollywood abound. A constant flashing of press cameras, a red carpet entrance, and screaming female fans mimic Downey's real-world status as star. At the fundraiser, Stark learns from *Vanity Fair* reporter, Christine Everhart, that Stane is still supplying weapons to terrorists and takes action, signaling his newfound compassion and further deviating from the playboy persona implied at the film's outset. Stark uses the upgraded Iron Man armor to return to Afghanistan to attack the Ten Rings, the group of fighters who had captured him previously and who are now terrorizing villagers in Gulmira (the village where Yinsen's family lived) in scenes of slaughter resembling war-on- terror media footage. Iron Man saves the villagers and incinerates the weapons depots in spectacular fireballs. The sequence which details the insurgents' attacks on locals is extended and invites viewer sympathies through close-ups of children screaming for their father. As Stark, in the guise of Iron Man, kills the insurgents, a medium close-up lingers on a young boy embracing his father, thereby accentuating their father-son relationship (reiterating a common thread throughout the franchise). On completing his mission, Stark is attacked erroneously by the U.S. military, and when he returns home, Potts inadvertently observes him as his Iron Man armor is being removed. "Are those bullet holes?" she asks, appearing horrified, to which Stark quips, "Let's face it, this is not the worst thing you've caught me doing," his response seeming to allude to Downey's personal life. As David Carr of the *New York Times* observes, "That running dialogue—between audience and actor, between Mr. Downey's past and present—gives the film a symbolic power not usually found in comic book movies." The film's closing scenes appear to correspond even more closely with Downey's own past when he makes an "unscripted" announcement at a press conference, declaring, "I'm just not the hero type. Clearly. With this laundry list of character defects, all the mistakes I've made, largely public," reflecting ironically on Downey's own life. Even though Rhodes instructs him to 'just stick to the cards, man," Stark declares, "The truth is… I am Iron Man." This latter sequence reflexively comments on the film's improvisation and the convergence between Downey as star image and real person, as well as his refusal to conform.

Iron Man 2

The second film follows in a similar vein and the show-time aesthetics recur as Stark appears in another celebrity role at an expo in New York. Indeed, his opening speech seems autobiographical for Downey: "I'm not saying that from the ashes of captivity, never has a greater phoenix metaphor been personified in human history." The theme of bodily wounding also continues in the second film, which begins where the first ends, with Stark now being slowly poisoned by the palladium that powers the arc reactor in his chest. We therefore see him regularly monitoring the palladium toxicity of his blood. A close-up of the monitoring device reveals the words "blood toxicity" and inevitably summons analogies with Downey's history of substance abuse. He also needs to drink a chlorophyll concoction to counter the effects of the palladium (reflecting Downey's own rehabilitation and his preoccupation with vitamin and health pills), and he learns from Jarvis that "the device that is keeping [him] alive is also killing [him]."

Because of Stark's continuing work on the Iron Man suit, he is handed a subpoena to attend the Senate Armed Services Committee where, in its allusion to the war on terror, the film essentially parodies the justification for the invasion of Iraq. Stark's contempt for authoritarian figures is apparent when he responds to Senator Stern's (Garry Shandling) questions with "Yes, dear." While the sequence parodies the Colin Powell interview when the case for invading Iraq was put forward, it simultaneously continues to evoke Downey's disregard for authority as Stark then remotely commandeers the video screen. He summons up images of destruction caused by malfunctioning Iron Man copies in North Korea and Iran, and points out to the Senator their obviously greater threat. The excessive "playboy" characterization of Stark amplifies the implied criticism of the Iraq invasion even more, and he makes the politicians' claims seem ridiculous, summarizing his senate committee appearance with the words, "If there's one thing I've proven, it's that you can count on me to pleasure myself."

Even as he faces the prospect of his demise caused by the palladium contamination, Stark throws a party to which he invites dozens of girls, gets drunk, and dances in his Iron Man suit, presenting an unpalatable aspect of the Stark persona (possibly responsible for the fact that *Iron Man 2* is rated as the least popular of the trilogy). During the course of the party, he partially destroys his luxury Malibu home and, because he is facing imminent death, gives away his entire art collection and hands over the company to Potts. Although he saves himself by creating a new element to substitute for palladium (trying it out in a high-inducing test probably reminiscent of the actor's past experimentation with different drugs), *Iron Man 3* completes Stark's reformation from playboy persona to compassionate individual because he relinquishes his Iron Man armory and personal possessions. At the same time, the theme of bodily wounding and contamination gives way to more profound psychological vulnerability and Stark suffers regular anxiety attacks, chiming with reports of such disorder in soldiers returning from Iraq and Afghanistan, while also reflecting Downey's own history.

The overall trajectory of the trilogy therefore represents Stark as a changed character who realigns his moral compass. He becomes caring, compassionate, and less materialistic, seeming untroubled by the fact that he is stripped of his possessions. Yet he is able to recover and begin again, the motif of regeneration being persistent within the trilogy, and resembling Downey's equally remarkable recovery from drug addiction and imprisonment. Certainly, the explicit parallels with Downey's life imply that the trilogy is about Downey discovering his own identity as distinct from his Iron Man role. Stark's final words in *Iron Man 3* of "You can take away my house, and all my tricks and toys. One thing you can't take away … I am Iron Man" (which mirror those at the end of the first film), suggest that although Downey's behavior and situation may have changed, he is basically still the same person whose destiny was to become a star.

Conclusion

While the Iron Man trilogy's success partly reflects the more generalized popularity of filmic superheroes in the new millennium, there can be no doubt that Downey's portrayal of Tony Stark is a significant factor. This characterization, often improvised by Downey himself, mirrors his personal life and Stark's reformed morality parallels Downey's "reformation" following his respective film successes after *The Singing Detective* in 2003. In a related way, Downey's dedication to yoga, martial arts, and a generally healthy lifestyle is echoed in Stark's attempts to detoxify his body. The journey for Stark continues in *Iron Man 3* about which director Shane Black comments, "Downey's Tony Stark character is stripped of his suit's powers and his technology and must recover using his own strength and wits. It is a journey in some ways similar to Downey's own recovery from addiction and other troubles earlier in his career" (qtd. in "*Iron Man 3*"). This convergence suggests that all the aspects of Downey's image fit with the traits of Stark's character. Additional appeal for audiences may arise from the tension between Downey as star and Downey as ordinary person. Dyer suggests that one of the problems of debating the concept of stardom concerns the gap between "stars-as-ordinary and the star-as-special" (*Stars* 49). Arguably, this gap is explored in the character of Tony Stark through his physical and psychological vulnerabilities, which resemble those of Downey, and a trajectory that sees him lose his home and possessions. Downey's appeal arises precisely because of his "ordinariness" and the fact that he has transcended his personal difficulties. In short, Downey closes the gap between ordinariness and specialness. Dyer also states that "the selective use of a star's image is problematic in that it cannot guarantee that the particular aspects of a star's image that it selects will be those that interest the audience" (143). However, by selecting traits for Stark's characterization that parallel those of Downey, particularly his history of incarceration, drug-taking, and alcoholism, the *Iron Man* films have clearly struck a chord with audiences and critics alike. As Chris Heath comments, "[Downey's] resurrection has all the characteristics of an origin story for a Hollywood superhero. A gifted young actor loses his way, cheats death again and again, then straightens himself out just in time to conquer the world."

Works Cited

"Actor's Toughest Role: Beating Addiction a Struggle for Troubled Star." People in the News. *CNN,* 2004. Web. 18 Oct. 2013.
"All Time Box Office—Opening Weekends." *Box Office Mojo.* IMDb, n.d. Web. 9 Nov. 2013.
Ambrose, Thomas. "The Man in the Iron Mask." *Empire Magazine* Sept. 2007. 70–82. Print.
Ansen, David, and Ramin Setoodeh. "Inside the Actors' Studio." *Newsweek,* 2 Feb. 2009: n.p. *Proquest.* Web. 31 Oct. 2013.
Buck, Joan. "An Exceptional Talent." *Vogue,* 1 Apr. 2006: 370–73, 408. *Proquest.* Web. 31 Oct. 2013.
Carr, David. "Been Up, Been Down. Now? Super." *New York Times,* 20 Apr. 2008. Web. 19 Oct.2013.
Chaplin. Dir. Richard Attenborough. Maple Pictures, 1992. DVD.
Collins, Robbie. "Review of *Iron Man 3*." *Telegraph,* 19 Apr. 2013. Web. 5 Nov. 2013.
Dahl, Sophie. "It's Elementary: From Superhero to Sherlock, Robert Downey Jr. Has Been on a Tear, Propelled by a Tireless Work Ethic and a Dedication to the Simplest Details." *Vogue,* 1 Apr. 2009: S18-S21. *Proquest.* Web. 31 Oct. 2013.
The Dark Knight. Dir. Christopher Nolan. Warner Bros., 2008. Film.
"Destroying Lives 'For Their Own Good.'" Letters to the Editor. *Wall Street Journal,* 11 May 2001: A15. *Proquest.* Web. 31 Oct. 2013.
Dyer, Richard. *Heavenly Bodies: Film Stars and Society.* London: Routledge, 2004. Print.
_____. *Stars.* London: BFI, 1979. Print.
French, Philip. "*Iron Man 3*." *Guardian,* 28 Apr. 2013. Web. 5 Nov. 2013.
Fur. Dir. Steven Shainberg. New Line Cinema, 2006. DVD.
Fussman, Cal. "The Complete Robert Downey Jr." *Esquire,* 1 May 2012. Web. 5 Nov. 2013.
Gilbey, Ryan. "Robert Downey Jr.: From Lost Cause to Highest-Paid Hollywood Actor." *Guardian,* 17 July 2013. Web. 18 Oct. 2013.
Good Night and Good Luck. Dir. George Clooney. Sony Pictures Home, 2006. DVD.
Hampp, Andrew. "*Iron Man 2* Sparks $100M Marketing Bonanza as Partners Flock to Summer Blockbuster,

Ad Age Looks at Who's Getting What—and How Many Brands Are Too Many." *Advertising Age*, 19 Apr. 2010. Web. 4 Nov. 2013.

Heath, Chris. "RD3." *GQ*, Apr. 2013. Web. 2 Nov. 2013.

Home for the Holidays. 1995. Dir. Jodie Foster. *The Robert Downey Jr. Collection*. Fox Home Entertainment, 2009. DVD.

Indiana Jones and the Kingdom of the Crystal Skull. Dir. Steven Spielberg. Paramount, 2008. Film.

Iron Man. Dir. Jon Favreau. Paramount, 2008. DVD.

Iron Man 2. Dir. Jon Favreau. Paramount, 2010. DVD.

Iron Man 3. Dir. Shane Black. Disney, 2013. Blu-Ray.

"*Iron Man 3* Premiere." *Telegraph*, 25 Apr. 2013. Proquest. Web. 16 Oct. 2013.

Kiss Kiss Bang Bang. Dir. Shane Black. Warner, 2005. DVD.

Ndalianis, Angela, and Charlotte Lenry, eds. *Stars in Our Eyes: The Star Phenomenon in the Contemporary Era*. Westport, CT: Praeger, 2002. Print.

Newman, Kim. "*Iron Man*." *Sight and Sound* 18.7 (2008): 61–62. Print.

Pomerantz, Dorothy. "Robert Downey Jr. Tops Forbes' List of Hollywood's Highest-Paid Actors." *Forbes*, 16 July 2013. Web. 16 Oct. 2013.

Ressner, Jeffrey. "From Hollywood to Hell and Back." *Time*, 151.16 (1998): 66–68. Print.

Riva, J. Michael, prod. des. "*Iron Man*: Special Features." *Iron Man*. Dir. Jon Favreau. Paramount, 2008. DVD.

"Robert Downey Jr. to Star in *Iron Man*." *Breaking News*, 2 Oct. 2006. Web. 4 Nov. 2013.

Robey, Tim. "Iron Man with a Light Touch: Robert Downey Jr. Is a Mischievous Treat as the Playboy-Turned-Superhero in This Exuberant Big-Budget Special." *Daily Telegraph*, 30 Apr. 2010: 31. Proquest. Web. 16 Oct. 2013.

A Scanner Darkly. Dir. Richard Linklater. Warner Bros., 2006. DVD.

Scott, Paul. "The $100m Man: From Washed Up Addict to.... How *Iron Man* Star Robert Downey Jr. Turned His Life Around from Prison and Cocaine—Thanks to the Iron Will of His New Wife." *Daily Mail*, 24 May 2013: 60. Proquest. Web. 16 Oct. 2013.

Sherlock Holmes. Dir. Guy Ritchie. Warner, 2009. DVD.

The Singing Detective. 2003. Dir. Keith Gordon. Paramount Home Entertainment, 2004. DVD.

Smith, David. "The Star Who Came Back from the Depths." *Guardian*, 24 Aug. 2008. Web. 17 Oct 2013.

Stanley, T.L. "Tie-Ins: LG, BK, 7-Eleven to Pump Paramount's *Iron Man*." *Brandweek*, 12 Jan. 2008. Web. 4 Nov. 2013.

Udovitch, Mim. "The Sobering Life of Robert Downey Jr." *New York Times*, 19 Oct. 2003: SM34. Proquest. Web. 31 Oct. 2013.

Wilde, Jon. "More than Skin Deep." *Guardian*, 8 Nov. 2003. Web. 17 Oct. 2013.

Zodiac. Dir. David Fincher. Paramount, 2007. DVD.

Fragmented Relationships: Father-Son Dynamics in *Less Than Zero*, *A Guide to Recognizing Your Saints* and *Iron Man 2*

Jennifer Harrison

"If my father were less of a pioneer, he probably would have been more of a father, but I wouldn't be who I was."—RDJ qtd. in Diamond

A son lives his life assuming his father loved his best friend more than him.... A father is hurt by his son's sudden departure from the nest.... A son learns the father who pushed him relentlessly to succeed loved him after all.... A father and son recommit to forming a relationship after years of drug abuse.... Each of these story lines reflects a fragmented and strained father / son relationship, but ultimately, in three Robert Downey Jr. films, *Less Than Zero*, *A Guide to Recognizing Your Saints*, and *Iron Man 2*, the son learns that the father loved him dearly, although that discovery came too late for Julian Wells in *Less Than Zero*, nearly too late for Dito Montiel in *A Guide to Recognizing Your Saints*, and long after his father's death for Tony Stark a.k.a. Iron Man, in *Iron Man 2*. In each, Downey portrays characters from vastly different backgrounds, and in each, he brings a poignancy and versatility as viewers watch a grown man realize the depth of his father's love.

In *Iron Man 2*, Tony notes, "My father never told me he loved me—he never even told me he *liked* me." In *A Guide to Recognizing Your Saints*, the adult Dito asks his dying father, "Did you love me or not? Daddy, I've got to know." In *Less Than Zero*, Mr. Wells tells his son, "I'll do everything I can to help you, but I need you to help me, too." Both Tony and Dito are surprised by what they learn in the aftermath of death and / or dying; in both cases, the characters learn that their fathers were proud of them. Julian realizes that only he can make changes in his life. Each film indirectly explores the father-son context, and each son, as an adult, realizes that his misperception impacted a significant portion of his adult life. In *Iron Man 2*, for example, Tony confides at one point in Nick Fury, S.H.I.E.L.D. director, that his father was relieved to send him to boarding school, and while Fury attempts to encourage Tony to realize that his father loved him, years of hurt have depleted his ability to see his father as anything other than an effective, yet cold, businessman. It is this exploration of the human spirit for which Downey has an uncanny knack. What is it about Robert Downey Jr.'s ease of portraying torn characters that has created such a loyal following of eager viewers? This essay will take the perspective that it is Downey's ability to embody a character with whom viewers can relate and empathize, as in the characters of Dito and Tony, and even addict Julian, that has created such an interest in his film career. Journalist Scott Raab writes of Downey,

> You know he's crazy. I know he's crazy. He knows he's crazy. Onscreen, over the course of twenty years and dozens of movies, Downey, whatever his character, is a bolt of human lightning, the most labile and accessible unacting actor alive. His physical gifts are stunning. His work in 1992's *Chaplin* was uncanny, and even in his fifth decade, he's lithe, fluid, panther-quick. But it's his rogue tongue and seemingly unmediated heartspring that make it almost impossible not to like him. Everything boils over; nothing is repressed. Intense, exhilarating—all artifice, yet done so well it feels like life ["Quiet One"].

It is this "unmediated heartspring" that Downey breathes into the characters of Julian, Dito, and Tony. In 2007, Downey noted in an *Esquire* interview, "I'm not an actor. It's my day job, and I learned how to hustle it really good, and I have a love for it, and I get it, but I don't know what I'm doing…" (Raab, "The Quiet One"). This same self-deprecation permeates the characters Downey portrays in *Less Than Zero*, *A Guide to Recognizing Your Saints*, and *Iron Man 2*.

The Importance of Fathers

The father-son relationship is not the central theme in any of these films, but the impact of the father-son relationship on each character and the son's quest for redemption from a father perceived as aloof are powerful undercurrents in each film. In *Iron Man 2*, interestingly enough, both the hero and the villain, Tony Stark and Ivan Vanko, respectively, are defined by relationships (or lack thereof) with their fathers. In *Less Than Zero*, the opening high school graduation scenes establish the tone for what may have previously been a contentious father-son relationship, as Mr. Wells notes that he did not think Julian would graduate. Father and son hug with what appears to be relief on the part of the father, jubilation on the part of the son, with very little foreshadowing of what will unfold in just a few brief months. In *A Guide to Recognizing Your Saints*, it is evident from the first scene with Dito Montiel, his father, and his older best friend, Antonio, that Dito feels that his father does not love him, at least not the way he loves Antonio. This misperception on the part of Dito establishes a cycle of anger, partly fueled by outside events, that characterizes teenage Dito's relationship with his father, and his lack of communication, as an adult, with his father for nearly 15 years. All three men lead, or will eventually lead, very public lives: Tony Stark is the potent face of Stark Industries who takes a risk, at the end of *Iron Man*, to proclaim that he is Iron Man; Julian Wells is a well-known fixture on the Hollywood elite party circuit; and the teenage-to-adult Dito Montiel becomes an author who reads his work in coffee shops and bookstores. And, yet, all three men are fighting a personal demon, one that claims the life of Julian Wells and saves the lives of both Tony Stark and Dito Montiel.

All three father-son relationships reflect the son's disillusionment with the father, and in the cases of Dito and Julian, the reverse as well. Although Tony Stark famously notes in *Iron Man 2* that he thought his father hated him, he soon discovers that his father dedicated his life's work to his son; the younger Stark's disillusionment appears to diminish somewhat as the message from his father reinvigorates his mission to find a replacement for the Palladium core that is keeping him alive. In Julian's case in *Less than Zero*, the mutual disillusionment ends with rejection of home and family, a rejection that is perpetuated each time Julian tries, unsuccessfully, to return home and seek support from his father, who has wearied of the cycle of addiction. Dito's disillusionment leads him to depart for California without the blessing of his father who had admonished him, "You're not going anywhere"; his father, in turn, becomes disillusioned as a result of his son's abrupt departure and a lack of understanding of how Astoria, Queens could not be enough for his son. Although all three characters reconcile with their fathers, Julian's reconciliation will remain forever unfinished, and Tony's occurs years after his father's death; only Dito has the opportunity to reconcile in person and visibly embrace that reconciliation—one that promises to endure throughout whatever time his very ill father has left.

Wolfgang Lepschy, in his dissertation on the father-son relationship in the work of Ernest Hemingway and Ernest Gaines, contends, "The identity crises of their various male protagonists are almost always related to or can be traced back to a problematic or non-existing relationship to their father." This perceived imbalance or troubled relationship impacts the "perspective of the sons who grow up deprived of the parental guidance they need" (39). In the case of Julian Wells, his post-high school life represents a distressed father-son relationship, whereas with Dito, his father was a constant presence; however, Dito perceived his affection as one-sided and directed more toward his best friend than him. On the other hand, Tony Stark grew up believing his father felt he was a nuisance, and, like Julian, his world of wealth revolved around other caregivers due to an absent, workaholic, father. Lepschy posits, "To make his peace with the past, [the son] needs to recognize that his inability to own up to his feelings…" presents challenges for "coping with emotionally difficult situation(s)" (163). This recognition represents the culmination of *A Guide to Recognizing Your Saints*; progress toward that recognition in *Less Than Zero*, a progress cut short by the son's death; and a recognition that his father had left an undeniable legacy for the future in the case of Tony Stark in *Iron Man 2*.

The father-son dynamic is a consistent theme in American cinema; Rattigan and McManus argue, more in reference to 1980s films due to the time period of their article, that "motion pictures … have demonstrated a virtual obsession with father-son relations…." Guilt is often a subsidiary, but no less significant, component of the relationship, often "resulting from some unspecified wrong committed by either or both" (15). Does the relationship between the two individuals, "father" and "son," necessitate opposition, simply by virtue of the generation gap? That appears to be plausible in *A Guide to Recognizing Your Saints* and *Less Than Zero*, while in *Iron Man 2*, the guilt may be one-sided, the guilt of a workaholic father who considered his son his "greatest creation" but was incapable not only of expressing that emotion in a reciprocal manner but also of pulling himself away from his work. Interestingly, it is only when Tony Stark is at one of his lowest moments that he learns how much his father loved him (*Iron Man 2*). Each father and son relationship reflects a distinct impediment in terms of misunderstanding of each other's personalities, emotions, and qualities.

All three sons "carry the burden of being, or believing themselves to be, inadequate sons, of not measuring up to their respective fathers' requirements" (Rattigan & McManus 16). Dito is unable to forgive his father, and it takes a plaintive call from his mother and repeated calls from his Astoria friends for him to return, 15 years after his departure, to see his very ill father, and perhaps seek forgiveness from his father for his abrupt departure. The reconciliatory actions in *Less Than Zero* are too late for Julian and his father, while for Dito and his father, the conversation at the end of the film occurs just in time. Psychologist Lennox Thomas contends, "Human attachment is key to psychological development and personality; we are born relationship seeking.... From the earliest attachment relationship, we continue through life, learning from and experiencing others. These various relationships from our past have affected and shaped us..." (Thomas 73). For example, *A Guide to Recognizing Your Saints* depicts the estranged relationship between the adult Dito and his father, and the origins of that estrangement when Dito was a teenager; as viewers, we seek some sort of a positive conclusion for both men, and that conclusion occurs when, after angry words expressing 15 years of repressed emotion, both father and son express their love. Similarly, Tony Stark is able to see the emotion on his father's face when watching the film reel of outtakes from the 1970s. Julian and his father in *Less Than Zero* take an emotional step toward resolution, but the sought-for-resolution leaves viewers frustrated when Julian dies from an overdose orchestrated by his pimp, Rip.

Each film explores an underlying theme—specifically what it means to be an effective father and a good son. Social scientists refer to three elements that characterize a "good" father: engagement, accessibility, and responsibility (Pleck 33); by the 1970s, society began to clamor for more egalitarianism in child rearing, with the father equally responsible for raising children. The sons in all three films are products of the late 1960s / early 1970s. The 1970s and 1980s, the time period of the childhoods of each of the sons in these films, represented societal concerns about the absent father, especially in reference to the amount of time a father spent with his child (Pleck 42). *Less Than Zero* represents typical 1980s films in the sense that the characters are on a quest to find meaning in their lives (Jordan 185). In *Iron Man 2*, Nick Fury (S.H.I.E.L.D.) is a pseudo-father figure for Tony Stark; even in spite of his brief appearances in the film, he is the voice of reason. The father-as-provider, in this case, financial provider (Kelly 111), is all that Tony saw of his father—until he was able to watch the film reel indicating how much his father loved him. He saw his father as the stereotypical "head of household" with little family involvement and a stilted emotional connection. In *A Guide to Recognizing Your Saints*, Dito feels as if he is an accoutrement at times, as opposed to his father's son. Each film explores the pain and shame that psychologist Frank Pittman posits may accompany a failed father-son relationship. If, as Floyd contends in reference to father-son relationships in general, "Men's and boy's relationships with their fathers might be among the most influential and socially significant same-sex relationships that they form in the life course" (599), then the failed father-son relationships experienced by the sons in *Less Than Zero*, *A Guide to Recognizing Your Saints*, and *Iron Man 2* must have had an enormous impact on the development of Julian, Dito, and Tony, despite the fact that fathers are not the central theme in any of these films.

Downey as Auteur

The fragmented father-son relationships in *Less Than Zero*, *A Guide to Recognizing Your Saints*, and *Iron Man 2* are not a far cry from Downey's own experiences. The role of Julian, he told *Mademoiselle* in 1988, caused him to "di[g] into [his] duffle bag ... [of] repressed ideas." He explained, "Maybe there's a family crisis, but you think, 'I've got to put this to the back of my head because I've got other things to think about.' Until finally there's this pile of dirty, mismatched socks at the bottom. I started to mentally pick them out and fluff and fold them." He had been repressing (mainly through drugs) his fear, sadness, and resentment over the breakup of his parents' marriage and his strained relationship with his father, who was something of an absentee dad who moved the family frequently for his own work and introduced his young children to drugs. Senior and Junior worked out their issues in therapy (Garbarino, "Star"), and today Robert Jr. does not blame his father for his own mistakes. On the contrary, he seems to proudly hold his father up as an example of artistic integrity—the kind that he often sacrificed, himself, in the quest for commercially successful work.

His self-deprecation at his often very public debacles and personal and professional turnaround in the last decade may not be all that surprising and is particularly evident in the characters he selects to play (including the sons in the films that are the subject of this chapter). Downey himself noted, "Bad form, self-deprecation, another character flaw" (Hedegaard 58). Similar to the characters in these three films, he recognizes his flaws and, also like these characters, took time in accepting them. The actor's relationship with his own father had a huge influence on him. As Downey notes,

> Looking back, the best thing on my dad's side was that he never capitulated ... there's still this part of my dad that lives in me.... Moving forward, there's this sense that if you capitulate to try to conform the seed of an idea that you have that excites you, then it's never just going to stop.... And, I think, particularly if you're a father who has gained, or gained and lost and regained any sort of success, the likelihood and the odds of replicating anyone else's successes are nil. And so the real definition of success is essentially, How comfortable are you in your own skin, and are you heading in a direction that gives you a sense of hope for the future, or a sense of, at least, engagement with life? And that has nothing to do with all these outward trappings [Fussman 83].

It may be this fatherly influence that impacts each of his career roles—both from his own experiences as the son of a filmmaker, and now as a father of two.

Downey noted a similar point in a 2010 *GQ* UK interview:

> My life, personal and professional, I've always had these big themes to do with fatherhood and taking responsibility for my own actions. The first day of shooting *Less Than Zero*, I'm on a tennis court with the director Marek Kanievska, and I really have no idea what I'm doing. So I started thinking, 'Do fathers and sons ever really connect? Are they ever truly able to love each other and accept each other?' At this point, I'm getting really choked up.... When the scene was done, Marek said, 'You know you're a real actor and I'm going to craft this whole movie around you. People are going to see who you are [Heaf].

All of the central characters in these three Downey films are boys and men who have both lost and gained over the course of their lives, and each is uncomfortable, at various points in the films, in his own skin. Viewers are treated to the evolution of Dito Montiel as he discovers the depth of his father's love as an adult, and similarly, recognition on the part of Tony Stark that he brought meaning to his father's life. The untimely death of Julian Wells occurred just as that realization had begun.

Less Than Zero

As has been noted by various film critics and purportedly intimated by Downey himself, art imitated life (and, perhaps, vice versa) with the filming of *Less Than Zero*. Already an

The tennis court scene: Downey as Julian Wells embracing his estranged on-screen father, played by Nicholas Pryor, In *Less Than Zero* (1987).

inveterate actor by the time the movie was made, having first acted in his father's movie *Pound* at age five, Downey's role in *Less Than Zero* garnered him critical acclaim. *People* magazine correspondent Michael Fleeman notes in a 2004 article, "How much of his personal life did he bring to that character? Probably quite a bit. The thing about Robert is, like lots of actors, there isn't much of a barrier between his subconscious and his emotions" ("Actor's Toughest Role"). Downey has commented that his work in *Less Than Zero* prompted his troubles off camera: "Until that movie, I took my drugs after work and on the weekends. Maybe I'd turn up hungover on the set, but no more so than the stuntman. That changed on *Less Than Zero*.... The character was an exaggeration of myself. Then things changed and, in some ways, I became an exaggeration of the character. That lasted far longer than it needed to last" (Wilde). The film affected him so profoundly that, in 1993, he buried the clothes he had retained from Julian's wardrobe in a symbolic grave in his backyard (Schneller). Nonetheless, in spite of a chaotic life off camera, his ability to portray poignancy in a fragmented father-son relationship is what continues to attract legions of devoted fans.

The father-son relationship in *Less Than Zero* may be only an underlying theme in the film, but the tattered relationship between Julian and his father impacts many of Julian's actions after his music producer career fails following high school graduation. Father and son share repartee after the graduation ceremony that is little more than foreshadowing; their discussion revolves around the gift of an investment in his son's music business plans for Tone Def Records, and his father notes, "You can consider it a graduation gift. The truth is, I never thought we'd get this far." Julian's retort, "Uh, I'm speechless," is classic Julian Wells, to which his father comments, "That's another surprise," as he hugs Julian. Julian parts ways with, "all right, I'll be home much later.... Keep you on your toes. Nobody likes a complacent parent." This humorous repartee will be the last positive exchange between father and son until almost the end of the film.

In a series of flashbacks, viewers learn that friend Blair has opted to model rather than attend college; Clay leaves Blair behind only to return home at Thanksgiving to find Julian in bed with her. When Clay goes home again at Christmas, tension exists between the three. Blair has been worried that Julian is in trouble, to which Clay objects, contending that Julian has been a drug user since he was ten. It turns out, however, that in a matter of months, addict Julian has acquired a debt of $50,000 to drug dealer/pimp Rip, and he appears to have burned the last bridge with his father.

This burned bridge has resulted in a strained relationship between father and son; Julian is no longer welcome at home. When Julian breaks into the family home just before Christmas, his father tries to get him to leave: "We talked about this. You can't stay here. Live your life any way you want, but not here." Julian's retort is a combination of exhortation and exhaustion: "Just give me a second—You're a father and I'm a son. I'm your son...." Julian is near his breaking point, and even though he is eager for reconciliation with his father, his addiction takes precedence. He gets high again, this time with a fix provided by Rip, the man to whom he already owes a significant amount of money. After Clay and Blair help him detox, it appears that Julian has finally realized that he needs help, and that this time, those words are not empty ones. He goes to talk with his father, a man shattered, and his father, at first icy, thaws somewhat. When Julian asks to come home, his father refuses, the quintessential response of a father who has been through this conversation one too many times with his addict son. He tells him, "Julian, we've been through this a hundred times.... You conned your way through rehab—you lied, you stole. Look what you've done to our family." Julian retorts, "I just need you to be my father for one god damn day. Just help me.... Can't you tell when I'm telling the truth?" These, on the surface, might appear to be the cajoling words of an addict looking for respite before another binge, but Julian manages to convince his father that he is serious this time. His father responds with sorrow, "No, trust was the first thing you ruined." Julian turns to go, choked up, but adds,

"Yeah. Oh, I'm gonna go. There's this guy I owe a large sum of money to—I know, big surprise. I'm gonna talk to him, and try to ... try to do something right for once. I mean it. So, I just want you to wish me luck—whether you believe me or not." His father asks him if he could stay sober for one week, and offers, "I'll do everything I can for you. I'll do everything I can to help you, but I need you to help me, too." Julian's response, "I could try," appears to be believable; they hug and cry. The father and son reconciliation, while in its incipient stages, shows immense promise, and while it is important not to forget that Julian is an addict, it seems that fulfillment of Julian's desire for demonstrable love from his father may be on the horizon.

Julian is resolute when telling Rip about his desire to be clean, but that desire is overcome by addiction when Rip's bodyguard Bill puts drugs in front of Julian; Rip forces him to prostitute himself again, and it is in this state that Clay discovers him and rescues him. The last high, though, was too much for Julian, and he succumbs to the overdose, an inevitable climax to the tumultuous journey of an addict seeking love and fulfillment in a shallow and hollow environment.

The production notes for *Less Than Zero* refer to Julian as one with a "devil-may-care" approach to life, and that is the Julian viewers see at first, but differentiating between the man and the addict is an essential component of this film; underneath the layers of addiction is a man looking for connections in a world that is devoid of them, whether familial, friendly, or otherwise. This film is about isolation; ironically, in death, Julian is not isolated, as he is surrounded by two of the people who love him the most, Blair and Clay. Jami Gertz, who plays Blair, said of the film, "When you have a family that doesn't work, you find a new family, and what most young people find is their friends." Screenwriter Harley Peyton expresses in the same production notes his own take on the main theme of *Less Than Zero*: "...for Julian, dealing with love is something that he has completely put aside, because it has been painful for him: You see that with his father, rather than with his friends. It's fairly hard for any of them to express it.... In a funny way I really think that this is a love story about three friends." Julian's quest for love and companionship seems to have reached a fulfilling conclusion toward the end, in spite of his untimely, yet unsurprising, death; the film's conclusion depicts the three friends together in the end, even if one is only there in spirit.

Downey's charisma makes Julian seem real. His portrayal of Julian's self-destructive behavior, not atypical of an addict, invites sympathy; he makes viewers care about what happens to Julian. The reality of this film is that only Julian can help himself, foreshadowing, perhaps, Downey's own life 15 years later. The title alone, *Less Than Zero*, with its hints about how much value human beings attach to one another and to life, is reflective of the lack of real connection between father and son, a connection that appears to be on the horizon, and yet is taken away in the very poignant sunrise outside Palm Springs. Downey notes, "I think this really is a movie about change. People are afraid of change. They say things like, 'We're moving to Seattle—God I'm scared!' But all the characters in Less Than Zero change, whether it means changing by leaving this physical plane or doing a serious transition..." (*Less Than Zero* production notes). Julian and his father appear to be on the path toward redemption toward the end of the film, and all three friends, Julian, Clay, and Blair, have realized the value of the love they have for one another; each has transformed throughout the film, even though Julian's transformation ends with his death. The specter of death and resulting transformation is also a part of *A Guide to Recognizing Your Saints* as the adult Dito Montiel returns home to his dying father.

A Guide to Recognizing Your Saints

If change is the key to the father-son relationship in *Less Than Zero*, it is also the key to *A Guide to Recognizing Your Saints*. The story of the connections between seven friends, Dito, Antonio, Mike, Guiseppe, Nerf, Laurie, and Diane and their associated teenage angst abuts the story of Dito's relationship with his father, Monty. Downey portrays Dito as an adult, the troubled man who has to make amends with his dying father. The events of the summer of 1986, the summer that changed forever the relationship between father and son, are conveyed via a series of flashbacks featuring Shia LeBeouf as the teen Dito. Film critic Robert Koehler, in his review of the film, notes, "Monty respects Antonio as the oldest and toughest of the bunch, but unconditionally loves Dito, who displays both rowdy and softer sides.... But along with Laurie, newly arrived Scottish kid Mike offers Dito a counterpart to the brutalized world of Antonio; Mike writes poetry, and inspires Dito to consider forming a band with him. Dito is gradually forced to make life-changing choices."

The relationship between Monty and Dito focuses on anger, betrayal, and abandonment, with Dito's concern that his father loves Antonio more than him ultimately leading to Dito's departure for California and Monty, a man who loved his son unconditionally, being frustrated by his son's inability to accept a life in Astoria, Queens or his love. "The failure of communication between father and son is one of the painful elements in *A Guide to Recognizing Your Saints*," contends A. O. Scott in his September 2006 review of the film. The film's opening warning from Dito, circa July 1986, "My name's Dito. I'm gonna leave everybody in this film," foreshadows the events of that tumultuous summer, and the closing remarks at the end from the adult Dito, "In the end, just like I said, I left everything and everyone—but no one, no one has ever left me," are both oddly disconcerting, but both remarks demonstrate the power of change and the theme of connection in this film.

The exchanges between father, son, and truly, between each of the characters, are often angry and rarely quiet. Monty's temper often gets the best of him, although, unlike Antonio's father, he is not physical with Dito; his profession, typewriter repair, is a solitary one, and he seems to enjoy the loud, often erratic, disruptions from his son and his friends. Monty is a man, though, who is confident that all will be all right; Dito's friend, Mike, captures Monty completely when he says, about halfway through the film, "He's scared." At the same time, Monty warns Dito that if he were to leave, it would negatively impact the family; in other words, his departure would be the ultimate betrayal. The traditional expectation of a child's role as caregiver is one the Montiels share, and one against which Dito fights; in the last few days before Dito leaves for California, his father, whether consciously or not, pushes him away in his anger. They share a hostile exchange, tinged with years of betrayal, anger, and misunderstanding, that begins with a reference to Antonio:

> DITO: Why don't you ever listen to anything I ever say?
> MONTY: I'm listening to you.
> DITO: You're not listening. [Monty reaches out and touches his hand.]

> Dito: Don't fucking touch me.
> Monty [yelling]: Don't you talk to me like that. Don't you raise your voice to me. You're my son.... What's the matter with you? It's going to be all right. Do you hear what I'm saying? ... You don't raise your hands to your father. It's okay. Don't you raise your hands to me again. I'm your father. You're not supposed to hate your father.
> Dito: When are you my father?

This scene provides the cataclysmic element that prompts Dito to leave for California. The argument ends with no closure; both father and son shout insults at one another, the son's peppered with expletives, both taking a monstrous tone in their efforts to outdo the other.

In an interview included in the production notes for *A Guide to Recognizing Your Saints*, Montiel notes, "Robert brought realness to the role.... He brought this sense of indifference to the role that played out as a slow awakening..." (12). This "slow awakening" is driven home in an exchange between the adult Dito and his mother, Flori, in which she reminds him of how much his father loves him:

> You know, if you hooked your father up to a lie detector test, and asked if he was the best father ever, he'd pass with flying colors. That's because he loved you.... People used to think he was your grandfather. He thought that was funny.... We needed you probably more than you needed us.... Your father was so crazy about you. I never saw nothing like it. You were more his buddy than his son. He couldn't wait for you to come out and play.... You can't come back with hatred for your father. You can't. How could you love him so much in that book and not see him for so long?

In a similar exchange between adult Dito and Laurie, she tells him, "You want it straight? You killed him when you left.... Go home and take care of your father. Go home and take care of your mother. That will make you a fucking man." These two reminders are all that the adult Dito needs to confront his father:

> Dito: Did you love me, ever? [Monty tells him to leave.] Dad, did you love me or not? Daddy, I got to know. Come on—lie to me.... Did you love me or not? Answer me.
> Monty: Of course I did.... I told you I love you the last time I saw you. I love you, Dito, all right? You're my son. I'm very proud of you....

A Guide to Recognizing Your Saints ends on a positive but torturous note as the son reconciles with his dying father; it also marks the true transformation of father and son, as both try to atone for 15 years of separation and guilt. The son had begun the path toward healing with the writing of his book, but ultimately, it took a father's poor health to bring the son home to seek redemption. By the end of the film, both are finally on the path to putting words to emotions that had been simmering for 15 years.

Iron Man 2

The tortured exchange and reconciliation with a dying father is something that Tony Stark in *Iron Man 2* is not able to experience. The production notes for the film contend, "Overwhelmed on all fronts, while facing his own personal demons, Tony must finally call on his allies—old and new—to help him confront the gathering forces that threaten to destroy him and all of mankind." Stark is a combination of pure genius and self-deprecating humor, and a man on a personal mission to not only save the world, in true hero fashion, but chase away the demons from his past as well. He is temporarily blindsided by alcohol and the thrill of adoring fans as a celebrity and public figure, but it is Nick Fury of S.H.I.E.L.D. who reminds him of his humanity (despite the palladium in his chest keeping him alive), and of his father's love. They share an intense conversation in reference not only to the technology in his chest, but also to Howard Stark:

> FURY: That thing in your chest is based on unfinished technology.
> STARK: No it was finished. It's never been particularly effective until I miniaturized it and put it in my....
> FURY: No. Howard saw the arc reactor as a stepping stone to something greater. He was about to kick off an energy race that was going to dwarf the arms race. He was on to something big—something so big that it was going to make the nuclear reactor look like a triple A battery.
> STARK: Just him—or was Anton Vanko in on this, too?
> FURY: Anton Vanko was the other side of that coin. Anton saw it as a way to get rich.... When the Russians found out he couldn't deliver, they shipped his ass off to Siberia. He spent 20 years in a vodka-fueled rage, not quite the environment you want to raise a kid in— the son you had the misfortune of crossing paths with in Monaco.
> STARK: You told me I hadn't tried everything. What do you mean—I haven't tried everything? What haven't I tried?
> FURY: He said that you were the only person with the means and knowledge to finish what he started.... Are you that guy? Hmmm, are you? 'Cause if you are, then you can solve the riddle of your heart.
> STARK: I don't know where you are getting your information, but, uh, he wasn't my biggest fan.
> FURY: What do you remember about your dad, huh?
> STARK: He was cold, he was calculating. He never told me he loved me. He never even told me he liked me. So, it's a little tough for me to digest when you're telling me he said the whole future was riding on me, and he's passing it down. I don't get that. We're talking about a guy whose happiest day was when he shipped me off to boarding school.
> FURY: That's not true.
> STARK: Well, then, clearly, you knew my dad better than I did.
> FURY: As a matter of fact, I did. He was one of the founding members of S.H.I.E.L.D.

This conversation may just have been the impetus Tony needed to end his self-destructive streak.

Iron Man 2 opens with a television somewhere in Moscow playing the interview with Tony Stark from the end of *Iron Man*, in which Stark admits, "Let's face it; I'm not the heroic type ... laundry list of character defects, all the mistakes I've made. The truth is [pause]—I am Iron Man." It is to this admission that the father of the main antagonist in the film, Ivan Vanko, dies, and this fact sets in motion for Vanko a delirious desire to exact revenge upon Tony Stark, the son of the man whom Vanko feels wronged his father, Anton Vanko. Both men, Stark and Vanko, have now lost their fathers; while both hero and villain have different goals in life, they share two common elements—both are now fatherless, and both inherited the brilliance of their fathers.

Fury wants to ensure that Tony understands that his father was more than brilliant, that he was a man who deeply loved his son; the box Fury left for Tony contains a series of film reels, one of which contains a message specifically for Tony. Howard notes,

> Tony, you are too young to understand this right now, so I thought I would put it on film for you. I built this for you [looks at the models on the table].... It represents my life work. This is the key to the future. I am limited by the technology of my time, but one day you will figure

this out, and when you do, you will change the world. What is, and always will be, my greatest creation is you.

This message, one that reveals his father's humanity, leads Tony to the original 1974 Stark Expo diorama, a nearly-lost molecular structure diagram. Tony's reaction is that of a man who seems to have acquired something he had always desperately wanted; it could be argued that it is this message from his father that helps to reinvigorate Tony Stark, and also provides the impetus for the development of the palladium alternative, the new triangular chest arc.

Screenwriter Justin Theroux notes, "We ... had to rectify what to do when a private citizen, even a really rich and powerful one, comes up with something that has the ability to tip the balance of power, not just nationally, but globally.... Tony has to balance that line of celebrity and hero, and what happens when you say to the world, 'I am Iron Man.' What does that statement buy you and what problems does it present?" ("*Iron Man 2* Production Notes" 9). For Tony, this new hero status comes with a price—an increased volatility and a drinking problem, not unlike that of his father; the meeting with Nick Fury and the viewing of the film reel with his father's message help to curb those proclivities, and mark his recognition that he can move away from the shadow of his father.

The exploration of the father-son relationship in *Iron Man 2* is relatively minor, but this understated emphasis on the father-son dynamic might actually be one of the most compelling elements of the film. Like many people with brilliant minds, Tony Stark is conflicted; he has always assumed his father hated him, and yet he discovers that his father considered him his greatest creation. While watching the clip his father had recorded for him, Tony also, quite passively, observes a film clip in which he, as a young child, had interrupted his father's filming of the introduction for the 1974 Expo; Howard appears quite irritated by the interruption, and snaps at Tony. While this is the only interaction between father and son depicted while Howard was alive, it does not indicate a positive relationship, although it could also be a glimpse into the life of a brilliant man, consumed by alcoholism, and frustrated by the limitations of 1970s technology—a man who, although he loved his son, was loathe to express emotions other than irritation and anger. In perhaps another instance of art imitating real life in the relationship between Downey and his own father, the lack of attention Tony receives from his work-obsessed, alcoholic father may have driven him to seek the attention of others and may even explain his eagerness to reveal himself as Iron Man at the end of the first film. He seeks approval from others, even in spite of his brilliance, and thrives on the audience participation, for example, in the 2010 Stark Expo. The superhero is on a crash course to self-destruction, and yet his father's long-hidden film reel message conveys not only Howard's humanity, but reminds Tony of his own. The film clip depicts the love of a father for his son, but also a father's desire to pass on his life work to his son via the diorama / model of a new element; Howard has provided Tony with a key to not only his own future, but, potentially, the future of science and of the world. Tony, acknowledging the presence of his father's legacy as he creates the new palladium alternative, later notes, "Dead for almost 20 years ... still taking me to school" (*Iron Man 2*).

Downey's career rejuvenation began with *Iron Man*, but his career, like the lives of the sons in each film, has experienced a series of highs and lows. Then, along came *Iron Man*— the film that many believe resurrected Downey's career. He had continued to act even in spite of very public events—public intoxication, arrests, jail time,—and yet, his career, despite successes, often took a backseat to his profligate drug use. Journalist Raab notes in a 2009

Esquire article, "Downey's forty-four years old, with hard miles on the odometer, a blown gasket or two thwapping in his head, and a lead foot on the gas, still gunning it to make up for all that time lost." This description may not be too different from that of the characters he plays with uncanny likeness: Julian Wells in *Less Than Zero*; the adult Dito Montiel, a man who has to come to terms with his past, in *A Guide to Recognizing Your Saints*; and Tony Stark in *Iron Man 2*, a man who realizes that his father's ambitions included not only the acquisition of money but an intense love for his son, and a vision of what his son could accomplish. That latter point may also not be too far from autobiographical, as Downey Sr. also had a vision for what his son would accomplish as an actor. In a November 2010 *Playboy* interview, Downey noted, "Dad's shadow is still there. I'm sure that's part of some metamorphosis" (Fleming). The previous year, Downey noted, "...there are a bunch of other things I've always wanted to do that remain very, very much unrequited. And no matter how you slice it, I am still executing the wishes, thoughts, themes, titles, and stories coming from elsewhere. I feel like they're mine, because I really invest myself in them—but there are some interesting things out there" (Raab, "The Back-Deck View"). Downey's ability to invest himself in his films is a central part of the viability of his work in *Less Than Zero*, *A Guide to Recognizing Your Saints*, and *Iron Man 2*; in each, he effectively portrays a son yearning for his father's love and support, and in each, the sons ultimately find both.

Works Cited

"Actor's Toughest Role: Beating Addiction a Struggle for Troubled Star." People in the News. *CNN*, 2004. Web. 22 Nov. 2012.

Aitken, Stuart C. *The Awkward Spaces of Fathering*. Ashgate, 2009. eBook Collection. *EBSCOhost*. Web. 22 Dec. 2012. 229–233.

"Celebrating Fatherhood and the Role of Fathers." *Harvard Extension Hub*. Harvard University. 15 June 2012. Web. 22 Dec. 2012.

Cohen-Shalev, Amir. "Beyond Reconciliation: Filial Relationship as a Lifelong Developmental Theme in Bergman's Films." *Style* 43.1 (2009): 86–108. *MasterFILE Premier*. Web. 7 Feb. 2013.

Diamond, Jamie. "Robert Downey Jr. Is Chaplin (on Screen) and a Child (Off)." *New York Times*, 20 Dec. 1992. Web. 1 Aug. 2013.

Fleming, Michael. "The Real Robert Downey Jr." *Playboy*, Nov. 2010. Web. 30 Mar. 2013.

Floyd, Kory, and Morman, Mark T. "Human Affection Exchange: II. Affectionate Communication in Father-Son Relationships." *Journal of Social Psychology* 143.5 (2003): 599–612. *MasterFILE Premier*. Web. 22 Dec. 2012.

Fussman, Cal. "Robert Downey, Junior (Cover Story)." *Esquire* (2012): 82–89. *MasterFILE Premier*. Web. 22 Dec. 2012.

A Guide to Recognizing Your Saints. Dir. Dito Montiel. First Look Studios, 2006. DVD.

"*A Guide to Recognizing Your Saints* Notes." Filmography. *Downey Unlimited Forever*. Web. 22 Nov. 2012.

Guy, Raz. "'Less Than Zero' Addicts Reach Middle Age." *NPR*, 2010. Web. 22 Dec. 2012.

Heaf, Jonathan. "Robert Downey Jr. Has the Cure." *GQ* (UK), Dec. 2010. Articles and Interviews. *Downey Unlimited Forever*. Web. 1 Aug. 2013.

Hedegaard, Erik. "The Man Who Wasn't There (Cover Story)." *Rolling Stone*, Aug. 2008: 56–61. *MasterFILE Premier*. Web. 7 Feb. 2013.

Iron Man 2. Dir. Jon Favreau. Marvel Studios, 2010. DVD.

"*Iron Man 2* Production Notes." Filmography. *Downey Unlimited Forever*. Web. 22 Nov. 2012.

Jordan, John W. "Good and Bad Fathers as Moral Rhetoric in Wall Street." *Fathering: A Journal of Theory, Research, & Practice About Men as Fathers* 7.2 (2009): 180–195. *Academic Search Premier*. Web. 22 Dec. 2012.

Kelly, Janice. "Fathers and the Media: Introduction to the Special Issue." *Fathering: A Journal of Theory, Research, & Practice About Men as Fathers* 7.2 (2009): 107–113. *Academic Search Premier*. Web. 22 Dec. 2012.

Koehler, Robert. "A Guide to Recognizing Your Saints." *Variety*, 401.12 (2006): 99–100. *MasterFILE Premier*. Web. 22 Dec. 2012.
Lepschy, Wolfgang. "Of Fathers and Sons: Generational Conflicts and Literary Lineage—The Case of Ernest Hemingway and Ernest Gaines." Dissertation, Augsburg University, 2003. Web. 22 Nov. 2012.
Less Than Zero. Dir. Marek KanievskaTwentieth Century–Fox, 1987. DVD.
"*Less Than Zero* Notes." Filmography. *Downey Unlimited Forever*. Web. 22 Nov. 2012.
Morice, Laura. "Acting—Or Just Acting Up?" *Mademoiselle*, Nov. 1988: n. pag. Articles and Interviews. *Downey Unlimited Forever*. Web. 4 July 2013.
Pleck, Elizabeth H. "Two Dimensions of Fatherhood: A History of the Good Dad—Bad Dad Complex. Included in Lamb, Michael E. *The Role of the Father in Child Development*. Wiley, 2004. eBook Collection. *EBSCOhost*. Web. 20 Nov. 2012.
Pittman, Frank. "Fathers and Sons." Sept. 1993. *Psychology Today*. Oct. 2009. Web. 22 Nov. 2012.
Raab, Scott. "The Back-Deck View from the A-List." *Esquire* 152.6 (2009): 108–115. *MasterFILE Premier*. Web. 22 Dec. 2012.
_____. "The Quiet One." *Esquire* 147.3 (2007): 148–212. *MasterFile Premier*. Web. 22 Dec. 2012.
Rattigan, Neil, and Thomas P. McManus. "Fathers, Sons, and Brothers: Patriarchy and Guilt in 1980s American Cinema." *Journal of Popular Film & Television* 20.1 (1992): 15–23. *Academic Search Premier*. Web. 22 Dec. 2012.
Schneller, Joanna. "What a Tramp!" *GQ*, Jan. 1993: n. pag. *Downey Unlimited Forever*. Web. 4 July 2013.
Scott, A.O. "The Old Neighborhood Never Looked So Grim." *New York Times*, 29 Sept. 2006. Web. 22 Dec. 2012.
Thomas, Lennox K. "Relational Psychotherapy: The Significance of Father." *Psychodynamic Practice* 16.1 (2010): 61–75. *Academic Search Premier*. Web. 22 Dec. 2012.
Wilde, Jon. "More Than Skin Deep." *Guardian*, 7 Nov. 2003. Web. 24 Mar. 2013.

"Welcome to the movie factory": *Tropic Thunder* as Postmodern Comedy

Brian S. Reinking

"Start the cameras; this is Vietnam: the movie!" says Sgt. Cowboy as a film crew walks through Hue City as it burns and crumbles in *Full Metal Jacket*. "Don't look at the camera! Just go by like you're fighting. Like you're fighting. Don't look at the camera. This is for television. Just go through. Go through," Director Francis Ford Coppola barks at soldiers landing on a beach in *Apocalypse Now* as he appears in a cameo as a television director. Moving to cover away from sniper fire in Hue, a wounded marine says, "I *hate* this movie" to combat correspondent Michael Herr. Herr calls *Dispatches,* a 1977 book of Vietnam reportage, his Vietnam movie which he, like other correspondents, had been compelled to make in the absence of any real movies—*Green Berets* notwithstanding—about the war at the time. Shortly after *Dispatches*, beginning with *Deer Hunter* and *Apocalypse Now*, Hollywood began making Vietnam movies.

In the 2008 film *Tropic Thunder,* Jack Black's soldier character Fats says, "I fucking hate movies … I don't want be in this shitty movie," echoing the marine in *Dispatches*. *Tropic Thunder* is continuously intertextual: the film draws on many previous Vietnam films, some of the processes behind making them, and other literary, nonfiction, and filmic sources, in creating its own product. The postmodern qualities of self-referentiality and a blurred line between fiction and nonfiction are clear in the tagline for *Tropic Blunder*, "The true story behind the making of the most expensive fake true war story ever" (*Tropic Thunder*). The "real" Sgt. Four Leaf's discovery as impostor and the actors' struggle to discover who they really are when they "may be nobody" embodies the postmodern quality of "simulacra," a term used by theorist Jean Baudrillard to mean a representation of something for which no original exists.

A hyper-reality, the continuous use of pastiche and parody, the pervasiveness of the media's effects on consumer desire, the presence of machines of reproduction, the discussion of theory, the blending of high and low culture, the critique of identity, and the controversy surrounding the film mark *Tropic Thunder* as more than mere spoof, but rather its own independent, postmodern (re)product.

Simulacrum and Hyper-Reality

The Vietnam War films alluded to in *Tropic Thunder* make various claims to authenticity. Oliver Stone, the writer/director of *Platoon*, served a tour of duty as an Army grunt. Coppola claims to have experienced his own Vietnam in making *Apocalypse Now* (*Hearts of Darkness*). *Full Metal Jacket* was co-written by combat correspondents Michael Herr and Gustav Hasford, and the film *Hamburger Hill* claims to be "the most realistic portrayal of the Vietnam War ever filmed. Because it's the only one that's true" (front cover). Jean Baudrillard in "The Precession of Simulacra" defines the final stage of simulation as "the generation by models of a real without origin or reality: a hyperreal. The territory no longer precedes the map..." (1732). The Vietnam scenes in *Tropic Thunder* aim to represent the reality of Vietnam based on earlier fictional film versions of Vietnam, not the Vietnam War itself.

The characters of *Tropic Thunder*, especially Tugg Speedman (Ben Stiller), live in a hyper-reality. Director Damien Cockburn (Steve Coogan) throws a group of actors into the jungle without cell phones or assistants. Cockburn is the only link to civilization, but he steps on a landmine and is splattered all over the jungle. Speedman, who has experience making effects-driven films, attempts to convince the other actors that Cockburn's obliteration was a simulation only and that their reality is still being staged for the film. Reality plays like the movie was scripted to play. Michael Herr in *Dispatches* describes the effect the media has in creating a hyper-reality:

> You don't know what a media freak is until you've seen the way a few of those grunts would run around during a fight when they knew that there was a television crew nearby; they were actually making war movies in their heads, doing little guts-and-glory Leatherneck tap dances under fire.... We'd all seen too many movies, stayed too long in Television City, years of media glut had made certain connections difficult [209].

Robert Downey Jr.'s Kirk Lazarus playing Sgt. Lincoln Osiris is the voice of reality after Cockburn explodes. He says, "Ain't no *Criss Angel Mindfreak* David Blaine trapdoor horseshit jumping off here." However, Lazarus has his own problems with recognizing reality: as a serious actor he refuses to give up the illusion and break character "until he make[s] the DVD commentary!" (He also says in defense of quoting *The Jefferson*'s theme song as advice to Alpa Chino, "Just because it's a theme song doesn't make it not true.") Lazarus can not convince the others that their situation is no illusion because a squad from Flaming Dragon's heroin army fires on them. Like some of the soldiers Michael Herr observed performing absurd war moves in Vietnam, Stiller as Sgt. Tayback and his squad spray blanks one-handed from the hip, while turning somersaults, breaking out dance moves, and yawping war cries. They are convinced, for the time, that they're actors in a movie. As "Baudrillard suggests ... we all live our lives as if within quotation marks, as if playing a part in a movie" (Leitch 1731).

Tugg Speedman plays Sgt. Four Leaf Tayback when in the movie-within-a-movie. He becomes the lone holdout believing they're still making a film. He goes off on his own, and Flaming Dragon eventually captures him. At their compound, Tran, their leader, interrogates and beats Speedman. His plea, "P-p-p-p-please, don't hurt me" makes Tran realize that Speedman is Simple Jack, a mentally handicapped farm hand from a film Flaming Dragon has come to love. (The VHS tape of *Simple Jack* is the only film they have.) Tran forces Speedman to perform the character of Simple Jack continuously. At first Speedman balks, but he begins to like his role. He exists in a hyper-reality in which he's living the life of a fictional character which he helped create. Speedman is in his own "head movie," a phrase Simple Jack uses to describe his dreams. Speedman as Simple Jack at the Flaming Dragon compound embodies the concept of simulacrum. Fredric Jameson defines simulacrum as "the identical copy for which no original has ever existed" (*Postmodernism, or, The Cultural Logic of Late Capitalism* 321).

The movie Speedman and Kirk Lazarus (Robert Downey Jr.) and others are attempting to make is also a simulacrum because the "real" Sgt. Four Leaf Tayback, played by Nick Nolte, is a charlatan. The "real" Tayback admits to Cody, the pyrotechnic expert (Danny McBride), that "[he's] never been outside the States." The man who reportedly lost his hands, became a POW, was liberated by an extraction team, wrote a book about the experience, and secured a movie deal actually has hands, has made the whole thing up, and—as Pyro Cody says—is "the Milli Vanilli of patriots," referring to the lip-synching pop duo who were exposed as "fakes" in the early Nineties. Cody had revered Tayback and his book *Tropic Thunder* as his personal *Catcher in the Rye*, but Cody learns that Tayback is as phony as the adults in Salinger's book. As Baudrillard explains, "it is dangerous to unmask images, since they dissimulate the fact that there is nothing behind them" (1735).

Media Penetration and Machines of Reproduction

The media creates images that fail to correspond to reality. Fredric Jameson observes in "Postmodernism and Consumer Society" that advertising, television, and the media have penetrated far deeper into society than ever before (1974). *Tropic Thunder* begins with advertisements and trailers that help establish the characters of the five members of the squad. Alpa Chino (Brandon T. Jackson) is advertising Booty Sweat and Busta Nut Bars. Trailers for Tugg Speedman's action *Scorcher* films, Kirk Lazarus' drama *Satan's Alley*, and Jeff Portnoy's (Jack Black) comedy *The Fatties: Fart 2* run before the film begins. The trailers set a satiric tone for the film and establish typecast roles for the actor-characters which become difficult for them to break. In the jungles of Vietnam after Damien Cockburn has been blown apart, Alpa Chino as Motown begins his march. He looks shiftily over his sunglasses, cracks open an energy drink, and says, "Man, I'm thirsty. Might as well have some of this Booty Sweat I got back in Da Nang." Alpa Chino's cavalier self-promotion—although he later says he donates two million dollars from his revenue streams to charities in his community—is shameless product placement. The stock image of a pack of Marlboro Red cigarettes tucked under a helmet's scrim band in most Vietnam films is the equivalent. The well-loved *Simple Jack* VHS tape in the remote Flaming Dragon compound also shows the long reach of the Western media.

The videocassette, like Speedman who is featured in the medium, is obsolescent. The VCR, like the Wii and the TiVo, are all machines that present simulations of real life. Fredric Jameson in *Postmodernism, Or, The Cultural Logic of Late Capitalism* writes, "that home appliance called television ... articulates nothing but rather implodes" (328). Like the television, the Wii on which Speedman's agent Bill Peck (Matthew McConaughey) is constantly playing simulated sports and the TiVo that he so myopically fights to get for Speedman are both "machines of reproduction rather than production" (Jameson 329). Kevin Sandusky who plays Brooklyn in the movie-within-a-movie (Jay Baruchel) explains how "Hollywood was split into schisms, some studios backing Blu-Ray Disc, others backing HD DVD..." to which Kirk Lazarus as Sgt. Osiris replies, "You talking to me this whole time?" More than a set up for a great line and smash cut, Brooklyn's recapitulation of the battle between Blu-Ray and HD DVD is a reference to the newest "machine of reproduction," the emblematic technological achievement of our age.

Parody, Pastiche and Bricolage

Tropic Thunder has been called a satire or a spoof; however, Ben Stiller, who, in addition to playing Tugg Speedman, directed the film and co-wrote the screenplay, feels the film is more than a send-up. He says, "No, I feel the tone of the movie is its own thing.... I think there are elements of satire, but I don't think it should be categorized just as that. There are elements of parody in it, but obviously I don't think it's just that. I feel like hopefully it's its own thing, which has a lot of familiar stuff that we are playing off of." The presence of the past in the film and the charge that it is mere spoof reflect the position Jameson believes modern artists find themselves in: "all that is left is to imitate dead styles, to speak through the masks and with the voices of the styles in the imaginary museum" (1965). The movie's strongest "own thing" is its critique of how Hollywood presents subjects like war, race, drug addiction, and mental handicaps for profit and shapes the viewer's perception of those subjects. Jameson argues that modern art "tends to turn upon itself and designate its own cultural production as its content" ("Postmodernism and Consumer Society" 1970). *Tropic Thunder* uses references to Vietnam War films and other Hollywood films in order to critique what goes into the making of a film—its actors, directors, agents, and the bigger behind-the-scene movers and politics of Hollywood.

Parody dominates *Tropic Thunder*. In the first scene after the movie trailers, Ben Stiller's Tugg Speedman playing Sgt. Four Leaf Tayback falls to his knees, raises his hands to the air in a Christlike pose, and absorbs a ridiculous amount of rounds from the enemy behind him. The scene plays exactly like Sgt. Elias' death in *Platoon* (1986). This exaggerated scene is clearly parodic, mocking the excessiveness of the original. The Vietnam film genre's heyday spanned the late Seventies to late Eighties, so making *Platoon* (1986) and other Vietnam films from the era the subject of parody is a stale exercise. Fredric Jameson in "Postmodernism and Consumer Society" argues that "writers and artists of the present day will no longer be able to invent new styles..." (1965). He identifies pastiche as "one of the most significant features or practices of postmodernism..." (1960) and explains that pastiche is "like parody, the imitation of a peculiar or unique style ... but it is a neutral practice of such mimicry ... without the satirical impulse..." (1963). In *Tropic Thunder*, the pervasive imitation of scenes and plots from earlier films—at times clearly parodic of the particular film and at other times neutral or nostalgic—creates the foundation from which the film is able to comment on the current excesses of the movie factory: Hollywood. *Tropic Thunder* draws upon a rich store of Vietnam films, including *Platoon, Hamburger Hill, Full Metal Jacket, The Deer Hunter,* and one of Robert Downey Jr.'s own films, *Air America,* set in Laos. *Rambo I* (set in Vietnam but after the war), *The Nutty Professor 2, The Jeffersons, The Odyssey,* and the documentary *Hearts of Darkness,* a film about the making of *Apocalypse Now*, are part of the film's sources as well.

Vietnam Films, Michael Herr and The Odyssey

The scene in which Tugg Speedman is bowed to his knees with the enemy bearing down on him (this time Flaming Dragon forces, not the NVA) plays again near the end of the film. The reworking of *Platoon*'s most dramatic scene—the scene where Sgt. Barnes (Tom Berenger), the bad soldier, leaves Elias (Willem Dafoe), the good soldier, for dead—ties into the parallel plot structures of *Platoon* and *Tropic Thunder*. Soldiers split into two camps in *Platoon*: half support Barnes and half support Elias. In *Tropic Thunder,* Tugg Speedman is the delusional, bad actor because he thinks the action is fake when it is not. Robert Downey Jr.'s character Kirk Lazarus is the sane, good actor because he is sure the action is real. The names Elias and Osiris sound similar. Speedman and Lazarus also pull Kevin Sandusky in opposite directions. Sandusky is the only one who can read the map when the actors are actually lost because he's the only cast member who went to the film's boot camp. As Roberts and Welky explain, Oliver Stone put the actors of *Platoon* through a "two-week-long boot camp in the Philippine jungles" where long marches, a diet of cold rations, and "uncomfortable nights in foxholes" were "punctuated by sudden bursts of explosions" (290). Stone's boot camp that was orchestrated by Captain Dale Dye is much like the "real" Sgt. Four Leaf Tayback's insistence that director Damien Cockburn "put those boys in the shit" and that Cockburn give him and "that pyromaniac Cody all the smoke bombs, charges, explosives, and detonators [he's] got." Stiller actually first got the idea of making a mock Vietnam War movie in the 1980s when he heard about actor friends going through rigorous boot camps for *Platoon* and *Hamburger Hill* (CanWest). Exact quotations like "I got a baaaad feeling on this one" and "If the machine breaks down, we break down" (*Tropic Thunder*) are reproductions of Sgt. Barnes' and Sgt. O'Neill's original lines in *Platoon.* Lines from other Vietnam films are mimicked in *Tropic Thunder* as well.

Recycled images are a hallmark of postmodernism. Donald Crimp notes of postmodern art, "the fiction of the creating subject gives way to the frank confiscation, quotation, excerptation, accumulation and repetition of already existing images" (qtd. in Hutcheon 251). *Hamburger Hill* (1987), a low-budget film about the battle for Hill 937, came out amidst the slew of Vietnam films in the Eighties, and *Tropic Thunder* appropriates parts of the film as a source of its pastiche. Robert Downey Jr.'s Vietnam character Sgt. Lincoln Osiris says "ain't nothin' but a thang" to the horribly injured Sgt. Four Leaf Tayback played by Speedman. The chant "Don't mean nothin.' Not a thing" is featured in *Hamburger Hill.* Three black soldiers chant the refrain as they mourn the death of another black soldier who died with only a few days left in his tour. Private Motown is one of the three who mourns. Alpa Chino's Vietnam character's name is Motown in *Tropic Thunder. (*The name Al Pacino, in fact, connects *Tropic Thunder* to another Vietnam War film, *Apocalypse Now,* to be discussed later.) Robert Downey Jr.'s great line, "I'm a dude playing a dude disguised as another dude" is ripe for many interpretations, but at one point in the film Kirk Lazarus who is playing Sgt. Osiris is disguised as a rice farmer who is bringing the captured Jeff Portnoy/Fats (Jack Black) to the Flaming Dragon Compound. Part of Robert Downey Jr.'s disguise as farmer is heavy eyeliner around his eyes. *Hamburger Hill* ends with a forty second clip of Private Beletsky, whose eyes are heavily outlined to simulate war grime, but the makeup has the effect of making actor Tim Quill appear effeminate—even pretty. Other images from *Hamburger Hill* appear in *Tropic Thunder*.

In *Tropic Thunder*, Tugg Speedman's abandoned "son," Little Half Squat, who crawls onto the bank of the river after Speedman escapes the Flaming Dragon compound, mirrors the image of a Vietnamese toddler dressed in silk pajamas sitting abandoned on a roadside at the beginning of *Hamburger Hill*. (Little Half Squat also connects *Tropic Thunder* to *Apocalypse Now*—to be discussed later.) The gore of *Hamburger Hill* and other Vietnam War movies is parodied in the opening fight sequence of *Tropic Thunder*. Like Speedman's Sgt. Tayback who has lost his hands, Lt. Eden in *Hamburger Hill* temporarily issues commands even though his arm is blown off. The stock Vietnam War film image of a soldier whose intestines are spilling out of him appears briefly in *Hamburger Hill*. In the earlier film *Apocalypse Now*, a VC soldier suffers the same wound and "about the only thing holding his guts in is that pot lid." In *Tropic Thunder*, Kevin Sandusky as Brooklyn holds his exaggerated entrails in his hands and says, "What am I looking at? What is this?" Karl French notes that the spilled guts image as it is seen in *Apocalypse Now* comes from a photograph in *Vietnam Inc.*, Phillip Jones Griffith's 1972 book of photoreportage, of a real VC soldier "with a three-day-old wound" who had placed "his intestines in an enamel bowl" (180).

Another work of reportage on Vietnam, Michael Herr's 1977 *Dispatches*, provides many of the images for Vietnam War films, particularly *Apocalypse Now*, for which Herr wrote the narrative voice-over, and *Full Metal Jacket*, which Herr co-wrote with Stanley Kubrick and Gustav Hasford. For example, "Born to Kill" written next to the peace symbol on Private Joker's helmet was a paradox from a real soldier's helmet described in *Dispatches*. The Vietnam films Michael Herr's work contributed to are a part of *Tropic Thunder's bricolage*, the process of creating something from a variety of available things. Jean-Francois Lyotard sees the creation of postmodern works as "a sort of *bricolage*" ("Defining the Postmodern" 1613). The parody and pastiche of Vietnam and other films are the available materials with which *Tropic Thunder* is put together. Gunnery Sargent Hartman, played by former marine drill instructor R. Lee Ermey, harasses the marine recruits at boot camp on Parris Island in *Full Metal Jacket*. His obscenity-laden threats about what violence he'll do to the recruits by manipulating their body parts are unforgettable. In *Tropic Thunder*, Damien Cockburn adopts the affect of a drill instructor just before he is blown apart by a vestigial land mine. He calls the actors "maggots" (one of Sgt. Hartman's favorite put-downs) repeatedly and also uses his own less-forceful variation of it, "wriggly worms." Cockburn slaps Fats around like he's Leonard Lawrence (Gomer Pyle). His self-conscious, serio-comic imitation of the original drill instructor is generally the approach *Tropic Thunder* takes. Tom Cruise as media mogul Les Grossman also echoes Sgt. Hartman. He threatens Director Cockburn, Agent Bill Peck, and a member from Flaming Dragon (thought to be a competing production agency). Grossman oftentimes threatens sexual violence inflicted by the victim's own body parts. Grossman's line, "I will f*#$ you up" and its delivery are nearly mimetic to Drill Instructor Hartman's warning to Gomer Pyle in the second scene of *Full Metal Jacket*.

Tropic Thunder also pulls from *Rambo II*, particularly in a scene that only takes a second or two in which Tugg Speedman is captured and tortured by Flaming Dragon. Speedman's arms are tied to a yoke, and he is repeatedly dunked in pond water like Rambo who plunged into a leech-ridden sewer. Scenes from *The Deer Hunter* (1978) also appear in *Tropic Thunder*. The pigs squealing in the open ground of Flaming Dragon's compound, the "real" Sgt. Four Leaf's use of the flamethrower, Speedman's thick headband, and his torture by Trang are all reproductions of images from this first (other than *The Green Berets*)Vietnam film. *Air America,* a 1990 film co-starring Mel Gibson and Robert Downey Jr. is also a source for *Tropic Thunder*. The focus on the Laotian heroin trade is the strongest resemblance. Downey's character pilot Billy Covington says, "No need to give up on a good theory just because it isn't true," which sounds a lot like Downey's line as Sgt. Osiris, "Man, just cause it's a theme song don't make it not true" (*Tropic Thunder*). Some of the uses of earlier films in *Tropic Thunder* are so quick or obscure that they are easy to miss. Fredric Jameson writes of postmodernism, "The allusive and elusive plagiarism of older plots is, of course, also a feature of pastiche" ("Postmodernism and Consumer Society" 1966).

The Odyssey, too, is one of the sources of *Tropic Thunder*. Jeff Portnoy, Jack Black's character, wants to kick his addiction before the squad of actors infiltrates the Flaming Dragon compound where there is a "mother lode" of heroin. He tells Sandusky, "If you guys want to make it through this, you gotta strap me to a tree." He tells them not to untie him no matter what and that anything he says will be a lie. Portnoy is a version of Odysseus who ordered his men to strap him to the mast so he could listen to the sirens (Homer 186). Portnoy uses his own kind of cunning, promising sexual favors to Alpa Chino if he unties him, to no avail. John Milius who wrote the original screenplay for *Apocalypse Now* drew as primary sources Conrad's *Heart of Darkness* and *The Odyssey* (*Hearts of Darkness*). *Tropic Thunder* makes its own allusion to *The Odyssey* with Portnoy's scene on the tree.

Apocalypse Now, Hearts of Darkness *and* Heart of Darkness

Both *Apocalypse Now* itself and the making of the film are the most obvious sources of *Tropic Thunder*'s pastiche and parody. *Tropic Thunder* draws on *Apocalypse Now* from the beginning of the film until the end. Early in *Tropic Thunder*, the pyrotechnic Cody gyrates sensually as he detonates explosions along the tree line to simulate a napalm strike, crying ecstatically, "Mother Nature just pissed her pant suit" (*Tropic Thunder*). *Apocalypse Now* begins with the image of helicopters flying in front of an impenetrable jungle. Behind the helicopters, napalm explosions destroy the natural scene. Stephen Hunter remarks of director Francis Ford Coppola, "He loved the smell of napalm" (147). Another connection to *Apocalypse Now* early in *Tropic Thunder* occurs when the "real" Sgt. Four Leaf Tayback tells director Cockburn who is having trouble controlling his actors, "when the herd loses its way, the shepherd must kill the bull that leads them astray." The quotation makes sense when considered as a reference to Colonel Kurtz who in *Apocalypse Now* has gone rogue and insane in Cambodia. In the remote outpost, he's leading an army of followers (some U.S. military and some native) who worship him like a god. Captain Willard's mission is to terminate Kurtz's command, which he eventually completes. Images of the ritualized slaughter of a real water buffalo intermix with images of Willard chopping down Kurtz with a machete. E. N. Dorall in "Conrad and Coppola: Different Centres of Darkness" sees an "intrusive symbol of the scapegoat" in *Apocalypse Now* beginning early in the film with a chaplain conducting communion while in the background a helicopter transports a cow. The scene that follows shows Kilgore and his troops dining on beef (307). The "real" Four Leaf's cryptic advice to Cockburn is an oblique reference to the sacrificial bovine motif in *Apocalypse Now*. A water buffalo also physically appears in *Tropic Thunder* and Portnoy is strapped to it.

As the platoon members who have separated from Speedman stop to rest in *Tropic Thunder*, Robert Downey Jr. as Sgt. Osiris says, "You know back before the war broke out I was a saucier back in San Antone." He sounds exactly like Chef in *Apocalypse Now*. Hailing from New Orleans, Chef's lines are only slightly different. Ben Stiller, Justin Theroux and Etan Cohen's decision to include the saucier line from *Apocalypse Now* reflects the film's postmodernism because "the [postmodern] work of art" is "now a virtual grab bag or lumber room of ... random raw materials and impulses of all kinds" (Jameson, *Postmodernism, Or, The Cultural Logic of Late Capitalism* 325). Drug use by soldiers appears as a stock feature of many Vietnam films. Chef smokes marijuana on the boat with Clean and Lance in *Apocalypse Now*. Lance, however, goes further and drops acid as the patrol boat approaches the Do Long Bridge. The film *Tropic Thunder* inverts a character's drug use with Jeff Portnoy's forced withdrawal from heroin while in the backcountry away from his "jellybeans."

The working through past references goes deeper than *Apocalypse Now*. The crew's attempt to recover Tugg Speedman from the Flaming Dragon compound plays much like the end of *Apocalypse Now*, which takes as one of its sources Joseph Conrad's 1902 novella *Heart of Darkness*. This part of the ending of *Tropic Thunder* is an imitation of an imitation of the original fictional work which, as Adam Hochschild discusses in "Mr. Kurtz, I Presume," could have been based on actual contemporaries of Conrad. The agent Kurtz, in Conrad's work, does not want to leave his Inner Station where he is a god to his followers. Marlow, the loose model for Captain Willard in *Apocalypse Now*, "trie[s] to break the spell ... of wilderness that seem[s] to draw him to its pitiless breast..." (64). Colonel Kurtz also is entrenched at his outpost. Tugg Speedman tells Kirk Lazarus, "Home? But I'm doing five shows a day for a standing-room-only crowd. Don't you get it? I already am home." Speedman's deliberate bathing of his head, which is cast half in shadow and half in light, is parodied imagery taken from *Apocalypse Now*. Unsettling high string music plays in the background as the camera pans across Speedman's room and captures Little Half Squat, the toddler in silk pajamas, who performs *tai chi* in the background. The same shot occurs in *Apocalypse Now* with similar music, but a woman—presumably one of Colonel Kurtz's mistresses—is seen doing *tai chi*. Coppola's ending for *Apocalypse Now* takes its cue from James Frazer's work on comparative mythology, *The Golden Bough*, which "conjures up the sacred grove at Nemi..., where a priest-king held uncomfortable sway aware that at any moment another priest-king would spring on him to slay him and take over as king" (Hunter 152). A similar tension exists throughout *Tropic Thunder* between Kirk Lazarus as the hot new star who threatens to usurp the cooling Speedman, who "was once the highest-grossing star in the world."

The making of *Apocalypse Now* is also a source for *Tropic Thunder*. In *Tropic Thunder*, Maria Menounos reports for *Access Hollywood*, "The film is already rumored to be one month behind schedule just five days into shooting." The 1991 documentary *Hearts of Darkness* recounts the troubles that plagued the making of Coppola's film. *Apocalypse Now* was supposed to take five months to shoot, but it required "238 days of principal footage" (*Hearts of Darkness*). The recasting of Willard from Harvey Keitel to Martin Sheen affected the schedule. William Hagen notes that "the role of Willard was offered to ... Al Pacino" among others (298). (*Tropic Thunder*'s hip hop star is therefore an oblique reference to *Apocalypse Now*.) Typhoon Olga wrecked some of the sets and set filming behind. The presence of Filipino rebels as close as ten miles from the shooting also disrupted the Flight of the Valkyrie scene as some of the Filipino helicopters Ferdinand Marcos had made available for the film were needed by the army. *Tropic Thunder* mirrors this element of the film's making closely, with Flaming Dragon patrols running into the cast. Also, Coppola invested much of his own money earned by the huge successes *Godfather I* and *II* to keep the filming moving forward after running over budget; he admits he began to feel a little like Kurtz as he presided over various underlings in a remote location as director in "one of the last dictatorial posts left" (*Hearts of Darkness*). Damien Cockburn fleetingly feels a similar power—"I am Jesus Christ ... and you are my chosen disciples" as he's the only one to possess the means of communicating with the chopper. A landmine ends Cockburn's brief reign.

Problems with the cast of *Apocalypse Now* also bogged down the filming. Martin Sheen had a heart attack and had to return to the U.S. Dennis Hopper who plays an American journalist who has become a kind of disciple to Kurtz was not learning his lines. Marlon Brando who plays Kurtz arrived for the filming excessively overweight when Kurtz is described in *Heart of Darkness* as sick and so thin his rib cages are visible (Conrad 59). *Tropic Thunder*'s "director" Damien Cockburn complains about his actors acting like prima donnas; Les Grossman threatens to shut production down if the director can't get them in line. Brando had not even read *Heart of Darkness* before coming to the Philippines, and Coppola read it to him on the set. In *Tropic Thunder*, Kevin Sandusky explains to Portnoy, Alpa Chino, and Lazarus how they'll use a rescue scene from *Tropic Thunder*, the book the film is based on, to pull Speedman out of the Flaming Dragon compound: "Did you guys read the book? You guys all read the script, right?" Robert Downey Jr.'s character Kirk Lazarus replies, "I don't read the script; the script reads me." Lazarus' line reflects the state of affairs at the end of the filming of *Apocalypse Now*. Coppola wasn't sure in what direction he wanted to take the ending. Instead of halting forward progress while he wrote and reworked the script the way he wanted it, he had Brando, Sheen, and Duvall do guided improvisation and let the cameras roll (*Hearts of Darkness*). The script read them. Maria Menounos describes *Tropic Thunder* as "the most expensive war movie ever made" and as "a bungle in the jungle"; Coppola worried, "this film is a twenty million dollar disaster. Why won't anyone believe me?" (*Hearts of Darkness*).

In 2008 a mockumentary titled *Rain of Madness* became temporarily available for free through *iTunes*. In the thirty-minute film, Justin Theroux (one of the writers of *Tropic Thunder*) poses as German documentary director Jan Jurgen who is making a movie about the making *Tropic Thunder*. *Rain of Madness* is a send-up of *Hearts of Darkness* (Wortham). As Linda Hutcheon writes about postmodernism, "the most important boundaries crossed have been those between fiction and nonfiction" (251). *Hearts of Darkness* details how Francis Ford Coppola became in a way a kind of Kurtz and how for the cast and crew their filming in the Philippines was like the Vietnam War. As Coppola explained at the 1979 Cannes film festival, "My film is not a movie. My film is not about Vietnam. It is Vietnam.... The way we made it was very much like the way the Americans were in Vietnam. There were too many of us. We had access to too much money. Too much equipment..." (*Hearts of Darkness*). In *Rain of Madness*, studio executive Rob Slolom played by Bill Hadler says, "The only difference between this film [*Tropic Thunder*] and Vietnam is that with this film we're going to win." Not only does *Tropic Thunder* draw from the documentary *Hearts of Darkness* about the making of *Apocalypse Now*, *Tropic Thunder* also has its own mockumentary about its own fictional production process that sends up a documentary about the making of a fictional movie. *Tropic Thunder* and its mockumentary create an echo chamber of the postmodern quality of "metafictional reflexivity" (Hutcheon 258). Justin Theroux said of *Rain of Madness*, "It's a black hole of metaness" (qtd. in Wortham).

Nostalgia, High and Low Culture and Theory

When asked what he thought about *Tropic Thunder*, Francis Ford Coppola said, "Ben Stiller and those guys were obviously affected or impressed or in some way inspired by *Apocalypse Now* and the process of making the film that they went and did their comedy" (qtd. in Duralde). Fredric Jameson describes the nostalgic mode in "Postmodernism and Consumer Society." He believes viewers enjoy watching movies that capture some part of their viewing past. He uses the example of the style of *Star Wars* (1967) employing many of the same devices of the "afternoon serial of the Buck Rogers–type" from the 1930s-1950s: "*Star Wars*... satisfies a deep (might I even say repressed?) longing to experience them [the serials] again" (1965–66). For Stiller and Downey who were both born in 1965, *Apocalypse Now* would have hit theaters when they were fourteen. Justin Theroux and Etan Cohen would have been young teens when *Platoon, Hamburger Hill*, and *Full Metal Jacket* came out. It's not unreasonable to wonder if the writers and actors of *Tropic Thunder* were drawn to the idea of a Vietnam War film even if it was part spoof because of a nostalgic longing for the genre. The younger actors in *Tropic* express their nostalgia to the older actors. Sandusky says, "You're Kirk Lazarus ... I memorized every single monologue you ever did when I was in theater school." Alpa Chino says, "Look, Tugg, I saw *Scorcher I* twenty-four times when I was in eighth grade. I got high to that shit. You the man." It's clear that the postmodern features of intertextuality, parody, and pastiche are part of *Tropic Thunder*. The nostalgic mode may be at work as well. Other postmodern elements, like the melding of high and low culture, the creation of theory, the politicization of art, a critique of black identity, and a cooptation of subordinate culture round out the film.

The juxtaposition of a trailer for a serious film with a serious actor (Kirk Lazarus' *Satan's Alley*) side by side with *The Fatties: Fart 2*, a flatulence comedy parodying *The Nutty Professor 2*, demonstrates the postmodern "bridging the gap between elite and popular art" (Hutcheon 262). Robert Downey Jr.'s Kirk Lazarus, still speaking like Sgt. Osiris, schools Ben Stiller's Tugg Speedman on acting theory: "This a science man—this is high art ... I've always found mere observation in and of itself a tad rudimentary. Sometimes we gotta dig deeper to mine the true emotional pay dirt. Thus we can diagram the source of the pain and live it...." Lazarus as an actor is clearly talking theory, something he does often in the film. (While Alpa Chino and Lazarus observe Speedman performing as Flaming Dragon's Simple Jack, Alpa Chino slaps Lazarus who's in the middle of a theoretical acting lesson.) In his pretentious way Lazarus attempts to practice his own theorization. Jameson explains that "theoretical discourse is ... itself very precisely a postmodernist phenomenon" (*Postmodernism, or The Cultural Logic of Late Capitalism* 317).

Controversy and the Creation of Black Identity

Postmodern art is also "inescapably political" as Linda Hutcheon explains (245). Tugg Speedman tells Tran, the leader of Flaming Dragon, that he was not nominated for an Oscar for his role as Simple Jack because "it's very political ... you have to take out ads..." *Tropic Thunder* the film itself became politicized because of its use of the word "retard" and the character Simple Jack. The film tries to satirize the actors (Lazarus' list in the film includes Tom Hanks and Sean Penn) who may be exploiting the mentally handicapped or people with other mental disorders by portraying them for acclaim, but *Tropic Thunder* deeply offended groups like the American Association of People with Disabilities whose president Andrew J. Imparato said the film was "offensive start to finish" (Abramovitch). Protests against the film's insensitivity to the mentally handicapped overshadowed African American objections to Robert Downey Jr.'s character, Sgt. Lincoln Osiris. Downey earned an Academy Award nomination for best supporting actor for his characters in *Tropic Thunder*. (Heath Ledger won posthumously for *The Dark Knight* that year.) Some African American critics were offended that a nomination went to a white actor for putting on blackface, but Johnathan Pitts-Wiley, an African American critic, allows "for a good in-poor-taste jest" and believes that "Robert Downey Jr. pulled it off" and that he "hilariously and skillfully played an actor trying—poorly—to play a black man" ("Best Actor in Black Face"). *Tropic Thunder* makes a nod to the process of blackface going on in the movie. Flaming Dragon's Simple Jack puts on a whiteface for his performances at the compound. Also, when two Flaming Dragon soldiers chuckle at Jeff Portnoy's unintentional flatulence, he smothers their faces with pure heroin, in effect covering the two Asians with yellowface.

Within the film itself, Alpa Chino voices potential objections African Americans might have with Kirk Lazarus playing Sgt. Lincoln Osiris. After Lazarus goes into a particularly jivey, soul brother routine, Alpa Chino mocks him and says, "Hell, yeah. That's how we all talk? We all talk like this, suh. Yes, suh. Ha. Yeah, um-hmm. Get some crawfish and some ribs. Ah-ha. Yeah." Alpa Chino's criticism of Lazarus' portrayal can be interpreted as also critiquing how media presents stereotyped versions of African Americans. Later in the film Alpa Chino imitates a stereotypical Australian, which offends Lazarus, who fails to see how his imitating an African American is equally offensive. Alpa Chino defends the parleying of his rap career into acting against Lazarus' criticism by saying, "I just knew I had to represent, because they had one good part in it for a black man, and they gave it to Crocodile Dundee." His video for Booty Sweat, however, works to further negative stereotypes about African Americans, and his use of the "n word" offends the white man in blackface, Lazarus/Osiris. African American critic bell hooks writes in "Postmodern Blackness," "We have too long had imposed upon us from both the outside and the inside a narrow constricting notion of blackness" (2481). The portrait of blackness that Lazarus as Osiris presents is a composite of the character King in *Platoon* with his semi-literacy and jive combined with television's George Jefferson and, as Alpa Chino points out, Benson and Chicken George. Osiris is Hollywood's notion of blackness imposed from the outside. The image that womanizing, jewelry-flaunting hip hop star Alpa Chino presents in the Booty Sweat video is a notion of blackness imposed from within.

Conclusion

Tom Cruise's media mogul character—who was so popular with audiences that a spinoff featuring him is rumored to be in the works—tries to convince Speedman's agent, Bill Pecker, to abandon Speedman to his Flaming Dragon captors and collect on the star's insurance policy. Grossman dances to T-Paine's "Apple Bottom Jeans" in the seclusion of his ImagiCorp office as he makes the proposition to Peck. Grossman explains what's in it for the agent if he plays along: "... I'm talking G5 for the Pecker. That's how you're going to roll. No more frequent flier bitch miles for my boy.... Playa. Playa." Seeing a bald, bearded, overweight CEO with neck hair and hairy knuckles dance to hip hop and use Black English is a reminder of how the media can co-opt "forms which originally expressed the situation of 'popular,' subordinate, or dominated groups." The hip hop words Grossman uses are examples of how "vital sources of production (as in black language) are reappropriated by the exhausted and media-standardized speech of a hegemonic middle class" (Jameson, "The Political Unconscious" 1949) or, in Grossman's case, the upper class. Luckily, Tugg Speedman is not left to perish in Laos. Kirk Lazarus and the crew come to his rescue. Bill Peck's eleventh hour arrival with the TiVo (the latest machine of reproduction) saves the chopper from Tran's RPG. Speedman goes on to win Best Actor for his part in a movie about the failed making of a movie about a mission in Vietnam that never actually happened.

Ben Stiller offers an explanation and defense of *Tropic Thunder*: "The whole vibe of the movie is that we're saying, 'Look how ridiculous this world is.' It's a very tough world to navigate, in which to maintain your equilibrium" (CanWest). The world of *Tropic Thunder*, like ours, is a postmodern world where artists work through previous layers of film, literature, image, and style in an attempt to create something of their own; where we bowl and play tennis on game consoles; where satire doesn't come with a user's manual; where the line between fiction and nonfiction has become blurred to the point that war seems like a movie and movies have their own boot camps and documentaries; where we "may be nobody" because of our mimicry of the stereotypes the media presents to us that have no basis in reality; and where larkish cameos by megastars who play the hands that control our media may spin off to become the main characters of new movies.

Works Cited

Abramovitch, Seth. "*Thunder* Premiere Showdown Pits Megastars Against Disabled Who Obviously Don't Get the Joke." *Gawker*, n. p., 12 Aug. 2008. Web. 10 Mar. 2013.
Air America. Dir. Roger Spottiswoode. Artisan, 1990. Film.
Apocalypse Now. Dir. Francis Ford Coppola. Omni Zoetrope. 1979. DVD.
Baudrillard, Jean. "From The Precession of the Simulacra." *The Norton Anthology of Theory and Criticism*. Ed. Vincent B. Leitch. 1732–41. New York: W.W. Norton & Co., 2001.
Canwest News Service. "Stiller Pushes Boundary with War-Film Farce *Tropic Thunder*." *Montreal Gazette*, 12 Aug. 2008. Web. 10 Mar. 2013.
Conrad, Joseph. *Heart of Darkness*: *An Authorized Text Backgrounds and Sources Criticism*. 3d ed. Ed. Robert Kimbrough. New York: Norton, 1988. Print.
The Dark Knight. Dir. Christopher Nolan. Warner Bros., 2008. Film.
The Deer Hunter. Dir. Michael Cimino. Universal, 1978. Film.
Dorall, E. N. "Conrad and Coppola: Different Centers of Darkness." *Heart of Darkness*: *An Authorized Text Backgrounds and Sources Criticism*. 3d ed. Ed. Robert Kimbrough. New York: Norton, 1988. Print. 301–11.

Duralde, Alonso. "Francis Ford Coppola on New Apocalypse Now, Influencing *Tropic Thunder* and the Downside of CGI." *Movieline*, 19 Oct. 2010. Web. 10 Mar. 2013.
French, Karl. *Apocalypse Now: A Bloomsbury Movie Guide*. New York: Bloomsbury, 1998. Print.
Full Metal Jacket. Dir. Stanley Kubrick. Warner Bros., 1987. Film.
The Green Berets. Dir. Ray Kellogg, John Wayne. Warner Bros./Seven Arts, 1968. Film.
Griffiths, Philip Jones. *Vietnam, Inc*. 1971. Paris: Phaidon Press, 2001. Print.
Hagen, William. *"Heart of Darkness* and the Process of *Apocalypse Now."* Heart *of Darkness*: *An Authorized Text Backgrounds and Sources Criticism*. 3d ed. 293–301. Joseph Conrad. Ed. Robert Kimbrough. New York: Norton, 1988. Print.
Hamburger Hill. Dir. John Irvin. Paramount, 1987. DVD.
Hearts of Darkness: A Filmmaker's Apocalypse. Dir. Fax Bahr and George Hickenlooper. ZM Productions, 1991. VHS.
Herr, Michael. *Dispatches*. New York: Knopf, 1977. Print.
Hochschild, Adam. "Mr. Kurtz, I Presume." *The New Yorker*, 7 Apr. 1997: 40–47. Print.
Homer. *The Odyssey of Homer*. Trans. Richmond Lattimore. New York: HarperCollins, 1991. Print.
hooks, bell. "Postmodern Blackness." *The Norton Anthology of Theory and Criticism*. Ed. Vincent B. Leitch. 2478–2484. New York: W.W. Norton & Co., 2001.
Hunter, Stephen. *Now Playing at the Valencia: Pulitzer-Prize Winning Essays on Movies*. New York: Simon & Schuster, 2005. Print.
Hutcheon, Linda. "Beginning to Theorize Postmodern." *A Postmodern Reader*. Ed. Joseph Natoli and Linda Hutcheon. Albany: SUNY Press, 1993. Print.
Jameson, Fredric. "The Political Unconscious." *The Norton Anthology of Theory and Criticism*. Ed. Vincent B. Leitch. 1937–1960. New York: W.W. Norton & Co., 2001.
_____. "Postmodernism and Consumer Society." *The Norton Anthology of Theory and Criticism*. Ed. Vincent B. Leitch. 1960–1974. New York: W.W. Norton & Co., 2001.
_____. *Postmodernism, Or, The Cultural Logic of Late Capitalism*. Durham: Duke University Press, 1991. Print.
The Jeffersons. Dir. Don Nicholl. Embassy Television, 1975–1985. DVD.
Leitch, Vincent, ed. *The Norton Anthology of Theory and Criticism*. New York: Norton, 2001. Print.
Lyotard, Jean-Francois. "Defining the Postmodern." Leitch 1612–1614.
_____ *The Postmodern Condition: A Report on Knowledge*. Trans. Geoff Bennington. Minneapolis: University of Minnesota Press, 1984. Print.
The Nutty Professor 2: The Klumps. Dir. Peter Segal. Universal, 2000. Film.
Pitts-Wiley, Johnathon. "Best Actor in Black Face." *The Root*, 18 Feb. 2009. Web. 10 Mar. 2013.
Platoon. Dir. Oliver Stone. Hemdale, 1986. VHS.
Rambo aka *First Blood*. Dir. Ted Kotcheff. Orion, 1982. Film.
Rambo: First Blood Part II. Dir. George P. Cosmatos. TriStar, 1985. Film.
Roberts, Randy, and David Welky. "Coming to Terms with the Vietnam War: A Sacred Mission: Oliver Stone and Vietnam." *Hollywood's America: Twentieth Century America Through Film*. Eds. Steven Mintz and Randy W. Roberts. Malden, MA: Wiley-Blackwell, 2010. 281–300. Print.
Salinger, J. D. *The Catcher in the Rye*. 1951. New York: Little, Brown, 1991.
Star Wars. Dir. George Lucas. 20th Century–Fox, 1977. Film.
Tropic Thunder. Dir. Ben Stiller. Dreamworks, 2008. DVD.
Tropic Thunder: Rain of Madness. Crea. Justin Theroux and Steve Coogan. iTunes, 2008. Video.
Wortham, Jenna. "Get *Tropic Thunder* Mockumentary Free on *ITunes*." Underwire. *Wired*, 25 Aug. 2008. Web. 10 Mar. 2013.

Layers of Lazarus:
Robert Downey Jr. Hits "true emotional pay dirt" Through Blackface

Derek Adams

In his *Chicago Sun Times* online review of the 2008 box-office smash *Tropic Thunder*,[1] renowned film critic Roger Ebert offers up a moderate endorsement—"It's the kind of summer comedy which rolls in, makes a lot of people laugh and rolls on to video." The somewhat complimentary review awards the film 3.5 stars for its artistic merits, the same rating bestowed on *Gran Torino* and *The Hurt Locker*, two powerful, award-winning films produced that same year. Much of his praise for *Tropic Thunder* is linked to the stellar performance of one of its most notable co-stars: "When it's all over, you'll probably have the fondest memories of Robert Downey Jr.'s work." Ebert writes, "All but stealing the show, Robert Downey Jr. is not merely funny but also very good and sometimes even subtle as Kirk Lazarus [...]." Little more than a decade ago casual movie fans likely would not have predicted the acclaim being heaped on Downey for his acting prowess. His brilliant performances in films like *Less Than Zero* (1987) and *Chaplin* (1992) were being overshadowed by repeated run-ins with law enforcement officers between the mid–1990s and the early 2000's. Drug use, weapons possession, parole violations, and a one-year prison sentence were part of a well-documented public spectacle that cast a pall over the star's career. He continued making films and working in television during that span, but it became increasingly difficult to divorce the quality of his work from the messiness of his personal life. Rather than being appreciated for his superb acting talents, his illicit behavior turned him into a media caricature of recklessness and vulgarity devoid of self-awareness that obscured the figure that has recently reemerged as one of Hollywood's finest. An inverted dynamic is at work in the resurrection of his career at the time *Tropic Thunder* is released. His meteoric rise correlates with his blackface performance, a seemingly defunct, satirical form of racial caricature that is impossible to divorce from the messiness of its historical implications. Reviving his career in large part through this satirical role as Kirk Lazarus, Downey not only positively transforms his public image, but also causes viewers to contend with their own latent racial anxieties that are resuscitated through blackface.

Iron Man and *Tropic Thunder* are equally responsible for Downey's sudden career resurrection in 2008. Since the release of these films, Downey has become a central figure in two incredibly successful film franchises (*Iron Man* and *Sherlock Holmes*) and another (*The Avengers*) whose star is rising. His appeal as eccentric, playboy, billionaire-genius superhero Tony Stark (*Iron Man*) was foreseeable; as evidenced by the financial success of superhero film franchises of that decade (*The Incredible Hulk, Spiderman, The Dark Knight*), most everyone loves superheroes. His layered complexity as Kirk Lazarus offers a much more interesting case study for his career resurrection. Certainly one of his more memorable roles to date, Downey's portrayal of Kirk Lazarus, the critically acclaimed, Australian-born Method actor whose cinematic success (he has won 5 Oscars) comes from fully and authentically embodying the lives of the characters he portrays, steals the show. His lines are unforgettable and nearly all are rife with irony and humor that leave viewers breathlessly laughing. In fact, they seem perfectly suited for a film whose storyline is equally unforgettably comic; ultimately *Tropic Thunder* is a movie about the making of a movie (coincidentally titled Tropic Thunder) based on a memoir written by a man who hears the story that is the premise for the memoir from another man. This quixotic narrative layering undermines what would otherwise be a rather solemn story of the rescue of an American POW from an internment camp during the Vietnam War. In fact, so farcical are many of the film's elements (it introduces viewers to the cast of the film within the film through hyperbolic movie trailers and an over-the-top rap music video promoting an energy drink called Booty Sweat) that *Tropic Thunder* cloaks itself in satire from head to foot to mock the culture of unoriginality and egotism currently pervading Hollywood cinema.

Considering the satirical nature of the film, it is not surprising that Downey's performance as Kirk Lazarus is regarded with fondness. His "subtle" prodding at celebrity culture through this character—Lazarus is shown in one scene physically assaulting a member of the paparazzi and in another standing naked on a hotel balcony flipping off television cameras—is a refreshingly hilarious caricature (and in some ways a self-caricature of his own celebrity) that can be appreciated by casual moviegoers and film critics alike. However, most of what viewers revere about Downey's role in the film has little, if anything, to do with Lazarus and more to do with the character Lazarus portrays in the film within the film, that of Sgt. Lincoln Osiris, a black man.

Immersing himself completely in every role he takes on, Lazarus undergoes a controversial skin-darkening procedure to embody the identity of the black Sergeant. It is this character, the man with the black face, who stirs fondness in viewers whenever they recollect Downey and his lines. Most movie covers including the original depict Downey as Sgt. Osiris and not as Kirk Lazarus (IMDb). Downey, then, for all intents and purposes, is acting black. In playing a white man who darkens his skin to portray a black character, he is engaging in a layered form of blackface, a practice by which individuals, usually white, use makeup to darken the features of their skin to give them a stereotypically black appearance. The literal black face that is produced as a result of the procedure Lazarus undergoes is merely a more technologically advanced version of "blacking up," the process of applying blackface makeup to an actor's skin (Toll). In concert with his newly darkened epidermis, Lazarus manipulates his mannerisms and patterns of speech to complete the prescription for what he purports to be an authentic black identity, but is really nothing more than a blackface performance.

A practice long considered dead, or at the very least outdated, blackface is rooted in

From the back: Jay Baruchel as Kevin Sandusky, Brandon T. Jackson as Alpa Chino, and Robert Downey Jr. as Kirk Lazarus as Sgt. Lincoln Osiris in Ben Stiller's *Tropic Thunder* (2008).

the institution of chattel slavery in the United States and the racial animosity embedded in its power relations. The practice was an integral part of staged productions known as minstrel shows, in which actors performed what had been collectively determined as the foundational elements of black culture. Many of these staged elements include an exaggeration of the perceived physical attributes of black men and women (i.e. kinky hair, large white eyes, massive red lips, raggedy attire, and, of course, dark skin) reminiscent of the Sambo figure. Too, they are equally invested in the stereotypically-regarded demeanor and mannerisms of black folk, such as the use of black vernacular, a propensity for laziness, soulful musicality, childish ignorance, and a general playfulness properly suited for lampoon. Acting legends like Bert Williams, most notable for becoming the first black man to headline a Broadway production (*In Dahomey*, 1903) and Lincoln Perry, who brought to life the iconic character Stepin Fetchit onscreen, popularized the practice of burnt cork blackface on stage and in cinema during the early stages of the twentieth century. Each of these men is considered the comic genius of his day, although their performances raise important questions about the social consequences of reinforcing black stereotypes for popular consumption. Many critics have argued that the continuation of these forms of representation was an extension of the racial power hierarchy that disempowered black Americans.[2] Alexander Saxton reminds his readers, "Blackface minstrelsy epitomized and concentrated the thrust of white racism" as it permeated American popular culture. It afforded largely white audiences a forum to ridicule figures of the slow-witted "plantation darky" and the "northern negro dandy" that were legacies of racial fantasy in the white American imagination. The valorization of blackface as an artistic production faded over the course of the century, especially as social movements for racial equality such as the Harlem Renaissance of the 1920s and the Black Arts Movement of the 1960s redirected authority to black men and women to represent themselves through artistic mediums. C. Thomas Howell's controversial film *Soul Man* (1986), despite box-office success, was sharply criticized for its white protagonist's explicit use of blackface to move the narrative forward (Attanasio). With the exception of a few rare films like Spike Lee's *Bamboozled* (2000), a wonderfully insightful examination of minstrel performance as a gateway into the world of Hollywood, blackface virtually disappeared from public attention.

How convenient, then, that the resurrection of Downey's stardom coincides with a role that revives, albeit satirically, controversial racial performances connected to one of the most contentious legacies of American history. Because of slavery's perversely violent and psychologically demeaning components, the majority of Americans today, presumably, would characterize neither the institution of chattel slavery nor the practice of blackface minstrelsy stemming from it as "funny," or would recall it with "fondness." Yet, a majority of *Tropic Thunder* reviewers applaud Downey's cinematic portrayal of Lazarus/Osiris in this way with little mention whatsoever of the controversial racial performances it harkens to. This essay enters the dialogue at this fissure. More specifically, it is interested in the implications of a white actor resurrecting his acting career through blackface and achieving A-list success as a result. The analysis forecasts a series of interrelated considerations: the director's (Ben Stiller's) intentional use of satire to rekindle discussions of race; the various performative layers of white and black characters; the capacity of current postracial sentiment pervading American society to mask racial anxieties that continue to be experienced individually and collectively; the treatment of race in American popular culture in the twenty-first century; and the intricacies of Osiris' actions and mannerisms as brought to life by Downey and the way they might color a viewer's perception of the history behind the role. Although he brings the practice of blackface back from the world of the dead to execute his role in the film, the important questions about the meaning of such a performance have seemingly been left behind. This chapter brings those forgotten questions to the fore as a tool for framing an examination of the significance, and insignificance, of Downey's success once he goes black.

Question 1: What Are the Consequences of Satire?

Satire is parody with a point. Satire is never innocent, as it requires satirists to dip their hands into the messiness that the genre takes as its subject. *Tropic Thunder* is no different, wading through a muck of disingenuous political correctness at the center of identity politics. Downey's journey through the world of buried racial anxiety, however, yields unanticipated consequences. The film gave rise to a maelstrom of pandemonium over controversial remarks made by Downey's character about "going full retard." In the film, type-cast action hero Tugg Speedman, who is looking to resurrect his career as the lead in Tropic Thunder, debates with Lazarus his decision to play the role of Simple Jack, a young boy struggling with mental challenges. Speedman possesses virtually no dramatic talent (he lacks the ability to cry at one of Tropic Thunder's most emotional scenes) and accepted the role with the expectation that audiences would see him as a more complex thespian much like Lazarus. He earnestly believed that film critics would award him an Oscar for his portrayal of the less fortunate. *Simple Jack* tanked, pulling Speedman's acting career down with it. Unfortunately for Speedman, his portrayal was poorly received by critics and viewers alike, and is ridiculed on a segment of *Access Hollywood*. The problem with his portrayal, Lazarus tells him, was "going full retard":

> Everybody knows you never go full retard [...] Check it out. Dustin Hoffman, *Rain Man*, look retarded, act retarded. Not retarded. Count toothpicks, cheat at cards. Autistic, sho. Not retarded. Then you got Tom Hanks, *Forrest Gump*. Slow, yes. Retarded, maybe. Braces on his legs, but he charmed the pants off Nixon and he won a ping pong competition. That ain't retarded. Peter Sellers, *Being There*. Infantile yes, retarded no. [long pause] You went full retard man. Never go full retard. You don't buy that? Ask Sean Penn 2001 *I Am Sam*. Member? Went full retard, went home empty handed.

Through this spiel articulated in his characteristically comic black vernacular, Lazarus raises a serious issue concerning the nature of performing roles representative of members of an underrepresented population. The problem is that he glosses over the greater ethical implications of the issue, specifically the impact such a performance has on the underrepresented population being portrayed and how they are treated in turn. Instead, he focuses on the degree to which fully embodying such a role influences Academy Award decisions. Lazarus is privileging artistic integrity above the plight of real, and in this case, marginalized people. His principled integrity is ironically hypocritical considering he is attempting to occupy the skin of a member of an underrepresented group in his own portrayal as Osiris. He is lecturing Speedman about "going full retard" when he has himself undergone a medical procedure that allows him to go full black. This irony demonstrates the self-absorption at the heart of Lazarus' hyper self-awareness.

Unfortunately, much of this potentially productive conversation about Lazarus' hypocrisy as it relates to issues of the representation of the underrepresented gets overshadowed by a focus on political incorrectness. Speedman and Lazarus's conversation, although satirically intended, sparked mass protest in the world outside of the film by individuals and groups such as the Special Olympics and the American Association of People with Disabilities. These groups argued that the film intentionally caricatures the mentally challenged in demeaning ways and that it should be boycotted. In an NPR interview with host Melissa Block on *All Things Considered*, Chairman of the Special Olympics, Timothy Shriver, equates the conversation between Speedman and Lazarus to "hate speech" that is "an affront to dignity, hope, and respect" (Block). What became known as the "'R'-word protest" dominated headlines during the film's premiere and for weeks following, prompting both Stiller and co-writer Etan Cohen to address the issue through interviews with the media. They encouraged protestors not to disparage the film as a maliciously-intended satire that grossly misrepresents the life experiences of the mentally handicapped. Their intent in using the R-word debate between Speedman and Lazarus, the co-writers attest, is to reveal to viewers the moral decline in Hollywood cinematic culture resulting from its exploitation of the mentally handicapped in the quest for individual accolades. Cohen confesses, "[W]e're really trying to make fun of the actors who use this material as fodder for acclaim. The last thing you want is for people to think you are making fun of the victims in this who are having their lives turned into fodder for people to win Oscars" (Adler). The substance of the 'R'-word controversy has ignited a meaningful discussion that, considering the wide viewership of the film, is far-reaching. The intrigue inherent in this debate between 'R'-word protestors and *Tropic Thunder* enthusiasts resonates well beyond the confines of the film. Aside from decrying the film, protestors were calling for a collective reconsideration of the historical significance of the term "retard." In particular, they were focused on the ways it gets used in acts of bullying to belittle and dehumanize others, which, they argue, is precisely what was occurring through its "liberal employment" by Stiller and Downey.

This call for viewers to pay attention to the historical implications of labels and stereotypes is intriguing precisely because of the failure and/or inability to do so in regard to Downey's blackface performance. Unlike national associations in support of disabled individuals, civil rights groups like the NAACP did not organize official protests of the film. Jessie Jackson, Al Sharpton, and Benjamin Jealous were not condemning its release. Prominent black ministers were not preaching against it to their congregations. No groups of black men and women concerned with the film's racial content were found picketing in front of movie theaters during its release. With the exception of one incredibly thoughtful online reviewer to whom no other commenter responds,[3] even the comment boards were silent on the issue of race and its relationship to the film's employment of blackface. The intensity of critical attention paid to the R-word controversy presents another possible explanation for the indifferent response to the film's racial elements. In a special commentary piece to CNN, Shriver writes, "...I am disappointed that we were not consulted in the same manner as other minority groups depicted in the film and that there are 17 mentions of the R-word to 1 mention of the N-word." The comment conceivably encourages a comparison between these two marginalized groups that privileges the concerns of people with disabilities and their supporters above those of the individuals impacted by blackface. Although certainly unintended, the comparison invokes a hierarchy of oppression that indirectly discourages anyone from taking up the cause to question the film's blackface element. This unintentional marginalizing of one underrepresented group by another—our plight is worse than yours so you have no grounds for complaint—is an unfortunate consequence of Shriver's statement, much like the R-word protest is the unintended consequence of Stiller's attempt at satire through the conversation between Speedman and Lazarus. Nonetheless, the elevation of the importance of the R-word protest above all other concerns functions as a possible explanation for the unconcern with which Downey's blackface is received. It contributes to its implications being swept under the metaphorical rug.

More optimistically, it is quite possible that the performance is so poorly received by protestors precisely because Speedman is such a terrible actor, a fact made explicit throughout the film. Lazarus' subtlety and nuance in performing blackface assuages feelings about the controversial aspect of his performance. In an interview with *Playboy*, Downey admits that once he nailed down the voices for his characters, he felt he "could do no wrong" (Fleming). If Speedman had possessed any measure of Lazarus' qualities when acting as Simple Jack, he might be considered with the likes of Hanks, Hoffman, and Sellers. Perhaps then Stiller's character could do no wrong—then again, perhaps not.

Question 2: To What Degree Is the Film Self-Aware as Satire?

The film's overt self-awareness as a medium of satire is integral to the audience's celebration of Downey's blackface performance. This self-awareness as satire is manifest in a variety of the film's aspects. For instance, the production team for the film within the film is so entirely inept that they are one full month behind schedule after only five days of shooting, a temporal quandary. Further evidence of this self-awareness involves the name of Downey's characters. Lazarus and Osiris are both figures of legend notable for their respective emergences from the world of the dead. In the Bible's gospel of John, Jesus restores Lazarus to life and regenerates his health four days after he has died. Similarly, Osiris, god of Egyptian myth, is indirectly connected to the trope of resurrection and the conquering of death. As a god, Osiris transcends mortality, making it impossible for him to be resurrected. However, as renowned Egyptologist John Ray explains, "[Osiris'] true realm was not of this world, since he sat in perpetual rule over the dead. In this aspect, he is nothing less than the sun at night, giving life and sustenance to the netherworld" (Ray 156). Downey's Lazarus/Osiris character aligns closely with both legends. His racially-manipulated body represents the regeneration of racial anxieties attached to blackface practices that have supposedly vanished from this world. He is "the sun at night," shining light on one of humanity's greatest fears in the twenty-first century—race. He gives "life and sustenance" to a world of racial contention that is not past. Possessing only one of these names might be considered coincidence. However, the combination of the two suggests that Stiller and his co-producers are aware of the potential of this character to dredge up racial anxiety from the netherworld. The name might also hold personal meaning for Downey, who can be said to have resurrected himself, in a sense, by getting sober. When paired alongside Jack Black's heroin-addicted character, Jeff Portnoy, viewers encounter another layer of the film's self-awareness.

The strongest evidence of this self-awareness, however, is embedded in the dialogue written into the script, specifically that of the Lazarus/Osiris character. Lazarus stretches the boundaries of what viewers understand as self-awareness throughout the film. In one scene, Tropic Thunder director Damien Cockburn, frustrated with his selfish actors, scuttles them to the heart of the Vietnam jungle to break them of their celebrity vanity and pettiness in hopes that they will experience real fear. On arrival, he demands that his actors hand over their cell phones to him. When he gets to Lazarus, he is told in Osiris' black vernacular, "Weren't no cell phones in '69, man. I'm head to toe legitimate." On a literal level, there is nothing satirical about Lazarus' statement. There were no cell phones in 1969 (the year in which Tropic Thunder is set), so it makes sense that in embracing the role he would not have one on him. On another level, his statement is so absurd that it can be nothing other than satirical. Head to toe, Lazarus is a white man pretending to be a black man, the very definition of racial illegitimacy. Too, the legacy of blackface is to offer up a representation of blackness that scholars have accurately identified as anything but racially legitimate. His statement has the added dimension of coming from an actor acting out a role, which in and of itself is a staged performance. There is nothing "legitimate" about any aspect of Lazarus at that moment, yet he uses that specific term to characterize himself in much the same way that Tropic Thunder/*Tropic Thunder* characterizes itself as a war drama even though it is really a satire. Both characterizations are satirically intended.

Shortly after disposing of their cell phones and launching into an explanation of his intentions to shoot the film guerrilla-style with an assortment of hidden cameras, Cockburn steps on an old French landmine and is blown to pieces. Speedman, thinking this is a cinematic special effect (it is not!) meant to energize him and his co-stars, takes command of the "mission" and demands that they press on. Much more doubtful, Lazarus, in his characteristic Osiris black vernacular, contests the point with Speedman that Cockburn is not really dead:

> LAZARUS: "Yo asshole, this mutherfucka's dead. Ain't no Criss Angel mind freak, David Blaine, trapdoor horseshit jumping off here."
> SPEEDMAN: "Hey, you wanna get on the train here or do you want to ruin another take, huh?"
> LAZARUS: "Ain't no goddam takes. Ain't no goddam motion picture."
> SPEEDMAN: "You sure?"
> LAZARUS: "Oh yeah."
> SPEEDMAN: "Yeah."
> LAZARUS: "For certain, man."
> SPEEDMAN: "Then why are you still in character? Hmm?"
> LAZARUS: "I know, but I don't have to tell you."
> SPEEDMAN: "You don't know."
> LAZARUS: "Man, I don't drop character till I done the DVD commentary."

Notorious for never breaking character, as the last line of their back-and-forth suggests, Cockburn's death presents Lazarus with a unique problem. No director means no film; therefore, acknowledging his death virtually necessitates that Lazarus break character and drop his performance as Osiris, an action that violates his sense of artistic integrity. He values his dedication to craft to such a high degree that it actually trumps the life of the director of the film his character is part of. Cockburn's death is not enough to draw him away from his performance and back to the world outside of the film within the film. Choosing instead to latch on to the possibility that the film is still under production even without a director, he engages in a type of hyper self-absorption that stretches the limits of self-awareness. He is so entirely self-aware as Osiris that he is willfully, blindingly oblivious to his circumstances as Lazarus. The irony of this obliviousness is that Cockburn is the one man in the film who can finish production on Tropic Thunder and get it through the stage of DVD commentary at which point Lazarus can drop character without violating his artistic principles. Without him, Lazarus' artistic integrity would theoretically entrap him in a state of perpetual black performance from which he would never break free. True to form, Downey delivers the cast commentary for *Tropic Thunder* with his co-stars in character as Osiris, further emphasizing the film's self-awareness.[4]

The stereotypical nature of Downey's dialogue further magnifies the sharpness of the film's satirical self-awareness. Frustrated with the refusal of his four co-stars to continue following his orders after hours of blindly stumbling through the jungle, Speedman tells them all, "I don't believe you people!" Without pause, Lazarus, still fully invested in his identity as Sgt. Osiris, accusingly responds, "Hey, what do you mean *you* people?" After a brief pause, rap mogul co-star Alpa Chino (Brandon T. Jackson), the only "legitimate" black member of the cast, looks directly at Lazarus and angrily asks him, "What do *you* mean you people?" This moment is significant because it is one of only two instances in which Lazarus is called out for performing blackness. He is repeatedly criticized and mocked for never breaking character, but, as is the case with commentary outside of the film, rarely are the racial dimensions of his performance challenged within it. Through his response, Lazarus indirectly accuses Speedman of stereotyping all black men and women through the generalization "you people," a designation Speedman does not intend on a racial level. Alpa Chino directly accuses Lazarus of reinforcing the racial implications of Speedman's unintentional generalization by lumping himself in with "you people," something that he, as Osiris, intends on a racial level. He is an opportunist, intentionally misinterpreting Speedman's phrase in order to marginalize a group of individuals so that he may identify with them, even as he challenges the idea of their being marginalized. It is another example of the hypocrisy with which Lazarus adds to his black legitimacy.

Lazarus' stereotypical behavior continues to wear on Chino to the point that he eventually calls him out as a fraud. Chino yells, "I'm sick of this koala-hugging nigga, telling me..." and then is slapped hard in the face by Lazarus. Trying to retaliate, he is drawn in a tight embrace by Lazarus who slowly, dramatically whispers in his ear, "For four hundred years, that word [nigga] has kept us down. Took a whole lotta tryin,' just to get up that hill. Now we up in the big leagues getting our turn at bat. Long as we live, it's you and me baby." His consoling words of wisdom for Chino are hilarious. Not only is Lazarus using the word "us" in relation to "nigga" to draw racial connections between himself and his co-star, he is also reciting the lyrics from the theme song for *The Jeffersons*, a sitcom running from 1975–1985 about a black family that moved from Queens to a Manhattan high-rise. The seriousness behind the weight of the word "nigga" and all of its historical implications, which presumably triggers Lazarus' physical reaction, is completely undermined by his reliance on the theme song from a sitcom that itself has received criticism as a caricature of black life. It is a beautifully engineered invocation of caricature in the employment of caricature to validate legitimacy that is actually illegitimate.

The bulk of what Lazarus says and does as Osiris is comically self-reflexive without ever eliciting a moment of true self-reflection from him. His most famous line from the film—"Me? I know who I am. I'm a dude playing a dude disguised as another dude"—is the pinnacle of his hypocrisy. He is so deeply enmeshed in the various layers of the identities he is performing that he lets go of any true sense of self. He is a completely de-centered, nondescript dude in disguise, played by another de-centered, nondescript dude who may also be in disguise. And even when Lazarus stops performing, the satire does not end. In a moment of existential angst during the film's climax, Lazarus breaks character and confesses, "I think I might be nobody." This is the brilliance of the satire written into the script—a character so self-aware that he is actually unaware of his self at the most basic level. Manohla Dargis of the *New York Times* writes, "Though Mr. Downey's character [...] has been cut from moldy Fred Williamson cloth,[5] he's also the most recognizably human character in a lampoon rife with caricatures." This "recognizably human" attribute Dargis describes legitimizes the film's self-awareness in the way that it makes its most illegitimate character the most believably human one. Bringing this caricature of a character performing caricatures to life through dialogue is a stroke of artistic genius. The magnificence of the satirical performance, though, has the effect of softening its racial implications, even to the point that they may be greatly diminished or easily dismissed.

Question 3: How Does the Quality of Downey's Portrayal Affect the Reception of His Character?

The earlier comparison between *Tropic Thunder* and *Iron Man* is intended and requires further explanation. The two films were released in the same year and both entail Downey playing a character playing another character. In *Iron Man*, he is the aforementioned eccentric, playboy, billionaire-genius Tony Stark who, after a near-death escape from imprisonment at the hands of armed militants, creates and effectively becomes the superhero Iron Man. He convincingly plays a man who, to the viewer's knowledge, has a superhero alter ego distinct from that of Stark. As previously described, a similar layering dynamic is at work in *Tropic Thunder*, in which Downey acts as Lazarus acting as Sgt. Osiris. This type of role poses a unique challenge for Downey. To bring these characters to life onscreen, he must effectively become two distinct individuals who are individually recognizable, but who also share enough similarities to eventually be associated as the same person.

Downey's exceptional skill in negotiating the one-man-plays-two-distinct-yet-interconnected-roles-in-the-same-film character labyrinth is affirmation of his acting greatness. He captures the intricacies of black speech and mannerisms through Lazarus to a degree that makes Sgt. Osiris believable as a black character. In fact, so believable is this performance of blackness that it has the potential to fool the unsuspecting. One contributor to the NYTimes.com comment board writes, "All [my 16-year-old daughter] could say after the movie was 'I can't believe that was Iron Man, he really looked like a black man with that makeup'" (744888 CA). The young woman's near disbelief (she is aware of the role's requisite blacking up) points to how persuasively Downey performs as Lazarus playing as a black man, even though the film goes out of its way to make explicit that it is a role being acted out by a white man in the film within the film. The daughter's reflection skips this connection; Downey is not playing Lincoln Osiris, but rather playing Kirk Lazarus who plays Osiris. Jumping past that middle step is a convenient reminder that Downey is most commonly associated with Sgt. Osiris. The role he convincingly plays as a white man in the film (who is easily recognizable as Iron Man) is greatly overshadowed by the way that character brings Osiris to life through blackface.

Dana Stevens' review in *Slate* magazine likens Downey's acting skills in *Tropic Thunder* to those of Robert DeNiro, one of the greatest actors of a generation. Known for epic roles as Travis Bickle (*Taxi Driver*), Jack La Motta (*Raging Bull*), Master Chief Billy Sunday (*Men of Honor*), and James Conway (*Goodfellas*), to name a few, DeNiro (who himself has been nominated for five Oscars) is one of the most fiercely passionate actors of his generation. Stevens writes that Downey performs in *Tropic Thunder* with "DeNiro-like intensity." To make the comparison is rather complimentary although somewhat unconventional. Because of the nature of each genre, comparisons are rarely drawn between satirical and dramatic performances. It is akin to comparing apples and oranges. DeNiro's most intense and memorable performances are dramatic, not satirical. Ascribing this type of intensity to Downey for a satirically-intended role in a satirical film suggests that his performance transcends the expectations of the genre.

The greatest measure of Downey's brilliance as Sgt. Osiris might be most accurately measured by critics of *Tropic Thunder*. Despite its financial success, there is a relatively large number of individuals who openly deplore the film, characterizing it as "superficial," "classless," "a terrible movie," and most often, "a waste of time and money." Internet message boards and blog posts are littered with similar comments detesting what the commenters deem to be a cinematic flop. Still, despite these unsavory reviews hundreds of contributors who find the film detestable exalt the excellence of Downey's performance at the same time. One commenter writes, "If it weren't for Robert Downey Jr. Danny McBride ... and Tom Cruise's outrageous character, this movie would have been a total waste of time" (cab38). Another skeptic posts, "quite possibly one of the worst movies of all time. Ben Stiller just aint done much since *Something About Mary*.... Robert Downey was the only one keeping me in the theater" (cornett, TN). Another professes, "[T]he theater had very nice seats with lower back support. The air conditioning was at just the right temperature. I followed the 'film' long enough to enjoy Robert Downey's blackface pitch. I had a great nap and left" (ghhugh3). This last review is particularly interesting, since the phrase "blackface pitch" suggests that the viewer had some foreknowledge of Downey's roles going into the movie. Not only does it also skip the middle phase of the layered blackface, but the phrase suggests that it is solely the exceptionality of the racial performance that attracts this viewer to the film. Collectively, they all abhor or are bored by the film and yet also revere Downey's role in it. Even more credentialed critics who assign the film a marginal rating share similar sentiment for Downey's role. Rene Rodriguez of the *Miami Herald*, who gave the movie a "rotten tomato," praises Downey: "Cruise and particularly Downey are something to behold: they give this Thunder its lightning." For them, Downey steals the show, even if they claim there is not much of a show to be stolen, but the show stealing is perceived to be done by the black man Osiris, not by his white counterpart. Hundreds of blog posts and online comment boards critiquing the film offer commentary that focuses almost exclusively on Downey's role as Sgt. Osiris. Rarely ever is his identity as Lazarus referenced or are his lines as Lazarus repeated. It is his blackface performance that registers as phenomenal at every level and for nearly every viewer. This cinematic exceptionality, his show-stealing performance, may potentially relegate the racial dimensions of the Lazarus/Osiris blackface performance to the margins of their critical attention. For these viewers, the excellence of the performance either obscures or transcends the need to discuss the racial implications of benefitting from blackface.

Question 4: What Place Does Race Hold in a Postracial World?

To be clear, the premise of this question is absurd. In fact, it is so monumentally absurd that in many ways it reads satirically. "Postracial" implies that race holds no place in a world that has supposedly transcended racial anxiety. In conjunction with colorblindness ("I don't see race anymore"), postracial sentiment dominates the current national dialogue on all issues that are directly or indirectly linked to race. Postracial frames the sociopolitical context in which the film is produced and received, making the dynamics of a role replete with so much racial baggage even more interesting. In the world of 2008 in which postracial dogma dictates that racism is vehemently dismissed as antiquated, Lazarus' unconventional blackface is casually accepted as an element of humor, a product of good screenwriting seemingly divorced from an ugly history of racial tension deeply entrenched in the social fabric of American culture. To suggest otherwise is to invite the wrath of the masses for challenging the prevailing postracial attitude.

The release of the film coincided with two momentous postracial phenomena: the rising political star of Senator Barack Obama, and the growing fervor of the Birther Movement, a group of extreme "constitutional conservatives" alleging a conspiracy to cover up then–Senator Obama's national origin. Both play significant roles in the insistence that we have moved beyond race as a substantive topic, and both offer indirect evidence explaining the positive reception of Downey's blackface. On March 18, 2008, on his way to receiving the Democratic nomination for the Presidential ticket, Senator Obama delivered a speech at the Constitution Center in Philadelphia, PA titled "A More Perfect Union." His speech, commonly termed "Obama's race speech," was an attempt to positively transform the way Americans think about the highly controversial subject of race. Advocating for the transcendence of petty racial difference in the quest for a national and in some ways global utopia elevated the candidate to a level of prominence that dramatically altered the nature of U.S. political and racial discourse. With his eventual nomination on August 28, 2008 (a mere two weeks after the release of *Tropic Thunder*), the first visibly racial individual became frontrunner for the Executive Office. Almost three months later, this same man was overwhelmingly elected to serve as President of the United States, marking one of the most epic moments in the nation's history. The election of Obama ushered the American public into an era of postracialism in which they believe they have moved beyond issues of race. After official calls declaring Obama's electoral victory, pundits from across the political spectrum fell over one another proclaiming the significance of the victory. Television and radio personalities on all networks, even those stations that openly opposed Obama and his politics, were quick to note the historic implications of this election. Overcoming historically entrenched racial barriers to hold an office previously never held by a visibly racial individual, President-elect Obama metaphorically destroyed race as an impediment to individual achievement. If the problem of the twentieth century was the problem of the "color line,"[6] postracial logic mandated its resolution in the early stages of the twenty-first century with the election of Obama.

The Birther movement, rather less enthralled with Obama's political celebrity and arguably his racial identity, began advancing claims alleging the intentional falsification of Obama's status as a natural-born U.S. citizen. Their claim offers a direct challenge to his legitimacy as an American citizen. One line from their website reads, "[Under the Fourteenth Amendment] there is nothing that would grant natural born citizenship to Barack Hussein Obama, II. The man occupying the Oval Office is not qualified to hold that office by virtue of the U.S. Constitution and the intent of our founding fathers who wrote it."[7] As evidence, they cite exaggerated theories that his father had incentives to declare his son a citizen of the "Brittanic Majesty" and/or of Kenya to catalyze a regime of Islamic world domination more than four decades later. Even Donald Trump emphatically supported the movement, demanding the release of Obama's birth certificate to the general public and sending his own investigators to Hawaii to discover the "truth" behind his heritage.[8]

The Birther movement is as important to the rise of postracialism as is the figure of Obama because of what it reveals about the nature and the consequences of a supposed transcendence of race. The most obvious revelation is that race is as significant a factor in the twenty-first century as it ever was in previous centuries. Postracialism merely facilitates the creation of a collective psychological space in which race no longer matters, so long as the real world effects of racial difference can be willfully ignored. In 2009, renowned novelist Colson Whitehead wrote an op-ed piece for the *NY Times* titled "The Year of Living Postracially," mocking this sentiment. Its forcefully ironic opening line—"One year ago today, we officially became a postracial society"—plays on the fanaticism with which Obama's ascendance to the White House is regarded. Race, Whitehead emphasizes, still matters so greatly that he nominates himself as Secretary of Postracial Affairs to deal with the lingering effects of a culture of race that have yet to disappear.

The less obvious revelation is much more catastrophic. The Birthers' theory illuminates the dominant racial group's appropriation of the capacity of postracialism to empower racially marginalized groups. In 2008, Liliana Herakova and her fellow researchers at University of Massachusetts, Amherst conducted a study to assess possible connections between the foundational premise of colorblindness (a term they use analogously with postracialism) and the relative silence surrounding the issue of race on the part of their students. They write, "On our campus the predominant sentiment was that the acknowledgment of race as a marker of inequality was in and of itself the enactment of racism, as it obliterates faith in everybody's individual capacity to succeed." As they rightly point out, "Such logic produces a morality that absolves systemic racism while pointing a finger at those individuals that acknowledge racial inequality as racists" (Herakova 373). In essence, postracialism invites the inversion of racial logic—pretending race doesn't exist and remaining silent about its effects is racial transcendence; acknowledging the real world effects of race, or even just its existence as a category, is racist.

We see the inversion of this logic at the heart of the Birther movement. Certain groups and individuals accused Birthers and their supporters of forwarding a racist agenda through the fabrication of their racially-driven, discredited theories about Obama's illegitimacy. The Birthers' desire to invalidate Obama's American heritage, they argue, was the result only of his dark complexion. Birthers responded by leveling their own accusations of racism against their accusers, suggesting that anyone who discusses race is inherently racist. Under the "FAQ" section on the Birther website is the following exchange:

> **Question**: Are you racists, because Obama is black?
> **Answer**: We are not racist, many of our supporters and members are people of different skin colors. The question of Constitutional eligibility transcends color. Those who call us racists can offer no conclusive proof that Obama, II is in fact a natural born citizen. The fact is that 96% of people who describe their ancestry as coming from Africa voted for Obama, while 43% of those whose ancestry can be classified as Caucasian voted for him, this was about the same percentage that voted for McCain. Looking at these numbers *it is clear that those who identified themselves as having African ancestry were those who demonstrated that they are racists* [emphasis added]

Birthers answer the accusation of racism with non-contextualized percentages to validate their own accusation of racism against their critics. Implicit in their "Answer" is the idea that anyone raising issues of race and racism in relation to the political philosophy of the movement is racist. They forward their claim despite the fact that a number of independently funded, scholarly studies demonstrate the persistence of oppressive racial practices that negatively affect underrepresented, primarily black populations in the twenty-first century.[9] Too, leveling claims of racism or accusing others of being racist, regardless of the situation, illustrates reliance on the very formulation of race and racial significance claimed to have been left behind in a postracial world.

Americans clearly are not over their racial anxieties, at least not collectively. And yet, when it comes to Robert Downey Jr. and his role in *Tropic Thunder*, viewers act as though they are. Downey and his blackface performance demand (much like Obama himself) an acknowledgment of the contentious racial history that American culture is striving to evade in the quest for postracial enlightenment. His performance serves as an inconvenient reminder of the grotesque and horrific racial practices instrumental in the relations of power that shaped this nation's history. The postracialism espoused by groups like the Birthers through their political platform and the film's viewers through their silence thrives on the suppression of this history. In this sense, the satirical nature of Downey's performance has an effect similar to the election of Obama. (The two are not substantively equal, simply analogous.) Both are exploited by dominant groups as tools to mask the tangible effects of modern day racism in the name of racial transcendence. The symbolism of their bodies has been appropriated to advance an agenda of silence concerning prevailing racial antagonisms. Even more disheartening are the social consequences for individuals within this postracial space who do not blindly accept the mask. Reading into the racial dimensions of Lazarus/Osiris is to openly question the central tenet on which this postracial enlightenment is founded—the meaninglessness of race. Characterizing the performance as racially significant virtually assures a racially-oriented retaliation (i.e. You are racist for talking about it!), hence the reluctance to talk openly about Downey and blackface. In fact, based on Herakova's findings it is quite likely that even subtle, thoughtful suggestions concerning the historical implications of blackface or treating it as anything other than comedic and/or satirical would invite similar accusations.

Premise 1: Performing Blackface Is Tricky, Accepting It as Satire Even More So

The switch from a series of questions to this premise is important, as phrasing it otherwise would simply be to ask a rhetorical question with a predictable answer. Assuming that *Tropic Thunder* screenwriters created the Lazarus/Osiris character as a direct response to the postracial controversy stoked by a fascination with Barack Obama and Birthers is inaccurate. It often takes significant amounts of time to complete huge cinematic projects, and Stiller and his production team would have written scripts and begun filming months before Obama's Constitution Center speech. It is, then, nothing more than timely coincidence that Downey's career is resurrected, in large part, through a racially polarizing figure at the same moment that Obama's political presence catalyzes a dramatic shift in the tenor of the national conversation about race. Lazarus/Osiris operates as a gateway for the audience to participate in this discussion of race in relation to questions of history, legitimacy, anxiety, artistry and representation. Yet, there is a reluctance to step through that gateway. Blackface is a controversial enterprise tangled in a sticky web of racial antagonisms, but its reality is trumped by an intense appreciation of the brilliant humorousness Downey injects into it.

Nonetheless, the uncritical celebration of Downey's blackface performance and the disregard for its historical significance by millions of viewers is confounding. Characterizations of either *Tropic Thunder* or Robert Downey Jr.'s Lazarus/Osiris performance as overtly racist are unjust. The convincing mockery with which Lazarus' claims to legitimacy are treated makes it difficult to argue otherwise. It is also quite possible that an uncritical audience is simply unaware of the history of and behind blackface. Much more likely, though, is the idea that viewers are reluctant to acknowledge that history. In his research on African American humor Mel Watkins attests, "[Blackface] minstrelsy was a critical and complex phenomenon that revealed more about our national character and concerns than we would like to admit or have heretofore adequately assessed. This avoidance is in part attributable to our lingering unease with openly confronting and examining the shadowy and ineluctably ambivalent issues comprised by the paradigm of race" (Bean, et al.) The collective uneasiness at the heart of discussions of race makes it a subject that, at best, is difficult to negotiate in a postracial world. Most are not up to the task and those who are must often deal with harsh consequences.

This very uneasiness makes Downey's role in the film so important. His performance is powerful precisely because viewers feel compelled to shy away from conversations about its historical implications. Were Lazarus simply an uncomplicated caricature like Simple Jack, or any other satirized by the film (i.e. shallow, drug-addicted celebrities), his role would be reductive and would invite overly simplistic conversations about race.[10] But his greatness in blackface dictates otherwise, insisting on an engagement of the complexities of blackface history with the highest possible level of adroitness, care, and accuracy. Viewers unwilling to engage at this level attempt instead to turn the film's satire into a mask under which they can bury racial anxieties they no longer feel comfortable openly expressing in a postracial world. To do so is to miss the point of the film's satire and its capacity to challenge otherwise unchallenged assumptions about race. Lazarus tells Speedman, "I've always found that mere observation, in and of itself, is a tad rudimentary. Sometimes we got to dig deeper to mine the true emotional pay dirt." His comment adds to the layers of self-awareness. Although this line resonates for both Speedman and Lazarus within the film, it also functions as a critique of the uncritical viewer. Merely observing the racial elements of Downey's performance without digging into the "true emotional pay dirt" is trite. This is, perhaps, the most important idea viewers can take away from *Tropic Thunder*'s racial dimensions: self-awareness. The film, and especially Downey's role, resurrects blackface to immerse viewers in the chaos of racial self-awareness buried beneath the smooth veneer of postracial superficiality. Viewing the film without this critical lens, we are as tragically self-absorbed as are the very individuals we find ourselves laughing at for their egotism. Through a more critical perspective, we peel back the layers of Lazarus only to find our own layers falling away and our racial biases exposed.

Notes

1. Worldwide, the film grossed more than $188 million (*Box Office Mojo*).
2. Recent critical scholarship contests the long held claim that all blackface was a means of racial domination devoid of any potentially positive impacts on black culture. Both Eric Lott's *Love and Theft* (2006)

and Annemarie Bean's *Inside the Minstrel Mask* (1996) offer much more comprehensive descriptions of blackface minstrelsy, the history behind the practice, and the variety of its resonances amongst members of the American working classes.

    3. The random comment is so insightful in comparison, it is worth citing in full: "The difficult question is whether irony, or an ironic parody, performed by a white actor is the best manner to pose a critique of such a painfully entrenched signifier as Blackface…. Blackface is not just imitation or impression, it is an entrenched signifier with a particular representational intent, namely that of deforming the body for the purpose of maliciously mocking black Americans—historically, slaves on plantations. To take the position that 'we should all just get over it' or somehow transcend ourselves and our history is not generous nor thoughtful enough. It also upholds the constant that the colonizers, once again, get to tell/represent history" (Problematic irony—*esten80*).

    4. Interestingly, Downey's co-stars Black and Stiller oscillate back and forth between referring to him as Osiris and as Robert during the cast commentary. They go so far as to ask Downey directly which he should be referred to as. Too, Osiris refers to them by both their character names and real names, although neither of them are in character during the commentary.

    5. Fred Williamson is an actor and director known primarily for his work with the "blaxploitation" genre, a term used to characterize television and cinematic portrayals of hypersexual, hypermasculine black males as depicted in *Shaft* (1971) and *Boss Nigger* (1975). See *Baad Asssss Cinema: A Bold Look at 70's Blaxploitation Films* (2002).

    6. In his address "To the Nations of the World" in London at the first Pan-African conference, July 1900, social intellectual W.E.B. DuBois famously proclaims, "…the problem of the Twentieth Century is the problem of the color line." His claim becomes one of the most important principles for the push for civil rights. For more, see *The Souls of Black Folk* (1903).

    7. Since the reelection of President Obama on Nov 6, 2012, the Birthers have suspended any further posts on their site (http://birthers.org/) concerning his citizenship status.

    8. Trump's relationship to the Birther Movement was chronicled extensively by the *Christian Science Monitor* (http://www.csmonitor.com) throughout their campaign to discredit Barack Obama's citizenship status.

    9. One example includes the results of a sociological study reported in *USA Today* on April 27, 2011 that reveals racial prejudice plays a significant role in views on President Obama's citizenship status four years after the Birthers began espousing their theories that rely on postracial rhetoric (Vergano).

    10. The complexity of this type of racial satire is perhaps best illustrated in Dave Chappelle's sketch comedy *Chappelle Show* (2003–2006). Touré's discussion of *Chappelle Show* in his book *Who's Afraid of Post-Blackness?* (2012) offers a compelling analysis of Chappelle's own inability to negotiate the oversimplification of the racial elements of his comedy.

Works Cited

Adler, Shawn. "'Tropic Thunder' Director/Star Ben Stiller Says Disability Advocates Planned Boycott Is Unwarranted." *MTVNews*, 11 Aug. 2008. Web. 1 Apr. 2013.
Attanasio, Paul. "Soul Man." Rev. of *Soul Man*, dir. Steve Miner. *Washington Post*, 25 Oct. 1986. Web. 1 Apr. 2013.
The Avengers. Dir. Joss Whedon. Paramount, 2012. Blu-ray.
Bamboozled. Dir. Spike Lee. New Line Cinema, 2000. DVD.
Bean, Annemarie, James V. Hatch, and Brooks McNamara, eds. *Inside the Minstrel Mask: Readings in Nineteenth-Century Blackface Minstrelsy*. Hanover: University Press of New England, 1996. Print.
Chaplin. Dir. Richard Attenborough. Maple Pictures, 1992. DVD.
Dargis, Manohla. "War May Be Hell, But Hollywood Is Even Worse." *New York Times*, 12 Aug. 2008. Web. 18 Jan. 2013.
The Dark Knight. Dir. Christopher Nolan. Warner Bros., 2008. Film.
"Disabled Group Calls for *Tropic Thunder* Boycott." *All Things Considered*. Narr. Melissa Block. *NPR*, 12 Aug. 2008. Radio.
DuBois, W.E.B. *The Souls of Black Folk*. Chicago: A.C. McClurg, 1903. Print.
_____ "To the Nations of the World." Pan African Convention. Westminster Hall, London: 25 July 1900. Speech.
Ebert, Roger. "Tropic Thunder" Rev. of *Tropic Thunder*, dir. Ben Stiller. *Chicago Sun Times*, 11 Aug. 2008. Web. 2 Feb. 2013.

Ellison, Ralph. "Change the Joke and Slip the Yoke." *Shadow and Act*. New York: Vintage, 1964. Print. 45–59.
Fleming, Michael. "*Playboy* Interview: Robert Downey Jr." Nov. 2010: n. pag. Institute for Robert Downey Jr. Studies—Required Reading. *Robert Downey Jr. Film Guide*. Web. 3 May 2013.
Goodfellas. Dir. Martin Scorsese. Warner Bros., 1990. Film.
Gran Torino. Dir. Clint Eastwood. Matten Productions, 2008. Film.
Herakova, Liliana, et al. "Voicing Silence and Imagining Citizenship: Dialogues About Race and Whiteness in a 'Postracial' Era." *Communication Studies* 62.4 (2011): 372–388. Print.
The Hurt Locker. Dir. Kathryn Bigelow. Voltage Pictures, 2008. Film.
In Dahomey. Dir. McVon Hurtig and Harry Seamon. New York Theater, New York. 18 Feb. 1903: 53 performances. Performance.
The Incredible Hulk. Dir. Louis Leterreri. Universal Pictures, 2008. Blu-ray.
Iron Man. Dir. Jon Favreau. Paramount, 2008. DVD.
The Jeffersons. Dir. Don Nicholl. Embassy Television, 1975–1985. DVD.
Less Than Zero. Dir. Marek Kanievska. Twentieth Century–Fox, 1987. DVD.
Lott, Eric. *Love & Theft: Blackface Minstrelsy and the American Working Class*. Oxford: Oxford University Press, 1993. Print.
Men of Honor. Dir. George Tillman Jr. Fox 2000 Pictures, 2000. Film.
Mettinger, Tryggve N.D. *The Riddle of Resurrection: "Dying and Rising Gods" in the Ancient Near East*. Stockholm: Almqvist & Wiksell International, 2001. Web. 20 Jan. 2013.
"Nap." Reader Review: Ghhugh3. *New York Times*, n.d. Web. 22 Jan. 2014.
Obama, Barack. "A More Perfect Union." Speech. Philadelphia, PA, March 18, 2008.
Raging Bull. Dir. Martin Scorsese. United Artists, 1980. Film.
Ray, John. *Reflections on Osiris: Lives from Ancient Egypt*. New York: Oxford University Press, 2002. Print.
Rodriguez, Rene. "Tropic Thunder (R): Some Sparks but No Fire." *Miami Herald*, n.d. Web. 22 Jan. 2014.
"See 'Pineapple Express' Instead." Reader Review: Cab38. *New York Times*, n.d. Web. 22 Jan. 2014.
Sherlock Holmes. Dir. Guy Ritchie. Warner, 2009. DVD.
Soul Man. Dir. Steve Miner. Balcor Film Investors, 1984. VHS.
Spiderman. Dir. Sam Raimi. Columbia Pictures, 2002. Film.
Stevens, Dana. "There's Something About Robert Downey Jr." *Slate*, 13 Aug. 2008. Web. 22 Jan. 2014.
Straussbaugh, John. *Black Like You: Blackface, Whiteface, Insult & Imitation in American Popular Culture*. New York: Penguin, 2006. Print.
Taxi Driver. Dir. Martin Scorsese. Columbia Pictures, 1976. Film.
Taylor, Yuval, and Jake Austen. *Darkest America: Black Minstrelsy from Slavery to Hip-Hop*. New York: Norton, 2012. Print.
Toll, Robert C. *Blacking Up: The Minstrel Show in Nineteenth-Century America*. New York: Oxford University Press, 1974. Print.
Touré. *Who's Afraid of Post-Blackness?: What It Means to Be Black Now*. New York: Free Press, 2011. Print.
Tropic Thunder. Dir. Ben Stiller. Dreamworks, 2008. DVD.
"Tropic Thunder." *Box Office Mojo*. IMDb, n.d. Web. 24 Jan. 2014.
"*Tropic Thunder* Movie Poster." IMDb, n.d. Web. 3 May 2013.
Vergano, Dan. "Study: Racial Prejudice Plays Role in Obama Citizenship Views." *USA Today*, 27 Apr. 2011. Web. 24 Jan. 2014.
Whitehead, Colson. "The Year of Living Postracially." *New York Times*, 3 Nov. 2009. Web. 20 Mar. 2013.
"Worth Every Penny!" Reader Review: CA, Pasadena 744888. *New York Times*, n.d. Web. 22 Jan. 2014.
"WOW." Reader Review: Cornett, TN. *New York Times*, 1 Sept. 2008. Web. 22 Jan. 2014.
Zimmerman, Johnathan. "Donald Trump, the 'Birthers,' and the GOP's Moment of Truth." *Christian Science Monitor*, 26 Apr 2011. Web. 3 May 2013.

Language and Power in *The Soloist* and *A Guide to Recognizing Your Saints*

Sam Lundberg

The motor-mouthed wit, typically played by a non-white actor who acts as the protagonist's sidekick, has a long history in Hollywood, such as Eddie Murphy in the *48 Hrs.* films and Chris Tucker in the *Rush Hour* films. Traditionally, they form a counterpoint to the protagonist: While the hero honestly believes in whatever ideals are motivating him on his journey, the sidekick is usually in it for personal gain and mocks those institutions, allowing the film to be both idealistic and cynical simultaneously. Slovene philosopher Slavoj Žižek described this particular model of belief in *The Sublime Object of Ideology*: "Cynical distance is just one way ... to blind ourselves to the structuring power of ideological fantasy: even if we do not take things seriously, even if we keep an ironic distance, *we are still doing them*" (Žižek 33). Robert Downey Jr.'s characters after 2008's *Iron Man* also follow this model, with an important twist: In his protagonists, particularly Sherlock Holmes and Tony Stark, the believing protagonist and mocking sidekick are combined into one figure, who shoulders both the ironic detachment and earnest faith simultaneously.

However, there is one aspect in which the fusion of the two character types is imperfect: that of racial and economic difference. The quick and slang-heavy speech of the sidekick represents affluent white anxieties about the loss of control over language and culture in general, allowing the narrative to heal those anxieties by having the protagonist and sidekick reconcile; the scene in *Rush Hour* in which Jackie Chan and Chris Tucker's character bond over the Edwin Starr song "War" exemplifies this symbolic reconciliation. Without this scene of racial harmony, the traditional depiction of the non-white poor person sticks out strangely. In most of Downey's later films this issue is avoided by avoiding the poor, through focusing on the rich in *Iron Man* and *Iron Man* 2 and in whitening England for the *Sherlock Holmes* films, but in one film, it is unavoidable: the 2009 film *The Soloist*, directed by Joe Wright and starring Jamie Foxx and Downey. The film's portrayal of a friendship between Downey's character, Steve Lopez, and Foxx's character, Nathaniel Ayers, leaves little room for the filmmakers to avoid the issues of language and power.

Through an in-depth analysis of *The Soloist*, I will explore how the film struggles with but ultimately avoids the issues resulting from the clash between a traditional portrayal of

Robert Downey Jr. (left) as Steve Lopez helps push Nathaniel Ayers' (Jamie Foxx) cart of worldly possessions in Joe Wright's *The Soloist* (2009).

the poor population and Downey's fusion of believing white protagonist and cynical non-white sidekick. I will then briefly contrast it with his earlier performance in 2006's *A Guide to Recognizing Your Saints*, a film from before *Iron Man* which offers a much more honest portrayal of language and poverty.

The Soloist

The narrative of *The Soloist* is simple: Downey's character, Steve Lopez, is a successful newspaper columnist for the *L.A. Times* who meets Nathaniel Ayers, played by Jamie Foxx, a homeless musician playing in the park who, he discovers, was at one point a promising student at Juilliard. The bulk of the film consists of Lopez attempting to convince Ayers to reintegrate himself with society by visiting a homeless center and accepting an apartment. These scenes primarily serve, however, to create a stage on which issues of capitalism, race, and language can attempt to work themselves out.

The complex relationship between language and capitalism is encoded into the structure of the narration of the film, which serves as its opening lines. Unlike in *Kiss Kiss Bang Bang*, in which Downey's narration is both stream-of-consciousness and omnipotent, capable of rewinding the film, summoning title cards, and ordering characters around, *The Soloist*'s narration is carefully constructed and completely impotent. This dichotomy comes from their diegetic locations: *Kiss Kiss Bang Bang*'s narration is, until the final moments, positioned outside the cinematic world, whereas *The Soloist*'s narration is merely the text of Lopez's articles read aloud.

The ramifications of this shift are much clearer when it is considered in the context of a recurring theme in the film: the decline of the newspaper industry. In an early scene, Lopez's coworker complains that young, college educated people no longer care about what is happening in the world at large, a fear repeated implicitly later: While Lopez gets blood taken, his nurse, who, between her outfit and non-standard hair color, is clearly meant to stand in for the coworker's specter of the twenty-somethings the newspaper is losing, tells him how her "dad is gonna freak when he finds out" she met him, but that she doesn't "really read the newspaper." Together, these strands point to a much deeper insecurity than the mere obscelesence of a medium—specifically, the perennial fear of losing control of the discourse.

The term discourse does not refer merely to the set of literal statements made, but to the unspoken meanings and ideas that cause people to make one statement instead of another. Necessarily, the discourse is pre-rational, and this is precisely what causes the fear: if the dominant discourse is founded only on the acceptance of it, and one's acceptance is not instantly sensible, it is constantly in a highly precarious position, as it is always under potential threat from others' discourses. To this extent, Lopez represents the absolute apex of the upper class control of the discourse. Repeatedly, smaller scenes appear, often just brief clips of dialogue, that serve no purpose but to show Lopez using language to undermine another member of his class: In one scene he interviews and undermines an atheist because of his unbelief, and he, in the process of trying to purchase coyote urine to scare raccoons from his lawn, mocks the seller's choice of words. In these scenes he is established as the Platonic ideal of the person currently in charge; he is completely one with language—at least, with the linguistic system that is currently dominant.

In their first encounter, Lopez finds Ayers in a park, playing scales on a two-stringed violin. Immediately, Ayers subverts the dynamic Lopez has had with other characters by failing to acknowledge him as an interviewer. He launches a torrent of speech, completely ignoring Lopez's questions. The film tries to soften this blow by having Ayers speak in near-gibberish, as a discourse can only be threatened by another coherent one. However, this does not completely remove its threat, as gibberish is always at some level the threat of another model of understanding whose cohesiveness is not immediately obvious.

Ayers begins to talk about the statue of Beethoven near which he stands, foreshadowing another way in which he will subvert capitalist expectations. He obsesses about the constituent materials of things, whether they are the components of the statue, his violin, or the letters that make up the names he hears. By focusing on the object itself and not its larger symbolic meaning, he specifically ignores the exchange-value of the objects, another aspect of the discourse that exists only through mutual acceptance. Thus, from their first scene Ayers is challenging the fundamental tenets of essentialist capitalist thought. This first scene serves to state explicitly, in terms of physical people, the conflict that was stated earlier in terms of the society as a whole, with Ayers representing the hole in the discourse, those that refuse to acknowledge the newspaper, those whose logic is fundamentally different and thus destabilizing, and with Lopez representing the old discourse's attempts to reintegrate this remainder into itself.

After his first attempt at reintegration—writing a newspaper column about Ayers—Lopez tries to do it in an even more traditionally capitalist way: pride of possession. Lopez offers him a new cello, but stipulates he can only play it at a local homeless shelter, which Ayers refuses to go to because people smoke cigarettes there. Lopez offers Ayers the ability to play it immediately, on the street, and a remarkable thing happens: While Ayers plays the introduction to Beethoven's Symphony No. 3, the film cuts away from Ayers and Lopez to an impressionistic montage of other scenes, both from earlier in the film and entirely new. In essence, music has taken the place of Downey's narration from *Kiss Kiss Bang Bang* discussed above, taking over the film at large. However, this narration is not reliant on the verbal signifier, which can be undercut; unlike speech, music is non-representative, unshakable. Here, the threat is not just of an alternative discourse which has equal claim to truth, but an unshakable discourse that can overcome any competitors.

By making the connection between Ayers and the non-linguistic discourse explicit, instead of the implicit connection earlier in the film, the process of positioning him as the Other is complete. The Other represents the one who enjoys totally, the one whose enjoyment is so complete it stretches beyond the bounds of language, depicted at this point through the poetic shots of cities and animals and later in the film as pure bursts of color on the screen. The pleasure always belongs to the Other, someone other than the perspective character; as Lopez tells another character later, "I've never loved anything the way he loves music."

Significantly, however, Ayers' pleasure is not free from the conventional discourse, in that his secret pleasure revolves around Beethoven, perhaps the single greatest symbol of the bourgeoisie ideology. Even that point, then, which is supposed to be that which escapes ideology, that which is transcendent, is still deeply based on centuries of cultural history. This fact is most evident in Ayers' instrument; in the real-life, he was in fact a double bass major at Juilliard (Lopez 12). By shifting the instrument he played from double bass to cello to fit more properly the image of the tortured musician, the filmmakers reveal to what degree the presentation of that which escapes the symbolic realm is still only a symbol.

What does it mean to say that Ayers' character is not a contingent threat from outside, but is instead a necessary symbol within it? In the Lacanian model, the mind is structured entirely around absence and the promise of a future presence. The true pleasure instead happens not when the anticipated object arrives, but in the act of anticipation itself. In this film, the anticipated moment is the removal of the threat originally represented by the growing failure of the conventional meaning-producers, such as the press, and then specifically embodied in Ayers and his music. Thus, the transition from Ayers being a random man speaking nonsense to a classic example of the tortured genius originally appears as movement from being outside the system in his own world to inside the system, but is instead simply movement from one location in the system to another.

At this point, the film is on track for the traditional Hollywood "white person helps non-white person through adversity" film, like 2009's *The Blind Side*. Social conflict has been invoked in spectral form, then incarnated into a specific physical figure who rejects mainstream capitalist society. From this point, the genre dictates that the rejection is reducible to a simple cause, which can be absolved or fixed, and the representative of capitalism and the Other can unite, symbolically healing society. Of course, this narrative is only possible in the realm of fiction, as another Other must always take the place of the last. In this way, the traditional structure can be likened to that of a cartoon character who runs off the cliff and hovers impossibly over the chasm; the film must end before the inevitable realization and the fall.

However, *The Soloist* is based on a true story, and because the filmmakers were attempting to stay to some degree truthful to it, even using actual L.A. homeless people as actors in the film (Wright, "Commentary"), this simple path is not available. Instead, when Lopez goes to drop off Ayers' cello, he meets David, the head of the local homeless shelter. When Lopez asks him about Ayers' specific illness, he responds that he "doesn't know" and that he doesn't "get too hung up on diagnosing." Referring to the homeless population, he explains that "every one of them has been diagnosed more than [Lopez] can imagine, and as far as [he] can tell it hasn't done them any good." These lines, which come almost verbatim from the book, where they are spoken by Dr. Mark Ragins (Lopez 50–52), cut off this traditional progression by pointing out how much more complex real mental illness is than is often presented. This theme of the complexity of mental illness is strengthened by the intercut scenes showing Ayers' past; his supportive family undercut the idea that mental illness can simply be reduced to childhood trauma, and an intensely shot sequence shows that his issues became worse despite what would be considered capitalist stability.

The next roughly half-hour of the film centers around Lopez coming to terms with the fact that there is no simple fix to mental illness, and it is in this section that the narrative can be seen as subversive. Lopez here steps in for not simply the protagonists of other similar films, but for the capitalist perspective that cannot understand why poverty is about more than a literal lack of opportunity. Ayers' mental illness stands in for all failures to act in what are defined as acceptable ways, and the issue is tied directly into the issue of language, of the difference between Lopez's wit and Ayers' deluge of words.

It is crucial to capitalism that its structure seems completely self-evident and natural, that enjoyment comes from the consumption of commodities, and that the trade of labor-hours for those commodities is the next logical step. Similarly, failure according to capitalist standards can only be the consequence of rejecting the self-evident trade of commodities for labor-hours. Ayers' symptoms—a constant litany of voices that prevent him from being able to focus—serve to prevent him from making this self-evident trade; the self-evident logic of capitalist life is not obvious to him, because the constant chatter prevents him from working through it. Thus, Lopez's desire is to free Ayers from the voices, allowing him to reach the end of thought—the point where capitalism is self-evident—and his new life of owning an apartment and living traditionally.

At this point, then, the filmmakers face an issue: their accurate depiction of mental illness means that the traditional resolution, the discovery of the simple cause and the healing of it, is not available. Their solution, ultimately, is to abandon the traditional ending of these films which would unite Ayers and Lopez in freedom from language and instead to make Ayers' character completely Other, completely alien to comprehension and understanding, and to have the ultimate unity with the system be exclusively Lopez's.

This section begins when Ayers' character, encouraged by Lopez to perform, can't handle the pressure and runs into the night. Lopez tries to find him, and wanders through an urban wasteland that, for the first time in the film, threatens his well-being. While the danger is never explicit, the scene is shot in a much more ominous way than Lopez's earlier visits to where the homeless live; smoke and haze covers the area, there is constant shouting, and Lopez looks around nervously and begins to jog through. Recognizing another person from the homeless shelter being arrested, he argues with the police for his release, but is treated rudely. He finds a crime scene, assumes the victim of the crime was Ayers, and rushes to a hospital. The atmosphere there is no better than on the street: Constant shouting from everyone means he has trouble being heard, and he is shunted from one desk to another, all of whom have never heard of Ayers. Lopez here crucially mirrors his first scene with Ayers, in which Ayers obsessively spells out both his own name and Lopez's name repeatedly; at each desk Lopez is forced to spell out Ayers' name in exactly the same way, copying his diction exactly.

These scenes reposition the entire map of the film. Lopez is no longer the representative of capitalist society, trying to reform the Other; he is instead being treated as a marginalized figure, ignored and lost. Crucially, the constant chatter in these scenes functions in exactly the same way as the chatter in the scenes depicting Ayers' illness, again showing how mental illness here is not a special case but is in fact just one particular explicit explanation for the only logical explanation within capitalism to fail to succeed: an excess of language.

Lopez finally finds Ayers, who never was in the hospital to begin with, but after further arguing and unpleasantness ends up on his ex-wife Mary's sofa, having given up on Ayers. The pivotal scene of the film, in which Ayers aggressively lashes out at Lopez for calling him Nathaniel while Ayers has always respectfully called Steve "Mr. Lopez," brings up the little-mentioned but omnipresent double–Othering of race that also separates the two men and effectively destroys Lopez's assumption of his own powerful, privileged position. Lopez leaves, afraid for his safety but also convinced that he overstepped his presumed authority. Finally, the film can reach the catharsis it has been attempting; after Ayers' refusal to be "fixed" and reintegrated by a speech revealing his problems' simple cause, Lopez must accept the position of the one who is "fixed," by realizing his own powerlessness to intervene in the world of the Other. Mary's speech, whose content, advising Lopez to stop trying to fix everyone, is less relevant than its structural placement as the revelation of the solution to his sudden descent from a privileged position, finally allows the film to end in the traditional transcendent way.

The final narration positions Ayers as completely Other, a man with completely opaque thoughts that cannot be fit inside the conventional discourse, but Lopez has, crucially, learned from him "being loyal to something you believe in, holding on to it, and above all else believing without question it will carry you home." These comments are crucial, as this absolute certainty is exactly the first step at the base of the discourse that was threatened by the appearance of the Other; thus, by passing through the world of the Other, Lopez has brought back that certainty in himself, symbolically tethering the teetering discourse with his own new appreciation for the importance of belief. It is crucial that while, like all of Lopez's narration, the final narration is the text of his newspaper, thus embedding it in a conditional world, it is the first narration since the earliest moments of the film that is not merely a draft that constantly repeats and edits itself; instead, the narration is totally confident and presented as complete and unthreatened. In other words, the problem is solved and the day is saved; capitalist meaning-producers, represented by the newspaper industry, have recovered their place as unthreatened and the Other has been, if not absorbed and fixed, at least de-fanged.

A Guide to Recognizing Your Saints

To some degree 2006's *A Guide to Recognizing Your Saints*, written and directed by Dito Montiel, follows the same model as *The Soloist*. Again the Other is represented by the poorer class, and their world is depicted as highly dangerous and to be avoided. The underprivileged, non-WASP teens in Astoria, Queens have no power but through the macho threat of violence which they communicate through their speech, their physicality, and even their graffiti. Ultimately, the plot tracks the protagonist—played by Shia LeBeouf as a teenager and Robert Downey Jr. as an adult—trying to make the same development himself that Lopez was trying to get Ayers to make in *The Soloist*: the state of freedom from the constant babble, where conforming to conventional capitalist wisdom is self-evident. However, there is one key difference between the films: their depiction of the language of the Other.

In *The Soloist*, the Other was depicted as being one with his language, and this unity constituted its threat: The loss of a central control over the conventional discourse was mirrored by the lack of a need for a central control in the Other's. *A Guide* shares some aspects of the depiction of the Other in *The Soloist*, primarily that the Other is constant and enveloping, almost irreducible to individual words; the sounds of the city simply wash over the viewer. However, unlike *The Soloist*, the Other is not in control of its discourse in *A Guide*, and in this lies the difference. Ultimately, the plot consists of little more than a series of attempts by the teenage protagonists to pretend that they have control over the symbols that they use, that the symbols are, in fact, one with themselves, natural extensions of their desires, instead of social constructs they must deal with as they find them. As Montiel says in his commentary, "This is a whole movie about people saying nothing, going nowhere." Even the adults, particularly Dito's father, are trying to grasp hold of what they already pretend to have. Ultimately, though, their social world comes from beyond them.

Giuseppe's death halfway through the film depicts this desire and failure in microcosm. He is hanging out near a subway track with his friend and brother, trying to prove their masculinity to each other. He jumps onto the tracks to retrieve something that has fallen, and stays to grandstand, bragging that he would be able to step onto the electrified rail of the subway and stay safe. His brother's attempts to depict himself as an uncaring and complete figure begin to bother him, and he lays on the track, threatening to get hit by the train if his brother refuses to admit he cares about him. The brother refuses, and Giuseppe accidentally fails to get out of the way before the train reaches him and he is killed. In this scene, which sets the tone for the violent last third of the film, the pattern of all the violence in the film is represented symbolically: Desperate attempts to express one's inner feelings—in this case, Giuseppe's desire to express his desire for his brother's affection and care—can only be stated in the language of violence and masculinity. Giuseppe is merely using the language of bragging and dangerous acts, but the necessarily violent character of that language, the danger that is assumed to only be rhetorical, turns out to be real.

This pattern is explored in a much larger form as one of the main plot threads of the movie, which is instigated by the language of graffiti. A Puerto Rican teenager tags Dito's parents' house, claiming it as his territory. In the confrontation, Dito's friend, who is unable to avoid yelling at and threatening anyone she encounters, escalates the situation until the point where the tagger threatens to kill Dito. This ultimate threat is merely a way for the tagger to walk away from the conversation without losing face, but like Giuseppe's attempt to use the threat of death rhetorically to elicit a response, which leads to the threat being carried out, this threat has consequences that are implicitly unintended—the threats are only meant as posturing—even if they seem explicitly to follow. Graffiti offers the teens in this neighborhood the same type of symbolic power that their verbal threats do. Only an outsider (the new student from Scotland who writes poetry) ventures further with the written word, until Dito finds his own voice as a writer years later.

After the first graffiti incident, Dito finds the same person tagging his friend's mother's store. Dito's friends threaten the tagger's brother; in response, the tagger repeats his threat to Dito's life. After his brother's death in the train accident, Antonio attacks and accidentally kills the tagger. Finally, a relative of the tagger shoots another of Dito's friends. Every act of escalation, and the final acts of violence, are intended first and foremost as statements, as violence without violence—in other words, as pure language. If there is one specific cause behind all of these acts, it is the characters' inability to admit that there is anything to what they are saying that is more than its explicit content. In this way, the characters of *A Guide* are trying and failing to fit the depiction of the Other in *The Soloist* specifically, but any films that feature the quick-talking clever urban character, and the tragic events of the film are the natural result.

This excess—that thing the characters cannot express—comes out in Montiel's unique directorial style which mixes experimental sequences into the traditional content of the rest of the film. Having been called "impressionistic" and compared to Robert Altman in reviews, Montiel explains in the DVD commentary, "[E]verything about this film that is people talking over each other, cut to black, the voices echoing, typing on the wall—it was painful to put it up there. It wasn't like ah, this is a good gimmick, you know. It was—it felt right, and that's it." Dito still cannot express in words the feelings he tries to communicate in the film, but instead lets the style speak for itself. For example, the screen fades intermittently to black during Dito's father's seizures; phone conversations are sometimes depicted with just audio, a black screen, and subtitles; and in one sequence, each of the teenaged characters turns and talks directly to the camera, expressing the inner content he is seeking to express. Their inability to express their feelings with each other—especially Channing Tatum, whose line, "I'm a fuckin' piece of shit, and that's who I am," expresses the self-loathing that leads to his murder of the tagger—means these emotions have to come out in other ways. These cinematically unconventional uses of language (visual and verbal) underscore the teenagers' inability to master their world.

Finally, Dito decides to escape to Los Angeles, where he becomes a successful musician and author. He eventually returns as an adult played by Downey in scenes intercut with the film revolving around his father's illness and meeting back up with his former friends who are still in the same neighborhood, living in various states of economic success. Dito is there to convince his father to go to a hospital, but instead argues with him about their relationship, bringing to a head many of the issues regarding language the film raises. Dito insists that his father say explicitly that he loves him, but his father can only respond "a father always loves his son," echoing his comments on what a father does or a son does earlier in the film. Instead of going through the realm of the Other and returning, as Downey did in *The Soloist*, Dito here leaves the realm of the Other and returns, and his time outside has allowed him to realize that these symbolic attempts to communicate will always fail because of the necessary gap they place between people as abstract signs and people as physical beings.

Both of the attempts to force other characters to move past posturing and into honest statements of their feelings—Dito with his father and Giuseppe with his brother—mistake a key step toward unraveling these systems: They move around the symbols, trying to force the characters to say the opposite, instead of examining the symbols themselves and why those particular forms were picked. Thus, the film ends without any catharsis or completion; Dito's father says he loves him, but Dito does not seem to believe it, and he ends on narration, the first narration since the earliest moments, with Dito visiting Antonio in prison but unable to resolve anything ("I don't know what I thought was going to happen," he says). Thus, while the film provides a fascinating depiction of the language of the Other, it does not offer any final simple explanation.

Conclusion

In a remarkable way, the two films fit each other: *The Soloist* sets up the idea of the Other, who is at one with language and may not ultimately be able to be reached by the viewing subject—that is, the white observing subject; *A Guide* exposes *The Soloist*'s fundamental naiveté about the Other, showing that the Other has no more direct access to language itself than Lopez does to Ayers.' The shared failure to provide true and thorough catharsis implies a path that avoids the mistakes of both ideological worlds, one that accepts that language is perpetually a faulty device for communication and acknowledges the extent to which any figures of power are merely presenting an image, an image in which much of society is complicit. It is not the easy answer expected of the inspirational film, but it is a true one nonetheless.

Works Cited

The Blind Side. Dir. John Lee Hancock. Warner Bros., 2009. Film.
48 Hrs. Dir. Walter Hill. Paramount, 1982. Film.
Iron Man. Dir. Jon Favreau. Paramount, 2008. Film.
Iron Man 2. Dir. Jon Favreau. Paramount, 2010. Film.
A Guide to Recognizing Your Saints. Dir. Dito Montiel. First Look International, 2006. DVD.
Kiss Kiss Bang Bang. Dir. Shane Black. Warner Bros., 2005. Film.
Lopez, Steve. *The Soloist*. New York: G.P. Putnam's Sons, 2008. Print.
Montiel, Dito. "Director's Commentary." *A Guide to Recognizing Your Saints*. First Look International, 2006. DVD.
Rush Hour. Dir. Brett Ratner. New Line Cinema, 1998. Film.
Sherlock Holmes. Dir. Guy Ritchie. Warner Bros., 2009. Film.
The Soloist. Dir. Joe Wright. DreamWorks, 2009. DVD.
Wright, Joe. "Director's Commentary." *The Soloist*. DreamWorks, 2009. DVD.
Žižek, Slavoj. *The Sublime Object of Ideology*. London: Verso, 1989. Print.

Robert Downey Jr. as Detective: Sherlock Holmes Redux

Linda Ledford-Miller

The fictional Sherlock Holmes was born in 1854 and born in print to the reading world in 1887 in *A Study in Scarlet*. As his 160th birthday approached in January 2014, scholars and fans were planning conferences and celebrations from New York (the Bakers Street Irregulars) to London ("Sherlock Holmes: Past and Present") and beyond. Though Sir Arthur Conan Doyle attempted to dispose of his annoyingly popular sleuth during a struggle with Professor Moriarty at Reichenbach Falls in "The Final Problem" (1893), the unhappiness of Sherlock's fans (and perhaps Conan Doyle's own interests) forced Doyle to revive him in "The Adventure of the Empty House" (1903). Since his resurrection, Holmes has never been out of print. He first appeared in film in 1900, in a thirty second short, *Sherlock Holmes Baffled*, but the first film based on a Conan Doyle story was an American silent film adaptation of 1905, *Adventures of Sherlock Holmes; or, Held for Ransom*.

Sherlock Holmes stories have been adapted for film and television with great regularity since 1908, and include the famous Basil Rathbone series of fourteen films (1939–1946) and the revered Granada television series starring Jeremy Brett as Holmes, spanning ten years (1984–1994) and forty-one episodes, ending prematurely with Brett's death from a heart attack and only eighteen of the stories left untold. More recent interpretations include the popular and critically acclaimed BBC *Sherlock*, with three episodes in 2010 and 2012, and three more planned for 2013. CBS opened its fall 2012 season with *Elementary*, with a modern-day Holmes who has recently moved to New York City, played by the English actor Jonny Lee Miller, and a female Dr. Watson played by Lucy Liu. With his roles in the 2009 film *Sherlock Holmes* and the 2011 film *Sherlock Holmes: A Game of Shadows*, Robert Downey Jr. joins a pantheon of actors and interpretations of the iconic detective.

Both Downey films were directed by Londoner Guy Ritchie, best known for the heist film *Lock Stock and Two Smoking Barrels* (1998) and the crime comedy *Snatch* (2000). Critical response to Ritchie's Sherlock Holmes films, and Downey's performance in them, varied greatly, with Sherlock Holmes generally faring better than the sequel two years later. Richard Roeper, for example, reviewer for *The Chicago Sun Times*, gave *Sherlock Holmes* a grade of B+, and *Sherlock Holmes: A Game of Shadows* a C+. Audience response was strong for both films, with a rating of 81 percent for the first film and 78 percent for the sequel (www.rot

tentomatoes.com). *Sherlock Holmes* was nominated for two Oscars, Art Direction and Original Score, taking in a domestic gross of $209,028,679 and a foreign gross of $315,000,000, for a worldwide total of $524,028,679, and at $24.6 million setting a record for a film opening on Christmas Day (Subers). Robert Downey Jr. earned a Golden Globe for Best Performance by an Actor in a Motion Picture—Comedy or Musical (2010). Though more harshly critiqued and not nominated for any Oscars, *Sherlock Holmes: A Game of Shadows* fared even better financially, with $186,848,418 gross domestic earnings and $357,000,000 foreign, for an even higher total of $543,848,418 worldwide earnings. DVD sales added another $47 and $45 million, respectively. Whatever their shortcomings, both films were clearly very popular with audiences.

Critiques of the films tend to focus on two areas: the question of authenticity, or faithfulness to the "real Holmes" of Arthur Conan Doyle, and the issue of (homo?) sexuality.

Authenticity: Sherlock Holmes as Action Hero?

Bob Mondello comments that "Ritchie's come up with precisely what you'd expect of him—a pumped-up, anachronistically modern Sherlock Holmes designed for the ADD crowd," while Roger Ebert sees Holmes as "yet another classic hero [who] has been fed into the f/x mill, emerging as a modern superman." J.R. Jones complains that "Arthur Conan Doyle's master detective became one of the great heroes in genre fiction precisely because he was so freakish ... his intellect so overdeveloped that he couldn't relate to anyone. The very idea of handing him over to professional lad Guy Ritchie ... to be played as a punch-throwing quipster by Robert Downey Jr., is so profoundly stupid one can only step back in dismay." The essential complaint among critics is that Ritchie's approach depends too much on advanced technologies and action sequences, and that Downey-as-Holmes is too slapstick and overly physical, and not adequately cerebral, thus distancing the character from his origins and identity in the Conan Doyle canon.

Yet the canon itself provides evidence of Holmes' physical prowess. In the first of the original tales, *A Study in Scarlet*, Watson comments that Holmes is an "expert singlestick player, boxer, and swordsman" (14). In *The Sign of Four* (1890) Holmes has a conversation with the porter of Pondicherry Lodge with whom he had once boxed, the porter noting that Holmes "has wasted [his] gifts [and] could have aimed high, if [he had] joined the fancy," and even been a professional boxer (151–152). In "The Adventure of the Yellow Face" (1893), Watson asserts that Holmes is "undoubtedly one of the finest boxers of his weight" (547). Holmes suffers a minor injury in a barroom brawl in "The Adventure of the Solitary Cyclist" (1903), calling the "few minutes" of the fight "delicious" and the day "enjoyable" (842). In "The Adventure of the Empty House" Holmes explains to Watson how he managed to survive the battle with Moriarty in "The Final Problem," in which he seemed to die along with his nemesis: "I have some knowledge, however, of baritsu, or the Japanese system of wrestling, which has more than once been very useful to me. I slipped through his grip..." (764–765). Barton-Wright, the inventor of the mixed martial art known as baritzu or bartitzu and popular in turn-of-the-century England, claimed it could be effective "against every possible form of attack, whether armed or otherwise"(qtd. in Godfrey, note 20, 171). Holmes states in "The Adventure of the Illustrious Client" (1924), "I'm a bit of a single-stick expert, as you know" (528). In short, there is ample evidence in the canonical texts for the physical prowess of the original Sherlock Holmes character. The "reinvention" of the iconic detective owes as much to a return to origins as to the anachronism of currently available modern technologies.

The opening scene of *Sherlock Holmes* manages to combine the intellectual with the physical skills of the great detective. As Lestrade and Watson ride in a police hansom toward their destination, Holmes runs along the street, leaping over obstacles, rolling and landing on his feet like a gymnast. As he starts down a long flight of curving stairs, he encounters a sentinel, a man much larger than himself. His calculator brain processes his strategy, in a voice-over narration accompanied by slow motion action:

> HOLMES: Head cocked to the left.
> Partial deafness in ear.
> First point of attack.
> Two. Throat. Paralyze vocal cords. Stop screaming.
> Three. Got to be heavy drinker. Floating rib to the liver.
> Four. Finally, drag the left leg. Fist the patella.
> Summary prognosis: Conscious in 90 seconds.
> Martial efficacy: Quarter of an hour at best.
> Full faculty of recovery, unlikely.

The sequence then repeats in real time, Holmes using martial arts to quickly incapacitate his enemy. Ritchie uses this technique of "Holmesavision" to demonstrate both the Holmes of rational calculation as traditionally understood, and the" kinetic," "more visceral" Holmes

Jude Law (left) as John Watson and Robert Downey Jr. as Sherlock Holmes demonstrate their fighting skills in Guy Ritchie's 2009 film, *Sherlock Holmes*.

("Holmesavision on Steroids"). When he reaches the bottom level, Holmes finds a beautiful young woman dressed as a bride, writhing upon an altar of sacrifice and about to stab herself. He engages in battle with the cloaked dark priest officiating over the evil ritual killing, using two sticks against Lord Blackwell and his supporters—two short hard sticks similar to unlinked nunchucks, or to the sticks used in several Asian martial arts. With Lord Blackwood in custody, Holmes expertly spins his short sticks and tucks them neatly, even jauntily, one under each arm.

Holmes demonstrates his boxing acumen in a later scene. To the lively Irish tune of "Rocky Road to Dublin," about an Irishman in Liverpool who gets in a fist fight with some English, Holmes fights bare knuckled against a man much larger and heavier than he. Initially Holmes seems to be merely slapping his opponent and dancing out of his grasp to avoid injury, playing more than fighting, at one moment even clapping at his opponent's success in tossing him to the ground. But a handkerchief with an embroidered red "A" suddenly appears on the railing behind him. He looks up and sees the enigmatic Miss Irene Adler, who winks at him, places a bet, and disappears. Holmes wants to end the fight, giving the win to the giant fighting him, but the giant, and the excited audience, do not agree.

> HOLMES: That's it, big man.... We're done. You won. Congratulations.
> OPPONENT: Oi, we ain't done yet.
> HOLMES: This mustn't register on an emotional level.
>> First, distract target.
>> Then block his blind jab.
>> Counter with cross to the left cheek.
>> Discombobulate.
>> Dazed, he'll attempt wild hay maker.
>> Employ elbow block, and body shot.
>> Block feral left. Weaken right jaw.
>> Now fracture.
>> Break cracked ribs.
>> Traumatize solar plexus.
>> Dislocate jaw entirely.
>> Heel kick to diaphragm.
>> In summary: Ears ringing, jaw fractured, three ribs cracked, four broken, diaphragm hemorrhaging, physical recovery, 6 weeks.
>> Full psychological recovery, 6 months.
>> Capacity to spit at back of head ... neutralized.

Once again Holmes calculates his strategy mentally before implementing it physically, and once again the audience sees the event in slow motion during the thought process, followed by the real-time version in which Holmes attacks and overcomes his opponent, leaving him severely injured in the space of ten or twelve seconds, precisely as calculated. Holmes the dispassionate intellectual uses his powerful intellect to command his highly trained body.

Downey embraced the physicality of the Holmes role as interpreted by Ritchie, as he said in an interview, "I love his take on it. We're both martial arts enthusiasts and historically, in the real original stories of Sherlock Holmes, he's kind of a bad-ass and a bare-knuckle boxer and studies the rare art of baritsu" (Mueller). Downey shares these interests with his character. Since 2003 Downey has practiced the martial art of Wing Chun made famous by Bruce Lee, which requires both mental and physical training, combining scientific movement with mental and spiritual development. His trainer, or Sifu, Eric Oram, describes Downey's training: "This shotgun mind of his channeled it into a single point of focus and turned it into a laser" (Dehority). Downey worked hard with his personal trainer to prepare for his first action hero role as Tony Stark in *Iron Man* (2008), adding weight training and weight gain to his martial arts practice. That role established him as a bankable action hero for the first time and no doubt led to his role as an "action hero" Sherlock Holmes.

Sherlock Holmes: A Game of Shadows continues and expands the action theme, with Holmes' arch nemesis (or dark twin) Moriarty using his own "Moriarty-avision." In addition to granting equal powers to equally matched protagonists, Ritchie adds some uncertainty to Holmes' use of Holmesavision. That is, Holmes calculates his strategy, the audience sees the plan in slow motion, but in real time the strategy on occasion "doesn't work as well as expected. There's different endings" (Ritchie, "Holmesavision"), and Holmes must counter for the unexpected interference with his plan.

The Reichenbach Falls scene near the end of the film exemplifies this difference. Holmes and Moriarty are playing a game of chess. The two antagonists call out chess moves, each expecting to beat the other. But Holmes has the upper hand: his colleagues in London are deciphering Moriarty's stolen notebook containing all his financial information, confiscating Moriarty's fortune as he and Moriarty parry moves. Moriarty threatens "to find the most creative of endings for the doctor. And his wife." The thought process and voice-over narration of Holmesavision and Moriarty-avision begin:

> HOLMES: His advantage, my injury. My advantage, his rage.
>   Incoming assault, feral, but experienced. Use his momentum to counter.
> MORIARTY: Come now. You really think you're the only one who can play this game.
>   Trap arm. Target weakness.
>   Follow with haymaker.
> HOLMES: Ah. There we find the boxing champion of Cambridge.
> MORIARTY: Competent, but predictable. Now allow me to reply.
> HOLMES: Arsenal running dry. Adjust strategy.
> MORIARTY: Wound taking its toll.
> HOLMES: As I feared. Injury makes defense untenable. Prognosis increasingly negative.
> MORIARTY: Let's not waste anymore of one another's time. We both know how this ends.
> HOLMES: Conclusion, inevitable. Unless....

Holmes blows ash into Moriarty's face and grapples with him. As Dr. Watson steps out on the balcony, Holmes gives him a meaningful look and tumbles over the bannister with Moriarty in his grasp, falling far below to their deaths, clinging together in a slow motion sequence, then separated and falling quickly in real time. Holmes appears to sacrifice himself in order to assure Moriarty's death and spare Dr. Watson and his wife the gruesome end Moriarty intended for them. And unlike previous Holmesavision sequences, the real-time event at the Falls does not correspond to Holmes' or Moriarty's mental preview of it. As a result, this pivotal action sequence simultaneously meets and deceives audience expectations.

Bromance or Romance?

According to Conan Doyle in a letter to Joseph Bell, "Holmes is as inhuman as a Babbage's Calculating Machine, and just about as likely to fall in love" (qtd in Graham and Garlen 24). Conan Doyle positions his hero as a kind of asexual computer. Holmes himself prizes logic and scientific thinking above all else: "Love is an emotional thing, and whatever is emotional is opposed to that cold, true reason which I place above all things, I should never marry myself, lest I bias my judgment" (*The Sign of Four* 235). Holmes makes several comments regarding his attitude toward women. "Women are never to be entirely trusted— not the best of them," for they are "naturally secretive," Holmes believes (*The Sign of Four* 188). In fact, according to Watson, the great detective has an "aversion to women" ("The Greek Interpreter" 682). The only woman to truly interest Holmes is Irene Adler. Yes, like so many other women she is beautiful, but more importantly she is exceedingly intelligent and clever, and the only woman to best Holmes at his own game. She first appears in "A Scandal in Bohemia" (1891), where his Majesty the Grand Duke Wilhelm Ormstein describes her: "she has a soul of steel. She has the face of the most beautiful of women, and the mind of the most resolute of men" (248). Dr. Watson begins his tale by introducing Irene Adler and her importance to Holmes:

> To Sherlock Holmes she is always the woman. I have seldom heard him mention her under any other name. In his eyes she eclipses and predominates the whole of her sex. It was not that he felt any emotion akin to love for Irene Adler. All emotions, and that one particularly, were abhorrent to his cold, precise but admirably balanced mind. He was, I take it, the most perfect reasoning and observing machine that the world has seen, but as a lover he would have placed himself in a false position.... And yet there was but one woman to him, and that woman was the late Irene Adler... [238–239].

Critical opinion is somewhat divided on the issue of Holmes' sexuality. For June Thomson, Holmes was an inveterate bachelor and "almost certainly remained celibate all his life,"

"Beneath this pillow lies the key to my release." Downey as Holmes in Guy Ritchie's *Sherlock Holmes* (2009).

given the limited options in the Victorian period for sex outside the bonds of matrimony (17). Joseph Kestner goes a step further and sees Holmes as the model of masculinity in his time, "radically gendered as masculine in Victorian culture: observation, rationalism, factuality, logic, comradeship, daring and pluck," and believes that "Doyle indisputably aligns Holmes with manliness by linking his character to science, practical application, exact knowledge, logic and system, all elements gendered masculine in the nineteenth century" (2, 29). Critics and reviewers of the two Ritchie films focus more sharply on the possible homosexual overtones of the relationship between Holmes and Watson, despite Holmes' admiration for Miss Adler and despite Watson's fiancée and then wife, Mary, sometimes expressing disappointment that Ritchie did not go further toward the queering of the film (Rossiter Drake).

Though it is true that the Holmes of page and film resists Watson's marriage plans, does it necessarily follow that he resists out of (sexual) love for Watson, however unconsummated? After a period of Holmes' bad behavior, locked in his flat experimenting noisily with a way of silencing gunfire, even Mrs. Hudson asks Watson to extend his engagement to Mary Morstan. In *Sherlock Holmes* Robert Downey Jr. replaces the gentlemanly asexuality of the stories with male banter between Watson and Holmes, but his Holmes also has explicit sexual interest in Irene Adler. He visits her in her ample and luxurious hotel room, watching her as she undresses behind a screen. She invites him to come away with him, drugs him with doctored red wine, but kisses him passionately just before he falls asleep. In the next scene, the chambermaid enters the room and finds him in a seated position, handcuffed to the bed, naked but for a small pillow covering his male essentials. He attempts to instruct the chambermaid with a provocative double entendre, "Beneath this pillow lies the key to my release," but she runs for help. As Graham and Garlen so aptly observe, "Ritchie and his screenwriters develop Holmes' sexuality in several directions simultaneously," noting that "the sexualization of Sherlock Holmes began almost as soon as the first stories went to print, but the cultural appropriation of Holmes as a romantic hero has only increased since then.... Today, Sexy Sherlock is almost a given..." (31, 25). Downey's disheveled, quasi-bohemian appearance may seem somewhat antithetical to the staid, restrained Holmes perhaps better known to fans through previous interpretations—particularly the iconic Jeremy Brett in his carefully tailored and fitted suits—but Downey's Holmes is in keeping with contemporaneous interpretations for television such as the much tattooed Holmes of *Elementary*. Despite the setting of Victorian London, this Holmes is anything but Victorian in behavior.

Ritchie said he wanted to make a Sherlock Holmes "along the lines of Butch and Sundance" (Bentley). *Butch Cassidy and the Sundance Kid* (1969) is a Western and a quintessential buddy movie. Critics have compared the relationship of Holmes and Watson to Butch and Sundance as well as to police partners Riggs and Murtaugh of *Lethal Weapon 2* (1989), a buddy cop movie. Like the Sherlock Holmes films, one partner has a love interest (Sundance's girlfriend Etta) and even a wife and family (Roger Murtaugh's wife and two children), while the single partner seems less settled and more eccentric (Butch Cassidy and Martin Riggs). Despite the amorous and clearly heterosexual relationships of the more stable man of the duo, the friendship between the two men often seems to take precedence, with each ready to die for the other, each eager to sign on to the next dangerous adventure.

Our detective and his "loyal dog" (as Lord Blackwood calls Watson) face just such a second adventure together in *Sherlock Holmes: A Game of Shadows*. Notwithstanding his apparent reluctance to lose Watson to his chosen domestic bliss, Holmes delivers him to his wedding ceremony, though in a rather battered state after a night of gambling and brawling. Holmes stands apart from the wedding crowd, a solitary figure observing the newlyweds, clapping lightly and unconvincingly at their happiness. He soon meets with Professor Moriarty at the latter's invitation. During their conversation, Moriarty inquires about Dr. Watson's marriage. Holmes replies that the ceremony was "Definitive. He'll no longer be party to my investigations.... I trust you'll take this into consideration." But Moriarty reveals that Irene Adler has recently and unexpectedly died of a rare and virulent strain of tuberculosis (after having tea with him), and lays her handkerchief in the center of his chess board, and then refuses any "consideration" for Watson. "Are you sure you want to play this game?" Moriarty asks. Holmes thus understands that Watson and his new bride are in danger. Meanwhile, the happy couple boards a train for their honeymoon in Brighton. Snuggled into their first class cabin, the newlyweds accept a bottle of champagne as a gift, but the delivery turns into an attack on Watson. Mary astutely grabs the small pistol she had noticed tucked into the back of Watson's trousers, and points it at the villain, telling her husband to open the exterior door. Watson pushes the attacker out the door to his death. Another knock on the door reveals a "woman" deftly elbowing and shooting several "soldiers" about to attack the Watsons. Holmes comes to the rescue, telling Watson, "I agree it's not my best disguise, but I had to make do." He warns the Watsons that the enemy will be back. To Mary he says, "Do you trust me?" "No," she replies. "Then I shall have to do something about that," responds Holmes, just before pushing her out the open exterior door of the train. When Watson realizes his wife is missing, he attacks Holmes, ripping off his shirt. Holmes puts Watson's head in a scissor lock with his legs. The return of their common enemy breaks up the fight. Watson assumes that Holmes is the target and has brought revenge upon him and Mary, but Holmes says, "They're not here for me. They're here for you. Fortunately, so am I."

HOLMES: Our relationship...
WATSON: Relationship?
HOLMES: Very well, partnership—has not yet run its course. My dear fellow, if you could be bothered to see this through to the end, I shall never again ask you to assist me.
WATSON: [with repressed anger] *Once more* unto the breach [Emphasis added].

Though it is true that Holmes dresses as a woman for these scenes and that some of their interactions might seem ambiguous, such as when Holmes insists that Watson lie down with him in the train car, it is also true that Holmes takes each action as part of a plan to save Watson's life, and by extension, the life of Mary Watson as well. Mary's reaction to the first attacker, with her quick thinking and threatening pistol, fundamentally makes her an addition to the duo. Though Holmes throws her off the train, where she lands in the river and soon gets rescued by Sherlock's equally eccentric brother Mycroft, near the end of the film she and Inspector Lestrade work together to deplete Moriarty's fortune. Mary assists Holmes and Watson in the destruction of the criminal mastermind that threatens them all.

Ritchie's adaptations of the Sherlock Holmes stories evidence many of the "elements common to the bromance...: back-and-forth banter, a love-hate dynamic, codependency, masculine physicality and action, male camaraderie and loyalty, and potential homoeroticism" (Thomas 38). Yet all definitions of "bromance" eliminate sex: "bromance designates a significant bond between men" (Thomas 38); "a relationship or friendship between two men that is extremely close but does not involve sex" (*Random House*); "a close nonsexual friendship between men" (*Merriam-Webster*). Despite any potential and probably purposeful ambiguities in their actions, both films highlight "the heteronormative exploits of Robert Downey Jr." and his soldier-doctor partner, John Watson (Nicol 138). Holmes' and Watson's relationship exists in a time in which schools were single sex, gentlemen's clubs (no women allowed) were common, and male bonding was not unusual. Holmes and Watson share the bonds of a profound (heterosexual) friendship. "I am lost without my Boswell," Holmes declares in "A Scandal in Bohemia" (243), which is literally true, given that Watson is Holmes' biographer and "creates" him in print. Furthermore, Holmes has no other friends; his eccentricities and his astonishing brilliance isolate him even if he were not antisocial and thus isolating himself.

Authenticity: The "Real" Sherlock Holmes?

Has Guy Ritchie got it wrong? Does his comic, physical Sherlock Holmes lack authenticity? Is Downey's Holmes a mere antic clown without the deductive powers that Holmes is known for? A kind of slapstick detective more akin to Inspector Clouseau than the canonical Holmes? The actors themselves weighed in on this issue. Jude Law stated in an interview, "there's loads to be interpreted from the originals *and loads that we've locked in our minds that's wrong*" (emphasis added; "Sherlock Holmes Reinvented"). Robert Downey Jr. made his views clear as well: "The more I look into the books, the more fantastic it becomes. Holmes is such a weirdo" (qtd in Nicol 128). Furthermore, "authenticity is inherently and cripplingly subjective, with the process of adaptation entailing such a vast array of competing agendas and circumstances as it seeks to transcend the social, cultural and political divide between the context of the originating texts and that of the moment of adaptation" (McCaw 39). The Holmes of text is such a "weirdo" that any adaptation of the stories must wrestle with how to present such a weirdo in a manner that will appeal to the viewing public. Holmes is excessive is so many ways: excessively knowledgeable, excessively skilled at martial arts, and certainly excessively brilliant. From the original texts to the myriad interpretations for television and film, his ferocious intellect serves as a useful tool for deciphering crime and bringing criminals to justice, but it also makes those around him very uncomfortable, almost fearful. Surely if Holmes can be a threat to criminals, if he can read the world in a tiny clue, he might be dangerous to the law-abiding as well. His deductive skills startle; his thought processes are uncanny. The police he works with need him, but resent him. The Ritchie films soften the cutting edges of Holmes' intellect by incorporating more humor and placing more emphasis on his physical skills.

Robert Downey Jr.'s interpretation of Holmes is both modern and canonical. His Holmes is true to the chemist-adventurer of the Conan Doyle stories. He experiments on himself (and Watson's dog), he uses cocaine, smokes a pipe, and plays the violin, and he tends to be almost anti-social. He is also what Downey called "the first martial artist in Western culture" ("Sherlock Holmes Reinvented"). Like the original consulting detective, his Holmes makes use of costumes and disguises, though his disguise as a woman in *A Game of Shadows* is rather more slapstick and disappearing by matching the fabric of furniture is a new turn in costuming. Like all interpretations of Holmes, this Holmes is brilliant, logical, and scientific. But with the use of "Holmesavision," the audience sees in slow motion the nearly mathematical calculations that Holmes makes before he attacks, followed by the actual attack at normal speed, and how the brilliant mind commands and controls the body.

Though the first film is not based on a Conan Doyle story, many of the characters come directly from the originals, including Irene Adler. The second film takes much from "The Final Problem," the story in which Conan Doyle killed off his famous detective: Holmes struggles with his arch enemy Dr. Moriarty and they both seemingly fall to their deaths. In the story, Holmes claims that he used his knowledge of baritsu to survive; in the film, Holmes survived by using his brother Mycroft's small personal oxygen supply. In fiction, Holmes returns to life and consulting in "The Adventure of the Empty House." In film, Downey's Holmes returns to Watson's office, just as Watson finishes his "final" Sherlock Holmes adventure for publication, writing of Holmes, "I shall ever regard him as the best and wisest man whom I have ever known." He and Mary are preparing for a trip to Brighton; a small package arrives. Within the package is the personal oxygen dispenser that Holmes used to survive Reichenbach Falls. Watson is shocked and immediately suspicious. He leaves the room to question Mary about the postman who delivered the package. Disguised as the fabric of an armchair, perfectly invisible, Holmes removes his head covering and rises to place a question mark at the end of Watson's telling of his death. "The End?"

Works Cited

Bentley, David. "Sherlock Holmes: Does It Survive Guy Ritchie's Action-Hero Reinvention?" *The Geek Files*. Blog. *Coventry Telegraph*, 4 Jan. 2010. Web. 17 May 2013.
Butch Cassidy and the Sundance Kid. Dir. George Roy Hill. Twentieth Century–Fox, 1969. Film.
"bromance." Dictionarywww *Unabridged*. Random House, Inc., n.d. Web. 27 May 2013.
"bromance." Merriam-Websterwww, 2013. Web. 27 May 2013.
Conan Doyle, Sir Arthur. *Sherlock Holmes: The Complete Novels and Stories*. New York: Bantam, 1986. Print.
Dehority, Sam. "Robert Downey Jr.: 'He Was Skinny.' How the 150-Pound Star of Sherlock Holmes Trained Up (and Down) to Become Hollywood's Top Action Hero." *Men's Fitness*, 15 Dec. 2011. Web. 15 May 2013.
Drake, Rossiter. "Prelude to a Kiss? Robert Downey Jr. Jude Law Share an Intriguing Romance in Sherlock Holmes." *7x7SF*, 24 Dec. 2009. Web. 22 Apr. 2013.
Ebert, Robert. "Sherlock Holmes." Review. *Roger Ebert.com*, 23 Dec. 2009. Web. 10 May 2013.
Elementary. Crea. Robert Doherty. CBS, 2012+. Television.
Godfrey, Emelyne. "Urban Knights in the London Streets." *Masculinity, Crime and Self-Defence in Victorian Literature*. New York: Palgrave Macmillan, 2011. 128–146. Print.
Graham, Anissa M., and Jennifer C. Garlen. "Sex and the Single Sleuth." *Sherlock Holmes for the 21st Century: Essays on New Adaptations*. Jefferson, NC: McFarland, 2012. 24–34. Print.
"Holmesavision on Steroids." Special Features. *Sherlock Holmes: A Game of Shadows*. Dir. Guy Ritchie. Warner Bros., 2011. DVD.
Iron Man. Dir. Jon Favreau. Paramount, 2008. DVD.
Jones, J.R. "Sherlock Holmes." Review. *Chicago Reader*, n. d. Web. 20 May 2013.
Kestner, Joseph A. *Sherlock's Men: Masculinity, Conan Doyle, and Cultural History*. Aldershot: England: Ashgate, 1997. Print.
Lethal Weapon 2. Dir. Richard Donner. Warner Bros., 1989. Film.
Lock Stock and Two Smoking Barrels. Dir. Guy Ritchie. PolyGram,1998. Film.
McCaw, Neil. "Sherlock Holmes and the Authenticity of Crime." *Adapting Detective Fiction: Crime, Englishness and the TV Detectives*. London: Continuum, 2011. 19–39. Print.
Mondello, Bob. "'Sherlock Holmes'—A Smarty-Pants Sleuth Aims For An Action-Hero Hit." *NPR*, 23 Dec. 2009. Web. 22 May 2013.
Mueller, Matt. "Robert Downey Jr. Q & A: Sherlock Holmes." *Matt Mueller*, N. p., Aug. 2008. Web. 9 May 2013.

Nicol, Bran. "Sherlock Holmes Version 2.0: Adapting Doyle in the Twenty-First Century." *Sherlock Holmes and Conan Doyle: Multi-Media Afterlives*. Eds. Sabine Vanacker and Catherine Wynne. New York: Palgrave Macmillan, 2013. 124–139. Print.

Roeper, Richard, "Sherlock Holmes." Video Review. *Richard Roeper & the Movies*, 25 Dec. 2009. Web. 10 May 2013.

_____ "Sherlock Holmes: A Game of Shadows." Video Review. *Richard Roeper & the Movies*, 11 Dec. 2011. Web. 21 Jan. 2014.

Sherlock. Crea. Mark Gatiss, Steven Moffat. BBC Worldwide, 2010. Television.

Sherlock Holmes. Dir. Guy Ritchie. Warner Bros., 2009. DVD.

Sherlock Holmes: A Game of Shadows. Dir. Guy Ritchie. Warner, 2011. DVD.

Sherlock Holmes Baffled. Dir. Arthur Marvin. American Mutoscope & Biograph, 1900. Short Film.

"Sherlock Holmes: Past and Present." Conference. Institute of English Studies, University of London. 21–22 June 2013.

"Sherlock Holmes Reinvented." Special Features. *Sherlock Holmes*. Dir. Guy Ritchie. Warner Bros., 2009. DVD.

Snatch. Dir. Guy Ritchie. Sony, 2000. Film.

Subers, Ray. "End-of-Run Report: Case Closed on 'Sherlock Holmes.'" *Box Office Mojo*. IMDb, n.d. Web. 2 May 2013.

Thomas, Kayley. "'Bromance is so passé': Robert Downey Jr.'s Queer Paratexts." *Sherlock Holmes for the 21st Century: Essays on New Adaptations*. Ed. Lynnette Porter. 35–47. Jefferson, NC: McFarland, 2012. Print.

Thomson, June. *Holmes and Watson*. 1995. New York: Carroll & Graf, 2001. Print.

The Avengers in Post–9/11 America

Mike Hernandez

> "If al–Qaeda could do to the Marvel Universe what Doctor Doom, Magneto and Kang the Conqueror had failed to do, surely that meant the biggest challenge yet to the relevance of superhero comics."
> —*Grant Morrison, Supergods*

In the years following the September 11, 2001, terrorist attacks, American culture has been increasingly preoccupied with—even desperately obsessed with—violence and the idea of heroism. The death and destruction in New York made Hollywood action movies and heroes look ridiculous, naive, and disrespectful by making their outlandish disaster fantasies eerily and disturbingly real. The violent imagery of Hollywood blockbusters, as Jean Baudrillard famously noted, was invading the real world (Baudrillard 6), unaccompanied by real world counterparts to the Bruce Willis and Arnold Schwarzenegger characters that the movies had always provided to save the day. Heroes like that exuded a kind of confidence—even invulnerability—that just wasn't sustainable anymore. In the months following the attacks, some of these naive-seeming movies were kept from release, reworked, quietly released, and critically ignored; others in development were simply cancelled. One thing seems clear more than ten years after real terrorists destroyed two iconic American buildings in New York with no Hollywood hero, secret agent, rogue cop, commando, or otherwise, to stand in their way: American escapism isn't what it used to be.

Meanwhile, studios and moviegoers spent millions and billions of dollars on movies based on superhero comics, full of good-versus-evil escapism—not simply childish, but originally created for American children. Not only were the heroes more fantastic in these movies, but villains were outlandish enough for audiences to safely feel menaced by. These movies often employed serious tones with varying degrees of success; while a film like *Batman Begins* needed an element of gritty realism to recover from the camp of the 1990s franchise, others only embraced what Charlie Jane Anders of *io9* has called a lazy cynicism (Anders) that had already plagued the superhero genre in its original medium for twenty years. Since the late 1980s, the superhero genre had been deconstructed repeatedly and continually, darkened and problematized, often made edgy without any of the innovation that made seminal serious superhero stories like *Watchmen* or *The Dark Knight Returns* so innovative in the first place (Morrison 216). Even Frank Miller and Alan Moore, the originators of this trend, have lamented this stagnation, the crisis that engulfed a genre rooted in optimism and idealism (Wolk 235).

Enter the subject of this book, Robert Downey Jr., whose portrayal of Tony Stark/Iron Man restores the sense of adolescent optimism and adventure that the superhero genre was built on. Downey's portrayal of Tony Stark in 2012's *The Avengers*, like his performances in *Iron Man* and *Iron Man 2*, blends flippant charisma and self-conscious humor with a measured seriousness that helps the movie overcome the tendency to routine darkness and often unearned seriousness that has overwhelmed the superhero genre since 9/11 and the 1980s before that. More than ten years after the September 11 attacks, Marvel's blockbuster brought viewers a newly imagined, 3D attack on Manhattan, aborted in the end by Downey's Iron Man. And, while Downey's performance restores a kind of optimism to the superhero movie genre, it and the Marvel franchise in general also engage with complex contemporary issues including plutocracy, deterrence, American exceptionalism, and altruism. All these issues, which revolve around Downey's character, have occupied the American imagination, popular culture, and political consciousness since 2001. They are part of an ongoing American identity crisis, reflected most tellingly in the escapist fantasies that meet with the most commercial success. *The Avengers* and Downey's contribution to it reflect a desire in post–9/11 America to be safe while maintaining certain ideas, illusions, and reassurances about the nation's identity.

While this chapter's main context is America after 9/11, it is important first to look back to another troubling time, the one that gave birth to the fantasy of the superhero. One of the superhero genre's formative influences is Hugo Gernsback's science fiction pulp magazine *Amazing Stories*, whose seminal August 1928 issue features on the cover a man soaring into the air wearing a jetpack and contains another story about a ray gun-wielding space soldier. Comics writer Gerald Jones explains the magazine's significance best:

> In newsstands filled with dread, here suddenly was joy, a safe but unbounded future. Here in the hearts of children who saw that cover was a soft, exhaustless lift into the open, golden sky ... both [stories] presented universes of violence containable by gadgetry and American know-how. They left behind the barbarian nostalgia of Edgar Rice Burroughs and the apocalyptic fears of H.G. Wells and reassured American boys that the future would be theirs and would be wonderful [Jones 30–1].

This description of pulpy optimism exemplifies the American desire for technologically-assured safety and excitement, particularly in the economic hard times during which Gernsback's magazines were published and characters like Superman were conceived. Even the combination of jet pack and ray gun seems to anticipate the centrality of a hero like Iron Man to the genre. These are the same desires that *The Avengers* answers today, thanks in part to Downey's ability to sell both the seriousness of the violence and the fantasy of containment. The kind of heroes American audiences decide to celebrate with billions of dollars in ticket sales says a great deal about what kind of fantasies they want to embrace, as well as what kind of self-image they want to embrace as a nation. Superheroes are, after all, an American creation.

What They Desire, but Not What They Deserve?

Critics seem to agree that *The Avengers* succeeds in its goal of providing audiences a fun, well-made superhero movie that gives viewers what they want; it has to be profitable, after all. Whether the movie's efficient gratification of audience desires is an entirely good thing, a fulfillment of what such a movie can and should do, however, has also been asked by the same critics. In a review for *NPR*, Bob Mondello compares the movie to the more serious *Dark Knight* trilogy by Christopher Nolan, saying that "[the trilogy] reminds us a caped-crusader movie can aspire to greater things. But nobody says it has to, and [director] Joss Whedon just wants *The Avengers* to be fun. Which it is" (Mondello). Similarly, Roger Ebert writes that "'The Avengers' is done well by Joss Whedon, with style and energy. It provides its fans with exactly what they desire. Whether it is exactly what they deserve is arguable" (Ebert). Ebert isn't the only writer to ask whether viewers are well-served by how effectively their fantasies are being produced for them. In many ways, this complaint brings to mind of the peak of the action movie genre before reality caught up with its violence and destruction. The September 11 attacks really shook the destruction-preoccupied genre of action movies because they fulfilled a fantasy viewers didn't want to admit to. Hollywood had rehearsed the destruction of the city, even the buildings which were eventually to be destroyed. Jean Baudrillard controversially compared the pleasure of those movies to that of pornography (Baudrillard 7). In order to be enjoyable again, movies in the action genre had to be darker and feel less like they used disaster for pleasure.

The Avengers, however, manages to provide enjoyable banter, gratifying brawls, and captivating 3D action that culminates in the near-destruction of Manhattan, ending right at the top of a skyscraper. Roaring, bird-faced aliens on flying chariots terrorize fleeing New Yorkers while enormous armored eels thrash into and around buildings. The newly-formed Avengers have their hands full fighting off alien invaders, but the final—and more troubling—threat of destruction is the nuclear missile fired at Manhattan in order to contain the invasion. The order for the strike comes from a council of ominous and (literally) shady bureaucrats shown on monitors, while salvation from the nuclear annihilation comes from a reckless egotistical billionaire whose fortune comes from his military weapons contracts. While *The Avengers* may not be as overtly political or intellectual as Nolan's movies, it undeniably bears some connections to American politics and ideology that are worth looking at closely.

Post–9/11 superhero movies often put forth the idea that noble, unproblematic heroism is a luxury that can't be afforded, a trope that's unsurprising in the post–9/11, post–Guantanamo torture, post-drone strike American political climate. Note, for example, the accusation leveled at Batman in *The Dark Knight Rises* that despite his best efforts "the only victory [he] achieved was a lie" (*The Dark Knight Rises*) or Dr. Manhattan's reaction in *Watchmen* (2009) to his former teammate Ozymandias' use of a nuclear disaster to scare world powers into making peace: "without condoning or condemning, I understand" (*Watchmen*). Even if morally questionable actions in the name of peace or security are not championed in these movies, the idea of their necessity is definitely entertained. These heroes sacrifice their morals or souls for the greater good, thereby embodying a higher, less glamorous heroism in keeping with a decade of unpopular American wars.

While this is certainly one reflection of American self-image since 9/11, the one *The Avengers* shows is ultimately supposed to be as optimistic and reassuring as Gernsback's jet-pack cover was in its time, which is why it features imperfect characters who become greater instead of idealists who sacrifice their morals. It is simultaneously a return and revision of the classic hero's journey structure. This strategy is most obviously and extensively employed in the story of Tony Stark in the *Iron Man* movies and *The Avengers*. Redemption is a dominant, but comically offset theme in these movies, which begin with an arms manufacturer and war profiteer quitting the weapons business to fight global crime on his own and culminate with his embrace of self-sacrifice. That representation of American heroism, as the villainy of the past twelve years has shown, is effective for good reason.

Real World Counterparts

A character like Tony Stark gradually embracing altruism is a truly intoxicating fantasy today, considering today's pervasive image of military contractors profiting from unpopular wars and greedy corporate executives escaping economic recession with hedge funds intact. It is no coincidence that the two most successful superhero franchises in recent years have featured rich men who use their power in an earnest attempt to make the world a safer place, one compelled by a desire for justice or the other feeling that he owes a debt to the world. The success of Batman and Iron Man in Hollywood is symptomatic not only of the fear of terrorism, but also a national fantasy of trustworthy government, upper class, and military defense industry.

A look at public opinion today quickly shows that these are major issues troubling American society. In 2011, a *New York Times/CBS* poll reported that "89 percent of Americans say they distrust government to do the right thing" (Zeleny and Thee-Brenan), while a study of Gallup polls from the early 1970s to 2011 showed that "over the course of the past 60 years, overall trust in [the government, the courts, the media, and big business] has been in steady decline—even in good times" ("Trust in America"). It is no wonder American audiences turn to such unlikely heroes in fantasy when they have such difficulty trusting leaders or institutions in real life. Economist Justin Wolfers, the author of this study, goes on to report that in the 1950s 4 out of 5 Americans trusted government, which had gone down to 1 in 5 by 2011 ("Trust in America."). By this logic, 2012 American audiences should despise a character like Tony Stark, who represents private business, the upper class, and defense technology. Marvel's Stan Lee claims that making Iron Man a character readers like despite these factors was a deliberate challenge in his creation in 1963; the troubling figure of Howard Hughes, famously accused of being a shameless war profiteer, was a formative influence at that time (*Iron Man*).

The contemporary problem of war becoming an unstoppable commercial industry, reflected in a character like Stark, was warned against by Dwight Eisenhower in his 1961 presidential farewell address, in which he popularized the now ubiquitous phrase "military industrial complex." While Eisenhower wasn't arguing that the military industrial complex was inherently bad, he predicted the conflict between safety and freedom that comes from such an arrangement, saying,

> We recognize the imperative need for this development. Yet we must not fail to comprehend its grave implications. Our toil, resources and livelihood are all involved; so is the very structure of our society. In the councils of government, we must guard against the acquisition of unwarranted influence, whether sought or unsought, by the military-industrial complex. The potential for the disastrous rise of misplaced power exists and will persist [Eisenhower].

This potential, many would say, has been fulfilled. For instance, an article in *The Atlantic* cites this fact as evidence: "To train, equip, and maintain one American soldier in Iraq or

Afghanistan for just one year costs a cool million dollars. Meanwhile, according to 2010 census figures, the number of Americans falling below the poverty line has swollen to one in every seven" (Bacevich). The challenges to making a likeable Tony Stark must have seemed substantial enough in 1963, when the United States was mired in the Vietnam War. Yet today, the challenges seem at least as great if not greater, with more than ten years of war in Iraq and Afghanistan and an economic recession placing more and more strain on the country's economy.

Thanks, however, to the charm of Robert Downey Jr.'s portrayal and other production decisions in the first two *Iron Man* movies, it's easy for viewers to overlook, forgive, or simply miss things like the similarity between Stark's reckless partying in *Iron Man 2* and the outrageous behavior of defense contractors in Afghanistan in 2012, which were caught on cellphone video and released online by *ABC News* to understandable public scandal. Employees of the defense contractor Jorge Scientific fired their weapons while drunk, wrestled on the floor, and even got high on ketamine, all while their compound in Afghanistan could have been attacked (Galli, Schwartz, and Ross). It's not simply that Downey's charm as Tony Stark makes it possible to ignore the character's flaws, it's also the element of parody he brings to the role in the worst excesses and the seriousness he brings to the heroic parts that make the character likeable.

Even Justin Hammer, Tony Stark's grinning, unironic wannabe in *Iron Man 2*, finds his real world counterpart in Erik Prince, founder of the defense contractor Blackwater who, according to Jeremy Scahill's book-length investigation of the mercenary army, "liked to position Blackwater as a patriotic extension of the U.S. military" (Scahill xxii). Suddenly, perhaps, Hammer's jingoistic display of patriotically-decorated attack drones at the Stark Expo, complete with fanfare, doesn't seem entirely fantastic. It shouldn't. Prince is reported to have told a military panel that the company's corporate goal is "to do for the national security apparatus what FedEx did for the postal service" (Scahill xix). It's troubling in real life, yet amusing in *Iron Man 2* when Tony Stark proclaims that he has privatized world peace and struts out of a government hearing reminiscent of Howard Hughes' senate hearing. No children went trick-or-treating as Jorge Scientific employees that Halloween, yet many certainly knocked on doors dressed as Iron Man, for more reasons than the obvious ones.

Selling Stark

Iron Man director Jon Favreau realized the risk of unlikeability and the contradiction that holding Tony Stark up as a hero might require. Explaining the *media res* opening of *Iron Man* in a commentary track, he said that although some involved in production thought that a linear structure would be better, it was harder to like Stark when the film opened at the earliest chronological point in the movie, with Stark gambling away more money than most viewers can ever hope to have and then arrogantly selling a new weapon of mass destruction to the military, describing it as "the weapon you only have to fire once" (*Iron Man*). Instead, Favreau thought it would make it easier to like Stark to get directly to the point where he is a prisoner of a terrorist organization and then cut back, saying,

> [it] allowed us to play Tony Stark in a much different way than if we had done it linear. We had actually done linear cuts ... what happened is Tony Stark would just not be a very likeable

guy ... he was forgiven much more because you knew that he was gonna end up in a really compromised position, probably the worst position that you could think of, which was basically in a hostage video [*Iron Man 2*].

However, viewers also owe the rehabilitation of a potentially repulsive character to Downey, who made it possible with his charisma to like a character with such easily loathsome real-world counterparts. Reviewers have repeatedly noted that the self-awareness Downey brings to the role saves it, making Stark more like a parody of people like Prince than actually like him.

One reviewer of the first movie said that Downey "puts the much needed irony in *Iron Man*" (Keough). Another reviewer said of the second movie that "Downey takes unwinking self-consciousness to heights where he can only be visited by Bill Murray" (McCarter). This necessary irony comes from another of Downey's frequently cited skills, what Steve Vineberg calls "the actor's trick of making lines sound as if they were newly minted" (Vineberg), which strips away the affectations of a routine performance, making Stark less of a corporate archetype than a send-up of one. Vineberg explains the effect of Downey's delivery style this way: "what we pay attention to are Mr. Downey's wit and vocal style: the weird, accelerated vocal rhythms; the way he reconfigures punctuation, ramming together sentences and throwing in odd, unexpected breaks" (Vineburg). The mechanics of this irony, in turn, may be an outgrowth of Downey's method of preparation, memorizing his lines, then learning them all as one run-on sentence, and then finally reducing them all to an acronym ("Robert Downey Jr."). It makes sense in this light that Downey's performances, though well-memorized, should seem fresh; at that level of abstraction, lines that might be played in some routine or cliché way can take on other possibilities that might otherwise be overlooked—such as a charmingly arrogant arms manufacturer.

Of course, another factor in the self-consciousness and nuance of Downey's performances is his energetic personality. He often speaks quickly and cleverly in interviews as well as his performances, and the connection should not be dismissed as too obvious. This brings up an important aspect of discussing any of Downey's performances: the relevance of biographical details, particularly in roles that resonate with his history or public persona. Downey has played multiple roles involving various elements of addiction, excess, and the ensuing turmoil that invite biographical connections in criticism and commentary. Roles like the drug addicted teenager in *Less Than Zero*, the recovering alcoholic principal in *Charlie Bartlett*, and the excessive and heavy drinking Tony Stark, among others, have prompted some thoughtful commentary on how Downey's life informs his performances. Stark's character resonates with Downey's public persona in the way both have undergone a reinvention of sorts, the former undergoing a moral reformation and becoming a superhero while the latter has achieved sobriety and a career renaissance. There's an evolution from excess to responsibility in both that has often been noted. It is important to keep this in mind while also avoiding biographical analysis that discounts Downey's skills as an actor. The relevant skill here is probably the ability to channel the useful parts of one's personality to effectively portray a volatile, yet charming superhero like Iron Man.

Furthermore, Downey's ability to charmingly play hard-to-like characters has been noted as far back as 1993, in the movie *Hearts and Souls*; director Ron Underwood needed and found this ability in Downey, saying, "'We had to have someone with very great personal charm, who would make you root for this guy even when he's pretty abrasive toward the beginning, ... 'I honestly don't know if the film could have been made without him'" (qtd Falk 201). As in post–9/11 film, so in Downey's portrayal of Tony Stark: self-consciousness is key. Superheroes didn't have to go to war themselves after 9/11, but the more successful stories often took a darker, more serious approach, self-aware to some degree and infusing the obligatory victory with a cost or consequence for the hero. As Tom Pollard notes in *Hollywood 9/11*, "Pre–9/11 films now appear naive and optimistic compared with today's pessimistic genres, which include revenge thrillers, violent combat films, torture porn, and dark sci-fi" (Pollard 2). While the avoidance of naiveté is necessary, the tendency toward darkness is not as necessary as it is common. Downey's portrayal of Stark is the most successful superhero portrayal to incorporate optimism without the naiveté that might easily accompany it by default. Unlike the pulp escapist fantasy of Gernsback's day, the *Iron Man* movies and *The Avengers* don't derive their optimism from the technology they feature. The optimism comes from the characters, including (but not limited to) Tony Stark.

Stark's significant challenges to overcome are more related to emotional and moral development than physical or technological issues. The invention of the Iron Man suit is standard; the viewers know it has to happen, but the idea that someone like Tony Stark would decide to dedicate himself to this kind of effort is extreme fantasy. In *The Avengers*, Stark's contributions to the battle to save New York are certainly impressive, but his acceptance of self-sacrifice in a situation in which there is no other option is built up to throughout the film in his arguments with Captain America, Steve Rogers. A person like Stark, who— even after he has decided to become a hero—fights for his own glory, is really a fantasy because he becomes selfless, not because he has an amazing suit of armor or an unreal intellect.

The balance between ironic self-awareness and necessary seriousness comes from Downey's ability to balance verbosity and well-used silence. The excesses written into the character are successful because Downey underplays them; Stark is supposed to be effortlessly larger-than-life. Lines that are outrageous by nature are played tongue-in-cheek, quickly and self-consciously. After casually explaining the complicated science behind the villain Loki's plan in *The Avengers*, Stark is asked, "When did you become an expert in thermonuclear astroyphysics?" His reply of "Last night" comes matter-of-factly from Downey, who moves on quickly to his next line, keeping the scene going. Stark's achievements are impressive because they seem so easy, so natural to him. His impressive quips are— and should be—casual to him, an effect that is enhanced by Downey's oft-mentioned ability to imbue memorized lines with a feeling of spontaneity. (Another factor, of course, is Downey's ability to improvise when scripted lines don't work.) Whedon and directors of other movies Downey has been in have noted how he can make scripted lines sound like he just came up with them; this is important because Tony Stark should rarely look like he's trying at all, in order to highlight the scenes that are supposed to feature real emotional growth.

This emotional growth, contrasted effectively with the irreverence and flippancy Downey brings to his lines, is often played with either subtlety or silence. The restraint of the performance in moments that could be more violently emotional comes from Downey's preference. Whedon notes that Downey objected to a scripted angry outburst at Captain America after the death of their friend Agent Coulson (*The Avengers*). When Rogers asks Stark if this is the first time he's lost a soldier, Stark turns on him and says seriously, "We are

NOT soldiers." Whedon says in his DVD commentary that Downey's scripted reaction was more extreme, but after discussion, they decided that they "hadn't earned it" emotionally. This is a key line in the self-sacrifice story running through the movie, yet not one that needs to be made any more obvious than it already is. If the fantasy of Tony Stark is the maturation or improvement of a flawed and powerful person, the fact that he eventually will embrace self-sacrifice can't be so obvious that even Stark seems to know that he will soon face a moment of truth. It's important not to parody the genuine emotions—this isn't the place for irony.

Even in a scene in which he sits and says nothing, Downey adds to the emotional conflict over responsibility within his character. As Stark and Rogers sit around a table, S.H.I.E.L.D. spymaster Fury talks about the idea for the Avengers, saying the plan was to see if the extraordinary people they put together could "become something more. To see if they could work together when we needed them to, to fight the battles that we never could" (*The Avengers*). Sitting with his back turned, Downey turns to look back and then stops, facing forward again, angrily taking his eyes away from Fury's direction. He keeps his hands in his lap, one hand around a fist. Fury goes on to say, "Phil Coulson died still believing in that idea, in heroes" (*The Avengers*). At the word "heroes," Downey rises quickly and silently from his chair, still staring forward. He stops and moves his eyes in Fury and Rogers' direction without facing them and then walks out. Not only are the retorts gone, but so is the confident swagger and direct eye contact. He flees the room, his ideas of heroism and the merits of his previous feats truly shaken. Agent Coulson's death prompts Stark to finally face the idea of self-sacrifice, the eternal escapist unable to run from a truth that comes with heroism. The gravity Downey gives to his reaction in this scene, both in execution and in contrast with the rest of the performance, is key.

The restrained effect is intensified in the silence of Stark's final heroic act, when he carries a nuclear missile away from Midtown Manhattan and into a portal. The selflessness of the action is highlighted by the fact that Downey says nothing. There is simply a close-up shot on his face, watching the missile destroy the enemy, and then closing his eyes as he falls helplessly through space. The altruistic sacrifice of a hero who represents the wealthy and the powerful in America speaks to a virtue the country ostensibly lacks. It embodies both a contradiction and a fantasy of American self-image. Downey's Stark, however, isn't the only character in *The Avengers* who holds up a mirror to American identity fantasies.

"We're not a team... We're a time bomb."

One of the most significant scenes that shows *The Avengers'* roots in American ideology and fantasies of heroism comes in between some of the most gratifying fight scenes of the movie. While arguing over the morality of advanced weaponry developed by the supposed good guys at S.H.I.E.L.D., the members of the Avengers fall into criticizing each other personally, highlighting the different facets of the American idea of heroism the characters represent. The temporarily captured villain Loki berates agent Natasha Romanov/Black Widow, for thinking she can balance out the lives she's taken in the past by rescuing her fellow agent Clint Barton/Hawkeye. Those remarks, however, also speak very directly to the ethos of the Avengers as well. The peak of Loki's speech is played over shots of Stark, Rogers, and Bruce

Banner/the Hulk, reacting to their discovery of S.H.I.E.L.D.'s secret weapons project and Nick Fury's realization that his secret is out:

> Your ledger is DRIPPING—it's gushing red—and you think saving a man no more virtuous than yourself will change anything? This is the basest sentimentality. This is a child at prayer. Pathetic ... you pretend to be separate, to have your own code, something that makes up for the horrors. But they are a part of you, and they will NEVER go away [*The Avengers*].

The speech resonates with the faces of the flawed heroes as they are faced with upsetting revelations; Captain America, standing for patriotism and idealism and World War II nostalgia in his spangled uniform, finds a crate containing large and intimidating-looking weapons and the scientists, Stark and Banner, find computer files with models of missiles engineered from alien technology. Fury storms in, upset that his questionable actions in the name of safety have been exposed. Thor and Romanov enter and a standoff immediately ensues in which the major characters turn on each other, resorting to accusations and self-justifications that revolve around the issues of deception, surveillance, war profiteering, nuclear deterrence, self-sacrifice, and, ultimately, the definition of heroism that some of the characters settle for.

Fury tells the angry Avengers that S.H.I.E.L.D. had to make more powerful weapons because after Thor's initial appearance on Earth destroyed a small town, they realized how vulnerable Earth really was. Thor retorts that stronger weapons won't result in greater safety, but simply signal to other worlds that Earth is ready for a "higher form of war." When Stark also criticizes the strategy of nuclear deterrence, Fury stares at Stark and reminds him that he made his money from selling deadly weapons. The camera pans from character to character as they exchange their accusations, finally closing in on the captured Loki's mind-influencing scepter on the table in the room, moving toward and flipping over it, showing the movie's heroes arguing upside-down behind a glowing weapon. This movement of the camera is, as Whedon has admitted, intended to make the point that the world has been turned upside-down (*The Avengers*). Logic falls to emotion as well-meaning people argue over the solution of weaponry to deter and face threats. As the initial conflict reaches a peak, Romanov asks, "Are you really that dense? S.H.I.E.L.D.. monitors potential threats," to which an incredulous Banner replies, "Captain America is on threat watch?" (*The Avengers*). When Romanov says "We ALL are!," the overarching theme that our protectors can be as dangerous as any attacker is explicitly spelled out for the viewer. And, of course, no character in this scene is more definitive of that idea than Bruce Banner, whose calm detachment hides an angry and unreasonable beast, the Hulk.

Like Captain America with his optimistic World War II era nostalgia and Nick Fury with his argument for the necessity of hard choices, the Hulk also represents an aspect of American self-image: the sleeping beast, the reluctant and guilty superpower. The Hulk's origin in a radioactive experiment gone wrong evokes a Cold War theme of the weapon that can neither be unmade nor really controlled. S.H.I.E.L.D. thinks the way to handle this weapon is through monitoring and containment, watching his movements from afar and keeping a special cell strong enough to hold him in their Helicarrier. Banner initially prefers the idea of suicide, though this strategy of self-destruction—or disarmament, if you will—fails, and eventually he manages to hold his rage monster at bay by embracing the fact that he is always angry. Stark, in his irreverent mode, encourages Banner to embrace the Hulk, saying that he "need[s] to strut" (*The Avengers*). What Stark's position amounts to is that deliberate, strategic gratification of the Hulk's destructive impulse would be preferable to hapless explosion; it's also worth noting that the only other character in the movie who wants this power unleashed is Loki, the ambitious god of mischief. That Banner finally does use the Hulk for good during an alien invasion represents the promotion of Stark's view by the movie—as well as the fact that this is what gratifies the commercial audience the most. If the Hulk represents a violent impulse in the American consciousness, the good, intentional Hulk is representative of this American self-image: that of a power capable of annihilation which prefers to live in peace if only outside aggressors would allow it to.

It's an optimistic, if also vain fantasy, that the Hulk embodies in general, and in *The Avengers* the statement that fantasy makes may concern the issue of choice and the necessity of self-control. Banner's first transformation into the Hulk evokes the look of a monster movie, like the helpless anguish of a person about to become a werewolf. The lighting is dark as Agent Romanov lies trapped under a fallen pipe and a shaky handheld shot focuses on Banner's fist pounding on the floor as he struggles to maintain control. Emotionally shaken by the team's argument over S.H.I.E.L.D.'s weapons and then knocked down by an explosion on the ship, Banner's voice deepens and he begins to grow in size. As he completes his transformation, the camera closes on the Hulk's expression as he has his last rational thoughts: fear and regret. The viewer sees his eyes, sad and briefly conscious-looking before he becomes only dumb, roaring muscle, destroying much of the Helicarrier. In his commentary to the movie, Whedon compares this transformation to Banner's second transformation in the final battle: "You have two different Hulks in this movie: the one he becomes unwittingly and the one he decides to be. And the difference is palpable" (*The Avengers*). In this movie, a major aspect of the heroes' heroism is their overcoming of their very prominent flaws. The fact that the story is one of improvement shows the movie's optimism and rejection of darkness for its own sake. The fantasy is the improvement of these people for the good of others. It reaches for a positivity that doesn't exist in typical post–9/11 superhero movies.

While the name makes the symbolism of Captain America too obvious to even state, it's important to list some of the details of his story all the same. Before he was given the elusive super-soldier serum, Rogers was a scrawny kid who only had guts, rejected by the U.S. Army for service in World War II multiple times for his frailty. He now has superhuman strength and endurance thanks to the same science that reassured readers of Gernsback's pulps. His glory is rooted in his self-sacrifice in World War II, a greatness America still looks back on longingly, romanticizing this greatness throughout popular culture. While Rogers makes a valid jab at Stark about the self-centeredness of his heroism, Stark reminds him of the importance of technology, telling him, "everything special about you came out of a bottle" (*The Avengers*). Stark doesn't value the passive reception of power over ingenuity, and evokes the self-righteous entrepreneur or inventor who feels entitled to do as he likes—again evoking Howard Hughes. Although Stark and Rogers' confrontation is interrupted by an enemy attack, their aborted argument leads to a recurring theme in the most popular post–9/11 superhero movies: wealth and power.

"Genius, billionaire, playboy, philanthropist"

Stark may claim to privatize world peace, but he and Bruce Wayne also work to solve another major problem in Post–9/11 America in their 2012 movies: the growing global energy crisis. It is no coincidence that both Batman and Iron Man put their money and

Tony Stark (Downey) casually confronts the villain Loki in Joss Whedon's *The Avengers* (2012).

effort (apart from crimefighting) into free clean energy projects. This is the American fantasy of the benevolent rich that the most popular superheroes of the past decade reflect. They solve not only the problems of crime and war, but also the energy crisis. They do everything that the government and the corporate powers of the real world do not. Iron Man even saves New York from destruction in an act of near-self-sacrifice, righting a wrong of more than ten years ago and fulfilling the fantasy of the altruistic wealthy savior. It says even more about the American mindset that the final villain of this fantasy, from whom Tony Stark has to save New York, isn't an alien invader or a Norse demigod. It is a shady government cabal who decide to nuke Manhattan just to be sure the alien threat is neutralized. In these movies, we are kept safe not only by superheroes' abilities to keep us safe, but also by their moral compasses, which rival those of the legal authorities.

As this essay has argued, the fantasy is effectively constructed, thanks in no small part to Downey. Yet is the fantasy inherently beneficial or harmful to viewers? Ebert's question of whether viewers are too well served comes to mind again. Downey's flippant, sometimes parodic performance makes it possible for us to like a billionaire who profits from death and destruction despite ourselves. The profiteers behind companies like Halliburton and Blackwater should be so lucky. His portrayal of a billionaire weapons manufacturer plays to an American desire—two American desires, actually—to trust businesses and to believe in American ingenuity's ability to save them. This troubling realization reflects another growing drive in American culture to worship and defend celebrity. This worship applies, of course, to celebrities in the entertainment industry, but also increasingly includes political leaders; the trend goes as far back as John F. Kennedy's televised debates with Richard Nixon, is exemplified in the election of former movie star Ronald Reagan in the 1980s, and even worked briefly for John McCain during his 2004 presidential campaign.

Today though, critics like Chris Hedges go so far as to liken the support of Barack Obama in America to the purchase of a brand ("Buying Brand Obama" 24). The idea of branded leadership is closely connected to American self-image; audiences buy the Iron Man brand as well, thanks in large part to Downey's performance. Since the beginning of the *Iron Man* series, Stark's opposite number in DC Comics and main box office competitor is also a rich man who acts outside the law, problematically, but necessarily so. Does this mean post–9/11 America has a newfound fascination with or desire for plutocracy? It may, but it is a fantasy version of plutocracy, one altogether more altruistic than anything one could expect in America today, where some might say a plutocracy already exists. Although Hedges rightly points out the negative effect that celebrity culture has of distracting from the important issues, it is important to consider the real virtue celebrated in the popularity of Iron Man: selflessness and self-sacrifice.

Consider Downey's ad lib in conversation with Banner about how the Hulk is actually a gift. Whedon notes that Downey added the line "it's a terrible privilege" to his description of the arc reactor in his chest. The line is played, like the rest of the conversation, seriously. He hesitates in the middle of the line to emphasize the effort of naming his gift. He says, "it's a terrible ... privilege." The fact that he says "privilege" and not "burden" or "gift" or "curse" is appropriate, given the class situation of Downey's character. The arc reactor, the source of both his life and his power, is something he realizes no one else has. It makes him special, gives him something no one else can have, but it's also terrible. The fact that something so terrible is a privilege despite being terrible implies an acknowledgment of responsibility. It helps emphasize that in a moment of seriousness, this vain and difficult rich person realizes that he also has a duty. It enhances what's already in the plot of the movie, heroic self-sacrifice from an unlikely part of post–9/11 America; that audiences respond to it says that they want to see those unlikely sacrifices in the post–9/11 age. As Downey says in a recent trailer for *Iron Man 3*, "since New York, nothing's been the same."

American democratic society requires such self-sacrifice as Hedges also explains in his book *Empire of Illusion*, providing a perfect counterpoint to the potentially negative reading of Stark in *The Avengers*: "Democracy is not an outgrowth of free markets. Democracy and capitalism are antagonistic entities. Democracy, like individualism, is based not on personal gain but on self-sacrifice" (*Empire of Illusion* 185). Some viewers might find it problematic that charm can make a character like Tony Stark so popular, but ultimately something that makes selflessness seem iconic, like Downey's portrayal of Stark, is an admirable use of talent that makes an enjoyable movie also a movie worth paying attention to.

Works Cited

Anders, Charlie Jane. "Several Reasons Why Avengers Kicks Ass (That You Haven't Already Heard)." *io9*, 4 May 2012. Web. 4 Feb. 2013.

The Avengers. Dir. Joss Whedon. Paramount, 2012. DVD.

Bacevich, Andrew J. "The Tyranny of Defense Inc." *The Atlantic*, 4 Jan. 2011. Web. 5 Feb. 2013.
Baudrillard, Jean. *The Spirit of Terrorism and Other Essays*. New York: Verso, 2003. Print.
The Dark Knight Rises. Dir. Christopher Nolan. Warner Bros., 2012. DVD.
Ebert, Roger. "The Avengers." *Chicago Sun-Times*, 2 May 2012. Web. 16 Dec. 2012.
Eisenhower, Dwight. "Dwight D. Eisenhower: Farewell Address." *American Rhetoric*, n.d. Web. 2 Feb. 2013.
Falk, Ben. *Robert Downey Jr: The Fall and Rise of the Comeback Kid*. London: Portico, 2010. Print.
Galli, Cindy, Rhonda Schwartz, and Brian Ross. "Video Shows Drunk, Stoned U.S. Defense Contractors." *ABC*, 18 Oct. 2012. Web. 22 Dec. 2012.
Hedges, Chris. "Buying Brand Obama." *The World as It Is: Dispatches on the Myth of Human Progress*. New York: Nation, 2010. Print. 24+
_____. *Empire of Illusion: The End of Literacy and the Triumph of Spectacle*. New York: Nation, 2009. Print.
Iron Man. Dir. Jon Favreau. Paramount, 2008. DVD.
Iron Man 2. Dir. Jon Favreau. Paramount, 2010. DVD.
Jones, Gerard. *Men of Tomorrow: Geeks, Gangsters, and the Birth of the Comic Book*. New York: Basic Books, 2004. Print.
Keough, Peter. "Iron Man." *Phoenix*, 1 May 2008. Web. 10 Feb. 2013.
McCarter, Jeremy. "The Brainy Blockbuster." *Newsweek* 155/156.26/1 (2010): 80–81. Business Source Elite. Web. 1 Mar. 2013.
Mondello, Bob. "'The Avengers': Slick Summer Superheroics." *NPR*, 3 May 2012. Web. 4 Feb. 2013.
Morrison, Grant. *Supergods: What Masked Vigilantes, Miraculous Mutants, and a Sun God From Smallville Can Teach Us About Being Human*. New York: Spiegel & Grau, 2011. Print.
Pollard, Tom. *Hollywood 9/11: Superheroes, Supervillains, and Super Disasters*. Boulder, CO: Paradigm, 2011. Print.
"Robert Downey Jr." *Inside the Actors Studio*, 15 Dec. 2006. Narr. James Lipton. *YouTube*, 15 May 2013. Web. 2 Aug. 2013.
Scahill, Jeremy. *Blackwater: The Rise of the World's Most Powerful Mercenary Army*. New York: Nation, 2007. Print.
"Trust in America: Recovering What's Lost." *NPR*, 30 Oct. 2011. Web. 2 Feb. 2013.
Vineberg, Steve. "Delivering Something Real To 'Ally McBeal.'" *New York Times*, 18 Mar. 2001. Web. 2 Jan. 2013.
Watchmen. Dir. Zack Snyder. Warner Bros., 2009. DVD.
Wolk, Douglas. *Reading Comics: How Graphic Novels Work and What They Mean*. New York: Da Capo, 2008.
Zeleny, Jeff, and Megan Thee-Brenan. "New Poll Finds a Deep Distrust of Government." *New York Times*, 25 Oct. 2011. Web. 4 Feb. 2013.

Biography

Robert Downey Jr. has frequently cited Carl Jung and Joseph Campbell when attempting to explain the story of his life. He mentions archetypes and myths, uses words like "path" and "destiny," and references a variety of philosophies from Buddhism to the 12-step program, but always ultimately admits that he "still [hasn't] figured it out" (Heath 93). Robert John Downey was born in Manhattan on the fourth of April, 1965 to actress-singer-comedian Elsie Ford and underground filmmaker Robert Downey, who changed his last name from Elias to his stepfather's to get into the army underage (*Inside the Actor's Studio*). Downey Sr. served three years in the army, playing baseball and spending eighteen months in the stockade for getting into a drunken brawl with his lieutenant. With time on his hands, he discovered a love for writing, completed an unpublished novel, and, after working as a waiter, decided to go into screenwriting ("Ups and Downeys"). Junior's grandfather had also been in the army, as "a captain in World War Two" (*Good Morning America*, 2013) and his father's mother had been a model and magazine editor (*Talk Talk*). Coming from a mixed cultural and religious background including Irish Catholics and Russian Jews on the Downey-Elias side and Germans and Scots on the Ford side, the Downey kids (Robert Junior's sister, Allyson, had been born two years earlier) grew up surrounded by Greenwich Village artistic types who encouraged diversity and experimentation.

Although Elsie's brilliance, humor, and confidence in him inspired young Robert to perform (Diamond), Robert Downey, Sr.'s influence arguably had the most impact. Feeling that hiding his bohemian lifestyle and anti-establishment views from his children would be hypocritical, he sat his son on his lap while he wrote, took drugs, and screened the dailies (*Talk Talk*). He also took his son to movies, some of them R-rated. Little Bobby, as he was then called, particularly liked *The Bad News Bears* "because the weirdos win" (Hofler). He always stood out among others his age because he came from a "weird" background, with a father who made strange films that were usually funny, often political (anti-racist or anti-capitalist), and always avant-garde and an actress mother who picked him up from school wearing an outlandish quilted cape (Diamond). As a kid, he was both embarrassed by and proud of his parents. Even though it meant being a misfit, Robert was "just really grateful that [he] was born into a family that put its art first…. The downside is that when you put art first, it doesn't always pan out so well" (qtd. in Hofler). By the time he was fifteen, Bobby had appeared in four of his father's films, beginning with *Pound* (1970) when he was just five. At seven, he appeared in *Greaser's Palace* (1972), in which he "got his throat cut by God" and saw his mom "killed." Robert's father said, "It could have been too much to expose him to. It was traumatic for him to see that kind of violence. He didn't comprehend that everybody comes back again" (Diamond). Downey told James Lipton on *Inside the Actor's Studio* (*IAS*) that growing up with an underground filmmaker and an actor-singer as parents "was just conducive to believing that this was what you were supposed to do, you were supposed to try to push the envelope and it was very natural to have no interaction with, you know, mainstream anything."

He attended Stagedoor Manor, a summer acting camp in the Catskills, when he was eleven and twelve, spending his time smoking and making out with a seventeen-year-old girl named Rhona (*Tonight Show*, 2004). Some of the other campers saw him as a cocky boy, always bragging about his father the filmmaker (Falk 19). He was a hyperactive child, unable to be still for long and needing to entertain himself and others. His first wife Deborah said that he thought he had to always be "on" (Garbarino, "Star"), like a clown compelled to amuse others even if it affected him negatively. Not being tall or particularly athletic and possessed of the long, dark eyelashes of a girl, Robert was picked on by larger boys but came to be admired by females. Although he describes himself as an awkward youth trying to be cool and failing miserably, driving his bicycle into a bush at the sight of a girl he favored ("Restoration"), his sister remembers seeing him constantly surrounded by young women. One time when he was sick and called her for help, she arrived at his apartment to find a roomful of girls "rubbing his feet, feeding him through an eyedropper" (Schneller). Nevertheless, he was no doubt drawn to performance partly because his insecurities stemming from his outsider status and his unstable upbringing drove him to seek attention and praise. In 1998, he told Mike Figgis that he got into acting because he was looking for a "connection" with others—even with strangers who had nothing invested in him but money (*Projections 10*).

Robert Downey Jr.'s childhood had a lasting traumatic effect on him. Although he recalls his parents being very loving and affectionate, they did not seem able to balance their artists' lifestyle with providing a stable home life for their impressionable kids. As a boy, Robert had nightmares about "pirates coming in the window" (Schneller) and "spent a lot of time 'waiting for Dad to come home...'" (Schneller). Downey Sr. and his friends introduced Robert to illegal drugs at a shockingly early age—at least as young as eight years old (*IAS*) and possibly as early as six (Garbarino, "Star"). Downey is reluctant to blame his parents: "Well let me put it this way. It was such a permissive time and um, it was that culture and so we were not discouraged from it" (*IAS*). The family moved often for his father's film projects and yo-yoed between near-poverty and careless spending, depending on the inconsistent success of these films. He told *WOW* magazine in 1987 that his parents were incredibly supportive of whatever he chose to do, but that their transient, unstable lifestyle caused problems for him emotionally—he hated being constantly "uprooted." His father moved them frequently to get a new environment for writing, admitting, "Junior was born in Manhattan. Then we moved to Forest Hills. Then a loft in Greenwich Village. London. New York again. New Mexico. Los Angeles. Connecticut. Woodstock. New York. Los Angeles again. Back to New York. Back to Los Angeles. It was crazy" (Garbarino, "Star"). Downey Sr. became a cocaine addict when, despite receiving underground critical acclaim for films like *Putney Swope* (1969), the pressure to balance art and income became too much. He shared this habit with his son, using it, according to Jr., as a means of bonding and showing love (Gliatto). Downey admits he was regularly doing hard drugs by the time he was a teenager (Fleming, "Candid"). "A lot of what we did to ourselves, he's done too," his father admits in *The Last Party* (1992): "It was an idiot move on our parts, a lot of us, to share that with our children." Sr. was worried "many times" that his son would succumb to a drug-related death.

Allyson Downey recalls their childhood somewhat differently from Robert's happy image of an artsy, liberal family, characterizing it as "'a nightmare' wholly lacking in adult guidance" (Garbarino, "Star"). She also struggled as a young adult with cocaine addiction, as well as bulimia (*Talk Talk*). She remembers times spent with her brother in the family Volvo, listening to the radio and "mimicking their parents' fights" (Schneller). Downey may have later forgiven "Pops" for the chaos he caused in their lives, but according to his sister, "Robert was openly upset and remained angry at his father for years, until they started making movies together in the late Eighties" (Schneller). Allyson guessed that he may have developed low self-esteem because "Robert was good at so many things, we were hard on him: 'This is good, but you can do better.' There was no unconditional confirmation" (Schneller). Downey does remember his parents arguing, such as the time his father threw a milkshake and it landed on the ceiling of their hotel. He lay in bed staring at the mess that had formed into a nipple-like drip, thinking how "uncomfortable it was to see [his] parents in serious conflict, ... that weird hate, hate, hate thing" (Felperin). Those memories of impotent rage would come in handy later, whenever he needed to use his own pain for a role. Before he got sober, Elsie Downey said she had never seen her son happy: "I've never seen him enjoy life. He enjoys lives" (Garbarino, "Star"). Although his father, who the younger Downey obviously admired for his artistic chutzpah if not his parenting abilities, was able to leave his alcohol and drug problems behind years earlier, Robert's own battle with addictions to alcohol, cocaine, heroin, and various other drugs like Valium, marijuana, and magic mushrooms, would last, by his own admission, from about age 13 to 38—a long twenty-five years (*GMTV*).

Elsie and Robert Sr. finally split when Robert Jr. was twelve or thirteen (sources vary). In the 1992 political documentary *The Last Party*, he offers an emotional description of his own reaction to his parents' separation:

> My mom and dad were the kind of couple that people always said would never split up; they'd always be together and they were the perfect couple. And then when I was twelve, um, well, I'll never know why. It's really, I guess, none of my business—I have my own ideas—but they split up and my sister went with my father I think out to California and I moved to New York with my mom.

He moved from Woodstock, where he had taught himself how to play the piano (*IAS*), and lived for a time with his mother in a small apartment in New York City. In the documentary, Downey tells a young boy who is facing his parents' divorce that when his own parents split up, he "felt like [he] ... had to do everything all of a sudden.... It was a drag." He told Scott Raab in 2009 about that time, during the late 1970s in New York:

> [T]here I am, and it's *Rocky Horror Picture Show*, Friday and Saturday night at the Eighth Street Playhouse, and there's my buddy Frank Hall—who I've known since I was five—and there are these kids from a local club calling us Rocky Horror freak-outs, and we get our asses kicked. And there's my mom, fresh out of doing these movies with my dad, and they've broken up, and we're living in a nasty walk-up place on Forty-eighth and Madison. There we were—there were those times and those trials—and now.

Whether that pressure or simply the desire to party and entertain girls led him to leave his mother's house, Robert soon decided to join his father in California, instead.

When he arrived in L.A., he found that the other kids expected him to be "tough" because he came from New York, so he took to riding his bike around with a knife stuck into his sock (Hedegaard) so as not to disappoint. He created a carefree punk image for himself, complete with spiky hair and edgy clothes, but in some ways, "[i]t was all a front. Robert didn't really like punk rock. His personal favourites included the likes of Genesis, Supertramp and Steely Dan. He'd enjoyed singing Schubert in choral competitions and also sang in the mall during holidays. He was really a theatre brat, but he kept all this quiet in order to impress his new pals and score trendy girlfriends" (*Talk Talk*). "I wanted to fit in, to be a bit of a gadfly *and* be the center of attention," he told *Harper's Bazaar* in 1992: "I tried anything that was going on—drugs, casual sex..." (Bishop). He attended Santa Monica ("San-Mo") High, walking the halls with the likes of Charlie Sheen and Emilio Estevez. In fact, Downey made friends with the middle Estevez brother, Ramon, who taught him "about punk rock and tap dancing and introduced [him] to the rigors of various aspects of theater arts" (Raab, "Second Greatest"). Robert cared little for the boring, disciplined confines of school and usually preferred to bum around smoking pot, turning up only to appear in theater arts productions including *Oklahoma!*, *Detective Story*, and *The Rivals*, or to sing madrigals with the geekiest school club he could find (Turan). He always felt like an "oddball" (Heath).

In 2009, he told Scott Raab, with great nostalgia, all about those years as a teenager living in L.A. with his dad, in the early Eighties, getting beaten up, buying alcohol under age, getting drunk in Douglas Park and eating burgers at Jack in the Box. He once worked at a Thrifty's, where he and his buddies "ran a counter scheme" for extra money. This was also around the time that he "got [his] first DUI—although [he] didn't have [his] license yet." He took his friend Chris Bell's mother's Mercedes for a joy ride and asked a policeman for directions (Raab, "Second Greatest"). In the same interview, Downey describes himself as a "latchkey kid" who "grew up on the streets." At the end of grade eleven, a guidance counselor told Robert that he would need to take summer makeup courses in order to graduate with a high school diploma the following year, and even phoned Mr. Downey in an attempt to use a parent's authority to pressure the teenager. However, Robert Sr. reportedly told his son to either go back to school or get a job—the choice was his. When Robert remembers this story now, saying that his was "the wrong dad to call" (*IAS*), he seems to be torn between still thinking it was "cool" that his dad let him quit school and that he grew up with the freedom that he did, and feeling like his parents should have provided more structure and guidance for him. He recently told *The Sun*, "I wish I'd had proper discipline in my life at 18" (Showbiz). That incident marked the end of Downey's formal education until he fulfilled the requirements for his G.E.D. in prison, achieving the highest marks of any inmate to that point (Garbarino, "Star").

After quitting school, the teenager moved back to New York City to pursue acting seriously, at first living with his sister on Edgar Allan Poe Street (*IAS*). To make ends meet, he worked at Area night club as living art, "sending Gumby dolls down a conveyer belt" for ten dollars an hour, dressed in an "orange dayglo jumpsuit" ("Biography, Famous"); sold shoes (which he was fired for stealing); and bussed tables at Central Falls, where he served tea to Sting (*Ellen*, 2006). He appeared in several theater productions including the Norman Lear musical *American Passion* (1983) and went to auditions whenever he could. Between telling roomfuls of hopeful actors that they could go home because he was getting the job (Schneller) and telling off directors who asked him stupid questions, he managed to land a bit part in *Baby It's You* (1983), only to have most of his scenes cut (Hirschberg). Cynical from an early age, he told *Rolling Stone* in 1988 that his bad attitude cost him a few jobs and won him a few more: "It doesn't matter whether or not you can act. If you can go into a room and make these sweaters want to have you around for six or eight weeks, that's what will really get you a job." Natural talent, ambition, and charm combined to make Downey one of the few New York busboys to actually make it into show business.

In April 1984 he met Sarah Jessica Parker on the set of *Firstborn*, only his second non–Downey Sr. film, and the young couple moved in together almost immediately (Diliberto and Evans). They were so conscious of how their fast-moving relationship would be viewed by others that they took pains to keep their living arrangement a secret until the film had wrapped (Diliberto and Evans). She persuaded the impractical youth to do logical things like open a bank account and without her, Downey's father said, "Robert would go at 100 miles an hour into a brick wall" (Diliberto and Evans). In 1987, Robert said of Sarah Jessica, "She's smart and well-spoken and funny" ("What's up")—qualities he would admire in his future wives, as well. After cohabitating since both were nineteen years old, at twenty, Parker was wearing what she called "kind of a hanging-out-together ring" from Downey, although a marriage never materialized. Both teens had emerged from broken homes and been forced to fend for themselves early (Diliberto and Evans). From the beginning of their relationship, he was not only drinking and smoking pot like most of the other youths their age but had also developed a serious cocaine habit. Parker, who never got into drugs herself, spent much of her time nursing him back to health and getting him out of bed and to the set on time. His dishonesty with her would eventually lead to their breakup.

Just after meeting Parker, Downey travelled back to L.A. to film the 1985 James Spader movie *Tuff Turf*, in which he plays a punky-looking drummer who befriends Spader's outsider character. He also joined the cast of a George C. Scott TV series about Mussolini, as Mussolini's son, but it was *Weird Science* that first brought Robert Downey Jr. fame. When John Hughes cast him in 1985, Robert was a young twenty years old and already fully immersed in L.A. party life. Hughes, the force behind Eighties teen classics like *The Breakfast Club* (1985) and *Pretty in Pink* (1986), saw something in the funny boy that audiences would respond to and he was right—immediately after the film's release, fans began to recognize "Ian" on the street (*IAS*). It was his widest-reaching film to date.

Weird Science paid off in other ways as well. On the Universal lot, he met Anthony Michael Hall and began a lifelong friendship with him as well as with Joel Silver, who produced the film. Hall got him an audition for *Saturday Night Live*, and Robert thought it would be a breeze but entered a room full of executives—"thirty shirts" (*Letterman*, 1990). He put his shirt over his head and played an Iranian guy he saw at a club in L.A. (*Letterman*, 1990). He only lasted on *SNL* as a cast member for one season (1985–86), playing a variety of roles including husband to guest star Madonna, then Sean Penn's wife. In 1986, he filmed the Rodney Dangerfield vehicle *Back to School* at the same time as *SNL*, flying between L.A. and New York: "LIVE FROM NEW YORK—IT'S A TIRED YOUNG MAN!" (Hirschberg). Downey, Parker, Billy Zane, and Kiefer Sutherland shared an L.A. apartment during these early years when they were all beginning their Hollywood careers (Falk 51). He would later say, "When I came to L.A., everything that I thought I wanted happened for me. And I think that what kept me from really looking at myself, and growing, was my success" (Figgis). All that success didn't match up with his low opinion of himself and only sent him spiraling further out of control, ashamed of his inability to find a balance between his dark and light sides (Schneller).

The Pick-Up Artist (1987) was Downey's first leading-man role. The film, co-starring Brat Pack princess Molly Ringwald and directed by James Toback (Warren Beatty, who Downey said made Ringwald and himself kiss "like forty times" for one scene, produced) was criticized for being a "sexually irresponsible" film (Hirschberg) because of its casual treatment of promiscuous sex during the height of AIDS awareness. After *The Pick-Up Artist*, Downey had finally made enough money to get the gap between his teeth fixed.

Also in 1987, Downey received his first critical acclaim for the role of Julian Wells in *Less Than Zero*, a Hollywood version of Bret Easton Ellis' slim novel. While Andrew McCarthy played the romantic lead, Robert threw himself headlong into the part of a disaffected drug addict who is disowned by his family and driven to prostitution to pay off a hefty drug debt. The role's unconventionality appealed to him, since he "couldn't see many of [his] peers being able to handle playing a crack-whore" (Hoban). He did push-ups on set to get his heart rate up enough to play a coke addict but didn't need the calisthenics when he went out partying after each day of filming. In his review of the film, Roger Ebert called Downey's acting "so real, so subtle and so observant that it's scary." Others called his performance "painfully honest" (Weinberg) and "desperately moving" (Maslin). From then on, his unique talents were in high demand in Hollywood.

In 1988, *YM* interviewer Stephen Schaefer described Downey as "smart, funny," and "jaded," "with a mocking self-awareness that's as charming as it is surprising." Robert said at the time, "I believe in self-imposed destiny," and he doesn't seem to have changed his mind on that. He seems to believe, for example, as did his friends and relatives (Tresniowski), that his drug problem continued because he allowed it to. *Johnny Be Good* (starring buddy Anthony Michael Hall), *Rented Lips* (his father's movie in which Jr. played the role of a Method-acting porn star named Wolf Dangler), and *1969* (a touching anti-war teen drama co-starring friends Kiefer Sutherland and Winona Ryder) were all released in 1988. Downey was not living with Parker at the time of the *YM* interview but they were still in love and still seeing each other. He told Schaefer, "I just bought a house and she might move in. If I'm good." He may or may not have been good, but they did move in together again. Their pink stucco house in the Hollywood Hills was originally built for Charlie Chaplin. Downey bought a red lacquer piano and played "depressing" songs for guests (*Early Show*, 2005). He appeared with Parker in a Rock the Vote campaign ad against music censorship and the couple toured several cities as members of Young Artists United. After being urged by Parker and his then-manager, Loree Rodkin, he also in 1988 served his first stint in rehab for cocaine addiction shortly after proclaiming to the press that his alcohol and drug problems were over (Hirschberg).

The year 1989 saw the release of two very different films, *True Believer* (a courtroom drama starring James Woods, who took a liking to "Binky" as he called Downey on set (Hoban), and *Chances Are*, a Cybill Shepherd romantic comedy with a twist—in it, Downey's character dies and is reincarnated as a young man, who then falls in love with his own daughter. He also filmed *Air America* (1990) with Mel Gibson and remained sober the entire time despite being on location in Thailand, where he was offered and rejected everything from drugs (Gliatto) to child prostitutes (Sanello). This dedication as well as an impromptu, Fred Astaire–like tap dance impressed writer and co-producer John Eskow, who expressed his admiration of Downey's myriad talents to the actor. Downey shrugged off the compliment: "You know how it is, man. When we hate ourselves, we learn to do a lot of things well, don't we?" (Commentary). The film began a friendship with Mel Gibson that would serve him well in 2003 and would serve Gibson well years after that. When Robert appeared in another of his dad's movies, *Too Much Sun* (1990), he also wrote and sang the humorous title song, which was played during the end credits. *Soapdish* (1991), starring Kevin Kline, Sally Field, and Whoopi Goldberg, was Downey's first movie with Michael Hoffman, who also directed him in 1995's *Restoration*. Playing a producer of a cheesy soap opera who is prompted by a rival actress to sabotage the career of the lead (portrayed by Sally Field), Downey is competent if underused as David Seton Barnes but some of Kline's scenes are still funny today.

Robert Downey Jr. in costume in his Academy Award-nominated role as Charlie Chaplin in Richard Attenborough's *Chaplin* (1992).

As a young actor, Downey would vacillate between dismissing himself as a fraud and bragging that he was the best around, saying, "There's no stopping me!" (Hirschberg). Hedegaard wrote in *Rolling Stone* in 2008, "he used to say, 'There's no one that can act better than me. There's no one that will go places that I will go.' Today he calls this the bleating of 'an egomaniac with an inferiority complex' but then feels compelled to add, 'even if at times it were true.'" In 1991, he got the chance to prove that he could play a role that no one else could.

As soon as he heard that famed *Gandhi* (1982) director Lord Richard Attenborough was planning to film a biopic about Charlie Chaplin, Downey went after the role like a madman. He trained diligently and tried as hard as he could to keep his personal problems from affecting his work. While Robert was preparing for his role in *Chaplin* (1992), Parker had finally had enough of being a glorified babysitter to a grown man and the two parted ways. Sarah had been his safety net, his home base, but he was so dishonest with her for so long that that breach of trust could never be repaired. Depressed over the breakup, he nevertheless threw himself into the new challenge of acting a part that would have been intimidating even for seasoned pros like Robin Williams and Billy Crystal, who were both considered for the role (Fleming, "Candid"). According to Diana Hawkins in Attenborough's autobiography, Robert eventually reached a point during filming when he couldn't sleep and would get up in the night to score drugs, return home, and try to get a couple of hours of rest before rolling out of the car for the morning set call (234). This most demanding performance of his career to date received a great amount of critical praise, although the film overall was considered flawed. Downey was nominated for a Best Actor award at the 1993 Oscars, losing to Al Pacino (*Scent of a Woman*) in what some considered a miscarriage of justice. He did, however, take home a BAFTA (British Academy of Film and Television Arts) award for his physically stunning and emotionally insightful portrayal of the cinema god.

In 1992, Robert began a 42-day courtship with model/actress/singer Deborah Falconer that culminated in their wedding on May 29. He explained that he decided to marry Falconer because didn't want to be a "goat" to her: "Men are goats; we can't help it. Unless we really decide to, and then something changes in our eyes and things are just a little different forever. I address women differently now. Before, there was always some part of me that subconsciously was cruising them" (qtd. in Schneller). Despite protestations to the contrary, however, Downey mainly remained a goat until he met his second wife. He wanted to consciously avoid repeating the mistakes of his father, using his family as "a home base ... and expect[ing] things to work" (Schneller), but soon found himself unable to sustain the marriage. He also fronted the presidential campaign documentary *The Last Party* in 1992. In this mix of political commentary and character analysis, Downey and his new, pregnant partner can be seen cuddling on the couch, but other scenes showcasing his erratic behavior and highlighting his father's fears for Robert's physical and emotional health reveal how psychologically troubled he was at this point in his life. Indio Falconer Downey was born September 7, 1993, but despite Robert's obvious devotion to his son (in 2008 he told *Rolling Stone*, "My entire life is a love note to this little prick!"), family life did not put an end to his drug addictions. He had told an interviewer in 1992 that "drugs are a symbol for a spiritual deficiency" (Bishop). He'd hoped that *Chaplin* would heal his spiritual wounds, but it could not. *Heart and Souls* (a sweet film in which Downey plays several characters at once) and *Short Cuts* (featuring director Robert Altman's award-winning ensemble cast) rounded out the year.

Downey endured heavy metal music and dripping sewage to shoot Oliver Stone's *Natural Born Killers* (1994) with Woody Harrelson and Juliette Lewis (*Charlie Rose*, 1995). As Wayne Gale, the over-the-top, Australian TV journalist who accompanies the killers on their final spree, Downey demonstrates his incredible range. The romantic *Only You* (1994), directed by Norman Jewison, failed to challenge him but at least he was able to work with his friends, Marisa Tomei and Billy Zane.

In 1995, Downey reunited with Michael Hoffman to make the period dramedy *Restoration*, playing a doctor who is ordered to marry the king's favorite mistress to keep her out of the sight of the queen. Speaking in an English accent, wearing a long, heavy wig, scampering about in nothing but a feather and rolling around in bed with British actor Polly Walker didn't faze him, but not-so-behind-the-scenes, Robert was having "a personality meltdown" (*Charlie Rose*, 1995) which required all of cast mate Ian McKellan's tenderness to overcome. Hoffman was also aware of his young star's drug problem but was willing to overlook it since it didn't seem to impair his ability to show up on set and produce a high quality performance (Kennedy). Having begun a friendship with Downey, Sir Ian asked Robert to join him in his modernized version of Shakespeare's *Richard III*, a clever re-envisioning through the iconography of Nazi Germany that took some liberties with the original, including having

Downey's character, Lord Rivers, stuck through with a blade while receiving oral sex. *Home for the Holidays* (1995), directed by Jodie Foster, who, like Attenborough, let him do as he pleased but expressed her concerns about his drug use in a letter, allowed Downey to play his joking, manic self while stretching his wings in his role as Holly Hunter's gay brother. This was the first film on which he used heroin on set, resulting in "one of the most relaxed performances in the history of cinema" (Fleming, "Candid"). Downey later commented that he knew he was in a downward spiral as soon as he started smoking heroin and crack instead of just snorting coke: "It finally tied my shoelaces together" (Kirn 49). Not content to switch one drug for another, he started using both in the extra-dangerous combination of "speedballs" that killed actors John Belushi, Chris Farley, and River Phoenix. His thirtieth birthday was spent "curled up outside on the ground in drug withdrawal while his wife glared down at him, shivering with fury" (Kirn 47).

By 1996, he was in a bad state. Around this time, Mike Figgis, the award-winning director of *Leaving Las Vegas* (1995), met Downey, who infamously showed up for the interview barefoot, high, and carrying a gun. Nevertheless, Figgis cast the addict in *One Night Stand* (1997), as Wesley Snipes' character's best friend, a gay choreographer dying of AIDS. In April, Deb had had enough. She left him, taking Indio with her. Less than two months later, in June 1996, Robert was arrested: "In one wild four-week period, police nabbed Downey with coke, heroin and an unloaded .357 Magnum in his car; he staggered into a neighbor's Malibu home and fell asleep in a child's bed; and [in July] he fled after four days from a detox center a judge had ordered him to attend" (Tresniowski). He was given three years' probation (Tresniowski) during which he was expected to appear for mandatory drug tests. During his initial incarceration, he was allowed a week's leave to host *SNL* in a painfully self-satirizing episode that nevertheless showcased his versatility as a performer. *People*'s Tom

Downey as Peter Wright attempting to charm Faith Corvatch (Marisa Tomei) in Norman Jewison's *Only You* (1994).

Gliatto wrote at the time, "Downey's nightmarish predicament suggests a personal hell at odds with his devil-may-care affability." In a 2004 *Good Morning America* interview with Diane Sawyer, Downey calls these "the 'cry-help' days" during which he was "full of crap" every time he said he was finished with drugs. In the same interview, he attributes his addiction in part to narcissism and a desire to play with "hopelessness" and "romantic self-destruction": "It was imprinted" by heroes like James Dean "and that was [his] loop, pretty much." He came of age in an environment, a family and a culture, that encouraged and romanticized self-destructive behavior.

Despite Downey's desperate condition during the late Nineties, he kept working. After seeing him in an orange jumpsuit on Court TV, James Toback quickly wrote *Two Girls and a Guy* specifically for him (*Biography*). Required to take mandatory drug tests during filming, he stayed sober for those two weeks but didn't remain clean for long, failing to show up for a court-ordered test in September, 1997 and therefore violating his probation. He spent 113 days in a Los Angeles County jail, where he received a gash to the face during a fight with other inmates (Garbarino, "Star"), but was temporarily allowed out to film *U.S. Marshals* (1998), a sequel to the enormously successful *The Fugitive*. Its failure was a low point for Downey, who wasn't particularly interested in "Johnny Handgun" movies at the time but thought "what [he] really needed to do was to be in one of those films that [he] love[d] taking [his] kid to" (qtd. in Figgis). Downey also appeared that year in *Hugo Pool*, directed by his father. In it, he appears horribly emaciated, makes a sly reference to being "out on bail," and when his sadly over-the-top character is finally accepted by the other characters, admits, "I'm happy to be a part of anything." He put on weight for *The Gingerbread Man* (1998), starring Kenneth Branagh, but his physical state didn't bother director Robert Altman, anyway. Altman, whose own improvisational style meshed well with Downey's, said that the actor's drug use had no effect on his performance and that he would hire him again "on the spot," whether he was clean or not (Garbarino, "Last Party").

Although Downey released *Friends and Lovers*, *Bowfinger*, *Black and White*, and *In Dreams* all in 1999 and filmed the critically acclaimed *Wonder Boys* (2000) and *Auto Motives* (2000), "Another missed [drug] test in [June] 1999 landed him in the California Substance Abuse Treatment Facility and State Prison in Corcoran" (Tresniowski). Downey told the judge, "It's like I have a shotgun in my mouth, and I've got my finger on the trigger, and I like the taste of the gunmetal" ("Actor's Toughest Role"). This behavior was more an expression of his unresolved issues than a suicide attempt, though, as friend Josh Richman said, "Robert was never a guy with a death wish" (qtd. in Schneller). He went first to rehab at Cedars-Sinai, then to prison, when Judge Mira sentenced him to three years; however, he was allowed to finish filming *In Dreams* and was released after 11 months. At the premiere of *Black and White*, fans, friends, and his sister protested Downey's incarceration, holding banners demanding "Rehab—Not Prison" (Klingman).

Sources claimed that the actor kept to himself at first but "[e]ventually Downey began interacting, making his cellmates laugh with Hollywood horror stories. By Christmas he was even leading an inmate chorus in the Yuletide caroling" (Garbarino, "Star"). He survived by doing artwork, listening to Sting's new album *Brand New Day* (*Ellen*, 2006), reading mail from mostly female fans, and writing more letters and poems to his mother and sister than he had in the rest of his life previously (Garbarino, "Star"). Friends such as Sean Penn "(who [had previously] staged 2 failed drug interventions on his friend's behalf)" visited him and commented on his ability to display a sense of humor in the face of tragedy (Garbarino, "Star"). Downey wasn't laughing, though, after his son's first visit to the prison, when "Indio asked his mother, Is Daddy a bad man?" (Garbarino, "Star").

According to Michael Douglas, who had starred with Downey in *Wonder Boys*, those who knew him were "heartbroken" (Garbarino, "Star") to learn that the gentle actor would be going to prison. Douglas said, "In his sobriety, you can sense how painful simple alertness is for him. He feels it all—watching him, you can understand the notion of self-medication" (Garbarino, "Star"). Allyson Downey agreed, telling Garbarino in 2000, "The world Robert lives in, his emotional reality, it's so overwhelming for him just to function. He's like an idiot savant. He's a brilliant actor, a brilliant person, and a really good friend. But he has handicaps in dealing with day-to-day situations.... [He uses drugs] to block out all the emotions—just so he can function." Most people who knew him didn't believe he deserved to be in jail, since he was such "a sweet guy" (Toback qtd. in Howden 167) and didn't hurt anyone but himself, but Downey later said, "Drug abuse is wrong. It's not okay. I let down everyone who ever cared about me" (Howden 168). In a *Vanity Fair* interview, Downey called himself an insecure exhibitionist who planned to stop using his dysfunctional family background as an excuse for his behavior (Garbarino, "Star").

After his release from prison in 2000, he spent time in a live-in rehab community in L.A., attempting to rebuild his relationship with Indio (Tresniowski). Although he seemed committed to a sober life, singing at a charity concert with Sting two weeks after his release and being back in the middle of the Hollywood lifestyle again was "too much too soon" (Tresniowski). When he started filming *Ally McBeal* almost immediately, he was unprepared. Downey asked, "Do you know what it's like to come straight out of jail and onto *Ally McBeal*? I was still wondering if we were playing handball in the prison yard at lunch time. They asked me if I was going to be okay while offering $115,000 a week. I just nodded" ("On *Ally McBeal*"). Although the show's ratings soared after he joined the cast, Downey took the part of Larry Paul not because he was desperate to be in a TV show but to be close to Indio and because Indio wanted to see him play "a good guy" (Snierson). He briefly dated star Calista Flockhart, who proved unable to resist the chemistry they generated on set, although she eventually broke up with him in favor of Harrison Ford, which he totally understood (Howden 172). He played with Indio on the set, leading the crew to believe that he was very affectionate with and committed to his son (Tresniowski). Sometimes singing and playing piano in his episodes, the actor impressed viewers with scenes like the one in which his performance of Joni Mitchell's anti–Christmas song "River" "transcend[ed] the proper, socially recommended response, and le[ft] you grateful for whatever combination of talent and vulnerability that led to that moment" ("'River' Keeper"). Despite being highly praised for his work on the show, Downey was stressed by the taping schedule and not entirely happy being on TV instead of film (Tresniowski). He was nominated for an Emmy and won Golden Globe and Screen Actors Guild awards for his portrayal of Larry Paul but, as Downey said in 2004, he was "very, very unhappy—unhappy at that point in [his] life, but also with the whole TV thing. There is no way out of a series until your contract is up. It was like 'Groundhog Day' being on that" (De Vries).

Less than four months after being released from Corcoran, on November 25, 2000, an anonymous phone tip brought police to Downey's suite at Merv Griffin's Resort in Palm Springs, where he let them in without a fight and they discovered cocaine, Valium, and a now-infamous Wonder Woman costume left behind by a friend. According to *People*, "Downey had turned down several Thanksgiving invitations from friends and family and instead chose to spend the holiday weekend with strippers, barflies, limo drivers and other strangers, leading up to the arrest that seemed at once inevitable and surprising" (Tresniowski). Being stuck in *Ally McBeal*, upset over the breakup of his family, and no longer on probation, Downey had quickly slid back into his old habits. He reportedly told police after being assured that he'd receive no special treatment from them, "I'm not a movie star. I'm just a guy with a drug problem" (Smolowe).

Downey was released on bail and showed up for work on the Tuesday after his arrest but the seeds for his exit from the show were already being sewn (Tresniowski). Mel Gibson's plans for his friend to star in a stage production of *Hamlet* had to be cancelled, as did his role in *America's Sweethearts* (2001), with John Cusack taking his part alongside Julia Roberts (Tresniowski). Although he was always "incredibly professional" on set according to directors, "It is away from movie and TV sets that Downey is a mess. His on-the-edge lifestyle ha[d] left him in a financial bind, in debt to the IRS and on the hook for mounting legal fees" (Tresniowski). When he was arrested again in 2001, wandering around Culver City barefoot and under the influence of cocaine, he was sent to rehab instead of prison but the producers of *Ally McBeal* had had enough. In 2013 he admitted, "My attitude was always, 'Fuck it, I don't care. I don't care about fame. I don't care if I fuck up my career. It's not important to me'" (Showbiz).

During moments of self-reflective sobriety, however, he realized that his career did mean something to him, even if it diverged from the conventional movie-star path. His next job after being written out of *Ally McBeal* was the 2001 video for Elton John's song, "I Want Love," directed by Sam Taylor-Wood, in which the camera follows Downey walking through an empty house, lip-synching lyrics that could easily apply to his own life. At a 2004 Kennedy Center Honors presentation to the pop star, Downey called John a "lifesaver" and a "mentor" who helped him through a "desperate time in [his] life," not only by giving him work but also by sharing empathetic words of wisdom about his own addiction, primarily during a short plane ride the two men shared ("Presentation").

In 2002 he started filming *The Singing Detective* after being given the script by friend Mel Gibson, who thought that the parallels between protagonist Dan Dark's skin disease and Downey's addiction would be therapeutic for the actor to work out on screen (*Charlie Rose*, 2003). Downey said at the Toronto International Film Festival press conference in 2003 that it's about "real everyday miracles, when you allow them to occur." The movie was directed by Keith Gordon, who had become friends with Robert during the making of *Back to School*. Based on Dennis Potter's critically acclaimed British TV series, the screenplay (written by Potter himself, who specifically wanted Downey for the role (TIFF)) focuses on the noir fantasies of writer Dan Dark, who is confined to his hospital bed by crippling psoriasis and whose belief in "all clues and no solutions" is reflected not only in his novels but also in the film itself. Gordon helped Downey get over his "self-consciousness, fear, and mistrust" (TIFF) by building up his confidence and allowing him to improvise radically different takes as much as he wanted to (Gordon, "Commentary").

After *The Singing Detective*, which Downey felt was a personal triumph despite its lukewarm reviews (Pevere), he met Susan Levin, then Vice-President of Joel Silver's production company, while filming *Gothika* with Halle Berry in Montreal. Although he was drawn to Levin's competence, he told Oprah, "She's got a great sense of humor and she's a little bit crazy, too. Because, look, she's sitting right here next to me." Susan told *Harper's Bazaar*, "He's this incredible amalgam of contradictory traits that is never boring.... He's completely eccentric but grounded. He's someone who has lived so much life yet has almost a Peter Pan kind of never-grow-up quality" (Cutter). Levin was naïve about the extent of Downey's addiction but when "Darth Vader" reared his head after *Gothika* wrapped, she gave him an ultimatum: me or the drugs (Cutter). In July of 2003, threatened by Levin and scared for his life after eating a greasy cheeseburger, he threw his drugs into the ocean and apparently never touched them again (Cutter). He told the *New York Times* in 2004, "I'm a pretty easy read. I'm either doing well or I'm having a sidebar conversation with the valet at your party and we disappear and come back 45 minutes later looking very alert.... I'm a lab rat at heart and I miss that 'whoopee' feeling, but I've found other ways to get that" (De Vries).

One of those ways is music. Since his late teens, Downey has been writing songs—well over 50 (Fleming, "Candid"). *The Futurist*, his debut album, achieved #1 bestselling new artist of 2004 status (*IAS*). It includes eight original songs written and performed by Downey (covering such themes as hope, fear, and rage) and two covers including Charlie Chaplin's classic, "Smile" and "Your Move," a portion of a Yes song featuring Jon Anderson on backup vocals. "Broken," "clearly an exorcism" which began as a duet with Downey's first wife, singer Deborah Falconer ("Broken") and added to by Mark Hudson is sadistically lovely if over-produced, while the simple beauty of the songs written entirely by Downey, such as the jazzy "5:30" ("probably one of the first things that [he] ever wrote"—"5:30"), "Details," and "Hannah" shines through. The title track, "The Futurist," began as an instrumental called "Snakes" (referring to those who tempt a person away from monogamy) which he played in a moving scene in *Two Girls and a Guy*, was redone as a synth-pop version with hilariously suggestive lyrics for an *Ally McBeal* soundtrack, and evolved into a celebration of the singer's commitment to his future wife, Susan. One reviewer noted that "he seems to bring all the highs and lows of his life and career to bear on his trio version of Charlie Chaplin's 'Smile,' featuring legendary jazz bassist Charlie Haden" (Collar). He performed the singles "Man Like Me" and "Broken" on TV shows such as *Oprah* and *The Tonight Show*. In a *New York Times* interview, Downey says, "every one of the songs is influenced by my experience, but I hope it's a little obscured" (De Vries). Typically self-aware and self-deprecating, he tells the interviewer,

> Look, it's not like I'm pushing schlock, but nowhere on God's green earth would I be a new recording artist who would be getting on *Oprah* without *Weird Science* and the penitentiary. It's the perfect combination, pretty divine. But it's a gross-out too. Beyond nepotism. No way would I ever get to express myself musically if I wasn't an actor of ill repute. You don't get on *Oprah* if you lead a gleaming life and then just happen to cross over into music. So yeah, I'm a little bit uncomfortable about it [De Vries].

Although there's a definite spiritual element to the album, when asked what he thinks of religion, Downey says, "I'm not above it. But like Jung said about people using religion to avoid a religious experience, I have managed handily to avoid a religious experience. I don't know where I fall. Spiritual Green Party? There were times when I was into the whole Hare Krishna thing, which is pretty far out. Now I would call myself a Jew-Bu, a Jewish-Buddhist. But there were many times when Catholicism saved my butt" (qtd. in De Vries).

Downey's next film, *Kiss Kiss Bang Bang* (2005), features "Broken" in the end credits. He gained confidence with this film, on which Susan was a producer and Shane Black, who wrote the script for *Lethal Weapon*, wrote and directed. Downey told Michael Fleming, "It was a practically perfect script, and we played with it a little bit and made some improvements. I liked the way it felt. My energy was even. Val [Kilmer] and I synced nicely, and Shane did a great job directing" (so great, in fact, that he was asked to direct the 2013 release, *Iron Man 3*). Black said on *Larry King Live*, "It's the anti-action action movie.... What isn't in it are a lot of very cool, tough, slick, mythic archetypes that just go about their business and they're the best in the world at what they do. What is in it is a bunch of normal people trying to be much tougher" ("Kiss Kiss Bang Bang").

Robert married Susan in August 2005 in Amagansett, New York, in a Jewish ceremony. Sting and Billy Joel played at the wedding, as did Robert himself. Also in 2005, he gave up a chance to tour with Duran Duran to be part of a stellar ensemble cast in George Clooney's *Good Night, and Good Luck* (*Conan O'Brien*, 2005). Then, Downey and producer Trudie Styler convinced Styler's husband, Sting, to help them finance *A Guide to Recognizing Your Saints*, filmed in 2005 and released in 2006, based on his friend Dito Montiel's memoir. Montiel also helmed the film, winning Best Director at Sundance. Also released in 2006, *The Shaggy Dog* was a remake featuring Downey as an evil scientist. He told David Letterman that he wanted to do a Disney movie to prove he was "all right now" (*Letterman*, 2005). *A Scanner Darkly* (2006), directed by Richard Linklater (*School of Rock*), was based on a novel by Philip K. Dick, author of the book that inspired another dystopian tale, *Blade Runner* (1982). Co-starring Keanu Reeves, Woody Harrelson, and Winona Ryder, the film used a technique called rotoscoping, in which the performances are animated after being filmed. *Fur* (2006) with Nicole Kidman, a fictional representation of photographer Diane Arbus' development as an artist, features Downey as her freak-show darker side, covered head-to-toe in hair. Like *The Singing Detective*, *Fur* seems slightly ludicrous at first but actually amounts to quite a moving avant-garde experience. The film was not widely seen, however, and was not even heard of by most audiences, as Downey pointed out in a 2008 interview with Jonathan Ross. He was excited to work with David Fincher (*Fight Club*) on *Zodiac* (2007), playing the role of smart-assed, hard-partying San Franciscan journalist Paul Avery alongside Jake Gyllenhaal's cartoonist and Mark Ruffalo's detective. *Charlie Bartlett*, directed by Jon Poll and starring newcomer Anton Yelchin, also came out in 2007. It offered him a chance to play a supposedly straight character—a vice-principal who lectures a student on responsibility to others, while privately falling apart because of his own alcoholism, low self-esteem, and tendency to play with guns.

Although he had accumulated quite a list of quirky, respectable, and enviable roles between quitting drugs in 2003 and realizing, five years later, that those days were behind him, *Iron Man* was definitely the turning point in Downey's career. Despite the confidence he'd gained with films like *The Singing Detective* and *Kiss Kiss Bang Bang*, Robert said,

> Probably the person resisting it the longest was me. I resisted being open to thinking of myself in that framework, that I could do the superhero thing. But maybe I could look like I was six feet tall, in the right boots. I could get my arms a little bigger and not move my face so much when I talked. I could be in a jeep with a bunch of military guys cracking jokes and then not look like a bitch when the bomb goes off. I might even look like the kind of guy who designs those big bombs. By the way, that's more likely me. He's not a hero in the beginning and has no intention of becoming a hero. He's injured by his own creations. I just love that [qtd. in Fleming, "The Real"].

When he got the part in 2007, he answered for Scott Raab, "Why am I the guy for this job? Because the story is the most duplicitous and conflicted of all the Marvel characters, because he's really just a guy who gets put in an extraordinary set of circumstances—partially due to his own character defects and partially due to his lineage—and you can pick a fucking million Joseph Campbell myths and look 'em up, but none of them apply more to me, and there's nothing I could bring more to than this job and this story" ("Quiet One"). He told Michael Fleming, "I prepared for the screen test so feverishly that I literally made it impossible for anybody to do a better job. I had never worked on something that way before; I was so familiar with six or nine pages of dialogue, I had thought of every possible scenario. At a certain point during the screen test I was so overwhelmed with anxiety about the opportunity that I almost passed out ... just an unadulterated fear of failure" ("The Real").

Far from failing, he aced the superhero role and it rocketed him to superstardom. Much like Downey himself, Tony Stark was a character "who went through all these transitions and was for years considered a second-tier superhero" (qtd. in Fleming, "The Real"). The actor "still get[s] all choked up just remembering" that, after having been told there was no way Marvel would hire him for *Iron Man* (2008) under any circumstances, telling director Jon Favreau that he'd prefer to hold out hope (Hedegaard), and finally screen testing for Tony Stark, Favreau called to tell him he'd gotten the part. Marvel was so pleased with the film's (and Downey's) performance that they gave him a Bentley: " 'My door prize after the two-week total of Iron Man proceeds,' he says, sheepishly" (Raab, "Second Greatest").

That summer, when filming *Tropic Thunder*, Ben Stiller's 2008 satire of Hollywood war movies like *Apocalypse Now*, *Platoon*, and Downey's own *Air America* (1990), Downey did not take his role as the black-faced Kirk Lazarus lightly. He worried about "squandering all the good will he'd built up with *Iron Man*" ("On 'Thunder'") but said,

> I also thought about my dad's film *Putney Swope* and how that was about a creative black man who, only by accident in 1968, finds himself in a position of true influence and power. And then I thought about all the years following that and how many black entertainers, more so than even my own pigmented brethren, had influenced me. I thought about struggle, and then I thought about my own struggle. And without imagining I could draw any realistic parallels, I decided to invest myself in it. I just had all these references guiding me and [laughs]—you know, forget everything I just said. My heart was in the right place, and when the character's voice happened, I could do no wrong [Fleming, "The Real"].

His instincts about the controversial role proved correct when he was nominated for a Best Supporting Actor Oscar at the Academy Awards (the award went to the late Heath Ledger).

Filmed in 2008, *The Soloist*'s release was delayed until 2009. This seriously underrated true-story drama directed by Joe Wright (*Atonement*) saw both Downey and co-star Jamie Foxx give Oscar-worthy performances as *L.A. Times* columnist Steve Lopez and homeless musician Nathanial Ayers, respectively. Not wanting to rest, Downey followed up the successes of *Iron Man* and *Tropic Thunder* with *Sherlock Holmes* (2009), a Guy Ritchie re-envisioning of the great detective as an action hero more closely aligned with Arthur Conan Doyle's stories of the bare-knuckle boxer than with pop culture's idea of Holmes as a pipe-smoking armchair genius. Downey won a Golden Globe for his eccentric, martial-artist take on the British sleuth and made a good friend in co-star Jude Law, who played Dr. Watson.

The box office successes of both *Iron Man* and *Sherlock Holmes* made *Iron Man 2*'s outstanding profits in 2010 no surprise. Putting more of his own "character defects" (Rottenberg) into Tony in the second Iron Man outing should also have come as no surprise given that Downey told Michael Fleming in 2010 that he could still relate to his earlier self

> [a]bsolutely and entirely. But sometimes it's necessary to compartmentalize the different stages of your evolution, both personally and objectively, for the people you have to love and tolerate. And one of those people, for me, is me. I have a very strong sense of that messed-up kid, that devoted theater actor, that ne'er-do-well 20-something nihilistic androgyne and that late–20s married guy with a little kid, lost, lost in narcotics—all as aspects of things I don't regret and am happy to keep a door open on. More than anything I have this sense that I'm a veteran of a war that is difficult to discuss with people who haven't been there.

Although the makers of *Iron Man 2* decided not to run with the "Demon in a Bottle" storyline of the comic series, the parallels between Downey's past and Stark's poisoned system and resulting irresponsible behavior are obvious. A Gene Siskel Film Center Renaissance Award helped him celebrate the successes of both of his franchises.

A slightly dark comedy, *Due Date* (2010); a very successful *Sherlock Holmes* sequel, *A Game of Shadows* (2011); an American Cinematheque Award (2011); and the birth of his second son, Exton (2012) kept Downey happily busy between *Iron Man 2* and his next outing as the armored hero, 2012's much-anticipated and record-breaking *The Avengers*. As part of an ensemble cast, Downey's wit, charm, and ability to be a team player helped make director Joss Whedon's the most-loved superhero film since *The Dark Knight*. *Iron Man 3*, released one year after *The Avengers* in May of 2013 and making over a billion dollars in its first month, took the subversion of the superhero genre even further, representing Stark as an emotionally wounded man beset by panic attacks and relying on his army buddy James Rhodes (Don Cheadle) to help him out of a jam. Downey doesn't want to give up his most successful role to date, but doesn't want to overstay his welcome, either (Heath). Whether his run as Tony Stark ends with *The Avengers 3* or not, it's clear that Robert Downey Jr. has made an impression on the world, and will continue to for as long as he can. *The Judge*, a Team Downey production co-starring Robert Duvall, is slated for release in October 2014 and he helped friend Jon Favreau out a few months earlier with a minor role in *Chef* (2014), a quirky comedy starring the director himself.

Finally happy and at peace, financially successful, and able to choose whatever projects interest him, Downey is content to work alongside his wife and others in their production company, Team Downey. A large support network that includes the love of an uncompromising woman, his family, several assistants including the loyal Jimmy Rich, a multitude of well-connected friends, weekly therapy sessions, 12-step AA meetings, Wing Chun Kung Fu, yoga, Chinese herbal supplements, and, above all, self-discipline have kept him from sliding back into those old habits. Downey says, "Discipline for me is about respect. It's not even about self-respect; it's about respect for life and all it offers. And not indulging. I have happily reconsidered my position on a bunch of things I didn't want on my 'no' list despite all evidence that I couldn't handle them. At the end of the day, anything I think I'm sacrificing I'm just giving up because it makes me feel better" (Fleming, "The Real"). He still believes that acting is easy, at least compared to the real-world problems that many people, including himself, have had at one time or another: "[I]f you've had a life as difficult as anyone's and your most stressful times had nothing to do with being powdered for your fucking close-up, then the reality of a day spent on a relatively safe film set is not daunting at all" (Fleming,

"The Real"). Although casual observers may think, based on his talk-show showiness, that he is supremely confident, even arrogant, that pose is just a mask, one of many he still uses to cover some leftover insecurity. By 2013, he was able to tell Jimmy Kimmel, "I've migrated from no self-esteem to low self-esteem."

Like many of his peers, Downey spent years making movies, making money, making women, and doing drugs, yet his is not the typical Hollywood experience. Although he was always able to maintain a reputation as an incorrigible but amiable, genuinely nice guy ("maybe too sensitive to live in this world," according to John Eskow) and a brilliant improvisational actor, he went through more than even the usual dysfunctional star upbringing. An early sensitivity and inferiority complex, avant-garde unstable home life, sense of himself as a misfit, taste of fame and respect, public humiliation, physical and mental suffering, sixteen months in prison, getting clean, getting humble, and devoting himself to his family, his friends, and his health all before reaching A-list status have combined to make him a very self-aware, down-to-earth, self-deprecating, yet confident man who knows the difference between the business of Hollywood and the business of life. While he may not always believe that everything happens for a predetermined reason, he seems to have hope that a person who remains open to the positive possibilities of life has a greater chance of finding them. In 2010 he said, "I have such an overwhelming sense that if you're in the right state of heart, which I have been for a little while, the next right thing appears to you" (Fleming, "The Real"). Although he's now "in the right state of heart," Downey is still an eccentric—a fear of bugs, of both the insect and virus variety, has survived the end of his cocaine-fueled paranoiac period (Diamond) and he still likes to wear odd outfits such as the custom-made *lederhosen* he wore to the German premiere of *Iron Man 3*. Having finally overcome his inherited demons and those he created all on his own, Robert Downey Jr. may still be the same crazy-talking, hyper, attention-seeking kid he's always been, but he has learned the key to survival: "There's somewhere you're supposed to go and if you get quiet enough, you'll make it" ("*Fur*: HBO").

Works Cited

"Actor's Toughest Role: Beating Addiction a Struggle for Troubled Star." People in the News. *CNN,* 2004. Web. 3 Aug. 2013.
Air America. Special Edition. Dir. Roger Spottiswoode. Lions Gate Home Entertainment, 1990. DVD.
Ally McBeal. Crea. David E. Kelley. 20th Century–Fox Television, 1997–2002. Television.
America's Sweethearts. Dir. Joe Roth. Columbia, 2001. Film.
Atonement. Dir. Joe Wright. Universal, 2007. Film.
Attenborough, Richard, and Diana Hawkins. *Entirely Up to You, Darling*. London: Hutchinson, 2008. Print.
"Auto Motives." 2000. Dir. Lorraine Bracco. *Love & Distrust*. Phase 4 Films, 2010. DVD.
The Avengers. Dir. Joss Whedon. Paramount, 2012. Blu-ray.
Baby It's You. Dir. John Sayles. Paramount, 1983. Film.
Back to School. 1986. Extra-Curricular Edition. Dir. Alan Metter. Fox Home Entertainment, 2011. Blu-ray.
The Biography Channel Presents: Robert Downey, Jr. A&E Television Networks. New Video, 2007. DVD.
"Biography, Famous." 2006. Audio and Video Index. *Downey Unlimited Forever*. Web. 2 Aug. 2013.
Bishop, Kathy. "A New and Improved Robert Downey, Jr. Takes on the Role of a Lifetime and Grows Up in the Process." *Harper's Bazaar*, Dec. 1992: n. pag. Articles and Interviews. *Downey Unlimited Forever*. Web. 1 Aug. 2013.
Black and White. Dir. James Toback. Columbia TriStar, 1999. DVD.
Blade Runner. Dir. Ridley Scott. Warner Bros., 1982. Film.

Bowfinger. Dir. Frank Oz. Universal, 1999. DVD.
The Breakfast Club. Dir. John Hughes. Universal, 1985. Film.
"Campaign Ad." *Rock the Vote 88*. 1988. Audio and Video Index. *Downey Unlimited Forever*. Web. 8 Aug. 2013.
Chabon, Michael. *Wonder Boys*. 1995. New York: Random House, 2008. Print.
Chances Are. Dir. Emile Ardolino. TriStar, 1989. Film.
Chaplin. 15th Anniversary Edition. Dir. Richard Attenborough. Maple Pictures, 1992. DVD.
Charlie Bartlett. 2007. Dir. Jon Poll. *The Robert Downey, Jr. Collection*. Fox Home Entertainment, 2009. DVD.
The Charlie Rose Show. PBS. 20 Dec. 1995 and 23 Oct. 2003. Television.
Chef. Dir. Jon Favreau, Open Road, 2014. Film.
Collar, Matt. "*The Futurist*." Review. *All Music Guide*. 2004. Downey Review Archive— Music Reviews. *Downey Unlimited Forever*. Web. 7 Aug. 2013.
Cutter, Kimberly. "Susan Downey: Iron Woman." *Harper's Bazaar*, 9 Dec. 2009: n. pag. Web. 21 May 2013.
The Dark Knight. Dir. Christopher Nolan. Warner Bros., 2008. Film.
De Vries, Hilary. "Robert Downey Jr.: The Album." *New York Times*, 21 Nov. 2004: n. pag. Web. 3 Aug. 2013.
Diamond, Jamie. "Robert Downey Jr. Is Chaplin (on Screen) and a Child (Off)." *New York Times*, 20 Dec. 1992: n. pag. Web. 1 Aug. 2013.
Dick, Philip K. *A Scanner Darkly*. 1977. New York: Vintage, 1991. Print.
Diliberto, Gioia, and Hilary Evans. "Sarah and Robert Play House." *People*, 30 Sept.1985: n. pag. Articles and Interviews. *Downey Unlimited Forever*. Web. 3 Aug. 2013.
Downey, Robert, Jr. *The Futurist*. Sony Classical, 2004. CD.
Due Date. Dir. Todd Phillips. Warner Bros., 2010. DVD.
The Early Show. CBS. Jan. 2005. Television.
Ebert, Roger. "Review of *Chaplin*." *Chicago Sun-Times*, 8 Jan. 1993: n. pag. Downey Review Archive— Chaplin. *Downey Unlimited Forever*. Web. 2 Aug. 2013.
Ellen. NBC. 27 Sept. 2006. Television.
Ellis, Bret Easton. *Less Than Zero*. New York: Simon & Schuster, 1985. Print.
Eskow, John. "Director's Commentary." *Air America*. Special Edition. Dir. Roger Spottiswoode. Lions Gate Home Entertainment, 1990. DVD.
Falk, Ben. *Robert Downey Jr.: The Fall and Rise of the Comeback Kid*. London: Portico, 2010. Print.
Felperin, Leslie. "Robert Downey Jr.: Marlon Brando on Acid, Anyone?" *Independent News* 2003: n. pag. *Downey Unlimited Forever*. Web. 6 June 2013.
Figgis, Mike. *Projections 10: Hollywood Film-Makers on Film-Making* (Excerpt). 2000: n. pag. Institute for Robert Downey, Jr. Studies—Required Reading. *Robert Downey Jr. Film Guide*. Web. 8 Aug. 2013.
Fight Club. Dir. David Fincher. Twentieth Century–Fox, 1999. Film.
Firstborn. Dir. Michael Apted. Paramount, 1984. Film.
Fleming, Michael. "A Candid Conversation." *Playboy*, Dec. 1997: n. pag. Articles and Interviews. *Downey Unlimited Forever*. Web. 3 Aug. 2013.
_____ "The Real Robert Downey, Jr." *Playboy*, Nov. 2010: n. pag. Articles and Interviews. *Downey Unlimited Forever*. Web. 3 Aug. 2013.
Friday Night with Jonathan Ross. BBC. 2 May 2008. Television.
Friends and Lovers. Dir. George Haas. Lions Gate Home Entertainment, 1998. DVD.
The Fugitive. Dir. Andrew Davis. Warner Bros., 1993. Film.
Fur. Dir. Steven Shainberg. New Line Cinema, 2006. DVD.
"*Fur*: HBO First Look." *Fur*. Special Features. Dir. Steven Shainberg. New Line Cinema, 2006. DVD.
Gandhi. Dir. Richard Attenborough. Columbia, 1982. Film.
Garbarino, Steve. "Robert Downey's Last Party." *Detour*, Feb. 1999: n. pag. Articles and Interviews. *Downey Unlimited Forever*. Web. 8 Aug. 2013.
_____. "The Star in Cell 17." *Vanity Fair*, Mar. 2001: n. pag. Institute for Robert Downey, Jr. Studies—Required Reading. *Robert Downey Jr. Film Guide*. Web. 3 Aug. 2013.
The Gingerbread Man. 1998. Dir. Robert Altman. Universal, 2002. DVD.
Gliatto, Tom. "Hitting Bottom." *People*, 19 Aug. 1996. Web. 4 Aug. 2013.
GMTV with Lorraine. You Tube, 17 Dec. 2008. Web. 8 Aug. 2013.
Good Morning, America. ABC. 2004. Television.
Good Morning, America. ABC. 29 Apr. 2013. Television.
Good Night and Good Luck. Dir. George Clooney. Sony Pictures Home, 2006. DVD.

Gordon, Keith. "Director's Commentary." *The Singing Detective*. 2003. Dir. Keith Gordon. Paramount Home Entertainment, 2004. DVD.
Gothika. Dir. Mathieu Kassovitz. Warner Bros., 2003. DVD.
Greaser's Palace. Dir. Robert Downey [Sr.] Cinema 5 Distributing, 1972. Film.
A Guide to Recognizing Your Saints (2006). Dir. Dito Montiel. First Look Home Entertainment, 2007. DVD.
Heart and Souls. 1993. Dir. Ron Underwood. Universal, 1998. DVD.
Heath, Chris. "RD3." *GQ*, May 2013: 90–97, 144–146. Print.
Hedegaard, Erik. "The Man Who Wasn't There." *Rolling Stone*, Aug. 2008: n. pag. Articles and Interviews. *Downey Unlimited Forever*. Web. 3 Aug. 2013.
Hewitt, Chris. "A Farewell to Armour." *Empire*, Apr. 2013: 76–85. Print.
Hirschberg, Lynn. "Robert Downey's Weird Science of Acting." *Rolling Stone*, May 1988: n. pag. Articles and Interviews. *Downey Unlimited Forever*. Web. 1 Aug. 2013.
Hoban, Phoebe. "Hollywood's Newest Golden Boy." *Premiere*, Apr. 1989: n. pag. Articles and Interviews. *Downey Unlimited Forever*. Web. 5 Aug. 2013.
Hofler, Robert. *Variety's The Movie That Changed My Life*. Philadelphia: Da Capo Press, 2009.
Institute for Robert Downey, Jr. Studies—Required Reading. *Robert Downey Jr. Film Guide*. Web. 5 Aug. 2013.
Home for the Holidays. 1995. Dir. Jodie Foster. *The Robert Downey, Jr. Collection*. Fox Home Entertainment, 2009. DVD.
Howden, Martin. *Robert Downey Jr.: The Biography*. London: John Blake, 2010. Print.
Hudson, Greg. "The Man in the Iron Mask." *Sharp*, May 2013: 66–71. Print.
Hugo Pool. 1997. Dir. Robert Downey, Sr. Wellspring, 2002. DVD.
In Dreams. Dir. Neil Jordan. Dreamworks, 1999. DVD.
Iron Man. Ultimate 2-Disc Edition. Paramount, 2008. DVD.
Iron Man 2. Dir. Jon Favreau. Paramount, 2010. DVD.
Iron Man 3. Dir. Shane Black. Disney, 2013. Blu-Ray.
Jimmy Kimmel Live! ABC. 2 May 2013. Television.
John, Elton. "I Want Love." 2001. Dir. Sam Taylor-Wood. *You Tube*, 1 Sept. 2010. Web. 6 Jan. 2014. Music Video.
Johnny Be Good. 1988. Dir. Bud Smith. MGM Home Entertainment, 2003. DVD.
The Judge. Dir. David Dobkin. Warner Bros., 2014. Film.
Kamin, Dan. Message to Erin E. MacDonald. 14 Jan. 2013. E-mail.
Kirn, Walter. "Robert Downey Jr.: Hardass, Flake, Superstar. He's Anything You Want Him to Be, and an Iron Man, Too." *Rolling Stone*, 1104 (13 May 2010): 42–49. Print.
Kiss Kiss Bang Bang. 2005. Dir. Shane Black. Warner Bros., 2006. DVD.
"Kiss Kiss Bang Bang." *Larry King Live*. 17 Oct. 2005. Audio and Video Index. *Downey Unlimited Forever*. Web. 6 Jan. 2014.
Klingman, Mark. "Rehab—Not Jail for Robert Downey, Jr.!" moogymusicwww, N. p., Apr. 2000. Web. 6 Jan. 2014.
The Last Party. 1992. Dir. Mark Benjamin and Marc Levin. Live Home Video, 1993. VHS.
Late Night with Conan O'Brien. NBC. 10 Nov. 2005. Television.
The Late Show with David Letterman. CBS. 1990 and 2005. Television.
Leaving Las Vegas. Dir. Mike Figgis. MGM/UA, 1995. Film.
Less Than Zero. 1987. Dir. Marek Kanievska. Fox Home Entertainment, 2001. DVD.
Lethal Weapon. Dir. Richard Donner. Warner Bros., 1987. Film.
Maslin, Janet. "Young Lives." Review of *Less Than Zero*. *New York Times*, 6 Nov. 1987: n. pag. Downey Review Archive. *Downey Unlimited Forever*. Web. 5 Aug. 2013.
Montiel, Dito. *A Guide to Recognizing Your Saints: A Memoir*. New York: Thunder's Mouth Press, 2003. Print.
Mussolini: The Untold Story. NBC, Nov. 1985. TV Mini-series.
Natural Born Killers: The Director's Cut. 1994. Dir. Oliver Stone. Warner Bros., 2009. DVD.
1969. 1988. Dir. Ernest Thompson. MGM Home Entertainment, 2002. DVD.
One Night Stand. 1997. Dir. Mike Figgis. New Line Home Video, 1998. DVD.
Only You. Dir. Norman Jewison. TriStar, 1994. Film.
The Oprah Winfrey Show. 23 Nov. 2004. Television.
Pevere, Geoff. "Robert Downey High on Praise." *Toronto Star*, 14 Sept. 2003: D02. *LexisNexis*. Web. 8 Mar. 2013.

The Pick-up Artist. 1987. Dir. James Toback. Fox Home Entertainment, 2009. DVD.
"Presentation for Elton John." *The Kennedy Center Honors*. 2004. Audio and Video Index. *Downey Unlimited Forever*. Web. 8 Aug. 2013.
Pretty in Pink. Dir. Howard Deutch. Paramount, 1986. Film.
Pound. Dir. Robert Downey, Sr. United Artists, 1970. Film.
Putney Swope. Dir. Robert Downey, Sr. Cinema V, 1969. Film.
Raab, Scott. "The Quiet One." *Esquire*, Mar. 2007: n. pag. Articles and Interviews. *Downey Unlimited Forever*. Web. 4 Aug. 2013.
_____. "The Second Greatest Actor in the World." *Esquire*, Dec. 2009: n. pag. Articles and Interviews. *Downey Unlimited Forever*. Web. 4 Aug. 2013.
Rented Lips. Dir. Robert Downey, Sr. International Video Entertainment, 1987. VHS.
Restoration. Dir. Michael Hoffman. Miramax Home Entertainment, 1995. DVD.
"Restoration." *Larry King Live*. 1995. Audio and Video Index. *Downey Unlimited Forever*. Web. 6 Jan. 2014.
Richard III. 1995. Dir. Richard Loncraine. *The Robert Downey, Jr. Collection*. Fox Home Entertainment, 2009. DVD.
"'River' Keeper." *Entertainment Weekly*, 5 Dec. 2000: n. pag. Downey Review Archive— Music Reviews. *Downey Unlimited Forever*. Web. 7 Aug. 2013.
"Robert Downey Jr." *Inside the Actor's Studio*. 15 Dec. 2006.. *You Tube*. N. p., 15 May 2013. Web. 2 Aug. 2013.
"Robert Downey Jr.—Biography." *TalkTalk*, n.d. Web. 8 May 2013.
"Robert Downey Jr.—Broken." *You Tube*, 7 Mar. 2008. Web. 5 Aug. 2013.
"Robert Downey Jr.—5:30." *You Tube*, 7 Mar. 2008. Web. 2 Aug. 2013.
"Robert Downey—Flirting with Disaster.." *Entertainment Weekly*, 9 Aug. 1996. Web. 4 Aug. 2013.
"Robert Downey Jr. on Ally McBeal." Institute for Robert Downey, Jr. Studies—TV Studies. *Robert Downey Jr. Film Guide*. Web. 5 Aug. 2013.
"Robert Downey Jr. on 'Thunder.'" *The Early Show*. CBS. 18 Aug. 2008. Web. 8 Aug. 2013.
Rottenberg, Josh. "*Iron Man 2*: The New Iron Age." *Entertainment Weekly*, 30 Apr. 2010. Web. 8 Aug. 2013.
Sanello, Frank. "Natural Born Talent." *Cosmopolitan*, Jan. 1994: n. pag. Articles and Interviews. *Downey Unlimited Forever*. Web. 5 Aug. 2013.
Saturday Night Live. Season 11. NBC, Nov. 1985-May 1986. TV Series.
A Scanner Darkly. Dir. Richard Linklater. Warner Bros., 2006. DVD.
Scent of a Woman. Dir. Martin Brest. Universal, 1992. Film.
Schaefer, Stephen. "Robert Downey Jr. Succeeds in Show Business Without Really Trying." *YM*, Oct. 1988: n. pag. Articles and Interviews. *Downey Unlimited Forever*. Web. 5 Aug. 2013.
Schneller, Johanna. "What a Tramp!" *GQ*, Jan. 1993: n. pag. Articles and Interviews. *Downey Unlimited Forever*. Web. 11 July 2013.
School of Rock. Dir. Richard Linklater. Paramount, 2003. Film.
The Shaggy Dog. Dir. Brian Robbins. Disney Home Entertainment, 2006. DVD.
Sherlock Holmes. 2009. Dir. Guy Ritchie. Warner Bros., 2010. Blu-Ray.
Sherlock Holmes: A Game of Shadows. 2011. Dir. Guy Ritchie. Warner Bros., 2012. Blu-Ray.
Short Cuts. Dir. Robert Altman. FineLine Features, 1993. Film.
Showbiz, Bang. "Robert Downey, Jr—Robert Downey, Jr: 'I wish I'd had discipline.'" *Contactmusic*, 10 June 2013. Web. 2 Aug. 2013.
The Singing Detective. 2003. Dir. Keith Gordon. Paramount Home Entertainment, 2004. DVD.
The Singing Detective. BBC, 1986. TV Mini-series.
"*The Singing Detective* Toronto International Film Festival (TIFF) Press Conference." Sept. 2003. Audio and Video Index. *Downey Unlimited Forever*. Web. 8 Aug. 2013.
Smolowe, Jill. "Repeat Offender." *People*, 11 Dec. 2000. Web. 5 Aug. 2013.
Snierson, Dan. "The Ups and Downs of Ally McBeal." *Entertainment Weekly*, 3 Nov. 2000. Web. 5 Aug. 2013.
Soapdish. Dir. Michael Hoffman. Paramount, 1991. DVD.
The Soloist. Dir. Joe Wright. Paramount, 2009. Blu-Ray.
The Tonight Show with Jay Leno. NBC, 2004. Television.
Too Much Sun. 1990. Dir. Robert Downey, Sr. RCA/Columbia Pictures Home Video, 1991. VHS.
Tresniowski, Alex. "Bad to Worse." *People*, 18 Dec. 2000. Web. 4 Aug. 2013.
Tropic Thunder. Dir. Ben Stiller. Dreamworks Home Entertainment, 2008. DVD.
True Believer. 1989. Dir. Joseph Ruben. Columbia, 2008. DVD.

Tuff Turf. 1985. Dir. Fritz Kiersch. Image Entertainment, 2012. DVD.
Turan, Kenneth. "Cinema Scion." *Interview Magazine*, Apr. 1989: n. pag. Articles and Interviews. *Downey Unlimited Forever*. Web. 1 Aug. 2013.
Two Girls and a Guy. 1997. Dir. James Toback. Fox Home Entertainment, 2000. DVD.
Tyley, Jodie. "The End of the Iron Age." *SciFi Now* 79 (Spring 2013): 22–27. Print.
"Ups and Downeys." *Interview Magazine*, Nov. 1990: n. pag. Articles and Interviews. *Downey Unlimited Forever*. Web. 3 August 2013.
U.S. Marshals. Dir. Stuart Baird. Warner Bros., 1998. DVD.
Weinberg, Scott. Review of *Less Than Zero. Apollo Movie Guide, 1998–2008*. Downey Review Archive. *Downey Unlimited Forever*. Web. 4 Aug. 2013.
Weird Science. 1985. Dir. John Hughes. P Universal, 2008. DVD.
"What's Up with Robert Downey, Jr.?" *WOW*, Aug. 1987: n. pag. Articles and Interviews. *Downey Unlimited Forever*. Web. 4 Aug. 2013.
Wonder Boys. Dir. Curtis Hanson. Paramount, 2000. DVD.
Zodiac. Dir. David Fincher. Paramount, 2007. DVD.

Filmography

1970 *Pound,* Puppy
1972 *Greaser's Palace*, Boy
1975 *Moment to Moment* aka *Two Tons of Turquoise to Taos*, Himself
1980 *Up the Academy*, Boy on Soccer Team
1982 *America* aka *Moonbeam* (released 1986), Paulie Hackley
1983 *Baby It's You,* Stewart
1984 *Firstborn,* Lee
1985 *Girls Just Want to Have Fun*, Punk Party Crasher
1985 *Deadwait* (short), Delivery Boy
1985 *Arrival* (short), Eddie
1985 *Tuff Turf,* Jimmy Parker
1985 *Weird Science,* Ian
1985 *Mussolini: The Untold Story* (TV mini-series), Bruno Mussolini
1985–1986 *Saturday Night Live* (TV series), Various
1986 *That's Adequate* (released 1989), Albert Einstein
1986 *Back to School,* Derek Lutz
1987 *The Pick-Up Artist,* Jack Jericho
1987 *Less Than Zero,* Julian Wells
1987 *Dear America: Letters Home from Vietnam* (documentary), Soldier (voice)
1988 *Johnny Be Good,* Leo Wiggins
1988 *Rented Lips*, Wolf Dangler
1988 *1969,* Ralph Carr
1989 *True Believer,* Roger Baron
1989 *Chances Are,* Alex Finch
1990 *Air America,* Billy Covington
1990 *Too Much Sun,* Reed Richmond
1991 *Soapdish*, David Seton Barnes
1992 *Chaplin,* Charles Spencer Chaplin
1992 *The Last Party* (documentary), Himself, Narrator
1993 *Heart and Souls,* Thomas Reilly
1993 *Short Cuts,* Bill Bush

1993 *Luck, Trust & Ketchup* (documentary, released 1996), Himself
1994 *A Century of Cinema* (documentary), Himself
1994 *Hail Caesar,* Jerry
1994 *Natural Born Killers,* Wayne Gale
1994 *Only You,* Peter Wright
1995 *Restoration,* Robert Merivel
1995 *Richard III,* Lord Rivers
1995 *Home for the Holidays,* Tommy Larson
1995 *Mr. Willowby's Christmas Tree* (TV short), Mr. Willowby
1996 *Danger Zone,* Jim Scott
1996 *Saturday Night Live* (TV series), Guest Host
1997 *One Night Stand,* Charlie
1997 *Hugo Pool,* Franz Mazur
1997 *Two Girls and a Guy,* Blake Allen
1998 *The Gingerbread Man,* Clyde Pell
1998 *U.S. Marshals,* Special Agent John Royce
1999 *Friends & Lovers,* Hans
1999 *Bowfinger,* Jerry Renfro
1999 *Black and White,* Terry Donager
1999 *In Dreams,* Vivian Thompson
2000 *Wonder Boys,* Terry Crabtree
2000 *Auto Motives* (short), Rob
2000–2002 *Ally McBeal* (TV series), Larry Paul
2001 "I Want Love" (music video), Himself
2001 *The Making of "I Want Love"* (documentary), Himself
2002 *Lethargy* (short), Animal Therapist
2003 *Whatever We Do* (short), Bobby
2003 *The Singing Detective,* Dan Dark
2003 *The Life and Art of Charles Chaplin* (documentary), Himself
2003 *Gothika,* Pete Graham
2004 *Tangled Up in Blue* (TV movie), Himself
2004 *Eros,* Nick Penrose (segment "Equilibrium")
2004 *A&E Between the Lines* (TV documentary series), Narrator
2005 *The Outsider* (documentary), Himself
2005 *Game 6,* Steven Schwimmer
2005 *Kiss Kiss Bang Bang,* Harry Lockhart
2005 *Good Night, and Good Luck,* Joe Wershba
2005 *Family Guy* (TV series), Patrick Pewterschmidt (voice) (episode "The Fat Guy Strangler")
2005 *Hubert Selby Jr.: It'll Be Better Tomorrow* (documentary), Narrator
2006 *Me, Miami & Nancy* (shown 2011), Himself
2006 *A Guide to Recognizing Your Saints,* Dito Montiel (as an adult) (also co-produced)
2006 *The Shaggy Dog,* Dr. Kozak

2006	*A Scanner Darkly,* James Barris
2006	*Fur: An Imaginary Portrait of Diane Arbus,* Lionel Sweeney
2007	*Zodiac,* Paul Avery
2007	*Lucky You,* Telephone Jack
2007	*Charlie Bartlett,* Nathan Gardner
2007	*The Modern Warrior* (TV documentary), Himself
2008	*Iron Man,* Tony Stark/Iron Man
2008	*Iron Man* (video game), Tony Stark (voice)
2008	*The Incredible Hulk,* Tony Stark
2008	*Tropic Thunder,* Kirk Lazarus
2008	*Tropic Thunder: Rain of Madness* (video short), Kirk Lazarus
2009	*The Soloist,* Steve Lopez
2009	*Sherlock Holmes,* Sherlock Holmes
2010	*Iron Man 2,* Tony Stark/Iron Man
2010	*Love & Distrust* (video), Rob (segment: "Auto Motives")
2010	*Due Date,* Peter Highman
2011	*Sherlock Holmes: A Game of Shadows,* Sherlock Holmes
2012	*The Avengers,* Tony Stark/Iron Man
2013	*Iron Man 3,* Tony Stark/Iron Man
2014	*Chef,* Marvin
2014	*I Am Steve McQueen* (TV documentary), Narrator
2014	*The Judge,* Hank Palmer (Team Downey produced)
forthcoming 2015	*The Avengers 2: The Age of Ultron,* Tony Stark/Iron Man

About the Contributors

Derek **Adams** is an assistant professor of English at Ithaca College. He specializes in 20th-century African American literature. His research is centered on non-traditional forms of racial passing in literature and film that challenge the presumed desirability of heteronormative whiteness.

Nils **Bothmann** studied English, media, and history at the University of Cologne. His master's thesis was published as *Terrorist Thrills: The Depiction of Terrorism in U.S. Mainstream Cinema Since the 1980s*. He works as a film journalist, lecturer, and media scholar while writing his dissertation, "DetAction: The Works of Shane Black."

Thomas **Britt** is an assistant professor of film and video studies at George Mason University in Fairfax, Virginia. His areas of research include film ethics and screenwriting. His writing has been published in *Americana*, *Cinephile*, and *Bright Lights Film Journal*, among others, and he is a staff writer, columnist, and interviewer for *PopMatters*.

Jennifer **Harrison** is a professor of history at Kaplan University, teaching courses in American women's history, art and culture, and world history. She received a bachelor's degree in history and French from Virginia Wesleyan College, and a master's degree in history, with an emphasis on women's history, from the University of Richmond.

Mike **Hernandez** is a writing instructor at DePaul University in Chicago. He has published an essay on shifting racial identity in *Doctor Who and Race*, and another on L. Frank Baum's influence on T.S. Eliot in *The Baum Bugle: A Journal of Oz*.

Linda **Ledford-Miller** has a Ph.D. in comparative literature from the University of Texas at Austin. She teaches language, literature, and culture at the University of Scranton. Her most recent publication is the journal article "Gender and Genre Bending: The Futuristic Detective Fiction of J.D. Robb" in *Reconstruction: Studies in Contemporary Culture*.

Christian B. **Long** lives in Christchurch, New Zealand, and is the coeditor, with Jeff Menne, of *Film and the American Presidency* (Routledge, 2014) and the author of articles in *Post45*, *Senses of Cinema*, and *Canadian Review of American Studies*.

Samuel **Lundberg** is an undergraduate at Judson University in Elgin, Illinois, focusing on film studies and philosophy. His work will be published in the forthcoming *The Child in Post-Apocalyptic Cinema*, *The Women of James Bond*, and *Shattering Release*.

Erin E. **MacDonald** received a Ph.D. in English from the University of Waterloo. A professor at Fanshawe College in London, Ontario, she has recently published a literary companion book on mystery author Ed McBain and is writing one on Ian Rankin. Her articles have appeared in *The Journal of American and Comparative Cultures* and *Clues*.

Ruth **O'Donnell** is a film scholar whose research interests include star studies, psychoanalysis, and representations of race and masculinity in Hollywood film. Her first book, *Tom Cruise: Performing Masculinity in Post-Vietnam Hollywood*, is slated to be published by IB Tauris.

Karen **Oughton** is a lecturer in film and media at Regent's University London. She is a freelance film journalist with outlets including *Ain't It Cool News* and *Fangoria* and has contributed materials to Lionsgate releases and the Russian World Service.

Fernando Gabriel **Pagnoni Berns** is a graduate teaching assistant in the Facultad de Filosofía y Letras at the Universidad de Buenos Aires (Argentina). He has published articles in *Undead in the West*, *Horrofilmico: Aproximaciones al Cine de Terror en Latinoamerica y el Caribe*, and in *The Culture and Philosophy of Ridley Scott*.

F.E. **Pheasant-Kelly** is an M.A. course leader, reader in film and television studies, and co-director of the Film, Media, Discourse and Culture Research Centre at the University of Wolverhampton, UK. Her research centers on fantasy, 9/11, abjection, and space.

Tony **Prichard** is a senior lecturer at Western Washington University in Bellingham, and a doctoral candidate at European Graduate School. His research interests include continental aesthetics, critical theory, visual culture, science fiction, cinema and televisual studies, contemporary fiction, and Afrofuturism.

Brian S. **Reinking** is a candidate in the English literature and criticism doctoral program at Indiana University of Pennsylvania. He teaches composition at Harrisburg Area Community College and Penn Manor High School in South Central Pennsylvania.

Jason Davids **Scott** is an assistant professor at Arizona State University where he teaches film and theatre. He has been a film publicist and a feature film development executive, and is the vice president of publications for the Mid-Atlantic Popular/American Culture Association, where he also serves as film studies area chair.

Index

Numbers in ***bold italics*** indicate pages with photographs.

A&E Between the Lines 292
acting style ***8***, 10–12, 40, ***41***, 43, 46, 48, 53–56, 60, 86, 88, ***95***, 99, 103–104, 117, 122, 127, 131, 225, 227–228, 232, 256, 259–262, 265–266, 271, 283
addiction *see* drug addiction
Adventures of Sherlock Holmes, or, Held for Ransom 244
AIDS 43, 100–103, 274, ***277***
Air America 3, 11, 126, 162, 208, 211, 274, 283, 291
Allen, Woody 125
Ally McBeal 4, 38, 125, 128, 279–280, 281, 292
Alms for the Middle Class 3
Altman, Robert 1, 4, 7, ***8***, 10, 34, 242, 276, 278
America 3, 291
American Anthology of Folk Music 69
American Passion 3, 273
American Psycho ***90***; *see also* Ellis, Bret Easton
America's Sweethearts 4, 125, 280
Anderson, Jon 281
Apocalypse Now 205, 206, 209, 210–214, 283
Arbus, Diane 128, 131–***132***, 282
arrests 4, 36, 102, 108, 124–125, 137, 140, 148–149, 176, 180–181, 185, 218, ***277***–280, 284
Arrival 291
art ***13***, 53, 56, 89, 184, 195, 202, 222, 225, 270
Atkins, Tom 159
Atonement 283
Attenborough, Sir Richard 4, 7, 10–11, 34, 40, ***42***, 44–45, 47–48, 52–53, 55–59, 61, 136, ***275***, ***277***
Auto Motives 4, 278, 292
The Avengers 5, 9, 12, 75, 162–163, 218, 255, 256–258, 261–***265***, 284, 293

The Avengers 2: The Age of Ultron 5, 293
Avery, Paul 81–84, 282; *see also* Zodiac
awards 3–5, 7, 34, 59–60, 93, 96, 103, 112, 121, ***129***, 176, 222–223, 227, 245, 276, 279, 282–284
Ayers, Nathaniel 238
Ayers, Nathaniel (character) 235, ***236***–239, 243, 283

Babo 73 69
Baby It's You 3, 273, 291
Back in Action 162
Back to School 3, 67, 87, 273, 280, 291
The Bad News Bears 269
Bamboozled 66, 221
Bandler, Richard 19
Banner, Bruce 9, 262–264, 266
Baranski, Christine 33
Barry, John 59
Baruchel, Jay 208, ***220***
Batman 257–258, 264, 266; *see also* The Dark Knight
Batman Begins 255
Baudrillard, Jean 205–206, 255, 257
Beatty, Warren 66, 274
Beckett, Scotty 124
Beethoven, Ludwig van 237–238
Beetlejuice 130
Being There 222
Belushi, John 123, ***277***
Bening, Annette 4, 108, ***110***
Benn, Krystal ***110***
Berenger, Tom 209
Bernsen, Corbin 155
Berry, Halle ***129***, 280
Bettany, Paul 183
Bibb, Leslie 184
Bill and Ted's Excellent Adventure 130
The Birth of a Nation 65

Birther Movement 229–231, 233*n*7*n*8*n*9, 234
Black, Jack 205, 207, 209, 211
Black, Shane 1, 7–***8***, 10, 51, 53, 138, 142–144, 153–***154***, 157–***158***, 159–164, 189, 281–282, 295
Black and White 4, 18, 36–37, 107, 124, 278, 292
Black No More 68–69
Black Widow 262–264
blackface 12, 68, 73, 132, 215, 218–233, 283
Bladerunner 282
Blaine, David 206, 225
The Blind Side 238
Block, Melissa 222
Bogart, Humphrey 121
Bond, James ***154***, 182, 295
Bowfinger 4, 124, 278, 292
Boyer, Charles 124
Branagh, Kenneth 43, 278
Brando, Marlon 213
Brat Pack 29, 50, 91, 122, 274
The Breakfast Club 273
Brecht, Bertolt 33
Brett, Jeremy 244, 250
Bridges, Jeff 184
Broderick, Matthew 43
Brown, Jim 18, 30–31, 33, 38
Bruce, Lenny 123
Bugsy 18, 34
Bulworth 66
Burroughs, William S. 66
Burton, Richard 124
Butch Cassidy and the Sundance Kid 118, 250
Butler, Judith 76, 79–81, 87, 107, 112–113, 115

Cabin in the Sky 69
Cagney, James 121, 133*n*1
Campbell, Joseph 269, 283
Canby, Vincent 57–58, 61
Captain America 261–264

Index

Casablanca 25
Catcher in the Rye 207
celebrity *see* stardom
A Century of Cinema 292
Chabon, Michael 112–113
Chafed Elbows 69
Chan, Jackie 235
Chances Are 3, 12, 274, 291
Chandler, Raymond 160
Chaplin (film) ix, 1, 4, 7, 11–12, 34, 40, *41*–61, 64, 93, 122–124, 127, *129*, 133, 136, *139*–140, 145–146, 176, 218, **275**, 276, 291
Chaplin, Charles ix, 4, 7, 11–12, 34, 40, *41–42*, 43–44, 46–58, 61, 89, 107, 136, 146, 274, **275**, 281
Chaplin, Geraldine 44, 48, 57, 59, 98
Chaplin, Michael 44, 55, 58
Charlie *101*–104; *see also* One Night Stand
Charlie Bartlett 5, 12, 166–174, 260, 282, 293
Cheadle, Don 162–163, 284
Cheers 130
Chef 5, 284, 293
childhood 50–53, 88, 108, 136, *139*, 176, 269–272, 285
Chinatown 142
Christ pose 77, ***101***–102, 104, 208
Christie, Agatha 147
Christmas 4, 32, 82, 89, 91–92, 141, 159, 197, 245, 278–279, 292
Clancy, Tom 162
class 17, 20, 24, 27, 31, 50–51, 68, 76, 91, 155, 235–241, 266
Clooney, George 282
Cochrane, Rory **129**
Cohen, Etan 212, 214, 223
Cole, Nat King 46
Conan Doyle, Arthur 117, 148–149, 244–245, 248, 250, 252–253, 283
Conrad, Joseph 211, 212; *see also* Heart of Darkness
Coogan, Steve 206
Cooper, Gary 121
Coppola, Francis Ford 205, 211–214
Corcoran/Corcoran II 4, 108
Coulson, Agent 261–262
Crabtree, Terry 112; *see also* Wonder Boys
Crichton, Michael 162
Crowe, Russell 64, 72
Cruise, Tom 210, 216, 228, 296
The Crying Game 107
Crystal, Billy 43, **275**
Cumberbatch, Benedict 117

Curry, Tim 119
Curtis, Tony 43, 60, 118
Cusack, John 280

Dafoe, Willem 209
Dandridge, Dorothy 123
Danger Zone 4, 124, 292
Dangerfield, Rodney 273
Dangler, Wolf 92, 274; *see also* Rented Lips
Dark, Dan 11, ***13***, 89, 125–127, 138–***139***, 140–141, 150, 280; *see also* The Singing Detective
The Dark Knight 178–***179***, 215, 218, 257, 284
The Dark Knight Returns 255
Davis, Betty 121
Davis, Hope 169
Deadwait 3, 291
Dear America 291
The Deer Hunter 205, 208
Dekker, Fred 159
Deleuze, Gilles 168, 173
DeNiro, Robert 122, 227–228
Dennings, Kat 167
detective 1, 11–12, 125, 136–151, 155, 160–161, 244–***246***, 252–253
Detective Story 3, 272
The Devil's Advocate 130
Dick, Philip K. 128, 282
Die Hard 32, 155
Dispatches 205, 210
Donner, Richard 144
Dostoyevski, Fyodor 29–31, 34–35
Double Impact 162
Douglas, Michael 279
Downey, Allyson 3, 65, 269, 271, 278, 279
Downey, Elsie 3, 52, 65, ***139***, 269, 271
Downey, Exton Elias 5, 284
Downey, Indio Falconer 4, 93, 142, 276, ***277***, 279
Downey, Robert, Sr. 3, 31, 52, 65–66, 68–72, 93, ***139***, 176, 184, 195, 203, 269–273, **275**, 276, 278
Downey, Susan 5, 38, 60, ***129***, 280–282
drug addiction 3, 4, 5, 9, 11, ***13***, 30–31, 34–38, 44, 47–48, 51, 60–61, 84, 88–95, ***101***–104, 123–126, 128–131, 133, 136–137, 140, 144, 146, 149–150, 166, 173, 176–178, 183, 185–186, 187–189, 195, 197–198, 202, 211, 212, 218, 224, 252, 260, 269–283, 285
Due Date 5, 7, 60, 162, 284, 293
Dunbar, Rockmond 156
Duran Duran 87–88, 282

Duvall, Robert 213, 284
Dyer, Richard 176–177, 180, 182, 189

Eastwood, Clint 138
Ebert, Roger 38, 42, 92, 122, 127, 128, 218, 245, 257, 265, 274
Eisenhower, Dwight 258
Elementary 244, 250
Ellis, Bret Easton 3, 31, **90**, 91, 274
Entertainment Weekly 97, 165, 288
"Equilibrium" 5; *see also* Eros
Erasmus 21
Ermey, R. Lee 210
Eros 5, 292
Eskow, John 11, **275**, 285
Estevez, Emilio 43, 272
Estevez, Ramon 272
Exposed 31

Factor, Davis ***13***
Falconer, Deborah 4, 5, 53, 93, 270, 276, ***277***, 281
Family Guy 5, 292
Farley, Chris 123, ***277***
Farrell, Colin 64, 72, 142
Favreau, Jon 5, 7, 176, ***179***, 183, 185, 259–260, 283, 284
Feige, Kevin 180
Field, Sally **275**
Figgis, Mike 10, 43, 55, 88, ***101***–104, 270, 274, ***277***, 278
Fight Club 282
film noir 125, 137–138, 140–142, 148, 150, 153, 160–161, 280
Fincher, David 5, 7, 75, 83, 282
Fingers 17–18, 21, 27, 31
Firstborn 87, 273, 291
Fleming, Michael 7, 14, 51, 56, 62, 203, 224, 234, 270, 275, 277, 281, 282, 283, 284, 285, 286
Flynn, Errol 124
Forbes 7, 15, 28, 152, 184, 190
Forest Gump 222
48 Hrs. 235
Foster, Jody 10, 48, 94–96, 99–100, ***277***
Foucault, Michel 170
Foxx, Jamie 235, ***236***, 283
Fraternity 3
Frazer, James 212
Freud, Sigmund 136–138, 149–151
Friends and Lovers 4, 124, 278, 292
Fry, Stephen 147
The Fugitive 278
Full Metal Jacket 205–206, 208, 210, 214
Fur: An Imaginary Portrait of

Index

Diane Arbus 5, 55, 121, 128–130, *132*–133, 178, 282, 293
Fury, Nick 191, 194, 201, 202, 262–263
The Futurist 5, *13*, 140, 281

Gale, Wayne 75–78, 82, 276; see also *Natural Born Killers*
The Gambler 18, 31, 34
Game 6 5, 292
Gandhi 40, *275*
Garbarino, Steve 8, 10–11, 15, 88, 105, 108, 112, 119, 120, 150, 151, 195, 270–272, 278–279, 286
Garber, Marjorie 108, *111*–112
Gardner, Nathan 12; see also *Charlie Bartlett*
Garland, Judy 25, 122–123
Garrick, David 121
gayness see homosexuality
gender *8*, 12, 18, 32, 67–68, 75–82, 85, 86–89, 93, 97–98, 102, 107–*114*, 117–118, 136–138, 141–150, 153–159, 161, 163–164, 250–252; see also homosexuality; queer theory
Gernsback, Hugo 256–257, 261, 264
Gertz, Jami 31, 91
Gibson, Mel 3, 4, *13*, 38, 125–127, 138–*139*, 144, *154*, 211, 274–*275*, 280
The Gingerbread Man 4, 124, 278, 292
Girls Just Want to Have Fun 3, 291
Gleiberman, Owen 97, 105
Gliatto, Tom 31, 39, 270, *275*, 278, 286
The Godfather I and II 213
Goldberg, Whoopi *275*
The Golden Bough 212
"Goldilocks" incident 4, 141, 144, 150
Goldman, William 57
Good Morning America 269, 278
Good Night, and Good Luck 5, *129*, 133, 178, 282, 292
Goodfellas 227
Gordon, Keith 10, 13, *139*, 280
Gothika 5, *129*, 280–281, 292
GQ 61, 62, 63, 106, 180, 190, 195, 203, 204, 287, 288
Graham, Heather 34
Gran Torino 218
Grauman's Chinese Theater 5
Graysmith, Robert 83–84
Graysmith UNMASKED 83–84
Greaser's Palace 3, 65, 269, 291
Green Berets 205, 211
Griffith, Phillip Jones 210
Grodin, Charles 66

Gugino, Carla *139*
A Guide to Recognizing Your Saints 5, 10, 191–194, 199–200, 203, *236*, 240–242, 282, 292
Guttenberg, Steve *95*, 98
Gyllenhaal, Jake 83, 282

Haden, Charlie 281
Hadler, Bill 213
Hail Caesar 4, 124, 292
Haim, Corey 124
Hall, Anthony Michael 3, 273, 274
Hall, Arsenio 94
Hall, Rebecca 9
Halliday, Brett 160
Hamburger Hill 206, 208–210, 214
Hamlet 4, 125, 280
Hammer, Justin 259
Hammett, Dashiell 160
Hanks, Tom 215, 222, 224
Hansen, Maya 9
Hanson, Curtis 112
hard-boiled see film noir
Harrelson, Woody 130, 276, 282
Harris, Jared 148
Harvard Man 18
Hasford, Gustav 210
Hawkeye 262
Hawkins, Diana 11, *42*–43, 46–47, 57, 59, *275*
Heart and Souls 4, 12, 60, 64, 66, 72, 124, 260, 276, 291
Heart of Darkness 211, 212, 213; see also Conrad, Joseph
Hearts of Darkness 206, 209, 212–214
Heath, Chris 61, 62, 181, 189, 190, 269, 272, 284, 287
Heathers 130
Hedegaard, Erik 38, 39, 195, 203, 272, *275*, 283, 287
Hedges, Chris 266, 267
Hepburn, Katharine 121, 133n3
Herr, Michael 205, 206, 209, 210, 217
Hillis, Ali 157
Hilton, Tyler 170
Hoffman, Dustin 43, 222, 224
Hoffman, Gaby 37
Hoffman, Michael 10, *275*, 276
Holmes, Katie 113
Holmes, Sherlock 5, 7, 52, 73, 75, 89, 107, 117–118, 122, 137, 140, 146–151, 235, 244–*246*, 247–*249*, 250–253; see also *Sherlock Holmes* (film)
Home for the Holidays 4, 10, 86, 94–*101*, 104, 124, 186, *277*, 292
homosexuality 36, 86–87, 89–94, 96–104, 107, *114*–119, 141, 144–149, 153–157, 163, 245, 250–252, *277*; see also gender; queer theory
hooks, bell 215, 217
Hopkins, Anthony 52, 57
Hopper, Dennis 23, 33, 213
Houston, Allan 36
Howard, Terence 162, 184
Howell, C. Thomas 221
Hubert Selby Jr.: It'll Be Better Tomorrow 292
Hudson, Mark 281
Hudson, Rock 116
Hughes, Howard 258, 264
Hughes, John 273
Hugo Pool 4, 124, 278, 292
The Hulk see Banner, Bruce
Hunter, Holly *95*–96, *277*
Hurt, John 156
The Hurt Locker 218
Hutcheon, Linda *13*, 213–215, 217

I Am Sam 222
identity *8*–9, 11–*13*, 14, 35, 40, *41*, 65, 67, 72–73, 79–80, 86, 88, 93–94, 97, 100, 102, 107, 114–117, 119, 121, 131–*132*, 150, 164, 174, 183, 205, 214–215, 219, 222, 226–228, 256, 261–262, 270, 272, 280, 283, 285; see also gender; race
The Immigrant 44
improvisation see acting style
In Dahomey 221
In Dreams 4, *8*, 75, 78–81, 85, 86, 107–112, 124, 278, 292
The Incredible Hulk 5, 218, 293
Indiana Jones and the Crystal Skull 178–*179*
Iron Man 1, 7, 9, 12, *41*, 73, 112, 121–122, 162, 180, 183, 186, 227, 256, 258, 260–261, 266, 284
Iron Man (film) 5, 7–*8*, 10, 27, 38, 54, 56, 60, 75, 124, 133, 137–138, 162, 174, 176–179, 181–189, 192, 202, 218, 227, 235, *236*, 248, 256, 258–260, 266, 282–283, 293
Iron Man 2 5, 162, 176, 178, 180, 182, 187–189, 191–194, 200–203, 235, 256, 259, 283–284, 292
Iron Man 3 5, *8*, 10, 14, 53, 157, 159, 162, 164, 178, 182, 188, 189, 266, 282, 284, 293
Iron Patriot 163

Jackson, Brandon T. 207, *220*, 226
Jackson, Michael 43

Index

Jackson, Victoria 23
Jameson, Fredric 207–208, 211, 212, 214, 216
Jarecki, Nicholas 32, 38
The Jazz Singer 68, 73
The Jeffersons 206, 208, 215, 226
Jeffries, Ross 17–22
Jericho, Jack 17–*26*, 27, 32–33, 35–36; see also *The Pick-up Artist*
Jewison, Norman 60, 276, ***277***
Joel, Billy 282
John, Elton 4, 280
Johnny Be Good 3, 274, 291
Johnny Mnemonic 130
Johnson, Arnold 70–72
Jolson, Al 68–69, 73; see also *The Jazz Singer*
Jordan, Neil ***8***, 75, 78, 107–108, ***110***–112
The Judge 5, 9, 284, 293
Jung, Carl 269, 281
Jurassic Park 98

Kamin, Dan ix, 43–47, 55, 59–60, 107
Kanievska, Marek 29, 195
Kassar, Mario 57, 59
Kehler, Jack 159
Keitel, Harvey 17–18, 23, 33, 212
Kelly, Moira 51
Kidman, Nicole 55, 131–***132***, 282
The Kids Are All Right 93
Killian, Aldrich 9
Kilmer, Val 5, ***129***, 141, 153, 282
Kimber, Shaun 75–76
Kimmel, Jimmy 285
King, B.B. 67
King, Larry 282
Kingsley, Sir Ben ***8***, 14, 43, 182
Kinski, Natassja ***101***
Kirby, Jack 64
Kiss Kiss Bang Bang 5, ***8***–9, 12–***13***, 53, ***129***, 133, 136, 138, 140–141, ***143***–145, 148–150, 153–***154***, 155–163, 178, ***236***, 238, 281–282, 292
Kline, Kevin ***41***, ***275***
Knox, Mallory 75–78
Knox, Mickey 75–78
Kubrick, Stanley 210

Lacan, Jacques 238
language 82–83, 138, 140, 216, 219, 221–222, 225, 235–243, 261
Larson, Tommy 94–100, 104; see also *Home for the Holidays*
The Last Action Hero 153, 162
The Last Boy Scout 153, 159–160, 162
The Last Party 4, 48, 52, 94, 271, 276, 291

Law, Jude 87, 107, 117–118, 147–148, ***246***, 252, 283
Lazarus, Kirk see Osiris, Lincoln
Lear, Norman 3, 272
Leaving Las Vegas ***101***, ***277***
LeBeouf, Shia 199, 241
Ledger, Heath 123, 215, 283
Lee, Spike 66, 221
Lee, Stan 64, 258
Leer, James 113–115; see also *Wonder Boys*
Leno, Jay ***13***
Less Than Zero (film) 1, 7, 11, 29, 31–32, ***41***, 49, 86, 88–89, 94, 97, ***101***, 103, 112, 191–***196***, 197, 199, 203, 218, 260, 291
Less Than Zero (novel) 3, 31, ***90***, 91
Lethal Weapon 144, 153, 155, 159–160, 162, 164, 281
Lethal Weapon 2 144–145, 160, 162, 250
Lethargy 4, 292
Letterman, David 118, 147, 273, 282
Levin, Susan 5
Levinson, Barry 34
Lewis, Juliette 276
The Life and Art of Charles Chaplin 292
Limelight 46
Linklater, Richard 1, 128–130, 133, 282
Lionel 131–***132***; see also *Fur*
Lipard, George 66
Lipton, James 45, 55, 88–89, 270
Little Miss Sunshine 87
Liu, Lucy 244
Lloyd, Harold 145
Lock Stock and Two Smoking Barrels 244
Lockhart, Harry 12–***13***, 138, 140–142, ***143***–146, 153–***154***, 155–***158***, 162–163
Lohan, Lindsay 124
Loki 261–262, 264, ***265***
The Long Kiss Goodnight ***154***, 159, 162
Lopez, Steve 235, ***236***–239, 243, 283
Love & Distrust 293; see also *Auto Motives*
Love and Money 31
Luck, Trust & Ketchup 292
Lucky You 5, 293
Lyotard, Jean-François 210, 217

Macklin, Charles 121
Madonna 273
Maguire, Toby see Leer, James
Mailer, Norman 29–33, 38
The Making of "I Want Love" 292
The Mandarin ***8***

March, Fredric 121
Marlowe, Philip 160
martial arts 60, 245–***246***, 247–248, 252–253, 284
Marvel 9, 133, 180–181, 255, 256, 258, ?82, 283
masculinity see gender
Maslin, Janet ***90***, 92, 105, 274, 287
Matheson, Chris 159
The Matrix 130
McAdams, Rachel 148
McAvoy, May 68
McBride, Danny 228
McCarthy, Andrew 31, 91, 274
McConaughey, Matthew 207
McDermott, Dylan 97
McDormand, Frances 113
McGrath, Derek 171
McKellan, Sir Ian 276
McTiernan, John 32
Me, Miami & Nancy 292
media 9, 50, 56, 66, 73, 75–78, 82–85
Meet Me in St. Louis 25
Melinda and Melinda 125
Men of Honor 227
Menounos, Maria 212, 213, 222
Method acting 12, 40, 46, 54, 65, 72, 121, 132, 140, 146, 274
Michael Collins 107
Mihok, Dash 148
Milius, John 211
Miller, Frank 255
Miller, Jonny Lee 244
Milli Vanilli 207
Minnelli, Vincente 69
Mira, Judge Lawrence 4, 36, 278
Mr. Willowby's Christmas Tree 292
Mitchell, Joni 279
Modern Times 52
The Modern Warrior 293
Moment to Moment 291
Monoghan, Michelle 141, 153
Monroe, Marilyn 121, 123, 113–***114***, 123
Montiel, Dito 200, 240–242, 282
Montiel, Dito (character) 191–195, 199–200, 203, 241–243
Moore, Alan 255
Mumbo Jumbo 65–66
Muni, Paul 121
The Muppets see *Mr. Willowby's Christmas Tree*
Murphy, Brittany 124
Murphy, Eddie 235
Mussolini: The Untold Story 3, 273, 291
My Own Private Idaho 130

The Natural 157
Natural Born Killers 1, 4, 9, 34, 75, 81–82, 85, 104, 124, 276, 292
The New York Times 15, 20, 28, 39, 48, 57, 90, 105, 181, 187, 189, 190, 203, 204, 226, 233, 234, 258, 267, 281, 286, 287
Nicholson, Jack 142
Night of the Creeps 159
9/11 12, 183, 185, 255, 256–257, 261, 264, 266
1969 3, 274, 291
Nixon, Richard 19, 20, 222, 266
Nolan, Christopher 257
Nolte, Nick 207
Northam, Jeremy **139**
The Nutty Professor 2 208

Obama, Barack 229–231, 233–234, 266, 267
The Odyssey 208, 209, 211
Oklahoma! 3, 272
One Night Stand 4, 43, 86, 88, 100–**101**, 124, **277**, 292
O'Neal, Ryan 156
O'Neill, Oona 51, 136
Only You 4, 60, 124, 276, 292
Oprah see Winfrey, Oprah
Oram, Eric 60, 247
Osiris, Lincoln 11–12, 64–65, 69, 72–73, 121, **132**–133, 146–147, 206–212, 214–216, 218–219, **220**–231, 283; *see also Tropic Thunder*
the Other 79, 147, 155, 164n4, 238, 240–243
The Outsider 32, 38, 292

Pacino, Al 59, 209, 212, 276
Palmer, David 17–18, 27
Paltrow, Gwyneth 52, 163, 177
Parker, Sarah Jessica 3, 47, 273, 274, **275**
Partners 156
Pastorelli, Robert 124
Paul, Larry 4, 279 see also Ally McBeal
Paymer, David 66
Pearce, Drew 162
Pearce, Guy 9
Penn, Christopher 124
Penn, Sean 4, 215, 222, 273, 278
Pennies from Heaven 126
People 39, 135, **196**, **277**, 280, 286, 288
The People vs. Larry Flynt 130
Perry, Lincoln 221
Peyton, Harley 198
Philips, Bijou 37
Phillips, Todd 7–**8**, 10
Phoenix, River 123, **277**

The Pick-up Artist 3, 10, 17–**26**, 27, 29, 31–35, 39, 274, 291
The Picture of Dorian Gray 115–116
Plato, Dana 124
Platoon 206, 208, 209, 215, 283
Playboy 7, 14, 50, 60, 62, 63, 203, 224, 234, 286
Point Break 130
Polanski, Roman 142
Poll, Jon 166, 174, 282
Pollock, Jackson 184
postmodernism **13**–14, 146, 160, 166, 205–217
Potter, Dennis 126, 128, 280
Pound 3, 64–65, 73, **196**, 269, 291
Powell, Colin 188
Presley, Elvis 20, 66, 69, 123, 160
Pretty in Pink 273
The Private Life of Sherlock Holmes 117
Pryor, Nicholas **196**
Psycho 107–108
Pulp Fiction 148
Putney Swope 65, 70–72, 270, 283
Pyle, Gomer 210

The Quaker City 66
queer theory 10, 78–81, 86–87, 91, 93, 96–97, 104, 107–112, 115, 117–119, 146–147, 149–150
Quill, Tim 210

Raab, Scott 56, 62, 119, 120, 192, 202, 203, 204, 271, 272, 282, 283, 288
race 7, 12, 18, 29, 36–37, 65, 67–71, 73, 102, 144, 146, 155, 157–159, 162–163, 209, 214–216, 218–233, 235, **236**, 240–241, 243, 283
Raging Bull 227
Rain Man 222
Rambo I and II 208, 210
Rapace, Noomi 147
Rathbone, Basil 244
Reagan, Ronald 17–20, 23–24, 27
Redford, Robert 157
Reed, Ishmael 65–66
Reeves, Keanu 130, 282
Reid, Wallace 123
Reilly, Kelly 148
Reisz, Karel 31
Rendall, Mark 170
Rented Lips 3, 92, 274, 291
Restoration 4, 11, 102, 124, **275**, 276, 292
Rich, Adrienne 93
Rich, Jimmy 284

Richard III 4, 124, 276–**277**, 292
Richman, Josh 278
Riley, Thomas 66–68; *see also Heart and Souls*
Ringwald, Molly 3, 10, 17, **26**, 33, 274
Ritchie, Guy 5, 7, 60, 117–119, 146–147, 244–247, **249**, 250, 252, 283
Riva, J. Michael 184
The Rivals 3, 272
River's Edge 130
Robbins, Brian 7
Roberts, Julia 280
Robinson, David 40, 44, 46
Rocky Horror Picture Show 88, 119, 271
Rolling Stone 54, 57, 62, 63, 88, 89, 105, 203, 273, 275, 276, 287
Rose, Charlie **13**, **41**, 56, 276
Ross, Jonathan 282
Roth, Joe 125
Rowe, Ryan 159
Rudin, Scott 11
Ruffalo, Mark 282; *see also* Banner, Bruce
Rush Hour 235
Ryder, Winona 130, 274, 282

Safety Last! 145
Salinger, J.D. 207
Santa Monica High School 3, 272
satire 12, 64, 65, 71–73, 208, 215–216, 219, 221–233, 283
Saturday Night Live 3, 4, 273, **277**, 291, 292
Sawyer, Diane 278
A Scanner Darkly 1, 5, 11–12, 121, 128–**129**, 130, 133, 178, 282, 293
Scent of a Woman 276
Schiffer, Claudia 36
School of Rock 282
Schroeder, Joyce 5
Schuyler, George S. 68–69
Scott, George C. 273
Seberg, Jean 124
Secretary 130
Sedgwick, Eve Kosofsky 87, 119, 147, 155–156
Sedgwick, Kyra 66
Sellers, Peter 222, 224
serial killer 1, 11, 75–76, 78, 82–84, 107
sexuality **8**, 29–33, 36, 86, 88, **90**–94, 97, 102–103, 112, 117–119, 146, 148, 150, 250, 272; *see also* gender; homosexuality; queer theory
Shaft 97
The Shaggy Dog 5, 10, 12, 60, 121, **129**, 282, 292

Shainberg, Steven 55, 130–*132*
Shandling, Gary 188
Sheen, Charlie 272
Sheen, Martin 212, 213
Shepherd, Cybill 3, 274
Sherlock (TV show) 117, 244
Sherlock Holmes (film) 5, 7–*8*, 9–10, 38, 60, 86–87, 92, 124, 136, 138, 145–150, 162, 178, 218, 235, 244–*246*, *249*–250, 283, 293
Sherlock Holmes: A Game of Shadows 5, 60, 86, 92, 107, 117–118, 147–150, 162, 244–245, 248, 250–251, 284, 293
Sherlock Holmes Baffled 244
Shields, Brooke 36
Shoot to Kill 155
Short Cuts 4, 34, 124, 276, 291
Shriver, Timothy 222–223
The Sign of Four 245, 249
The Silence of the Lambs 82, 107
Silver, Joel 273, 280
Simpson, O.J. 125
The Singing Detective 4, 10–*13*, *41*, 54, 89, 121–122, 125–130, 133, 136, 138–*139*, 140–142, 150, 178, 188, 280, 282, 292
Sizemore, Tom 66
Smith, Anna Nicole 124
Smith, Harry 69
Snatch 244
Snipes, Wesley *101*, 104, *277*
Soapdish 3, *275*, 291
The Soloist 1, 5, 10–11, 235, *236*–243, 283, 293
Solomon, Ed 159
Some Like It Hot 118
Soul Man 221
Spader, James 89–*90*, 273
Speed 130
Spiderman 218
Spy Magazine 18–19
Stagedoor Manor 3, 270
Stane, Obadiah 184, 186–187
Stanislavski, Constantin 54
A Star Is Born 122
Star Wars 214
stardom, star persona/theory 7–9, 29, 31, 47, 49, 58, 61, 64, 82, 119, 121–125, 127, 130, 136–137, 139–141, 144, 146–151, 153, 166–167, 174, 176–189, 201–202, 218–219, 221, 224, 229, 260, 265–266, 283, 285
Stark, Howard 191–194, 200–203
Stark, Tony *8*–9, 12, 14, *41*, 56, 75, 89, 112, 121–122, 137–138, 162, 174, 176–177, *179*–189, 191–195, 200–203, 218, 227, 235, 248, 256, 258–*265*, 266, 283, 284; see also Iron Man

Stern, Howard 10, 96–97
Stevens, Inger 124
Stevenson, Cynthia 97
Stiller, Ben 5, 56, 64, 73, 146, 206, 208, 209, 212, 214, 216, *220*, 221, 223, 228, 232, 283
Sting 272, 278, 279, 282
Stone, Oliver 1, 7, 9, 34, 75–77, 209, 276
Streep, Meryl 122
Strong, Mark *8*, 147
A Study in Scarlet 244–245
Styler, Trudie 282
Sunday Morning Shootout 47, 59
Sunset Boulevard 140
Superman 256
Sutherland, Keifer 3, 273, 274
Sweet Smell of Sex 65

The Talented Mr. Ripley 148
Tangled Up in Blue 292
Tatum, Channing 242
Taxi Driver 227
Taylor, Dylan 170
Taylor-Wood, Sam 280
Team Downey 5, 9, 60, 284
That's Adequate 3, 291
therapy 9, 133, *139*–140, 163, 170, 195
Theroux, Justin 202, 212, 214
Thompson, Vivian 78–81, 108–112; see also In Dreams
Thor 263
Three of Hearts 93, 118
Thunderball **154**
Toback, James 7, 10, 17–19, 22, *26*, 29–39, 107, 274, 278, 279
Tomei, Marisa *42*, 276, *277*
Too Much Sun 3, 93, *275*, 291
Top Gun 141
Tracy, Spencer 121–123
trauma 9, 38, 51, 92, 122, 125–128, 131
Travers, Peter 55, 57–58
Tropic Thunder 1, 5, 7, *8*, 11–*13*, 40, 64, 66, 69, 72–73, 92, *132*, 146–147, 205–217, 218–233, 283, 293
Tropic Thunder: Rain of Madness 5, 213–214, 293
True Believer 3, 51, 162, 274, 291
Trump, Donald 229
Tucker, Chris 235
Tuff Turf 3, 67, 273, 291
Two Girls and a Guy 4, 12, 30, 34–38, 278, 281, 292
Tyson (film) 18
Tyson, Mike 18, 37–38

Udovitch, Mim 13, 15, 181, 186, 190
Underwood, Ron 12, 66, 260–261

Up the Academy 3, 291
U.S. Marshals 4, 11, 124, 278, 292

Vanity Fair 151, 184, 187, 279, 286
Vanko, Ivan 192, 201
Vineberg, Steve 7, 260
Vogue 180–181, 189

Wagner, Natasha Gregson 34
Walker, Polly 276
War Machine 163
Watchmen 255
Wayne, Bruce *see* Batman
Wayne, John 121
Weird Science 3, 67, 87, 273, 281, 291
Wells, Julian 3, 11, 31–32, *41*, 89–94, 191–*196*, 197, 203, 274; see also Less Than Zero
Whatever We Do 4, 292
Whedon, Joss 257, 261, 263, *265*, 266, 284
White Men Can't Jump 130
Widen, Gregory 159
Wigdor, Geoff 80
Wilde, Oscar 115–116, 147
Wilder, Billy 117, 140
Williams, Bert 221
Williams, Robin 43, *275*
Williamson, Fred 226, 233n5
Willis, Bruce *154*, 255
Wilson, Erin Cressida 130
Winfrey, Oprah 280–281
Wing and a Prayer 24
Wing Chun Kung-Fu *see* martial arts
Winter, Ariel 142
Wonder Boys (film) 4, 86, 107, 112–117, 119, 124, 128, 278, 279, 292
Wonder Boys (novel) 112–113
Wonder Woman 4, 280
Wood, Elijah 37
Woodard, Alfre 66
Woods, James 3, 51–52, 274
Wright, Joe 235, *236*, 238, 283
Wright, Peter *277*; *see also Only You*
Wright-Penn, Robin *139*
Written on the Wind 116
Wu-Tang Clan 36–37

Yelchin, Anton 167, 282
Young, Harrison 142
Young, Stephen 170

Zane, Billy 4, 273, 276
Žižek, Slavoj 235, 243
Zodiac 5, 75, 81–85, 178, 282, 293